GERMAN CAPITAL SHIPS OF WORLD WAR TWO

Below: Trondheim, probably on the afternoon of 11 June 1940. In the left foreground is *Gneisenau*; behind her is *Scharnhorst* with *Kondor* and *Lody* alongside. One of the destroyers in the rear is *Galster*, and the cruiser is *Admiral Hipper*. In the foreground are He 115 and He 56 floatplanes. (ECPA)

GERMAN CAPITAL SHIPS OF WORLD WAR TWO

M. J. WHITLEY

ARMS AND
ARMOUR

First published in Great Britain in 1989 by Arms and Armour Press, Artillery House, Artillery Row, London SW1F 1RT.

Distributed in the USA by Sterling Publishing Co. Inc., 387 Park Avenue South, New York, NY 10016-8810.

Distributed in Australia by Capricorn Link (Australia) Pty. Ltd, P.O. Box 665, Lane Cove, New South Wales 2066, Australia.

British Library Cataloguing in Publication Data
Whitley, M. J. (Michael J.)
1. Germany.   Kriegsmarine.   Capital ships, 1939–1945—
Illustrations
I. Title
623.8′252′0943
ISBN 0-85368-970-9

Jacket illustration: 'Sinking of *Bismarck*', by Claus Bergen. Reproduced by courtesy of Freundeskreis Marineschule Mürwick, Flensburg, Federal Republic of Germany.

Designed and edited by DAG Publications Ltd. Designed by David Gibbons; edited by David Dorrell; Layout by Anthony A. Evans; typeset by Asco Trade Typesetting Ltd, Hong Kong; printed and bounded in Great Britain by The Bath Press, Avon.

CONTENTS

PREFACE

This volume completes the story of the Kriegsmarine's surface warships that was begun with *Destroyer!* and continued with *German Cruisers*. After an introduction dealing with development up to the end of World War One, it opens with the events that led to the building of the so-called 'Pocket Battleships', progresses through the intermediate design of *Scharnhorst* and *Gneisenau*, then on to *Bismarck* and the '*H*'-class ships laid down just at the start of World War Two. The attempts by the German Navy to form an air arm in the 1930s and build an aircraft-carrier force are also discussed in detail and the reasons for their failure examined. However, no attempt is made to chronicle the various post-'*H*'-class design projects, as these were in reality merely political flights of fancy of grandiose proportions and could never have been constructed.

The format follows that of the earlier volumes, beginning with a technical section dealing with the various aspects of each class design. The technical section has, almost without exception, been compiled from primary official archive sources. These include the reports of many conferences, minutes and official correspondence unearthed by many hours of burrowing in both my own archive holdings and those of the British and German Ministries of Defence. The quoting of references for most of these individual items is meaningless but the major source documents are listed at the end of the book. An operational section follows, in which will be found details and accounts of the actions the ships participated in. It is inevitable that several of these actions have already been examined in the earlier books, but where this occurs this book deals with that action from the battleship's point of view. Thus it is possible in the case of the 'Channel Dash' (Operation 'Cerberus') in 1942, for example, to study the course of events from battleship, cruiser and destroyer participants.

As in the other books, all German accounts have been compared, contrasted and reconciled with the equivalent, contemporary Royal Navy accounts of the same action. In many instances RAF and Fleet Air Arm records have also been consulted. Times are German, unless otherwise stated and ranges have been quoted in metres, although contemporary practice was to use hectometres (100m). Likewise, gun calibres are always stated in centimetres, as was the practice at the time.

I should like to record my thanks and appreciation to the following individuals and organizations for their help in compiling this work. R.M. Coppock of the Naval Historical Branch, Ministry of Defence; D.K. Brown, Ministry of Defence, Bath; E.A. Munday, R.C.M. King and C. Morley of the Air Historical Branch; Dr. Hoffman, Herr Jamans and Frau Muller of the Bundesarchiv; Dr. J. Rohwer of the Bibliothek für Zeitgeschichte; Dieter Jung and Norbert Kelling; Paul Kemp of the Imperial War Museum; David Lees and Arnold Hague of the World Ship Society; George Moore, Ron Pankhurst and Ray Sturtivant, who helped with various aviation matters, as did Bob Layman in the U.S.A.; Frhr. von Müllenheim-Rechberg, who answered questions on *Bismarck* and Manfred Wilske who is an expert on the subject of *Graf Zeppelin*; Michael Bullen and David Ennor for help with photographs. Finally, I should like to express thanks to my wife Rita once again for the typing work.

Below: *Bismarck* sails for trials in peacetime paint scheme. Much gun control equipment is still missing. (Bundesarchiv)

INTRODUCTION

Modern Germany is a relatively young nation for it was not until 1870 that the individual German states banded together to counter-attack France, who had actually declared war only on the powerful Kingdom of Prussia. This feeling of national unity, despite the religious differences between north and south, led to official unification on 18 January 1871 when Kaiser Wilhelm I of Prussia became the first head of the new German Empire. Prior to unification those states on the North Sea and Baltic littoral—Oldenburg, Hanover, Schleswig-Holstein, Mecklenburg, Pomerania and Prussia— had maintained small numbers of armed ships for coastal defence purposes but, with the possible exception of Prussia, they were of little military significance. This became apparent in 1848 during the war with Denmark when the Danish fleet had little difficulty in blockading the north German ports. For example, a single Danish frigate stationed off Heligoland (then a British possession) was able intercept all traffic into and out of the Elbe and Weser rivers.

This caused a political storm and the National Assembly in Frankfurt voted six million Thaler for the establishment of a national naval force. Senator Duckwitz of Bremen was given responsibility for naval affairs while on the initiative of a Hamburg trading company, four ships were purchased— three paddle steamers and a sail frigate—to form the nucleus of the new fleet, whose base was to be Bremerhaven. On 15 October 1848 the 'Hamburg Flotilla' arrived at its base and became the Bundesmarine. During the following years, further ships were added, some being built to order in Great Britain while others were purchased locally. In addition, the Danish frigate *Gefion* was captured and taken into service as *Eckernförde*; her new name commemorated the action between shore batteries at that town and Danish warships, one of which was *Gefion* and the other *Christian VIII*, which was sunk. This early Bundesmarine lasted only until 1852 as the end of the war with Denmark quenched the the demand for national unity and the ships were soon paid off and sold. Two were bought by the Prussian Government but the remainder became fishing or merchant vessels.

After the dissolution of the Bundesmarine only Austria and Prussia of all the Germanic states continued to support naval forces. The Prussian Navy was founded in 1853 and in the following year Prinz Adalbert of Prussia assumed command. Its main function was little more than coastal defence and army support, but soon eyes were being cast further afield and between 1855 and 1869 five wooden frigates were built to serve on foreign cruises. They were the first Prussian ships with screw propellers and ventured as far afield as the Azores, the Suez Canal, China and Japan. Between 1859 and 1865 steam gunboats were put into service, 21 of which were

on strength when a new war broke out, this time between Schleswig-Holstein and Denmark. Both Prussia and Austria supported Schleswig-Holstein and a combined squadron under the command of the Austrian Admiral Tegetthoff raised the Danish blockade of the German Bight on 9 May 1864 after an action with Danish frigates. This squadron then assured the northern states free passage to the high seas until the armistice.

In 1866 Prussia and Austria were themselves at war and after the former's victory at Königgrätz, she absorbed both Schleswig-Holstein and Hanover who had sided with the Austrians. This resulted in Prussia controlling all the northern coast of the German Federation, together with the important base at Kiel, which she had held since 1865. The German Federation, which hitherto had included all Germanic states as well as Austria, was now disbanded and henceforth would not include the latter, at least until the formation of the Third Reich.

Under Prussian control the north German states became the North German Confederation in 1867 and the Prussian Fleet the North German State Navy. In a ten-year programme it was envisaged that the strength of the Navy would rise to sixteen armoured ships, twenty frigates or corvettes, eight 'avisos' and many lesser warships. In addition, a new base was established on the Jade river and named Wilhelmshaven, after the Kaiser. The war with France saw no noteworthy naval actions for the rapid advance of the Prussian Army quickly ended hostilities.

During the first ten years of its existence the Kaiserliche Marine, as the fleet was renamed after unification, concentrated its attention on coastal defence duties and although overseas bases were planned and a 'Flying Squadron' for distant waters was formed, there was initially no intention to rival Great Britain or France in naval superiority. Many of the fleet's new ships were built in British yards, but in 1872 the ironclad *Hansa* was launched at Stettin, the first such ship designed and built in Germany. This signalled a new era in which Germany was to become independent of foreign naval assistance for warship construction.

The most important epoch of German seapower began with the the ascent of Kaiser Wilhelm II to the throne of the German Empire in 1888, since he was greatly interested in seapower and naval affairs. For strategic reasons he built the North Sea—Baltic Sea canal, which was named the Kaiser Wilhelm Canal in his honour; more familiarly known as the Kiel Canal, it was opened on 21 June 1895. Together with Admiral Tirpitz, who had assumed the post of head of the Navy in 1897, the Kaiser embarked on a course of action which was eventually to lead Germany into conflict with

Great Britain. Under the leadership of Tirpitz, the Navy expanded quickly, much to the dismay of Britain, who mistrusted Germany's aims despite the close ties between the two countries at that time. The result was a race in warship construction which Germany could never win because her shipbuilding and industrial output were less than those of Great Britain, even though, for example, her steel output in 1910 was about double that of her rival.

In the last decade of the nineteenth century Germany laid down what could be considered her first really useful battleship design, as opposed to pure coast defence vessels. This was the *Kurfürst Friedrich Wilhelm* class of four ships displacing 10,670 tons. They were armed with six 28cm (11in) guns mounted in barbettes with full shields, one each forward and aft with the third amidships. Coal-fired with reciprocating engines, the ships could achieve just over 16 knots. All four were reconstructed between 1900 and 1905 and three of them served on foreign stations between 1900 and 1901. In 1910 the name ship of the class, together with *Weissenburg*, was purchased by Turkey, with whom they served during World War One; *Heireddin Barbarossa* (ex *Kurfürst Friedrich Wilhelm*) was sunk by the British submarine *E11* in 1915. Neither of the remaining pair was in German front-line service by 1914.

The next class, *Kaiser Friedrich III*, consisted of five ships which were contemporaries of the Royal Navy's *Majestic* class. Displacing about 10 per cent more than their predecessors, they had more powerful machinery and were faster. Unusually, they adopted a smaller calibre gun, 24cm (9.4in), and carried fewer of them, four, in two twin mountings. Compared with the *Majestics*, therefore, they were outgunned. None was in front-line service by 1914 and all were broken up in 1919-1921.

The 24cm gun was retained for the following five units of the *Wittelsbach* class whose dimensions did not differ greatly from those of *Kaiser Friedrich III* except for increased beam. The side and deck armour was reduced but speed was a knot or so better than the preceding class. Nevertheless, they were of no military value by 1914. Two of the vessels, *Wittelsbach* and *Schwaben*, were converted to motherships for minesweeping motor launches in 1918 and *Zähringen* to a target vessel in 1926/27.

The adoption of the 24cm gun was by this time very questionable because the standard calibre of the Royal Navy was the 12in gun (30.5cm), now carried by nine *Majestic*-class ships and twenty *Canopus* and sub-classes. Thus the new *Braunschweig* class, once more of five ships, reverted to the 28cm gun. Displacement continued to rise, due mainly to an increase in beam, and installed power was also raised to increase speed to about $18\frac{1}{2}$ knots. The ratio of length to beam is of interest for German warships were always designed as beamy gun platforms. Compared with the 1:5.7 of the *Canopus* class, the *Braunschweigs* had a ratio of 1:4.98. This trend was however limited by the constraints of the Kaiser Wilhelm Canal (or Kiel Canal) whose locks were the determining factor. During World War One none of the *Braunschweig* class saw much active service, expect for patrol duties in the early years. All survived the war. *Lothringen* and *Preussen* were converted to motor minesweeper motherships in 1918/19 and the class was retained after the Armistice to form the initial equipment of the newly formed Reichsmarine. By the 1930s only *Hessen* remained, converted into a radio-controlled target vessel, until 1945 when she was taken over by the Soviets and renamed *Tsel*. Also still extant at the outbreak of World War Two was a 63m-long remnant of *Preussen* retained for explosive tests.

The last class of German pre-dreadnoughts were the *Deutschland*s, a marginal improvement upon the previous *Braunschweig*s. Visually they were very similar to the earlier vessels, except for the absence of gun-houses for the upper deck guns. These were carried in casemates like the guns on the battery deck—rather a retrograde step—but their calibre was increased to 17cm (6.7in). Internally their protection was improved. All five ships were active until about 1916, when they formed the 2nd Squadron of the High Seas Fleet (*Deutschland* as flagship). *Pommern* was sunk but the other four had long careers in the Reichsmarine after 1919. The Royal Navy's last pre-dreadnoughts were the two *Lord Nelson*s, in comparison with which the *Deutschland*s did not fare well on paper. The British ships had much heavier side armour but their horizontal protection was weaker (25mm against 40mm). The 12in gun remained the British calibre, of which four were shipped, but they also had ten 9.2in (23.3cm) guns. There was little to choose in speed; both had reciprocating machinery.

When the Royal Navy revealed *Dreadnought*, with her all big-gun armament of ten 12in guns compared with the customary four, and quadruple-shaft turbine machinery giving a speed of 21 knots, the other major naval powers were forced to reconsider their plans; Germany in particular, for the large increase in dimensions forced on designers to produce a reply to *Dreadnought* necessitated, in turn, a widening of the Kaiser Wilhelm Canal. That the appearance of *Dreadnought* disrupted the plans of rival powers is illustrated by the two-year gap between the laying down of the *Deutschland*s and the first of Germany's dreadnoughts, the *Nassau* class.

Although this class carried twelve main guns as opposed to *Dreadnought*'s ten, their disposition was inferior in that only eight could fire broadside, only two turrets being mounted on the centre-line. The reason for this was that turbine design in Germany had not advanced far enough for this mode of propulsion to be adopted for capital ships. In consequence, bulky triple-expansion machinery had to be shipped, which dictated internal arrangements to some extent. The 28cm gun was also retained so that the *Nassau*s were both slower (although not that much) and under-gunned compared with *Dreadnought*. On the other hand, the protection of *Nassau* was heavier at 35.2 per cent of weight as compared with 28 per cent for *Dreadnought*, although differences in the ways of weight allocation make even this simple comparison misleading. All four ships were active during the 1914–18 war both in the North Sea and Baltic. They formed half of the 1st Squadron at Jutland, where all but *Posen* received a couple of shell hits. *Westfalen* was torpedoed by the submarine *E23*

later that summer but was repaired. *Rheinland* went aground in the Aaland islands at the entrance to the Gulf of Finland in 1918 and was salvaged only after almost 6,500 tons of shells, coal, crew and armour had been taken off; she was never repaired. Of her sisters, *Nassau* was allocated to Japan and *Westfalen* and *Posen* to Great Britain; all were scrapped in 1920/24.

The *Heligoland* class of the 1908 programme introduced the 30.5cm (12in) gun but retained the triple-expansion machinery, although they were the last German battleships to do so. This also forced the retention of the same gun layout as that of the *Nassau*s, but in order to increase speed by $\frac{1}{2}$ knot, the number of boilers had to be increased to fifteen, which required a third funnel uptake. Considerable alteration was made to the machinery spaces, allowing all three boiler rooms to be placed between the magazines for the wing turrets. Another modification was the shipping of four-cylinder triple-expansion engines in lieu of three-cylinder. All except *Oldenburg* (1912) were completed in 1911 and saw service with the High Seas Fleet throughout the war, including Jutland. They were scrapped after the war but not before *Ostfriesland* had been used in the famous aircraft-versus-ships trials in the USA in 1921.

The 1909 and 1910 programme ships, the *Kaiser* class, introduced turbine propulsion for German capital ships, and it was even intended to fit one of the class (*Prinzregent Luitpold*) with a large cruising diesel. This radical change allowed a redisposition of the heavy guns, with the after turrets superfiring and the wing turrets reduced to two, staggered (reportedly) to allow cross-beam fire. The value of this was questionable, however, because of hull straining and blast effects on the opposite turret. The weight saved by the reduction in turrets was used to increase protection over that of the *Nassau*s so that maximum belt armour was 350mm, deck 60mm and the torpedo bulkhead now 40mm thick. The main machinery, still a triple-shaft arrangement, developed 31,000shp for a maximum designed speed of 23 knots. Three different turbine designs were employed—Parsons, AEG-Curtiss and Schichau—to gain operating experience. In the event, the diesel for *Prinzregent Luitpold* was not judged to be sufficiently far advanced to be used operationally and was never fitted; as a result, she remained a two-shaft ship with only fourteen boilers (instead of sixteen) and a maximum designed speed of 20 knots. On trials the class averaged 22.4 knots, with *Prinzregent Luitpold* making 21.7 knots. During World War One all were used on raids against the East Coast of England and all were at Jutland. In 1919 all five were scuttled at Scapa Flow.

The following *König* class of four ships finally saw the adoption of all centre-line turrets and all were intended to have a cruising diesel but, because experience in *Prinzregent Luitpold* was not forthcoming, they received turbines instead.

On trials they were generally slower than the *Kaiser*s, averaging just over 21 knots. Used on the East Coast raids and at Jutland, this class had a relatively active career by High Seas Fleet standards. Only *Kronprinz* (later renamed *Kronprinz Wilhelm*) remained undamaged at Jutland, but she was torpe-

armour (40.6 per cent of total weight) was the same as that of *König*. However, although the maximum belt thickness was also the same as *König*'s, the remainder was distributed differently. The main machinery was naturally turbine-driven and advances in boiler design allowed a reduction in number to fourteen, of which only three were oil-fired. Great Britain on the other hand had gone over completely to oil firing in the *Queen Elizabeth*s but required no fewer than 24 boilers for their 75,000shp to give 24 knots. The *Baden*s, however, were designed for only 22 knots. Two ships, *Baden* and *Bayern*, were provided for under the 1912 programme, one in 1913 (*Sachsen*) and one more in 1914 (*Württemberg*). These last two were to be somewhat different and *Sachsen* was to have had a diesel on the centre shaft. The first to complete was *Bayern* on 18 March 1916, but she was not operational by the time of the Jutland action. She later saw service in the Baltic and was mined and badly damaged in 1917. *Sachsen* and *Württemberg* both remained incomplete but afloat at the end of the war and were broken up. The two completed ships were scuttled at Scapa Flow, although *Baden* was beached and salved, being sunk as a target off Portsmouth in 1921. This was the final design of battleship laid down by the Kaiserliche Marine.

The appearance of Admiral Fisher's brainchild *Invincible*, the world's first battlecruiser, in the Royal Navy naturally called for a suitable reply. The original reply resulted in the armoured cruiser *Blücher*, designed from false intelligence and not therefore an adequate counterpart. A more powerful design was therefore proposed. This was *Von der Tann*, laid down by Blohm und Voss five days after *Invincible* was commissioned. She was armed with the standard 28cm (11in) gun in four twin turrets with the midships pair staggered to give a theoretical cross-beam firing ability. Introducing turbines to German capital ships, *Von der Tann* was designed for 24.8 knots with 42,000shp but exceeded that when forced. She was more heavily armoured than *Invincible* and altogether a better fighting ship; after a distinguished war record, she became one of the Scapa Flow casualties.

Two more Schlachtkreuzer were provided for under the 1909 programme. An improved *Von der Tann* design, they had a fifth twin turret, superfiring aft. A new 50-calibre 11in gun was carried and their protection was also better, but displacement rose by about 4,000 tons. *Goeben* was one of only two German warships in the Mediterranean at the start of World War One and became quite a thorn in the side of the Allies thereafter. As the Turkish *Yavuz*, she lasted until the early 1960s. Her sister ship *Moltke* had an active life, being twice torpedoed (by the submarine *E1* on 19 August 1915 and then by *E42* on 25 April 1918) before being scuttled at Scapa Flow.

Seydlitz was the next battlecruiser, similar to *Goeben* but with protection once again increased, a factor which saved the ship at the Dogger Bank when she received two heavy hits and both after turrets burned out. At Jutland *Seydlitz* sank the British battlecruiser *Queen Mary* but received 21 hits herself, as well as being struck by two torpedoes. Nevertheless, the ship managed to get home with over 5,000 tons of

doed and badly damaged by the submarine *J1* in November 1916, as was *Grosser Kurfürst* on the same occasion. This class also saw service in the Baltic where *König* sank the Russian battleship *Slava* in October 1917. All four were scuttled at Scapa Flow.

Despite the introduction of the 34.3cm (13.5in) gun by the Royal Navy in its 1909 *Orion* class, Germany had adhered to the 30.5cm weapon. However, the jump in calibre to 38cm(15in) in the *Queen Elizabeth*s could not be ignored and a new German gun was therefore developed. The adoption of the 38cm gun, actually 38.1cm SKL/45, required an increase in displacement of about 12.5 per cent over that of the *König*s, even with a reduction in the number of heavy guns to eight. With this design, the *Baden* class, the Kaiserliche Marine finally went over to all centre-line turrets, with two each forward and aft, 'B' and 'C' turrets being superfiring. Hull dimensions were not greatly increased and the weight of

water aboard. Three and a half months later *Seydlitz* was back in service, but was eventually scuttled in Scapa Flow in 1919.

It was not until 1911 that further battlecruisers were provided for and two more in the following years, 1912 and 1913. These ships, *Derfflinger*, *Lützow* and *Hindenburg*, were the last German battlecruisers to be completed and were considerably larger than their predecessors. Displacement rose to 31,500 tons full load, but without any commensurate increase in beam (the canal limitations!). They were well armoured and fast, with an average speed of $26\frac{1}{4}$ knots. The main change was in the main armament, raised to 30.5cm (12in) guns, which were disposed in four twin turrets, superfiring forward and aft. In appearance, they were flush-decked and handsome vessels, but internally the absence of a torpedo bulkhead behind the underwater torpedo tube compartment contributed to the loss of *Lützow* at Jutland. Of her sisters, *Derfflinger* also fought at Jutland where her gunfire sank *Queen Mary* and *Invincible*, while she was hit by 21 shells of various calibres. *Hindenburg* was completed too late for Jutland and both she and *Derfflinger* were eventually scuttled at Scapa Flow.

One more class of battlecruiser was put in hand before the war ended, this being the *Mackensen* class, the name ship of

Right: *Württemberg* remained incomplete in 1919. (WBB)

which was laid down in 1915 under the 1914 programme. Three more ships, *Prinz Eitel Friedrich*, *Fürst Bismarck* and *Graf Spee* were also laid down in 1915, but the first two were never actually named as they were not launched by the war's end. These powerful ships would have displaced 35,300 tons and been armed with eight 35.56cm (14in) guns, disposed as in *Derfflinger*, but none was ever completed. A similar fate befell the even larger *Ersatz Yorck* design, of which four ships armed with 38.1cm (15in) guns were laid down in 1916. Work proceeded slowly and none was ever launched. Originally they were intended to be of the *Mackensen* design but the adoption of the 15in gun in the Royal Navy led to a recasting of their plans.

On the outbreak of World War One in August 1914 the *Kaiserliche Marine* possessed four capital ships armed with 11in guns and eleven with 12in guns with two more completing. Five battlecruisers with 11in guns were also in service. The Royal Navy on the other hand had ten 12in-gunned ships, twelve 13.5in-gunned and twelve battlecruisers, one-third of which had 13.5in guns. Two battleships and two battlecruisers were completing. Great Britain therefore had a considerable superiority in numbers and a decided advantage strategically because of geographical considerations. As a result, the Kaiserliche Marine was unable to break the British stranglehold on the North Sea and in fact never seriously challenged it. Atlantic operation was impossible even if they did break out because Germany possessed no overseas bases and the technology of the day did not allow continuous deep water operation in the absence of any means of replenishment at sea. Thus actions in the North Sea were few and far between, with Jutland the high point, and in the early years German activities were mainly of a short-ranged raiding nature. More offensive action took place in the Baltic against the Russians and *Goeben* was active in the Black Sea against the same adversary.

Wartime construction increased the disparity between the opponents for Great Britain added another seven battleships (ten of which had 15in guns) as well as two more battlecruisers armed with 15in guns. On the other hand, the High Seas Fleet received only five more battleships and three battlecruisers. However, no German battleship and only one battlecruiser was lost during hostilities (ignoring the large armoured cruiser *Blücher*, designed orginally as a reply to *Invincible*), whereas the Royal Navy lost two battleships (neither in a ship-to-ship action) and three battlecruisers, all at Jutland. Pre-dreadnoughts have not been considered.

The First World War at sea could not have been decisively won by the High Seas Fleet on its own but the U-boats came very close to it and the gradual escalation of the U-boat programme soon caused cut-backs in the large warships programme. It was the German Army which was eventually defeated and with it the Kaiser's Empire—in reality, the Navy could only sit back and watch. The surrender terms required the High Seas Fleet to be interned in a neutral port but they were actually sent to Scapa Flow where they languished until that fateful day, 21 June 1919, on which the scuttling took place.

1. REBUILDING THE FLEET, 1919–1935

With the scuttling of the High Seas Fleet and the distribution of the remainder of the modern ships among the victorious Allies, Germany was left with but a handful of over-age pre-dreadnoughts with which to police her coastal waters. Under the terms of the Versailles Treaty, Germany was permitted to retain only six battleships with two more in reserve, and there were similar restrictions upon other categories of warship; aircraft, aircraft-carriers and submarines were totally forbidden. There were also strict controls on man-power, methods of recruiting, length of service, etc, and other restrictions on fortifications. All in all, the Treaty of Versailles was a punitive document, but what else could Germany expect? Nevertheless, its very nature led to strong resentment in Germany and in the course of time to its circumvention, initially covertly but in later years more openly, until its final abrogation.

As far as battleships were concerned, there remained to the newly founded Reichsmarine only the pre-dreadnoughts *Braunschweig*, *Elsass* and *Hessen*, completed in 1904 and 1905, and three *Deutschland* class ships, *Hannover*, *Schlesien* and *Schleswig-Holstein*, completed between 1907 and 1908. *Preussen*, *Lothringen* and *Zähringen*, the latter dating from 1902, were also retained in subsidiary categories.

These elderly vessels could obviously present no threat to the Western powers but were probably intended as a bulwark against the designs of Soviet Russia to the east, a task with which they could possibly have coped, given the condition of the Soviet Fleet in 1921.

The ships of the older *Braunschweig* class had been paid off and disarmed even before the end of World War One and were being used as depot ships and accommodation hulks. However, in the absence of anything better, they were taken in hand for refit in 1923, when their superstructure was altered, part of the secondary armament landed and two single above-water torpedo tubes fitted forward and aft in casemates just below the main gun turrets. Little else was done and the ships recommissioned between 1924 and 1925, being used thereafter for training purposes. *Braunschweig* and *Elsass* were both finally paid off on 31 March 1931, but *Hessen* was not paid off until 14 November 1934; she was subsequently converted into a radio-controlled target ship at Wilhelmshaven Naval Yard on the lines of the earlier *Zähringen* (converted during 1926/27). *Hessen* differed from *Zähringen* in that she was given heavy armouring to absorb battle practice hits. Even this proved insufficient and in 1938 she was given an extra above-water belt 30–40mm thick from water-line to upper deck, composed of the new *Wh* armour. This new protection withstood heavy hits from the main armament of *Tirpitz* and other capital ships very well and *Hessen* survived World War Two. *Zähringen*, on the other hand, was sunk by air attack at Gotenhafen on 18 December 1944. Both ships were controlled by old torpedo boats converted for the purpose, *Blitz* (ex *T141*, ex *S141*) for *Zähringen* and *Komet* (ex *T123*, ex *S23*) for *Hessen*.

Hannover, the most elderly of the *Deutschland*s left to the Reichsmarine, was refitted in 1920-21 when, like the earlier class, she received torpedo tubes but in this case a pair of twin mountings in a casemate to port and starboard forward only. Otherwise she was little altered externally. Almost ten years later a second refit (1929–30) equipped her with a new bridge structure and tubular fighting mast with a heavy foretop. *Hannover* was eventually paid off in 1935 and stripped of her guns and equipment but she was not broken up. Instead, she was used for shock test work in connection with magnetic ground mines, her intended conversion for use as a target ship for aircraft having been rescinded on the outbreak of World War Two. Eventually she was broken up in 1944/46 at Bremerhaven.

The remaining two pre-dreadnoughts, *Schlesien* and *Schleswig-Holstein*, had much longer active careers. The former had been used as an accommodation ship in 1917 and by 1918 was in use as a cadet training ship. She was paid off for many years but in 1924 was taken in hand for refit at Wilhelmshaven. The bridge structure was rebuilt and a heavy tubular foremast and top fitted. The forward funnels were trunked into one after the conversion of eight of her

Below: *Hannover* in Reichsmarine days. Note the casement torpedo-tube forward. Compare this view with that of *Pommern*. (WBB)

boilers to oil-firing. Like *Braunschweig* she received four single trainable torpedo tubes. Finally, the secondary armament was modernized and new 15cm (5.9in) guns fitted. In a further refit in 1938/39 the remaining four coal-fired boilers were removed and their uptake as well. *Schleswig-Holstein* was similarly refitted but did not undergo the 1938/39 refit. Both ships were extensively used in the training role prior to 1939, making several long overseas voyages.

Among the conditions of the Versailles Treaty was that no ship could be replaced until twenty years after the launching date in the case of battleships and also that new vessels of this type must not displace more than 10,000 tons. By these means the Allies had sought to shackle the German Fleet and ensure that it could never again pose a threat to them. However, the very age of the ships left to the Reichsmarine negated much of this intention, for on the basis of completion dates *Preussen* could be replaced in 1922 and even the youngest, *Schleswig-Holstein*, in 1926. Had the Treaty condi-

tions been thought out in a better fashion and Germany been allowed to retain, say, three 1916 ships, no replacement could have been allowed in theory until 1936.

Some thought of the replacement of these old vessels was begun in the early 1920s, when a number of ideas were studied. Given the restriction of 10,000 tons, the options were of course limited, for these parameters were tighter than the ships they were to replace, in terms of displacement tonnage. What kind of ship was to be built naturally depended upon contemporary strategic thought, for the battleship was still the deterrent of the day. The Allies had intended that Germany's strategic horizons be limited essentially to the Baltic Sea and the German Bight, and certainly there was a good deal for Germany to consider in the former theatre. Here was her longest coastline, Poland and the Soviet Union represented very real enemies, and the existence of the 'Polish Corridor' cut off East Prussia from the Reich. Moreover, Poland had established naval forces on a new base, Gdynia, from where they could interrupt communication with East Prussia. France too was considered to be a possible enemy, not surprisingly in view of history; and the recent political ties between France and Poland, established in the 1920s, could not be ignored either, for an attack on Poland could conceivably result in an attack on Germany from the west.

During the course of a Flag Officer's conference in December 1922 the main tasks of the Navy were defined as follows:

(a) The priority was to secure Germany's trade routes to the outside world.

(b) When threatened by North Sea or Baltic powers, the fleet was to be concentrated in the Baltic as the chances of successful action were deemed more hopeful in this theatre. The defence of the North Sea coast was to be left to local forces.

However, it was acknowledged that the forces available precluded any real hope of fulfilling (a) if the enemy was a major power and that blue water operations were no longer a possibility. The strategic horizons were limited to a minor war in restricted waters for the foreseeable future.

Most of the Navy's planning and war game activities during the early 1920s was therefore centred around scenarios which either envisaged an enemy attempting to force its way into the Baltic via the Skagerrak, or localized conflicts with the Baltic sea powers. Thus France (whose political ties with Poland obliged her to be prepared to send a cruiser squadron into the Baltic to assist the Poles in wartime) featured strongly in these scenarios, as did various other permutations of France, Belgium, Poland, Russia and even Denmark being enemy powers. Poland, in fact, possessed little in the way of a navy in the early 1920s but her army was much larger than that of Germany. At the same time, the existence of the 'Corridor' separated East Prussia from the rest of Germany. This province was barred from sustaining any warlike industrial activities and stock-piles of military supplies were also limited under the peace treaty provisions. In addition, the whole of the Baltic coast from Schleswig-Holstein to the River Oder was disarmed. Thus, one of the duties of the Navy was to secure communications with and re-supply East Prus-

sia, in the event of hostilities with Poland. By the end of the 1920s studies were being made for attacks on Gdynia. The German Navy in the early and middle of the 1920s could in all probability have contained the fledgling Polish fleet but two factors were of great concern to Germany.

First, there was the already mentioned threat of a French squadron entering the Baltic in support of Poland. The strength of this French commitment under the terms of the Franco-Polish treaty was believed to amount to two armoured cruisers, four cruisers, four destroyers and three submarines. It was not believed that France would risk her larger battleships of the *Courbet* class in the shallow and restricted waters of the Baltic, so that the likely opponent would be no more powerful than a *Danton*-class cuirassé d'escadre (pre-dreadnought), *Voltaire* usually being the ship quoted. These ships, completed in 1911, displaced about 18,000 tons and were armed with four 30.5cm (13in) guns in two twin turrets and twelve 24cm guns. With a designed speed of about 19 knots, they had a maximum thickness belt armour of 270mm. Three remained to France out of a class of five, *Voltaire*, *Condorcet* and *Diderot*.

The second worry was the expansion planned for the Polish fleet, a building programme having been initiated in 1924. This envisaged the construction of two cruisers, six destroyers, twelve torpedo boats and twelve submarines over

a period of twelve years. In the event financial restraints curtailed this programme; only two large destroyers and three submarines materialized. Nevertheless, this was not known by Germany at the time, when a replacement for the elderly *Braunschweig*s was being considered. It therefore appeared possible that the small, weak and obsolete German fleet might well be caught between two enemy forces, one light, fast and modern to the east and the other slow, armoured and heavily armed to the west. Comparisons were drawn between the capabilities of the *Braunschweig* class and *Voltaire*, which demonstrated the inferiority of the former. It was considered that the French ship could deliver 6.25 tonnes of shells per minute to a range of 35km, while in reply, *Braunschweig* could fire 1.92 tonnes to a range of 23km. This comparison was a little vague and included both 30.5cm and 24cm guns for the French ship and was based on a possibly optimistic rate of fire and range on the part of the French guns. In terms of speed and protection there was probably little to choose between the two ships.

When it came to considering the replacement of *Preussen*, therefore, the first of the old pre-dreadnoughts to reach the age when the treaty allowed it, the decision as to what type of ship to build was not simple. Not only had economic, manning and strategic factors to be considered, but also the severe restrictions imposed by the Versailles Treaty. This

Above: The battle squadron in Reichsmarine days. *Hessen* is in the foreground. (WBB)

allowed replacement battleships to displace no more than 10,000 tons (i.e., less than that of the older ships), at a time when other nations were designing 10,000-ton *cruisers*. The Treaty did not, however, impose any limitation on the maximum gun calibre, it obviously being considered that any advance beyond the existing 28cm would entail such sacrifice in armour or speed to meet the 10,000-ton limit that no useful fighting ship could be developed. There were also the more practical aspects to be considered—the Danzig Navy Yard was no longer in Germany, Kiel dockyard had been closed down and that at Wilhelmshaven was in a state of chaos. In addition, only the rump of a Constructors Department remained, with many specialists having left.

When the Provisional Reichsmarine had been established on 16 April 1919, Konteradmiral (K.Ad.) von Trotha (a former Chief of Staff to Admiral Scheer) was appointed its chief. Unfortunately some of the effects of the Kapp *putsch* in the spring of 1920 tarnished this officer's reputation and he was forced to resign, being succeeded by K.Ad. Michaelis in July. His tenure of the post was brief, however, and his successor, Admiral Behncke (appointed on 31 August 1920), was therefore in command when the Reichsmarine was legally constituted by decree on 23 March 1921. Thus it had fallen to Behncke to initiate the first discussions on the ship replacement question in 1920.

These led initially to two schools of thought: (a) a well protected but slow monitor; and (b) a hard-hitting well armed cruiser type but with little armour. However, (a) was unpopular with the Navy as it would reduce the fleet to a coast defence force and it was desirable to retain at least a pretence of a high seas capability. In 1923 a sketch design (known as II/10) for option (a) envisaged a 10,000-ton vessel armed with four 38cm guns, powered by a twin-shaft turbine plant capable of 22 knots. The protection included a 200mm waterline belt and an armoured deck 30mm thick (see Fig. 1). This protective scheme was considered too weak but despite various permutations of guns, speed and armouring being juggled with, it was eventually decided that this avenue was not worth pursuing. As a result, the (b) option was examined and sketch design I/10 drawn up. This vessel was armed with eight 21cm (8.26in) guns in four twin turrets, two forward and two aft, and powered by a twin-turbine installation of 80,000shp to give a speed of 32 knots. The consequence of the increase in speed was a considerable reduction in the protective scheme, viz. 80mm belt and 30mm deck. In appearance this design was remarkably similar to the new light cruiser *Emden* (see Fig. 2). This option proved no more satisfactory than design II/10 and in the absence of any other ideas, design work lapsed in 1923.

On 1 October 1924 Admiral Behncke, who had headed the Navy in the difficult years since 1920, retired and was replaced by Admiral Zenker. This officer had had a distinguished career at sea, having commanded the battlecruiser *Von der Tann* at Jutland. He set about resurrecting the plans for replacement capital ships with enthusiasm. Re-examination of the previous monitor and cruiser options resulted in both being judged unsatisfactory. The monitor could fulfil some but not all of the required demands, while the cruiser was fast but poorly armed. Thinking once again turned to a proper battleship type.

The question of the main armament calibre remained open to discussion because it was not stipulated in the Treaty of Versailles. As a result, it had initially been believed in Behncke's time that 38cm (or 15in) might be possible. However, it now appeared unlikely that the Allies would permit this and instead the less politically explosive 30.5cm gun was chosen. This led to Entwurf II/30 which was a 132m long ship armed with six 30.5cm in three twin turrets, with the after pair being in echelon (see Fig. 3). Belt armour was 200mm maximum. The interesting feature of this project, however, was the adoption of diesel propulsion. It was a three-shaft design, having a maximum speed of 21 knots, diesels being chosen in anticipation of significant weight economies. Germany had a vast amount of experience with diesel propulsion for, in addition to having built many hundreds of U-boats during World War One, she had even planned the installation of a large cruising diesel in the battleship *Prinzregent Luitpold* well before that war. This was to have been a Germania six-cylinder double-acting engine driving the centre shaft. In the event, despite the engine undergoing shore trials, it was never actually fitted. From II/30 onwards all designs were intended primarily for diesel machinery, although a turbine-driven secondary alternative was usually sketched. Turbo-electric and diesel-electric options were also considered from time to time. In fact, II/30 was not popular because of its poor secondary armament (merely three single 8.8cm) and another proposal, IV/30, was put forward instead.

This proposal was unusual in that the three twin 30.5cm turrets were all forward, presumably to reduce the citadel length and thereby save weight. It also included two twin 15cm mountings. This was not acceptable either, nor were some other basically similar proposals with 10.5cm secondary armament. The side protection for these designs was 160–180mm. Another proposal, V/30, had 180mm belt armour, with 200mm on the conning tower. This had a triple 30.5cm turret forward and aft, as well as two twin 15cm and four 8.8cm guns.

Lengthy discussions took place between all interested parties without a consensus emerging, so that a major conference was called for 15 May 1925 to thrash out the various points of view. The military departments thought that the armour was too weak on all the proposals, and the Weapons Office demanded better turret and barbette protection. This the Construction Office could not agree to, as with three twin 30.5cm turrets there was insufficient reserve for improved protection. Two representatives from the Marinekommandoamt professed themselves satisfied with only four 30.5cm guns, on the grounds that with a rate of fire of 25 seconds per barrel, this was sufficient. Weight thus saved could obviously be used to improve protection. On balance it was agreed that Entwurf II/30 was the least unfavourable design and the Construction Office was asked to produce a sketch design based upon four 30.5cm guns. The secondary armament was to be four to six 15cm and three twin 8.8cm. With these parameters, the maximum possible armour thickness was to be ascertained.

In fact, these discussions were somewhat academic as the gun calibre question still remained unresolved. 30.5cm guns were allowed to Germany, but only for coast defence purposes; moreover, only one new gun could be built per year. However, it was pointed out that there were in existence three reserve guns which could be diverted to arm Panzerschiff A. Civilian ministry officials held the view that the Allies were most unlikely to allow anything other than 28cm but almost all the naval officers were opposed to this calibre. Nevertheless, practicality won the day and of the four new proposals tabled, two were armed with 28cm guns. These two, I/28 and II/28, differed mainly in the arrangments of the 28cm guns, the former having one triple turret fore and aft, and the latter design three twin turrets, of which the two after ones were in echelon. Both designs had two twin 15cm guns. I/28 had six to eight 8.8cm but II/28 only four in two twin mountings. Of the 30.5cm proposals, VI/30 had a twin turret forward and aft, while VII/30 had the turrets in echelon all forward. All four designs were three-shaft layouts for 21 knots.

By now it was becoming imperative that a decision be reached on the gun calibre if progress were to be made. Laying-down dates were already slipping back. Accordingly, Admiral Zenker was pressed for a decision and a further conference was called for 27 May 1925. That morning a preliminary discussion took place before the main meeting on the subject of the 30.5cm gun, when it was suggested that, as a last resort, perhaps the Allies could be asked for a ruling on the matter! It was also pointed out that with the French still in occupation of the Ruhr, Krupp could not deliver more than one gun per year. No agreement was reached at this preliminary discussion, so the whole matter was debated again. Zenker eventually opted for *II/30*, but further argument ensued over the flak armament; in the end, Zenker put off the decision until August. His basic view was that fire power was more important than protection. Meanwhile the Construction Office was fully occupied with light cruisers and torpedo boats, which were far easier to design within the constraints of the Treaty limits. It was, however, envisaged that Panzerschiff A be included in the 1926 budget. All this delay meant that the elderly Linienschiffe had to soldier on.

Political events now seemed to come to the aid of the Navy for in July France evacuated the Ruhr, whereupon Krupp's became available for naval work once more, from the beginning of August. On the other hand, Deutsche Werke and the Navy Dockyard at Willhelmshaven were about to lay off men due to lack of orders. This stimulated discussion again over the replacement question. Following the 27 May conference the Construction Office had worked out two new designs, I/35 (Fig. 4) and VIII/30 (Fig. 5). The former was smaller and slower but better armed and protected than the latter but was in reality only a monitor type. Once again, neither was acceptable and by 13 August Zenker decided to order a light cruiser (*Köln*) and a half flotilla of torpedo boats for the next year's construction, in lieu of a capital ship.

This delay and procrastination was especially unfortunate for the Navy because the economic position was becoming worse (naval construction was expensive) and the Navy had its own problems, culminating in the Lohmann incident in 1927. Lohmann was a naval officer who had the responsibility for promoting activities banned by the Versailles Treaty by means of support for thinly disguised 'commercial' undertakings. Although his affairs were in order financially—he had not made personal use of naval funds—the politicians were angry that funds were being diverted for purposes they knew nothing about. As a result, there was a noticeable reluctance on the part of officials and politicians to exert themselves in support of the Navy. This, together with the still considerable body of opinion against any form of rearmament, delayed the approval of any new capital ship. The Lohmann affair led to the resignation of the Defence Minister, Dr Gessler (a man with a keen interest in the Navy's policies), to the obvious detriment of the Reichsmarine.

Not only were there political problems, there were also severe financial restraints, for Weimar Germany was in the midst of horrific inflation. Nevertheless, the money allocated for naval expenditure had risen from 104 million Rm to 233 million Rm between 1924 and 1927, of which, 30 per cent was for new construction. It was hoped that this trend would continue—hopefully to 400–500 million by 1936—but inflation effectively defeated these plans for the moment.

The Fleet manoeuvres of 1926 brought a new twist to the discussions for as a result of these, K.Ad. Pfeiffer, an officer hitherto committed to 30.5cm as the minimum acceptable gun calibre, now asked for a design to be prepared based upon a fast battleship or a heavily armed cruiser. In response to this demand, two new sketches were drawn up, I/M26 and II/M26. The first carried six 28cm guns and eight 12cm flak at 28 knots with 100mm belt armour (see Fig. 6). *II/M26* differed in that it shipped six 3.7cm in addition. At a new conference on 12 January 1927 reference was made to the previous favourite, Entwurf II/30, and the advances in technology which promised better guns, protection and speed. This had led to the development of designs I/M26 and II/M26, of which the latter attracted some support. Zenker, although previously a proponent of guns over armour, now changed his views and declared that a 'battleship-cruiser' had only restricted possibilities. In his view this type was insufficiently protected to be able to defend the entrances to the Baltic. However, there were others who felt that this fast well-armed type might have political merit by thwarting the Washington Treaty restrictions and thereby forcing the Allied powers to invite Germany in from the cold and back to the conference table. This promising concept was unfortunately not pursued. Instead Zenker ordered a powerful battleship design to be drawn up. Matters were thrown into confusion once more. A decision was desperately needed, not least because it would dictate which yard was to lay down Kreuzer E (*Leipzig*). Both K.Ad. Oldekop, head of the Allgemeinen Marineamt, and the Yard departments pressed for a decision and wanted finance included for one ship in the 1928 estimates. However, Geheimrat Presse, Chief of the

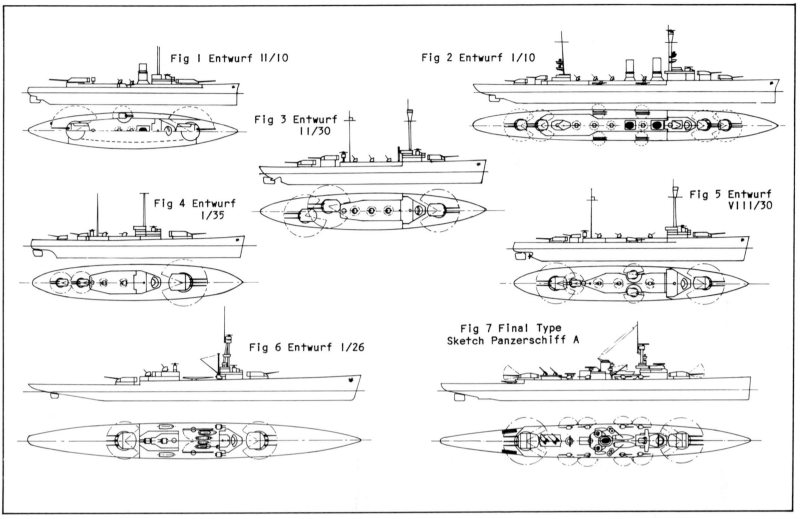

Fig 1 Entwurf II/10

Fig 2 Entwurf I/10

Fig 3 Entwurf II/30

Fig 4 Entwurf 1/35

Fig 5 Entwurf VIII/30

Fig 6 Entwurf 1/26

Fig 7 Final Type Sketch Panzerschiff A

Construction Office, pointed out that the money could be included pending a decision as the cost would be the same, the high cost of engines for the fast ship being offset by the extra cost of armour on the better protected project. Zenker therefore decided to include finance in the 1928 estimates.

At another conference, held on 7 March 1927, it was again attempted to decide on the gun calibre and type of vessel to be constructed. It would appear that by now there was a good degree of agreement as to what was required between the Construction Office and Marinekommandoamt—a fast type of vessel. Even so, a slow design of only 18 knots surfaced yet again, but the short hull length required by the diesels for this speed did not allow sufficient deck space to dispose of a useful armament. Only if both turrets were forward could the various demands be met without lengthening the ship. This was another monitor concept and in consequence was not acceptable. However, the Construction Office now put forward another proposal with good gun disposition an sufficient space to install 38,500shp for a speed of 24 knots. This met general approval, except that a higher speed was re-

quired despite the fact that only 18 knots was attributed to their possible French adversaries. For the first time now, the theory of out-gunning anything it could not escape from and being faster than any heavier gunned adversary, surfaced in the discussions. The line of development took a distinct step away from the battleship idea, towards a lightly armoured but fast ship with 28cm guns.

The choice of 28cm seems to have been decided mainly by the impossibility of producing a suitable design on 10,000 tons with 30.5cm guns; possible Allied objections were considered irrelevant. In June Zenker informed his senior Admirals that agreement appeared to have been reached. The requirements were:

(a) a ship capable of defeating the French battleships

(b) capable of superior speed over 10,000-ton Washington cruisers to be able to support the 15cm light cruisers

As both (a) and (b) could not be fulfilled on 10,000 tons, two separate paths could be pursued: a well-armoured heavily gunned ship of medium speed for (a), or a fast lightly armoured ship of good radius of action for (b). This latter ship was to be superior to the Washington cruisers and faster than any battleship. Four main design projects had previously been promulgated:

Type A:	4 × 38cm	Type B2:	6 × 30.5cm
	250mm armour		299mm armour
	18kt		21kt
Type B:	6 × 30.5cm	Type C:	6 × 28cm
	250mm armour		100mm armour
	18kt		26–27kt

The first three types had been exhaustively discussed and argued since 1925, which left only Type C as a viable option. Zenker proposed, therefore, that two such ships be constructed, after which the political situation could be reviewed, when it might be possible to build a more powerful type.

The Type C design (see Fig. 7) fulfilled only the minimum requirements as far as armour and speed were concerned. It was essentially design I/M26. Armour could not be increased because the hull was not strong enough and the speed could only be raised at the expense of either gun calibre or protection. Still unclarified was the secondary armament and the torpedo outfit, the latter being considered of importance. Submerged tubes were favoured but these could only be installed by reducing bunker space, with a consequent reduction in endurance. The preferred secondary armament was six or eight 12.5cm guns, either in shielded high-angle mountings or low-angle in twin turrets.

The problem of constructing a ship of 10,000 tons displacement was now well on the way to being solved, after some eighteen different sketch designs had been examined. The result was very much a 'political' ship but it reflected great credit on the head of the Construction Office, Dr (Ing)h.c. Paul Presse, and his colleagues that a design appeared at all. On 11 April 1928 Admiral Zenker and Presse signed their approval of the 'Tye Sketch', thereby clearing the way for construction to begin. Preliminary drawings and building data were passed to the yard only four months later, despite a heavy work load and shortage of man power in the Construction Office, and on 28 December 1928 the full drawings were released. The final design conformed in general with Proposal C of 1927, except that 100mm belt armour proved impossible to achieve. All the secondary armament was shipped in single shielded mountings with two 8.8cm SKC/25 mountings on the centre-line aft.

Admiral Zenker resigned his post in September 1928 because he felt some responsibility for the Lohmann affair referred to earlier. His successor was Admiral Raeder, who took over as Chef der Marineleitung on 15 October. Further development of the Panzerschiffe was now under his direction.

By the time that the third projected Panzerschiff came to be seriously discussed, in 1929, the question of the effects of Panzerschiffe A and B upon the world's naval powers, especially France, had to be taken into consideration. It was believed that France had a projected armoured ship under development for completion in 1930/31, which would displace 17/18,000 tonnes, carry six 30.5cm guns and have a 150mm armour belt. If this were the case, then the French ship

would outclass *Deutschland* and her sisters. Such a design was in fact mooted from 1924, but with eight 30.5cm guns in two quadruple turrets, which was to lead over ten years later to the completion of *Dunkerque*. There was a view within the German Admiralty in December 1929 that a repeat Panzerschiff B had some merits, but on the other hand France could not be ignored. However, if Panzershiff C were to be given the same speed as the projected French designs, then the German ship's armament would have to be reduced to only eight or nine 21cm guns—which was of course unthinkable. This led once more to consideration of the monitor type but this found little favour.

Two main possibilities were therefore envisaged. First, to build a repeat Panzerschiff B without regard to the French but give better protection to the secondary guns, heavier flak and fit her out as a fleet flagship, even at the cost of deleting the torpedoes. The advantages of this option were that little new design work load was involved; it was simple and cheap. On the other hand, the low speed was a disadvantage in comparison with the French designs and reduced the effectiveness of the ship.

The second option was to retain the existing armour but to reduce the main armament to nine 24cm guns, in three triple turrets (the weights being estimated as almost equivalent to two triple 28cm) and, because of the increased rate of fire of the smaller calibre gun, the secondary armament could be dispensed with, the weight saved being used to uprate the machinery. It was estimated that by this means speed could be increased by $1\frac{1}{2}$ to 2 knots. The advantages of this proposal were that the superiority over the Washington 10,000-ton cruisers would be retained, and that it might still be possible to strike an effective blow against an enemy battleship, but with her superior speed the ship could avoid contact if desired. The French 17,000-ton design could probably be outrun. Finally, fewer men would be required and fire control would be simplified. If one turret were disabled, then only one-third of the total fire power would be lost as opposed to 50 per cent with Panzerschiff B. The disadvantages were that the chance of an effective hit were reduced with the lighter calibre and that, while simplicity and a single ammunition calibre might indicate cheapness, the design would have to be re-cast at considerable expense. Also it was pointed out that the dangers of being overhauled by the French ship were only reduced, *not* eliminated.

The basic questions posed therefore were:

(a) Given a 10,000-tonne limit and nine 24 cm guns, was 30 knots plus possible with the same protection as Panzerschiffe A and B? If 'yes', should design work be started?

(b) If 'no', or if the speed of the French ship was found to be greater than 30/31 knots, then AIII, the Marineausbildungsabteilung*, favoured continuing the existing type.

These proposals set a few hares running and it would appear that some considered the reduced-calibre ship a proposal favoured by AIII. In fact, it was intended to stimulate

*Literally Training Office, but this department was actively concerned with military aspects of warship specification. Later it became AIV.

discussion as to the direction in which the Navy should proceed, and it was simply suggested that it might be worth while examining a lower calibre, if a speed in excess of 30 knots could be guaranteed. Any firm proposals were dependent upon obtaining more accurate details of just what type of ship the French were planning.

Political considerations had a great deal of consequence at this time as far as battleship construction was concerned, just as they have on the nuclear missile question today. During the decade following the end of World War One there was a strong movement to end all possibility of another holocaust and disarmament was the buzz-word. At the Washington Naval Conference in 1921/22, it was agreed to halt capital ship construction for ten years, a decision which did not affect Germany as she was not invited; and in any event, she was already bound by the Versailles Treaty. Subsequent conferences in Rome (1924) and Geneva in 1927 proved fruitless but in 1930, at the London Naval Conference, it was proposed by Great Britain and the United States that the ban on battleship construction be extended for another five years. Both France and Italy objected because Germany had begun the construction of Panzerschiff A. Britain, in an attempt to prevent the various agreements falling apart, sought to persuade Germany to abandon her battleship replacement plan until 1937. This Germany refused to do, but the political situation was nevertheless very delicate. It is in the context of this background that the discussions regarding continuance of the Panzerschiff design, particularly of 'C', should be seen. Not only had the German Naval Staff to be wary of being seen to flout the Versailles restrictions; they had also to take notice of the deliberations of the major sea powers and make guesses about what treaty limits might be defined, should international agreement ever come about.

In refusing to cancel the Panzerschiffe programme, Germany argued that, even with these ships, she could not consider herself defendable against even minor powers, who moreover were not denied submarines and aircraft. The existence of the Panzerschiffe should not, according to Germany, be seen as a threat to her neighbours. Basically Germany was not willing to cancel unless other powers abandoned submarines and bomber aircraft, which was highly unlikely.

Although Panzerschiff B had been laid down in 1931, the future construction programme remained unclear in 1932 because, not only was the international situation in disarray, but also the political stability of Germany was being undermined by the rise in strength of the National Socialist Party, led by Adolf Hitler. Further to confuse matters, the new Defence Minister of the von Papen government, General von Schleicher, had, during a radio broadcast on 26 July, intimated that Germany might well declare herself free of the Versailles restrictions if the major powers rearmed and prevented Germany from continuing her programme. All these factors bore upon the Ship Replacement Conference, held on 28 June 1932 and chaired by Admiral Raeder. It was re-established that replacement of the elderly Linienschiffe was necessary on several grounds:

(a) They were inferior to all modern battleships and even pre-dreadnoughts in terms of speed, guns and protection.

(b) They were capable of only 16–18 knots and therefore not fast enough to intervene and support hard-pressed cruisers.

(c) Their internal sub-division was poor; the instance of *Hannover*'s grounding in 1924 being cited.

(d) Repairs and modernization costs were unrealistic.

(e) Morale grounds.

They were not therefore up to their intended task, direct coastal defence and the prevention of enemy landings. As far as trade protection was concerned, they were useless. The general consensus was that the Panzerschiffe programme should be continued, but if 'C' could not, as intended, be ordered on 1 October 1932 on pressing political grounds, which direction should the Navy move? Initially it was suggested that the destroyer programme be brought forward, but a new cruiser could also be considered, possibly a repeat *Leipzig*. If, however, Germany were freed from the shackles of Versailles by 1 October, then the Navy would favour the construction of a much more powerful ship than the existing Panzerschiff design. This was because the new French design for *Dunkerque* completely outclassed it and rendered obsolete the reason for it—an ability to run away from anything it could not defeat. There were therefore strong military reasons for not continuing the Panzerschiff, a product solely of Versailles.

The possession of capital ships brought important political, economic and military advantages which cruisers and destroyers could not do to the same degree. Their existence raised the chances of political alliances; gave the ability to defend German neutrality in the event of a conflict between Great Britain and the USSR; strengthened Germany's position at the League of Nations; and were important for showing the flag as an advertisement for Germany industry. Furthermore, as was pointed out during the controversy over the question of Panzerschiff A, the ship would provide work for 3,000 men.

The pressure was therefore towards a third capital ship and Raeder favoured a bigger design of 15/18,000 tonnes, armed with three triple 28cm turrets, to avoid the construction of new guns. As an alternative, the emergency installation of four twin 20.3cm turrets in a Panzerschiff hull was ordered to be examined, presumably with an eye to any future treaty agreements and restrictions. The proposal to build a new light cruiser was discarded on the grounds that *Leipzig* did not compare well with current foreign designs. A break in capital ship construction was considered undesirable because replacement of the old pre-dreadnoughts would be delayed and there would therefore be a gap in construction until about 1937. In the end it was decided that if, by October 1932, the situation with regard to the Versailles Treaty was still unclear, the Navy would go ahead with Panzerschiff C as a repeat of the earlier designs with the type of machinery to be decided after experience with the motors of *Leipzig* and the first results of the minelayer *Bremse*'s diesel installation. Panzerschiff C, in fact, eventually retained the diesel propulsion.

2. THE PANZERSCHIFFE

Panzerschiff A: Deutschland

DESIGN AND CONSTRUCTION

Ersatz Preussen, the first of the Panzerschiffe and destined to be named *Deutschland*, was ordered on 17 August 1928 and laid down at the Deutsche Werke yard on 9 February 1929 (ship's book date). Supervising her construction was Schiffsbaudirektor Lofflund assisted by Ob. Marinebaurat Malsius and Marinebaurat Senst.

The hull, constructed mainly from Schiffsbaustahl II, was longitudinally framed, with a centre keel between frames $6\frac{1}{2}$ to 154 and between 169 to $173\frac{1}{2}$. In between these stations the main centre-line bulkhead formed the keel; five longitudinal frames were worked in either side of the keel. Longitudinal I extended from frame $6\frac{1}{2}$ to $15\frac{1}{2}$, $63\frac{1}{2}$ to $123\frac{1}{2}$, and $154\frac{1}{2}$ to $173\frac{1}{2}$ with the inner side longitudinal bulkhead forming the missing portions. Longitudinal II extended from frame $26\frac{3}{4}$ to $173\frac{1}{2}$ except between $136\frac{4}{10}$ and $144\frac{6}{10}$ in which area the turret

longitudinal bulkhead replaced it. Longitudinal III formed the edge of the side double bottom and, between frames 71 and 116, formed the side docking keel. This longitudinal was also partly continuous with the outer side longitudinal bulkhead. Longitudinal IV extended from frame $41\frac{4}{10}$ to 154 and V from 63 to $112\frac{3}{2}$. These longitudinals were welded variously oil- and or watertight, according to the requirements of the double-bottom bunkerage arrangements. Transverse frames were positioned every 1,500mm, welded to the longitudinal frames and the shell plating. On each side of the hull a bilge keel was fitted. This was 1,200mm high, of hollow section, fabricated from 8mm steel partly welded and partly riveted. It extended from frame $77\frac{1}{2}$ to $115\frac{1}{2}$.

Below the armoured deck there were two main longitudinal bulkheads, one inner and one outer. The inner extended from frame 31 to $149\frac{1}{2}$ in height from Longitudinal III or from the outer side longitudinal bulkhead up to the armoured deck. This bulkhead was 45mm thick, inclined

---

ARMOUR SCHEME: *DEUTSCHLAND*

Side protection	Thickness (mm)	Material
From frame:		
$6\frac{1}{2}$ to 16	30	
16 to $25\frac{3}{4}$	40	
$25\frac{3}{4}$ to 31	50	N
31 to 42.4	60	
42.4 to 136.4	50/80	
136.4 to 154	60	
154 to Bows	18	
Gun turrets		
Front	140	K.C.s
Side (to front)	80	K.C.s
Side (to rear)	75	K.W.s
Rear	170	N
Roof (incline to front)	105	K.C.s
Roof (horizontal)	85	K.W.s
Roof (incline to rear)	50	K.W.s
Roof (incline to side, front)	90	K.C.s
Roof (incline to side, rear)	85	K.C.s
Base (to front amidships)	80	K.W.s
Base (to front sides)	30	K.W.s
Base (to sides)	60	K.W.s
Base (to rear)	30	K.W.s
Barbettes		
Vertical plates	100	K.C.s
Straps	30	S
Conning tower		
Dome for 6m range-finder	55	N
Roof	50	N
Vertical plates	140	K.C.s
Base	30	N

Side protection	Thickness (mm)	Material
Shaft	60	N
Deck, forward gunnery position	10	SIII
Protected Positions		
After gunnery control:		
Roof	20	Ww n/A
Deck	20	Ww n/A
Walls	50	Wh n/A
Foretop gunnery control: roof, walls, deck	14	Ww n/A
After range-finder cupola:		
Roof and deck	20	Ww n/A
Walls	50	Ww n/A
Foretop R/F Cupola: roof, base, walls	14	Ww n/A
Forward and after flak control: roof and walls	14	Ww n/A
Searchlight controls	10	SII
Splinter protection-tubes	10	Wh n/A
8.8cm and 3.7cm shell hoists	20	N
Torpedo bulkhead	45	N
Side Splinter Protection		
From armoured deck to superstructure and forward turret to aft turret	10	SII
Armoured Transverse Bulkheads		
Bulkhead $6\frac{1}{2}$	30	
Bulkhead 31	60	N
Bulkhead $149\frac{1}{2}$	60	

Side protection	Thickness (mm)	Material
Bulkhead $173\frac{1}{2}$	30	
Deck Armour		
Armoured deck:		
Inside longitudinal side bulkheads	30	
Outside longitudinal side bulkheads	45	
Inside barbettes	15	N
Frame $6\frac{1}{2}$ to 31	30	
Frame $149\frac{1}{2}$ to $173\frac{1}{2}$	30	
Tween Deck:		
Frame 31 to $149\frac{1}{2}$, outside armoured deck	20	SII
Superstructure deck:		
Frame 33 to 154	18	
to frame $164\frac{1}{2}$	10	SIII
from frame $164\frac{1}{2}$	7	

Key to armour material abbreviations:
K.C.s	Krupp cemented (weldable)
K.W.s	Krupp unhardened (weldable)
N	Low nickel armour steel (Heft B Nr.29 der Materialvorschrift 1915)
S	Special steel (Heft B, Nr.15 der Materialvorschrift 1915)
SII	Shipbuilding steel II (Heft B Nr. 16 and 26)
SIII	Shipbuilding steel III
Ww n/A	Rolled armour plate, unhardened, new type
Wh n/A	Rolled armour plate, hardened, new type

outwards from the bottom to the top by $13\frac{1}{2}°$, fabricated from low nickel armour steel and formed the torpedo protective bulkhead. The outer longitudinal bulkhead extended between frames $42\frac{4}{10}$ and $136\frac{4}{10}$ and from the inner longitudinal bulkhead to the lower edge of the side protection. This bulkhead was only 10mm thick. The areas formed by these bulkheads and the shell plating were known as the inner and outer 'Wallgang', the outer being a bulge to the ship's hull. These spaces were sub-divided by transverse bulkheads, of which there were fifteen, fourteen or nineteen either side, depending on the deck level in question. Other longitudinal bulkheads included the centre-line bulkhead, which extended in height from the shell plating up to the lower platform deck.

The main watertight integrity of the hull was conferred by 28 transverse bulkheads which extended from the shell plating up to the armoured deck except for two, one forward and one aft, which extended only as far as the lower platform deck. Between frames $37\frac{1}{2}$ and $149\frac{1}{2}$, these bulkheads reached from inner or outer longitudinal bulkheads across the ship. Forward and aft of these stations, they extended to the skin plating. In thickness they varied from 5mm to 15mm, but at frame $6\frac{1}{2}$ and the upper part of $173\frac{1}{2}$ were 30mm thick; while at frame 31 from below the armoured deck to the upper edge of the side protection, and from $149\frac{1}{2}$ from the lower edge of the armoured deck to the upper platform deck, they were 60mm—i.e., they were the end transverse armoured bulkheads.

Also below the armoured deck were two pairs of longitudinal turret support bulkheads, spaced about 4,100mm from the centre-line, between frames $42\frac{4}{10}$ and $50\frac{6}{10}$ aft and $136\frac{4}{10}$ and $144\frac{6}{10}$ forward; they were of doubled fishplate riveted construction.

Above the armoured deck, which extended from frame $6\frac{1}{2}$ to $173\frac{1}{2}$, were two further longitudinal bulkheads which extended between the turrets from frame 50 to 136, spaced about 3,700mm from the centre-line. These bulkheads reached from the armoured deck to the upper deck and were of welded construction in the lower part, while the upper section was riveted with welded T stiffeners. It

was secured to the armoured deck by welding and to the superstructure deck by riveted angles.

The shell plating, which varied in thickness between 10mm and 20mm, was semi-welded but with riveted joints except that, forward of frame $149\frac{1}{2}$, all-welded construction was employed above the upper deck. The upper deck was overlaid with 55mm teak planking and the superstructure decks with 50mm Oregon pine.

Internally, the hull was divided into sixteen main watertight compartments, numbered according to standard German practice I to XVI from stern to bows.

PROTECTIVE ARRANGEMENTS

A detailed tabulation of the armour distribution and thickness is given in the table. The main protective belt consisted of two rows of armour plates, one above the other, with a tapered joint between the two rows, the upper being 80mm and the lower 50mm in thickness. This was fabricated from low nickel armour steel of a composition dating from 1915 and was inclined outwards from the bottom by $13\frac{1}{2}°$. It extended from frame $42\frac{4}{10}$ to frame $136\frac{4}{10}$. Fore and aft of the main belt was a 60mm section which protected the remaining magazine spaces. At the fore ends the belt was only 18mm thick, while aft of frame 31 (the forward end of the torpedo tubes) the belt reduced to first 40mm then 30mm. The main barbettes were 100mm KCs (Krupp cemented, hardened) armour and weighed 146,300kg each. This armour was also used for the conning tower but in a thickness of 140mm.

The main horizontal protection consisted of 45mm low nickel steel armour from the longitudinal bulkheads above the armoured deck, to the top of the 45mm torpedo bulkead. Inside the longitudinal bulkheads the armour was only 30mm thick, as was the deck aft of frame 31 and forward of frame $149\frac{1}{2}$. Thus the protective deck did not extend across the full beam of the ship and was not given the curved sides common in all post-Panzerschiff designs. Inside the barbettes the deck was only 15mm thick. Armoured transverse bulkheads were incorporated at frames $6\frac{1}{2}$ (30mm), 31 and $149\frac{1}{2}$ (60mm) and $173\frac{1}{2}$ (30mm), all of nickel steel armour. The total weight of armour and protective plating was 702,149kg.

MAIN MACHINERY

The main machinery chosen for Panzerschiff A was as already described, diesel motors in a twin-shaft configuration. There were six main machinery spaces, arranged from aft: Motor room 1 (Port shaft), Gearing room, Motor room 2 (Port shaft); and Motor room 1 (Starboard shaft), Gearing room, Motor room 2 (starboard shaft). These were identified as compartments VI to XI and occupied $61\frac{1}{2}$ metres (or about 34 per cent) of the ship's waterline length. The main motors themselves were supplied by MAN and were nine-cylinder, two-stroke, double-acting type M9Z 42/58 of 7,100bhp each giving a total of 56,800bhp. Two were installed in each motor room and coupled via a Vulcan geared drive to a second motor room, giving four motors per shaft.

Each motor room also housed an auxiliary diesel, which was also of MAN design, a five cylinder two-stroke, double-

ADMIRAL GRAF SPEE: MOTOR ROOM ARRANGEMENTS

VI   VII   VIII   IX   X   XI
No.1 Motor Room   No.2 Motor Room   No.3 Motor Room   No.4 Motor Room
M = Magazine   T = Thrust Bearing Space

acting type M5Z 42/58 (i.e., a bore of 420mm and of 425rpm). Motor rooms 2 and 4 (i.e., one port shaft, one starboard) also housed a main hull and fire pump. Each motor room also contained two 270kW diesel dynamo sets for a total generating capacity of 2,160kW. Two auxiliary water tube boilers provided steam for domestic and fire-fighting purposes. These were above the armoured deck. There was a motor room watch-keeping stand in Nos 1 and 3 motor rooms and an auxiliary position in the other two. The main engine control position was on the port side of the upper platform deck. Total weight of the main and auxiliary engines, including oils, etc., was 2,078,213kg. Independent rudder motors were provided and there was a reserve hand steering position on the starboard side of the lower platform deck, frame stations $22\frac{1}{4}$–$26\frac{1}{2}$.

The main steering position was on the command bridge, with a second in the conning tower. Three secondary positions existed, in the command centre, the forward rudder motor room and in the hand steering position. 3,200 tonnes of diesel oil were carried and about 200 tonnes of oil fuel for the auxiliary boiler.

ARMAMENT AND FIRE CONTROL

Six 28cm SKC/28 guns comprised the main armament, carried in two triple turrets (type Drh LC/28), one forward and the other aft. These had a maximum elevation of 45° and fired a 300kg projectile. The turret faces carried 140mm KCs armour. (Full details are given in Table I). This gun was a new model, developed for the Panzerschiffe and differed from the older model shipped in the pre-dreadnoughts.

The secondary armament comprised eight 15cm SKC/28 guns in single shielded pivot MPL28 mountings disposed four a side. This gun mounting allowed 35° elevation and the gun fired a 45.3kg projectile. Of the four guns on each beam, two were fitted each forward and aft of the midships heavy flak platform.

The heavy flak armament consisted of three 8.8cm L/45 guns of World War One vintage, carried in open shielded pedestal mountings port and starboard, abreast the funnel and on the centre-line, superfiring over the after 28cm turret. It is probable, however, that the unsatisfactory 8.8cm SKC/25 twin mounting had been intended and that the single guns were an interim measure until a new twin could be developed.

Light flak defence was provided by eight 3.7cm SKC/30 guns in twin LC/30 mountings, but these were not available on first commissioning. Their distribution was generally good, with one pair of mountings in the bridge wings at command bridge level and the second pair aft abreast the after range-finder. This gun was unfortunately not an automatic weapon and had a complicated gyro-stabilized mounting, which reduced its service effectiveness. Finally, four MGC/30 single guns made up the remainder of the flak outfit. Also carried aboard were eight MG08 and eight MG08/15 machine-guns and a 6cm Schnellbooteskannone KmLL.

The torpedo outfit comprised two quadruple banks of tubes for 50cm torpedoes, mounted on the quarterdeck, in-

ADMIRAL GRAF SPEE: ARMOUR BULKHEAD AT FRAME 29½

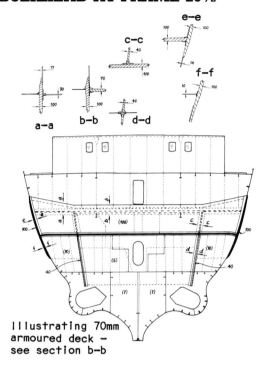

Illustrating 70mm armoured deck — see section b–b

DEUTSCHLAND: SECTION AT FRAME 114½/116, STARBOARD SIDE

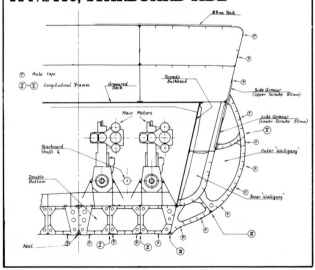

itially unshielded. Torpedoes and warheads were stowed or serviced under the after turret at the break of the forecastle, manoeuvred by means of hoists and overhead running tackle.

The fire control system continued the layout adopted by the 'K'-class cruisers, with three main gunnery control positions, one forward in the conning tower, one at the top of the

foremast tower and one on the after superstructure. Each of these positions was equipped with a stereoscopic range-finder, 6m base in the forward position, 10m base in the others. Within the conning tower itself were two gunnery bearing directors (*Art.*, *Rw.*, *Zg.*) in tandem on the centre-line. Outside on the Night Control Stand were two further gun director pedestals, (*Art. Zeilsaule*), to port and starboard at the forward end. Also protruding through the roof of the conning tower were four navigational periscopes, two each to port and starboard and one for the helmsman at the front end. At the foretop were a further pair of directors on the centre-line, fore and aft of the 10m range-finder. Once again, these were visible only by their periscope hoods above the armour. The after gunnery position was fitted with only a single gun director on the centre-line just aft of the rangefinder.

Range and bearing data were fed from these positions to a main fire control T/S on the lower platform deck directly below the conning tower or to an after position also on the lower platform deck below the aftermost 8.8cm mounting. For night actions, the night control position has already been mentioned, above the command bridge. At the forward end of this on the centre-line was a searchlight director with, either side of it, a starshell director. Two further searchlight directors were fitted on each side of the conning tower and another pair on the after gunnery position. These were used to control five Siemens-Schuckert 150cm searchlights which were fitted, one on the foremast tower, and two each to port and starboard of the funnel on heavy tubular support towers.

Fire control for the secondary armament was exercised by the use of any of the three main control positions and a separate T/S on the lower platform deck. This T/S was also intended for use with the heavy flak, but initially there was no effective independent control for the 8.8cm guns. Portable 1m base range-finders were provided for the 3.7cm guns.

The torpedo armament had its own fire control arrangements, with a 3m base range-finder to port and starboard at the base of the foremast tower at signal bridge level. Within the conning tower to port and starboard were two torpedo directors with periscope sights and two torpedo bearing pedestals with binocular sights in the open bridge wings at the after end of the command bridge adjacent to the 3.7cm mountings. Finally, right at the after end of the after gunnery control position was the torpedo rate of change of bearing instrument, the Torpedoauswandlungsmesser, or TAM. The tubes themselves were also fitted with basic sights and firing mechanisms for local control.

MODIFICATIONS

Shortly after completion, the tubes were fitted with protective armoured shields and the torpedo calibre altered to 53.3cm. In 1934 a stabilized high-angle director became available, model SL2, and two such equipments were fitted early that year. One was placed forward, above the signal bridge at the base of the tower mast, the second abaft the funnel, both on the centre-line. This director was fitted with a 4m base stereoscopic range-finder and could tilt about its

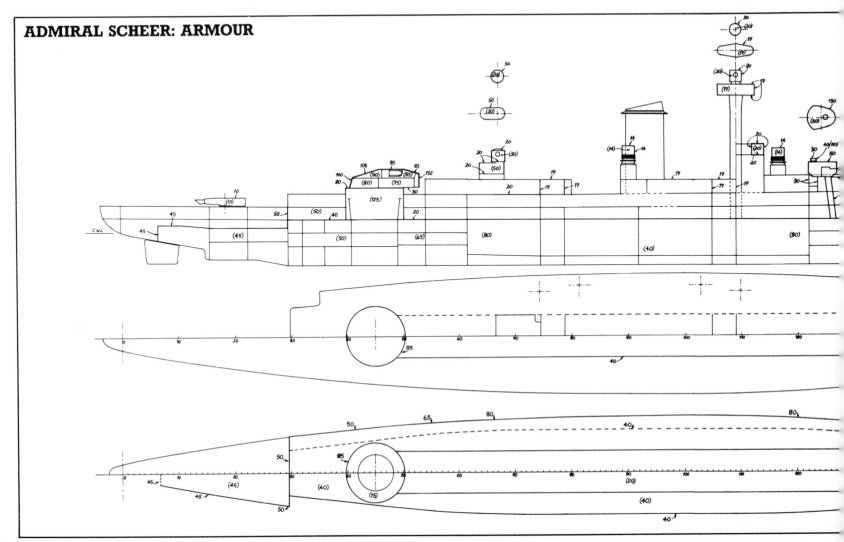

vertical axis by 12°. (While the ship's drawings dated for modifications as late as March 1944 confirm the size as 4m, comments in the ship's KTB during 1942 refer to 3m range-finders forward and aft.) At approximately the same time twin 8.8cm mountings reached service and three 8.8cm LC/31 twins replaced the old singles.

During a further refit between December 1934 and February 1935, a new auxiliary boiler was also fitted. The lower searchlight position was altered to face forward instead of aft and some rearrangements were made to the rigging. In November 1935 the ship returned to Wilhelmshaven for further dockyard attention and in the course of this refit, which extended until 11 January 1936, received a catapult and fittings to operate a second aircraft. A proposal to fit an armoured cupola to the forward gunnery position was not carried through.

In 1937, following *Deutschland*'s return home for repair after being bombed in the Mediterranean, a further period of refit and repair took place which extended until October. In the course of this refit the searchlight towers were landed and replaced by a platform around the top of the funnel upon which the four searchlights were repositioned. Finally in 1938 a shallow, raked funnel cap was added. Her light flak was in all probability not increased until after the 1939 Atlantic sortie, when four single 2cm MG C/30s were installed, on the forecastle and quarterdecks. Further additions may have been made during the short refit at the Danziger Werft between December 1940 and January 1941.

During the course of the repairs following torpedo damage incurred in April 1940, *Lützow* (as *Deutschland* had now been renamed) landed her 8.8cm guns and received in lieu 10.5cm SK/C33 weapons in adapted 8.8cm twin mountings (LC/31). Two single depth-charge traps were added and the bows altered to a slightly raked form, increasing her overall length by almost 2 metres. Her visual appearance was altered again in 1942 with the fitting of a much larger funnel cap. In that year she also received an Army-pattern 'Vierling' on 'A' turret and possibly a second at the break of the quarterdeck, for

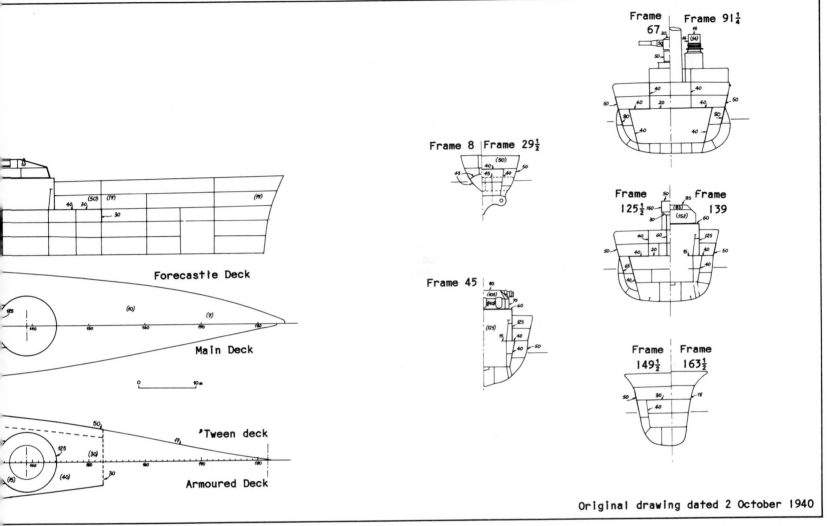

Frame 67   Frame 91¼

Frame 8 | Frame 29½

Frame 45

Frame 125½   Frame 139

Frame 149½   Frame 163½

Forecastle Deck

Main Deck

'Tween deck

Armoured Deck

Original drawing dated 2 October 1940

which the exercise loader had to be landed to compensate. In addition, the foremast searchlight was replaced by a single 2cm mounting. By March 1944 the light flak comprised eight 3.7cm guns in the original twin mountings and eleven of 2 cm, all in single mountings, the Vierlinge having presumably been landed to await replacement by the naval tri-axial version.

In August of that year the light flak was again altered, with two single 4cm Flak 28 Bofors replacing the forward pair of 3.7cm mountings. Reportedly, a further four were also fitted. Two of these may have been on the upper deck abreast the bridge, replacing the single 2cm. Two more were scheduled to be fitted aft, one in lieu of the TAM and the other on the quarterdeck, but it is uncertain if this was ever carried out. Six 2cm LM44 twins replaced six of the single 2cm. Three Vierlinge were now carried and two single 2cm for a total of twenty-eight 2cm guns. An extra 10 tonnes reserve of fuel of ballast was required to compensate for the heavier tri-axial Vierlinge. Shields were fitted to the twin 2cm but none to the

3.7cm or 4cm, but the remaining pair of 3.7cm mountings were landed at Gotenhafen on 4 November and reinstalled with shields fitted a few days later. The final intended flak outfit for 1945 was ten fully automatic 3.7cm and twenty-eight 2cm but this was never finalized.

Panzerschiff B: Admiral Scheer

DESIGN AND CONSTRUCTION

The second of the new Panzerschiffe, initially designated *Ersatz Lothringen*, was not authorized until 1931 and was ordered as yard No.123 from the Naval Yard at Wilhelmshaven. She was laid down on the No.1 slip on 25 June 1931 to essentially the same design as her predecessor. Supervising construction were directors Schulz and Lottmann, assisted by Marinebaurat Wischer.

COMPARISON OF MACHINERY WEIGHTS:
PANZERSCHIFFE

MI	Deutschland	Admiral Scheer	Admiral Graf Spee
Diesel motors	900,010	981,980	1,013,083
Refuelling gear	61,386	60,738	56,498
Pipework	36,713	67,347	109,273
Shafts	184,864	158,671	158,811
Propellers	26,483	27,092	27,159
Fan machinery	19,672	11,760	11,765
Deck plates	15,295	24,042	20,487
Cables	9,998	14,380	21,758
Fittings	6,056	3,240	4,308
Equipment	55,784	55,232	62,318
Total	1,316,261	1,412,852	1,482,868
Oil	102,900	232,000	230,500
MII			
Total	559,052	663,289	761,677
Total MI + MII	1,978,213	2,308,141	2,475,045

Weights in kilogrammes. When the weight of a design was being calculated, the various items of equipment and materials were grouped into classes for the purpose. Thus group 'S' covered the hull category, 'MI' the main and 'MII' the auxiliary machinery, 'A' the gunnery departments and so on. Different nations sometimes included similar items in different categories from those of other nations, making direct comparisons occasionally misleading. This was particularly true in the case of structural plating of a protective nature, which was classified by some as 'hull' and others as 'protection'.

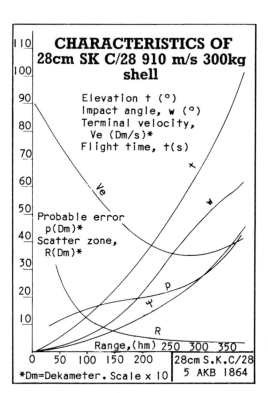

Some modifications had been made to the *Deutschland* plans; in particular, the beam had been increased by 0.7 metres, and instead of the tubular foremast this ship was to receive a heavy multi-sided tower. Displacement rose partly because of the larger dimensions but also because the weight of the main machinery had increased by 9 per cent, pipework doubled in weight, cabling was heavier and the weight of deck plating in the machinery spaces was well up on that in the earlier ship. In some compensation, the shafting was considerably lightened and further weight saved by lighter fan and ventilation machinery.

In the hull construction itself, not a great deal of weight was saved by the use of light alloys, which represented only 0.58 per cent of the weight worked in by the plating and fabrication shops (SI). For a bare hull weight of 5,705,787kg, it represented but 0.54 per cent, mostly aluminium, which was employed for minor bulkheads, walkways and fan trunking. The hull itself was mainly fabricated from Schiffbaustahl II, but the new steel ST52 was also employed. The other main difference was that this ship received a Frahm-type fluid transfer stabilizer system, between frames 109 and $113\frac{1}{2}$, with the tanks in the Wallgang between longitudinals IV and V.

MAIN MACHINERY
This was the same as that installed in *Deutschland*.

PROTECTIVE SCHEME
The armouring of this ship followed that of Panzerschiff A with certain differences. The main belt had the 80mm plating as the lower row of plates with the 50mm on the top row. Angle of inclination remained 14°. As with the earlier ship, the torpedo bulkhead did not extend to the bottom skin. On the other hand, the thickness of this torpedo bulkhead was reduced from 45mm to 40mm. Both main and torpedo bulkheads were fabricated from Wh/na armour and not the older Krupp cemented type. The horizontal protection once again comprised a single main armoured deck, 40mm thick outside the 40mm longitudinal bulkheads above the armoured deck and 20mm within them, except over the steering gear where it was 45mm. The after transverse armoured bulkhead at frame $29\frac{1}{2}$ was increased to 50mm, but the forward one remained 30mm.

There was a considerable increase in barbette armour thickness, to 125mm Wh/na, with straps fabricated from Ww/na. Each barbette was formed from ten rolled and curved plates, with an internal diameter of 10,200mm and a height of 5,560mm. Each plate weighed almost $17\frac{1}{2}$ tonnes. The two barbettes together weighed 358,426kg. The conning tower was of similar construction to that of *Deutschland*, with the vertical walls manufactured from KC n/a armour and the roof, floor and shaft from Ww/na. Its wall thickness was, however, increased by 10mm to 150mm and the armoured cupola for the range-finder doubled in thickness.

The result of these changes in the protective scheme was that the vertical armour totalled 413,285kg and the armoured deck itself 474,869kg. This gave a total of 898,154kg, or 20 per cent more than that of *Deutschland*. These figures exclude the main turret armour which totalled 192,000kg.

Opposite page: *Deutschland* completed but prior to commissioning. *Emden* is being commissioned in the foreground, and a *K*-class cruiser appears in the background. (USN)

Above: *Deutschland* as completed. View from the foretop. (WBB)

Above centre: *Admiral Scheer*, details of tower mast. (USN)

Above right: *Admiral Scheer*, Midships detail. Note flak director, folded 10.5cm gun platform and searchlights. (USN)

ARMAMENT AND FIRE CONTROL

The gunnery outfit was identical to that of *Deutschland* with the minor exception that ten 2cm MG C/30 guns were provided for, with fourteen mountings. Provision was also made for an aircraft and catapult, with the latter now positioned abaft the funnel, thus displacing the HA director. In consequence, two directors had to be fitted in lieu, one either side of the funnel, which benefited, fire control considerably. Six 150cm searchlights were fitted, four on the funnel platform and two on large sponsons, one either side of the tower foremast. This ship, completing late in 1934, was able to receive 53.3cm torpedoes, 8.8cm twins and 3.7cm guns from the outset.

MODIFICATIONS

Few outwardly noticeable modifications were made until 1936. Prior to this the crane arrangements had been altered and some changes made to the rigging. During March and early April 1936 the ship received some alterations at Deutsche Werke in Kiel when four ZAG (Zielanweisergeräte) were fitted in the flak control position. Two sponsons for 3m base night torpedo range-finders were fitted to port and starboard on the tower mast at command bridge level and two 2cm mountings were added on the funnel platform. In July 1939 during the course of an engine overhaul at Wilhelmshaven a new-style Demag crane was fitted.

It was not until after the outbreak of war that the ship's appearance was changed considerably by Wilhelmshaven dockyard; the heavy tower mast was removed and replaced by a lighter tubular structure of a similar pattern to that of

Deutschland (now *Lützow*) but with a different arrangement of platforms. The original gunnery control position was refitted at its top. The fore ends were rebuilt from frame 112 to the bows and a raked stem worked in, in an attempt to reduce the wetness forward—a problem with these ships. At the same time degaussing coils were fitted and a funnel cap added, the latter a little more prominent that that of *Lützow*. All main motor bearers were renewed, the aircraft landing mat was taken out and the stabilizer tanks were converted to bunkerage and store spaces. The 8.8cm guns were landed and replaced by 10.5cm SK C/33 guns in modified 8.8cm twin mounting. The boats positions were altered, the 2cm on the funnel platform landed and two Army-pattern Vierlinge fitted, one on 'A' turret and the second at the break of the forecastle, under 'B' turret.

In 1941 a second radar set was added to the after range-finder and the forward radar modified. Scuttles in the fore ends were blanked off and racks for reserve torpedoes installed to increase reserve capacity from two to four. Finally, the bakery oven from the aircraft-carrier *Graf Zeppelin* was appropriated and fitted aboard!

By 1942 the funnel had received an enlarged funnel cap, one searchlight being landed, with the odd one being moved to the after end of the funnel platform and the two 2cm guns reinstalled on this platform. As the war dragged on, *Admiral Scheer*'s flak outfit increased progressively until about mid-1944, when it comprised eight 3.7cm in the orginal mountings and twenty-nine 2cm in five Vierlinge and nine singles. Her intended outfit for 1945 was four 4cm flak 28 Bofors in single mountings, four 3.7cm in two twins and forty-two 2cm

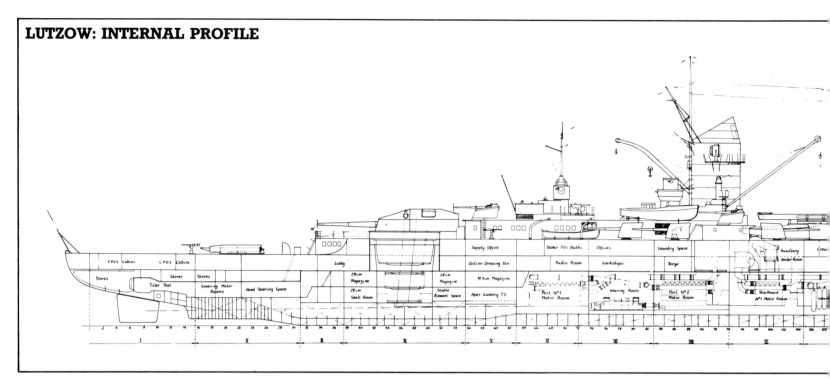

in six Vierlinge and nine LM44 twins, but this was never carried through.

Panzerschiff C: Admiral Graf Spee

DESIGN AND CONSTRUCTION

The order for this ship was placed on 23 August 1932 with the Naval Yard at Wilhelmshaven and she was laid down on 1 October that year as their yard No.124. As *Ersatz Lothringen* had not yet been launched, this ship was laid on the adjacent slip, number II. Construction was once again in the hands of Schiffsbaudirektor Lottmann, assisted by Marinebaurat Dykmann. The lengthy discussions which preceded the ordering of this ship have already been dealt with, so only those features which differed from the earlier two vessels will be examined. Initially designated *Ersatz Braunschweig*, she was essentially a repeat of *Admiral Scheer* as far as dimensions and method of construction were concerned; she too incorporated anti-rolling tanks and had a hull which was fully welded except for four riveted seams. Her hull was, however, some 10.3 per cent heavier than that of *Admiral Scheer*, partly due to her thicker armoured deck which was counted in the hull weight (as opposed to the vertical armour which was always quoted separately). Light alloys were again incorporated but only to the extent of 34 tonnes.

MAIN MACHINERY

By the time that the machinery for Panzerschiff C was being discussed, advances in machinery practice and design meant that the choice of diesel as main propulsion was no longer automatic for the new ship. Since the decision to equip *Deutschland* with this method of propulsion, boiler and turbine design had not stood still and in the meantime the first operating reports had been received from the installations aboard *Leipzig* and *Bremse*. On 13 August 1932 Admiral Raeder had these reports to hand, the essence of which was that both installations had shown defects and problems, which could be rectified in time but it could not be said when. The general opinion was that diesels should only be used for boost or cruising purposes. Two days later other departments put forward the entirely opposite view, holding diesels to be satisfactory but that further work was required on transmissions and noise. On 16 August Raeder attempted to reconcile these opposing views when the Construction Office stated that weight for weight, diesel was best but that further reports were required from *Leipzig* and *Bremse*, especially as regards underwater noise; they also suggested awaiting the first trials reports from *Deutschland*, even though these were some time away. Steam was not to be considered further because of its 50 per cent less radius of action.

The decision was therefore made that *C* was to receive diesels. Although the main engines were identical to those of the earlier ships, weights once again increased, this time by another 31 tonnes. On the other hand, 4 tonnes were saved in lighter refuelling equipment and a similar amount in lighter deck plates. However, increased electrical power demands resulted in nearly 6 tonnes extra weight, and internal pipework added yet another 42 tonnes. As the weight of the auxiliaries and their associated fittings also grew, the final machinery weights exceeded those of *Admiral Scheer* by 167

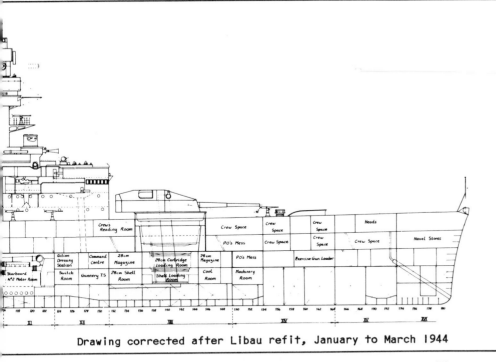

Drawing corrected after Libau refit, January to March 1944

off by armoured transverse bulkheads 29½ and 148, which were also 100mm in thickness, the former between the main armoured deck and the after lower armoured deck (see page 22). Like Panzerschiff B, this ship also had 40mm torpedo bulkheads but in this case these extended to the bottom shell plating between frames 49.1 and 134.9, where it replaced longitudinal III. Outside this length it extended to longitudinal III.

The main horizontal protection comprised a single armoured deck, 40mm thick, between the top edge of the torpedo bulkheads and the lower edge of the inboard longitudinal 40mm bulkheads between the barbettes. Outboard of the torpedo bulkheads to the ship's side the thickness was only 30mm, while the centre-line protection was only 20mm. Although a Panzerannordnung, or armour distribution drawing, for the ship has not so far come to light, there is evidence to suggest that at least some of her horizontal protection was 70mm thick. Certainly it was this thickness immediately forward of bulkhead 29½, but perhaps it only covered the magazine areas. Reference to the table will show that there was insufficient increase in deck weight over that of Admiral Scheer for the thickness to be a uniform 70mm, especially as the 30mm outboard plating was not present in Scheer. Aft of the bulkhead at frame 29½ the lower armoured deck of 45mm protected the steering gear. The main horizontal protection weighed 697 tonnes. Barbettes were 125mm in thickness, fabricated from ten plates of Wh n/A armour.

ARMAMENT

This was similar to Panzerschiff B except that this third ship completed with 10.5cm guns.

MODIFICATIONS

Admiral Graf Spee, as Panzerschiff C was subsequently named, had a relatively brief career, so that modifications were few. Practically all that was done was to remove the searchlights and sponsons from the forward tower mast in 1938 and to add a radar set.

In common with all Germany's Versailles Treaty designs, the Panzerschiffe were found wanting in many respects despite outward appearances. By December 1937, after service in the Atlantic, Mediterranean and the Bay of Biscay, as well

tonnes and those of Deutschland by 497 tonnes. The arrangement of the machinery spaces, compartments VI to XI, was similar to that of Admiral Scheer; i.e., with the Vulcan geared drive in the motor rooms, thus needing a smaller space for the thrust bearing rooms in compartments VII and X. In Deutschland the combined gearing and thrust bearing spaces were about 5½m longer, but the overall length of the machinery spaces was identical in all three Panzerschiffe.

PROTECTIVE SCHEME

There were again noticeable differences in the armour distribution and thickness in this ship compared with her earlier half sisters. The most significant of these was the increase in belt thickness to 100mm for its full depth. This extended from frame 29½ to frame 148 and was inclined 13° outwards from the bottom to the top. The ends of this belt were closed

No. of Main Motors	Power (bhp)	Speed (knots)	Rpm	Draught (metres)
2	358	5.38	45	5.8/7.27
2	1,659	10.06	79	5.8/7.27
2	3,775	13.52	105	5.9/7.24
2	4,590	14.69	114	5.8/7.27
4	9,770	18.34	142	5.8/7.27
4	15,130	20.68	164	5.9/7.24
4	19,125	22.22	176	5.9/7.24
6	24,675	23.50	190	5.8/7.23
6	31,015	24.87	204	5.8/7.23
8	36,125	26.00	213	5.8/7.27
8	53,650	28.50	240	5.8/7.27

PERFORMANCE TRIALS: ADMIRAL GRAF SPEE

STOPPING TRIALS: ADMIRAL GRAF SPEE

Speed (knots)	Order STOP: distance/time	Order FULL ASTERN distance/time
9	1,190m/8'49"	394m/2'38"
13	1,710m/9'00"	720m/2'40"
17	2,215m/8'38"	740m/2'35"
21	2,420m/9'20"	840m/2'22"
26	3,000m/9'30"	780m/2'20"

Conditions: wind force 3 to 4; depth of water 45m; ship's draught 5.6/7.4m

CONSUMPTION TRIALS: ADMIRAL GRAF SPEE

Run	1	2
Speed	18.69kt	26kt
Mean rpm	146	214
Main motors per shaft	2	4
Auxiliary motors/shaft	1	2
Horsepower	10,250	36,945
Consumption:		
1hp	248gm/hr	226gm/hr
Diesel generators	160kg/hr	160kg/hr
Auxiliary boiler	415kg/hr	415kg/hr
Total consumption	3,117kg/hr	8,925kg/hr
Range	16,300nm	7,900nm
Fuel per 100nm	16.80 tonnes	34.3 tonnes

Above: *Admiral Scheer*, showing details of catapult installation. (USN)

time when this major work should be started, he recommended some time after the completion of Panzerschiff D (*Scharnhorst*) and Panzerschiff E (*Gneisenau*).

Alterations considered necessary to the Panzerschiffe included:

30 tonnes for strengthening the main motors
3 tonnes for N.V.A. special equipment (radar)
10 tonnes for improved aerials
5 tonnes for improved aircraft facilities
19 tonnes for stabilization to the searchlights

Also desirable was splinter protection to free-standing guns, 20 tonnes. The total weight growths were estimated at 71,216kg for *Deutschland*, 71,699kg for *Admiral Scheer* and 76,699kg for *Admiral Graf Spee*.

The problems affecting the Panzerschiffe were discussed for the following twelve months and by November 1938 certain decisions had been made. The main intention now was to increase the beam but tank towing trials with form models showed that with only the beam increased, speed and seaworthiness would be reduced. Thus the plan to increase beam on its own (Entwurf B) with an increase in displacement of 200 tonnes was not on. The alternative plan, formerly Entwurf A of August 1938 but now Entwurf I, had an increase in beam and length. This had given very favourable tank trials and shown just how unfavourable the current ships' lines were. It was true that this plan would entail more work than the beam only plan, but it would take only three months more. This rebuild would allow the ships to have improved splinter protection, better stability, seaworthiness and strength, as well as a 2 knot increase in speed. Thus the work was well worth it from the technical point of view. Displacement would rise by some 750 tonnes, made up of 500 tonnes for hull widening, lengthening and splinter protection using new steels, 100 tonnes for new equipment, 50 tonnes for machinery and a reserve of 100 tonnes.

If, however, this major refit was unacceptable on cost and/ or time grounds, then the only alternative was to remove the torpedoes, saving 45 tonnes because the Fleet Commander would not allow the 15cm battery to be reduced. Removal of the aircraft and associated equipment would save only 30 tonnes. The tower mast could be rebuilt as on *Deutschland*, splinter protection provided and a similar amount allowed for extra equipment. However, the bows could not be rebuilt, nor could many of the other desirable modifications be done. Admiral Raeder opted for the major rebuilding, taking *Admiral Scheer* and *Admiral Graf Spee* in hand in 1940 and *Deutschland* in 1942. However, this latter ship would receive extra splinter protection during her three- to four-month engine overhaul period in 1939.

The intention by December 1938 was that *Admiral Graf Spee* would be rebuilt between June 1942 and June 1943, *Deutschland* between December 1942 and December 1943, and *Admiral Scheer* between January 1941 and January 1942. In fact, yard overloading, shortage of raw materials and the outbreak of war prevented most of these plans being achieved, although the tower mast was altered in *Admiral Scheer*.

as cruises further afield, sufficient experience had been gained for the Fleet Command to make various recommendations to the Naval Staff at OKM. The essence of these were that some extensive rebuilding was needed. Flag Officer (Panzerschiffe), (Bdp), wanted a wider stern but the Fleet Commander, Admiral Carls, felt that only a major rebuilding of the bow and stern would confer any improvements in seakeeping properties. The OKM wanted to reduce top weights by reducing the 15cm guns to two per side but Carls would not hear of this—four was the minimum and in any event, the gains in weight and personnel would be slight. He was far more in favour of combining the heavy flak and 15cm guns by means of a dual-purpose battery of three twin 12.7cm guns on each beam, plus a fifth in lieu of No.3 10.5cm gun. This, it was felt, would produce a number of advantages, namely splinter-proof ammunition hoists, a reduction of 80 to 100 men and free the 8.8cm magazines for 3.7cm and 2cm munitions.

All the Panzerschiffe in fact needed improved sea-keeping properties and the last two ship needed better night action control positions, as spray rendered the existing ones useless. Carls pondered on the merits of a knuckle bow to reduce the spray problem, but on balance concluded that it would not. He proposed that the bows of the ships be rebuilt and the tower foremast altered to that featured in *Deutschland*. In addition, it was necessary to continue the bulges further toward the upper deck and to work in some splinter protection to the latter. In compensation for the increased weights, certain items could be removed or altered; for example, the stabilizer space could be utilized for fuel oil, the forward tower could be reduced in height, the searchlights repositioned, and the aircraft landing mat removed. In his judgment, a reduction of $2\frac{1}{2}$ per cent on the speed of 28 knots was acceptable, if good open Atlantic properties were thereby achieved. One of his more novel suggestions was to recommend the possibility of using the Fieseler Storch aircraft for deck landing, although he did not suggest removal of the catapult. As to the

3. SCHARNHORST AND GNEISENAU

DESIGN HISTORY

Panzerschiff C had been proceeded with by the Navy with some reservations as the appearance of the new French capital ship design (which became *Dunkerque*) rendered it obsolete. Political circumstances had prevented the construction of anything larger although, as we have seen, larger designs had been discussed. Germany's medium-term objective was to build six replacement capital ships, of which three were completed or under construction by 1933. Two more were now under consideration, known as Panzerschiff D and Panzerschiff E, or *Ersatz Elsass* and *Ersatz Hessen* respectively.

During 1932 and early 1933 discussions were held to decide the most desirable parameters of these new replacement ships from a basic idea that the Panzerschiff A concept had to be expanded, despite the Versailles restrictions. The starting point being Raeder's earlier suggestions for a 15,000–18,000 tonnes project with three triple 28cm turrets, which he had favoured for Panzerschiff C.

In November 1932 Raeder and General Groener, the Defence Minister, had come to an agreement as to the future size of the fleet. This envisaged the following strength, to be attained in three stages, by 1938: six battleships or Panzerschiffe, six cruisers, six destroyer and torpedo boat half flotillas, three S-boat half flotillas, and, when the political situation permitted, sixteen U-boats.

The most pressing problem was the form which Panzerschiff D was to take. A decision had to be made by October 1933 by the latest and a conference was held in Berlin on 9 March 1933 to examine the matter thoroughly. At that time Britain and the USA were ruled out as possible enemies and in any case were not building any of the sort of ships Germany was considering. The pace-setter in German eyes was France and most design parameters were discussed with her

in mind. Comparisons with earlier wartime German designs were not considered valid as in that era armour belt was all and deck protection of lesser importance. Now, the growing power of aircraft also had to be accepted as a threat. Thus, given the known details of *Dunkerque*—a speed of 28 knots and a 33cm main armament—the basic parameters were set at 28 knots continuous speed and a belt strong enough to defeat 33cm armour-piercing shells.

It was estimated that a 320mm belt would be required to baulk a French shell of this calibre but this would only confer protection above 18,000m. Outside 25,000m, where shells would have a plunging howitzer-like effect, the armoured deck was the important protection. This established a known zone of protection. If the armour belt were less than 320mm, this zone would be reduced and vice versa. It was decided that if 320mm was not possible on whatever grounds, then

Right: *Scharnhorst* under construction. (WBB)

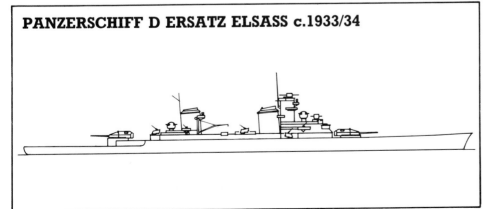

PANZERSCHIFF D ERSATZ ELSASS c.1933/34

the basic minimum requirements would be immunity to 33cm HE shells and 20.3cm AP shells. To achieve this, 220mm would be necessary which, it was judged, would give protection against 20.3cm AP shells at ranges of over 9,000m. The armoured deck had to resist AP shells which had penetrated the belt and its thickness was set at 80mm over the magazines, the remainder being 70mm with the sides 80mm (curved).

An upper armoured deck was also desirable, designed to give protection from aircraft bombs, but it was accepted that no protection could be guaranteed against the heaviest bombs, as this deck could never be thick enough. It was decided then to aim for immunity from the most common bomb weight of the period (50kg) and against high-explosive ordnance with or without a delay, for which purpose 50mm was considered the desirable minimum. It was estimated that if it were thinner, a bomb penetrating it could put a hole 1 metre square in the armoured deck. There would also be little protection for the crew below decks. It was therefore agreed that 50mm should be demanded, at least for the citadel area.

The conference now considered the vexed question of calibre. As always, there was the demand for the maximum calibre = maximum penetrating power = maximum explosive effect. On the other side of the coin was the lower rate of fire of large-calibre weapons. Six 28cm guns were considered superior to six 33cm from the rate of fire point of view; the larger calibre would be better only if eight guns could be carried. On the question of turrets, it was considered that the best layout and design still had to be established, but there were only triple turrets available at present. Quadruple turrets had the disadvantage that a hit on a turret would disable a larger percentage of the main battery so that if eight guns were in two quadruples, 50 per cent of the fire power would be lost. The advantages lay in weight-saving (about 25 per cent over triples), better salvo firing (i.e., 4 & 4 instead of 4 & 5), and lower cost (estimated at about 5 million Reichsmarks less for 33cm guns). It was also pointed out that the known advantages of a four twin turret arrangement should not be forgotten.

In the end, three basic sketch designs were considered, one of 18,000 tons, one with 28cm guns and one with six 33cm. K.Ad. Dr O. Groos, head of the Marinekommandoamt, favoured a 26,000-ton design with 33cm guns, stressing that parity with France was paramount. Basic costs were given as 120 million RM for the 18,000-ton ship, 150 million for 22,000 tons and 180 million for 26,000 tons. The Construction Office was forced to point out that the building of a ship of 26,000 tons was only feasible on No.2 slip at Wilhelmshaven and it would only be possible to dock her in the Kaiserdock at Bremerhaven or in Hamburg. If several ships were to be built, then additional floating docks would also have to be constructed.

Admiral Raeder eventually ordered a number of projects to be examined: (a) four twin 33cm; (b) two quadruple 33cm; and (c) three triple 33cm—all being of 26,500 tons. If 33cm guns proved impossible, then 30.5cm should be considered.

Finally, probably with the political question in mind, he ordered a fall-back project to be examined (Projekt XIII) of 22,000 tons and 28cm guns. Design work had to be completed by late 1934 so as to lay down in the autumn of that year.

About four months later, at another conference on 23 June, when the subject was again Panzerschiff D, it was evident that political considerations were forcing the Navy along a path contrary to its real desires for Raeder announced that the new ship was to be as *Deutschland* (formerly Panzerschiff A), but with the protection envisaged for the 26,500 tons project. The protection of this new proposal would be 220mm main belt, 70mm deck with 80mm over the magazines and 80mm curved deck. The upper armoured deck would be 35mm with 50mm in the citadel area. During the debates, it became evident that certain departments preferred the armoured deck at waterline level, while the Construction Office did not like the curved armour from a shipbuilding point of view; but this view was not generally concurred with. Questions were also raised over the design's performance against underwater explosions.

Armament provoked a good deal of discussion as usual, the Marinekommandoamt wanting 160rpg, while the Construction Office felt that this would be difficult and suggested 150rpg instead. The Weapons Office wanted the 15cm guns in four twin turrets for better ammunition supply and crew protection and was prepared to accept the extra weight incurred. This proposal met with general approval. The heavy flak outfit also came in for some discussion, mainly from the point of view of how many 8.8cm guns were to be shipped. Three, as in *Deutschland*, were suggested because they had a good field of fire, but there was also a demand for a fourth gun fitted abaft 'A' turret. As this would entail an increase in length of about 5 metres, a proposal to twin the existing three was also discussed. Ammunition hoists were required, ready-use lockers not liked and 200rpg demanded.

The Construction Office reported that, with the demands of the protection laid down, the displacement would be 17,000 tons and draught 7–8 metres. They also pointed out that space enhanced protection as well as armour thickness and that this could be better achieved in a larger ship. The Marinekommandoamt saw no objection to an increase to 18,000 tons, taking the view that every centimetre more of armour was a gain, suggesting that both size and protection be increased.

The question of the main engines required further investigation but the ship was to be fitted as a fleet flagship and with torpedoes as in *Deutschland*. It was envisaged that the ship could be ordered by 1 April 1934, to lay down on the slip vacated by Panzerschiff C.

During the autumn of 1933 further evaluations and calculations were made and another conference took place on 11 October. At this meeting the Weapons Office criticized the 15cm arrangements (turrets now, not centre pivot mountings); in particular, the fact that the barbettes of these were not set directly on the armoured deck. This was seen as an error which allowed the possibility of a shell which passed

Top: *Scharnhorst* as completed. Note the catapults. (Author's Collection)

Above: *Gneisenau* as completed. Note the detail differences from her sister, such as the foremast. The forward rangefinder is not yet fitted. (Author's Collection)

over the armour belt exploding under a turret with devastating effect. The Weapons Office considered these turrets undesirable if the ammunition was endangered. However, the Construction Office thought that these demands could be accommodated and would investigate the matter. The Marinekommandoamt confirmed the heavy flak as three twin 8.8cm but requested consideration of four twin and four directors disposed as in the light cruiser *Nürnberg*. The earlier proposal of a fourth gun abaft 'A' turret was out of the question. Now the Weapons Office suggested that the after centre-line gun be retained for five twins with two mountings on each beam, a proposal which the Construction Office agreed to look into. Some discussion also took place regarding the torpedoes, their exposed position and their value in a capital ship. The Weapons Office view was that torpedoes were of little importance in the design.

The question of the tower foremast was discussed, with the choice being taken between that of *Deutschland* or the square tower of her later sisters. The Construction Office favoured the circular tower, while the Weapons Office took the view that this provided insufficient rigidity for the upper fire control station. The point was also made that the principle of similarity in silhouette had already been broken so that the choice was wide open. Other points criticized were the restricted arcs of view of the forward range-finder and forward flak director. It was suggested that to improve matters, 'A' turret could be moved forward, but it was quickly pointed out that this would involve recalculation of much of

the design. The Weapons Office wanted the 40mm armour between the longitudinal bulkheads increased to 60mm and the 28cm gun barbettes increased to the same thickness as the side belt (i.e., 220mm). This would add some 36/37 tonnes per turret, and decisions on this and the 15cm turrets had to be taken very soon, so that the 15cm turrets could be ordered by 15 January 1934 and those for the 28cm guns by 1 November 1933.

Finally, the main propulsion method had still not been decided, so that the action radius could not be estimated, although the speed was reckoned to be equal to that of *Deutschland*. A week after this conference, on 18 October, it was decided to order two ships of 19,000 tons (but this was stricken out and by hand was written in as 17,000 tons), to be announced as 10,000-ton sisterships to *Deutschland*, and every effort was made to camouflage this breach of the Versailles limits.

By December the main calibre question had reared its head again. 1.4 million Reichsmarks had been budgeted in 1933 to develop a new 33cm gun, but it was felt that political events had reduced the need for this weapon, as it was believed that Britain was preparing a treaty proposal based on 25,000 tons and twelve 30.5cm guns for 1935/36. Raeder therefore felt that a 30.5cm gun should be developed by Germany for the ship to be built in 1935. The Weapons Office were of the view that it was the turret design which was the critical factor as regards timing—one year to design and $3\frac{1}{2}$ years to build—and it was easily possible to build a proof gun of either 30.5cm or 33cm in that time. For the moment, however, the new ships would still receive the 28cm gun.

It appears that two ships were ordered as Panzerschiff D and Panzerschiff E from the Naval yard at Wilhelmshaven and Deutsche Werke, Kiel respectively, on 25 January 1934 to the improved Panzerschiff concept—i.e., 18,000 tons, two triple 28cm, four twin 15cm and four twin 8.8cm. They were laid down on 14 February 1934 as yard numbers 125 and 235.

Admiral Raeder was not completely satisfied with these two ships, which were more political designs than anything else, especially compared with *Dunkerque*. He wanted parity with the French ship and pressed Hitler to allow the designs to be altered to accommodate a third 28cm turret. Hitler was still at this stage reluctant to involve Germany in political rows with the major powers and would not at first allow this change. Eventually, though, Raeder got his way and on 5 July 1934 Hitler gave his consent to the third turret. Construction of the two ships on the slips was immediately stopped pending a review of the design. This decision was looked upon with some dismay by the Construction Office who pointed out that, with current staff levels and work loads, a redesign could not be completed before October 1935 and other construction would be considerably delayed. The Marinekommandoamt thought that the Führer's intention was to authorize the investigation if a third turret was possible, rather than a direct order to redesign the ship at once. The full score of advantages and disadvantages had to be weighed up. Not least it would delay the 10,000-ton cruisers, the aircraft-carriers and put the fourth and fifth Panzerschiffe back a year and a half. It was in fact suggested that 'D' be continued as intended but that 'E' would be suspended pending the redesign.

A conference was called the next day, 6 July, to thrash out the various points of view on the redesign. The Marinekommandoamt laid down a basic proposal based upon 28 knots (continuous), 30 knots maximum speed, and sufficiently well armoured to give protection from 33cm shells between 15,000–20,000 metres. As armour belt of 300–350mm was demanded, with citadel armour, bow and stern splinter protection of 50–60mm, 350mm conning tower, etc. The main armament was to be disposed one turret forward and two aft, the 15cm guns in twin turrets as previously and no torpedoes were envisaged. The 33cm gun was again suggested in twin turrets but because of the design and construction period necessary, the ships could not complete before May 1939 if this calibre were chosen. The question was raised, however, could such a turret be fitted at a later date if the design were made to accommodate it? It could, but the Construction Office reported that it would require a nine months refit.

On 20 July the Marinekommandoamt reported to Admiral Raeder that it conceded the need for the third turret and parity with *Dunkerque*, but pointed out that accurate and reliable data for the protective scheme of the French ship were not available, unsurprisingly! They cited the differences in the figures quoted by '*Jane's*' and '*Weyer's*', the two foremost naval annuals, but the Construction Office thought 225mm about right from agents' reports; Italian reports put *Dunkerque*'s belt at 280mm. Various other reports put the main belt at 300mm maximum, with 300mm turrets and 320mm turret faces. Eventually it was decided to opt for the figure in *Jane's Fighting Ships*—275mm (actually it was 241mm at its maximum). As far as the Germans were concerned, the problem was to protect a 28cm-gunned ship against 33cm AP shells. According to their calculations, such a shell would penetrate 350mm armour up to 15,000m and 300mm armour up to 19,000m at a 70° impact angle. Thus 350mm was specified for the main belt. Improvements were necessary to the armoured deck over the magazines and on the curvature from 80mm to 95mm; the side above the armour was to be 45mm, while the armoured deck over the rudder was to be 95–100mm. Two sketch designs were prepared, Neuentwurf I and Neuentwurf II (new designs I and II).

Neuentwurf I with 125,000hp had the same installed power as that quoted by *Weyer* for 30 knots in *Dunkerque*, but would appear to have been rated at 28 knots and had thinner armour than Neuentwurf II. Neither design was liked because the 28cm gun could not penetrate *Dunkerque*'s armour at the ranges that she could penetrate the German ship's protection. Thus it was again considered if, at a later stage, three twin 33cm guns could be shipped. The Construction Office wanted turbine propulsion and did not favour an alternative of turbo-electric generation on weight grounds. On military grounds therefore, there was little enthusiasm for the two choices but the Marinekommandoamt, if it had to have one or the other, plumped for 'I'. Three days later Raeder decided on Neuentwurf I, ordering that nothing further was to be altered and that the 33cm gun was not to be shipped becaused of the delay entailed and the possibility of some future treaty limitations.

Another critical aspect of the design which still produced considerable discussion was the question of the main propulsion. Diesels had been adopted for the first of the Panzerschiffe, on the grounds of good radius of action and lower weights than a steam installation, although the latter aim proved false. Panzerschiff C had received diesels only after considerable doubts, which were even more evident when Panzerschiff D was discussed. The installations in *Leipzig* and *Bremse* were not altogether satisfactory and preliminary reports from that in *Deutschland* indicated similar problems. Thus, while diesels were at first considered for Panzerschiff D, its increase in size to 17,000 tons, and later 31,800 tons, ruled out this type as the motors of the day could not produce enough power. This left only new high-pressure steam turbine propulsion in consideration, and on 12 September 1933 it was decided that this would be employed. Diesel still had its proponents, however, and there was a demand that the design be such as to allow either steam or diesel to be installed, when the best method had finally been established. By 4 November 1933 steam had definitely been decided upon by the design and construction offices, but Raeder was still unsure and ordered two sketch designs prepared, one diesel, one turbine. In addition, there were to be two special high-pressure steam projects set up in private works. The advantage of one over the other was by no means clear-cut and many held the view that there was little to choose between the two, except that diesel did confer a greater radius of action. The operating experience gained with *Deutschland* led to some of the problems being solved and Panzerschiffe B and C would benefit accordingly. This led to the proposal that D should receive diesels but if E were to be built at the same time, it should be given turbines, presumably for comparative purposes. The Construction Office saw the HP steam project very much in the development stage and wanted one ship for evaluation purposes. Whether this was correct for such a large and valuable ship was questionable and the proposal met with little favour with the Marineabteilung, who certainly did not want two sisterships with different propulsion units. They took the view that the difference in radius of action was not much and plumped for the steam turbine installation. The power requirements were so great that fighting power and protection would have suffered if diesels had been chosen, despite the reservations of Raeder. However, encouraging results from the pilot shore trials plants in Hamburg and Bremen eventually helped to tip the balance towards steam. The difference between these results and operational experience at sea only became evident later (see the author's book *Destroyer*!).

Despite Raeder's decision in July 1934, the question of the ship's main armament was again the subject of discussion in March 1935. Five alternatives were tabulated:

(a) Nine, 30.5cm (three triple)
(b) Nine, 33cm (three triple)
(c) Six, 38cm (three twin)

PENETRATIVE POWER OF 28cm P.SPR L/3.7, 300kg SHELL (HOMOGENEOUS ARMOUR)

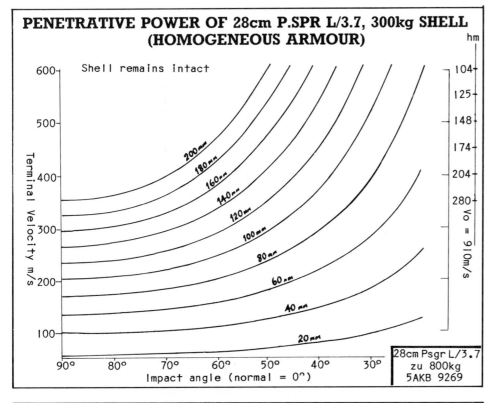

(d) Six, 33cm (three twin)

(e) Six, 35cm (three twin)

The first three would necessitate a new ship of 34,000–37,000 tons as opposed to the planned 31,500 tons. A re-design could be done but at considerable cost in terms of time, something like 1½ years, which would result in a gap of 3¾ years in capital ship construction. It was also likely to have a delaying effect on Schlachtschiff F. As far as (d) and (e) were concerned, these were possible either by an immediate change to the new calibre, or by designing them to allow a later up-gunning. The first option would entail a delay in the construction of D of 17 months and 23 months in that of E. Also, 11 million Marks would have been lost on 28cm guns and turrets then under construction. This option was therefore judged unacceptable on grounds of cost both financial and fiscal. The option of allowing a later increase in calibre by alterations at the design stage was the one preferred and if possible, the main armament was to be 35cm after up-gunning. A later re-gunning with three twin 35cm guns would entail an increase in weight of around 650 tonnes and a consequent increase in draught of 15cm. This was acceptable but the size of existing docks and locks had to be kept in mind. The new turrets would not cause a stability problem. Ammunition stowage would be reduced from 150rpg for the 28cm to 130rpg for the 35cm guns. The main problem was that the ships would be out of service for about fifteen months and the cost would be something like 35 million Marks!

PENETRATIVE POWER OF 28cm PSGR L/3.7, 300kg SHELL (FACE-HARDENED ARMOUR)

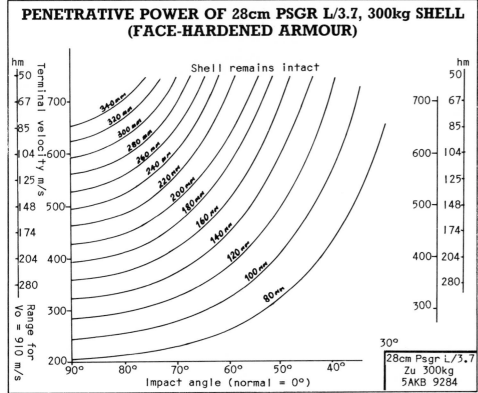

CHARACTERISTICS OF 28cm SK C/34, 890m/s 330kg SHELL

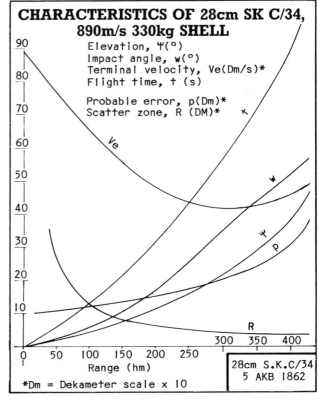

SCHARNHORST: ARMOUR ARRANGEMENTS

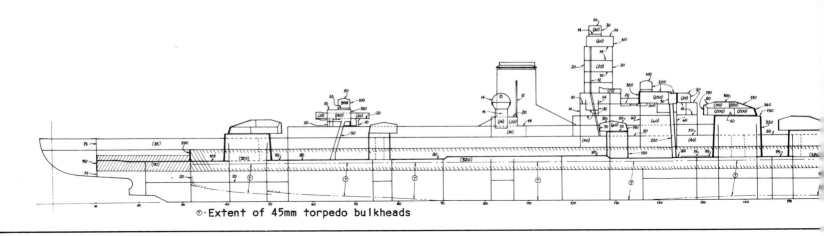

ⓣ·Extent of 45mm torpedo bulkheads

Comparative estimated performance figures were quoted:

	9 × 28cm	6 × 35cm	6 × 38cm
Vo (muzzle velocity)	890m/s	875m/s	865m/s
Shell weight	330kg	625kg	800kg
RpBM	3.5	2.3	2.0
Broadside weight/min	10,395kg	8,625kg	9,600kg
Broadside weight	2,970kg	3,750kg	4,800kg

Armour penetration 70° impact angle:

	10,000m	15,000m	20,000m	25,000m
28cm	348mm	280mm	225mm	194mm
35cm	490mm	418mm	354mm	229mm
38cm	545mm	465mm	392mm	333mm

As *Dunkerque*'s armour was now suspected to be 225mm, it would therefore be pierced by 28cm shells up to 20,500m, 35cm up to 35,000m and 38cm up to 40,000m. However, six 35cm guns were considered too few for good salvo firing, although it was acknowledged that the effect of a hit would be greater than a 28cm shell. Eventually it was agreed that a 28cm armament would be sufficient against *Dunkerque* and that construction would proceed with three triple 28cm turrets but allow for future rearmament with 35cm guns. This latter calibre was chosen on the grounds that it was more effective than the 33cm, it was more suited to the existing 28cm barbettes and would also reduce the variation in battleship main armament calibres (Schlachtschiff F was at that time planned with 35cm guns).

Towards the end of May 1938 the possibility of bringing forward the proposed rearming of *Scharnhorst* (D) and *Gneisenau* (E) was discussed. This had originally been scheduled for 1945 by which time it was anticipated that six H-class battleships would be in service and the older ships could be spared. However, advancing this plan would entail delay in the construction of the first two H-class ships. Any orders for rearmament had to be put out at least 2½ years before completion was required, some twelve months would be needed for the actual conversion, and the crews would have

to be retrained. The new armaments factory to be built in central Germany was scheduled to deliver the first 38cm gun on 1 July 1944, but this assumed that work on the factory had begun as scheduled on 1 April 1938—which it had not. Even so, by Christmas 1938 the refits were being scheduled for *Scharnhorst* between 1 January 1942 and 1 December 1942 at the Wilhelmshaven Naval Yard and her sister by Deutsche Werke, Kiel between 1 July 1941 and 1 June 1942. Eventually, however, it was decided not to bring the plans forward.

The two ships were eventually re-laid down to the enlarged design at the same shipyards, on 15 June 1935 and 6 May respectively, at a time when events were beginning to speed up in the world of treaties, rearmament and politics. The Führer had unilaterally abrogated the Treaty of Versailles on 16 March that year, whereupon Britain quickly moved to impose some limits upon German naval rearmament in the absence of any coherent international policies. The result of this initiative was the signing of the Anglo-German Naval Agreement on 18 June 1935, which limited the strength of the German Fleet to 35 per cent of that of the Royal Navy. This came too late to affect the design of Panzerschiffe D and E in any major fashion, but it obviously removed any worries about the usual 'growth' during the construction of new ships. The Royal Navy had 474,400 tons of capital ships at this time, which allowed Germany 166,000 tons. At the *declared* 'Washington' displacements of existing and new ships, this left Germany with 83,000 tons approximately, to use for post-Panzerschiffe D and E designs.

CONSTRUCTION

This class was 43.8m or 23.55 per cent longer and 9.3m more beamy than *Deutschland*. It is of interest that the extra beam was approximately that proposed for the rebuilding of the *Deutschland* class discussed earlier, which would have made the latter very 'short and fat'. The main constructional steel was ST52 except for plates and components less than 4mm in thickness or those which needed hot bending or a sharp angle, when ST42 was specified.

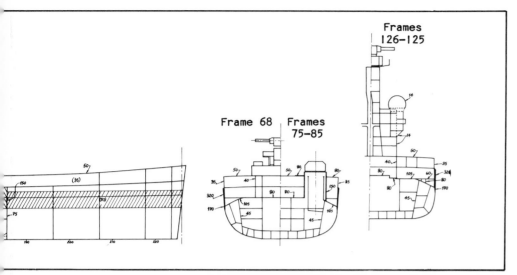

Frames
126-125

Frame 68   Frames
75-85

SCHARNHORST: SECTION THROUGH 'B' TURRET

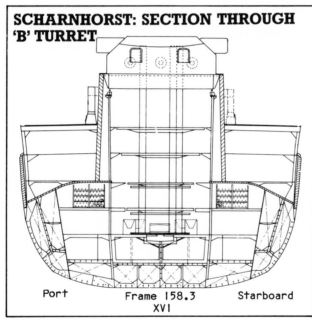

Port   Frame 158.3   Starboard
              XVI

Longitudinal construction was again employed. The main keel comprised a centre keel and a flat keel extending between frames 21.5 to 32, 54.5 to 139.25 and 207 to the stem. From frame 40.85 to the bows, the keel was oil- and watertight. Six longitudinal frames were worked in on each side of the hull. Longitudinal I extended from frame 10.5 to 21.5 and 54.5 to 185.7; II between frames 35.9 and 40.85, 62 and 139.25; III between 49.55 and 162.65; IV between 62 and 153.95; V between frame 32 and 49.55, 185.7 and 207; VI between frames 32 and 217.5. Above longitudinal frame VI the hull was stiffened with longitudinal beams. These longitudinal frames were welded variously oil- and watertight, depending upon their position. Bilge keels extended from frame 75.6 to 143.25. Transverse strength and rigidity was imparted by transverse frames spaced 1,500mm apart, many of which were welded oil- and watertight in the double bottom spaces, which extended from frame 21.5 to 229.5, bounded at the side as far as frame 62 by the side longitudinal bulkhead and forward of this by the torpedo bulkhead. Within this double bottom area was a complex maze of bunkers for fuel oil, feed water, washing and potable water, etc.

There were five main longitudinal bulkheads within the system of internal sub-division, known as the Wallgang bulkhead, torpedo bulkhead, turret support bulkheads, side bulkheads and centre-line bulkheads. The Wallgang bulkhead extended from frame 32 to 185.7 and in height from the torpedo bulkhead to the upper edge of longitudinal frame VI and the armoured deck. It was welded oil-tight. The torpedo bulkhead extended over the same area as the Wallgang, in height from the skin plating to the armoured deck and was inclined outwards from bottom to top by 10°. This was also oil-tight. It was continued as a side longitudinal bulkhead from frame 30 to 10.5 between the skin and the armoured deck. Turret support bulkheads took the weight of each of the three 28cm triple turrets between frames 40.85 and 49.55 ('C' turret), 153.95 and 162.65 ('B' turret), 171 and 179.85 ('A' turret). These extended from the bottom plating to the armoured deck and were spaced about 4,500mm each side of the centre-line. The main armoured deck extended from frame 10.5 to 185.7, 9,200mm above the bottom plating, except over the boiler spaces where it had to be raised 600mm to clear the tops of the boilers. Internal watertight integrity was conferred by 21 watertight compartments, I to XXI from aft to forward, of which compartments VI to XII accommodated the main machinery for the triple-shaft turbine installation. Compartments III and IV aft, and XV to XVIII on the lower deck levels, were associated mainly with magazine and shell room spaces, turret handling rooms, etc.

Two balanced rudders were fitted with separate electric rudder motors, either one of which could be rigged to steer both rudders if necessary. In addition, there was a hand steering position fitted with a triple wheel. The two helmsman's positions were on the command bridge and in the conning tower. Reserve positions were incorporated in the command centre on the 'tween deck, in each tiller flat and in the emergency hand steering position. Light alloys were once again employed to save weight, but although this totalled some 103.5 tonnes it still represented only 0.66 per cent of the hull weight (excluding the vertical armour and turrets).

PROTECTIVE ARRANGEMENTS

The horizontal armour comprised an upper deck of 50mm Wh n/a material which was designed to give protection from general-purpose (GP) bombs and to trigger the fuse of any delayed-action AP bomb which penetrated so as to ensure that it exploded above the main armoured deck. This deck armouring weighed 1,989 tonnes. Two decks below was the main armoured deck, 105mm thick KC material which extended from frame 10.5 to frame 185.7. This deck was horizontal inboard, where it commenced at the longitudinal splinter bulkhead but was rolled to a downwards curve so as

Above: *Gneisenau* about 1938 with an Ar 95 on 'C' turret and an He 114 on the midships catapult. (USN)

to meet the belt armour above its lower edge at 25° to the horizontal. The thickness of this was uniform from inboard to outboard. Bridging the midships section between the 20mm longitudinal splinter bulkheads was an area of 80mm plate seated on the upper edges of the 105mm armour. This 80mm plate was bounded fore and aft by bulkheads 185.7 and 54.5. Fabricated again from Wh n/a material, some 3,252 tonnes was worked into this deck. 150mm armoured bulkheads at frames $10\frac{1}{2}$ and 185.7 closed off the armoured carapace. The barbettes, slightly conical in form, were 350mm thick of Krupp Cemented (KC) armour and seated directly upon the main armoured deck.

Vertical protection consisted of a main belt 4.5m deep extending between frames 10 and 185.7, which was 320mm KC armour (*not* 350mm as often quoted). Its lower edge was seated on a step in the hull with the belt itself being backed by teak and secured to the hull with armoured bolts. This belt was full thickness for over 70 per cent of its depth, having a chamfered top and tapering over its bottom 30 per cent to 170mm at the lower edge. Forward of frame 185.7, 70mm plating extended to the bows, while aft a 90mm belt protected the rudder area. Above the main belt was the citadel armour belt, 35mm thick. Inboard of the main belt ran the torpedo bulkhead, 45mm thick, between frames 32 and 185.7. This was inclined outwards from bottom to top by 10°. Full details of the protective arrangements are shown on page 36.

MAIN MACHINERY

The choice of propulsion had not been easy at first but the increase in size of these ships to a nominal 26,500 tonnes led to steam being the only choice. An experimental programme begun in 1929 to develop a high-efficiency low-weight and space-saving high-pressure steam plant had, by the mid-1930s, shown sufficient promise for it to be installed in a new ship, the gunnery training ship *Brummer* (launched in February 1936) and for it to be specified for the new Type 34 destroyers. It was also to be installed in Panzerschiffe D and E, but not with such extremes of pressure.

Twelve Wagner boilers were installed in three boiler rooms, four in each. The boilers for both ships were built by Deschimag. These boilers operated at a pressure of 58 atmospheres (52kg/cm²) and 450° with a maximum rated output of 55 tons/hr. They were of three-drum type, the earlier experimental five-drum Wagner boiler with two superheaters and two economizers having been discarded as too complicated. Instead, two three-drum units were fitted side by side. These were also fitted with superheater and economizer, the latter being fed from the HP turbine exhaust and the middle of the IP turbine drum. They were single cased with a closed boiler room. Their height, 6,685mm, dictated a dome in the armoured deck over the boiler room spaces (compartments IX to XII). Natural circulation was employed and they were equipped with the now obligatory Askania automatic control of the double Saake burners.

GNEISENAU: TURBINE ARRANGEMENTS (SCHEMATIC)

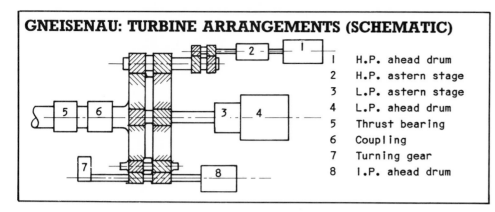

1   H.P. ahead drum
2   H.P. astern stage
3   L.P. astern stage
4   L.P. ahead drum
5   Thrust bearing
6   Coupling
7   Turning gear
8   I.P. ahead drum

SCHARNHORST: SPEED/POWER CURVE

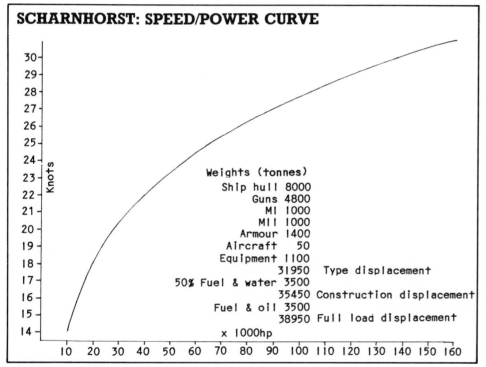

Weights (tonnes)
Ship hull 8000
Guns 4800
MI 1000
MII 1000
Armour 1400
Aircraft 50
Equipment 1100
31950   Type displacement
50% Fuel & water 3500
35450   Construction displacement
Fuel & oil 3500
38950   Full load displacement

Gneisenau, on the other hand, received Deschimag turbines (not Germania as has usually been quoted); all OKM documents of construction data 1935–1939 show this ship's machinery as being manufactured by Deschimag A.G. These also incorporated a cruising turbine which comprised a Curtis wheel and four single stages connected via a Vulcan coupling and developing 12,000hp per shaft. The HP turbine was unique in the Kriegsmarine in that it consisted of a Curtis wheel and three single Rateau stages driving through double-reduction gearing. (The Kriegsmarine distrusted double-reduction gearing, which resulted in less economical turbine designs.) Like all German turbine designs, there was a separate drum for each turbine, with the IP turbine of the first single Rateau stage and seventeen reaction stages driving via a pinion on to the top of the main wheel. The LP turbine consisted of five single and two double Rateau stages and drove on to the main wheel via an intermediate idler pinion. All the turbine drums were forward of the main wheel. The HP astern turbine, in series with the HP ahead turbine, consisted of one double-row Curtis wheel and drove through the double reduction gearing. A separate LP astern turbine was incorporated in the after end of the LP drum and was single flow with two Rateau stages. The astern turbines developed 19,000hp per shaft. The HP turbine ran at 6,725rpm at maximum power, with the cruising turbine shut down.

In both ships the cruising turbines were similar to those in the Type 34 destroyers—i.e., separate and driving via a Vulcan clutch. They were therefore afflicted with similar problems in that the drag of the clutch greatly reduced efficiency. In consequence, tests were carried out both with and without the cruising turbines, and the result was their removal. At the same time the admission of auxiliary exhaust steam into the LP turbine was also abandoned. The removal of the cruising turbines led to a 25 per cent increase in steam rate at powers of less than 10,000hp, but this did not outweigh the dislike of the cruising turbine, particularly as the disconnecting couplings on the propeller shafts allowed low power operations on one shaft with good turbine loading, when the lack of a cruising turbine made little difference. The total installed power was 53,360shp maximum per shaft—i.e., 160,080shp.

Comment has already been made on the weight complication, bulk and relatively low efficiency of German turbine and boiler design in the earlier volumes. Those of the battleships were little different. Weights were high because of the separate turbine drums, and their lower speeds increased unit size. Speed was too low because of the retention of single-reduction gearing, which led to low efficiency. For legal reasons, machinery designers also incorporated numerous safety measures in their equipment. These caused steam valves to trip if the following conditions existed: (a) shaft overspeed, (b) loss of lubrication pressure, (c) loss of condenser vacuum, (d) overpressure in turbine inlets, and (e) excessive axial movement.

This was acknowledged as being overdone and, in action, shock frequently caused one of these safety features to trip and immobilize the machinery. The three turbine spaces

While the steam plant was the same in each ship, the turbines differed. Panzerschiff D (*Scharnhorst*) received Brown-Boveri turbines which had impulse-reaction cruising and high-pressure (HP) stages with straight reaction intermediate-pressure (IP) and low-pressure (LP) turbines, with hollow rotors. The cruising and HP turbines were on the after end of the main wheel, while the IP and LP turbines were on the ahead side. The astern turbine was incorporated in the forward end of the IP turbine, separated by a diaphragm from the ahead blading. A second astern element was a double-flow reaction stage in the centre of the LP casing. This LP turbine sat directly on the underslung condenser and was supported by sprung feet to absorb shock. Drive from the gearing to the shafts was by means of Brown-Boveri toothed couplings. The weight of the main and auxiliary machinery is given as 4,000 tonnes.

GNEISENAU: INTERNAL PROFILE AFTER PROJECTED RE-ARMING WITH 38cm GUNS

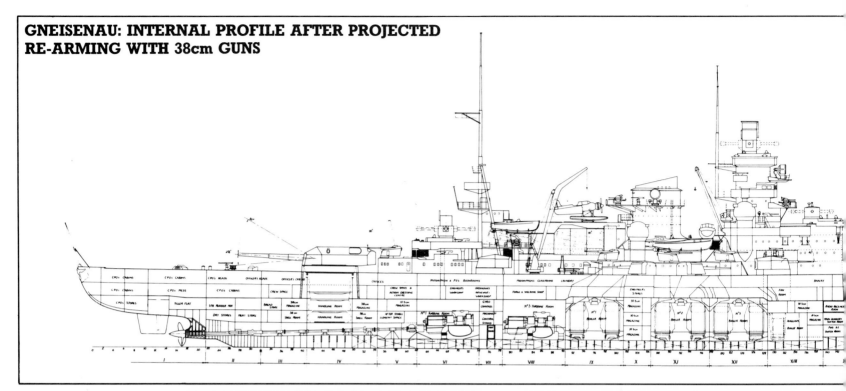

Right: Method of ammunition supply for the 10.5cm guns. (Bundesarchiv)

Centre: 10.5cm mounting at full elevation. (Bundesarchiv)

Far right: *Gneisenau.* Midships detail showing 3.7cm gun, crane and catapult tower. (Bundesarchiv)

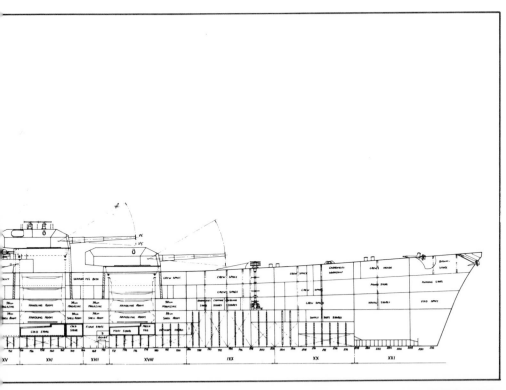

were arranged with No.1 aftermost in compartment VI driving the centre shaft, No.2 driving the port shaft in compartment VIII and No.3 driving the starboard shaft, also in compartment VIII, which was divided by a centre-line longitudinal bulkhead.

The ship's generating capacity totalled 4,120kW, made up of 3,220kW by turbo-generators and the balance by diesel generators. There were six 460kW and two 230kW turbo-sets and four diesel sets, two each of 150kW and 300kW. The turbo-generators were disposed in four generator spaces, No.1 on the port side in compartment VI at upper platform level above the port shaft tunnel, No.2 on the starboard side in compartment IX, No.3 on the port side, compartment XI, and No.4 on the starboard side, compartment XII. The diesel generator space, No.5, was on the port side in compartment XIII. To starboard in this compartment was the auxiliary boiler space.

ARMAMENT AND FIRE CONTROL

The main armament of nine 28cm SKC/34 guns was carried in three triple turrets, two forward, one aft. These guns fired a 330kg AP shell with a maximum range of 40,930 metres. Each turret had its own magazine and shell rooms, the former on the upper platform deck, the latter on the middle platform deck. Four magazines and two shell rooms served each turret; 150rpg was the rate book outfit.

It had been hoped to ship all the secondary armament of 15cm SKC/28 guns in twin turrets (LC/34), but this proved impossible on weight grounds. Two such turrets were shipped on each beam, one forward, one aft; but the remainder were carried in single shielded centre-pivot mountings (MPL/35), on each beam between the fore and aft twin turrets. In practice they were a mixed blessing as with all open mountings they were liable to be washed out at sea, while serving them in arctic conditions was hazardous at the best of times. The 15cm SKC/28 was a low-angle weapon only.

These two ships therefore continued Kriegsmarine practice in having separate low-angle secondary guns and high-angle heavy flak guns. The heavy flak was the 10.5cm SKC/33 gun carried in adapted 8.8cm twin mountings (LC/31), and the increase in size of Panzerschiff D over that of Panzerschiff A allowed the heavy flak to be more than doubled. This was achieved by siting three twin mountings on the superstructure deck amidships, where they had a very good field of fire, and a seventh mounting on the centre-line aft where it commanded the after arcs.

There was still little other choice for the close-range or light flak as the 3.7cm SKC/30 in twin mountings had not been superseded. Once again, however, the number of mountings could be doubled to eight—two abreast 'B' turret on the upper deck, two on the foremast tower above the command bridge, and four grouped around the after gunnery control position. Finally, there were ten 2cm MGC/30 guns in single mountings, of which only eight were carried in peacetime—two abreast 'B' turret on the shelter deck, two in the foretop, two on the funnel platform and two on the quarterdeck.

Above: *Gneisenau's* catapult with Ar 196. (USN)

No torpedo outfit was fitted but the ships were equipped with aircraft and catapult facilities. In contrast to the earlier Panzerschiffe these new ships were fitted with two catapults, one of which was on the roof of 'C' turret. This latter feature caused some problems, especially in the handling of the aircraft, which was by means of a collapsible derrick.

Main armament fire control followed the usual German pattern with three gunnery control positions, the forward position fitted with a 7m stereoscopic range-finder and the other two with 10m instruments. All three positions were fitted with armoured cupolas. The Gunnery TS and associated switch rooms and amplifier rooms were grouped on the upper, middle and lower platform decks in compartment XIV, together with the Action Command Centre. A reserve group of similarly equipped compartments was incorporated aft in compartment V. These two ships introduced the new C30 fire control equipment which would be further developed and refined in the later heavy cruisers and battleships.

A more sophisticated HA fire control system was fitted, the type 1933 SL6 director which, once again, was fully stabilized and fitted with the distinctive spherical shield. Compared with the 21 tonnes of the earlier SL1 however, it weighed over 40 tonnes. These were linked with two flak T/S's adjacent to the main gunnery T/S's. The Zielanweisergeräte (or ZAG) target indicator sight made its appearance in these ships.

Searchlights remained an essential element of night defence and to that end five 150cm equipments were fitted. One was on a platform on the forward face of the tower mast, two were fitted on the funnel platform and the final pair were on sponsons abreast the catapult base.

MODIFICATIONS

Early trials having demonstrated once again the general wetness of German ships forward, the leading ship *Gneisenau* was taken in hand by her builders in the autumn of 1938 for alterations to the fore-ends. This entailed the fitting of the so-called 'Atlantic Bow', a graceful curved prow to alleviate the spray problem. At the same time a large raked funnel cap was added. The bow alterations were not entirely successful and further to improve matters, the anchors were repositioned on the upper deck and the former hawse pipes welded closed a month or two later. In addition, the radio mast formerly fitted atop the upper range-finder was removed and replaced by a pole mast stepped abaft the tower mast. In February 1940 the after catapult was removed from 'C' turret. Its weight affected the turret's training, there was a serious danger of aviation spirit spilling on to the turret due to accident or battle damage, and the aircraft itself was very difficult to service in such an exposed position.

Radar was fitted in October 1939, the mattress aerial being fitted on to the foretop range-finder. At the same time, an office was installed on top of this range-finder for the operators. This was found to overload the training motors of the range-finder—a common problem. In January 1941 the slow-firing 2cm C/30 weapons were replaced by the C/38 model and a 2cm Vierling was fitted on the lattice tower, which had been stepped between the catapult and funnel during the major refit (July to November 1940). A second radar set was installed in 1942 while the ship was in Brest, as were two triple banks of torpedo tubes, the latter being the direct result of experience during Operation 'Berlin' and of the *Admiral Hipper* sortie. At least fourteen torpedoes could be accommodated. During the time the ship spent immobile in France, the hangar was extended and rebuilt with the catapult now inside it. The sides of this hangar could be lowered and the catapult trained for launching the aircraft. This modification displaced the tower-mounted Vierling but in its place three more were fitted, one on 'B' turret, one on the funnel platform and one on the hangar itself. It had also been intended to ship a tripod mainmast similar to that on *Scharnhorst* but this was never fitted, despite being available in Brest.

After being badly damaged by bombs at Kiel in February 1942, *Gneisenau* was paid off with the intention of starting the long planned rearmament with three twin 38cm turrets. This was never completed and the ship saw no further service.

Scharnhorst had her bows altered to 'Atlantic' form during July and August 1939, the hangar and catapult modified, funnel cap fitted and a new tripod mast shipped. She too had her anchor stowage modified. Radar was fitted at the same time as *Gneisenau* and she received a second set aft in Brest, as well as torpedo tubes. Six Vierlinge were fitted, four of which were biaxial Army-pattern weapons. One was shipped on 'B' turret, one on each of No.1 15cm turret roofs, one on the funnel platform and one each on the forecastle and quarterdeck. Those on the 15cm turrets and the main deck were the biaxial mountings. Ten single 2cm C/38 guns were also carried at this time. The Army-pattern guns were landed after Operation 'Cerberus' (the 'Channel Dash'). In 1942, after the ship had returned to Germany, the Admiral's bridge was closed in and its wings shortened, but little else was done prior to her loss in December 1943.

4. BISMARCK AND TIRPITZ

DESIGN HISTORY

When Adolf Hitler unilaterally abrogated the Treaty of Versailles on 16 March 1935 it resulted in a flurry of diplomatic activity, culminating in the signing of the Anglo-German Naval Agreement three months later on 13 June. By this agreement Germany undertook to restrict her fleet to 35 per cent of that of Great Britain which meant, as far as capital ships were concerned, that she was allowed 184,000 tons in this category. The three Panzerschiffe and the two *Scharnhorst*s accounted for some 83,000 tons, leaving about 101,000 tons available for new construction. However, the Washington Treaty of 1922 and the First London Naval Conference agreements and limitations still remained in force, which restricted capital ship displacement to 35,000 tons maximum. Germany could therefore legitimately construct three new ships of this displacement on the remaining tonnage.

In fact, Germany had for some time been working towards total disregard for the Versailles Treaty, for even when the preliminary discussions for Schlachtschiff F were begun in the spring of 1934, 35,000 tons was the specified displacement. The initial staff requirement called for a 35,000-ton ship armed with eight 33cm guns and twelve 15cm in twin turrets, sixteen 10.5cm and with protection as follows:

Main belt	350mm (as D and E)
Bow and stern	150mm
Armoured deck (horizontal)	100mm
Armoured deck (curved)	120mm
(and over magazines and rudder)	
Upper deck	50mm
Barbettes	350mm
15cm barbettes	150mm
Conning tower	400mm
Torpedo bulkheads	60mm
Side splinter protection	60mm

It quickly became evident that it was impossible to achieve this scale of protection and remain within the 35,000 tons limit, so the main belt had to be reduced to 320mm, bow armour to 70mm and the stern to 90mm. The main propulsion method had still not been decided, various options being under consideration. Sketch designs 3–6 detailed these options. By the autumn of 1934 the Construction Office had worked out the approximate dimensions based on eight 33cm guns, armour, secondary armament and flak outfit as '*D*' and '*E*', with a speed of 30 knots. However, on 2 November, during a conference on the design, it was stated that in order to have superiority over *Dunkerque* and *Strasbourg*, as well as equality with future battleships of other nations, it would be necessary to demand speeds of 33 knots (max.), 30 knots (continuous) and 21 knots (cruising). This was not concurred with by the head of the General Office, Viz. Ad. Guse, who reduced the figures to 29/27/21 knots respectively. These figures were accepted for the first and second sketch designs but reduced again on 26 November to 28 knots maximum on the measured mile—i.e., trials condition and 27 knots at sea. The estimated type displacement came out at 37,200 tonnes.

However, on 10 November Admiral Raeder instructed that under no circumstances must the design exceed 35,000 tons and that the hull dimensions must conform to the limitations of the existing locks, docks and harbour facilities. With this in mind, the military demands were re-examined but not reduced and it was recognised that a design always 'grew' during development and construction. This led to the conclusion that it was impossible to reduce the displacement below 37,200 tonnes. Re-examination of the calculations by the Construction Office confirmed this. On 21 December 1934, as a result of proposals from the General Office with the support of the Weapons and Construction Offices, Admiral Raeder agreed that:

(a) The type displacement could be exceeded provided that a considerable increase in fighting power was obtained thereby.

(b) Turbo-electric propulsion be investigated.

(c) That separate sketch designs be prepared for four twin

Below: *Tirpitz* completed up to the armoured deck. (IWM).

33cm turrets with turbo-electric drive and four twin 35cm turrets with steam turbine propulsion.

After calculation, the Construction Office reported that if the demanded military characteristics were to be met, neither of these two proposals under (c) could be achieved without seriously exceeding the specified type displacement; moreover, that this would eliminate Deutsche Werke at Kiel as a possible building yard. This was considered during a conference on 17 January 1935, when it was concluded that neither the slip length at Deutsche Werke nor those at the Naval Yard in Wilhelmshaven were to be allowed to dictate hull dimensions. It was reiterated that the limitation would remain locks and water depth off Germany's naval ports.

The main armament was also discussed—33cm or 35cm—and the speed given as 28 knots. This was actually intended as a maximum speed but was interpreted by Raeder as continuous and led to later disagreement as to what the design requirements actually were.

Two days later, on 19 January, Admiral Raeder decided to develop design 'F' with 35cm guns and geared turbines in mind. Armour thickness was to be as previously planned except that the main barbettes were to be 350mm in thickness above the upper deck and 320mm below it.

Maximum continuous speed was to be 28 knots. This, it was accepted, would require exceeding the 35,000-ton limit but it was stressed that the design was always to be referred to as '35,000 tons'. By this time the type displacement had

Opposite page, top left: *Tirpitz* in the fitting-out basin. (IWM)

Opposite page, centre: The armour belt being fitted to *Bismarck*; note the bolt holes. (Bundesarchiv)

Opposite page, bottom: The gun platform for 'B' turret is lowered onto *Bismarck*. (Bundesarchiv)

Near left: A turret loading complex is lifted into *Bismarck*. (Bundesarchiv)

already grown in fact to 39,000 tons, but recent accurate and exact recalculation of the hull weights of *Scharnhorst* and *Gneisenau* (Panzerschiffe D and E) now showed that even this figure was insufficient to meet the specified demands and that some of the armour would have to be reduced again. Further increase in displacement could only be achieved at the cost of exceeding the hitherto maximum draught of 10m, when fully equipped. In the meantime, investigations by the Construction Office and other departments into the requirements of using Wilhelmshaven as a base, and the use of the Kiel Canal, had shown that the hull dimensions were limited to 242m in length, 36m beam and 10m draught.

In March 1935 the question of using 38cm guns arose, presumably as a result of the abrogation of the Versailles Treaty. This could be done but the additional weight would be about 1,500 tons, pushing the displacement up to 42,000–42,500 tons. If this considerable excess over 35,000 tons were to be avoided, speed and/or protection would have to be greatly reduced. As the design already exceeded the Washington limits by 6,000 tons, and in view of the shallowness of German ports, the General Office decided against going beyond a 35cm gun. A 41,000-ton ship, armed with 35cm guns, having a maximum draught of 9.25m, could use the largest lock at Wilhelmshaven but 38cm guns would increase draught to 9.40m and prevent transit of this lock. If armour were reduced to compensate, then the ship would be at a disadvantage versus *Strasbourg*. Triple 38cm were considered (i.e., three triple turrets) but it was decided that 38cm guns were not possible on the current displacement. The options considered are detailed below:

The locks at Wilhelmshaven were 250m long, the north one 38m wide, the southern 33m with a depth of 10m.

On 1 April 1935 Raeder, in consultation with the heads of the main departments, decided that the displacement was now to be 41,000 tons with a main armament of eight 35cm guns in four twin turrets. The intention was to place an order with Blohm & Voss at Hamburg on 1 April the following year. If the current Naval Conference between the major powers permitted it, an increase to 38cm guns could be accommodated which, reported the Weapons Office, would entail a delay of about six months. Raeder in fact sanctioned 38cm as the main armament calibre on 9 May 1935.

Meanwhile, the Construction Office had investigated four alternatives for main propulsion arrangements. These were:

(a) High-pressure steam geared turbines, twelve boilers in six boiler rooms forward of the turbine rooms.

(b) As (a) but with the boilers in three boiler rooms all forward of the turbine rooms.

(c) As (b) but with one of the boiler rooms between the turbine rooms.

(d) Turbo-electric drive.

The Construction Office considered (b) the best solution. (d) was ruled out on weight grounds. The four arrangements and various options for the secondary armament, including the use of casemates, were detailed in sketch designs A3–A6. Further sketches A7–A9 detailed options for relocating the generator room (TE versions) and after turrets in the designs with 15cm casemates.

Entwurf A2 was one of the steam turbine designs, a three-shaft 115,000shp layout for 28 knots. Bunkerage was 8,000

Armour	Eight 35cm guns		Eight 38cm guns	
	Specified	Reduced	Specified	Reduced
Belt	320	290	320	260
Bows	70	70	70	70
Stern	90	80	90	80
Main barbettes	320	290	320	255
15cm barbettes	150	125	150	125
Conning tower	350	350	350	350
Torpedo bulkhead	45	45	45	45
Longitudinal b/h	40	40	40	35
Armoured deck:				
Sides	120	95	120	95
Between longitudinal b/h	100	60	100	60
Over magazines	100	80	100	90
Over rudder	100	95	100	85
Sides above belt	35	30	35	30
Upper deck	50	45	50	45
Type displacement	41,000 tons	39,000 tons	43,000 tons	39,800 tons
Draught (½ oil)	9.25	8.8	9.4	8.8
Length (wl)	243	243	250	250
Beam	36	36	36	36
Speed	27–28kts	28kts	27–28kts	28kts

SUMMARY OF HULL WEIGHTS

Category	Admiral Scheer	Admiral Graf Spee	Scharnhorst	Tirpitz
SI (Shipbuilding shop)	5,288,673	5,744,292	14,528,886	19,221,171
SII (Forging shop)	265,375	344,626	649,310	827,935
SIII (Joiners shop)	88,623	136,764	219,354	323,358
SIV (Paint shop)	63,116	73,373	140,350	168,347
Additions	5,705,787	6,299,055	15,537,900	20,540,811
Vertical armour (excluding turrets)	40,432 43,682 413,285	83,186 425,947	6,325 6,517,853	8,136,532
	6,159,504	6,768,684	22,138,939	28,683,668
Later additions	80,690	36,852	89,952	10,823
Total	6,240,194	6,805,536	22,228,891	28,694,491
Light alloy in SI	30,869	34,013	103,489	114,907
Armour comparisons:				
Upper Deck	—	—	1,989,915	2,248,053
Main Armoured Deck	474,869	697,083	3,252,381	4,293,264
	474,869	697,083	5,242,296	6,541,317

Weights in kilogrammes.

tonnes. The waterline length was 241.5m, 245.2m overall, with a beam of 36m. The secondary armament was four twin 15cm in C/34 gunhouses and four single 15cm in MPL C/20 mountings. Entwurf A3 had twelve 15cm C/28 guns, all in casemates; while Entwurf A4 showed all 15cm guns in LC/34 twin mountings of which the centre one was located on the superstructure deck. Entwurf A5 was A2 with turbo-electric drive.

The question of casemates generated considerable discussion, rather surprisingly in view of the obsolete nature of this feature. In the end it was decided that, to improve protection, 150mm armour would be worked in above the main belt up to the upper deck to provide a closed citadel and that the secondary armament would be mounted in turrets. This would avoid one of the major drawbacks to casemates—being washed out in heavy weather. The citadel question was examined in depth and various options were considered, mostly associated with its length. Thus proposals were studied for the citadel extending sufficiently far to encompass not only the four main turrets but also their magazines, as well as shorter options covering 'A' and 'D' turrets and one between 'B' and 'C' turrets only.

A further conference on 7 June 1935 addressed various options for the secondary armament and continued discussion about the main propulsion. At this time encouraging results with the turbo-electric machinery in the Lloyd liner *Scharnhorst* reopened consideration of this method, despite an extra 600 tons weight compared to geared turbines. The Construction Office, however, had its reservations and wished to conduct a detailed evaluation. Raeder decided that the current type displacement and measurements were not to be exceeded and intimated that he was satisfied with the protection scheme. It was desirable that all secondary guns be in turrets and the extra weight incurred by the turbo-electric drive had to be saved by economies elsewhere.

On 23 August 1935 the Construction Office presented Admiral Raeder with sketch design A13 (Entwurf A13), a three-shaft turbo-electric layout which he approved. Details still had to be finalized, including flak outfit, bridge shape, command stands and aircraft installations. The Algemeineamt demanded, and got, sixteen 3.7cm guns in eight twin mountings instead of only eight and, to improve habitability, obtained a reduction in citadel length to only between 'B' and 'C' turrets, thereby reducing the number of spaces without scuttles. Re-examination of the plans later proved it possible to position living spaces outside the main armoured areas, so that the citadel length was restored to its original length. (This was agreed on 23 January 1936.) At the same time, the barbette thickness was reduced to 220mm inside the citadel and part of the armoured deck from 100mm to 80mm. Further improvements in protection were obtained by using 20mm armour for splinter protection on the upper platform deck and increasing the armoured deck over the main magazines to 95mm. In addition, the main end armoured bulkheads 32 and 202.7 were extended to the upper deck. At the suggestion of the Weapons Office and Construction Office, Admiral Raeder agreed on 23 November

1935 that the intended upper taper of the belt armour be dispensed with and its thickness reduced to 300mm.

It was intended in October 1935 that 'F' be laid down on 1 July 1936 but it was hoped that she could be laid earlier. The political situation prevented this and it was therefore decided to press completion so that the ship would be in service by 1 October 1939 instead of 1 December 1939 as planned. 'G' was to be laid on the same slip as 'D' (*Scharnhorst*), but this slip would have to be extended so that only a part keel would be laid at first, as had been done for *Gneisenau*. 'G' was provisionally to be laid down on 1 January 1937, four months earlier than planned, for completion on 1 February 1940.

By June 1936 the Construction Office had finally decided against turbo-electric drive and proposed to Raeder that geared turbines be adopted instead. Raeder agreed to this on 6 June, but it meant that much of the calculation and drawing work had now to be redone—a situation which had happened before with Panzerschiffe D and E. The change in machinery weight did not lead to a reduction in displacement because the opportunity was taken to re-increase the main armour belt from 300mm to 320mm. However, the adoption of welded armour on the upper deck instead of riveted did save weight, allowing the deck above the main magazines to be increased from 95mm to 100mm and the sloped part in the same area from 110mm to 120mm. By December 1936 any further increase in the armoured deck thickness was impossible because the plates had already been rolled.

CONSTRUCTION

The final design hull dimensions were 241.6m waterline length and 36m beam. A centre keel extended between frames 47.6 to 154.6 and from frame 224 to the bows. Between frames 154.6 and 224, the keel was replaced by the centre-line longitudinal bulkhead and aft of frame 47.6 by the longitudinals. Docking stresses were taken by welded plate reinforcements to the centre keel between certain stations, at 500mm intervals. The double bottom extended for 83 per cent of the ship's length and was 1,700mm deep (1,200mm in the fore-ends). It was all welded, oil- and watertight as required, according to the liquid stowage arrangements. The ship was of longitudinal construction with nine longitudinal frames each side of the keel. Longitudinal VIII was continuous with the torpedo bulkhead, while III took the docking pressure up to frame 112.3. A bilge keel was worked in either side from frame 88.8 to 141.1, which was about 1,000m deep amidships, with a surface area of 55m². These were welded to the ship's side. Hull strength was calculated on a basis of wave length L/20. The torpedo bulkhead extended from frame 32 to 202.7 from the shell plating to about 1,400mm above the armoured deck. In the area of the barbettes of the after pair of 15cm turrets, it extended 2,400mm above the armoured deck. This bulkhead was riveted oiltight. Of the bulkheads within the outer Wallgang, those under longitudinal IX were oil-tight, those above, watertight. All the inner Wallgang bulkheads were oil-tight.

Main transverse bulkheads, with the exception of the turret support bulkheads, were interrupted by the side and centre longitudinal bulkheads. They extended from the inner bottom or shell plating to the armoured deck in the vertical plane and across the ship from torpedo bulkhead, extended bulkhead, longitudinal bulkheads or skin. Bulkhead 10.5 closed off the end of the armoured deck aft.

Longitudinal bulkheads were worked in aft, below the armoured deck from frames 10.5 to 32, which extended from the shell plating or the centre propeller shaft up to the armoured deck. Nos. 2 and 3 turbine rooms were separated by a centre-line bulkhead between frames 98.3 and 112.3, this bulkhead reaching from the inner double bottom to the armoured deck. An extension of this between frames 98.3 and 91.3 extended from the inner double bottom and the lower armoured deck. In the bows another longitudinal bulkhead between frames 154.6 and 224 over the vertical keel plate reached up to the lower or upper platform decks and was stiffened for docking stresses.

The weight of the turrets was taken by transverse support bulkheads at frames 41.8, 50.5, 60, 68.7, 169.98, 178.7, 188.8 and 196.9. These extended from shell plating to the armoured deck.

Above the armoured deck, the torpedo bulkhead was extended upwards as a side splinter protection bulkhead between frames 32 and 202.7. This reached up to the upper deck and was formed round the 15cm barbettes where necessary. In addition, there was a pair of side longitudinal bulkheads between 'B' and 'C' barbettes about 4,800mm from the centre-line, which also reached from armoured deck to upper deck. There were 34 transverse bulkheads above the armoured deck, whose height depended upon their position in the ship's length. Watertight integrity and damage control were conferred by the sub-division of the hull into 22 separate watertight compartments. Of these, the machinery spaces occupied compartments VIII to XIII. The upper deck was covered with 75mm teak planking from the stern to frame 233.

PROTECTIVE SCHEME

Vertical armour generally followed the layout adopted for Schlachtschiff E, the main difference, apart from the individual plate thickness, being the use of a vertical torpedo bulkhead instead of an inclined one. The side armour belt was fabricated from case-hardened KC n/A material and comprised an upper and lower row of plates. The lower row (320mm in thickness) had its top edge 100mm below the battery deck and extended down to 7,800mm above the keel (i.e., 1,600mm below the designed waterline). These plates were chamfered and stepped at their upper edge to accommodate the upper row of armour plates and were full thickness for 70 per cent of their depth before tapering down to 170mm at the lower end. The upper row was also of KC n/A material, 145mm in thickness, and reached to the upper edge of the upper deck plating. Behind the armour was a 60mm wood backing, the whole being secured to the hull plating by armoured bolts 50mm or 70mm in diameter. The main belt extended from frame 32 to 203 and was 4.8 metres in depth. Within the area of the main belt, the hull plating was 16mm thick in the lower and middle regions, 18mm along the upper edge and 25mm in the region of the after 15cm gun group.

Forward and aft of the main belt were thinner armour belts fabricated from Wh n/a material. These were lower and shallower in depth than the main belt. That aft was 80mm in thickness from frame 10.5 to 32, 2,100mm in depth, and reached 1,500mm below the designed waterline. The forward belt, 60mm thick, reached from the end of the main belt to

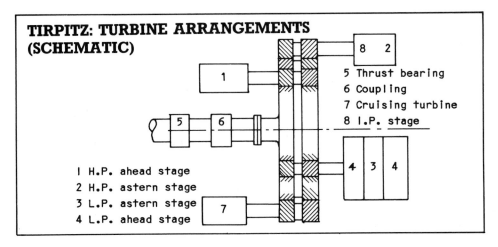

TIRPITZ: TURBINE ARRANGEMENTS (SCHEMATIC)

5 Thrust bearing
6 Coupling
7 Cruising turbine
8 I.P. stage

1 H.P. ahead stage
2 H.P. astern stage
3 L.P. astern stage
4 L.P. ahead stage

the stern and was 3,895mm in depth. These lower belts fore and aft of the main belt formed the shell plating in these areas. The butts had an inside strap and were riveted. Connections to the shell plating above and below these belts was rebated and riveted, there being no shell plating behind them.

Inboard of the main belt was an outer torpedo bulkhead, extending from longitudinal IX up to the armoured deck. The space between the side armour and this bulkhead was normally kept void but could be used for counter flooding in emergency. The inner or main torpedo bulkhead was fabricated from 45mm Wh n/a steel, with butts scarfed and riveted as well as having double butt straps of varying width. Between the inner and outer torpedo bulkheads were fuel and water stowage bunkers. At the midships section, the distance from shell plating to the main torpedo bulkhead was 5,300mm and to the outer bulkhead, 2,347mm. The width of the anti-torpedo protection was 5.8 metres. Total weight of vertical protection was 8,136,532kg.

Horizontal protection was endowed by two armoured decks, the upper deck and the main armoured deck. This was mostly fabricated from Wh n/a material. The upper deck armour extended from frame 10.5 to 224 and was 50mm in thickness except in the way of the openings for the 15cm barbettes, where it was increased to 80mm. Seams and butts were all welded. Some 2,248,053kg of armour was worked into this deck. The main armoured deck was generally 80mm thick inboard of the torpedo bulkhead and, outboard of it, sloped at 22°, 110mm in thickness, to join the side armour. Aft of frame 32 there was a lower armoured deck 110mm thick to frame 10.5. 4,293,264kg of armour was worked into the main deck.

The armoured citadel was closed off at either end by armoured bulkheads on frames 32 and 202.7, with another at frame 10.5, closing off the steering gear protection. The thickness of these bulkheads varied between 180mm and 220mm below the armoured deck. Above it, generally only 12mm plating was used. All armour over 100mm thickness was KC n/A; below it, Wh n/a was used.

Main barbettes were formed from two rings, the lower

from armoured deck to just below the upper deck being 220mm thick, while the upper ring was 340mm KC N/A. 15cm barbettes were 80mm Wh n/a. Conning tower armour was 340mm, fabricated from five plates bolted and butt-strapped. A 200mm-thick trunk allowed communication with the command centre.

MAIN MACHINERY

The main steam plant comprised twelve boilers arranged in pairs fore and aft in six separate boiler rooms. These were housed three abreast in compartments XI and XIII, being separated by auxiliary and control spaces. The boilers themselves were of Wagner pattern (built by Blohm & Voss for *Bismarck* and shared between Wilhelmshaven Naval Yard and Deschimag for *Tirpitz*), with an evaporation rate of 50,000kg/hr, operating at a pressure of 58kg/cm^2 and 450°C. Their steaming weight was about 54 tonnes (50 tonnes dry). Although fitted with Askania automatic regulation superheaters and a horizontal streamlined air pre-heater, no economizers were fitted and, like many German boilers, their efficiency at 80 per cent was on the low side. Two auxiliary exhaust steam ranges were fitted. One was at 1.5kg/cm^2 and supplied the de-aerator; the other exhaust, from feed pumps at 8kg/cm^2, supplied the second-stage feed heater, raising the feed temperature to 350°C. Two Saacke burners were fitted at one end of each boiler.

The geared turbine installation was a three-shaft layout with the centre turbine room furthest aft and the side turbines in separate compartments aft of the boiler rooms. As in the previous ships, Schlachtschiffe F and G adopted turbines of different manufacture and design. 'F' (later *Bismarck*) used Blohm & Voss manufacture and 'G' (later *Tirpitz*) shipped Brown-Boveri. Those aboard *Bismarck* were similar to the set aboard *Admiral Hipper* but because length was not so critical, the radial flow input impulse stage was not used. The HP turbine comprised a Curtis wheel and 40 reaction stages, while the IP turbine was a double-flow reaction arrangement with fifteen stages. An HP astern turbine, a single Curtis wheel, was carried in a separate drum on the other side of the pinion from the IP ahead turbine. The LP ahead turbine had nine reaction stages and, as usual, supported the main condenser, which was slung underneath it. The LP astern turbine was a divided double-flow type. No cruising turbine was fitted. Normal full power rating was 38,300hp per shaft, 46,000hp at maximum power. Maximum revolutions were 265rpm and disconnecting couplings were fitted on each shaft.

The turbines installed in *Tirpitz* were of the impulse-reaction type in the cruising and HP drums, straight reaction in the IP and LP drums, with hollow rotors. As shown on page 50, the cruising and HP drums were on the after end of the main wheel, the IP and LP drums on the ahead side. The HP astern turbine was contained in the IP ahead drum at its forward end, separated from the ahead stages by a diaphragm. The LP astern turbine was a double-flow reaction stage in the centre of the LP ahead turbine casing. All gearing was single-reduction, double-helical pattern.

TURRET PLAN AND PROFILE OF 38cm GUN

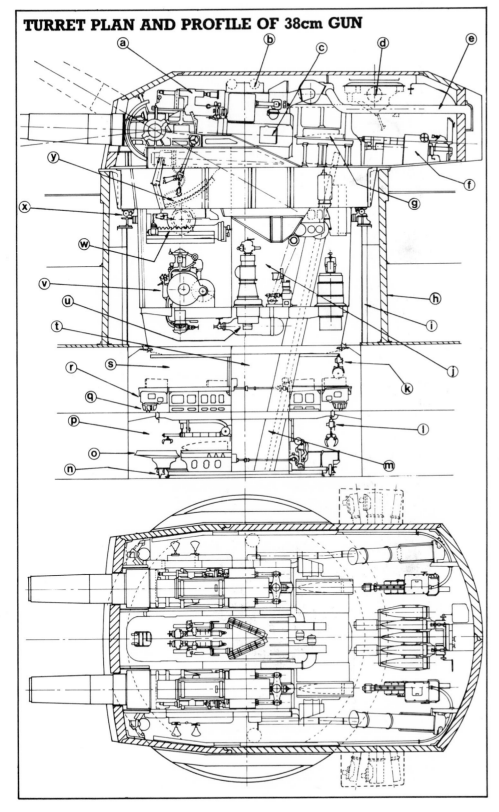

Auxiliary power was supplied by an auxiliary boiler on the lower platform deck immediately forward of centre No. 2 boiler room. Electric power was supplied by four main generator rooms, also on the lower platform deck. Nos. 1 and 2 generator spaces were to starboard and port respectively in compartment VIII, each housing four diesel generator sets of 500kW. Nos. 3 and 4 generator spaces were similarly arranged in compartment XIV but housed three 690kW turbo-generators each.

These ships were considered by Admiral Raeder to be the first in which the machinery spaces were of adequate size.

Bunkerage capacity for *Bismarck* was 7,400 tonnes, *Tirpitz* 7,780 tonnes maximum, these being the usable quantities; *Tirpitz*'s actual capacity was 8,297 tonnes. The remaining quantity could not be pumped. The designed action radius was 14,000 nautical miles at 15 knots but as early as October 1936 it was realized by the OKM that these calculations had been made on favourable peacetime conditions. As a result, the matter was re-evaluated, *halving* the radius to 7,000nm at 15 knots. This drastic step led to an examination as to whether it were not too late to install diesel propulsion and if it were not, what effect would it have on radius? No further action was taken on diesel machinery but in August 1941, as a result of evaluation of captured Royal Navy 'Fleet Tactical Instructions', which detailed the fuel consumption of all British warships, the matter of endurance was looked into once more. At this time the endurance figures for *Bismarck* were given as 8,600nm @ 15kts/ 8,150nm @ 21kts/ 5,200nm @ 27kts and 3,750nm @ 30kts. (No figures had as yet been established for *Tirpitz*). Fuel represented 15 per cent of displacement at 75 per cent full load. Based on fuel used per 100 tonnes of displacement per 100 nautical miles steamed, the figures quoted for *Bismarck* were 1.7m³ @ 15kts/ 1.8m³ @ 21kts/ 2.9m³ @ 27kts and 3.9m³ @ 30kts. The figures quoted for *Scharnhorst* and *Gneisenau* indicate that their lower pressure installations were not as economical as that of *Bismarck*; respective figures for these two ships at 27 knots were 3.4m³ and 4.0m³.

ARMAMENT AND FIRE CONTROL

The 38cm guns mounted in these two ships were a new design and not the 38cm L/45 weapon fitted in the *Bayern*-class battleships of World War One. Some comparisons were made before 1939 between the two weapons but this appears to be the only reference to *Bayern* in the *Bismarck* design history, so the new ship was not developed from the earlier one. It is possible that consideration was given to the use of the old 38cm SKL/45 gun in the new ship but it did not match up to the demands of the 1930s. Its turret weighed about 873 tonnes and had a maximum elevation of only 20° (originally 16°). This gave a maximum range of 23,200m with a 10° list but only 15,000m on the immersed side. In contrast, the 28cm guns of *Deutschland* ranged 31,900m on the *unfavourable* side of a 10° list. Training speeds were also inadequate, being 3°/sec. All in all, the older weapon was not suitable for a new capital ship. The new gun, known as the 38cm SKC/34 under the new designation system, was a pro-

SCHLACHTSCHIFFE F AND G: ARMOUR

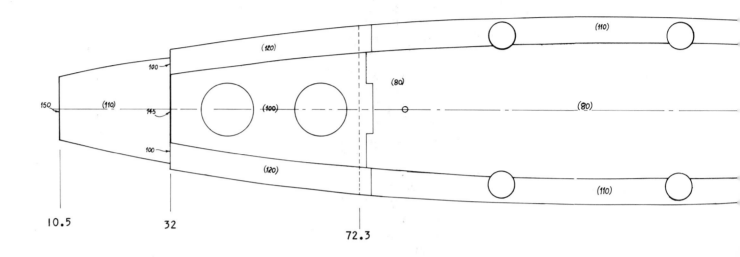

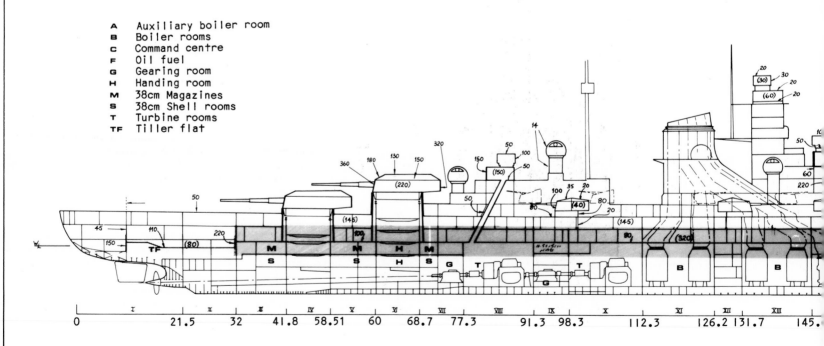

A   Auxiliary boiler room
B   Boiler rooms
C   Command centre
F   Oil fuel
G   Gearing room
H   Handing room
M   38cm Magazines
S   38cm Shell rooms
T   Turbine rooms
TF   Tiller flat

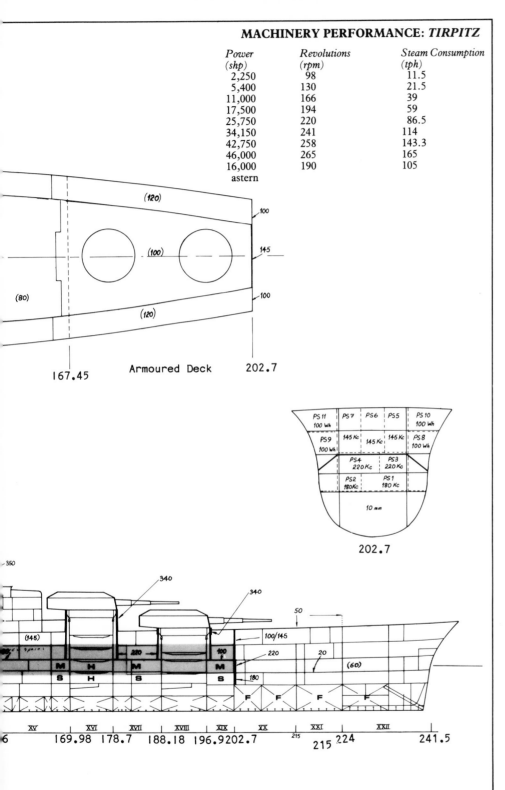

Power (shp)	Revolutions (rpm)	Steam Consumption (tph)
2,250	98	11.5
5,400	130	21.5
11,000	166	39
17,500	194	59
25,750	220	86.5
34,150	241	114
42,750	258	143.3
46,000	265	165
16,000 astern	190	105

duct of the Krupp company and fired an 800kg projectile with a muzzle velocity of 820m/sec. (See page 53 for a comparison between new and old 38cm guns.) The new charge was in two parts, the main one being brass-cased, weighing 112kg, the secondary 99.5kg; 130 rounds per gun were carried.

The main turrets (originally all fitted with 10m rangefinders) were disposed two forward, two aft with 'B' and 'C' superfiring. Training was electric as well as the auxiliary elevation system, auxiliary hoists and some other reserve systems but the main power system was hydraulic. Elevation/depression limits were +30°/5½°. 'A' and 'B' turrets had fields of fire 215° – 0 – 145°, 'C' and 'D', 35° – 180° – 325°. The turrets weighed 1,056 tonnes, or 1,048 tonnes less rangefinder. Armouring was extensive, the turret faces being 360mm, sides 150–220mm, roof 180mm and rear 320mm. All armour was bolted. There were six working levels in the turret system: the gun platform within the turret, the training platform, machinery platform and intermediate platform (all within the barbette and below the armoured deck), the magazine and shell rooms. 'B' and 'C' turrets had an extra intermediate platform in the barbette.

Within the turret, sights were fitted on the left-hand side of the left gun, the right-hand side of the right gun. Electric fans were fitted at the rear of the turret for smoke and gas extraction. Two C/6 periscopes were fitted in the roof.

The secondary armament, twelve 15cm SKC/28 guns in Drh LC/34 twin mountings, was shipped three turrets per side, the centre mounting being equipped with a 6.5m rangefinder. Turrets I weighed 150.3 tonnes, II 131.6 tonnes and III 97.7 tonnes. The forward turrets (I) had barbettes which reached the upper platform deck, the aperture between the revolving mass and the main armoured deck being sealed by a leather apron. The barbettes of the other turrets only extended to the armoured deck. The gun itself was the same as that mounted in *Scharnhorst* and *Gneisenau*, firing a 45.3kg projectile to a range of 23,000m with an elevation of 40°.

The forward turrets had five working levels, of which the gun platform was within the gun house. Inside the barbette were the training platform, engine intermediate platform and, below the armoured deck, the loading platform for shell and cartridge. Turrets II and III had no intermediate platform and the loading platform was within the barbette. The guns were hand-served, with cartridges being ejected below the turret. Main and reserve training motors were electric, elevation hydraulic with emergency hand operation. Turrets not fitted with a 6.5m range-finder were equipped with a C/4 periscope capable of rotating +90° from the gun direction. Protection included 100mm face, 40mm sides, 20–35mm roof and 40mm rear—thinner than those aboard *Scharnhorst*. Each turret had a field of fire of between 153° and 158°.

The 15cm guns were not dual-purpose weapons so the Kriegsmarine followed its, by now, customary practice of also fitting a heavy flak battery. The standard weapon for this task was now the 10.5cm SKC/33 gun, which had been fitted in *Scharnhorst* and her sister as well as being retrospectively fitted to the Panzerschiffe. This gun fired a 15.1kg shell in a fixed round weighing 27.35kg with a muzzle velocity of

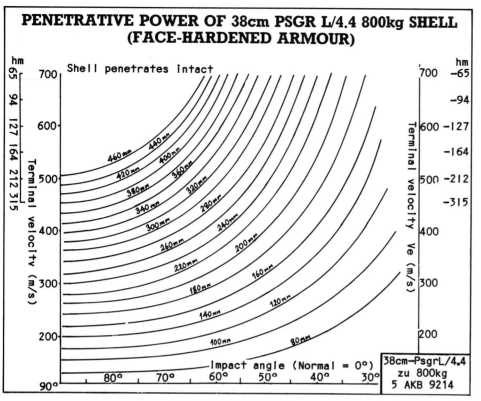

PENETRATIVE POWER OF 38cm PSGR L/4.4 800kg SHELL (FACE-HARDENED ARMOUR)

Shell penetrates intact

Terminal velocity (m/s) — left axis: 700, 600, 500, 400, 300, 200, 90°

hm (left): 65, 94, 127, 164, 212, 315

Terminal velocity Ve (m/s) — right axis: 700, 600, 500, 400, 300, 200

hm (right): -65, -94, -127, -164, -212, -315

Penetration curves: 460mm, 440mm, 420mm, 400mm, 380mm, 360mm, 340mm, 320mm, 300mm, 290mm, 260mm, 240mm, 220mm, 200mm, 180mm, 160mm, 140mm, 120mm, 100mm, 80mm

Impact angle (Normal = 0°): 80°, 70°, 60°, 50°, 40°, 30°

38cm-PsgrL/4.4 zu 800kg 5 AKB 9214

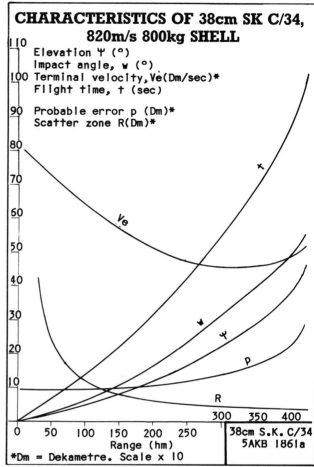

CHARACTERISTICS OF 38cm SK C/34, 820m/s 800kg SHELL

Elevation Ψ (°)
Impact angle, w (°)
Terminal velocity, Ve(Dm/sec)*
Flight time, t (sec)

Probable error p (Dm)*
Scatter zone R(Dm)*

Curves labelled: t, Ve, w, Ψ, p, R

Range (hm): 0, 50, 100, 150, 200, 250, 300, 350, 400

38cm S.K. C/34 5AKB 1861a

*Dm = Dekametre. Scale x 10

900m/sec. Its maximum range was 17,700m. Eight twin mountings were fitted on the superstructure deck, on either beam. This was a fully stabilized tri-axial mounting, originally designed to carry the 8.8cm gun and hence classified as 8.8 Dop. LC/31. However, only *Bismarck* received these and then only for the four forward positions, as in the meantime a stronger mounting had been designed for the 10.5cm Dop LC/37. *Bismarck* therefore completed her outfit with this pattern and *Tirpitz* was fully so equipped. Training was by means of a Pittler-Thoma electric drive with emergency hand wheels, elevation being electric with hand emergency. Loading was manual but an electric loading mechanism was fitted for use at high angles of elevation.

Light flak comprised sixteen 3.7cm SKC/30 guns in eight LC/30 twin mountings grouped about the fore and aft superstructure and twelve 2cm MG C/30 (later C/38) single weapons.

No torpedo outfit was originally envisaged but the ships were fitted for aircraft, having two fixed athwartships catapult amidships. Abreast the funnel were two single hangars while under the mainmast and boat stowage was a larger hangar. Maximum designed aircraft capacity was six, the standard catapult aircraft being the Arado Ar 196 seaplane. However, this would necessitate two of the aircraft being kept on the catapults, as only four could be stowed in the hangars. These ships were not fitted for minelaying.

The fire control system followed the layout of the earlier *Scharnhorst* and *Gneisenau*, with three main surface gunnery control positions. The forward position occupied the after half of the conning tower at navigating bridge level, another was positioned at the top of the foremast tower and the third aft on the superstructure deck. The forward position was equipped with a 7m base stereoscopic range-finder, the other two with 10m pattern equipments. Each of the two forward positions was also fitted with three ZG C/38S directors equipped with periscope hoods projecting above the armoured roofs. One was on the centre-line, the other pair sited to port and starboard. In the after position, however, there were only two, one each port and starboard. For control of night actions, there were two positions, one forward, one aft, equipped with two Zeilsaule C38s and a starshell director. Target data for range, bearing and inclination, etc. were fed to the main gunnery TS on the middle platform deck compartment XV. A similar space aft in compartment VII acted as a reserve position and was fitted out like the forward room, except that the shore bombardment computer was omitted. These spaces housed the computers necessary for gunnery purposes, both for the main and secondary armaments. Adjacent spaces housed the associated switch rooms, amplifier rooms and other fire control equipment. There were two main gyro rooms for the provision of stable element data to

GUNNERY WEIGHTS—'F' and 'G'
(17 February 1938)
(tonnes)

Part I

Eight 38cm SK C/34 in four Drh. L.C/34e mountings	4,232.0
Twelve 15cm SK C/28 in six Drh. L.C/34 (2 × 110t, 4 × 108t)	652.0
Sixteen 10.5cm SK C/38 in eight Dopp.L.C/38	216.0
Sixteen 3.7cm SK C/30 in eight Dopp.L.C/30	29.6
Twelve 2cm MG C/30 in twelve LC/30	4.8
Low-angle fire control	195.0
Searchlight equipment	75.0
Flak fire control	390.0
Range-finders	69.0
Gunnery communications	45.0
Acoustic signalling equipment	3.0
RPC for main armament	10.0
RPC for light armament	45.0
RPC for fuse setting	4.0
RPC for turret range-finders / RPC for range-finder cupolas	7.5
Stable element equipment	30.0
Gyro power supplies	100.0
Director firing	25.0
Warning equipment	10.0
Power supplies	7.7
Muzzle velocity measuring equipment	10.0
Turret loud speakers	4.0
38cm ammunition hoists	130.0

Part II

Gunnery equipment	96.8

Part III
Ammunition:

8 × 108 rounds of 38cm	1,022.1
12 × 105 rounds of 15cm	110.1
16 × 400 rounds of 10.5cm	218.4
16 × 2,000 rounds of 3.7cm	95.4
12 × 2,000 rounds of 2cm	11.2
Saluting munitions	5.0
Small arms	2.4
Special items	1.0
Pyrotechnics	0.7
Practice ammunition	24.0

Totals:

Part I	6,294.4
Part II	96.8
Part III	1,490.3
	7,881.5

COMPARISON OF 38CM GUNS

	38cm SK C/34 (Bismarck)	38cm SK L/45 (Bayern)
Muzzle velocity (m/sec)	820	800
Shell weight (kg)	800	750
Mean turret weight, less barbette	1,052	868
Rate of fire (rpm)	2.4	2.3
Weight of broadside (kg/min)	15,360	13,800
Maximum elevation (°)	30	20
Range (metres)	34,200	23,200
Range with unfavourable 10° list	27,200	15,000
Maximum training speed (°/sec)	5	3
Maximum elevating speed (°/sec)	6	4
Penetration performance:		
at 10,000m	510mm	390mm
at 20,000m	364mm	265mm
at 25,000m	308mm	220mm
350mm of armour penetrated at	21,000m	12,500m

Right: The conning tower of *Bismarck*. Three director periscope hoods and several navigational periscopes are visible. (Bundesarchiv)

Far right: *Tirpitz* in the Baltic in 1941. Note the absence of *Wackelkopf* flak director and after 38cm range-finder cupola. (IWM)

(fwd stb), B (fwd pt), C (foremost after) and D (aftermost). The main flak TS was on the upper platform deck, compartment XV, more or less on the centre-line. Adjacent to it were radio room B and the flak switch room. Immediately aft of it on the other side of the watertight bulkhead was the main action command centre. A reserve position was to be found on the middle platform deck aft, compartment IX.

Two 3m base night range-finders were also fitted in the wings of the Admiral's bridge and eight portable 1.25m instruments were carried for the 3.7cm guns. All range-finders were supplied by Zeis Jena.

Seven 150cm Siemens-Schuckert searchlights were fitted, one on a sponson on the forward face of the conning tower, four on the funnel platform (of which the forward two were equipped with folding hemispherical shields) and two abreast flak tower 'C'. For control purposes, three C38 searchlight directors were fitted on the port and starboard sides of the forward night control position and one each port and starboard in the after position under the after main range-finder.

MODIFICATIONS

Bismarck received radar sets before completion whose aerials were fitted on the front faces of the foretop range-finder and after range-finder. No spherical shields were ever fitted to flak towers 'C' or 'D' in this ship before her loss. The 10m range-finder fitted to 'A' turret was removed during or after her trials.

Tirpitz completed without the range-finder in 'A' turret and also carried the after flak towers with spherical shields. Experiences in the Atlantic by *Admiral Hipper*, *Scharnhorst* and *Gneisenau* during 1940/41 led to the installation of two quadruple banks of torpedo tubes on the main deck just abaft the catapult. These were installed before the ship left for Norway in 1942. By that time she had also received four Vierlinge, two on sponsons on the foremast and aft on the superstructure between flak tower 'C' and 'D'. The single 2cm guns displaced were repositioned just abaft 'B' turret on the navigating bridge and on the quarterdeck. The 2cm outfit was now fourteen single and four quadruple guns for a total of 30 2cm weapons. A new radar set and radar office was built on top of the foretop main range-finder tower and another set fitted to the forward range-finder. The two range-finders on the Admiral's bridge were given protective hoods, possibly in anticipation of the Arctic cold.

Shortly after the ship's arrival in Norway, two further Vierlinge were added. One replaced the two single 2cm guns on the navigating bridge and the second was fitted to a new bandstand on the roof of 'B' turret. As the war progressed, further augmentation of the light flak took place, by the addition of further Vierlinge. Two replaced the singles on the funnel platform and two more were fitted on the quarterdeck just abaft 'D' turret. By 1944 official records give *Tirpitz*'s light flak as sixteen Vierlinge and sixteen singles, giving a total of 80 2cm guns.

Radar was improved during 1943/44 by the fitment of a *Würtzburg* height-finding radar at the base of the mainmast, but this had been removed by the time that the ship was lost.

the fire control computers. The forward room was on the port side of the lower platform deck in compartment XV, the after one to starboard on the middle platform deck compartment VIII.

The flak fire control system was a further advance on the earlier battleships. A main control position was sited at the highest point in the ship, the foretop gallery. Here were fitted four Zeilanweisergeräte, or ZAG (Target Information Sights). Reserve positions were fitted on the fore and aft night control stands. Range data were supplied by four tri-axially stabilized SL6 high-angle range-finders with their distinctive spherical tops. These were fitted with 4m base stereoscopic night range-finders. They were identified as A

5. BEYOND TIRPITZ

Schlachtschiff H

DESIGN HISTORY

Germany still had enough tonnage allotment left after the programming of Schlachtschiffe F and G to construct another 35,000-ton battleship. Discussions about what form this ship was to take began in 1935, but no clear design ideas emerged until the autumn of 1936. Hitherto it would appear that the ship was intended as a repeat Schlachtschiff G. At the time the main armament under consideration was 35cm but on 5 October 1936 Germany informed Britain that, if the USSR were to arm ships with guns greater than 14in, she would arm 'H' with 38cm guns. The Soviet Union was indeed at this time actively considering new capital ship construction in association with various Western concerns, notably Ansaldo in Italy. It is not surprising therefore that, given the sympathy between Italy and Germany, the latter got wind of such plans. In addition, the Soviet Union approached the USA for 40.6cm guns and equipment as early as November 1936. Germany was convinced that the USSR would go for larger calibre weapons and as a result decided that 'H' would be designed from the outset for 38cm guns but in such a manner that, if this became politically impossible, 35cm guns could be quickly installed instead. High-performance 35cm guns were at this time under active development.

Thus on 23 October 1936 the Marineausbildungsabteilung AIV, or Development Office, promulgated the required military parameters for 'H' to generate discussion and to expedite finalization of the design parameters. This called for a 35,000-ton ship armed as *Bismarck*. A torpedo armament had been foreseen since 1935 but it was not clear if above- or below-water installation was the more favourable. However, recent developments in torpedo technology, notably gyro angling, opened up new possibilities for the positioning of the tubes. Both the Development Office and the Construction Office discussed the use of diesel propulsion, it having been established by the New Installations Department in the Construction Office that space should be available without increase in the ship's dimensions. The advantages of diesels have already been discussed in respect of the Panzerschiffe, but the Development Office required the speed of this new ship to be in excess of that of *Bismarck* and *Tirpitz*—it was designed to be superior to the French 35,000-ton ships under development. A minimum continuous speed of 30 knots was demanded with a radius of action of not less than the 16,000nm at 16 knots of the Panzerschiffe. Armour was to be the same as *Bismarck*.

In response to these parameters, the Operations Office stated that Atlantic operation was the intention and wished endurance to be 16,000nm at 18 knots; continuous speed was to be high enough to bring the French ships to action and this required 30 knots minimum (continuous). Armament was to be superior to *Dunkerque*'s and at least equal to *Richelieu*'s, for which 38cm guns were needed with a good turret disposition for the best salvo arrangement. Protection was to be better than *Richelieu*'s and improved splinter protection was wanted for the foretop, which might be subject to 40mm cannon firing aircraft (an interesting suggestion in 1936). On the other hand, due recognition had to be taken of the restricted nature of German ports and waterways. This limited draught to 10m at full load displacement. Four reconnaissance aircraft were required and two catapults. Ammunition outfit was concurred with, except that 150rpg were demanded for the 15cm guns, in lieu of 100rpg, and it was also suggested that the number of 15cm guns could safely be reduced as, in the intended sphere of operations, destroyer attack would be unlikely. Torpedoes would be useful but not mandatory.

As a result of these opinions, the Development Office amended the secondary armament ammunition to 130rpg plus 20rpg star shell and increased the foretop protection from 20mm to 30mm. The general requirements were confirmed on 11 December 1936—Type displacement as 'F' and 'G', armament similar except eight 38cm guns in four twin turrets with 125rpg. Two M5 triple banks or four M5 twin banks of torpedo tubes were to be installed behind the citadel armour. The decision as to triples or twins was to be taken on the basis of available space. Machinery was to be a three-shaft diesel installation using twelve nine-cylinder double-acting two-stroke MAN engines of 13,500–16,200bhp. Maximum continuous speed was 30 knots and endurance 16,000nm at 19 knots. Protection was as follows:

Side	320mm
Upper deck	50mm
Armoured deck	80mm/120mm
Conning tower	350mm
Citadel	145mm
Longitudinal bulkhead	30mm
Torpedo bulkhead	45mm
Mast	60mm
After conning tower	150mm
Barbettes	340/260/350mm

Two catapults were sited amidships and four aircraft allowed but splinter-proof accommodation was available for only two of the aircraft in individual hangars. Draught was not to exceed that of 'F' and 'G'; indeed any reduction would

SCHLACHTSCHIFF H: INTERNAL PROFILE

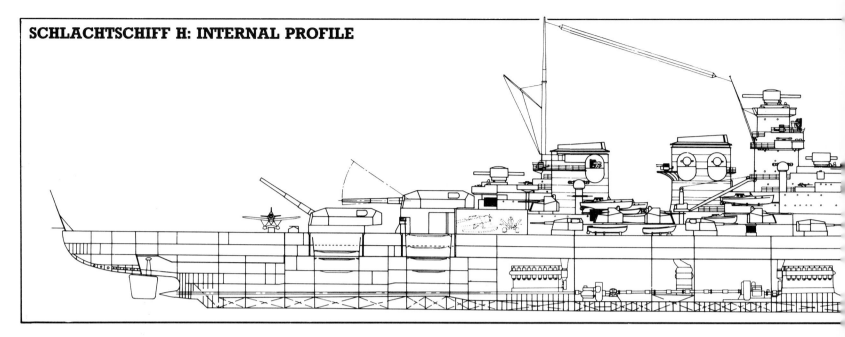

have been very welcome. The use of diesels was expected to increase machinery weight by about 1,400 tonnes; on the other hand, bunkerage could be reduced to about 4,500 tonnes for the same radius. It was expected that the saving would result in less draught than 'F' and 'G'.

In January 1937 Admiral Raeder notified his staff that because Britain had announced three further 35,000-ton ships (the last three *King George V*'s), it was expected that another ship could also be built by Germany. Accordingly, he ordered that all efforts should be made to lay down *J* on 1 May 1938, for completion in 3½ years.

It would appear that some time early in January 1937 the Soviet request to the USA for 40.6cm guns became known to Hitler; suddenly the parameters for 'H' became too weak and a larger calibre gun was needed. Hitler therefore ordered Raeder to design the new ships with 40.6cm guns. Another conference was called immediately, on 29 January, where it was announced by the Construction Office that only three projects were now being worked upon, out of the original seven: two with eight 40.6cm guns in twin mountings (Entwurf 3 and 3a) and one other Entwurfe 4 with twelve 38cm guns in four triple turrets. The ships were designed as very heavy gun platforms but heavy guns were not all-important. They were useless if they could not bring the enemy to battle; the ship had to be at the right place at the right time, a point which was made at the conference. Triple turrets were not favoured and the action radius of the steam turbine sketch design was held to be insufficient. Armoured protection layout drew little comment, except perhaps a slight improvement of the armour at the ends of the ship. The secondary armament was wanted in two groups of four guns on each beam, and the lack of protection for the crews of the heavy flak drew adverse comment, with the suggestion of the development of a splinter-proof gunhouse for the 10.5cm guns.

The Construction Office reported that, given the above demands, a speed of 30 knots was impossible to attain, so the Development Office opted for Entwurf 3 with 27.8 knots. Even an increase to 29 knots would require an increase in displacement by 8,500 tonnes (Entwurf 3a). Displacement had by now, in any event, risen to 7,000 tonnes above the stipulated 35,000. The Development Office saw no real need to increase the gun calibre to 40.6cm as the 38cm gun met all the demands, and German harbour restrictions, as well as the bends on the Kiel Canal, were no small consideration. They saw the best solution as 'F' with diesels and a higher speed or, second best, a ship with better speed than 'F' armed with 40.6cm guns in twin turrets. However, the Führer wished for bigger guns!

In April 1937 the Weapons Office forwarded their ideas for the improvement of the design. As first priority, they wanted the reinstatement of the original barbette armour to 350mm and the citadel to 150mm. They also wished to see the 150mm waterline protection extended in sufficient depth to the bows and a forward armoured deck of 30mm. If the extension of the waterline belt to the bows was impossible, a forward armoured bulkhead of 150mm was desirable. If 38cm guns in twin or triple turrets were employed, then turret and barbette armour could be increased by 10 per cent. As second priority, it was desirable to improve the protection of the 15cm guns to the level of *Scharnhorst*, increase the protection over the machinery spaces to 100mm and the sloped deck to 120mm, as well as giving the rudders 80–150mm protection on the waterline. Finally, the splinter protection above the armoured deck should be increased to 40mm.

With all these comments and demands, the design displacement grew accordingly. 'H' was intended as part of the 1938 programme and as early as mid-October 1935 it had been planned to lay down on 1 October 1937 for completion

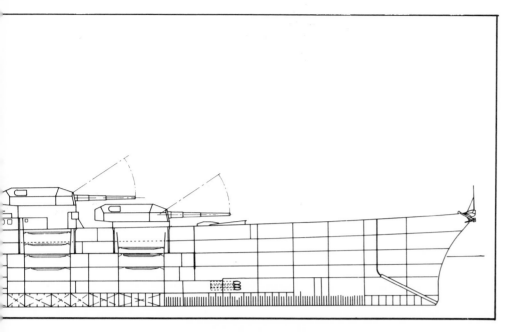

To return to the design development once more, Hitler approved Entwurf 3 armed with eight 40.6cm guns and of 58,000 tonnes on 24 July 1937. In August it was stated by the Development Office that, in the light of experiences in Spanish waters with the Panzerschiffe, together with comments by the Construction Office in December 1936, above-water torpedo tubes were probably not the best solution. As the laying down had been put back, it was probable that in the meantime the trials of new underwater tubes in *Hessen* would have borne fruit. Growth continued and a problem arose when it became necessary to publish some data about the new ship—nominally 35,000 tons as far as the outside world was concerned. By February 1938 displacement of the diesel-engined ship was 56,200 tonnes and as the Construction Office pointed out, if the correct hull dimensions were published with a 35,000-ton displacement figure, it would be an obvious falsehood! Also complicating matters was the hazy definition of responsibilities between the Construction Office and the Flottenabteilung who frequently did not see eye to eye. This resulted in considerable delay to both Schlachtschiff H and Kreuzer M.

Admiral Fuchs of the Fleet Office felt that his section had been kept somewhat in the dark by the Construction Office and had not been party to the decisions on the design subsequent to the establishment of the first parameters. When the news of the project reaching 58,700 tonnes displacement with a beam of 41m came to his attention, he was most critical. Its size was excessive, the beam far more than desirable (use of the Kiel Canal was impossible), the speed was too low and the draught too much. In his opinion, even the relatively low speed of this project could not be reached in depths of less than 100m. Despite voicing his objections, after a year's work, the only progress made was a reduction in beam by 1m and an increase in length by 12m, which raised the speed by 0.2 knot to 28 knots. It was beam which raised the the most problems—only the largest of the Russian *Popoffkas* had greater beam and they were hardly seagoing ships! Because of the beam, the machinery power was very inefficiently used. Fuchs was critical of the cause of this—the wide torpedo protection (6.5m), which was later reduced by the Construc-

by February 1941. Plans now began to go awry as Germany's limited yard capacity began to exert an influence. The only suitable slipway, IX at Blohm & Voss, would be occupied by 'F' (*Bismarck*) until winter 1937 and the alternatives, Wilhelmshaven Naval Yard and Deutsche Werk (Kiel), were ruled out as their slipways were either occupied or not long enough. Of the other yards, Deschimag's slip VI measured 300m × 39m but the water depth in the River Weser presented problems and the yard had no facilities for working armour plate. Either slip VII or VIII at Germania's Kiel yard could have been extended for larger ships by July 1936 if the go-ahead were given, but this would have necessitated the aircraft-carrier 'Flugzeugträger B' and 'Kreuzer J' (later *Prinz Eugen*) being transferred to other yards. In the event, this proved unnecessary, as even as early as November 1935 the laying down of 'H' had been put back a year, so Blohm & Voss could be used.

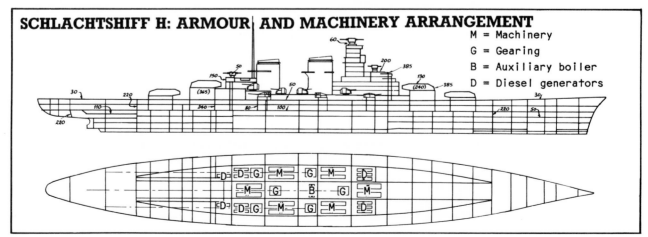

SCHLACHTSHIFF H: ARMOUR AND MACHINERY ARRANGEMENT

M = Machinery
G = Gearing
B = Auxiliary boiler
D = Diesel generators

tion Office to 6m, but no more than 5.4m had ever been demanded by the Fleet Office. The beam was also adversely affected by the machinery layout itself, which was considered to be 2m too wide.

In the course of considering the initial requirements for Kreuzer P (qv), discussions had been held between the Fleet Office and Constructor Driessen, during which the latter had suggested that by the adoption of a similar machinery layout to Kreuzer P, the beam of Schlachtschiff H could be reduced to 37m and a speed of at least 30 knots obtained. This could be done by reducing the Wallgang to 5.5m and the machinery width by 2m. At the same time, a considerable saving in displacement could be made; more if a few minor reductions were to be made in the military demands of the ship. As Driessen appeared sympathetic to the standpoint of the Fleet Office, the latter formally requested the Construction Office, on 15 September 1938, that he be given the task of developing the new battleship design. No answer to another, written, request on 19 September was forthcoming, probably due to the poor co-operation between the two offices. A repeated written request on 28 September eventually received a reply, which failed to answer the Development Office's request and merely pointed out that any possibility of improving the speed depended solely on reconsidering the basic military demands made upon the design.

The Construction Office offered only two alternatives, either to keep the displacement the same and increase speed, in which case, another 50,000hp would be required to give a 2 knots improvement on the measured mile or, if displacement were reduced by 1,000 tonnes, speed could be improved by 0.1 knot. This office was strongly against having to rework the design at such a late stage. Admiral Fuchs took a different view, believing that it would be possible to rework the layout without reducing the offensive power of the ship but at the same time obtain a smaller and faster vessel. Finally the Construction Office wrote to the Fleet Office on 10 November 1938 formally declining to allow Driessen to work on the design. They averred that for some time they had been examining whether, by minor alterations of the machinery layout, the ship's size could be reduced. They also stated that they had investigated the possibility of using the new V diesel of higher power to obtain a better speed. In the end they returned to the argument that the imminent laying down of 'H' prevented all further alterations.

By coincidence, that same day Admiral Fuchs had personally presented his opposite number at the Construction Office with a new sketch design for 'H'. This was of 51,000 tonnes, diesel-driven with four shafts and 193,000hp for a maximum speed of 30.5 knots. This led in turn to four new sketch designs being worked partly by AV and partly by the Construction Office.

By the end of 1938 the revised sketch designs were being considered in detail, Entwurf IV, which had a beam of 37m (cf. *Bismarck* at 36m), and Entwurf I also with 37m beam. The former was a pure diesel ship, the latter mixed turbine and diesel. They both drew the same amount of water, 10.35m with 7,500 tonnes of fuel, and carried similar armament—eight 40.6cm in twin turrets. Torpedoes were now included in the design, with six tubes being mounted below water in the bows. Aircraft installations comprised two hangars abreast the after superstructure, with two fixed transverse catapults on the quarterdeck, although catapults angled at 30° and 130° were another option. The protective scheme was similar in both designs, with a 300mm waterline belt (reduced from 320mm in earlier projects), 100/150mm bow armour (formerly 150/160mm) and stern armour unchanged at 150mm. The only other changes to the armour scheme was the reduced thickness of the armoured deck, now 90mm, and the sloped armour of 110mm (formerly 120mm). Turrets, barbettes, main and secondary armament protection remained as previously. The width of the torpedo protection was 5.5m (see page 55 for detailed table). It was, however, still to be decided if the former thickness of armour on the armoured deck could be restored; if so, draught would increase by 10cm and speed would be reduced by 0.1 knot.

The main discussion point was the machinery layout—should diesels or a combined diesel/steam system be preferred? Entwurf I had a total installed power unit of 220,000hp, comprised of eight diesels, each of 13,750bhp, grouped in two units of four and a two-shaft turbine installation each of three boilers with 110,000hp. Maximum speed was 32.5 knots and endurance 16,500nm at 19 knots (or 36 days), 5,250nm at 28 knots (or 9 days). Entwurf IV was a triple-shaft diesel layout, each having four 13,750bhp diesels for a total output of 165,000shp. Maximum speed was lower, at 30 knots, with endurance being 19,200nm at 19 knots (or 42 days) and 7,000nm at 28 knots ($10\frac{1}{2}$ days).

Both layouts were considered satisfactory for Atlantic employment. However, Entwurf I could maintain 22–28 knots even with one turbine out of action, while Entwurf IV needed all the diesels to make this speed. Up to 22 knots could be maintained by both designs on diesels alone, which it was acknowledged could be got in action quicker than a steam plant. The Development Office saw Entwurf I as the best solution if the ship had to break out into the North Atlantic at high speed, and if the fuel supply position on the ocean were difficult various fuels could be burned. Entwurf IV was better if the speed was considered acceptable for break-out, as no diesel supply difficulties were anticipated in the Atlantic. Moreover, the quicker readiness of diesels might be advantageous.

The New Construction Committee considered Entwurf IV the simplest and best solution but if speed was of the essence, then the choice would have to be Entwurf I. At cruising speed, I required 75 per cent of all motors, while IV required 50 per cent. It was also pointed out that steam plants were more vulnerable in action than diesels.

The Engineering Office considered both layouts of equal merit when it came to seaworthiness and action robustness, but noted that the mixed propulsion system would require some 4,000m³ more space than the diesel and would also require some 52 more engine room personnel than Entwurf IV. It would also be necessary to carry a greater range of spares and stores.

Above: *Schlachtschiff H* on the slipway, 8 September 1936. (WBB)

quoted for the draughts of Entwurf I and IV, on the grounds that the greater weight of armour in I (due to the armoured hangar) and its greater machinery weight (460 tonnes more). In their opinion, this had to result in a greater draught for I than IV. Their criticism continued! The quoted speed of 32.5 knots (Entwurf I) was not achievable nor would the endurance be anything like 16,500nm at 19 knots; it was more likely to be 15,000nm and then only when using the diesels with the steam plant cold. At 28 knots it was believed that range would be 5,000nm, not 5,250nm. As far as Entwurf IV was concerned, its endurance was likely to be 18,000nm at 19 knots and 7,000nm at 28 knots. The mixed propulsion designs would require all motors coupled up to achieve over 19 knots, while the pure diesel ship would have two motors in reserve on each shaft and would only need all motors at speeds greater than 24.5 knots. Thus the diesels on the mixed design would be much more highly pressed at cruising speed than those of the pure diesel version. If one turbine failed in Entwurf I, all diesels would be required for 28 knots. The speeds of the two main contenders were estimated as being 31.7 knots (I) and 30.4 knots (IV), and it was obvious that the Construction Office favoured the pure diesel version.

On 21 December 1938 Admiral Raeder made up his mind and authorized a design of 52,560 tonnes displacement, with a triple-shaft diesel installation of 165,000shp (i.e., essentially Entwurf IV). This had a number of merits, including a clear and uncluttered deck, with the hangars now below 'C' turret. The catapults were sunk into the quarterdeck and a Heinemat-type recovery system was included. The quarterdeck was broad enough to operate wheeled aircraft, specifically the Fieseler Storch. Other plus factors were a drier foreship, separate motor couplings and the ability to use the Kiel Canal. The only disadvantage compared with the old 'H' design was the reduction of two twin 15cm turrets.

Having lost so much time because of inter-department squabbles (see the Kreuzer M saga), it was now important to proceed with haste and to that end K.Ad. Fuchs was given special responsibility for 'H' and 'J' on 23 January 1939. He remained head of the Flottenabteilung. On 14 April 1939 orders were placed for the first two ships, 'H' with Blohm & Voss, as their yard No. 525, and 'J' with Deschimag at Bremen as yard No. 981. The following month further orders were placed for *K, L, M* and *N* on 25 May.

CONSTRUCTION

Only the first two ships were laid down, on 15 July and 15 August 1939 respectively. Work proceeded rapidly thanks to the single project authority, Admiral Fuchs, and the lead yard, Blohm & Voss. By the outbreak of war, some 766 tonnes had been worked into 'H' on the slipway and 40 tonnes into 'J', with 28,400 tonnes and 18,330 tonnes respectively ordered, delivered or in work in the slips. In addition, another 35,735 tonnes was in progress for 'K', although she had not been laid down. The immediate priority now was to complete warships and U-boats, which could be put into service during the present war, which was not expected to last long anyway. Thus, in compliance with pre-war plans, all

Admiral Schniewind considered that a faster ship than the old 28-knot 'H' design was needed. In his opinion the merits of the four-shaft mixed propulsion design had not been fully demonstrated and he opted for the triple-shaft pure diesel layout of 30 knots. However, he did order tank towing tests of the four-shaft layout of increased power and for full costs to be prepared for the two favoured options, whose designs were to be more fully drawn up in order that a decision could be reached. Turrets and barbettes were to be ordered for four ships.

A few days later the Construction Office reported to the New Construction Committee that they doubted the figures

construction was suspended on 30 September 1939. 'H' and 'J' lay rusting on the stocks until a decision was made on 25 November 1941 to scrap the incomplete hulls, such as they were, and to divert other materials and equipment to other uses. The orders themselves were not, however, cancelled until 29 and 31 August respectively.

PROTECTIVE SCHEME

The ship's protective scheme was an improvement upon that of *Bismarck*, although belt thickness was reduced to 300mm KC n/a. Above this was a 180mm belt and a third, reaching the upper deck, of 150mm. All the tapers for thickness trans-actions were on the inner side to allow a smooth low resis-tance outer face. Forward of the main belt, the waterline pro-tection reduced to 60mm as far as the bows, with 150mm in the area of the fuel bunkers. Aft, the belt varied between 30mm and 90mm. The torpedo bulkhead, of unhardened Wh n/a armour but fully welded, was 45mm thick and ex-tended from the bottom skin plating to the armoured deck. Above this deck it was continued to the upper deck as a 30mm longitudinal splinter bulkhead of Wh n/a hardened armour. Inboard of this was a further longitudinal bulkhead of 25mm hardened Wh n/a armour.

Horizontal protection comprised an upper deck of 50mm hardened Wh n/a armour to keep out low-calibre hits and to trigger the fuses of delayed-action AP shells or bombs. The main armoured deck was 100mm thick, increased to 120mm over the magazines, fabricated of Wh n/a hardened armour. Outside the torpedo bulkhead, the armoured deck was 120mm thick and sloped down to meet the lower edge of the side belt. Abaft the 220mm after armoured bulkhead, the armoured deck was continued one deck lower to protect the steering gear; this was 110mm thick. Similarly, forward of the forward armoured bulkhead the lower armoured deck was continued to the bows as 50mm.

MAIN MACHINERY

This comprised twelve MAN nine-cylinder double-acting two-stroke diesels, each of 13,750shp. They were arranged in six separate motor rooms, with four motors driving each shaft. Each motor room contained two diesels with an adja-cent gearing room Auxiliary power was provided by twelve diesel generators in six generator spaces, containing one, two or three diesels. Eight of the generators were of 920kW and four of 460kW. There were also two oil-fired auxiliary boilers between the midships gearing rooms below the armoured deck and two others supplied by exhaust diesel gases above the armoured deck.

ARMAMENT

These ships were the first German battleships to be designed for 16in guns. The gun was designated 40.6cm SK C/34 and fired a 1,030kg projectile with a maximum range of about 36,400m at 30° elevation. Like all other heavy guns, the charge was in two parts, the main one being brass-cased, weighing 91kg, and the 134kg fore charge (bagged). The twin turrets weighed 1,475 tonnes and were given 385mm

face armour, 240mm sides and 45mm roofs. No turrets were ever completed but several guns were and installed in coast defence batteries, notably in France, Norway and at Gotenhafen. Secondary armament was to have been twelve 15cm SK C28 in Drh LC/34 twin turrets, similar to those of *Bismarck*. The flak outfit was once again to have been a three-tiered one, with the twelve 10.5cm SK C/33 guns being car-ried in a new-type twin mounting. The usual complement of 3.7cm and 2cm guns was included. Also included were six 53.3cm torpedo tubes, three on either beam in fixed under-water bow positions.

Kreuzer P

DESIGN HISTORY

The original Panzerschiffe, as typified by *Deutschland*, were considered to be generally successful for their intended role, but by the late 1930s a better protected and faster version was desirable, now that the design parameters were no longer constricted by treaty limitations. The existence of more powerful French and British capital ships was also a factor. As a result, twelve such ships were proposed in the new ex-pansion programme of late 1938, known as the 'Z Plan'. The designs proposed for the new Panzerschiffe bear a strong re-semblance to that worked out for Panzerschiffe D and E be-fore they were given a third 28cm turret. Originally these ships were designated P1 to P12, but on 14 January 1939 it was ordered that they be referred to as Kreuzer P.

As usual, a number of different sketch designs were ex-amined, which had displacements of between 21,000 and 31,000 tonnes. Some designs had mixed steam and diesel propulsion systems, while others were pure diesel ships. Armament was generally two triple 28cm turrets, but 38cm armaments were also considered. By about September 1938 three ideas were being studied: Projekt II for a 21,000-tonne ship armed with two triple 28cm guns and having a main belt of 120mm; Projekt III was a variation of II but with belt armour increased to 180mm; and Project IIIa which was an enlarged design with two twin 28cm guns but with greatly increased protection. All three designs were diesel-driven.

Installed power and the protective schemes were discussed in depth. For example, if the barbettes on Projekt I were increased to 150mm at a cost of 200 tonnes, speed would not have been affected; but if the machinery weight were to be 32kg/hp instead of the planned 28kg/hp, then a penalty of 660 tonnes in weight would reduce speed to 33.6–33.8 knots. Similarly, if the heavier machinery were used in Projekt III speed would be reduced by 0.8 knot.

The first three ships were expected to utilize the six 28cm triple turrets surplus after the rearming of *Scharnhorst* and *Gneisenau*, but because this had been postponed there was an alternative suggestion of using two twin 38cm turrets (Pro-posal B). This was resisted because it would have made the ships too valuable for a commerce raiding role. This idea then progressed to a three turret 38cm design (Proposal C), which was the genesis of the Schlachtschiff O project.

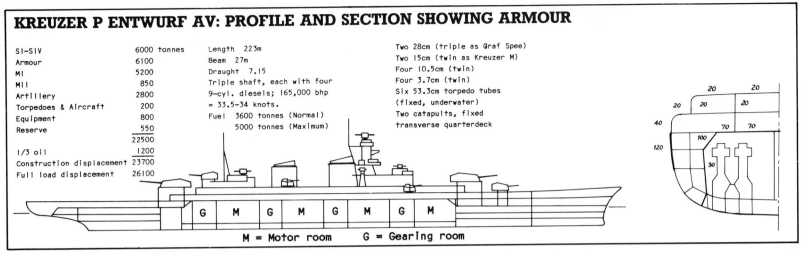

KREUZER P ENTWURF AV: PROFILE AND SECTION SHOWING ARMOUR

SI–SIV	6000 tonnes	Length 223m	Two 28cm (triple as Graf Spee)
Armour	6100	Beam 27m	Two 15cm (twin as Kreuzer M)
MI	5200	Draught 7.15	Four 10.5cm (twin)
MII	850	Triple shaft, each with four	Four 3.7cm (twin)
Artillery	2800	9-cyl. diesels; 165,000 bhp	Six 53.3cm torpedo tubes
Torpedoes & Aircraft	200	= 33.5–34 knots.	(fixed, underwater)
Equipment	800	Fuel 3600 tonnes (Normal)	Two catapults, fixed
Reserve	550	5000 tonnes (Maximum)	transverse quarterdeck
	22500		
1/3 oil	1200		
Construction displacement	23700		
Full load displacement	26100		

M = Motor room   G = Gearing room

By December 1938 the new Panzerschiffe were quite high in the Kriegsmarine's priority list, being regarded as an operational necessity; orders for three ships were authorized.

Towards the end of January 1939 the Fleet Office put forward a new sketch design (Entwurf A V). This was a triple-screw pure diesel design of 165,000shp with a speed of 33.5–34 knots. Armament was to be two triple 28cm turrets armoured as in *Admiral Graf Spee*, two 15cm LC/28 Kreuzer M twin turrets and the usual 10.5cm guns. Six underwater torpedo tubes were proposed.

The Fleet Office proposed the triple-shaft installation because in their view the merits of the four-shaft designs had not been fully proven. The machinery arrangements were the same as those to be used for Schlachtschiff H. However, the adoption of separate couplings for the diesels, of which there were four per shaft, necessitated four gearing rooms and a consequent increase in length. To avoid an increase in displacement over earlier projects, and to ensure that the forward turret was mounted sufficiently far aft to prevent spray problems, one of the 15cm guns was moved aft, astern of the after director where it displaced No. 5 10.5cm mounting. This allowed it a good field of fire with only 25° dead zone forwards either side of 'midships. Because the flak outfit was reduced by one twin, it was felt that the after flak director could also be dispensed with. A main mast was added, the bridge structure shortened and the forward 10.5cm guns on the main deck moved aft to avoid blast problems with the forward turret. The new motor arrangements also required a two-funnel layout which, it was felt, improved battleworthiness.

The protection of this design amounted to 6,100 tonnes—i.e., less than Projekts III and IIIa but greater than II. If, however, the desired speed could not be obtained with the proposed armour protection, then the thickness would have to be reduced. No reduction in speed could be countenanced. Cautious calculations of the speed gave it as $33\frac{1}{2}$–34 knots maximum with continuous speed about 1 knot less. Better motors could reduce the machinery weight and increase power. At the time H motors were being used but if the new V

motors were successful, an improvement could be expected. Time was now pressing—the Führer had decided that the first ship should be laid down on 1 February 1940 and the Construction Office required at least a year to get drawings to the shipyards.

At a conference on 4 April 1939 the SKL agreed the armour disposition in general but wished the deck increased and the belt thickness increased to 150mm, at the cost of a drop in speed of about 0.1 knot. Underwater torpedo tubes were considered the best arrangement, but if this were not possible they should either be in casements or on deck. It was not acceptable that they be deleted. The stern catapult arrangements were concurred with, as was the provision of both 15cm and 10.5cm guns. However, a demand from the Weapons Office for increased turret side protection was not agreed. The SKL maintained it necessary to have a construction reserve of 1–3 per cent to allow for the tempo of development during the ship's life. There was also a move to install the new V motors, instigated by the Construction Office, which was also agreed. The SKL accepted most of the improvements proposed, at the cost of $\frac{1}{4}$ knot speed, the maximum speed now being set at 33.75 knots.

The original intention to order twelve ships (P1–P12) was amended by May 1939, the programme now calling for only eight units. These were to be completed by 1943 (three ships), 1944 (one) and 1945 (four). Earlier, in December 1938, the twelve ships were to have been built between April 1940 (laying down of P1) and July 1948, the completion of P12. At one stage it had been proposed that P5 and P6 be given four twin 28cm guns but this was not proceeded with because of possible delays and difficulties.

None of these ships was ever laid down because of the outbreak of war and the general suspension of all long-term projects.

Schlachtkreuzer O

This project grew out of the Kreuzer P discussions and was an enlarged, faster and better armed ship altogether. It repre-

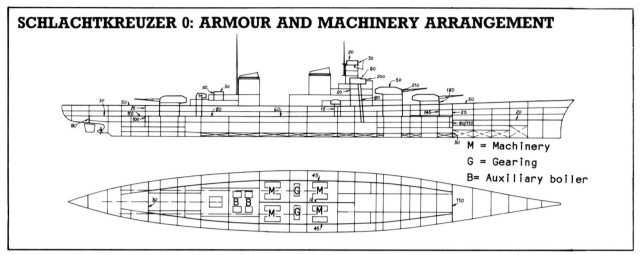

SCHLACHTKREUZER 0: ARMOUR AND MACHINERY ARRANGEMENT

M = Machinery
G = Gearing
B= Auxiliary boiler

sented a return to the *Hindenburg* concept of World War One and was a battlecruiser, being so designated by the Kriegsmarine. It developed from the earlier Kreuzer P discussions because of a proposal to use 38cm guns and it was felt that with such an armament, it required better speed and protection than the new Panzerschiffe. One of the earlier sketch designs envisaged two triple 28cm turrets on the lines of scheme 'B' for Kreuzer P, then a third triple turret on a design which approximated to scheme 'C' of the Kreuzer P project. This last scheme appears to have then received three twin 38cm turrets and had the belt armour increased to 180mm.

By July 1939 the design had gone almost unchanged from its first proposal, a somewhat unusual set of circumstances for the time. The engines and machinery installation were particularly liked. It was a combined steam and diesel layout, with four MAN 24-cylinder V engines on each wing shaft and four Bauer-Wagner boilers with a Brown-Boveri turbine on the centre shaft.

The original scheme had been to use four modified Benson-type boilers, of 60tph output and with operating pressure reduced to 64kg/cm^2. The modifications included changes in design to make it easier to replace failed tubes, and the inclusion of a circulating pump which forced feed water up the floor, roof and rear tube banks, similar to the La Mont design. This boiler had a vertical steam drum. However, with the development by Deschimag of the Bauer-Wagner boiler for the Spähkreuzer (*Z40–42*), this was adopted instead. It was a two-drum natural circulation type with five B & V atomizing burners at each end. The original design called for Saacke burners but the Kriegsmarine insisted on this change, probably for experience. It was fitted with economizer and pre-heater.

To conserve weight, it was desired to keep the machinery layout short and hence the armoured citadel also. This, however, led to the loss of some upper deck space, so that there was no longer any room to install the forward gunnery control position on the navigating bridge, as had been the practice hitherto. Instead, the bridge became part of the fore-

mast tower and there was only one main gunnery position, at its top. To compensate for the loss of the forward position, two range-finders were installed on the roof of the after hangar, which not only gave them a better field of control but it also allowed their use for HA control of the 15cm guns. The Weapons Office noted that the best distribution of the weight allowed for protection gave a belt thickness of 180mm which, they calculated, would defeat 20.3cm AP shells above 14,400m when fired from abeam, above 12,500–13,500m fired 20° from abeam and 7,500–8,500m if fired at 40° to the axis of the ship. The bow belt of 60mm extended to the stem and astern, 110mm protected the rudder by means of an armoured deck. Armour was above what was originally specified, the increase being some 50 tonnes.

Bunkerage was also increased to a figure in excess of 5,300 tonnes (normal) to give an endurance of 15,900nm at 18 knots. It was calculated that on one shaft in the Atlantic a speed of 16.5 knots would give a range of over 18,000nm. Standard displacement had risen from 29,100 to 29,250 tonnes, with the loss of 0.1 knot for a maximum speed of 33.8 knots. Full load displacement was 35,130 tonnes.

The final armament proposal was six 38cm guns in three twin turrets. There was some discussion as to the barbette diameter. This was 10m for the 38cm turrets but it would appear that there was a possibility of a future rearmament with 28cm triple turrets. This would necessitate 10.4m barbettes, which would incur a weight penalty of 32 tonnes. In the end Admiral Raeder agreed the type sketch for 'O' on 13 July 1939 and decided that later rearmament would not be possible. Barbettes were therefore confirmed as 10m diameter. The remainder of the armament was fairly light—three twin 15cm turrets and four twin 10.5cm guns, plus the usual light flak.

Orders were placed for three ships, designated O, P and Q respectively, on 8 August 1939, the building yards being Deutsche Werke (Kiel), Wilhelmshaven Naval Yard and Germania respectively. The outbreak of war a month later resulted in all three being cancelled without any work having been started on them.

6. AIRCRAFT-CARRIERS

DESIGN HISTORY

Despite the advanced state of aircraft development in Germany at the time of World War One, little progress had been made in the field of shipboard aviation, mainly because of the existence of the Zeppelin fleet, of which great things were expected. Even during hostilities the only real naval use made of the airships was for reconnaissance on a limited scale; they were used more for raids on the British Isles. The widescale use of fighter aircraft launched from platforms on the main gun turrets of the Grand Fleet battleships was never imitated by the German High Seas Fleet; and even the seaplane-carrier, of which the Royal Navy had put nine into service, appeared to hold little interest for the German Naval Staff. Only one ship was converted for this purpose, the light cruiser *Stuttgart*. Her conversion came late in the war and equipped her with two hangars aft to allow the operation of three floatplanes. As this work was not completed until May 1918, she saw no operational service and after the surrender was allocated to Britain and subsequently scrapped.

A further project to convert the obsolete cruiser *Roon* into an aircraft mother ship never left the drawing-board. Apart from *Stuttgart*, only the raider *Wolf* made operational use of a scout floatplane; but another brief use of shipboard aircraft does deserve mention, even though it was only of a temporary nature. In the summer of 1916 an air attack on the port installations of Reval in the Gulf of Finland could only be carried out by using torpedo boats to ferry the low-endurance seaplanes to a starting point offshore within their flying range. Four aircraft were so transported, one per torpedo boat, shipped on the after torpedo tubes. This was just one special operation and cannot truly be categorized as 'naval aviation'.

Only one attempt at producing a true aircraft-carrier was seriously made. This was to have been the conversion of the Italian liner *Ausonia* which had been lying incomplete at the Blohm & Voss yard since her launching in April 1915. Her reconstruction would have followed the lines of that carried out to produce the British aircraft-carrier *Argus*, except that the German ship would have had a proper bridge, funnel and superstructure on the starboard side. This was an advance on the *Argus* design whose retractable wheelhouse and horizontal smoke ducts in lieu of funnels led to problems in operational use. In another respect, however, the German design was behind the times for separate landing and flying-off decks were envisaged, despite the availability of a flush deck from stem to stern. A mixture of floatplanes and wheeled fighters, totalling about 30 aircraft, were to be accommodated. The ship was coal-fired, with twin-shaft 18,000hp geared turbine machinery, giving a speed of 21 knots. Curiously, both British and German conversions were from Italian liners. The German project came too late, however, for by late 1918 the war had been lost and it is doubtful if any work was actually carried out on the ship.

The collapse and surrender of Germany in November 1918 put an end to any further experiments and the Versailles Treaty of 1919 effectively killed any hope of future German naval aviation by prohibiting aircraft, their development and aircraft-carriers. Thus the situation remained until the late 1920s and 1930s, when, in a changed political climate, clandestine experiments with aircraft began again.

These undercover activities were directed mainly at the future formation of a land-based air force, but in October 1928 the Reichsmarine laid the foundations of a naval air arm, when it obtained government approval for a few seaplanes for 'experimental' purposes. The excuse for this was the fact that the Versailles Treaty allowed the Reichsmarine to retain anti-aircraft guns. This was interpreted as also permitting aircraft to tow the necessary targets for training purposes! In this way an organization known as 'Air Service Incorporated' was formed as a cloak for its illegal activities with the Fleet. Although eventually killed off with the advent of Hermann Goering and his 'everything which flies belongs to me' attitude, this service did constitute the basis of a naval air arm.

By the mid-1930s it had become evident that the aircraft-carrier could well have a place in the future Fleet plans, despite vigorous opposition from the proponents of the battleship and big gun. This argument was current in all the major sea powers of the period, except that the navies of the USA and Japan were more open-minded than those of Britain and France. Germany, however, was proscribed by the limitations of the Treaty of Versailles, as has been explained, but as the 1930s progressed political pressures to ignore or at least circumvent the restrictions mounted and active consideration was given to the construction of carriers and the formation of an air arm.

As early as March 1934 the question of fitting the Panzerschiffe and cruisers with aircraft installations for use in an Atlantic trade war was being discussed, together with the type of aircraft to be carried and how the ships' complements would be varied—depending on the presence or availability of a true aircraft-carrier or not. If such a carrier were not available, it was concluded that to guard against the sudden appearance of *Dunkerque* or *Strasbourg*, the Panzerschiffe and cruisers (including the auxiliaries) would have to carry one or more reconnaissance aircraft each. Any additional fitment for fighter/dive-bomber types was only possible if the probable

GRAF ZEPPELIN: DECK PLANS

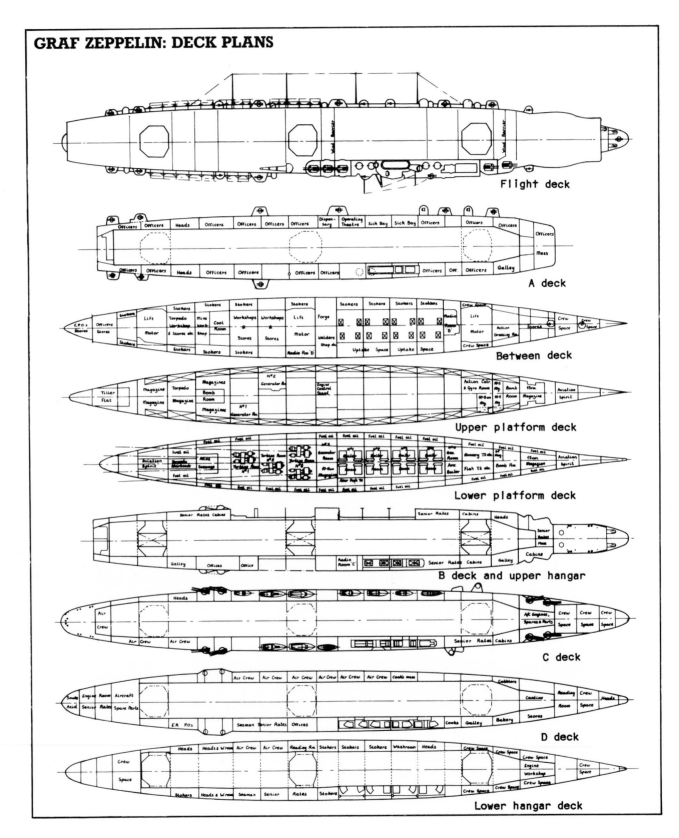

Flight deck

A deck

Between deck

Upper platform deck

Lower platform deck

B deck and upper hangar

C deck

D deck

Lower hangar deck

losses in this role could be accepted without endangering the main task, reconnaissance, and that sufficient aircraft could be carried, possibly six to nine, to ensure some chance of success. It was patently impossible to accommodate such numbers on the existing ships and, moreover, the fighter/dive-bomber types were fragile and not suited to conversion for open Atlantic employment. It was considered that they might be of use in areas where they could reach land after an operation, but this greatly limited their use and they became, in effect, a one-shot weapon, such as the later British CAM ships. In practical terms, therefore, the only option was to equip these ships with pure reconnaissance types. If a carrier were present, then the air complement of the raiders would remain the same but would be augmented by the carrier's own reconnaissance aircraft, whose operation would be relatively independent of the weather and augmented by her strike force of fighters and bombers. Air equipment of the auxiliary cruisers would be limited to one float reconnaissance aircraft handled by a boom. The proposed fitment was then established as:

Panzerschiffe and cruisers:	Reconnaissance aircraft to capacity
Carrier:	1 squadron reconnaissance
	2 squadrons multi-purpose
	3 squadrons fighter/dive-bombers
Auxiliary cruisers:	1 reconnaissance aircraft each

Also discussed at this time were the merits of the pure carrier versus the aircraft-carrying cruiser, probably as a result of the construction by Sweden of *Gotland*. This ship was a cruiser type of 5,500 tons full load displacement, armed with a twin 152mm turret forward and aft, with two further single guns in casemates below the bridge. Her long quarterdeck was equipped with a compressed-air catapult (of Heinkel manufacture) and could accommodate eight aircraft; three more could be stowed in a hangar below. With her speed of just over 27 knots and an ability also to carry up to 100 mines, this type of ship appeared an attractive proposition to Germany with ocean mercantile warfare in mind.

In the view of the Kriegsmarine Naval staff, the true aircraft-carrier would displace about 15,000 tons by 1937, given their observation of trends in Britain, the USA and Japan. General restraints were the Washington Treaty, which limited maximum displacement to 27,000 tons and the London Naval Conference, which stipulated that no carrier of less than 10,000 tons could be armed with guns above 15.5cm. They would be lightly armoured and have a cruiser's speed, guns would be well arranged, including astern, and they would be fully decked with an aircraft capacity of about 60. Lifts and catapults would be included.

On the other hand, it was noted that experiments with aircraft-carrying cruisers had been abandoned by Britain in 1918 and, although there had been much discussion and deliberation in the 1920s, none had been built. The concept envisaged all the guns forward with a free deck aft, fitted with two catapults, one on each beam. Aircraft complement was to be about 20. However, the necessity for a catapult launch restricted the size of the aircraft and slowed down the rate of launching. This could only be increased by more catapults. A ship of this type was not seen as an aircraft-carrier—its main use would be as a cruiser, but in this role it lacked astern fire and with a 180m long deck for aircraft purposes, would have been cramped and uneconomical in deck space. It was a compromise, neither a cruiser nor a carrier, and in the end was vetoed on these grounds. The solution, therefore, was a proper aircraft-carrier.

On 12 March 1934 the main design parameters for an aircraft-carrier were tabled and discussed on 19 March by a conference of the Ship Replacement Programme Committee. The basic requirements were:

(a) Theatre of operations—Atlantic and North Sea
(b) About 15,000 tonnes displacement
(c) Speed 33 knots (continuous)
(d) Armament nine 15cm or six 20.3cm guns with a strong flak outfit
(e) Endurance 12,000nm
(f) Cruiser protection
(g) 60 aircraft, a third of them with folding wings
(h) Two catapults
(i) The Air Ministry had indicated a minimum flight deck length of 180m.

Admiral Raeder's main criticism of this concerned the gun armament; he attached special importance to the astern fire power, being worried about a running chase, for which he considered two triple 20.3cm (8in) mountings the minimum desirable. This would have caused severe constructional problems, as no doubt he realized, for he was prepared to accept one triple 20.3cm with three more single guns each side in casemates. However, design calculations soon showed the 20.3cm armament to be impracticable; only the USA now had this calibre in aircraft-carriers. It was realized that there was insufficient space available to ship weapons for defence against heavy cruisers and flotilla leaders, and in any event a carrier would never operate alone. On the other hand, a good defence against aircraft and destroyers was a necessity. By April 1934, during a conference on future construction, it was proposed that an aircraft-carrier be included in the 1935 programme. The Treaty of Versailles remained a problem and in view of this, together with the fact that this was a completely new type of vessel for Germany, the head of the Marinekommandoamt proposed that preparations be started to allow an order to be placed by October 1935.

The formidable task of designing the new ship was entrusted to Marineoberbaurat Wilhelm Hadeler, formerly assistant to the Professor of Warship Construction at Berlin University. Hadeler gathered together a design team and made a start on the project, having obtained technical details of the USS *Lexington* and using the Royal Navy's *Courageous* design as a useful starting point. By June 1934 a sketch design had been prepared, which immediately attracted comments and demands for modifications from many sections of the Navy, who appeared to be unsure of their precise requirements for an aircraft-carrier. This bickering and indecisiveness was to be a feature of the design process of many a Ger-

Top: *Graf Zeppelin* under tow to Gotenhafen in the summer of 1940. (M. Wilske)

Top: *Graf Zeppelin* at Stettin in 1942. (Gröner)

Right: The carrier of Gotenhafen in 1941. (Gröner)

man naval vessel, with consequent long delays before construction commenced. The 'M'-type cruisers were a notable example of this and in the case of the carrier, this tortuous process were further complicated by the need to involve a second service, the Luftwaffe, whose C-in-C had no love at all for the Kriegsmarine.

In June 1935 the Anglo-German Naval Treaty was signed, in an effort by Britain to impose some form of control on Germany's rearmament, bearing in mind the Versailles restrictions' ineffectiveness. This agreement restricted the German fleet to 35 per cent of the British but, strangely, did not mention the forbidden category of aircraft-carrier—by which the Germans inferred a right legally to build 38,500 tons of this category! The Kriegsmarine then decided to build two vessels to utilize this tonnage, thus forcing Hadeler to recast his design, having by this time arrived at a legend displacement of some 24,000 tonnes, following changes in the staff requirements. It was initially believed that a large number of smaller ships would have been better, but the needs of the aircraft complement and the minimum flight deck length pushed displacement inexorably upwards. The major operators of aircraft-carriers were the USA, Britain and Japan, and Hadeler was fortunate that relations between his country and Japan were improving steadily (the Anti-Comintern Pact was signed in November 1936); in consequence, he was able to send a team to Japan to inspect the Imperial Navy's *Akagi*. As a result of this visit, numerous alterations were made to the German design, including the provision of a third lift and an extension of the flight deck. Later still, following the successful development of a catapult system by Deutschewerke, it was agreed during a conference on 10 April 1937 to install two such equipments at the forward end of the flight deck.

The design work continued and led to the unveiling of a 12,250-ton (standard) displacement vessel, which was actually of 33,550 tonnes full load displacement, with a speed of 33.8 knots on 200,000hp obtained from a four-shaft geared turbine installation, utilizing the new high-pressure steam concept. An aircraft complement of about 40 machines was envisaged with a gun armament consisting of sixteen 15cm guns (capable of low-angle use only) and ten, later twelve, 10.5cm AA weapons. The 15cm guns were originally to number only eight, in single mountings, but a proposal to save weight by utilizing twin mountings was misinterpreted and led to eight twin casemates in lieu of the intended four twins. This complicated ammunition supply arrangements and required larger gun crews.

CONSTRUCTION

The basic design featured a hangar structure and flight deck built on to the hull after contemporary Japanese and US practice, rather than the current British 'all one' concept. The hull was longitudinally constructed and sub-divided into 21 watertight compartments. Because of the high speed demanded, diesels were unsuitable for the main machinery and high-pressure steam turbines were therefore adopted, in a three-shaft installation. There were two hangars, one above the other, of which the upper was 185m long and the lower

172m. Neither of these extended the full beam of the ship, being bounded on the outboard side by a longitudinal bulkhead. Both were 16m in width but the lower hangar had less headroom, with a deckhead height of 5.66m as opposed to 6m. Clearance height was about 30cm less. Outboard of the hangars were workshops and accommodation spaces.

The flight deck was 242m long and 30m wide, of steel construction reinforced at nodal points, in particular at the edges of the lift openings where doubling was employed. It was supported by the ship's side and the two longitudinal bulkheads, strengthened by 30mm transverse girders at 2m spacings and longitudinal at 400mm spacings. This deck was the upper strength deck. It was overlaid with wooden planking and equipped with four arrester wires. Two emergency barriers were positioned fore and aft of the centre lift and it was originally envisaged that there would be four more wires forward and aft of the foremost lift; these may have been intended for astern steaming aircraft recovery. The wires were designed with a braking system such as to stop aircraft with a deceleration of 2.2 to 2.6g in 20–30m.

The lifts were of interest because, unlike other contemporary carriers (including Britain's *Illustrious* class), they were armoured. As a result, they were heavy, weighing some 50 tonnes or about 55–60 tonnes with aircraft. They were rated at 0.75m/sec at 6.5 tonnes. As these lifts were raised, aluminium decks rose to bridge the hangar deck openings between upper and lower hangars, which were strong enough to allow a Junkers Ju 87C to be wheeled over. Electric power was employed for the lift motors.

At the forward end of the flight deck were two compressed-air catapults, capable of launching a $2\frac{1}{2}$-tonne fighter at 4.25g and 140km/hr or a 5-tonne bomber at 3.8g and 130km/hr. Each catapult could launch nine aircraft on its own reservoir of air, or at the rate of one every half minute. Following this, 50 minutes were required for recompression. A catapult originally envisaged on the forecastle was deleted.

Internally, there were four main deck levels, which were full beam, denoted from keel upwards, hold, lower platform, upper platform and 'tween deck, of which the latter was the main armoured deck. Above the 'tween deck, the lower and upper hangars effectively split all other decks up to flight-deck level into gallery decks, except at the extremities, where mess decks or workshops closed off the ends of the hangars. These gallery decks were known as decks 'D', 'C', 'B' and 'A' (moving upwards to the flight deck), with 'B' deck running the full length of the ship to form forecastle and quarterdeck for working the ship.

Much of the ship's company and all Luftwaffe personnel were quartered on these decks around the hangar spaces. Officers' accommodation in the form of single and double cabins was on 'A' deck with the officers' mess right forward under the leading edge of the flight deck. The mess could be divided into two parts—one Navy, one Luftwaffe! Also on deck 'A', to port, was the sick bay, comprehensively equipped with an X-ray room, operating theatre, isolation room, two wards, dispensary and ancillary facilities. The ship's complement numbered 108 officers (51 air force) and 1,612 other ranks (255 air force).

Below the 'tween deck or armoured deck, the largest spaces were occupied by the main propulsion machinery and magazines. Four boiler rooms and three turbine rooms, together with four generator rooms and an auxiliary boiler room, comprised the machinery unit, which extended from frame stations $66\frac{1}{2}$ to 176 (i.e., 44 per cent of the ship's length). On the platform decks forward and aft, the combined magazine and shell rooms for the 15cm guns served their respective guns via electrical bucket hoist systems, whose supply route was complicated by the need to serve guns on the beam and thus be deflected around the hangar spaces. Also at the fore-ends was a separate magazine for bombs from which a lift conveyed the ordnance to the lower hangar deck. Aft was a large magazine for torpedoes with its associated warhead room below it, a magazine for mines and another for bombs. Lifts again conveyed the mines and torpedoes up to the lower hangar deck, via the torpedo workshop on the 'tween deck. The after magazine spaces for aircraft ordnance could stow 80–90 torpedoes or 220 mines with a normal stowage of 66 torpedoes and 48 mines. No provision appears to have been made for bombing-up on the flight deck except by cross-transfer via the aircraft lifts.

PROTECTIVE SCHEME

The ship's main vertical protection consisted of a 100mm waterline belt 4m deep, extending from frame 57 to frame 177 (i.e., about 48 per cent of the waterline length), covering the machinery spaces and after magazines. Forward, this belt was reduced to 60mm in way of the forward 150mm magazines and then continued to the bows as 40mm, finally

Right: *Graf Zeppelin* under camouflage netting at Gotenhafen. (WBB)

30mm. Aft, the belt reduced only to 80mm to the stern as protection for the steering gear. Inboard of the main vertical belt was a secondary 20mm longitudinal bulkhead which served as a torpedo bulkhead. The main horizontal armour on the 'tween deck was 40mm thick, with the periphery increased in thickness to 60mm and inclined at 45° to join the lower side of the waterline belt. Closing off the armoured carapace so formed were transverse armoured bulkheads, 80mm thick. Above the steering gear, 60mm horizontal plate

was employed. No protection was given to the hangar sides, other than splinter protection, but the flight deck itself was given a degree of protection. This was predominantly 20mm, but thickened adjacent to the lift shafts, especially the centre one where it was 38mm. This was undoubtedly for structural strength as well as for protective reasons. Around the funnel uptakes the flight deck was 40mm, while the vertical uptake protection was 80mm. Other armouring was spread rather thinly, the casemates having 30mm, flak directors 14mm,

GRAF ZEPPELIN: ARMOUR

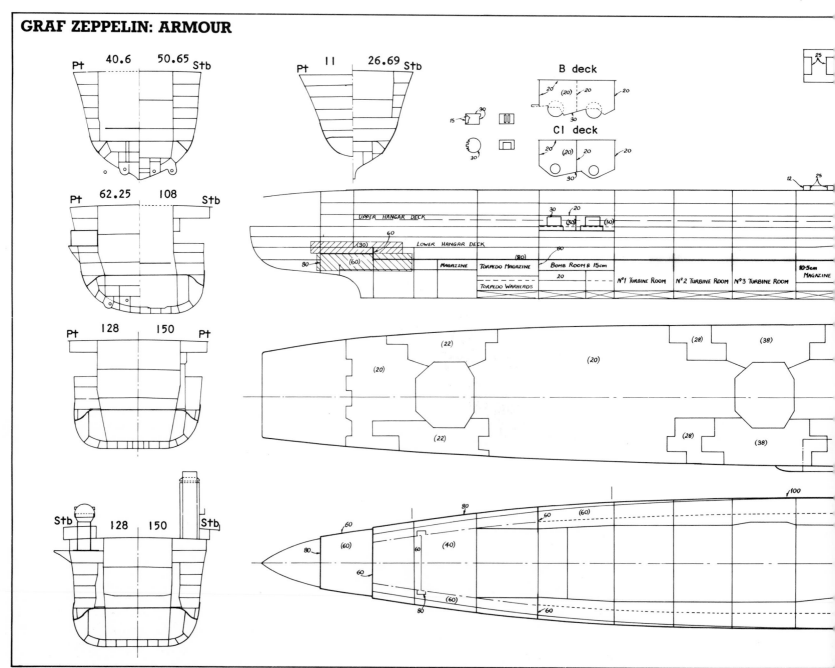

and bridge control positions 17mm protection. Total weight of armouring was approximately 5,000 tonnes.

MACHINERY

The steam plant comprised sixteen La Mont high-pressure boilers, four in each of four boiler rooms. Each boiler, operating at a steam pressure of 70kg/cm^2 (75kg/cm^2 max.) at 450°C, had a rated capacity of 60 tonnes per hour and was equipped with two Saacke ring oil burners, both at one end

of the furnance, under automatic Askania control. Economizers and air pre-heaters were fitted, with forced circulation for which an efficiency of 85 per cent was claimed. Although the boilers were never to steam at sea aboard the carrier, they were basically similar to those aboard *Admiral Hipper*-class heavy cruisers and would undoubtedly have suffered the same problems in service. Troubles experienced with the circulating pump and overheating of the air pre-heaters were eventually overcome, but excessive corrosion of the super-

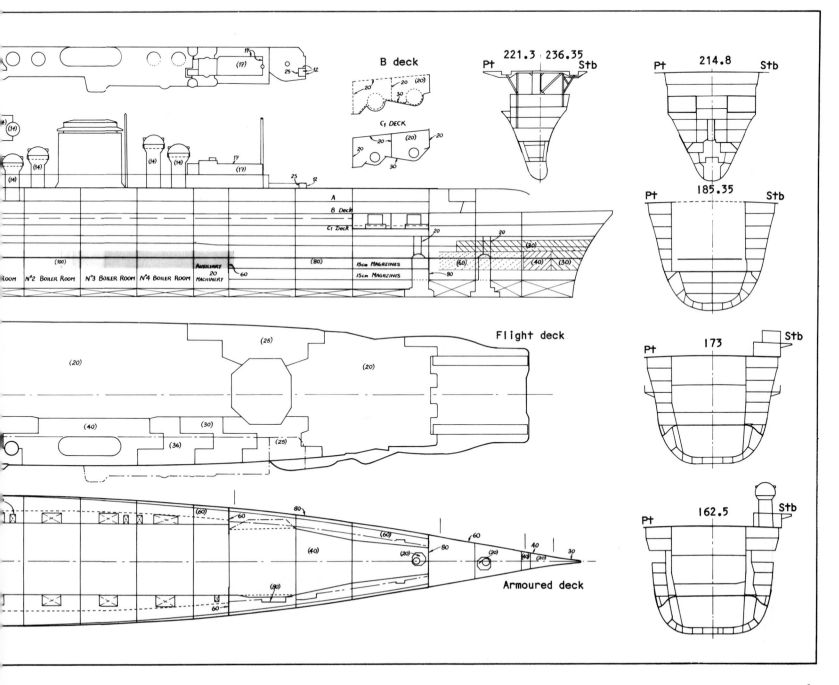

heaters caused by a carry-over of 1–3 per cent continued, despite alternations to the baffling in the steam drum. Corrosion also occurred in the economizers but the generator tubes themselves were relatively trouble-free. The boilers for Flugzeugträger 'A' (Aircraft-Carrier 'A') were built by Deutsche Werke, Kiel; those for 'B' by Germaniawerft.

The geared turbine installation had a designed power of 50,000hp per shaft on a four-shaft arrangement, in three separate turbine rooms. The forward turbine room housed two turbine sets driving the wing shafts, while the centre and aft turbine rooms contained the inner starboard and port turbines respectively. The turbines differed slightly between the two ships scheduled to be built, although initially, both were to be identical. Those for Carrier 'A' consisted of Brown-Boveri impulse/reaction type cruising and high-pressure stages with straight reaction type intermediate turbines. Astern power was provided by a stern element in the forward end of the IP turbine, separated from the ahead blading by a diaphragm, while the astern element of the LP turbine was a double-flow reaction stage at the centre of the casing. Like all German turbine designs, separate casings were employed for each turbine stage due to the retention of single-reduction double-helical gearing, leading to layouts which were extremely wasteful in terms of weight and space. Efficiencies too were generally low.

Turbine design therefore was very conservative and, if this method layout had been selected to give good safety margins in high seas operations where Germany had no bases or repair facilities, why was the same technique or thinking not applied to boilers as well?

The turbines for 'B' were built by Germania and were somewhat modified, being similar to those of *Prinz Eugen* except that the astern element in the IP turbine was removed and installed as a separate Curtis wheel on the forward end of the IP pinion. Comb-type disengaging couplings were fitted to each shaft and could be operated at speeds up to 18 knots by synchronizing turbine speed with trailing shaft speed.

Four boilers for 'B' had been completed by Germaniawerft at Kiel and underwent trials ashore in May 1940, some time after the ship was cancelled. The electrical generating capacity of the design incorporated four generator rooms using both turbo- and diesel generation. These were distributed as follows:

Generator Room	Location	Diesel Sets	Turbo Sets
1	No.1 Turbine Room Upper platform Dk. Stb.		2 × 460kW
2	No.2 Turbine Room Upper Platform Dk. Pt.	2 × 350kW	2 × 460kW
3	Lower Platform Deck Pt. amidships		1 × 460kW; 1 × 230kW
4	Fwd. of No.4 Boiler Room Lower Platform Deck	2 × 350kW 1 × 150kW	

AC power for control circuits, particularly gunnery fire control, was provided by one 400kW converter and four 100kW sets, the 400kW vertical-type motor alternator being in No. 2 Generator Room. Harbour steam supplies were provided by a separate auxiliary boiler room to starboard of No. 4 Generator space.

The main engine control stand and damage control centre was on the upper platform deck between No. 3 turbine room and No. 1 boiler room. Damage control arrangements were comprehensive, with the hull being divided into 21 watertight compartments. For fire-fighting purposes, besides the sea water lines supplied by the main hull and fire pumps and steam drenching, there were 20 gaseous extinguisher units that could flood compartments with 'Ardixine' gas to smother fire. This was not without its hazards, for it would also asphyxiate the crew and, moreover, could seep unnoticed through defective glands and seals into adjacent mess decks. This in fact occurred aboard *Admiral Hipper*, when a number of men were found dead in their hammocks one morning after fire-fighting activities in nearby spaces the previous evening.

An interesting feature of the propulsion plant was the provision of two Voigt-Schneider propeller rudders to assist berthing of the ship in harbour. These two units, powered by 450kW DC electric motors, were installed in the fore-ends on the centre-line and could be withdrawn through watertight doors in the ship's bottom when not in use. They could exert a lateral impulse of 7.7 tonnes and while not intended for use at sea, could, in emergency, be used for steering purposes at speeds not exceeding 12 knots. Furthermore, in the event of the main engines being destroyed, a speed of 3–4 knots could be obtained by using them to propel the ship.

The bunker capacity as designed was 5,000 tonnes oil fuel, which calculations showed to be sufficient for an endurance of about 9,600 miles at 19.1 knots steaming on two shafts (four boilers) with 10,500hp. At normal full power of 42,000hp per shaft and sixteen boilers on line, a speed of

Right: An RAF picture of the ship at Gotenhafen on 6 February 1942. (USN)

35.25 knots and an endurance of approximately 3,020 miles was anticipated. However, practical results on ships in service with similar powerplants later showed that the designed endurance figures for all classes of German warships were wildly optimistic. This was due to several reasons. First, the calculations included only the minimum number of boilers flashed up to make the desired speed and ignored the need to keep part of the powerplant at short notice for steam under war conditions. Second, for stability reasons, many ships could not consume all fuel stowed. Third, in service many of the high-speed steam-driven auxiliary turbines were extremely avaricious consumers of steam and grossly inefficient (this was particularly true of the Type 39 torpedo boats, for example). Thus it is unlikely that the endurance figures obtained on shore trials and design calculations given below would have been achieved in service:

Speed (kt)	36.5	24.2	19.15	15.3	15.3
Shafts (hp)	4 × 50,000	4 × 10,500	4 × 5,000	4 × 2,500	2 × 5,500
Endurance (nm)	2,645	6,750	8,340	8,800	11,480

FLUGZEUGTRAGER B: TURBINE ARRANGEMENT

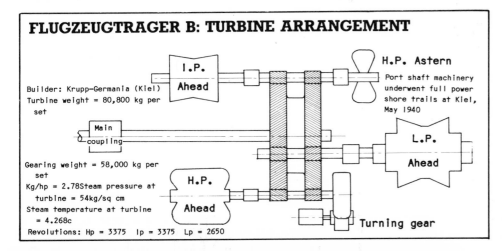

Builder: Krupp-Germania (Kiel)
Turbine weight = 80,800 kg per set

Gearing weight = 58,000 kg per set
Kg/hp = 2.78 Steam pressure at turbine = 54kg/sq cm
Steam temperature at turbine = 4.268c
Revolutions: Hp = 3375 Ip = 3375 Lp = 2650

I.P. Ahead

H.P. Astern

Port shaft machinery underwent full power shore trials at Kiel, May 1940

Main coupling

L.P. Ahead

H.P. Ahead

Turning gear

ARMAMENT AND FIRE CONTROL

The main armament consisted, most unusually for a late 1930s design, of twin 15cm SKC/28 in twin C/36 *casemate* mountings. These were at C deck level forward and aft, on frame stations 60, 68.1, 206.8 and 214.8, each mounting having a field of fire of 122°. Elevation was 35°, depression 10°. They were essentially low-angle weapons. Training and elevation was electric via Pittler-Thoma drive with emergency hand wheels. Two main ammunition hoists were provided for each mounting except the foremost one, together with electric emergency hoists. Shells and cartridges were delivered in the vertical position.

Secondary armament comprised the standard heavy flak gun, the 10.5cm SKC/33 in twin 8.8cm LC/31 mountings. Five mountings were included grouped about the starboard-situated island, two forward and three abaft it. Two mountings, at frame stations 109.2 and 196.6, were on the flight deck, two at 115.7 and 186.2 on the metre half decks and the fifth on frame station 122 on a deckhouse 2.17m above the flight deck. These mountings were converted 8.8cm mountings, tri-axially stabilized with 80° elevation. Each had a C37 setting machine at its after end.

Light flak was eleven twin 3.7cm SKC/30 mountings and eight MG C/30 2cm single weapons. The former were carried in sponsons to port and starboard at A deck level (six and three respectively), plus one on the island at frame station 162.5 and another on B deck centre-line, frame station 247. The 2cm weapons were on stations 66.6, 132.5, 144.5 and 206.8 (port), 66.6, 132.5 and 206.8 (starboard) and 1.5 on the centre-line.

The main 15cm gunnery control position was situated on the island, abaft the navigating bridge with a secondary position at the after end of the island. Only the forward position was equipped with a range-finder, a 6m base non-stabilized unit. The gunnery TS was situated on the port side of the lower platform deck and adjacent to it were the associated switch and amplifier rooms. No after 15cm TS was fitted. Stable element data were supplied from one of two gyro rooms on the upper platform deck. In addition, there were two 3m base stereoscopic night range-finders on sponsons at C deck level at frame space 170, port and starboard; these were stabilized for elevation only. Finally, in the island there were two night gunnery control positions, one forward and one aft. It was optimistically believed that these arrangements would afford the 15cm guns the ability to engage aircraft.

Flak fire control was exercised by the provision of two ZAG's forward and two aft, as well as four tri-axially stabilized 'Wackelkopf' towers with 4m base range-finders. There were two flak TS's, both on the lower platform deck, of which the foremost was in compartment XVII, immediately forward of the machinery spaces. The after room was on the starboard side, abreast No. 1 boiler room compartment XII. There were the usual comprehensive switching arrangements to allow each director to control various guns through either the forward or after TS. Five 150cm Siemens-Schuckert searchlights completed the fire control system.

When the design was reactivated in 1942, the armament remained essentially the same, except that the 10.5cm guns were now to be carried in 10.5cm LC/37 twin mountings equipped with electric RPC for training and elevation. An extra mounting was fitted ahead of the island on the flight deck. No change was made to the 3.7cm outfit but the 2cm outfit was increased to 28 guns in seven tri-axial naval-pattern mountings. Had the rebuilding been carried to completion, this outfit would undoubtedly have been further augmented.

CONSTRUCTION AND FATE

The contract for the hull of Carrier 'B' was placed with Germania Werft at Kiel on 11 February 1935 with 'A' being ordered from Deutsche Werke later on 16 November 1935, on which date a separate contract for 'B's' machinery was placed. German practice at the time was to keep the ship's name secret until the launching ceremony and as a result, at the time of their keel-laying, they were known only as 'A' and 'B' respectively. Two further units, 'C' and 'D', figured in forward planning but remained pipe-dreams. 'C' would have been built by Germania and 'D' by Deutsche Werke from July 1941 for completion in July 1944, according to plans dated May 1938, when it was anticipated that the orders would be placed on 1 April 1941. Five months later, this had slipped to 1 June 1943 for 'C', which was now to be built by Howaldt at Kiel and 1 January 1945 for 'D', for which Howaldt was also under consideration. The estimated cost of the carrier programme was 264 million Reichsmarks, spread over the period 1935 to 1942.

As it happened, due to slipway availability, 'B' was the first to be laid down, on 30 September 1936, as yard No. 555, with 'A' following on 28 December 1936 (yard No. 252), but construction of the latter made better progress subsequently. The main reason for this was yard capacity, for in this period of intense rearmament, shipyards, steel mills, foundries and factories were all over-loaded with orders and programmes were being continually put back. Even before the carriers were laid down, doubts about holding their scheduled completion dates ('A' 1 April 1939 and 'B' 15 November 1939) were being expressed in staff circles. While both yards had in hand a heavy cruiser and four or five destroyers each, Germania had, in addition, six F-boats and was more heavily engaged in the U-boat programme than Deutsche Werke. Already, their destroyer programme had been seriously delayed with construction times going out to almost four years, whilst Deutsche Werke were building the same ships in just over two years. Progress on 'B' was dependent on cruiser 'J' (later *Prinz Eugen*) whose construction had been delayed three months by the late completion of shore trials of her machinery, and she continued to absorb manpower badly needed on 'B'. In fact, Germania were forced to inform OKM that 'B' could not be completed until eleven months after *Prinz Eugen* left the yard. 'A' too was in trouble at Deutsche Werke, as unforeseen difficulties in the detailed construction of such a new type of vessel, combined with the late delivery of her turbines from Brown-Boveri led to a $10\frac{1}{2}$-month slip in her completion date. Further slippage occurred

as a result of the continuing alterations to *Blücher*, fitting out in the same yard and occupying resources needed on the new carrier.

By early 1938 a shortage of welders forced a halt on the construction of 'B' after about 500 tonnes had been worked into the hull and by autumn, when the figure had risen to 1,300 tonnes, the Algemeinesmarineamt (General Naval Office) was already suggesting to Raeder that the ship should be suspended and avoid committing a further 1,500 tonnes of material assembled but not yet worked in. The Algemeinesmarineamt already appeared to be having doubts as to the whole carrier programme and suggested that the design as it stood was not suitable for Atlantic employment; the machinery was considered suspect (possibly a reference to high-pressure steam propulsion) and could not be rectified or modified in 'B'. Yet the Atlantic was the very place the ship was meant to operate! Furthermore, the role of the carrier was to secure Germany's maritime lines of communication in conjunction with battleship groups, but it was not possible to build sufficient numbers of the size of 'A' on cost grounds alone, so the construction of larger numbers of smaller carriers would appear to suit Germany's requirements better. In fact, it was reported that the Development Office had made such a sketch design based upon 10,000 tonnes with fewer aircraft and the ability to catapult aircraft direct from the hangar. For the moment, however, no action was taken on the proposal but work continued on a very lethargic basis, partly due to the realization that aircraft-carriers were a new type for Germany and that it would perhaps be better to gain experience on one ship, so that any necessary modifications could be incorporated in the other.

After almost two years on the ways, 'A' was ready for launching at Deutsche Werke in December 1938. On 8 December the new ship was named *Graf Zeppelin* by the Gräfin Hells von Branesten-Zeppelin, daughter of the famous airship designer, and finally went afloat in the presence of Hitler and Goering, bedecked with swastika flags and bunting. She was towed to the fitting-out quay by the diminutive harbour tugs *Emil* and *Auguste* and their consorts. There, work continued both internally and externally with the funnel, mast and superstructure being erected. Unfortunately for the Kriegsmarine however, war clouds were gathering over Europe—four years ahead of schedule! The consequence of the actual outbreak of war in 1939 was that the impressive 'Z' plan fell into ruins with work proceeding only on those ships which could be completed within a short space of time. Although work continued on *Graf Zeppelin*, her unfortunate sister 'B' had all work stopped on 19 September, when she had been completed up to the armoured deck. The partly finished hull lay rusting on the stocks until, on 28 February 1940, Admiral Raeder ordered her to be broken up. Eisen & Metall A.G. of Essen were to be requested to tender for some 8,000 tonnes of scrap steel. A special decision was to be made as to the disposal of her machinery and generators. This was some five months before her planned launching date.

In October 1939 Hitler had agreed that, as well as the smaller ships, the completion of five large units under construction could be continued—*Bismarck, Tirpitz, Seydlitz, Prinz Eugen* and *Graf Zeppelin*—but for *Seydlitz*, and particularly the aircraft-carrier, the invasion of Norway in April 1940 finally sounded their death-knell. The acquisition of such a large coastline to defend absorbed huge numbers of men, weapons and small craft, much of which was purloined from other uses, so that during a conference with the Führer on 29 April 1940, Admiral Raeder himself proposed halting construction of the carrier, which was ordered the following day. The ship could have been commissioned by the end of 1940 but she would be without guns for a further ten months, and her fire control equipment had been seriously delayed by the sale of equipment to Russia under the German-Soviet Agreement. Her heavy flak had been diverted for other purposes, and the 15cm guns had been sent to Norway for coastal defence. Thus the ship would not be usable after trials until the end of 1941.

At a further conference at Obersaltzburg in July, Hitler acknowledged the usefulness of aircraft-carriers and saw the necessity for a 'flight-deck cruiser' as well as the resumption and completion of *Graf Zeppelin*. After this conference, the Construction Office suggested an 'M'-type cruiser, equipped to carry fourteen aircraft with a sacrifice in speed and gun power. But such ideas were a nonsense—why start a half-baked new project from scratch when an almost complete vessel of the true carrier type was already available? It is probable that this idea was merely the necessary response to a demand from the Führer and made with no intention of carrying it out, but the idea was resurrected some two years later.

All work on the ship stopped and on 12 July 1940 she left Kiel in tow for the port of Gotenhafen (formerly Gdynia) in East Prussia. Escorted by the old minesweeper *Nautilus*, the tow had reached Sassnitz by the 18th, where two twin 3.7cm guns were fitted before moving on to her final destination. There the ship lay until mid-1941, when Hitler's invasion of Russia caused the OKM to consider moving her in case of Soviet air attacks. The date of the invasion was set for 22 June 1941 and on the 16th the OKM ordered Gruppe (Nord) to have the ship out of Gotenhaften by the 19th at the latest. Flag Officer (Minelayers) was to provide an escort. Since it had earlier been decided not to move the carrier, this late change of plan was unwelcome to Vice-Admiral Schmundt, Flag Officer (Cruisers), who was in sea-going command of the Naval side of 'Barbarossa'. In the run-up to 'Barbarossa', his most important tasks were the laying of defensive minefields, particularly across the central Baltic between Memel and Oland (Operation 'Wartburg'), and the only tugs available were two already allocated as salvage tugs to this operation. These two vessels, *Danzig* and *Albert Forster*, left Gotenhaften with *Graf Zeppelin* in tow at midday on 19 June and by early afternoon on the 21st reported the carrier safely secured in Stettin. Later in the year, after the threat of Soviet attack had disappeared with the advance of the German Army into Russia, *Graf Zeppelin* returned to Gotenhafen once again. She left Stettin in tow on 10 November 1941 and arrived at Gotenhafen on 17 November.

The presence of the ship at Gotenhafen had duly been reported by RAF photo-reconnaissance aircraft and eventually a raid was mounted against her in the belief that she was in

Below: Raised again, the carrier awaits towing out of Swinemünde. This photograph was taken on 5 April 1947. (USN)

the final stages of fitting out. Photos obtained by a sortie on 2 June 1942 led to this assessment when it was observed that superstructure, masts and some light armament had been installed. The intelligence conclusions were that the ship might be ready for trials within the next two or three weeks. Ten Lancaster bombers of No. 5 Group, six from No. 97 Squadron based at Woodhall Spa and four from No. 106 Squadron at Coningsby, were rostered for the operation on the night of 27/28 August 1942. Only nine took off and of these only six claimed to have bombed the target. No hits were scored and no aircraft lost.

Used only as a floating warehouse, *Graf Zeppelin* remained at Gotenhafen until late 1942. Earlier that year a decision had been made to resume construction in the light of the usefulness of carriers in the sea war. The design was modified, giving her a slightly different appearance. In particular, a large funnel cap and tower mast structure were to be added, the searchlights removed and Vierling 2cm cannon were to replace the single weapons; radar was also to be installed. Apart from these cosmetic changes, it had been found after calculation that when fully loaded and equipped for service, the ship would have a list of $4\frac{1}{2}°$, which could only be compensated by the selective consumption of oil fuel over a period of 100 hours. As this was obviously excessive, it was decided to add bulges to the hull, compensating for the list by using thicker plate on the port bulge and incorporating some 300 tonnes of solid fixed ballast. This addition of bulges would also improve seaworthiness and range for they were divided horizontally, to form two separate fuel bunkers, increasing bunkerage to 6,740 tonnes.

The move from Gotenhafen back to Kiel for resumption of work was code-named 'Zander' and was under the command of F.Kpt. Remler from Kiel dockyard. The naval arsenal at Gotenhafen was ordered to arm the carrier with six twin 3.7cm and six 2cm Vierlinge, and install four searchlights for self-defence. Anti-submarine escort was to be provided by the minesweepers *M37*, *M3* and *M14*, together with boats of the 3rd VP flotilla, six boats from the UAS (*Damme*, *Stolpe*, *Spree*, *Pregel*, *Nogat* and *Brake*), and an air escort from Bd F Gr 1/196. The transfer was to start on 26 November 1942, using the tugs *Eisbar*, *Cappella* and *Passat*. By the evening of the 25th the carrier was ready to move but the following day weather conditions deteriorated, with high winds preventing the tow from leaving Hela Bay. After anchoring east of Hela, the convoy finally sailed again on the 30th and, passing westwards, the incomplete carrier anchored in Heinkendorfer Bay off Kiel in fog during the evening of 3 December. *Graf Zeppelin* was then put into floating dock for the necessary alterations to be made.

On 13 May 1942 Hitler held a meeting at his Wolfschanze ('Wolf's Lair') Headquarters to discuss the best means of increasing the flow of supplies to and raw materials from Norway. Viz.Ad. Krancke and K.Ad. Kleikamp were present, as were Albert Speer and Kaufmann. The question of protecting this traffic arose and, at a meeting afterwards with Raeder and Speer, the Führer ordered the conversion of the liners *Europa*, *Potsdam* and *Gneisenau* into carriers, presumably

with this task in mind. Raeder pressed Hitler to instruct Goering to provide aircraft for the Navy but with little concrete success. The Führer also made it clear that there was no possibility of the Navy getting its own air force in the current war. Back at the Tirpitzüfer, the Construction Office informed him that the preparation of drawings would require three months' work and conversion itself some twelve months, after the delivery of materials. On 15 May Raeder ordered an immediate start on the plans but the Führer had already defined the priority list: U-boats, torpedo boats, escorts, so carriers were well down the order. However, experience at sea had already shown that the fleet could not operate without air cover, so Raeder was ordered to continue *Graf Zeppelin*. Then, on 28 May, Hitler let Raeder know that he also wished to have the almost complete heavy cruiser *Seydlitz* converted.

The SKL spent some time evaluating the Führer's demands and were not impressed. For long operations with *Admiral Scheer* (25 knots) or *Tirpitz* (30 knots) only *Europa* was fast enough, but she did not have sufficient radius of action. Also because of their size, these ships would need protection themselves. They saw only limited potential for their employment:

(a) Use on short forays against British 'PQ' convoys for fighter cover and reconnaissance.

(b) To increase the range of land-based aircraft.

(c) As auxiliary landing grounds if shore airfields were knocked out.

(d) Training ships.

Task (d) would be important for *Graf Zeppelin*, which the SKL considered could be ready by April 1943 and for first aircraft sea trials by August. It would be necessary also to discuss the aircraft question with the Luftwaffe—*Potsdam* and *Gneisenau* were earmarked for 24 fighters and 12 multi-purpose aircraft each.

On 2 June the Construction Office was forced to report that the projected twelve months for the completion of *Graf Zeppelin* could only be achieved at the cost of cancelling the Type VIIC, the U-boat programme at Deutsche Werke, which both Raeder and the SKL were against. It was therefore decided to obtain extra labour from Albert Speer, but this had been refused once already. As far as *Seydlitz* was concerned, the Construction Office considered her conversion extremely questionable, bearing in mind that she would have to be stripped down to the armoured deck—all for the sake of a capacity of 12 aircraft. When Raeder met Hitler again on 15 June at the Berghof, he promised sketch designs within a few days and would be ready to order materials in a month's time, but suggested that the 90 per cent complete *Seydlitz* was not worth the effort of conversion.

A week later when plans were laid before him, however, the conversion of the heavy cruiser was ordered. On 17 July 1942 the Construction Office placed orders for the conversion of the three liners and the cruiser; preparatory work was to be started by the end of that month and completed by October, to allow loft work to be started. The Kriegsmarine and Luftwaffe had now been ordered to build, man and equip five

Above: *Seydlitz* at Bremen on 8 May 1942 with Z32, Z33 and Z34 also incomplete. Construction is well advanced. (USN)

struction as either a 'cruiser with aircraft fitment' or 'aircraft-carrier with adequate armament'. It was certainly considered possible to build a cruiser/carrier, the problems in accommodating the flight deck being solved by detailed attention to the catapult and arrester arrangements. Such a ship would have the speed and armament of a cruiser and be able to utilize these features, together with her armour and aircraft complement in the scout, flak protection, convoy escort and mercantile warfare roles. The existence of such a design would not, in the opinion of the SKL, be the death-knell of the true aircraft-carrier, whose main role was seen in the context of the battleship task force.

In fact, the SKL envisaged two roles for carriers, whose size was dependent upon tactical considerations. Paralleling the role of the cruiser/carrier was a small aircraft-carrier of about 15,000 tonnes—a size which the Construction Office believed would permit series construction. This would have a high speed, good radius of action, be armed with 12cm guns but carry only a reduced number of aircraft, although sufficient for the tasks proposed. The second type was a large carrier which was seen as indispensable for operations with the fleet. A ratio of small to large types of 5:1 was proposed. Raeder, who liked the possibilities of the cruiser/carrier, ordered an investigation of its merits. These thoughts no doubt led to the designs to be described shortly.

By October the Construction Office was still intending all-out work on *Graf Zeppelin*, although the man-power situation was still not clear. When Admiral Raeder met the Führer on 2 December, he reported that the programme had been reduced to *Graf Zeppelin*, *Seydlitz* and the incomplete French light cruiser *De Grasse*. This latter conversion had been ordered by Hitler in August. *Potsdam* and *Gneisenau* were deleted on the grounds of their poor speed and inadequate internal damage control sub-division. Raeder did however suggest their use as training ships. The Construction Office remained unhappy and on 18 November reported that they also considered the conversion of *De Grasse* questionable because of its turbine design and the fact that all the boilers were in one space. A week later they also recommended that the incomplete French carrier *Joffre* (laid down on 26 November 1938) be broken up, presumably to prevent any further crackpot conversion ideas.

Matters were now approaching a climax, for on 1 December the head of the Weapons Office, Admiral Witzell, reported that the demanded figure of 182,000 tonnes of iron and steel supplies for the first quarter of 1943 would not be met—only 127,000 was likely—which would obviously affect such fringe projects as these. Nevertheless, on 3 December Hitler ordered the conversion of *Europa* and *Gneisenau* cancelled and their workers transferred to *Graf Zeppelin*, *Seydlitz* and *Potsdam*. *De Grasse* was also to be converted. All came to nought however because of the 'Regenbögen' debacle off North Cape at the end of 1942 when, as a result, Hitler ordered all capital ship construction stopped on 26 January 1943, the necessary orders being given on 2 February.

Although the new C-in-C, Admiral Dönitz, managed to avoid the execution of most of the order, the completion of an

carriers by the end of 1944. However, after a visit by Speer to Wilhelmshaven on 24 August, he made it clear that the extra 8,500 yard workers needed would not be forthcoming.

Also in August 1942 Raeder had informed Hitler of SKL's opinion that the centre-piece of a construction programme for a future fleet should be the building of aircraft-carriers. However, building of battleships was not yet to be abandoned and, in deference to the Führer's wishes, the gun calibre question was to be re-examined. Later in the year the SKL produced a treatise upon the use of aircraft-carriers with the fleet, in which it concluded that a battleship hybrid, equipped to operate aircraft, was undesirable, as the aircraft fittings would incur serious penalties in the battleship features. If aircraft-carriers were to accompany battleships in a task force, then the classic roles of shipboard catapult aircraft (reconnaissance, anti-submarine and fighter) could be assumed by the escorting carriers and shipboard catapult provision be dispensed with. If, on the other hand, carriers could not be built in sufficient numbers, then it would be necessary to allocate space and equipment for 6–8 aircraft on capital ships (i.e., twice the capacity of *Tirpitz*).

Although the battleship/cruiser hybrid was not favoured, an aircraft-carrying cruiser was a recurring theme in the Tirpitzüfer, the main contention being its description and con-

aircraft-carrier for which there would be no capital ship or cruiser support made no sense. Once again, on 30 January 1943, work stopped aboard *Graf Zeppelin*. Some makeshift work continued until March to prepare the ship for yet another move, for Admiral von Conrady at OKM had ordered her back to the East. Deutsche Werke at Kiel estimated that the ship would be ready for towing out on 15 April and OKM requested that a suitable berth be prepared at Pillau. The code-name for the tow this time was 'Zugvogel' and the ship would be part of the Naval Salvage & Service Command, towing Commander Kpt.z.S. Ritschel. The flak weapons and searchlights were reinstalled and two barrage balloons added for good measure. Anti-submarine and air escort was also provided. Towing speed was to be 6 knots, using tugs *Eisbar, Norder, Taifun* and *Passat*. 'Zugvogel' sailed late in the afternoon of 20 April and arrived in Swinemünde on the 23rd, before finally being berthed at Stettin. Her transfer further east to Pillau was cancelled in the face of opposition, particularly from the U-boat command, because a berth in Pillau could not have been provided without seriously disrupting existing berthing arrangements for U-boats and minelayers.

Polish underground members promptly reported the carrier's arrival to British intelligence and on 23 June photo-reconnaissance aircraft confirmed her presence moored to a wharf on the Parnitz river, opposite Grosskraftwerk, near the Danzig-Parnitz canal, some two miles east of Stettin. Allied naval intelligence had been interested in the ship's progress and whereabouts since 1940 and reports from both British and French sources had often suggested that her completion was imminent. In June 1942 the British had believed her to be nearing completion and anticipated sea trials in three weeks, but full operational capability not for at least a further three months. Almost eight months later *Graf Zeppelin*'s arrival at Kiel had led to new reports of her impending entry into service; it was then believed that she might become operational in June 1943. However, the ship's arrival at Stettin and her condition, as revealed by PRU photographs, as well as underground reports, now suggested the truth—her construction had been abandoned. British naval intelligence reports dated 29 June 1943 acknowledged this, speculating that the reason could have been due to lack of materials, shortage of manpower, major breakdown of machinery or other unknown causes.

Graf Zeppelin remained at Stettin, forlorn and abandoned until 1945, when, in the face of the Russian advance, a decision had to be made as to her future. Since the top priorities for the fleet were U-boats and minesweepers, there was only one answer—it was not worth while moving her. Thus on 25 April 1945, almost exactly two years after arrival in the port, the still incomplete carrier was scuttled in shallow water, her machinery wrecked and the town abandoned.

After the German surrender, the Allied Tripartite Commission divided the remaining warships of the former Kriegsmarine between the victors and made provision for unserviceable vessels to be scrapped. The provisions were scrupulously observed by the British and Americans but were largely ignored by the Soviets. *Graf Zeppelin*, being a category 'C' ship (i.e., damaged or scuttled) should, under the terms of the Commission, have been destroyed or sunk in deep water by 15 August 1946; but this was not done and local pilots reported in the middle of 1947 that she had been raised (possibly by March 1946) and would soon be loaded with captured equipment for towing back to the Soviet Union. She is believed to have sailed from Swinemünde on 14 August 1947.

The subsequent fate of the incomplete ship is still, 37 years later, something of a mystery. Various authors and naval historians have put forward differing views as to the end of this enigmatic vessel. The ship was removed from Swinemünde, for she was not scrapped there. Certain sources allege her arrival in, and later breaking up at, Leningrad; but there is no positive proof that she ever arrived in the port and the docking of such a large and unusual ship would surely have been noticed by Western intelligence. Thus, since *Graf Zeppelin* sailed from Swinemünde but never arrived in Leningrad, the obvious inference is that she was lost at sea. Lenton records her fate as being mined north of Rügen on 15 August 1947, a date which accords well with her reported sailing date, but unfortunately the position does not. Rügen cannot be said to be on a passage route between Swinemünde and Leningrad, for it lies well to the west of Swinemünde. A more likely answer is that the ship was lost either to a mine or due to stress of weather somewhere to the north, probably in the Gulf of Finland, where minefields remained in abundance and any surface wreckage would not be visible to prying Western eyes. Under tow, with no power supplies and only a small passage crew, the salvaged hull would be in a low damage control condition and, as a result, very vulnerable to weather or explosion damage.

Despite the resumption of work on *Graf Zeppelin* earlier, the Quartiermeisteramt of the SKL still had considerable misgivings as to the suitability of the design and in the course of a memorandum in 1942 on the subject of a build-up of the fleet after the war, saw the need for a complete recasting of the basic design. This would feature dual-purpose 12.7cm guns, have a radius of action similar to that of the battleships, with a cruiser's speed and good sea-keeping properties for Atlantic deployment. (This may have been the design specification code-named 'Lilienthal', which featured in the 1943 war games at the Kriegsakademie. It envisaged a 58,000-tonne vessel armed with twenty 12.7cm DP guns, able to carry 100 aircraft and incorporated a 100mm armoured flight deck.) Also envisaged was a 'Flight-deck cruiser' which was to be an aircraft-carrier with good armament and not merely a cruiser with a flight deck. This ship was intended for mercantile warfare, carrying 12 general-purpose and 9 fighter aircraft—its main armament. Up to 1943 sketch designs had been prepared for four flight-deck cruisers (Flugdeckkreuzer) of between 10,000 and 40,000 tonnes, with heavy cruiser type guns, two aircraft-carriers of normal type of 30,000 tonnes, simple escort type carriers and a flying-boat tender. This was in addition to the conversions of *Seydlitz* and various liners.

The design for a 'Grosseflugzeugkreuzer' (project AI and AII) envisaged a 40,000-tonne ship with a three-shaft 210,000hp machinery installation and capable of 34 knots. This incorporated a hangar 160m long and could accommodate 12 fighters and 16 bombers. A gun armament of four 20.3cm, sixteen 15cm and sixteen 10.5cm was provided, with the 15cm still being shipped in casemates. Armouring was fairly extensive, totalling 9,000 tonnes with a 150mm main belt and 60–100mm armoured deck. A variation of this project was a modification as a true aircraft-carrier with the 20.3cm guns being omitted and a consequent increase in the aircraft capacity. The hangar length was increased to 210m, allowing the operation of 26 bombers and 12 fighters. The dimensions, engines and hull were to be identical to the Grosseflugzeugkreuzer, but with the omission of the heavy

guns the weight breakdowns were differently arranged. This design was referred to as the Grosseflugzeugträger.

An even larger project was the 'Atlantikflugzeugkreuzer' (projects AIII and AIV) which displaced about 70,000 tonnes, carried 38 aircraft and was armed with four or six 28cm guns! With armoured deck and flight deck up to 150mm thick and a waterline belt of 250mm, this was indeed a heavily protected vessel. Once again a modification of the sketch design was a true aircraft-carried layout, which, by the omission of the 28cm guns, allowed the aircraft complement to rise to 38 bombers and 12 fighters.

At the other end of the scale, sketch designs were prepared for three small flight-deck cruisers (designs EIV, EV and EVI), which varied between 12,750 tonnes and 22,200 tonnes full load displacement. Protection varied between light cruis-

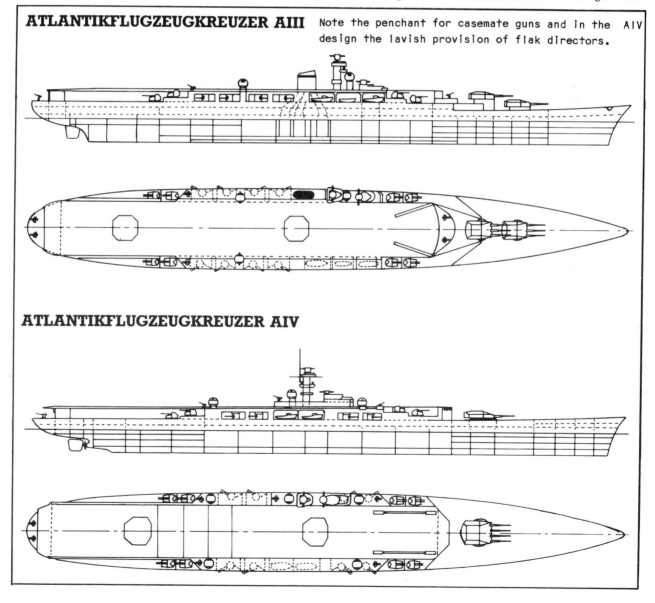

ATLANTIKFLUGZEUGKREUZER AIII Note the penchant for casemate guns and in the AIV design the lavish provision of flak directors.

ATLANTIKFLUGZEUGKREUZER AIV

er and heavy cruiser standards and the main armament comprised 15cm guns. Aircraft complements varied between 10 and 25. Two sketches were also prepared for flying-boat tenders (Flugbootträger). These two projects, IG and IE, envisaged ships of 13,000 tonnes or 36,500 tonnes able to carry seven or ten Blohm und Voss Bv 138 flying-boats. Finally, in March 1944, a meeting was called to discuss the conversion of freighters into auxiliary carriers, presumably on the same line as the British MAC ships. It was suggested that a 3,000-tonne ship could be equipped to operate two or three fighters and the 9,000-tonne 'Hansa' standard ship five or six aircraft; there was no great enthusiasm for the project and nothing came of it.

None of the projects described above (and detailed more fully in the tables) ever progressed beyond the preliminary stage and were merely 'quantified ideas' or design exercises. It has been suggested that they were intended to keep design staff occupied and to prevent their conscription!

POST-MORTEM

The unhappy story of *Graf Zeppelin* reflects the uncertainty and indecision within Kriegsmarine circles during the 1930s as to the future role of the Fleet itself. There were two main schools of thought: those who were battleship protagonists, and those who ardently favoured the build-up of the U-boat force. Under the command of Admiral Raeder, the battleship faction held sway, at least until the very end of that decade, but even with the emphasis on the surface fleet, there was little German recognition of the role of the aircraft-carrier. This was partly due to lack of experience with the type, but it

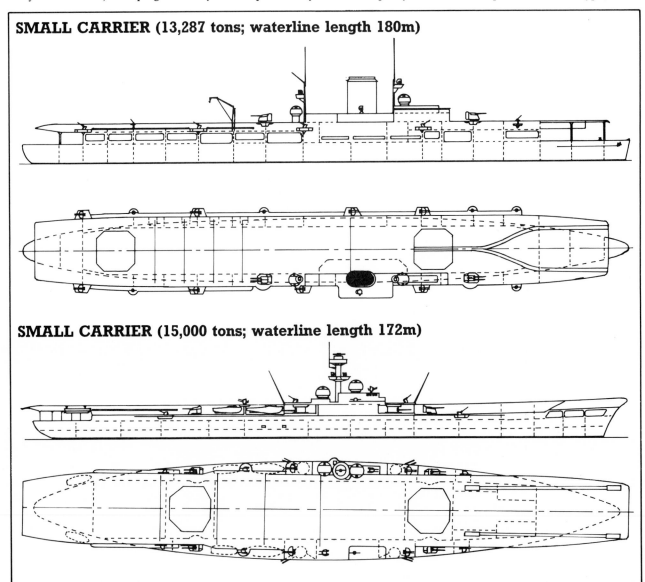

SMALL CARRIER (13,287 tons; waterline length 180m)

SMALL CARRIER (15,000 tons; waterline length 172m)

has to be admitted that the carrier's true potential did not come to be realized until 1940 with the Fleet Air Arm attack on Taranto, even within those navies experienced in carrier operation. Inside the North Sea operational area, carriers were not strictly necessary for Germany, nor were they of much advantage in the Baltic. The Atlantic, however, was a different matter but there such operations as were contemplated were of a cruiser warfare nature with independent operation of Panzerschiffe and light cruisers. The use of an aircraft-carrier in a task force was not initially envisaged.

In the 1930s war planning was based on the possibilities of France, Poland or Russia being the likely opponents in any future conflict, of which only France had an aircraft-carrier. As this ship, *Béarn*, was of dubious effectiveness, it was probably considered that in the Atlantic the threat of air attack could be discounted outside land-based aircraft range and that the ships' own catapult flights would provide adequate reconnaissance information. Then, with the growing likelihood of Britain becoming a future enemy and the intention of operating groups of ships as raiding forces in the Atlantic, the requirement for air cover became more pressing. The equipment of Britain's Fleet Air Arm may have been obsolete, but there could be no discounting the threat of its torpedo-bomber force. Thus the Kriegsmarine began its carrier programme, but with little priority and scant consideration in most of the plans for the build-up of the fleet.

Things did not progress smoothly even after the two ships had been ordered because of the chronic overloading of industrial capacity in 1937–39. Then, when war was certain, it was only possible to complete a few of the large surface ships—those which could be operational by 1941 at the latest, in the expectation of a short war. The resources allocated to the remainder were all diverted to more pressing needs, to the detriment of the carrier programme. This left the capital ships without any air cover at all, the dangers of which did not become apparent until the *Bismarck* sortie when it would not be unreasonable to suggest that, had *Graf Zeppelin* been present, her Messerschmitt Bf 109 fighters would have prevented the Swordfish torpedoes from ever reaching the battleship—and the sortie might not have ended so abruptly.

When it was decided to resume the completion of *Graf Zeppelin* in 1942, after aircraft-carriers of other nations had demonstrated the type's success at Taranto, Pearl Harbor and the Indian Ocean, the Kriegsmarine's requirement for the ship no longer actually existed for, apart from the independent Atlantic deployment of Panzerschiffe planned for 1942–43, no further Atlantic sorties were envisaged. The capital ships just did not exist to form a homogenous raiding squadron, and the abortive action in the Barents Sea in December 1942 finally killed all ideas of useful employment of an aircraft-carrier. Thus *Graf Zeppelin* was once again put into a backwater and all the plans, projects and schemes for further carriers were rendered unrealistic under the strategic conditions now prevailing. Like so many other projects, military, air force and naval, it was defeated by the attempts to produce far too many ship types on a limited industrial

base in too short a time. Contrary to general belief, despite the inter-Service squabbles, the Luftwaffe had produced the aircraft; it was the Kriegsmarine's lack of clear-cut policy for surface ships that led to the carrier's failure to achieve operational status.

AIRCRAFT

In January 1935 the Reichsminister der Luftfahrt, Erhard Milch, had laid down the agreed strength, composition and dispositions of the Naval Air Arm. Included among these was the provision for three carrier-borne Gruppen, one for reconnaissance (Träger Aufklärungsgruppe (M) 216), one general-purpose (Trägermehrzweckgruppe 286) and one dive-bomber (Trägersturzkampfgruppe 266). Each Gruppe comprised a staff flight and three squadrons (Staffeln), identified in the usual manner—(i.e., 1/216, 2/216, 3/216). Two Gruppen were to be based at Barge and the dive-bombers at Jever when disembarked. All were expected to form on 1 July (later October) 1938. Note that at this period naval aircraft duties were considered to be primarily spotter/ reconnaissance and torpedo-bomber, no pure fighter role being included. However, from 1935 onwards the small band of trained naval airmen were continually commandeered by the expanding Luftwaffe, with the result that the Navy ended up with a truncated force, capable of only a few duties. Moreover, despite this agreement with the Luftwaffe that the naval air arm would comprise nine squadrons of long-range flying-boats, eighteen multi-purpose squadrons, twelve carrier-borne and two shipboard catapult squadrons, such was the inter-Service bickering that only a fraction of this force was available at the outbreak of war.

The question of providing suitable aircraft for on-board use was being addressed by 1936 and it would appear that the Reichsluftministerium (RLM) was working quite closely with and co-operating with the Kriegsmarine at this time. Given the ignorance by the Construction Office as to the necessary characteristics of aircraft, it was essential that numerous technical queries be resolved if a workable design was to result. In July 1936, at a conference on carrier aircraft at the C Amt, a progress report was given. As far as the multi-purpose reconnaissance type was concerned, Arado had two aircraft under development, both powered by a BMW 132K radial engine, one a biplane and the other a monoplane. The monoplane was rejected as a solution to the problems of carrier operation but progress on the biplane depended upon the firm's overall work-load. This was the Ar 197. Another constructor, Fieseler, was developing a biplane, the Fi 167, powered by a DB 601 in-line engine; while Heinkel was also working on a DB 601-powered biplane. The latter design however failed to meet the demanded maximum take-off run and was deficient in the pilot's field of view. In view of this firm's work-load, it was decided that the Heinkel project would only be continued if the other two did not meet expectations. Mock-ups for these were ordered to be completed by September 1936.

The formation date set for the first carrier air group was 1 July 1938, by which time it was necessary to have 45 aircraft available and 45 more by 1 October. Because time was so short, it was decided to build both types in parallel, then decide on the final form after use at sea. Thus the first prototypes (V or Versuchs models) were required by 1 August 1937, the first pre-production model by new year 1938 and the first 45 ready for July. For the dive-bomber, there were also three types under consideration, the Ar 81 biplane, the Ju 87 monoplane, both of which were to be fitted with hooks, flotation bags and folding wings, and the He 118 which could not be fitted with folding wings due to weight and wing span. It was expected that aircraft could be provisionally available by the summer of 1937. The fighter type, the third category was not required to have folding wings, and for this task there were again three possible aircraft, the Messerschmitt Bf 109, Heinkel He 112 and Focke-Wulf Fw 159. They were required to be fitted with arrester hooks and flotation gear. The priority list was, first, the Trägermehrzweckflugzeug or multi-purpose type, second the fighter and third the dive-bomber.

While the actual aircraft were being developed, the RLM was ensuring that the necessary technical details were being forwarded to the Kriegsmarine to enable the ship design to proceed. On 4 August 1936 it was reported that a 5-tonne aircraft landing at 100km/hr would require 35m to land, given a deceleration of 2g. The same month Fieseler and Arado were requested to forward sketches of their designs to the Navy to enable the method of striking down and stowage to be worked out. In September there was another request for the weights of the various projects, and these too were supplied to the Navy:

	Height	Length	Span	(Wings folded)	Weight
Multi-purpose a/c	4.7m	12.0m	13.6m	6.0m	4,000kg
Bf 109	3.8m	8.6m	10.0m	(no)	2,100kg
He 112	3.75m	9.1m	11.5m	(no)	2,400kg
Ar 81	4.3m	10.5m	11.0m	6.0m	3,300kg
He 118	4.26m	11.8m	15.0m	(no)	3,800kg

In October 1936 the construction of a pontoon landing strip was proposed for test purposes afloat in connection with landing-on, but this was vetoed on grounds of cost. Instead, a landing strip had to be used which was faced with wood in the region of the arrester wires to simulate the carrier's deck. The Erprobungsstelle der Luftwaffe at Travemünde was engaged in this work, which was necessary to decide the optimum positions for the arrester wires and winches on the carrier's deck. Thus the OKM requested, on 22 December 1936, that wires and winches be ready for trials by May or June 1937, when it was proposed to conduct trials with a hook-fitted He 50 biplane. In response to this request, the RLM had already instructed Heinkel to fit hooks to an He 50, He 112T and one He 118T.

By 1937 the contenders for the various categories had been narrowed down. In the multi-purpose role, there were the Ar 195 and Fi 167, for the fighter role the Ar 197 and Bf 109, while the Ju 87 was now the only dive-bomber contender.

The Arado contender was a development of the Ar 95, a coastal patrol/reconnaissance/torpedo-bomber seaplane that had not been accepted for use by the Luftwaffe. The new model, the Ar 195, was a fixed-undercarriage two-seat biplane, powered by an 880hp BMW radial engine and capable of a speed of 280km/hr. Modifications included a cockpit canopy, arrester hook and catapult spools. Three prototypes were built, but unfortunately the Luftwaffe preferred the Fieseler contender, which was faster and possessed a better range.

The Fieseler Fi 167 was a lean-looking biplane of predatory appearance, powered by a 1,100hp Daimler-Benz 601B in-line engine. The two-man crew were seated in tandem and, like its rival, given the comfort of a covered cockpit, open at the rear to allow the operation of a rear defensive gun. In the clean condition (without bombs or torpedo) the machine could achieve a top speed of 325km/hr and it possessed, if anything, even better STOL characteristics than this firm's famous Fi 156 Storch, due to the ailerons and full-

span automatic leading-edge slats on both upper and lower wings; large trailing-edge flaps were fitted to the lower wings. Its defensive armament was limited to two 7.9mm machine-guns but the aircraft could carry a 1,000kg bomb or one torpedo. This machine more than met Luftwaffe requirements for a carrier-borne torpedo-bomber/reconnaissance aircraft and Fieseler were awarded a contract for twelve pre-production models (Fi 167A-O) to follow the two prototypes (Fi 167 V1 and V2). These pre-production aircraft featured a few refinements and the addition of a dinghy for the crew. A production order did not follow for the carrier herself was suspended in 1940 and the completed machines were used for a variety of trials before being formed into Erprobungsstaffel 167 and posted to the occupied Netherlands for advanced coastal service trials until 1942. When work was resumed on the aircraft-carrier, it was decided to use a modified Ju 87 (the Ju 87E) for the tasks originally intended for the Fi 167; the surviving nine aircraft, being surplus to requirements, were finally sold to Romania for operations over the Black Sea.

Arado persevered in the naval fighter requirement and produced the Ar 197, a single-seat fighter which could also carry 200kg of light bombs. This design, still a biplane type, had a maximum speed of 400km/hr and was armed with two machine-guns in the fuselage and two 20mm cannon in the upper wings. It was comparable with Britain's Gloster Gladiator fighter which, as the navalized Sea Gladiator, entered Fleet Air Arm service in December 1938. Unlike the British force, which had to made do with what it could get, and operated biplanes throughout the war, the Luftwaffe intended to go to sea with the best fighter available. It was once again unfortunate for Arado that Professor Messerschmitt had completed the first prototype of the Bf 109 fighter monoplane late in 1935, production versions of which began to enter service in 1937. The age of the biplane was at an end and the new monoplane far eclipsed the Ar 197's performance, with the result that only three biplane prototypes were flown and tested before the project was abandoned.

Not surprisingly, the aircraft eventually chosen for the fighter role was the Luftwaffe's premier machine, the Bf 109, modified for naval employment. (Whether the Luftwaffe would have been so generous if the Navy had had an independent air arm is very much open to doubt.) Nor were the machines to be obsolete marks—Messerschmitt had been ordered to produce a carrier-borne version of the Bf 109E ('Emil'), the best version available at the time. Messerschmitt began work on the project and built one pre-production aircraft, designated Bf 109T-0 (the 'T' referring to Träger or carrier) before concentrating on the Luftwaffe's own land-based fighters and turning the project over to the Fieseler company for final detail design work.

Fieseler were also to produce the production versions. The carrier version was powered by a Daimler-Benz DB601N twelve-cylinder engine of 1,200hp, giving the fighter a maximum speed (at 20,000ft) of 568km/hr. The 'T' version differed from the 'Emil' in having greater wing span, achieved by adding about 0.6m to each outer wing panel, folding

wings, which hinged just outboard of the gun bays, catapult points and an arrester hook. Armament comprised two 7.9mm MG17 machine-guns in the fuselage and two more (or 20mm cannon) in the wings. Ten new airframes were transferred from the parent factory production line to Fieseler and completed as Bf 109T-0s. Later an order was received for a production batch of 60 Bf 109T-1s, the definitive service version. After the suspension of *Graf Zeppelin*, the fighter order was also suspended but some time later production restarted with a modified design, the Bf 109T-2, with catapult points and arrester hook deleted for land service. These machines were issued for service in Norway, principally with I Gruppe of Jagdgeschwader 77 where their performance was well suited to the short exposed airstrips in that country. They were also used on the airstrip at Heligoland.

There was only one choice for the bomber role—the Junkers Ju 87 'Stuka', which was to become the standard Luftwaffe dive-bomber. Entering service with the land-based air force in 1937, the Ju 87 had been sent to Spain for operational testing during the Civil War and had since been honed into a highly effective weapon that was later to symbolise the blitzkrieg of 1939–41. The basis for the naval version was the Ju 87B, modified as the Ju 87C, which was fitted with catapult points and manually folding wings. A jettisonable undercarriage facilitated emergency ditching. The pre-production model was designated Ju 87C-0 and the production model Ju 87C-1. In the event, the carrier's suspension led to the cancellation of the production order and the majority of the airframes were converted to Ju 87B-2 standard. In 1942, following resumption of work on the ship, a new version, the Ju 87E, was proposed to combine the tasks of the Ju 87C and Fi 167, but the ship was cancelled again before this version left the drawing-board.

Despite the Navy's hopes and the grandiose plans of Milch nearly five years earlier, on the outbreak of war in September 1939 only one carrier-borne Gruppe had been formed—Trägergruppe 186 at Kiel-Holtenau; it comprised three Staffeln, 4/186 equipped with Ju 87s and 5 and 6/186 with Bf 109s. Nevertheless, they were available and even if their aircraft were not all fit for sea service, sufficient machines could probably have been scraped together to send a makeshift Gruppe to sea. Unfortunately, it was the carrier that was missing and the aircraft were therefore used for the land offensive against Poland, during which the Ju 87s of 4/186 sank the destroyer *Wicher* at Hela on 3 September.

The aircraft question has been dealt with in some depth because it is important to realize that, despite the attitude of Goering and his antipathy towards Raeder, much work was done to develop a suitable air group and it is possibly rather more the Navy's fault than the Luftwaffe's that it failed to reach fruition.

The other aspect of German shipboard naval aviation was the catapult reconnaissance aircraft. This role was initially fulfilled by the Heinkel He 60, which had been specifically designed for the task in 1932. It was a single-engined twin-float biplane, powered by a 660hp BMW engine. By the summer of 1933 fourteen had been delivered to the Navy's train-

Above: Ar 95A. (Bundesarchiv)

Above right: Ar 196.
(Bundesarchive)

ing schools as the He 60A. This was superseded by the main production model, the He 60C, in 1934, which retained the rather underpowered 660hp engine. It had a maximum speed at sea-level of 240km/hr and was armed with a single 7.9mm gun in the observer's cockpit.

About 250 examples were built by Heinkel, Arado and Weser. They served on all the Panzerschiffe and light cruisers (except *Emden*), including during the Spanish Civil War. By the outbreak of World War Two, they had become obsolete and were withdrawn from the Fleet but continued to give good service in the coastal reconnaissance role as late as 1943. Two designs were begun to replace the He 60, one by Heinkel themselves, the other by Arado.

The Heinkel machine, the He 114, was a twin-float two-seat sesquiplane with an all-metal fuselage and fabric-covered wings, designed in 1935. Various engines were tried in the prototypes, from the 640hp Jumo 210 of V2 to the 960hp BMW 132K of V4. The definitive versions had the BMW132K or 'N. Maximum speed was 335km/hr and the aircraft was armed with two 7.9mm machine-guns and a bomb load of 100kg. Like the He 60, it could also spray mustard gas from tanks in the floats. By September 1936 orders for 61 aircraft had been placed. The first deliveries were as follows: two '0' series (re-worked prototypes V4 and V5); V2 with a Jumo 210 in-line engine in August 1937; followed by 22 He 114As with BMW 132K and 'N engines between September and December of that year. The remaining 25 were to be expedited.

In service, the type did not fully reach expectations and although some 100 were eventually built, they saw only restricted shipboard use. *Gneisenau* carried one He 114 (V2) for a time in 1938/39 and the auxiliary cruisers *Atlantis*, *Widder* and *Pinguin* carried two each. Thirty-nine He 114s were exported to Sweden, Romania and Spain.

It was the Arado competitor, the Ar 196 monoplane, that was to provide the replacement for the He 60 in the Fleet. This aircraft was designed in 1937 and, to ascertain the best float layout, several prototypes were constructed of which

three, V3–V5, had a large centre float and small outrigger floats on the wings. The engine was an 880hp BMW 132Dc radial. After trials, the twin-float version was adopted and a more powerful 960hp BMW 132K engine installed for the Ar 196A-1 production version. It was of steel-tube construction, metal and fabric covered, with a crew of two. Catapult points were fitted to the floats and the wings could be folded at their trailing edge. Maximum speed was 310km/hr and the aircraft was armed with one 7.9mm gun in the observer's cockpit, as well as racks for two 50kg bombs. This version was the first to join the Fleet, serving with Bordfliegerstaffeln 1/196 and 5/196. Only 20 were built. Later a better armed version entered service, the Ar 196A-2, of which 24 were ordered to replace the A-1s. This new version was equipped with two 20mm cannon as well as two machine-guns. Total production of all types (mostly coastal patrol) was 546.

Admiral Graf Spee received the first example in 1939 and thereafter the Ar 196 served in all the ships of the fleet as well as the auxiliary cruisers. While generally a good aircraft, it did have the drawback of a high landing speed, which led to considerable amounts of spray being thrown on to the engine casing; cracked cylinder heads were a frequent occurrence.

One other aspect of German naval aviation deserves a mention, helicopters. These were under active development before the war and their use aboard ships was under consideration by 1940/41. In 1941 trials were begun using the Flettner Fl 265 V2 aboard the training cruiser *Köln*, and on 18 June a demonstration was performed in Travemünde in the presence of Fleet Commander, Admiral Schniewind, Generaloberst Udet of the Luftwaffe and others. No difficulties were experienced in landing the machine either on the cruiser's quarterdeck or on a platform on 'B' turret. Schniewind was extremely enthusiastic and pressed for further development with high priority, but he was to be disappointed. No helicopter was ever flown from the capital ships although some restricted operational use was made of the type in the Mediterranean.

7. PRELUDE TO WAR, 1936–1939

Panzerschiff A (*Ersatz Preussen*) was launched on 19 May 1931 after an address by Chancellor Brüning, the ceremony itself being performed by President von Hindenburg, naming the ship *Deutschland*. This was an important day for the Navy and marked the real rebirth of the Reichsmarine. However, it was not until 1 April 1933 that *Deutschland* was commissioned under the command of Kpt.z.S. Hermann von Fischel. April and May were taken up with final fitting out, storing and ammunitioning, before the ship undertook a trial cruise between 20 May and 1 June, which took her out of the Skagerrak up to the Faeroes and down to Wilhelmshaven. After a gunnery shoot, *Deutschland* went back into the yard for further attention before proceeding to the eastern Baltic on 31 July.

There she underwent a series of trials and evaluation by the New Ship Evaluation Command. On 23 August she reached 28.03 knots on the Neukrug mile, with 241 mean revolutions and 48,390bhp. The weather conditions were ENE Force 2, depth of water 60–65m and ship's draught 5.55–6.10m. A three-hour full power trial followed on 31 August and turning trials on 4 and 5 September, off Bornholm. In these latter trials it was found that the ship required 2min 51sec to execute a 16-point turn at 19 knots with hard starboard wheel on and a 760m diameter. At 25 knots, with hard port wheel, it took 2min 10sec. At full astern, the diameter was 2,320m in 5min 48sec, and the general comment was made that the ship steered well astern. However, under the prevailing weather conditions (NNE 5–6), it was also noted that a good deal of water came over the bows. The machinery was noisy but vibration was not a serious problem. The only vibration bad enough to prevent equipment working was experienced on the range-finder in the after turret at a critical speed of 21 knots, when trained right aft. The remainder of 1933 was taken up by training and various trials at Eckernförde, Flensburg, Kiel and Wilhelmshaven, where the ship gave Christmas leave.

Trials and training continued into 1934 but on 10 April *Deutschland* sailed for a short cruise to Norway, visiting Sognefjord and Hardangerfjord, with the Reichskanzler, Adolf Hitler aboard. This was followed by the spring manoeuvres in May and in June, and a deployment via the English Channel into the Atlantic for ocean gunnery trials, when a visit was made to Funchal.

In August the ship visited Gothenburg, after which the autumn manoeuvres took place. Flag Officer (Battleships), K.Ad. Carls hoisted his flag aboard on 1 October and made an official visit to Edinburgh between 16 and 20 October. On her return to Germany, *Deutschland* went into refit at Wilhelmshaven on 29 November with K.Ad. Carls lowering his flag on 13 December, when he inspected the new *Admiral Scheer*.

Admiral Scheer commissioned at Wilhelmshaven under the command of Kpt.z.S. Wilhelm Marschall on 12 November 1934 and began final storing and preparation for trials. Basin machinery trials were carried out between 3 and 6 December and a steaming trial on 12 December, followed by a gunnery shoot. The next day, Flag Officer (Battleships) came aboard to inspect the ship. He was the first of a series of distinguished guests, for on 14 December the Führer himself came aboard, together with the Defence Minister and Admiral Raeder. On 20 December *Admiral Scheer* proceeded to the Baltic for her trials and work-up training, running the measured mile off Danzig on 22–23 January and that off Neukrug in February and March. A recorded figure of 29 knots on the measured mile led to comparisons being made with *Deutschland*'s results, but the Construction Office stated that, while *Admiral Scheer* was larger and of better hull form than *Deutschland*, the increased displacement negated this and that she would probably have the same performance as the earlier ship; the 1 knot difference was put down as an error in the recorder. Turning trials showed that she was less handy than *Deutschland*, being slower in the turn and requiring a larger diameter at similar speeds. It was found that she did not steer well astern. On the other hand, the ship required only 3 knots to have steerage way on. The bilge keel, fitted after completion, was found to have a considerable beneficial effect.

Admiral Scheer was a very noisy ship, more so than her sisters, and vibrated between 21 and 23 knots, the critical speed being 22 knots. Less vibration was felt between No. IV 15cm and 'A' turret. Another factor criticized was the lubricating arrangements for the main motors when, should a list of 12° develop for any length of time, the lower motors had to be stopped because of insufficient lubricating oil supply. Trials and work-up training continued throughout 1935 and in October she sailed for the Atlantic via the Channel, visiting Madeira between 25 and 28 October, arriving back in Kiel by 8 November.

Deutschland spent the early part of 1935 in the North Sea area before leaving on a training cruise to South American waters on 16 March. She visited Port of Spain between 3 and 6 April and Aruba on 8 April, and remained in the Caribbean before returning home to give leave in Wilhelmshaven on 19 April. A period of dockyard time followed in June and July, after which an uneventful routine in home waters took place, until Kpt.z.S. Paul Fanger relieved von Fischel on 30

September. In October *Deutschland* proceeded to the central Atlantic with *Admiral Scheer* and visited Funchal at the same time as her sister was in Madeira. 1936 saw little change in this pattern of existence for either ship, except that *Admiral Scheer* made a cruise to the Irish Sea, English Channel and paid an official visit to Stockholm between 23 and 29 June, where she was inspected by King Gustav V.

In the meantime Panzerschiff C had been launched at Wilhelmshaven on 30 June 1934, when Admiral Raeder gave the customary launching address and the ship was sent down the ways by the daughter of Viz.Ad. Graf Spee of Coronel and the Falklands fame. Eighteen months passed before the ship began her first basin trials on 5 December 1935, followed by the official commissioning ceremony on 6 January 1936, when Kpt.z.S. Patzig formally took command.

Inclination trials followed when, in the fully equipped, half oil and water and no oil and water conditions, the MG was 0.67, 0.60 and 0.46 respectively; this was judged sufficient, although the comment was made that stability of the Panzerschiffe in general was poor, especially that of *Admiral Scheer*. In February *Admiral Graf Spee* made several runs on the Neukrug measured mile, when 28.5 knots was achieved on a displacement of 14,100 tonnes and 53,650bhp. Her manoeuvrability was not too dissimilar from that of *Admiral Scheer*, but the ship was found to be affected considerably by the wind. When stopped, she lay square to the wind and

drifted considerably, but with even a little way on the drifting was markedly reduced. As far as could be ascertained, the effect of the wind on the ship's speed was slight but depth of water did have an effect. In less than 30m of water, the loss of speed was 1–2 knots at high speeds.

Several features received criticism, including the design of the fore-ends, a complaint which recurred with every new German design thereafter. The unsatisfactory lubrication system of the main motors reported in *Admiral Scheer* was perpetuated in *Admiral Graf Spee*, with No.3 motor room especially singled out. Also criticized were the auxiliary watch-keeping platforms in the motor rooms—too small and badly ventilated. The position of the auxiliary boiler, above the armoured deck, also drew unfavourable comment because, should it be disabled, there was no alternative means of feeding the ship's company. The 100 per cent reserve of

electrical generating capacity of her predecessors was maintained but the fact that the generators had no submerged rating was judged poor. As far as noise was concerned, it was found that the stabilizer equipment was noisier than the main motors but the latter were some 6 to 9 Phon less noisy than those of *Admiral Scheer*. Vibration was also as unfavourable as that of *Scheer*. At sea, under poor weather conditions, with high sea and wind, spray from the bows hampered the bridge personnel and, in particular, the bridge design, both ship's and Admiral's, was poorly protected from the wind. Further criticisms concerned the field of view from the bridge periscopes, and another perennial—the chart room was too small.

The main motors drew little criticism, except for their noise and vibration, while fuel consumption was good compared with *Admiral Scheer*. However, the time taken to couple up a shaft (15min) was too long, mainly due to the slow speed of the electric turning motor. Uncoupling the claw coupling took only 5min. Bilge pumping capacities were too low and, in view of the vulnerability of the main generator plants and the auxiliary boilers' unprotected position, it was recommended that a 120kW harbour diesel set (or two) be installed in future construction. Finally, it was judged that an increase in engine room personnel was necessary if the ship was required to steam at more than 18 knots for any length of time, as four motors would be required. All in all, therefore, the design of the Panzerschiffe left something to be desired— hardly surprising in view of the design restrictions.

Nevertheless, despite these hidden problems, a fine new ship had joined the Kriegsmarine, as it was now known. And so it appeared when *Admiral Graf Spee* represented Germany at the Spithead Review between 15 and 21 May 1937.

When civil war erupted in Spain on 18 July 1936, Germany was quick to side with the 'White' or nationalist forces of General Franco, whose troops had crossed from Spanish North Africa to the mainland. The reason for this stance by Germany was the support by Soviet Russia of the Republican or 'Red' forces then in power in Spain. Italy also sided with Germany, while Great Britain and France adopted a neutral stance. At first all the major sea powers and a few minor ones despatched warships into Spanish waters to safeguard their own national interests and to protect their nationals in Spain.

For Germany, Italy and the Soviet Union, however, there were other reasons for their involvement. In the case of the two Axis partners, there was the undoubted opportunity to test new weaponry under active service conditions, a chance which benefited the Luftwaffe greatly and the Heer (Army) perhaps to a lesser extent; while the Italian Regia Aeronautica (Air Force), Army and Navy all played a role. On the other hand, the Soviet involvement was first and foremost political opportunism for long-term objectives, the arms supplied being merely a means to an end. The Axis partners also harboured strategic and political objectives but perhaps not in quite the same way as did Soviet Russia.

Hitler was initially lukewarm to the idea of the Kriegsmarine despatching a task force to Spanish waters as he feared an international incident. Earlier, during the spring of 1936, the re-militarization of the Rhineland had begun and it is quite possible that he wanted Germany to adopt a low profile for a period. Admiral Raeder, however, had other ideas and eventually persuaded the Führer to agree to his proposals. Hitler had in any case already decided to support Franco with arms after a secret meeting with Goering and General von Blomberg on 22 July. Later it became his policy to prolong the conflict in order to preoccupy the British and French governments, while at the same time drawing Italy closer to Germany because the latter's encouragement to Italian intervention led the Allied Powers to spurn Italy. Thus Italy joined the Axis camp. In fact, Italy was far more militarily active in Spain than Germany, with her submarines, for example, actively engaging in warfare on the side of the Nationalists. Nevertheless, the Kriegsmarine was to become involved and it welcomed the opportunity to do so because it allowed the stationing of task forces away from home waters and built up experience in keeping ships at sea under operational conditions without the support of base ports. This it had not been able to do since before 1914 and it was to become invaluable training in subsequent years.

On 23 July 1936 *Deutschland*, under the command of Kpt.z.S. Fanger, and her half sister *Admiral Scheer* (Kpt.z.S. Marschall) were both lying at anchor off Heligoland in preparation for manoeuvres when in the afternoon they were suddenly ordered into Wilhelmshaven to fuel and provision for a two-month cruise. Men on leave were hurriedly recalled and BdL, Vizeadmiral Carls (Flag-Officer—Battleships) shifted his flag from *Admiral Graf Spee* to *Deutschland*. Also hurriedly fitting out were the light cruisers *Köln* and *Leipzig*. For this sortie, both the heavy ships embarked aircraft, the flagship one He 60 from the Naval Air Station at Nordeney and her consort one from Holtenau. The squadron sailed the next day. Two days later the flagship anchored off San Sebastian where two British destroyers, *Verity* and *Veteran*, were already lying. *Admiral Scheer* on the other hand continued south, passed through the Straits of Gibraltar and reached Malaga around midday on the 27th. Several Spanish submarines and destroyers had been sighted on passage but no untoward incidents occurred.

This separation of forces set the pattern of operations for the Kriegsmarine for the remainder of the conflict. The northern part of the patrol covered the Basque coast where the important ports and bases of San Sebastian, Bilbao, Santander, Gijon, El Ferrol and Vigo were situated. The long southern coast of Spain, with the important ports of Malaga, Almeria, Cartagena, Alicante, Valencia and Barcelona, was covered later by units generally based in the Balearic Islands (Palma), while the Gulf of Cadiz on the southern Atlantic coast was watched by forces based on Tangier.

When *Scheer* reached Malaga, there were already substantial foreign forces present, including the US cruiser *Quincy*, the Italian cruiser *Muzio Attendolo* and the French contretorpilleur (heavy destroyer) *Maillé Brézé*. Also in port or in the bay were a number of Spanish warships, the cruisers *Miguel de Cervantes* and *Libertad*, as well as the old coast defence battleship *Jaime I* and a couple of destroyers. *Scheer* stayed only briefly, taking on a number of German refugees, before moving on to Barcelona. Thereafter she operated along the Mediterranean coast wherever German refugees were reported to be. There was considerable international co-operation in the matter of refugees, with all navies freely exchanging information and requesting assistance between themselves. On 1 August 1936 Admiral Carls ordered the painting of stripes in the national colours, black, white and red, on the forward and after turrets for aerial recognition purposes.

Deutschland herself joined *Admiral Scheer* at Valencia on 8 August and with the torpedo boats *Luchs*, *Leopard*, *Möwe* and *Kondor* covered evacuation operations in the Mediterranean, while *Köln* with the torpedo boats *Albatros* and *Seeadler* remained on the northern patrol. There were few serious incidents with Spanish naval forces, but the shelling of the steamer *Sevilla* by the destroyer *Almirante Valdes* and a similar incident involving the merchantman *Kamerun* and the cruiser *Libertad* led to a sharp protest from Marschall on behalf of Admiral Carls to the Spanish Government Naval forces. *Scheer* escorted *Kamerun* through the Straits of Gibraltar on 20 August, then returned to the Mediterranean until relieved by *Admiral Graf Spee* on 24 August, after which both *Deutschland* and *Admiral Scheer* set sail for home.

Overall, this first patrol had been a success, and much useful experience was gained. The main evacuation phase had been completed but now the OKM wished to maintain forces at sea off Spain for political purposes. Hence the despatch of *Admiral Graf Spee* (Kpt.z.S. Patzig) as well as the cruiser *Nürnberg*, wearing the flag of Befehlshaber der Aufklarungsreitkrafte, K.Ad. Boehm. Her patrol lasted until 5 October hen relieved by Admiral Carls once more, who had sailed from Germany on 1 October with his flag in *Deutschland*. Under his command were *Admiral Scheer* (now commanded by Kpt.z.S. Ciliax), the light cruiser *Köln* and the 2nd Torpedo-boat Flotilla (*Leopard*, *Luchs*, *Seeadler* and *Jaguar*), the oilers *Hansa* and *Neptun*, and the refugee ship *Oceana*. His force was divided into three components, the northern patrol, allocated to *Köln* for the duration of the deployment, the southern group with one Panzerschiff and two torpedo boats, and an eastern group with a similar strength. The ships allocated to the southern and eastern groups were to be

SPAIN

Above: *Deutschland* off Bilbao.
(USN)

to the red (Republican) forces, particularly those from Soviet Russia, and to report to the members of the London Non-intervention Commission.

The partisan approach of this mission is obvious, especially since *special* steamers was a cover word meaning ships carrying military supplies from Germany to the Nationalist forces. In fact, between 6 October and 14 November, seven ships were escorted into southern ports and three into northern, with another nine ships still under escort, when the station was relieved by Flag-Officer (Reconnaissance Forces) again. These supply ships were of the utmost importance to the Nationalist Forces—as indeed were the Soviet supplies for the Republicans—because Spain was not self-sufficient in arms manufacture and the chaotic conditions within the country added to the problems. Thus as early as September 1936 Germany had received long 'shopping lists' from Spain, requesting all manner of military hardware, from a 250-ton submarine, complete with crew and spare torpedoes, to binoculars! Anti-aircraft defences were particularly weak, both on Spanish warships and at naval bases. Hence the request for 10.5cm and 2cm guns for the old battleship *España*, similar weapons for the defences at El Ferrol and Cadiz; while the heavy cruisers *Canarias* and *Baleares*, then nearing completion, were short of AA guns, searchlights, range-finders and engineering equipment. Another major request was for six 60- to 80-ton MTBs armed with four 21in torpedo tubes. The greater part of this material came from Germany in the special steamers, under the protection of the Kriegs-marine but the U-boat was never supplied (although Italy transferred two). On their return voyage to Germany, many of these merchantmen carried valuable cargoes, such as copper, and thus needed escorting out as well as in Soviet aid came mostly out of the Black Sea into Alicante where, during November 1936, at least three ships arrived, including *Transbalt*, *Komsomol* and *Kursk*.

Admiral Carls turned over the patrol to Admiral Boehm for the second time on 14 November 1936 and returned to Germany. *Admiral Graf Spee* was the relief ship wearing the flag of K.Ad. von Fischel, operating in the south while Flag Officer (Reconnaissance Forces) looked after the northern sector, although the cruisers operated in the Mediterranean also. And so it went on into 1937 with Panzerschiffe and light cruisers doing alternate one to two month patrols, then a period in home waters. Few incidents of note occurred but during 1937 the Kriegsmarine forces became more closely involved. *Deutschland* and *Admiral Scheer* sailed for a new deployment on 10 May, relieving the light cruiser *Nürnberg* on the Spanish station on the 14th Spanish coastal waters, particularly off the main bases, were liberally sown with mines and watertight doors were kept closed on many occasions, particularly after the news of the mining of the British destroyer *Hunter* off Almeria. On 21 May *Deutschland* with the torpedo boats *Seeadler* and *Albatros* were at Palma; while *Admiral Scheer* and her escort, *Luchs* and *Leopard* were on patrol. Three days later there was a heavy Republican air raid on the harbour when eight aircraft bombed the cruiser *Baleares* but scored only near misses. Shore batteries, the

interchanged periodically. Responsibilities of the northern group extended between 40° and 45° N (i.e., from the centre of the Portuguese coast to the latitude of Bordeaux, with the focal point of operation being the northern coast of Spain). The southern group operated south of 40° and covered the Straits of Gibraltar. The ships of the eastern group would work in close co-operation with the German Embassy at Alicante and the consulate in Barcelona. Initially the southern group comprised *Admiral Scheer* with *Seeadler* and *Albatros*.

The objectives of Admiral Carls' mission were fourfold:

    (a) The escort and protection of *special* steamers.

    (b) To protect German interests in Spain.

    (c) Reconnaissance and intelligence-gathering for the white (Nationalist) forces.

    (d) To establish the nature and distinction of war supplies

cruiser and the British destroyer *Hardy* opened defensive fire, but the German squadron did not. After *Deutschland* sailed from Palma, a new attack resulted in numerous casualties aboard the Italian *Barletta*. As a result, *Deutschland* was ordered back to Palma to give flak protection, but this was countermanded by the OKM and Ibiza was specified as the new base.

Deutschland was lying at anchor in Ibiza bay on 29 May when a Republican naval force was sighted offshore, consisting of two cruisers and eight destroyers, obviously intent on a bombardment. While attention was diverted by this development, two trimotor bombers, which, according to eyewitnesses, carried *white* markings, flew out of the sun a few seconds later on bombing runs. *Deutschland* was struck by two bombs and a near miss sank a picket boat at her boom. The first bomb hit the upper deck in the vicinity of the bridge and exploded on the 'tween deck, in compartment XI. The second hit the gun deck by starboard No. 3 15cm gun. Serious fires broke out amidships, destroying the aircraft and causing a large number of casualties, both killed and wounded. At the same time, four of the Red destroyers turned inshore and opened fire. The German ship closed up action stations and shut all watertight doors, but did not herself open fire because of the fires raging amidships, and soon the destroyers were out of range. An urgent signal was despatched, recalling *Admiral Scheer*, and *Deutschland* put to sea herself as quickly as possible. Nineteen men had been killed and 81 injured, many being seriously burned. When the two ships met, doctors were transferred and *Deutschland* sailed for Gibraltar. There the dead, now 23, were landed with the wounded. After burying the dead, *Deutschland* returned to Germany.

The incident aroused very strong feelings in Germany—not surprisingly—and Hitler ordered immediate reprisals. *Admiral Scheer* received orders from the OKM to bombard Almeria and sink the Republican battleship *Jaime I*, but Kpt.z.S. Ciliax knew that this vessel was actually at Cartagena. Nevertheless, *Admiral Scheer* and four boats of the 1st Torpedo-boat Flotilla closed Almeria on the morning of 31 May to execute her orders. At 0515 action stations were closed up and 40 minutes later her aircraft was catapulted off for spotting purposes. The order to open fire, however, was delayed because of the receipt of a corrupt signal which it was feared might be a cancellation of the operation. It was not until 0650 that the signal was finally clarified—carry on the task. Even so, it was not until another 40min had passed that *Admiral Scheer* first fired her guns in anger. The sea was calm, with a haze over the coast as the Panzerschiff pounded the town with 28cm and 15cm gunfire. The flak guns were also employed against two patrol vessels off the harbour. Five minutes after *Scheer* opened fire, the shore batteries replied, one medium and one light battery, making very good shooting, near-missing *Seeadler* which with *Albatros*, had also opened fire. The German gunfire hit shore installations, barracks and defences, causing fires and damage. At 0745 *Admiral Scheer* ceased fire but then resumed firing at the northern shore battery, before finally ceasing fire at 0800.

Altogether, 91 rounds of 28cm, 100 of 15cm and 48 rounds of 8.8cm ammunition were expended. *Seeadler* fired five and *Albatros* 28 10.5cm shells. The British destroyer *Hereward* was a silent spectator of the action.

This retaliatory action by Germany drew considerable adverse reaction from foreign powers, with accusations of having bombarded an open (i.e., defenceless) city. Hitler was extremely agitated by these reports but in the end, when the Navy's official report came through, he could point to the fact that shore batteries had replied, so the city could not be described as defenceless. Germany's demands for stronger measures to be taken by the ships of the International Non-intervention Patrol were rejected, so that both Germany and Italy withdrew from it and therefore went their own ways.

Admiral Scheer was relieved by *Admiral Graf Spee* after the latter had represented Germany at the Spithead Coronation Review between 15 and 22 May 1937. Her deployment to Spain lasted until August and a fifth and final deployment followed in February 1938. *Admiral Scheer* completed seven patrols in Spanish waters, the last in June 1938. By 1938 General Franco's Nationalist forces were gaining superiority in the Civil War and German involvement was being scaled down, so that by the end of the year they could be withdrawn completely. With the fall of Barcelona and Catalonia, the war came to an end and on 28 March 1939 Franco's forces entered Madrid. Hostilities ceased officially on 1 April.

Back in home waters, *Deutschland* had completed her repairs while the two other Panzerschiffe underwent refits during the early and middle part of 1939. These refits introduced minor modifications to external appearance and the replacement of cranes by new types, etc. All three Panzerschiffe participated in the reoccupation of Memel on its reincorporation into the Reich in March 1939—Lithuania officially ceding the area to Germany in the face of overwhelming force on 22 March. The following month *Admiral Graf Spee* made an official visit to Spain for the first and in fact only time, after the end of the Civil War. Under the command of the Fleet Commander, Admiral Boehm aboard *Graf Spee*, the squadron consisted of the light cruisers *Köln*, *Leipzig* and *Nürnberg*, together with the 1st (*Beitzen*, *Thiele*, *Schultz*), 3rd (*Ihn*, *Steinbrinck*, *Eckoldt*) and 5th (*Von Roeder*) Destroyer Divisions, as well as U-boats and support ships. The opportunity was taken to conduct complex ocean exercises and was the largest German squadron to appear in Atlantic waters. It was also the last. The squadron visited various Spanish ports, both on the mainland and in Morocco, before returning home on 16 May. On her way home *Deutschland* joined the fleet on the return leg of a final long overseas training cruise.

During 1939 it was becoming obvious that war was looming once more and moreover, the unthinkable was becoming the probable—war with Great Britain. The German Navy, as is well known, was totally unprepared for a sea war with the Royal Navy, at least not until 1944 or 1945. Not in any category of ship could it hope to challenge British supremacy at sea and its hold over the exit routes to the Atlantic. Even in U-boats, the Kriegsmarine had too few and the crash-building programme had yet to bear fruit. The political

aspirations of the Führer, however, took little real cognizance of the Kriegsmarine's strength, for he was a land animal. His wars would be fought and won by the Army and the Luftwaffe. No sooner had Memel been occupied than a political campaign was mounted in the German press against Poland. On 28 April Hitler denounced the Anglo-German Naval Agreement and the Polish non-aggression Treaty. This was followed by a flurry of international political activity. Germany and Italy signed a pact on 22 May, while Britain signed the Anglo-Polish Treaty on 25 May. Given Hitler's designs on his eastern border, this latter pact was of the utmost significance and its affirmation by Chamberlain on 10 July made war inevitable. The Royal Navy mobilized its forces on 31 August and the stage was set for a new war. Germany had secured a non-aggression pact with Soviet Russia on 23 August, so neutralizing the major threat to her eastern provinces, and was herself allied with Italy. Ranged against her were France and Britain, as a result of their guarantees to Poland.

Thus, as the political house of cards collapsed, Admiral Raeder could only look at his available forces and make what plans he could. Instead of the forces expected from the grandiose 'Z Plan', the Kriegsmarine had available in the capital ship category only the three Panzerschiffe, together with the new battleships *Scharnhorst* and *Gneisenau*. The battleships *Bismarck* and *Tirpitz* were still only fitting out and of the new 'H' class, only the first two had been laid down, with little

progress on them. The situation was actually worse than this because *Admiral Scheer* was not fully operational due to engine defects, while the two new battleships had recently completed dockyard refits and were not properly worked up. Ranged against them were the twelve battleships and three battlecruisers of the Royal Navy and three old battleships and the new *Strasbourg* and *Dunkerque* of the French Navy. Under construction by the Allies were a further five battleships (*King George V* class) in Britain, as well as three battleships of the *Richelieu* class in France; Britain had also planned but soon cancelled four battleships of the *Lion* class.

Although this superiority of the Allies was not as great as it appeared, the Kriegsmarine was not in a good position. Certainly the older 'R'-class ships of the Royal Navy and the three *Lorraines* of the French were of dubious value, and the Italians in the Mediterranean would absorb the attentions of a greater part of the French forces. However, the battlecruisers *Repulse*, *Renown*, *Hood*, *Strasbourg* and *Dunkerque* could out-run and out-gun the Panzerschiffe and were superior in gun power to the *Scharnhorst* class; while the 15in guns of the modernized *Queen Elizabeth*'s and the 16in of the slow but powerful *Rodney* class could not be ignored by the Germans. Waiting in the wings were the new *King George V* class and *Richelieu* and her sisters. A direct challenge to the Royal and French Navies at sea was therefore out of the question and Raeder disposed his forces accordingly, aiming at a war against commerce at sea in the North and South Atlantic.

8. OCEAN RAIDING, 1939

With war now inevitable, Admiral Raeder needed to get what forces he could out into the open oceans before the Royal Navy closed the North Sea exits. As already recounted, there were only two capital ships available to him, *Deutschland* and *Admiral Graf Spee*, because the light cruisers—which type of ship had been so successful in World War One—had proved to be unsuitable for ocean employment (see *German Cruisers of World War Two*).

Deutschland, commanded by Kpt.z.S. Paul Werner Wenneker, was lying at Wilhelmshaven in late August 1939 and received orders to sail on a mercantile warfare cruise into the North Atlantic. The ship's main operational area was to be the seaways between Canada, the USA and Great Britain. A secondary objective was the traffic from the Gulf ports and the West Indies to the Azores. Having stored, provisioned and fuelled for a prolonged cruise, Wenneker took his ship out to sea on the afternoon of 24 August and shaped course northwards, a break-out through the English Channel having scant chance of remaining unobserved, and secrecy was of the essence if the German was to avoid acquiring a shadowing British cruiser. Even so, both sides were resigned to conflict in the very near future and patrolled accordingly.

Thus the warning of British aircraft received from a Luftwaffe machine of K.Fl.Gr 506 was timely and Wenneker judged it prudent to steam a feint course to the east as though making for the Baltic. Later that afternoon weather reports forecast a deterioration in visibility, just what the Panzerschiff needed in these essentially pre-radar days, whereupon course was altered to 270°. By 1600 visibility had indeed dropped to about 3 nautical miles and course was once again altered to 315° and speed increased as a result of the favourable conditions. The sailing of *Deutschland* had, it would seem, been seen by the aircraft earlier, for the B Dienst team reported a signal giving the ship's course as east, so that the feint course had served its purpose. Throughout the next few days *Deutschland* steamed northwards, carefully avoiding contact with merchant and fishing vessels for fear of being reported. During the 25th visibility closed down to as little as $\frac{1}{2}$ nm; this was convenient because by evening she was abreast Utsira on the latitude of Scapa Flow. The weather in fact was being kind to the Kriegsmarine and while crossing from Norway towards the north-eastern corner of Iceland, it was foggy as well.

Weather reports had forecast good visibility to the south of Iceland, so Wenneker decided to make his break-out via the Denmark Strait. Continually ensuring that all shipping was avoided, he took *Deutschland* around the north of Iceland and by the forenoon of 28 August was in the narrowest part of the Strait. This was transitted without problem except for the presence of some icebergs and a little difficulty with a hot bearing in the starboard engine. On the morning of the 30th the supply tanker *Westerwald* was sighted off the southern tip of Greenland, were she had been stationed to replenish the warship. Wenneker was a little disconcerted to be told that the tanker had sighted *Deutschland*'s smoke nearly 15 minutes before *Westerwald* had been spotted. Replenishment of fuel and provisions took a long six hours, after which he decided to remain south-east of Greenland while awaiting orders to begin operations. The alternative, south-west of Greenland, was discounted in view of the risk of detection by mercantile traffic to Hudson's Bay and from Greenland itself.

Events looked as if they might be beginning to move faster on 31 August, on receipt of a signal that hostilities would begin against Poland in home waters at 0445hrs on 1 September. As far as the Panzerschiff was concerned, the only other information was that the position of the Western Allies, Britain and France, was not yet known; but if they did declare war, then, for the moment, the German ships in the Atlantic were to defend themselves only if attacked. They and the U-boats were to await further orders and even Polish vessels were not to be attacked as yet. Signals concerning French and British mobilization were received on 1 September, with Italy remaining neutral but it was not until the morning of 3 September that the anticipated signal to commence hostilities against Britain was received.

Wenneker favoured an attack in the mid-Atlantic shipping lanes as giving the best chance of success and decided to move to a position 50° N, 30° W to intercept traffic between the USA and Britain. Should the weather conditions not allow searching of ships (the Prize Law was to be obeyed), then he was prepared to move further south to interdict the West Indies-Azores route. *Westerwald* was ordered to a waiting position in the Davis Strait to replenish *Deutschland* as necessary. However, Hitler still hoped to negotiate rather than fight and despite France's declaration of war, the SKL ordered the ships in the Atlantic to take only defensive measures for the present. *Deutschland* had hardly begun her search for shipping when a further signal was received from the SKL on 5 September, ordering a breaking off of mercantile warfare due to the political situation. Ships were to leave their operating area, lie low and maintain radio silence. Later that night the SKL sent further signals ordering French traffic to be left alone and to avoid incidents with French ships. As a result of this indecision, *Deutschland* was forced to loiter off Greenland for many days.

Wenneker's problem was twofold: first, he had no idea how long he might be held inactive and secondly he had little information about enemy dispositions. After considering if he should lose himself in the wastes of the South Atlantic, he decided to stay close to his supply ship. Fuelling occasionally and drifting much of the time, the long wait continued. News of the sinking of HMS *Courageous* meant that there was one less British aircraft-carrier which might detect her, but still no orders came. It was not until 24 September that a signal was picked up cancelling the veto on attacking French ships, but even now it still applied to liners unless they were clearly troopers. This signal, however, emanated from Befehlshaber der U-Boote and it was only the following day that the SKL ordered the Panzerschiffe to anticipate their release for action. The long-awaited signal finally arrived in the evening of 26 September, over three weeks after the ship had arrived on station.

Wenneker now decided to strike south, at the tanker traffic in the Gulf of Mexico–Panama area, which could also offer the possibility of refuelling himself. Three hours after her release, *Deutschland* altered course south, her company pleased to be freed from enforced idleness. The SKL still signalled restrictions on *Deutschland*'s freedom of action— Italian, Japanese and Soviet ships were only to be stopped to ascertain their cargoes. Later the SKL ordered no direct engagements with Royal Navy ships as a propaganda coup for the British was naturally undesirable. Nevertheless, the SKL expected maximum success!

On 29 September, as *Deutschland* steamed south on the latitude of Newfoundland, she heard of the first success by *Admiral Graf Spee*, making her even more eager to open her score. However, despite the use of her aircraft, no shipping was sighted and Wenneker decided to move towards the Panama–Aruba routes. After four days on the West Indies routes, not a single vessel had been seen, let alone stopped; and it could only be assumed that all traffic had been diverted north along the eastern seaboard of the USA and via Newfoundland. Consequently Wenneker resolved to remain only one more day in the south before returning north. This last day was 5 October and it saw *Deutschland*'s belated first success.

At 1100 that day, a ship was sighted and finally stopped two hours later, 600 miles due east of Bermuda. She proved to be the 5,044brt *Stonegate* owned by Turnbull-Scott of London on passage from Tocopilda to Alexandria with 8,600 tons of saltpetre. The victim got off a distress signal before being captured. Her crew were taken aboard and the ship sunk. In view of the previous lack of success and the fact that her presence had been made known, *Deutschland* signalled the SKL that she was returning north once more. She could not be aware of it, but the time wasted through no fault of her own at the start of her operation, probably robbed her of success, in that the Kingston (Jamaica)–UK route ceased to be used after 8 October 1939. Had she arrived earlier, her chances of success would probably have been greater. Halifax (Nova Scotia) was however a much more important starting point for convoys and it was to intercept these that she moved next.

The presence of an ocean raider became obvious to the British Admiralty after the sinking of *Clement* by *Admiral Graf Spee* but at first the presence of a second raider was not suspected. Nevertheless, a number of hunting groups were formed to track them down and bring them to action. Of these groups, only Force F was placed to deal with *Deutschland*. This consisted of the heavy cruisers *Berwick* and *York*, but when the presence of the second 'pocket battleship' (as the British dubbed the Panzerschiff) became known for certain, these two cruisers were ordered to cover the Halifax convoys. *Berwick* eventually made contact with a German raider, but this was the heavy cruiser *Admiral Hipper* at the end of 1940 (see *German Cruisers of World War Two*). *Deutschland* steamed north-east now, to position herself on the Halifax convoy routes, avoiding neutral shipping including the US coast-guard cutter *Campbell* on the 8th, and was not seen by the latter. The next day saw another success when *City of Flint* (4,963brt) was captured without signalling. Owned by NS Lines of New York, this vessel was found to be carrying a valuable mixed cargo bound for England. Taken in prize, a steaming crew was put aboard with orders to take her back to Germany and *Stonegate*'s crew with her. Wenneker's intention was to test the route home for prizes, using the coastal waters of Norway, and to take advantage of the cargo itself. Eluding the Northern Patrol, *City of Flint* reached Murmansk, then steamed southwards through the inner leads, but was eventually interned by the Norwegians and thus did not reach Germany—as yet.

On 12 October another ship was stopped, the Norwegian *Jacob Christensen*, bound for Oslo with coal from Baltimore. Heavy seas prevented her from being searched and since she was neutral she was released. Two days later a second Norwegian vessel, *Lorentz W. Hansen*, fell into the raider's hands 400 miles east of Newfoundland. This 1,918brt ship was found to be carrying 2,000 tons of timber bound for England and was sunk. Later that day the Norwegian tanker *Kongsdal* fell in with the raider and was stopped. A search revealed her cargo destined for Nyborg in Denmark, so she was released, but not before the crew of *Lorentz W. Hansen* had been put aboard. The tanker, relatively slow (and without radio or unwilling to use it), did not reach the Orkney Islands until 21 October, thus alerting the Admiralty to a second raider at large, positively identified as *Deutschland*. The raider moved to search south of the Newfoundland Bank the following day, avoiding the Japanese *Hakore Maru* without being seen, before Wenneker decided to find *Westerwald* again. Bad weather was forecast so that stopping and searching ships would be difficult, fuel was always important and lastly, it was believed his presence off Newfoundland was known. As we have seen, this last point was unfounded. *Westerwald* proved difficult to find and not having located her by the 22nd, Wenneker signalled to the SKL that he could only assume her lost. Shortly afterwards, the tanker made radio contact and steamed to the rendezvous west of Greenland. Between 25 and 29 October the two ships remained in company as replenishments were made. *Deutschland* was by this time having some engine problems, which required a few

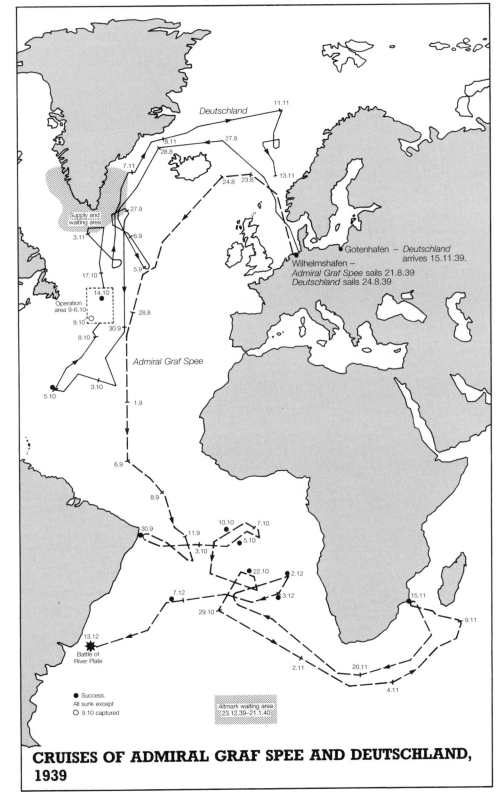

CRUISES OF ADMIRAL GRAF SPEE AND DEUTSCHLAND, 1939

Map labels:

Deutschland

Admiral Graf Spee

Supply and waiting area

Operation area 9-6.10

Gotenhafen – *Deutschland* arrives 15.11.39.

Wilhelmshafen –
Admiral Graf Spee sails 21.8.39
Deutschland sails 24.8.39

Battle of River Plate

● Success.
All sunk except
○ 9.10 captured

Altmark waiting area
23.12.39–21.1.40

Dates on map: 11.11, 27.8, 8.11, 28.8, 7.11, 24.8, 23.8, 13.11, 27.9, 3.11, 6.9, 5.9, 17.10, 14.10, 28.8, 9.10, 30.9, 8.10, 3.10, 5.10, 1.9, 6.9, 8.9, 30.9, 11.9, 10.10, 7.10, 3.10, 5.10, 22.10, 2.12, 7.12, 3.12, 29.10, 15.11, 9.11, 13.12, 2.11, 20.11, 4.11

days' work, preventing her from resuming operations before 2 November.

On 28 October the SKL had informed *Deutschland* of the intention to bring both her and *Westerwald* home between 11 and 19 November, but this was not made known aboard the ship until 1 November. Before he sailed home, Wenneker intended to make one more sortie into the North Atlantic between 2 and 5 November, then rendezvous with *Westerwald* before breaking through the Denmark Straits on the night of 9/10 November. A proposal to convert *Westerwald* to an auxiliary cruiser was vetoed by the SKL who then wished her to remain on station until the Panzerschiff reached home. On the evening of 2 November *Deutschland* began her new attack, but was only able to stop the 3,080-ton *Tyrifjord*, a neutral Norwegian homeward bound. By the evening of 4 November weather conditions deteriorated and the operation was broken off. The inability to use boats severely restricted activities under the Prize Law constraints.

Heavy weather continued throughout 5 November and the following day Wenneker decided against a new rendezvous with the tanker, intending to go north, aiming for the ice limit and to transit the Strait at high speed during daylight. This was successfully accomplished despite bad weather and ice. Late on 7 November course was altered to pass north of Iceland and the following day the wind rose and the temperature fell. Speed had to be reduced to 10 knots at times because of the gale force conditions, and by evening the ship was severely iced up. Only very slowly was ground gained to the east. By the forenoon of 9 November a north-easterly gale (Force 8) gusted to hurricane conditions at times with very poor visibility. It was unlikely that the ship would be detected under these conditions and even if it had been, all guns, directors and control equipment were iced up, with the exception of some of the secondary and flak weapons on the starboard (lee) side. The after 28cm turret was only provisionally operational, while the torpedoes, right aft on the quarterdeck, could not be manned at all. It was only on the morning of 10 November that conditions abated enough for men to be sent on deck to chip off the accumulation of ice.

Deutschland turned south on the 11th, passed the Shetland Narrows on the 14th, being met by the destroyers *Eckoldt* and *Ihn* off Kristiansand (South) later that day. She reached Kiel safely on 15 November. Her tally was not impressive, a total of 6,952 tons sunk and 4,963 tons captured; but it must be remembered that her time spent on offensive duty during this patrol was only a small proportion of that spent at sea through no fault of her own. She remained undetected for about two months, no small feat in itself, but as far as the Kriegsmarine was concerned, it would have been gratifying to have had more to show for it.

Admiral Graf Spee (Kpt.z.S. Langsdorff) left Wilhelmshaven on 20 August bound for a waiting position in the South Atlantic in preparation for the anticipated outbreak of war. Her main objectives were the Cape Town–Cape Verde Islands–Biscay routes or, as a secondary target, the sea lanes of the South and Central Atlantic and the southern Indian Ocean.

She sailed north along the Norwegian coast before breaking into the Atlantic undetected south of Iceland, the only raider actually to use this route. *Scharnhorst* and her sister ship *Gneisenau* tried a similar route later, but were forced to turn back and use the Denmark Strait instead. It was not until 6 September (i.e., after the outbreak of war) that the Royal Navy instituted the Northern Patrol, so that apart from a chance sighting by a merchant ship (and these were strenuously avoided) there was no way of knowing of the raider's passage. After passing the Iceland–Faeroes gap on 24 August, *Admiral Graf Spee* steamed south-west, then almost due south down the centre of the Atlantic, encountering very bad weather at first, which, while it helped avoid detection, also saw a Petty Officer lost overboard. By 30 August the Azores had been left to port and the weather became warmer. This began to cause problems with magazine temperatures because of faults in the cooling system; it also made conditions uncomfortable because of the darkened ship restrictions.

On the day war with Poland broke out (1 September 1939) the Panzerschiff stood some 1,000 miles north-west of the Cape Verde Islands, steaming due south. That morning her supply ship, *Altmark* (Kpt. Dau), hove into view, her light upperworks, yellow masts and black funnel being easily visible in the sun, but the tanker had sighted the Panzerschiff's superstructure long before. A busy period of stores transfers followed, while two 2cm guns, small arms and ammunition were passed to *Altmark*. As the two ships continued southwards in company, *Admiral Graf Spee* prepared for war, excess weight, useless equipment and unwanted inflammable stores (paint) being either ditched or transferred to the tanker. Also dismantled and ditched was the Landsegel mat for aircraft recovery, now no longer used. *Altmark* meanwhile was altered to acommodate prisoners from sunk and captured ships.

For the moment no orders had been received to begin operations and radio silence was maintained. Some information regarding enemy dispositions was received; one item of critical subsequent interest was a report on 7 October of the presence of the British light cruiser *Ajax* off the Brazilian coast. The equator was crossed with a small ceremony on the following day and on 10 October Langsdorff decided to go no further south but loiter in this relatively remote part of the South Atlantic, awaiting further orders. His B Dienst team were attempting to gain some insight into the strength of shipping traffic between La Plata and Britain, but without too much success. On 11 October the Arado Ar 196 seaplane was catapulted for reconnaissance and spotted a fast-moving warship, obviously British. Fortunately for the raider, her aircraft was not seen by the warship—actually the heavy cruiser HMS *Cumberland* on passage from Freetown to Rio de Janeiro. In this period of inactivity, further work was carried out aboard the Panzerschiff to make her more suitable for mercantile warfare.

One of the difficulties of operating in these latitudes was the weather, or more particularly, the good visibility. It had already become obvious from the meeting with *Altmark* just how far off the Panzerschiff's tall tower superstructure could be seen, a distinct disadvantage. Little could be done about this but to enable the speedy capture of enemy ships, it was essential to get an armed party aboard as quickly as possible. To this end, a good deal of work was done, re-siting the large power boats so as to be able to launch them in a shorter time. This also had the effect of giving numbers II and III 10.5cm guns a better field of fire.

Not until 25 September did her release come, whereupon Langsdorff decided to strike first towards the Brazilian coast in the vicinity of Recife. Releasing *Altmark* on 27 September, *Admiral Graf Spee* began operations and three days later, on the afternoon of 30 September, trapped her first victim. Despite the use of her aircraft, she failed to stop the merchantman sending a 'raider' signal, thus compromising her position. The captured vessel was the 5,051brt *Clement* out of Pernambuco bound for Bahia. As this was her final port of call, her cargo was not great but being a British vessel, she was scuttled. Actually there was an element of farce about this first 'kill', for despite the seacocks being opened, *Clement* refused to sink. Scuttling charges refused to go off, whereupon two torpedoes were fired. Both missed! Eventually she was sunk by gunfire. The skipper and Chief Engineer were taken aboard the Panzerschiff and the remainder of the crew left in the boats. Langsdorff, however, was a humane person and, despite the risks, signalled Pernambuco radio requesting a rescue mission. 'Thanks', replied the radio station, 'Hasta Luego'.

Later the same day, the Greek *Papalenos*, loaded with 5,705 tons of maize, was stopped but because she was neutral, with a neutral consigned cargo, she was released, after taking aboard the officers from *Clement*. This was probably a mistake, for these men had obviously seen things aboard the German ship and also, in the course of dealing with the Greek, the Panzerschiff's real name slipped out. For the express benefit of *Clement*'s crew, the ship had displayed the nameplate *Admiral Scheer*. Now alerted to the presence of a raider in the South Atlantic, the French and British Admiralties formed several hunting groups, of which the majority were aimed at the raider in the south, the presence of *Deutschland* in the north not yet being apparent. In view of the anticipated reaction, Langsdorff steamed east, combing the sea lanes in the area between St Helena and Ascension Island. While doing so, parts of the front and sides of the tower mast were painted white in an attempt to make it less visible and at the same time give it the appearance of a tripod mast. *Graf Spee*'s second victim was found on 5 October, *Newton Beech* (4,651brt), on passage from Cape Town to Freetown with 7,194 tons of maize. Once again, a 'RRRR' signal was despatched. Langsdorff decided to retain this ship for the moment and put a prize crew aboard. Searches of the ship unearthed some valuable documents, although the confidential books had been ditched. Thus he was able to reconstruct the British radio procedures in the event of an encounter with a raider. Deception signals were now a possibility and to this end, a standard British-pattern radio was taken out of *Newton Beech* and installed aboard *Graf Spee*.

These two successes were not enough to show for the time spent on the sea lanes in Langsdorff's opinion and, as with his consort to the north, the question of where the traffic had gone was a vital one. He knew that in September, for instance, more than sixty British merchantmen had visited Buenos Aires, so where were they now? A new success was gained on 7 October, the capture of *Ashlea* (4,222brt) out of Cape Town bound for England with raw sugar. After her crew had been transferred to *Newton Beech*, she was scuttled. The following day, Langsdorff searched the Cape–Canaries route towards the north-west, but sighted nothing. By now *Newton Beech* was becoming a millstone around the raider's neck and after transfer of the prisoners to the warship, she too was scuttled. The next victim was found on the evening of 10 October. This was the British *Huntsman* of 8,196 tons, on passage from Calcutta to England, with a mixed cargo, including 1,520 tons of tea. Her capture added another 84 prisoners to the tally, so Langsdorff decided to retain her as a prison ship.

However, using the previously mentioned radio, he despatched a signal 'SSSS SSSS SSSS, 7°20'S, 7°57'W, *Newton Beech*, torpedoed', to give the impression of a submarine attack, perhaps working in conjunction with the surface raider. He now moved to find *Altmark* once more, which was sighted on 14 October. Some cargo and all prisoners were transferred to the supply ship which remained in company until 18 October. Langsdorff now decided to search a new operational area on the Cape route, south-east of St Helena,

at a sufficient distance offshore that any distress signal could not be picked up by Walvis Bay radio station. While on route to his new area, the B Dienst team decyphered a signal from SNO Simonstown, warning shipping of two *Deutschland*-class raiders at large, operating aircraft and instructing merchant ships to be very wary of unidentified warships. This decrypt, together with possession of Admiralty instructions to merchantmen, gave Langsdorff considerable advantage in dealing with the approach to his victims. He had, for example, already painted out the national emblems on his reconnaissance aircraft.

The new operational area was reached on 22 October and almost immediately a ship was sighted by the Arado. After a burst of warning gunfire, the victim ceased radio-ing and an armed party was put aboard. The ship was the two-year-old *Trevanion* with 8,835 tons of zinc ore from Australia—a valuable cargo, which was soon on its way to the bottom. Her distress call had, however, been picked up by another ship, *Lanstephen Castle*, which relayed it to C-in-C Freetown, but despite searches the raider was not found. *Admiral Graf Spee* now steamed south-west, aware also from her B Dienst team that Simonstown had picked up *Trevanion*'s signal. They also heard and decyphered Simonstown's request to *Lanstephen Castle* to clarify the position given in the distress signal. It was obvious that defensive measures would have by now been taken on the Cape route and it was therefore pointless, indeed dangerous, to remain in the area. Hence the speedy exit to the west, at the same time signalling to the SKL of the

Below: *Admiral Graf Spee* with dummy 28cm turret. (WBB)

intention to be home for refit in January 1940. After meeting *Altmark* on 28 November and transferring the crew of *Trevanion*, *Graf Spee* fuelled before continuing operations.

A hornet's nest had obviously been stirred up in the South Atlantic, making it advisable to move on. Langsdorff opted for the Indian Ocean, where the valuable shipping routes to and from Australasia would probably produce rich pickings. After some hesitation, he decided to operate only at the south-western corner of the Indian Ocean, (i.e., south of Madagascar) to avoid risking *Altmark*'s double passage south of the Cape of Good Hope. This would still disrupt traffic across the whole of that ocean but at the same time would allow a rapid return to the South Atlantic.

Altmark was released once more on 28 October as the Panzerschiff set course for the Indian Ocean, rounding the Cape of Good Hope on 3 November. From 8 to 14 November a fruitless search was conducted south of Madagascar and the entrance to the Mozambique Channel. Heavy swells prevented full use of the aircraft and then, on 9 November, its engine suffered damage, making it unserviceable. As the only spare engine had already been used, the aircraft could no longer be flown. This severely restricted reconnaissance activities. By 14 November *Graf Spee* had closed the African coast enough for the mountains inland to be sighted—but still no ships. Eventually a small Dutch coaster was stopped but released, and it was not until the next day that another ship was stopped. This was *Africa Shell*, a small but brand-new motor ship in ballast for Lourenço Marques. Leaving the crew in boats, Langsdorff took the captain aboard and moved further south. Only the neutral Dutch *Mapia* was found, and released, before *Graf Spee* returned to the South Atlantic once more.

After rendezvousing with *Altmark* on 26 November, just south of the Tropic of Capricorn, some 1,500 miles west of the African coast, the raider refuelled and took on provisions, which extended her operation period until the end of February 1940. However the length of the cruise depended more on the state of her machinery than anything else. This was in need of overhaul and a few days were now spent on this task. Langsdorff decided that once ready again, he would try his luck in the area where *Trevanion* had been sunk, hoping that in his long absence from the area, shipping would be moving again. Here he would operate until about 6 December, after which he would either proceed home or try a strike against the River Plate area, depending on the ship's machinery conditions. By 1 December *Admiral Graf Spee* was en route for the Cape–St Helena and Cape—New York routes. Makeshift repairs to the Arado enabled reconnaissance flights to be made once more, a great advantage, as it considerably increased the search area.

The following day a smoke plume was sighted and after a chase, a new victim lay under her guns. This was the 10,086-ton turbine steamer *Doric Star* with a cargo of wool, grain and refrigerated meat from New Zealand to Britain. Her attempts at radio-ing were jammed by Langsdorff's captured transmitter, but not very successfully for it was heard being repeated in an essentially correct form by several other stations. At the

time of this interception, the raider's aircraft had not returned from its patrol and had actually come down, lost in the ocean, damaging the port float. In her concern to rescue the aircraft, *Admiral Graf Spee* sank the captured ship by gunfire and torpedo, taking aboard the crew and nineteen bars of silver from the cargo, before going to assist the aircraft. As a warship had been heard quite close, in communication with Simonstown, which had possibly heard the raider talking to her aircraft, it was obviously unwise to loiter in this area any longer. Then, on 3 December, the 7,983-ton *Tairoa* with wool and refrigerated meat bound for England from Australia was encountered and sunk. Two sinkings in 24 hours would be expected to suspend all traffic, so Langsdorff steamed for *Altmark* and refuelled on 6 December. He now intended to strike at the River Plate area, despite being aware (via SKL signals) of the presence there of the British cruisers *Exeter*, *Cumberland*, *Ajax* and *Achilles*. After exercises with his supply ship, which revealed the lack of training of the range-finder and director crews, resulting from the long period of mercantile warfare, Langsdorff moved westwards towards the coast of South America. His plan of campaign was to steam south-eastwards to Rio, then east and intercept a neutral with the object of fooling the British into believing that he had rounded Cape Horn and sailed into the Pacific.

After detaching *Altmark* on the morning of 7 December, the smoke of another ship was sighted that evening, some 400 miles south-east of the island of Trinidade. This turned out to be the 3,895-ton *Streonshalh* with a full cargo of wheat. She too was sunk by gunfire and her crew taken on board. Various papers were captured, among them a newspaper with a photo of *Cumberland* clearly illustrating her camouflage. This was of great interest to Langsdorff, for he intended to imitate it. Also of importance was the information from the local Attaché (via the SKL) of the presence of the large vessels *Highland Monarch*, *Marcony*, *Ashbury* and *Southgate*, which made tempting targets. Despite searches by the Arado, nothing was sighted and on 11 December the aircraft was damaged again, irreparably this time. As the intention was to build a false funnel on the catapult, the opportunity was taken to dismantle the aircraft at the same time. The ship continued on the course held throughout the night, with the intention of altering to 335° at 0600hrs on 13 December to sweep the sea lanes. The sky was cloudless, the sea calm, with visibility around 20 nautical miles. At 0552 look-outs reported mast-heads directly ahead, first two then four, at a range of 31,000m. Action stations were closed up as the right-hand ship was identified as the heavy cruiser *Exeter*. Two other smaller warships were initially identified as destroyers, giving Langsdorff the impression that they were the escort for a convoy. He decided to attack at maximum range—i.e., outside that of *Exeter*—before the enemy could react and get steam up for maximum speed. Almost immediately, the two smaller ships were identified as the light cruisers *Ajax* and *Achilles*. When they turned towards him, breaking out battle ensigns, the German captain realized that he had at last been brought to action by the Royal Navy.

9. RIVER PLATE, 1939

When the identity of the enemy forces became clear Langsdorff realized that he had no option but to fight, although the engagement of regular enemy naval forces was not part of his brief. All the enemy cruisers were faster than his ship, but none was individually a match for the Panzerschiff. Three together was a different matter, posing problems of gunnery control and target selection, which tasks were immediately addressed by her C.O. and the gunnery department. The men whose hour had now arrived were K.Kpt. Ascher, the senior gunnery officer who would fight the 28cm armament, F.Kpt. Fuchs who was the flak officer in charge of the 10.5cm guns, and Kpt.Lt. Meusemann, the third gunnery officer, in charge of the secondary (15cm) armament. Langsdorff elected to fight his ship from the foretop, where he had a good all-round view.

Admiral Graf Spee increased to full speed and at 0615 altered course to 115° to engage in a running fight to starboard. The British cruisers were now steaming in line ahead, working up to full speed, the range being about 18,000 metres. *Ajax* (Captain C.H.L. Woodhouse) led the line as flagship of Commodore Harwood, followed by *Achilles* (Captain W.P. Parry) with *Exeter* at the rear, under the command of Captain F.S. Bell. These ships formed the South American Division whose flagship was originally *Exeter* but be-

Below: *Admiral Graf Spee*, midships view showing wrecked Ar 196. (National Archives)

cause she had earlier gone to Port Stanley for repairs, Commodore Harwood had shifted his flag to *Ajax* where it still flew on *Exeter*'s rejoining the squadron. In *Exeter*'s absence, the New Zealand-manned *Achilles* had reinforced the squadron from the Pacific. Of the cruisers only one, *Exeter*, was a heavy cruiser with 20.3cm (8in) guns and even then she was an 'economy' version of the Washington Treaty type, as she had only three twin turrets. The other pair were *Leander*-class light cruisers with eight 15cm (6in) guns in four twin turrets. None of the British cruisers was armoured to any great degree, their only assets being speed and manoeuvrability. At the time of sighting the enemy, the cruisers were just standing down 'Dawn Action Stations'. Closing up once again, battle ensigns were broken out and action joined.

Admiral Graf Spee opened fire with her main armament at about 0617 and the first phase had begun. Her target was *Exeter*, the most dangerous of her adversaries. Both of the German's turrets concentrated on the heavy cruiser, firing four salvoes of base-fused AP. Initially short, Ascher soon corrected and straddled *Exeter* before switching to nose-fused HE ammunition to gain maximum effect against the lightly armoured adversary. Near misses would riddle the superstructure, bridge and turrets to cause casualties and hopefully slow her down as well. *Exeter* replied about two minutes later, having pulled out of the British line to port, under a prearranged plan designed to split the enemy's fire control in the event of meeting a pocket battleship. *Ajax* and *Achilles* meanwhile held their course, opening fire themselves at 0623 and 0621 respectively. They were in turn taken under fire by K.Kpt. Meusemann with his starboard 15cm (5.9) battery. Approximately four minutes after opening fire, *Exeter* received a hit in the bows, destroying the paint store; this was quickly followed by a second hit which struck the forecastle. It was the third shell which caused the most damage, however. This struck 'B' turret and unleashed a storm of shell splinters into the bridge, killing or wounding everyone there except for Bell.

The two light cruisers continued to engage, *Ajax* launching her Fairey Seafox seaplane for spotting purposes. As yet they remained only engaged by the Panzerschiff's secondary armament. At about 0625 Kpt.Lt. Brutzer, the torpedo officer, warned Langsdorff of a situation developing where the enemy might be in a favourable position to use torpedoes; *Exeter* did, in fact, fire her starboard tubes a short time later. To avoid any such torpedoes, Langsdorff altered course north, then north-west at about 0630, while at the same time shifting his ship's main armament on to the light cruisers who were attempting to relieve the pressure upon *Exeter*. Up

till now *Admiral Graf Spee* had received two 20.3cm (8in) shell hits, one on the 'tween deck in compartment XI and the second in the Admiral's bridge. A few 15cm (6in) had also found their target but had so far caused little damage. Langsdorff had been slightly wounded in this phase.

Both the British light cruisers were on the German's starboard quarter at a range of about 12,000m. Hitherto firing rapidly and independently, they now concentrated their fire as one unit under the control of *Ajax*'s gunnery officer, Lieutenant Dryer. After a brief period, in which they suffered the full attention of the German 28cm guns, *Exeter*'s reappearance forced Ascher to shift his forward turret back on to the heavy cruiser. A near miss at this time (approximately 0640) on *Achilles* sprayed her port side, bridge and director with splinters, causing casualties. With communication out between *Achilles* and the flagship, *Achilles* controlled her own gunfire again. At about 0700 *Exeter* was seen bearing 230° from *Admiral Graf Spee* at a range of about 29,000m (31,500yd), seemingly intent upon relieving the two light cruisers. Her 'B' turret was out of action and Captain Bell had been forced to regain control from the after steering position; this was little more than an open platform between the catapult and the mainmast. Conditions were difficult, with smoke swirling about, loose wires, petrol vapour from the aircraft and the concussion from the after turret adding to the bedlam.

After launching her port torpedoes without effect, *Exeter* was hit twice in quick succession. Listing about 7° to starboard with her bows down and fires raging, the British cruiser could take little more punishment. Only one gun in 'Y' (her aft) turret could now reply. Fortunately for her, *Admiral Graf Spee*'s attention was diverted once again by the light cruisers, which harried her from the starboard quarter, firing rapidly and well, hitting their target many times but still without inflicting serious damage. *Exeter*, heavily hit, turned away under smoke at about 0715 and a quarter of an hour later withdrew from the battle.

Admiral Graf Spee continued to engage the smaller cruisers, mainly with the 15cm guns but also, when conditions and observation allowed, with her 28cm guns. This had the effect of slowing down the cruisers' gunfire and rendering it less accurate. An attempt to fire torpedoes failed because at the moment of firing, a violent alteration of course to port to engage *Exeter* resulted in only one torpedo launching and that misfired.

The Panzerschiff turned north-west and at 0725 hit *Ajax* hard at short range with a 28cm shell, wrecking her 'X' turret and jamming 'Y' before ricocheting around the insides of the cruiser, inflicting serious damage before it burst. Also claimed were two 10.5cm hits on the bridge. A further shell carried away her main topmast. *Achilles* escaped hits. Torpedoes fired by *Ajax* missed as they were detected and avoided. Ascher was now having problems in engaging the light cruisers because of their rapid alterations of course and the smoke screens. The blast of the 28cm guns was affecting the 15cm guns and damage to the ammunition hoists caused supply problems to the secondary armament. Harwood too had his

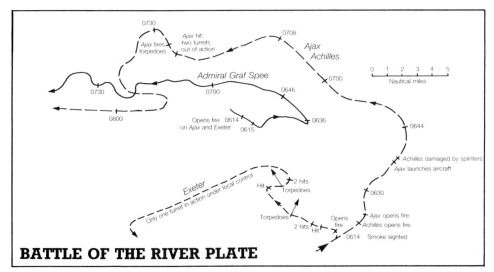

BATTLE OF THE RIVER PLATE

Diagram labels:
0730 — Ajax fires torpedoes
Ajax hit: two turrets out of action
0708
Ajax / Achilles
Admiral Graf Spee
0700
0646
0700
0730
0800
Opens fire 0614 on Ajax and Exeter
0615
0636
0644
Achilles damaged by splinters
Ajax launches aircraft
Exeter
Only one turret in action under local control
Hit
2 hits / Torpedoes
0630
Torpedoes
2 hits / Hit
Opens fire
Ajax opens fire
Achilles opens fire
0614 Smoke sighted

Left: *Admiral Graf Spee*, tower mast detail. (National Archives)

problems because his gunfire was having no appreciable effect on his adversary and his ammunition was becoming low, particularly for the forward turrets. At 0740 he turned away under smoke, intending to shadow until nightfall from the enemy's port and starboard quarters, then close up and use light guns and torpedoes under cover of darkness. Langsdorff surprisingly did not press his advantage and continued westwards, thus sealing his fate.

His ship had received two 8in (20.3cm) and eighteen 6in (15cm) hits, suffering one officer and 35 men dead so far, with another 60 wounded. Her armoured belt had been penetrated by one shell, and the armoured deck by one or two; but her fighting efficiency remained more or less intact. Internally, the galleys had been destroyed and a number of magazine hoists put out of action. In Langsdorff's opinion, the shell hits in the hull needed repair, before he could attempt to break back through the Atlantic to Germany. These were the reasons for his decision to seek respite in Montevideo, which he signalled to the SKL, receiving only the signal 'Agreed' in reply from Admiral Raeder.

Both light cruisers shadowed their adversary, occasionally coming under fire when they got too close, until it became obvious what his intentions were. Commodore Harwood then stood off the Plate and ordered the heavy cruiser *Cumberland* out from Port Stanley to replace *Exeter*; while at the same time reinforcements were despatched to the area from other commands, in order to bottle up the raider in this neutral port. The arrival of *Admiral Graf Spee* in the Uruguayan port caused something of a sensation and the eyes of the world were following events with great interest. Met off the harbour by a small warship of the Uruguayan Navy, the Panzerschiff was allowed to anchor and diplomatic machinations began.

Langsdorff, in conjunction with the German Ambassador, Dr Langmann, intended to ask for an extended stay of 72 hours (the Hague Convention allowed only 24 hours) in the neutral port, in order to effect the repairs necessary to make the ship seaworthy. This was granted, while the British and

French ambassadors naturally protested, pointing out quite rightly that the ship had already steamed over 100 miles at high speed since the action. In point of fact, it suited the Allies that the German ship be allowed to stay, because it allowed time for the necessary reinforcements to be collected and despatched to the mouth of the River Plate. A web of deception was now spun by the British, giving the Germans the firm impression that there were far more forces off the estuary than there really were. A detailed description of the political events surrounding the stay in Montevideo is outside the scope of this volume; suffice it to say that an attempt by Germany to get the 72 hours further extended did not succeed and Langsdorff was given an ultimatum that he must leave by 2200hrs on 17 December. Protests were to no avail, the die was cast.

Outside the estuary, the British force had been joined only by *Cumberland*. No other heavy forces could be in the area before 19 December, despite the propaganda claims. Some repair work was carried out aboard the Panzerschiff and all the crew were awarded the Iron Cross 2nd Class, with six receiving the 1st Class version.

After much communication between Montevideo and Berlin, it was eventually decided that the only courses open to Langsdorff were for him to scuttle the ship or be interned. Langsdorff decided to scuttle. Accordingly, on the evening of 17 December *Admiral Graf Spee* weighed and proceeded down river, followed by a German merchantship, *Tacoma* which had taken on board most of the crew of the Panzerschiff. Only 42 men of a scuttling party remained aboard, and at sunset, off Lobos Island, they were takken off by the Argentine tugs *Coloso* and *Gigante*, together with a lighter. In a spectacular explosion caused by six torpedo warheads, *Admiral Graf Spee* caught fire, burned and exploded for some time before settling on the bottom. As the depth of water here was only 8m, the upperworks and turrets remained above water, charred and twisted by the heat of the fires. Three days later, Kpt.z.S. Langsdorff retired to his hotel and shot himself.

What were the reasons for such an ignominious end to both ship and her commanding officer? There can be little doubt that the initial mistake was Langdorff's, not because he failed to destroy *Exeter* as Hitler believed that he should have done, but because he did not destroy or cripple the two light cruisers. *Exeter* was already out of the fight; her sinking could not extract Langsdorff from the predicament in which he found himself. His overriding need was to lose his ship in the wastes of the South Atlantic once more, and it was the light cruisers that stood in his way. He did not even need to sink them, only stop them from shadowing him. Once free of them, he had a reasonable chance of evading the hunting British and French warships, for this was the period when radar was in its infancy and few, if any, of the British warships were fitted with it. Aircraft could materially assist in the hunt but their range was limited and the only carrier anywhere near the area was *Ark Royal*, steaming south at speed but still many miles away. Had *Admiral Graf Spee* succeeded in getting away to the south, perhaps as far as Bouvet

Island at 55°, and rendezvous with *Altmark*, she might well have been able to lie low.

Operation of aircraft in those stormy southern latitudes would have made air searches for her exceedingly difficult. On the other hand, even from the River Plate area, it was a long and dangerous passage home with the Royal and French Navies fuly alert for her. From the southern ocean, it was a correspondingly longer passage, but it should be remembered that *Admiral Scheer* and some of the armed merchant raiders made such a passage, and after a repair period Langsdorff would have been able to choose his moment for return.

What induced Langsdorff to head for Montevideo will never be known for certain and the situation is further confused by the inadvertent destruction of all the Panzerschiff's action logs subsequent to the battle. The reasons given in his signal to the SKL appear to be flimsy but the psychological aspect should not be discounted. He had been at sea, as a fugitive, since the end of August and from eyewitness reports of the captured British merchant seamen, Langsdorff was, by December, living on his nerves. The tenacious attacks by inferior light cruisers may well have had a deep effect on his morale and in the heat of the battle forced him into a tactical error.

The loss of one of the much-vaunted Panzerschiffe so early in the conflict, and under such circumstances, naturally aroused a desire for explanations from the OKM. It was an event which resounded around the world, mostly to the discredit of Germany. The outward appearance of the ship as she lay in Montevideo gave no hint that she was either unseaworthy or not battleworthy, and many could not understand why she did not come out and give battle. Given the restrictions of the channels out of the estuary, and the presence of the waiting cruisers, this might well have been a suicide run, but the outcome was by no means certain. The correct decision would have been not to go up river in the first place. By the turn of the year, amplifying reports of the action were being received in Germany from all sources, both press and private. One retired officer even felt moved to write from Darien (in Manchuria!) complaining that while the Japanese could admire and understand Langsdorff's Hari-Kiri, they thought it a bit much to scuttle your ship because the galleys had been destroyed. American, South American and British press reports were studied avidly by a special group set up to investigate the matter. Among the information it received was a report from a disaffected stoker on the New Zealand cruiser *Achilles* giving details of the action from the British side, as well as detailed information concerning the defences of the Falkland Islands.

Just how badly damaged was *Admiral Graf Spee*? German records list her hits as 20, of which only two were believed to be 8in (20.3cm) hits. The order in which the hits were sustained cannot be stated with confidence but they were as follows:

(a) A 6in shell hit compartment X from the starboard quarter, passing through the starboard boat deck, crew's galley, the upper deck port side in the forward ammunition handling room (for the secondary armament), before exploding inside the splinter bulkhead. This disabled No. II ammunition hoist and cut all power for the forward group of 15cm guns, as well as damaging uptake and minor service steam lines.

(b) A 6in shell hit the starboard side from forward in compartment VIII, passing through the shield of the starboard 10.5cm mounting, the after boat deck and bakery, before exploding in the searchlight workshop. This knocked out the 10.5cm mounting and ammunition supply.

(c) An 8in shell hit compartment XI in the 'tween decks, passing through the side armour at about 90°, above the armoured deck. It continued through the splinter bulkhead, before exploding on the armoured deck inboard. This destroyed various store spaces and services, leaving a 25cm dent in the armoured deck directly between both No. 4 main motors in the engine room. Fire, smoke, water and firefighting gas swirled about in the area, with water leaking through small cracks into the motor room below.

(d) A 6in hit on the upper deck, compartment IV, passed from the starboard quarter to explode on the port side in the seaman petty officers wash-rooms, making a hole in the side.

(e) A 6in hit passed through the cutter and the port 10.5cm ammunition hoist, exploding on the ventilator shafts to No. 3 motor room.

(f) A 6in shell hit the 'tween decks, compartment III. This was an exercise round fired by *Achilles* and it bounced through several POs' cabins before coming to rest on the port side.

(g) & (h) 6in shell hits from the starboard quarter which caused minor internal damage.

(i) Another 6in shell which struck the deck-house in compartment VII. It passed through 3.7cm ready-use lockers before exploding in the base structure of the forward flak director. It knocked out the director, starboard 3.7cm gun and its crew.

(j), (k) & (l) 6in shells which ricocheted off the main gun turrets and exploded outboard with no damage.

(m) & (n) Hits which passed through the tower mast from starboard, damaging cabling.

(o) An 8in hit from the port beam which passed through the Admiral's bridge without exploding.

(p) A 6in shell from the starboard quarter struck the upper edge of the foretop screen.

(q) A 6in shell exploded on the left-hand side of PIII 15cm gun, disabling it and its crew.

(r) A 6in shell hit the night control stand but passed through without exploding.

(s) & (t) 6in hits with no real damage.

In addition, splinters from hits and near misses damaged director optics, searchlight mirrors and cables and jammed the catapult.

A detailed examination of this catalogue of hits reveals none of any serious nature, a fact which also struck the Uruguayan commission when they toured the ship while considering the time extension request; it is not certain if they were shown all damaged areas. The ship's main machinery remained undamaged and capable of full speed. Fuel would

not seem to have been a problem either. As far as her armament was concerned, both 28cm turrets were undamaged and
most of the secondary guns were in working order. Certainly
a number of ammunition hoists for the 15cm and 10.5cm
guns had been put out of action and some damage caused to
the fire control optics. Remaining ammunition included 306
rounds of 28cm (about 43 per cent of her original outfit),
some 50 per cent of 15cm ammunition and 2,477 rounds of
10.5cm. These figures surprised even the SKL, who
had assumed much less to remain. Also available were six
torpedoes.

The Kriegsmarine's investigations were seriously hampered by the unavailability of key witnesses to question—all
the surviving officers and men were still interned in Argentina. In January 1940 the SKL wired the Naval Attaché at
Buenos Aires, requesting that the 1st Officer, Kpt.z.S. Kay,
answer a number of questions. They were as follows:

(1) Why did *Admiral Graf Spee* not continue the action
until *Exeter* was sunk?

To which Kay replied that in the absence of Langsdorff, he
could only guess but there were a few possibilities:

(a) Uncertainty as to the speed and position of *Exeter* once
she was out of sight.

(b) A suggestion that more enemy ships were in the vicinity, deduced from B Dienst reports.

(c) The damage already sustained and the question of the
Panzerschiff's seaworthiness.

(2) On what grounds did *Admiral Graf Spee* decide to
make for Montevideo? Answer—After confirmation of battle
damage.

(3) Ammunition remaining and state of battleworthiness
on entering harbour?

Kay gave the figures quoted above and essentially the damage reported in the list of shell hits.

(4) Condition of engines? Maximum speed before and after the action? The answer was that the engines were still capable of maximum speed. Some damage had been caused to the uptakes and the auxiliary boiler had been destroyed.

A further question was posed on the remaining fuel levels, to which Kay replied at least *16 hours*. This surely must have been wrong, for *Admiral Graf Spee* had taken on 1,891 tons of diesel fuel on 26 November and topped up with a further 533 tons on 6 December. It is almost certain therefore that at that time her tanks were full—i.e., 2,800 tons. Given an average speed of 15 knots in the interim period until the morning of 13 December, she would have consumed about 441 tons. Manoeuvring at full speed during the battle for 18 hours would have burnt another 150 tons or so, leaving about 2,250 tons. Assuming escape to the South Atlantic at full speed, her remaining endurance would have been 16 *days* approximately, not hours.

So the mystery remains, with a number of unanswered questions. One not so far examined properly is Langsdorff's wounds. On his second wounding he was reported to be unconscious for some time, and when he resumed command it is not inconceivable that his judgment was in some way impaired.

But what of the ship's cruise itself, was it a success or not up to the point of action? The OKM was disappointed with the results of both Panzerschiffe for *Admiral Graf Spee* only sank nine ships of 50,000grt and *Deutschland* two of 7,000grt. Moreover, the hunt for the two raiders also netted the supply ship *Emmy Friedrich*. In addition, eight of Germany's merchant ships attempting to return home undetected also fell foul of the Hunting Groups (*Halle, Sante Fe, Uhenfels, Adolf Woermann, Watussi, Trifels, Adolf Leonhardt* and *Ussukuma*). Thus the losses probably outweighed the gains and it might well have been advisable to delay the operational release of the Panzerschiffe a little longer to give the blockade-runners a better chance of success. On the other hand, how long could the raiders have stayed undetected and what would have been the effect on their crews' morale?

Langsdorff and his men's efforts to destroy the ship and her equipment were not entirely successful, although it is probable that they did not know it, despite the fairly close watch kept on the wreck by the Germans over the following few months. Naturally the British Admiralty were interested in the wreck, even though the design itself dated back to the 1920s, for certain details were of modern design. They considered it unlikely that any major secrets would be revealed but expressed interest in a number of features, including fire control and range-finder systems, wireless and RDF equipment, armour, turret design, hull construction and the effect of shell hits.

To further this end, secret negotiations were put in hand to obtain the wreck by purchase, through the agency of an Uruguayan businessman, one Sen. Julio Vega Helguera. The Germans were quite prepared to sell the wreck, provided that they were allowed to remove or destroy military secrets; it is probable that they suspected just who the real interested party might be, especially as Helguera admitted that he might sell material to the ship-breakers T.W. Ward! Two Admiralty officials actually arrived in Montevideo on 29 March, Messrs Kilroy and Purvis, posing as employees of T.W. Ward. The former was a torpedo and ordnance expert, the latter the Assistant DNC. Over the next week or so this pair explored the wreck but found almost total destruction by fire, sea or weather. After a complete survey, a list of items for removal was drawn up, including armour plate from the main turrets and conning tower, samples of materials—i.e., welding, metals, glass, cables, etc.—three 11in guns and shells, a stabilized HA director, one each of the 3.7cm, 10.5cm and 15cm guns from the port side, a searchlight and other items of control equipment. Also snooping about on board was a Mr L.H. Bainbridge-Bell, sent by the Admiralty to examine the ship's FuMo22 radar set.

But before this work could be carried out, a severe storm raged on 14 and 15 April, during which the wreck keeled over to 50° and settled deeper into the mud. This precluded removal of the major items but what was obtained included a stabilized 10.5cm mounting, machine-guns, searchlight, armour plate and other equipment. All this was shipped to Britain aboard the Furness Houlder vessel *Princesa* in May and she sailed to join the convoy, SL34 (from Freetown), for the journey home. This convoy was attacked by *U46* (Endrass) off Cape Finisterre, leading to a rumour that the Germans, being aware of *Princesa*'s cargo, intended to sink it. Actually, Endrass's contact with SL34 was fortuitous, he was actually after US3, a troop convoy. *Princesa* and her cargo arrived at Milford Haven on 15 June, but the subsequent history of the *Graf Spee* parts is unknown.

Below: The scuttled wreck of *Admiral Graf Spee*. (Bundesarchiv)

10. HOME WATERS, 1939–1940

As the last few days of peace slipped away, Admiral Raeder could only view his situation with dismay, for the grandiose 'Z Plan' dream lay in ruins and Germany was faced yet again with a war against England, should Hitler's gamble in Poland not come off. His Kriegsmarine was but a shadow of the Kaiserliche Marine's strength during August 1914 and even if the Royal Navy's strength had also declined in the intervening period, it still far exceeded that of the Kriegsmarine. The two most powerful ships in home waters in August 1939 were the battleships *Scharnhorst* (Kpt.z.S. Ciliax) and *Gneisenau* (Kpt.z.S. Forster) which, together with the Panzerschiff *Admiral Scheer* (Kpt.z.S. Wurmbach), were in fact the only modern capital ships the Kriegsmarine possessed. There were of course two other big-gunned ships, the obsolete *Schleswig* (Kpt.z.S. Utke) and *Schleswig-Holstein* (Kpt.z.S. Kleikamp), but both these were pre-dreadnoughts, some thirty years old. The situation for the future was not rosy either because only four capital ships were actively under construction and of these, two had only been laid down in the last few weeks. The other pair, *Bismarck* and *Tirpitz*, were both fitting out but would not join the fleet for some time.

Of the available forces, *Scharnhorst*, *Gneisenau* and *Admiral Scheer* were in the Western Command area, the first two anchored off Brunsbüttel at the mouth of the River Elbe, the Panzerschiff en route for Wilhelmshaven to act as flak guard-ship. *Schlesien*, on the other hand, had left that base on 26 August, ordered to Kiel for duty with Befehlshaber der Sicherung (Ost). On 1 September she was sent to the yard at Kiel to be fitted with a prototype multiple MG34 2cm mounting (the effective Vierling) and on 13 September was attached to the training command. In the meantime, however, it had fallen to her elderly sister ship *Schleswig-Holstein* to open hostilities in the east against Poland. She sailed from Swinemünde on the forenoon of 24 August to make an official visit to the free port of Danzig (now Gdansk), or so it was intended to appear.

Until the end of World War One Danzig had been part of Germany and Hitler was determined that it should return to the Reich, by force if necessary. As early as October 1938 the German Government had approached the Poles with a view to its return but the response had been negative. Hitler's reaction to this rebuff was rapid. On 24 November 1938 he issued a Top Secret directive ordering preparations for a surprise occupation of the Free State of Danzig by German troops under the pretext of intervening in a quasi-revolutionary uprising by the Nazi elements in the city. The intention was to exploit a politically favourable situation *but not to start a war against Poland*. However, the possible repercussions of such an action had escalated since the plan was first mooted, for on 25 May 1939 the Anglo-Polish Treaty was signed. This raised the spectre of British intervention following any German attack on Poland. The question was, however, would Britain react any differently to this situation from the way she had to the annexation of Czechoslovakia and Austria? It was a gamble Hitler decided to take.

As the old pre-dreadnought steamed east, her gunnery department began to prime her ammunition in preparation for the task ahead. Passing the entrance to the Gulf of Danzig, Kleikamp headed for Memel (lately also reunited with the Third Reich), off which port he was joined by five ships (*M1*, *M4*, *M5*, *M7* and *M8*) of the 1st Minesweeper Flotilla. These ships were carrying 225 men of the 3rd Naval Artillery Division and their equipment, all of which were trans-shipped to *Schleswig-Holstein* and stowed below out of sight. Also aboard were a number of Press and film crews. The following day she arrived in the Neufahrwasser, to an ecstatic welcome from the Danzig Germans, as she came alongside, opposite the Westerplatte. While courtesy calls were being exchanged, the starboard 15cm battery was closed up, the flak weapons unobtrusively manned and the engines kept at 30 minutes' notice for 9 knots. The troops hidden below decks were alerted for an attack beginning that night. After dark the ship was closed up for action at 2200, but the order to attack was postponed, almost certainly as a result of political manoeuvring. This posed a problem for Kleikamp, for he could not keep so many men cooped up below decks indefinitely. So, the following day small numbers of men were allowed shore leave and at the same time the opportunity was taken to reconnoitre the Polish defences on the Westerplatte. Later that evening tugs moved the old battleship to a new berth by the Weichselmünde fortress, which caused some alarm to the Poles but eventually calm returned. There were still no orders for the attack.

The Westerplatte, a small neck of land on the seaward side of the Neufahrwasser, had been used as a munitions storage and transit depot by the Polish Government since 1920, with the agreement of the League of Nations Council. On 14 March 1924 the Council allocated the Westerplatte to Poland and the dump commenced operations in 1927. Its defences were negligible until about 1933–36, when the hostile attitude of Germany became apparent. Even so, the defences were then increased only by the addition of a few guard houses and barracks. In 1939 Poland realized the dangers from pro-German Danzig and decided to increase the number of troops on the Westerplatte to just over 200. When dawn broke on 1 September, however, there were no more than 182 regular soldiers in position. Their defensive power, apart from rifles, comprised one 75mm field gun, two 37mm anti-tank guns, four 81mm mortars and 41 machine-guns.

Schleswig-Holstein remained idle but keyed up. The Battle of Tannenburg was commemorated on 28 September but all thoughts were naturally on the new conflict ahead. Finally, on 31 August, the long-awaited orders arrived and at 2330hrs disembarkation of the troops began, being completed at 0145. The weather was good, with a light breeze and few clouds. The ship closed up to action stations at 0430, in preparation for moving to the bombardment position a few hundred metres up river. At 0447hrs permission was granted to open fire and a minute later the naval war had begun.

From 0448 to 0455 *Schleswig-Holstein* fired eight rounds of 28cm, 59 rounds of 15cm and more than 600 of 2cm in an attempt to breach the Polish defences which, despite the blazing wooden buildings and exploding fuel dumps, held firm. On seeing a breach in the perimeter wall, Kleikamp ceased fire to allow the shock troops to attack, but by 0707 the spirited Polish defence forced the Germans to withdraw. *Schleswig-Holstein* again opened fire but could not force a decision, as the Poles continued to repulse the German troops. Frustrated, Kleikamp was forced to call up air support, which did not arrive until 1805 on 2 September. The aircraft caused considerable damage, but still the Germans could not penetrate the defences. Strong reinforcements were brought up by the Germans, equally to no avail. Cut off and alone, the issue could have only one ending. Even so, it was not until the forenoon of 7 September that the Polish senior officer, Major Henryk Suchardski, was forced to capitulate after a very gallant defence. Her task finally completed, *Schleswig-Holstein* moved out into the Gulf of Danzig to bom-

bard other Polish shore defences, notably at Oxhoft and Hela, in which she was joined on 21 September by her sister *Schlesien* and other vessels, including *T107, Klaus von Bevern, M3, M4, T108* and *T111.* Between this date and the final Polish surrender, the old battleships fired many rounds against the shore batteries at Hela and Heisternest, without themselves being hit, although there were several near misses. The Polish defences on Hela were under the command of Rear Admiral Unrug, who managed to hold out until 1 October, after which the battleships returned to Swinemünde.

The attack on Poland brought Britain into a state of hostilities with Germany, as had been feared by Admiral Raeder. On 2 September Naval Command (West) ordered *Admiral Scheer* to 30 minutes' notice for 10 knots from 0900 on the 3rd, and *Scharnhorst* and *Gneisenau* to 2 hours' notice. On 3 September events moved faster, high-degree readiness for flak armament being ordered by Group (West) at 1147, followed almost immediately by the ordering of all ships to immediate notice for sea. Finally, at 1325 came the signal 'Commence hostilities with England.'

Admiral Scheer soon saw action for the Royal Air Force, prohibited at that time from attacking land targets, mounted an immediate strike against German warships lying in Wilhelmshaven, the Jade and off Brunsbüttel. Six Wellington bombers of No. 9 Squadron and eight of No. 149 Squadron took off to attack the ships located off Brunsbüttel (*Scharnhorst* and *Gneisenau*), and Blenheim IVs of Nos. 107, 110 and 139 Squadrons were ordered to attack ships in and around Wilhelmshaven. It was a misty autumn evening when three aircraft of No. 107 Squadron arrived in the Schillig Roads where, flying at a very low level, they were initially mistaken for Heinkel He 111s by the Panzerschiff. Caught unprepared, the ship's light guns failed to get into action until the aircraft had dropped their bombs and disappeared into the mist. A fourth aircraft, arriving a little later, attacked out of cloud from astern and was met by concentrated fire as it flew over the destroyer *Diether von Roeder,* anchored about 2,000m off the port quarter of *Admiral Scheer.* Heavily hit, the Blenheim crashed into the sea. Another machine was hit by 8.8cm gunfire and also crashed.

The mist and poor visibility caused problems in seeing targets early, but two more aircraft, flying parallel with the ship at maximum range of the 3.7cm guns, were engaged by these and the 8.8cm guns, and the lead aircraft was shot down. A last Blenheim attacked from ahead at low level where most of the 3.7cm flak was masked. Then, only 200 metres from the ship, it was hit by 2cm gunfire, which set the port engine alight and eventually the aircraft crashed astern. Several bombs, mostly duds, had hit the ship, probably dropped from too low a level for the fuses to arm; they caused light damage to the ship's Arado, catapult and one 8.8cm gun. The attack in, Wurmbach's words, was executed with appreciable cunning but resulted in disastrous British losses (Blenheims N6184, N6188, N6189 and N6240) for little return. No. 139 Squadron's aircraft did not find the target. *Admiral Scheer* also shot down one of her own defending air-

craft (whose pilot was killed) and later, while moving into the dockyard to effect repairs, a Junkers Ju 52, which failed to give recognition signals, received similar treatment.

The attack taught the Germans a number of lessons, one of which was that the ship had no effective defence against low-flying attacks from dead ahead. Also, the training speed of the 8.8cm guns was too slow and the rate of fire of the 3.7cm left a lot to be desired. The Wellington attack on *Scharnhorst* and *Gneisenau* was equally unsuccessful, and two No. 109 Squadron machines (L4268 and L4275) were lost.

Admiral Scheer quickly completed her repairs and on 23 September sailed for Kiel, escorted by the torpedo boats *Seeadler* and *Iltis*. Kpt.z.S. Krancke assumed command on 25 September. Her stay in Baltic waters was brief and after various exercises she returned to Wilhelmshaven on 18 December, just in time for an air raid. After another short Baltic deployment, the Panzerschiff started a major refit in Wilhelmshaven on 1 February 1940. Her crew transferred to the accommodation ship *Gravenstein*, leaving only essential watch-keepers and flak crews aboard. All guns were landed (including the 28cm) and the ship did not complete her refit until July 1940.

Scharnhorst and *Gneisenau* too were both ordered to Kiel and passed through the Canal on 8 September. In the Baltic both ships carried out battle practice against *Hessen*, on which occasion *Scharnhorst* suffered blast damage to her hangar and to the Arado, sitting on the midships catapult. This latter damage came as some surprise, as blast effects were not thought to be serious at this position, unlike that on the after catapult, sited on 'C' turret. She was also experiencing trouble with the centre turbine, necessitating some two weeks' repairs. During this spell in dock radar was fitted.

Kpt.z.S. Hoffmann relieved Ciliax as captain of *Scharnhorst* on the latter's promotion to flag rank and then the battleship returned to the North Sea for another operation. Kurt Caesar Hoffmann had joined the Kaiser's Navy in 1912 and had seen service during World War One. His previous command was the light cruiser *Königsberg*.

Gneisenau passed through the Kiel Canal on 5 October, wearing the flag of Konteradmiral Boehm. At 1900 on 7 October she sailed from the Jade and was joined by the light cruiser *Köln* and the destroyers *Heidkamp*, *Ihn*, *Roeder*, *Galster*, *Riedel*, *Schultz*, *von Arnim* and *Eckoldt*. The object of the sortie was a strike against enemy shipping off the south coast of Norway and to entice the Home Fleet across a U-boat patrol line. Their sailing had been detected by the British almost immediately and Admiral Forbes, C-in-C Home Fleet, put his battlecruisers and light forces at short notice for sea. A Hudson of No. 224 Squadron, RAF Coastal Command, made contact with the German ships after midday the following day and came under long-range flak fire from both *Gneisenau* and *Köln* but without effect. As a consequence of this, Boehm anticipated an air attack later and alerted his force to that eventuality. However, only further reconnaissance aircraft were sighted during the late afternoon and after sunset, by which time the German ships stood some 25 miles west of Boknfjord, just north of Stavanger.

To the British Admiralty, it appeared that this strong force was attempting to break out into the Atlantic. To counter this possibility the battlecruisers *Hood* and *Repulse*, with two cruisers and four destroyers, were sailed for a point north-west of Stadtlandet; the Humber Force put to sea to attempt to intercept the Germans if they reversed course and finally, *Nelson*, *Rodney*, the carrier *Furious* and screening forces, sailed from Scapa to cover the Shetland-Faeroes gap. All these manoeuvres were in vain. When darkness had fallen Boehm reversed course and after detaching *Köln* and four destroyers into the Skagerrak, *Gneisenau* and the remaining destroyers arrived back in Kiel by the early afternoon of 10 October. Twelve Wellingtons which had been sent to intercept them failed to locate their target.

In November both *Scharnhorst* and *Gneisenau* were ordered back into the North Sea for a further operation and after embarking aircraft (four in *Scharnhorst*) sailed from Kiel on the 8th. They lay at Wilhelmshaven until 21 November, when they put to sea at 1400hrs. Accompanying them were the light cruisers *Leipzig* and *Köln*, with the 4th Destroyer Flotilla (*von Arnim*, *Giese* and *Galster*). However, the cruisers and destroyers were detached to the Skagerrak the following day, while the battleships continued alone. The object of the sortie was to disrupt the British Northern Patrol—a cruiser line strung across the Iceland–Faeroes gap—and to make a feint into the Atlantic to draw off attention and resources of the Home Fleet from the activities of *Admiral Graf Spee* in the South Atlantic. In command of the operation at sea was the new Fleet Commander, Vizeadmiral Marschall, who had replaced Boehm following the latter's dismissal by Admiral Raeder after disagreements over operational questions. Boehm later took up the post of Admiral Commanding, Norway. The squadron was not detected either by the submarine patrols off the Skagerrak and German Bight, or by air reconnaissance, so the British Admiralty was unaware of the presence of these powerful ships on the high seas.

At the time the cruisers and destroyers were detached, the two capital ships were south-west of the Naze, steaming in line ahead, with 4nm between them, on a course of 320°. As dawn broke, the white ensign was hoisted, in accordance with operational orders. *Scharnhorst*, trimmed down by the bows by about one metre, was taking heavy seas over the bows under the prevailing conditions. As the day wore on the weather deteriorated, with a south-westerly wind blowing Force 7–8 and it was raining. Both ships were rolling heavily but the conditions were good for an undetected passage. By 1335 the squadron was clearing the Shetland Narrows north of the Viking Bank. The heavy weather in fact was causing some problems, in particular aboard *Scharnhorst* where port No. 1 15cm and port No. 1 3.7cm gun mountings went unserviceable as a result of water in the electrics. Similar problems affected the searchlights. Water also flooded into the ship through insecure openings and hatches, especially in compartments V and XIII. By evening even the main turrets reported the ingress of sea-water.

Throughout the afternoon and evening of 22 November the two ships forged on through the Shetland–Faeroes gap

and the following morning picked up the Faeroe Islands by radar at a range of 37,000m. Not only were they still undetected, the British Admiralty did not even know that they were at sea. They were now in the area where patrolling Royal Navy cruisers could be expected and the two German ships steamed in starboard echelon about 18,000m apart in order to sweep the widest possible area. On Northern Patrol duty this night were four light cruisers, the modern *Newcastle* and the elderly *Calypso*, *Ceres* and *Delhi*. Also on patrol was the armed merchant cruiser *Rawalpindi*. *Newcastle* was the most northerly and the auxiliary cruiser the most easterly of this loose patrol line.

Passing north of the Faeroes, Marschall steamed due west for some time, then at 0700 altered course to the north-west and in doing so avoided running into *Calypso*. For the remainder of the day the two battleships steamed a somewhat erratic but generally north-westerly course towards Iceland but sighted no enemy warships. Then, at 1607, the lookouts in *Scharnhorst* reported a vessel to starboard at a considerable distance. Seeing nothing from his bridge, Hoffmann climbed to the foretop to see for himself and identified the ship as one of the expected auxiliary cruisers. *Scharnhorst* closed up action stations and prepared for battle.

The British ship was *Rawalpindi* (Captain E.C. Kennedy), a 16,600grt former P & O liner, armed with eight 6in guns and two 3in AA. A German warship was first sighted from the crows-nest of *Rawalpindi* (at 1432), approaching at speed and identified as *Scharnhorst*. The enemy closed rapidly, then altered course parallel to the British ship, ordering her to stop as she did so. This Kennedy naturally ignored, while sending an 'enemy sighted' report: 'One battlecruiser brg 280°, 4 miles, course 135°. Position 63°41'N, 11°29'E. TOO 1545'. His signal was received by Admiral Forbes (C-in-C Home Fleet) at 1551, but it was quickly followed by a second stating the enemy's identity as *Deutschland*. This information was the first intimation of enemy ships at sea in northern waters and seemed to tie up with the recently disclosed activities of *Deutschland*. In fact, *Deutschland* was already back in German waters.

Kennedy now endeavoured to make for the safety of a fog bank about two points on the port bow but *Scharnhorst* realized his intention and cut her off, forcing Kennedy to make instead for an iceberg about 4 miles off to starboard. Commander Jokes reported all guns crews closed up as *Scharnhorst* put a shot across her bows (involuntarily as it was caused by a short-circuit). At this point one of *Rawalpindi*'s lookouts reported a second ship four points off the starboard bow, which was taken to be another ship of the Northern Patrol. However, on altering towards this ship for mutual support, it was quickly found that she was in fact *Gneisenau*.

Scharnhorst now ordered Kennedy to abandon ship but *Rawalpindi* opened fire with her 6in guns and at the same time attempted to screen herself with smoke floats. As dusk fell the range dropped to 10,500m and when it had closed further to 7,500m, K.Kpt. Dominik, *Scharnhorst*'s Gunnery Officer, opened fire in earnest. The first salvo struck the auxiliary cruiser on the boat deck just abaft the bridge, killing

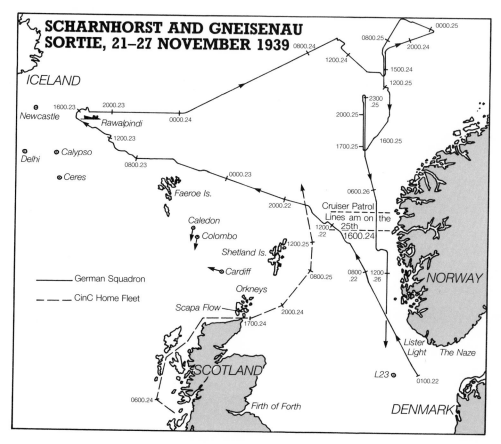

SCHARNHORST AND GNEISENAU SORTIE, 21–27 NOVEMBER 1939

ICELAND

Newcastle 1600.23 2000.23
Rawalpindi 0000.24
1200.23
Delhi Calypso 0800.23
Ceres

Faeroe Is. 0000.23
2000.22
Caledon
Colombo 1200.25
Shetland Is.
Cardiff
0800.25
Orkneys
Scapa Flow 1700.24 2000.24
SCOTLAND
0600.24
Firth of Forth

0000.25
0800.24 0800.25 2000.24
1200.24 1500.24
1200.25
2300.25
2000.25
1700.25 1600.25
0600.26
Cruiser Patrol
Lines am on the
1200.22 25th
1600.24
0800.22 1200.26
NORWAY
Lister Light The Naze
L23 0100.22
DENMARK

German Squadron
— — — CinC Home Fleet

---

all on the bridge except Kennedy, one CPO and a rating. The 15cm battery was also in action. *Gneisenau* also opened fire from long range. One salvo, thought to be from her, hit *Rawalpindi*'s main control room and destroyed it, as well as disabling S2 6in gun. All guns were now put into local control and ordered to continue firing. By now *Rawalpindi* was in a bad way, a shell had struck the engine room knocking out the dynamo, and all power to the ammunition hoists was lost. Hand-up parties were organized but the extensive woodwork in the former passenger apartments resulted in serious fires and much smoke throughout the ship. All guns except S2 and P1 were still in action but their fire was ineffective. At about 1510 Kennedy went aft with two ratings to try to get the smoke generator into action, but all three were killed a minute later by shell burst.

For most of the engagement *Rawalpindi* was out of control, both the bridge and tiller flat having been destroyed, but the engines remained capable of 21 knots throughout. Her guns were still firing fitfully while she was sinking. At 1712 Marschall ordered 'cease fire' after only eight minutes of action. During this brief action, the flagship fired 52 rounds from her main armament and 125 rounds of 15cm. *Scharnhorst* fired 89 rounds of 28cm and 109 of 15cm.

Rawalpindi was still under way slowly, but at 1730 a large explosion was seen. As the German ships stood by, a signal lamp in the stricken ship was seen to flash 'Please send boats'

and Marschall ordered survivors to be rescued— a gallant if dangerous task, bearing in mind the German's situation. In the darkness, with heavy seas running, the recovery of boats was no easy job nor a quick one and all the time the battleships lay stopped, the burning wreck illuminated their position with alarming clarity. Not until 1846, some 45 minutes after the start of the action, was a boat brought alongside *Scharnhorst* and it contained only six men. *Gneisenau* had just recovered 21 survivors. Then, just as a second boat was seen, Marschall abruptly ordered the rescue operation broken off. The time was now 1914hrs. Both ships worked up to 24 knots and steamed due east. The reason for the termination of the hunt for survivors was the lookouts' detection of a darkened ship faintly illuminated against the western horizon. Aboard *Scharnhorst* it was the fourth gunnery officer, Kpt.Lt. Fr. von Mullenheim-Rechberg stationed in the after director, who first saw the arrival at 1920. It appeared to be a warship of a fairly large size.

In fact, this was the light cruiser *Newcastle* which had received *Rawalpindi*'s enemy report at 1805. Also in receipt of this signal was the older *Delhi* and both ships altered course toward the position given by *Rawalpindi*. These two ships had been ordered by Vice-Admiral (Northern Patrol) to shadow *Deutschland* (sic) while the other pair, *Ceres* and *Calypso*, were ordered to concentrate off Kalso light to act as a strike force for a night attack. Note that *Newcastle*'s orders were specifically to shadow, *not* attack. The battleship *Warspite* was detached from an eastbound Atlantic convoy and sent to the Denmark Straits because it was still not clear if this enemy was breaking out or attempting to return home. Unfortunately the only long-range aircraft available, a single Catalina, went unserviceable after its first flight that day, so that all hopes of tracking the enemy rested on *Newcastle* and *Dehli*. The prospect of the other two elderly light cruisers attacking two battleships hardly bears thinking about. Their only real hope was to make an unobserved torpedo attack in the darkness, but both German ships had radar.

Newcastle sighted searchlights and gun-flashes after two hours' steaming and by 1916 her lookouts spotted a darkened vessel identified as *Deutschland*, bearing 70° at a range of 13,000yds broadside on. A minute later a second vessel was seen at a range of 11,700yds. The range closed rapidly and at 1922 Captain Figgins reduced speed and turned away, intending to shadow the enemy ships. *Newcastle*, however, had already been seen herself and caused the German ships to withdraw. Unfortunately for *Newcastle*, her attempt at shadowing was thwarted by the weather and her lack of radar (not fitted until the following year); after passing through a rain squall, she was unable to regain contact. Although she and *Delhi* searched for some hours afterwards, they could not relocate Marschall.

Newcastle was a *Town*-class light cruiser armed with twelve 6in (15cm) guns and commissioned in 1937. She was obviously outgunned and in any case her role in the situation was to shadow the German ships and to call up heavier forces to deal with them. Nevertheless, it is a little surprising that, having caught the enemy stopped and unprepared, Captain

Figgins did not launch a chance torpedo salvo. His ship was fitted with two triple banks of 21in torpedo tubes and it would have been disastrous for Marschall had one of his ships been damaged sufficiently to reduce its speed. On the other hand, it is also difficult to understand why Marschall made no attempt to destroy *Newcastle*, a task he could have accomplished with ease. This was to have consequences later within the German Naval Command.

The brief action had resulted in no damage to the German ships, apart from a single 6in hit on *Scharnhorst*'s quarter-deck, but once again the inadequacy of the aircraft installations had been demonstrated for blast effects from *Scharnhorst*'s guns resulted in both aircraft ('T3 + DH' and 'T3 + EH') on the catapults being damaged. Admiral Marschall withdrew east until midnight on the 23rd/24th as he quite obviously had stirred up a hornet's nest and British counter-measures would be considerable. In fact, Admiral Forbes had sailed from the Clyde on the evening of 23 November with *Nelson, Rodney, Devonshire* and seven destroyers for a position between the Shetlands and the Norwegian coast, but he was at some disadvantage as the Clyde was on Britain's west coast and the speed of his battleships was only about 22 knots at best. This illustrates clearly the impingement of one operation on another.

The reason why the Home Fleet was so badly placed was simply a very pessimistic assessment of Scapa Flow's defences against air attack on the outbreak of war, which led, after some argument, to the Fleet's base being shifted to Loch Ewe. Prien's sinking of *Royal Oak* by *U47* on 14 October further underlined the vulnerability of the main fleet anchorage at Scapa and the temporary base at Loch Ewe was equally undefended. The Admiralty now wanted the Home Fleet to be based in the safer waters of the Clyde, but this removed the fleet even further from the vital exits to the North Sea. Not surprisingly, Admiral Forbes objected and preferred Rosyth. Unfortunately, his view did not win the day and in consequence the Home Fleet could not reach the Shetland Narrows until 25 November. Other British counter-measures included stationing fourteen cruisers across the Shetland Narrows, plus a force of destroyers at 8–10 mile intervals in a line west to east. All available submarines were sailed from the Forth and Tyne to patrol off the Naze and Horns Reef. Twenty-four Whitley bombers of Nos. 10 and 51 Squadrons were moved to Kinloss and 24 Hampdens of Nos. 49 and 83 Squadrons to Wick under the command of No. 18 Group, Coastal Command.

Scharnhorst and *Gneisenau* steamed north-east from midnight on the 23rd/24th and for the next day loitered far to the north, to avoid the enemy. All this, however, gave extra time for the slow battleships of the Home Fleet to reach the scene. Marschall moved south once more on 25 November, but by the evening it was obvious that the weather was too good to be suitable for a successful breakthrough and he accordingly reversed course once more at 1700hrs. After steaming due north for six hours, weather reports became more promising and at about 2300hrs he reversed course southwards once

more. By this time the British cruiser patrol line had been established across the route home, while *Nelson* and *Rodney* with their supporting forces were patrolling an area north of the Shetlands on the latitude of the Faeroes, some 175 miles south-west of Marschall's 1100/25 position. It seemed as if the chances for his successful return home were slim.

At 0200 on 26 November both ships were ordered from the flag to have all twelve boilers on line from 0400 in preparation for a breakthrough from 0600. The expected poor weather now became fact and by 0930 visibility had reduced to only 1–2nm with an ESE gale rising to storm Force 10. Heavy seas washed the upper decks continuously and huge seas broke over the bridges. Fifteen minutes later the wind had risen to Force 11 and speed had to be reduced to 22 knots. Aboard *Scharnhorst* the weakness of the ventilator shafts was once again illustrated when water flooded into one boiler room and two boilers were put out. By 1044 conditions had eased a little, but under the circumstances it was not surprising that Marschall successfully passed through the British patrol line. Of the cruisers, only *Sheffield* was fitted with radar and that was an early air warning 79Y set. Heavy weather continued until 27 November, by which time *Scharnhorst*'s 'A' turret had been put out of action by the ingress of water. The submarine patrol line had also been evaded, and by early afternoon the German squadron was safely anchored off Wilhelmshaven.

The sortie was publicly proclaimed as a success but privately there were acrimonious criticisms of Marschall's hand-ling of the operation. Admiral Fricke, Chief of Operations, in particular, was scathing in his criticism of the fact that two powerful ships had turned and run from a lesser warship, maintaining that it too should have been sunk. It does seem odd that no attempt was made to sink *Newcastle*. Marschall's counter to this was that it had always been held that capital ships should avoid close contact with torpedo craft and reconnaissance vessels at night. Added to this was the fact that the operational orders issued for the sortie by Seebefehlshaber (West), Admiral Saalwachter, clearly stated that enemy forces were to be *avoided at night*. Inferior forces found in daylight were to be destroyed. Also criticized was the high level of ammunition expended in sinking *Rawalpindi*. Nevertheless, Marschall's conduct was judged too cautious and although he retained his post, the omens were not good for the future.

The two ships were an obvious target for RAF Bomber Command, indeed the only one because attacks against land targets were still banned, as were those against merchant vessels; there had been instances when pilots had been disciplined for attacking auxiliary naval vessels because they were not 'real warships', despite their having opened fire.

On 17 December 1939 No. 3 Group, Bomber Command, launched a strike by 24 Wellington I bombers drawn from No. 149 Squadron at Mildenhall (nine aircraft), No. 9 Squadron at Honington (nine aircraft) and six from No. 37 Squadron based at Feltwell. The strike leader was Wing-Commander Kellett of No. 149 Squadron. Each aircraft was armed with three 500lb SAP bombs. The operation orders ran in part: 'Task: to attack enemy warships in the Schillig Roads and Wilhelmshaven . . . great care is to be taken that no bombs fall on German soil and no merchant ships are to be attacked'. A naval officer accompanied Wing-Commander Kellett for the purpose of ship identification. The attack was to be carried out in daylight. Close formation and the bombers' own guns were held to offer sufficient defence according to the tactics of the day. The raid was a disaster. Not only was the target too close to the shore for bombs to be dropped without falling on land, but *Gneisenau* had already moved to the Baltic. There was no option but to return home without bombing, but the Luftwaffe prevented that. Bf 109 and Bf 110 fighters from JG 26 and ZG 76 respectively shot down two aircraft of No. 149 Squadron (N2691, N2692), five from No. 9 Squadron (N2940, N2939, N2872, N2983, N2941), and three from No. 37 (N2904, N2889, N2935). *Scharnhorst*'s light flak engaged for about eight minutes without effect, hindered by the adjacent cranes and buildings. The loss of life in this futile sortie was tragic, especially as the chances of hitting the ships were slight. At this stage of the war the RAF had not appreciated just how small a target a ship was, even to a trained attacker, and this force had no such skills.

Both ships required a period of repair and modification after their sortie, the heavy weather having demonstrated the weakness of deck openings and the effects of water on armament electrics. The ships' main machinery had, in general, performed well but the auxiliaries were found to be very

Bottom: *Scharnhorst* at Kiel during the harsh winter of 1939/40. (ECPA)

troublesome, a feature of German warship machinery, due mainly to their very high rotation speeds. After a short time in dock at Wilhelmshaven, *Scharnhorst* passed through the Kiel Canal and arrived at Kiel to join *Gneisenau* on 11 January 1940. The winter of 1939/40 was exceptionally severe and caused considerable difficulty for ships attempting post-refit work-up and of course normal training duties. Even the Kiel Canal was frozen and in Kiel Fjord itself communications with ships lying to buoys was usually on foot! By the beginning of February temperatures as cold as −15°C were common and this resulted in continual freezing up of fresh-water systems, in particular, the boiler feed water. Eventually *Gneisenau* was transferred west again on 4 February and her sister the following day. During this passage *Gneisenau* suffered some damage to her propellers, due to ice, and went into dock at Wilhelmshaven for repair. By 17 February both ships were operational and ready for sea.

The next day, both ships, accompanied by *Admiral Hipper* and the destroyers *Heidkamp* and *Galster*, sailed on Operation 'Nordmark', another strike against British shipping from Norway across the North Sea. By 1130 on 19 February they stood about 60nm west of Bergen but had sighted nothing. In fact, the presence of the ships in the ice off Wilhelmshaven had been reported by aircraft and had alerted the British Admiralty to just such an operation. Consequently normal convoy traffic was re-routed and ships of the Home Fleet put to sea. Marschall's blow therefore fell on empty sea and the only action seen was by *Heidkamp* which depth-charged a suspected submarine in the early hours of 20 February after the operation had been broken off. By that afternoon, the squadron was anchored in Wilhelmshaven once more. There they lay for the time being, Fleet Command having informed their captains that no further operations were planned for them until March. On 6 March one of

Scharnhorst's Arado Ar 196s crashed from low altitude and although the wreckage was recovered, both crew members were killed. The two battleships' next operation did not in fact begin until early April and in the meantime they remained in Wilhelmshaven.

Of the other capital ships in home waters, *Deutschland* had been renamed *Lützow* on her return from the Atlantic for fear of propaganda and political setbacks, should a ship bearing the national name be sunk. The name *Lützow* had until then been borne by a new heavy cruiser which had been sold incomplete to the USSR. The Panzerschiff underwent a refit period at Danzig until early December 1940 and then until the second week in March was engaged in post-refit trials, dockings and working up. Her Commanding Officer was now Kpt.z.S. August Thiele. Like all other Kriegsmarine units at this time, the winter hindered all her efforts and when on 12 March she sailed for Swinemünde with the cruiser *Emden* and the oiler *Nordmark*, the short passage took until 14 March. By 19 March *Lützow* lay at Kiel in readiness for further operations.

Schlesien (Kpt.z.S. Gunther Horstmann) was employed on mercantile warfare duties east of Gotland from 16 to 19 December 1939 before being ordered on 6 January 1940 to serve as a training ship for Station N in the western area. She was also to act as an icebreaker when required, but with the minimum possible disruption to the training programme. Leaving Danzig on 9 January, the ship reached Wilhelmshaven four days later. Thereafter she operated between Wilhelmshaven, the Elbe and Hamburg. Between 19 and 23 February she received two twin 3.7cm, one on the forecastle and the second on 'B' turret. However, on the 28th of that month she was ordered back to the Baltic where she was serving at the beginning of April.

Her sister, *Schleswig-Holstein*, having completed her part in the invasion of Poland, was also employed on mercantile warfare tasks in the Belts during December 1939. This duty was superseded by the need for icebreakers that winter, and on 6 January 1940 she received similar orders to her sister (as did *Hessen*). Two days later she sailed for Brunsbüttel but operated on the Elbe only until 12 January when relieved by *Schlesien*. After spending much of February in the Deutsche Werke yard at Kiel for hull repairs, she finally became operational again by 12 March, being employed thereafter as a target ship for the Torpedo School at Eckernförde.

As the two pre-dreadnoughts were outside the mainstream of the Kriegsmarine's capital ship operations, it will be convenient to review their subsequent careers as far as 1941 at this point. Both were included in the German Navy's all-out effort for Operation 'Weserübung', attached to the groups securing Denmark. *Schleswig-Holstein* led Group 7, tasked with the occupation of Nyborg and Kosor, the ferry ports on Funen and Sjaelland respectively, which straddled the Store Belt. Also under this command was a mixed bag of ships including the trials vessels *Claus von Bevern*, *Nautilus* and *Pelikan*, some tugs and a few trawlers. The old pre-dreadnought's part in this operation was somewhat inglorious as she ran aground on the Vengeance Bank due to compass failure and could not be refloated for ten hours. Eventually she returned to Kiel on 10 April and a few days later was transferred east to Swinemünde, where she was detailed as part of the escort for the incomplete heavy cruiser (formerly *Lützow*) which had been sold to the Soviet Union. This ship had been towed from Kiel on 20 April, escorted by *Saar* and *T139*, arriving in Swinemünde the following evening. However, the old ship's part in the operation was cancelled and she did not proceed to Libau (Liepaja in Latvia) where the actual transfer was to take place. Instead, she moved to Gotenhafen. The heavy cruiser left Swinemünde under tow of the tugs *Atlantik* and *Albatros* in the early hours of 27 April, escorted by *Schiff 23*. At 0100 on 29 April she was turned over to the Soviet destroyers *Lenin* and *Voikov* with the icebreaker *Krassin* at sea off Libau. (Her subsequent career is described in *German Cruisers of World War Two*.)

Schlesien operated out of Kiel during 'Weserübung' but saw no action. Both pre-dreadnoughts were used in training roles for the next couple of months and their operational capacity was limited. *Schlesien*'s engine power was reduced to 6,000hp and in June orders were received for each ship to land three 15cm guns, SIV, PIV and PV in the case of *Schleswig-Holstein* (OKM A Wa C11a 2755/40), the gun ports being plated in to preserve seaworthiness. *Schlesien* also lost her 3.7cm guns. Crews were reduced and sent to new billets in occupied France. For the remainder of June and July they acted as target and training ships but on 24 July the OKM ordered *Schlesien* laid up and on 30 July Günther Horstmann turned his command over to his First Officer, F.Kpt. Oehrl, who decommissioned the ship on 2 August. By the end of that month her sister was virtually inactive as a static training vessel because most of her crew had been posted away. On 29 August she was ordered to land all four 8.8cm guns, six 2cm and two or three range-finders for the defence of Hamburg.

In the event neither ship remained inactive for long because another hard winter threatened. *Schleswig-Holstein* was in Kiel dockyard by November, refitting for icebreaker duties once more, and her sister was in Deutschewerke for similar reasons. *Schlesien* recommissioned on 22 January 1941 under the command of F.Kpt. Isenlar and *Schleswig-Holstein* under F.Kpt. Roegglen two days earlier. Flak outfits had been strengthened by additional 2cm guns. By late March the need for these two elderly ships' services had gone and both were laid up as training hulks on 26 March, paying off on 31 March.

Yet again this lay-up was to be brief for the invasion of Soviet Russia—Operation 'Barbarossa'—was imminent. This time their heavy guns were needed as floating batteries. Kpt.z.S. Lindenau took over *Schlesien* on 24 May, ordered to overhaul and re-equip for duty from the end of May; while Kpt.z.S. Hennecke assumed command of her sister on 28 May. Their task was to act as floating batteries off the Danish coast to prevent any break-out by the Soviet Fleet after 'Barbarossa' had been launched. By about 12 June the two ships were on their respective stations, *Schlesien* in Segrö Bay on the western side near Aarhus and her consort off Drogden lighthouse in the approaches to Copenhagen. There they

Top: *Schleswig-Holstein* acting as an ice-breaker for a U-boat. (Bundesarchiv)

Above: *Schlesien* in heavy ice. (Author's Collection)

Another harsh winter, 1941/42, heralded their reactivation once more as icebreakers. On 12 January 1942 *Schleswig-Holstein* (Kpt.z.S. Stichling) ran aground off Mersagciens lighthouse while on this duty in the Irben Straits, which were badly iced up. She was holed in compartments V to IX and reported herself unable to proceed without escort and that tugs would probably be needed. The route into the Gulf of Riga was important as most of the German Army's supplies were sent this way and Gruppe (Nord) therefore ordered her sister, *Schlesien*, then at Kiel, to be prepared to replace her by the end of the week. The following day the casualty reported that only one boiler room was serviceable but that all generators were in order. However, the ingress of water could be contained although the draught was 2.5m greater at the bows and 1m less than normal aft. More important, she had only 120m³ of fuel oil and 47m³ of diesel oil. On 14 January *Schleswig-Holstein* signalled that there was more water in the ship than had been thought and that an attempt would be made to pump it out with the assistance of the icebreaker *Stettin*. Meanwhile the ship lay at anchor and was unable to proceed until patched up. The need for fuel was now pressing as she had only enough for her pumps to last for another three days. Because of the extra draught, scuttles on the 'tween deck had been smashed by ice and part of the armour belt had also been damaged, causing more leaks.

The stricken ship lay helpless for days despite the sailing by Gruppe (Nord) of ships to assist her. Not until 18 January could she report that the relief icebreaker *Castor* was in sight. The next day she resumed a slow passage west behind *Castor* but by evening she was fast in the ice once more off Domesnäs. This occurred several times for the next few days, so that it was not until the forenoon of 24 January that she reached Gotenhafen, now with a draught of 9.8m. Urgent repairs were sanctioned to the elderly vessel, as there remained a pressing requirement for icebreakers. In the meantime *Schlesien* had reached Gotenhafen and been ordered to escort a large convoy westwards. This comprised the depot ship *Wilhelm Bauer*, fourteen U-boats and four auxiliaries of the 27th U-boat Flotilla, *Schiff 28* and eleven minesweepers. By 28 January this convoy was stuck in the ice off Gedser and did not reach Kiel until 31 January, having taken 1½ days to proceed from Dornbush into that port.

It was intended that both ships be employed as batteries again in Danish waters when the thaw occurred in the event of any attempt by the Red Fleet to break out of the Baltic. Until the ice retreated, however, *Schlesien* continued her duties as an icebreaker. By 18 February 1942 she had brought two eastbound convoys from Gotenhafen, including the cruiser *Köln*. The cold continued and in March the ship was stuck fast several times, one passage from Swinemünde to Kiel taking *eighteen* days! In May *Schlesien* was stationed off Seelandsrev as a battery but her sister seems to have been still under repair. No action ensued and thereafter training duties were resumed. The winter of 1942/43 appears to have been relatively mild and the two old battleships' services were not required, so that it was not until the desperate days of late 1944 that they were active again.

remained for three months without incident, the Soviet Fleet having withdrawn into Leningrad. Towards the end of August, in view of the inactivity of the Russians, it was decided to withdraw the two ships to Aarhus and Copenhangen, but to keep them at three hours' notice.

No sooner had these orders been issued than reports emanating from Sweden indicated that the Red Fleet was about to break out and take shelter in Swedish waters. The Royal Swedish Navy was mobilized and the movement orders for the old German battleships were cancelled. However, it was a false alarm and on 1 September the battleships were ordered into the above-mentioned ports. The only other event to shake the calm was the suicide on 17 June of *Schlesien*'s First Officer, F.Kpt. Isenlar, who had had a nervous breakdown. By October the ships were back at Kiel; they then moved to Gotenhafen where they resumed their stationary training role once more.

11. 'WESERÜBUNG', 1940

When Operation 'Weserübung', the invasion of Norway and Denmark was planned, it was obvious to the SKL that to safeguard the passage of the occupying forces, the whole of the Kriegsmarine's strength would have to be employed. Even so, with such a disparity in size between the Allied and German fleets, surprise was an essential element in the planning of such a major undertaking. As far as capital ships were concerned, the only ships available were *Scharnhorst* and *Gneisenau* because *Admiral Scheer* was still under refit and the newly renamed *Lützow* (ex-*Deutschland*) was earmarked for an Atlantic operation. The two new battleships, *Bismarck* and *Tirpitz*, had still to be completed. Both *Scharnhorst* and *Gneisenau*, the latter wearing the flag of Viz.Ad. Günther Lütjens (standing in for Marschall who was on sick leave), were lying at Wilhelmshaven at the beginning of April and formed Group I, together with ten destroyers. The destroyers, however, were tasked with the occupation of Narvik* and were to be loaded with troops and equipment while the two battleships would provide offshore cover and diversionary tactics.

On the forenoon of 6 April Lütjens addressed the men of both ships' companies but without disclosing the full intentions of any forthcoming sortie, although it was obvious to most that something was afoot. The RAF was paying considerable attention to the port and over the past few days and nights air attacks had become a regular occurrence, although they seldom achieved anything. Even as the hours ticked away to the start of 'Weserübung', an air raid took place just before midnight on 6 April and *Scharnhorst* went into action against a low-flying aircraft in the roads. Although this was believed to be a minelaying mission, the first RAF minelaying was not until the night of 13/14 April. During the early hours of the next day the drone of aircraft could still be heard as the ships prepared to sail, but the big operation seems to have remained uncompromized. It was a still, clear night of a new moon as the two heavy ships weighed anchor and proceeded to sea. The Schillig boom was cleared at 0200, when the destroyers bound for Narvik joined from Cuxhaven, and an hour later the heavy cruiser *Admiral Hipper*, together with four destroyers, joined when the squadron reached lightship 'F'. The heavy cruiser's formation (Group 2) was bound for Trondheim but was to take passage in company with Group 1. Lütjens ordered his squadron to 25 knots and the great adventure had begun.

Dawn broke to a cloudless sky as the destroyers took up their screening positions. *Scharnhorst*, *Gneisenau* and *Admir-*

See Destroyer: German Destroyers in World War Two.

al Hipper steamed abreast about 2,000m apart. Visibility was very good, a factor which disturbed Lütjens, for he needed to remain undetected as long as possible. About two hours after dawn Bf 109 fighters arrived as air cover, followed by three He 111s after the Horns Reef had been passed. His fears were quite justified for Hudsons 'K' and 'M' of No. 220 Squadron had reported the German force at 0848 (British time), when 28nm to the north-west of Horns Reef. Course was now due north and at 1245 the Flag ordered speed increased to 27 knots. *Scharnhorst* immediately encountered problems as a steam valve on the port turbine shut off and stopped the engine. It was fifteen minutes before the defect could be cleared.

Visibility continued to be disturbingly good, about 10,000m in fact, as the squadron passed Hanstholm at 1330. Then an hour later when the ships were about 70 miles south-west of the Naze, they were attacked from the east by a formation of twelve Blenheims of No. 107 Squadron, RAF. The ships were still steaming in line abreast, with *Admiral Hipper* to the east, *Gneisenau* in the centre, and the attack seemed to concentrate on the heavy cruiser. All ships opened fire with heavy and light flak. It produced a good deal of noise and smoke but had little effect on the attackers. Similarly the bombers made little impression on the ships and their bombing was derisory. The Blenheims dropped forty 25lb SAP bombs! Seven more Blenheims of No. 21 Squadron failed to find the target, nor did two squadrons of Wellingtons (Nos. 9 and 115), which lost two aircraft (N2949 and P2524, both from No. 115 Squadron) to Bf 110 fighters. A sighting report by the aircraft did not reach the Admiralty until very much later. By 1441 it was all over and action stations secured.

As the afternoon wore on visibility reduced and radar sets were switched on. By evening the seas were rising, with forecast of worse to come. It began to drizzle and by the time Utsira was passed the wind had risen to Force 7. The big ships began to work badly but conditions aboard the destroyers were infinitely worse. Early in the evening orders came from the Flag in preparation for the risky break through the Shetland-Bergen narrows. In reality these narrows were not less than 200nm wide but any restriction in sea-room was unwelcome and aided the Royal Navy's search patrols. In the event the narrows were passed without incident between 2030 and 2330 that night.

The early hours of 8 April found the squadron abreast Bremangerlandet, rolling terribly in the pitch-black night. A south-westerly gale (Force 7 to 8) was blowing and large quantities of water came aboard because speed remained at

24 knots. As the middle watch wore on it began to drizzle, turning to rain by the time that the morning watch had closed up. Nevertheless, dawn broke with good visibility, but wind and sea remained unabated. During the forenoon the winds began to veer north-westerly, putting the seas on the port bow. At 0845 radio silence was broken by the destroyer *Lüdemann* reporting an unidentified destroyer. Half an hour later a second destroyer, *von Arnim*, signalled herself in action with an enemy destroyer and Lütjens immediately ordered *Admiral Hipper* to her assistance. The remainder of the squadron pressed on, punching through the heavy seas. Lütjens had been warned by Gruppe West that an enemy battle squadron was believed to be off Narvik and to reckon on its appearance the following day. If this were to prove true then he had a problem.

In the heavy seas and overloaded with troops, the destroyers were in no condition to fight; and in any event their main task was the occupation of Narvik, not the fighting of a sea battle. Lütjens was seriously concerned that *von Arnim*'s action could have compromised his position as he expected that the enemy destroyer would have reported the encounter. He also criticized *von Arnim* for opening fire counter to orders and stressed that she should have avoided the enemy. Whether this could in fact have been done was a moot point. Actually HMS *Glowworm* did not make a report, or if she did, it was not received; but Lütjens had to assume one made. In consequence, and in the knowledge of the enemy forces already reported off Westfjord, he decided to remain in close escort with Group 1 as far as the approaches to that fjord. This group was the largest force, wide open to attack under the prevailing conditions, as well as being badly overloaded. Theirs was the most important objective, which decided him on keeping both battleships with Bonte's destroyers and not splitting them between Groups 1 and 2. Fortunately no enemy forces made contact and Lütjens was able to detach the destroyers for their objective at 2102.

As midnight approached the west-north-westerly wind was reaching hurricane strength, with heavy seas breaking over the ships. Orders from the Flag detailed the intentions for the night; to steam westwards at 9 knots with one boiler on line per shaft. All precautions were to be taken to keep the armament dry (Don't get your powder wet!). *Scharnhorst*'s Commanding Officer, Kapt.z.S. Hoffmann, thought this imprudent under the prevailing conditions and ordered his Engineer Officer, F.Kpt. (Ing) Leibhard, to keep two boilers on line per shaft. This was a wise decision, as *Scharnhorst* was already suffering damage due to the heavy seas. Some structural damage had been incurred near Stb II 15cm gun and sea-water had flooded down the intake trunking into No.2 boiler room. As a result, *Scharnhorst* requested that speed be reduced, which was done, and passage continued at 7 knots. In the early hours of the next day, 9 April, sea-water flooded a vent shaft to a group of fuel bunkers in *Scharnhorst*, polluting some 470m³ of oil. At 0450 the two ships were about 50nm west of the southern tip of the Lofoten Islands, steering 310° at 12 knots. To the west visibility was intermittent with frequent rain squalls, while to the south

and east it was somewhat better. The wind and sea had abated slightly but the cloud base remained low and it was cold.

Now one of *Gneisenau*'s radar operators reported a contact astern at a range of 25,000m. Kpt.z.S. Netzband, who was somewhat sceptical of the radar's performance, was inclined to disbelieve this report but together with the gunnery officer, F.Kpt. von Buchka, went to range-finders to clarify the report although he could see nothing. When, 9 minutes later, a report from the foretop confirmed the radar's contact, Buchka was sent up to the Admiral's bridge to report to Lütjens . Meanwhile the object had become visible at bridge level and tentatively identified, first as a tanker and then as a *Rodney*-class battleship. *Scharnhorst*, on the other hand, did not detect the ship by radar but her lookouts saw the silhouette of a large ship to the west at 0505. Two minutes later it identified itself as an enemy by opening fire.

The British ship was the battlecruiser *Renown* (Captain Simeon) wearing the flag of Vice-Admiral Whitworth, who was actually in the area in support of a force of minelayers engaged upon Operation 'Wilfred'. This was an operation aimed at forcing shipping traffic (particularly the iron ore carriers bound for Germany) out of the sheltered inner leads and into the open sea, where the Royal Navy could attack them. The mines were to be laid off Horden in Vestfjord, off Stadtlandet and a dummy field off Bud. Although the strategic importance of Norway to both sides was recognized, neither was really sure of the other's intentions and in consequence both moved to pre-empt the other. It was expected that the Norwegians might oppose the minelayers with their ancient but well-armed coast defence ships, hence the presence of *Renown*. In addition, it was not inconceivable that the Germans might also interfere, as the ore route was of vital importance to them and the possession of the Norwegian coastline had quite obvious benefits to the Kriegsmarine— Admiral Raeder desperately wished to avoid being bottled up in the southern North Sea, as he had been 25 years earlier. To forestall a German invasion of Norway, the British prepared Plan R4, which aimed at occupying Stavanger, Bergen, Narvik and Trondheim, as soon as the enemy's intentions became clear. Troops for these landings began to embark in Scottish ports on 7 April but politics delayed their sailing, as well as the start of Operation 'Wilfred'.

Renown had actually sailed from Scapa Flow on 5 April, escorted by the destroyers *Greyhound*, *Glowworm*, *Hyperion* and *Hero*. Even before their departure, reports were filtering into the Admiralty, indicating that a major German operation might be under way, but it was far from clear if this was an Atlantic break-out or in connection with Norway. The details of the air attack on *Gneisenau* and the ships of combined Groups 1 and 2 by the RAF on the afternoon of 7 April had been greatly delayed in reaching the British Admiralty, with the result that the Home Fleet did not sail until 2015 that evening and, instead of cutting across the North Sea, Admiral Forbes (C-in-C Home Fleet) steamed north-east, to prevent a possible break-out into the Atlantic by the German force.

On the morning of 6 April one of *Renown*'s screening destroyers (*Glowworm*) lost a man overboard, turned back to look for him and was lost to view from the flagship. This ship was unaware of Admiral Whitworth's orders and had no idea where to rejoin the flag. In the event she fell in with the German destroyers of Group 2 and was eventually sunk by *Admiral Hipper* after a gallant but unequal battle as noted above. The battlecruiser *Repulse*, cruiser *Penelope* and the destroyers *Bedouin*, *Eskimo* and *Kimberley* were despatched to her aid but could not find the enemy cruiser. *Renown* meanwhile had detached *Hyperion* and *Hero* to oil in the Shetlands and by 0330 (British time) stood some 30 miles west of Skomvaer, having released the 'Wilfred' minelayers. At this time Admiral Whitworth was steering 130° at 12 knots, escorted by nine destroyers (*Hardy*, *Esk*, *Hotspur*, *Greyhound*, *Ivanhoe*, *Havock*, *Icarus*, *Impulsive* and *Hostile*). The wind had been a strong nor'westerly until midnight but had now abated to Force 5 and veered nor'nor'west. There remained a heavy sea and swell. It was overcast with snow showers as dawn lightened in the east. Because of the high seas, all the destroyers were stationed astern of the flagship.

At 0337 (British time) *Renown*'s lookouts sighted a darkened ship, bearing 070°, range 10 miles, silhouetted against the weak dawn, as she emerged from a snow squall. The enemy's course appeared to be approximately north-west and a second ship was thought to be in company. *Renown* got off an enemy report and prepared to engage. She altered course to 080° to close and increased speed to 15, later 20, knots. Twenty-two minutes after first sighting the German ships, *Renown* altered course to 305°, with the destroyers still astern. Under the prevailing conditions, the British seamen had considerable difficulty in identifying their target and believed it to consist of *Scharnhorst* and a heavy cruiser of the *Hipper* class. At 0405 *Renown* opened fire on the leading enemy ship bearing 018°, range 16,500m. She had been in contact with the enemy for some 23 minutes before they had realized her presence, which had enabled the slower British ship to gain position to

advantage. (The action which follows now reverts to German time, one hour ahead of British time.)

Renown's opening salvo landed short, some 300–500 metres abreast the bridge of *Gneisenau*, but it was not until 0510 that *Scharnhorst* replied, followed one minute later by the flagship. As soon as the British battlecruiser's gun flashes had been seen, Lütjens ordered a 40° turn to starboard on to 350° and increased speed, to clear the shell splashes. As this course led to 'A' and 'B' turrets being 'wooded', Kpt.z.See Netzbandt requested a better course from the flag and the German squadron therefore came back 20° to port on to 330°. *Renown* meanwhile maintained 305°, keeping the 'A' arcs just open. Heavy seas were breaking over the forecastle at 20 knots, causing serious problems to range-finder optics; and in fact a good r/f range was never obtained by *Renown* during the action. *Renown* was an old ship first commissioned in September 1916, which had 'grown' by some 5,000 tons since that time, with a consequent reduction in speed by 2 knots. Her last full power trial on the Talland mile gave a maximum of 30 knots, slower than her adversaries; but more importantly, her freeboard was 1ft less at the bows than formerly and in the heavy seas prevailing, took a lot of water over the bows and forward turrets.

Admiral Whitworth needed to close the range and gain bearing so at 0513 he increased to full speed but quickly found that the working of the ship and the amount of water coming over the turrets made conditions impossible; he was forced to reduce speed to 23 knots six minutes later. His destroyers, after gamely attempting to keep up and even engaging (although it is unlikely that they were ever in range!), were soon forced to reduce speed and they dropped back out of the action and were detached to Westfjord. The German ship's fire was also affected by weather and visibility and, according to *Renown*'s account, was very ragged for range and line with a variable spread. All three combatants' secondary armaments opened fire but with little effect at the ranges existing.

Renown, firing at *Gneisenau*, crossed her target with the fifth salvo, then straddled with the next, at a range of 17,000 metres. Continuing to fire with an inclination of 50°/70° left, the British ship made good shooting. Aboard *Gneisenau* a hit was reported on *Renown* at 0516, somewhere between the bridge and the bows. In fact, no hit had yet been registered but just as Netzbandt telephoned his senior gunnery officer to congratulate him, one of *Renown*'s sixteenth salvo struck the foretop of *Gneisenau*, killing F.Kpt. von Buchka and causing other casualties. This hit disabled the foretop rangefinder and director and also disrupted the secondary armament because its engaged director was damaged by splinters. Although the secondary gunnery officer transferred to the port director, the ship turned 60° to starboard on to 30° at 0519 on the orders of the flag, thus wooding the director. On this course and bearing, the flagship could only engage with 'C' turret and P IV 15cm gun. Even so, smoke from *Scharnhorst* obscured the range and it was probably for this reason also that *Renown* shifted target to the latter ship at 0520 after 23 salvoes, having hit her first target three times, the second

Below: *Gneisenau* in Norwegian waters. The turret tops are painted red. (USN)

two hits being on the left range-finder hood of 'A' turret and on the after flak deck near the port guns.

Renown opened fire on *Scharnhorst* at 0521 with the range estimated at 18,288 metres and was initially over but crossed with the first down ladder. Fire had to be checked four times between 0512 and 0557 because of snow squalls.

Lütjens was now attempting to disengage and had worked up to about 27 knots by 0530, engaging only intermittently with 'C' turret as and when visibility permitted. The heavy seas flooded *Gneisenau*'s 'A' turret through the gun ports and damaged range-finder hood; while aboard *Scharnhorst* both training engines had been put out of action in 'A' turret by the ingress of sea-water, as had both forward 15cm open mountings. At 0530 *Renown* switched to full broadsides to improve her chances but had fired only five when 'Y' turret ceased to bear. In the first phase of the action, she had received two hits but neither reduced her fighting power. The first hit aft, wrecking the gun-room bathroom and flooding the Admiral's, Captain's and Officers' baggage stores, before passing out of the ship without exploding. The second hit the foremast and disabled the W/T aerials, until emergency ones could be rigged.

Although the chase continued for some time, the German ships' superior speed enabled them gradually to draw ahead as *Renown* had been forced to reduce to 20 knots at 0540 to keep her forward turrets in action. The wind had freshened and veered NNE (Force 7) by now, as the participants traded shots through the squalls. *Renown* now steered 010° with the sea 25° on the starboard bow and, in one last effort to increase speed, altered course to bring the seas on the other bow at 0556. This allowed the speed to creep up to 25 knots and at 0615 fire was briefly reopened on *Scharnhorst*, which had suffered a machinery breakdown in the starboard engine room. No hits were obtained by any of the ships and at 0644, as the range was opening, *Renown* turned her forward turrets away from the seas and increased to 27 then 29 knots, but nevertheless lost contact with Lütjens' squadron. *Scharnhorst* ceased fire at 0641 but the flagship, generally in the lead, had fired her last salvoes at 0544, although she did reduce speed to close on *Scharnhorst* when the latter's speed had been reduced to 25 knots.

Renown had not been seriously hit and had fired about 230 rounds of main armament, rather more by 'A' and 'B' turrets than 'Y' due to the course of the action. In addition, the starboard 4.5in guns had fired 1,065 rounds but at ranges where it was ineffective. Sea-water had flooded into 'A' and 'Y' shell rooms due to severe blast damage caused to deck hatches and blast bags by her own guns. All director optics and turret range-finders had been washed out by the seas during the action.

Scharnhorst had not been hit but suffered defects in all her engines, as well as in Nos. I and III boiler rooms, which reduced her speed at embarrassing moments. All her aircraft were unserviceable. She had fired 195 rounds of 28cm, nearly all AP, and a handful of 15cm rounds. *Gneisenau* was hit three times, suffering two officers and four men killed and another nine wounded. Her guns fired only 54 28cm rounds,

mostly, for some reason, head-fused HE, and the 15cm guns ten rounds.

After successfully losing *Renown*, Lütjens continued north until midday on 9 April, when he altered course to the west on latitude 69°N. He had decided to break off the action on several grounds: (a) 'A' turrets of both ships were unserviceable (i.e., a third of their main armaments); (b) *Scharnhorst*'s machinery problems; (c) the damage to the flagship; (d) unserviceable fire control optics in the bad weather; and (e) the fact that *Scharnhorst* had fired almost all the AP shells in her after magazines. To replenish from the forward magazines would take some time. His plan to open the range (accepting the fact that only his after turrets would bear) and evade to the north however, left the approaches to Westfjord wide open. It would appear that Lütjens may now have had some doubts about this withdrawal, for he questioned *Scharnhorst* as to the number of enemy ships engaged. *Scharnhorst* reported only one seen at the start of the action, but after about 30 minutes she signalled her belief that *three* enemy had been seen. These would have been the futile shots from *Renown*'s screen, but it satisfied Lütjens.

By 2200 that evening Lütjens professed to being in something of a quandary. He felt that under the changed circumstances of the operation (quite how they had changed is not clear) he lacked clear orders as to what to do next. He was undecided as to whether he should return to Germany as close support for the destroyers of Groups 1 and 2, or let them proceed independently while his ships acted as a diversion for them. *Admiral Hipper* could not do this because of her damage, as well as being low on fuel, and he doubted if refuelling at sea was possible. He expressed particular concern over the pressures on the forces at Narvik and considered whether he should sweep for the enemy forces reported off the entrance to Westfjord. However, he soon discarded this idea on the grounds that they would be difficult to locate and bring to action under favourable conditions. In the end he decided that as his fuel situation was not critical, he would remain at sea to the north while repairing damage and awaiting developments. Finally, he opted to return home without the Narvik group.

Thus the destroyers in Narvik were left wide open to attack and it is possible that had Lütjens remained off the Lofotens instead of proceeding west, he might well have barred the passage of Warburton-Lee's 2nd Destroyer Flotilla. The fact that in doing so he drew off *Renown* is probably of little importance, as by this time the destroyers were inside the fjord and it was most unlikely that Admiral Whitworth could have risked pursuing them.

At Gruppe (West) Admiral Saalwächter concurred with Lütjens' decision to break off the engagement with *Renown*, on the grounds that his orders did not allow him to seek such an engagement and it was important that his ships remain undamaged for the return journey. However, Saalwächter was not in a position to order Lütjens to act in close support of the returning Narvik destroyers as he was somewhat in the dark as to the Fleet Commander's movements, intentions and, more important, damage state. There had been consider-

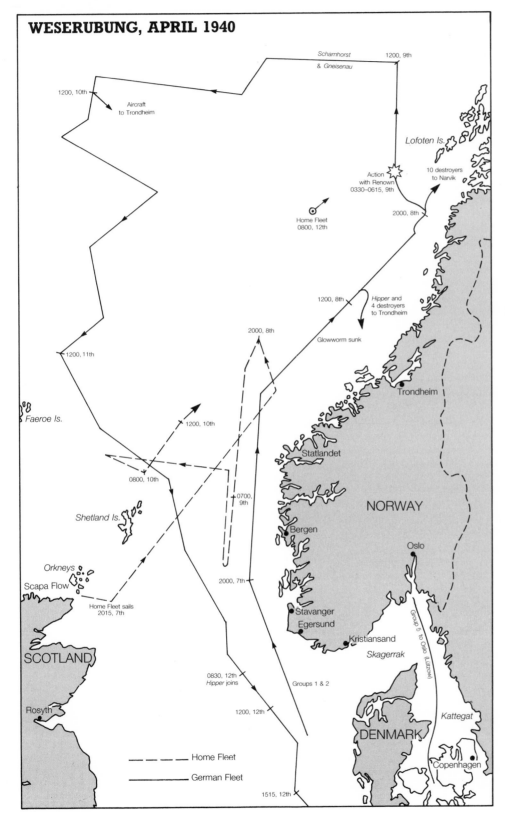

WESERUBUNG, APRIL 1940

Scharnhorst & Gneisenau   1200, 9th

1200, 10th

Aircraft to Trondheim

Lofoten Is.

Action with Renown 0330–0615, 9th

10 destroyers to Narvik

2000, 8th

Home Fleet 0800, 12th

Faeroe Is.

1200, 8th

Hipper and 4 destroyers to Trondheim

Glowworm sunk

1200, 11th

2000, 8th

1200, 10th

0800, 10th

0700, 9th

Trondheim

Shetland Is.

Statlandet

Bergen

NORWAY

Oslo

Orkneys

Scapa Flow

2000, 7th

Home Fleet sails 2015, 7th

Stavanger
Egersund

Kristiansand

Group 5 to Oslo (Lützow)

Skagerrak

SCOTLAND

0830, 12th *Hipper joins*

Groups 1 & 2

Rosyth

1200, 12th

Kattegat

DENMARK

- - - - Home Fleet

——— German Fleet

Copenhagen

1515, 12th

---

able difficulty with signals not being received by Gruppe (West) and others not being answered by the Fleet for operational security reasons. In consequence, it was only known ashore that the fleet's speed was restricted to 25 knots and that two turrets were unserviceable; it was not known if one or both ships were affected. In all probability this hampered Saalwächter in giving instructions to the commander at sea. Nevertheless, he acknowledged that it was appreciated that the return home would be the most risky part of the operation, particularly from Narvik, given the short endurance and poor sea-keeping properties of the destroyers. *Scharnhorst* still had machinery defects, although by this time the gunnery technical officer, Kpt.Lt.(W) Stetter, had managed to get 'A' turret functioning once more.

South of Jan Mayen island aircraft were flown off to Trondheim with reports and orders, while intentions for the break back through the Shetland-Bergen narrows were clarified. At this time, the seas were calm and visibility very good, the last thing Lütjens wanted. In mid-afternoon he signalled his captains of his intention to await an expected deterioration in the visibility and weather. A further problem was a signal from Gruppe (West) at 2219, warning of the presence of the carrier *Furious* somewhere off Norway. An obvious threat, this ship had embarked eighteen Swordfish torpedo-bombers of Nos. 816 and 818 Squadrons, but in fact her targets were the Norwegian ports and not the German battleships.

It was not until the afternoon of 11 April that *Scharnhorst* could report 'capable of 28.5 knots' to the flag and the return could begin. Lütjens now had intelligence that the main strength of the Home Fleet was between Trondheim and Westfjord, too far north-east to have much chance of intercepting him. Passing very close to the Shetlands, he forced the dangerous narrows and joined the homeward-bound *Admiral Hipper* on the forenoon of 12 April. Numerous aircraft had been sighted from about 0645 that morning, the first of which, Hudson 'F' of No. 224 Squadron from Leuchars, reported two battlecruisers and a cruiser off Egersund at that time. Another Hudson ('J' of No. 233 Squadron) took off to shadow the German force but nothing was ever seen of this aircraft again. Finally, two more Hudsons ('D' and 'G' of No. 224 Squadron) found and shadowed Lütjens' force throughout the rest of the forenoon. The German Admiral was not surprised, therefore, to be warned that four British bomber squadrons had been despatched against him and ordered a high degree of readiness in anticipation. A large force of Bomber and Coastal Command aircraft had been flown off to intercept, but poor visibility prevented their locating the German force. Of more than 90 aircraft participating in this strike, 48 were from Bomber Command comprising 36 Wellingtons of Nos. 9, 37, 38, 75, 99 and 149 Squadrons (of which four, P2520, P9246, P9266 and P9269, were shot down) and twelve Hampdens from Nos. 44 and 50 Squadrons; of the latter, No. 50 squadron lost four of its five machines (L4064, L4073, L4081 and L4083), while No. 44 Squadron lost two (L4099 and P1173), all to fighters. By 2212 the ships had anchored in Wilhelmshaven, unmolested.

Scharnhorst, in particular, needed a machinery overhaul but Hoffmann's expectation of docking was soon quashed, as the OKM ordered that no repairs be started which could not be completed in six hours! On 1 May *Scharnhorst* was ordered to Wesermünde and nine days later passed through to the Baltic, escorted by *Sperrbrecher 4* and accompanied by *Dithmarschen* and *Kamerun*. Although this move was intended for training and work-up, the commandeering of 87 senior and junior rates to other posts reduced the ship's efficiency. After spending a week in the eastern Baltic around Gotenhafen, the SKL ordered her to Kiel-Deutsche Werk, with immediate effect, for the much-needed machinery overhaul. The yard said twelve days were needed but the Fleet Commander said no later than 31 May! Repairs were duly completed by the stipulated day. *Gneisenau* too had been docked, partly due to grounding in the Elbe on 5 May. She then went to the eastern Baltic before returning to Kiel on 1 June.

The only other operational heavy unit at the beginning of April 1940 was *Lützow*, now re-rated Schwerekreuzer or heavy cruiser. She, however, was scheduled for a raiding cruise to the South Atlantic, where the Allied whaling fleets were the target. Her new Commanding Officer was Kpt.z.S. Thiele. August Thiele, 47 years of age, was a Berliner who had joined the Kaiserliche Marine in 1912. Between the wars he had commanded *Gorch Fock* and *Horst Wessel*, two of the sail training ships, as well as holding various shore command posts. He was to have a distinguished career in the Kriegsmarine.

This deployment was expected to be of about nine months' duration and *Lützow* had been stored to that effect. However, Hitler decided that instead she be employed as part of the naval forces allocated to 'Weserübung' and Raeder had no option but to agree. *Lützow* was therefore made flagship of the group tasked with the occupation of Oslo, from where Raeder intended that she break out into the Atlantic. Thiele prepared his ship for both these duties and although not entirely in agreement with his dual role, accepted it. Then, when the heavy cruiser *Blücher* was co-opted into the 'Weserübung' plan, it appeared that *Lützow* could be released for her raiding cruise; but unfortunately the Führer saw the new heavy cruiser not as a replacement but as an addition to the invasion force, insisting that *Lützow* participate in 'Weserübung' on her way out into the Atlantic.

Thus on 2 March Thiele was ordered to Wilhelmshaven as part of the group tasked with occupying Trondheim, from where an Atlantic break-out would be a better probability. Viz.Ad. Lütjens, the commander of this group, was less than enthusiastic about the addition of the slow former Panzerschiff to his fast group. To him and to Thiele, *Lützow* would be a square peg in a round hole and the Fleet Commander would have no option but to leave her behind if threatened by fast British forces en route. 'Weserübung' was, after all, the Fleet's main task, to *Lützow* it was only a side-show, each had different priorities. Thiele was extremely worried about the timing of sailing for Norway, which would involve a daylight passage in areas well patrolled by the RAF and, should

they be sighted, he could expect heavy forces of the Royal Navy north of the Shetland-Bergen narrows waiting to intercept him. With the whole of the fleet involved in 'Weserübung', he could not expect any support from them, should the worst happen. Even so, any extra British activity in Northern waters could well result in the interception of his supply oiler, already on station.

In the event, cracks were found in the foundation of *Lützow*'s No. 1 auxiliary motor, which needed dockyard repair. This precluded an immediate Atlantic deployment but after makeshift repairs, she was cleared for 'Weserübung'. At the same time, *Lützow* was transferred to Group 'Oldenburg', tasked with the occupation of Oslo, the Norwegian capital. Accordingly, *Lützow* re-embarked 400 mountain troops under Major von Poncet and 50 Luftwaffe ground staff, as well as 23 tonnes of stores, before proceeding east just before midnight, 6 April. In the early hours of the following day, she locked into the Kaiser Wilhelm Canal and while in transit received a decrypt of a British aircraft sighting report, which referred to the ships of Groups 1 and 2. Thiele considered this a foregone conclusion, given the good visibility conditions prevailing, and saw it as proof of his own doubts. *Lützow* reached Kiel early in the afternoon of 7 April.

The ships of Group 5, as the Oslo force was known, weighed and proceeded at 0300 on 8 April. In the van was the flagship *Blücher* (K.Ad. Kummetz) followed by *Lützow*, *Emden* and the torpedo boats *Möwe*, *Albatros* and *Kondor*. It was a light, clear and starry night as the ships cleared the boom at Kiel and set course northwards.

Halskov Rev lightship was passed at 0800, and at 1115 action stations closed up as the squadron proceeded at 18 knots in line ahead. During the early afternoon there were several alarms due to submarine sightings but all proved false. Several signals were received from Gruppe (Ost) concerning the operation, one of which stated that it seemed that no mines were present in the Drobak Narrows. Another gave instructions on how to respond to Norwegian delaying tactics—they should signal 'Entering with the approval of the Norwegian Government. Liaison Officer aboard'. The first quoted signal is of interest bearing in mind the later actions of Kummetz in *Blücher*. By 1906 the squadron had reached the latitude of Skagen and were about to enter the Skagerrak.

Now a genuine submarine alarm was raised as torpedo tracks were sighted, passing ahead of *Lützow*'s bows. Their assailant was in fact HMS/m *Triton* (Lieutenant-Commander E.F. Pizey), a unit of the 2nd Submarine Flotilla, which had sailed on 29 March for a patrol in the Skagerrak and Kattegat. Part of her patrol orders are of interest for she was to try a new method of intercepting enemy shipping. Prize Rules were still in force and when a ship was ordered to heave to, it was often scuttled by the crew. Pizey was ordered specifically to inform stopped ships that they would be given time to abandon in orderly fashion, in the hope that they would not in consequence scuttle their ships. This, it was hoped, would give a chance of putting a prize crew aboard. Such a scenario hardly applied to *Lützow* however! *Triton* had

Above: *Schleswig-Holstein* participated briefly in Weserübung. (Bundesarchiv)

in fact been put down by A/S trawlers already off the Skagen and was therefore south of her desired position.

By evening on 8 April she was off Laeso in the Kattegat when two heavy ships were sighted approaching from the west. Pizey soon realized that he would not be able to attain a suitable position to attack the leading ship, which he identified as *Gneisenau* but was actually *Blücher*; so he decided to attack the one astern, which he thought was *Nürnberg* or *Leipzig* (but was in fact *Lützow*), and chance a long shot rather than delay in the hope that the enemy would come close around the Skagen, when an attack opportunity might be missed altogether. *Emden* was correctly identified as the third ship. *Triton* was soon well abaft the beam of the leading ship but still in a position to attack the second vessel when, at 1855 *Gneisenau* (sic) altered more to port, thus putting the submarine on an 85° track. Pizey therefore decided to attack the most important target.

At 1858 he fired his full bow salvo of ten Mk VIII*E torpedoes at a range of 6,855m but almost immediately his asdic operator reported that the enemy had increased speed from 14 to 20 knots, when the firing data had been computed using 15 knots. All the torpedoes missed and the submarine was held ,8down by the torpedo boat *Albatros* while the squadron proceeded. Another British submarine, *Sunfish*, which had also sighted the German force, made a radio sighting report to the Admiralty. As darkness fell the German ships closed up for the night and continued northwards.

In the last hours before midnight Gruppe (Ost) informed Kummetz that two German merchantmen had been torpedoed and sunk at the entrance to Oslofjord that day (probably *Rio de Janeiro* by the Polish submarine *Orzel* and *Posidonia* by *Trident*), but he was already aware of the presence of submarines. The order by the Norwegian Admiralty for the dousing of all lights was also intercepted, leading Thiele to conclude that all chance of surprise was lost. Given the difficult navigational problems, he proposed to Kummetz that they should now proceed at high speed in the hope of transiting the Drobak Narrows before the lights were actually doused, but this was not concurred with. At 2353 Kummetz

entered the fjord at 18 knots and was illuminated by the searchlights on Raüoy and Bolarne, whose batteries opened fire on *Blücher*. It was now evident that suprise had been lost. Fortunately, visibility now closed in as the squadron hove to in order for troops to be disembarked to the R-boats and torpedo boats. On completion, the ships got under way once more at 9 knots as Kummetz intended to loiter north of Horten until dawn, then force the Drobak Narrows. Horten itself was shrouded in mist as the ships detailed for its occupation were detached at 0330. Reducing speed to 7 knots, the heavy ships awaited orders to proceed towards Oslo. The sky began to lighten at 0430 and about ten minutes later the squadron altered course to 358° and proceeded towards Kaholmen. All Army personnel were ordered below decks by the flagship.

In the fairway two Norwegian patrol vessels illuminated *Blücher* but otherwise took no action, although other searchlights in the Drobak Narrows now began to burn. As it slowly became light, the warships stood out clearly, while on land it was difficult to pick out any important features, especially defences. At 0520 *Blücher* ordered a reduction in speed, whereupon *Lützow* hove to, as the situation was far from clear. Five minutes later, while the flagship was bathed in ghostly light, the battery on Kaholmen opened fire (at a range of only about 1,800m), scoring immediate hits on *Blücher*. Another round from this heavy battery struck *Lützow* on the centre gun of her forward 28cm turret. This hit knocked out the gun and temporarily disabled the turret but the right and left guns were uncoupled after about five minutes; half an hour later the left gun was put back into service in makeshift fashion. A second hit was suffered in the 'tweendeck, compartment XIII, which caused fires in the sick bay and upper deck on the port side. Several casualties were incurred among the ship's company and embarked troops. A third shell struck the port boat crane, causing splinter damage and burning out some 8.8cm ready-use ammunition. P III and P IV 15cm guns suffered three dead and five wounded among their crews and ammunition handlers, while a number of other men at flak guns and searchlights were also wounded. In addition, many light calibre hits were received all over the ship.

Immediately the first shell had struck the flagship, permission was given to open fire and *Lützow* engaged with her port 15cm battery but the after 28cm turret could not bear. The light and heavy flak guns opened fire on Kaholmen but without any clear target. As *Lützow* now went full astern to extricate herself from the mess, the order to cease fire was given at 0523. *Emden*, however, was still proceeding ahead and there were a few anxious moments before a collision was avoided. The flagship was lost to view after an explosion, signalling that all her engines were out of action. A few minutes later she requested Luftwaffe support and, as *Lützow* turned south, ordered Thiele to assume command of the group. Nothing more was heard from the Flag.

Thiele was now in an extremely difficult situation, for with no forward guns he could not hope to force the narrows, guarded as they were by three old but obviously serviceable

Opposite page, top: *Lützow* torpedoed and helpless. Note the centre 28cm gun fully depressed; it had been disabled by the Norwegian shore batteries. (Bundesarchiv)

Centre: Further view of the crippled *Lützow*. Note two Ar 196 carried. (Bundesarchiv)

Bottom: The damaged stern of *Lützow*. (Bundesarchiv)

28cm guns. *Emden* was in no better situation for her 15cm guns were no match for the powerful shore battery, and as yet Thiele had no idea of the presence of the torpedo battery. Indeed, he did not even know if the flagship was afloat or not. Under the circumstances there was little that he could do except land the embarked troops along the fjord for them to get to Oslo by road or rail. *Emden* was ordered to land her troops north of Moss, the light forces in Sonsbukten, and *Lützow* hers in Verle Bay. Despite some trouble in *Emden*'s acceptance of Thiele's orders, and *Möwe*'s conflicting orders to close the flagship or land her troops, the Army forces were eventually disembarked at Sonsbukten by 0910.

The batteries on Bolarne and Rauöy were still holding out, however, and Luftwaffe strike forces had to be called up. Around midday the Norwegian steamer *Norden* was captured, a petty officer and radio operator were put aboard and the ship sent up through the narrows to establish the fate of the flagship. To cover her passage, *Lützow* moved up and for seven minutes bombarded the Kaholmen fort with 27 rounds of 28cm. Some twenty minutes later *Norden* radioed that *Blücher* had been sunk, probably as a result of two torpedo hits.

By mid-afternoon Rauöy and Horten were in German hands, leaving only Bolarne still holding out. Thiele now decided to clarify the situation in the Drobak Narrows by sending up the torpedo boats *Kondor* and *Möwe* as well as four R-boats, while *Lützow* and *Emden* provided cover. At 1725 Gruppe (Ost) signalled that aircraft of Fliegerkorps X had attacked Drobak and that the position was now favourable for the ships to break through. Thiele was more cautious, however, the Norwegian flag still flew over the fort, and he had no intention of proceeding until he knew that the danger of mines and torpedoes had been neutralized. A Norwegian Admiral was brought out from Horten in the hope that his influence could be used to persuade the fortress commander to surrender, but in the meantime Thiele received news that the latter wished to discuss terms. After an officer had been sent to talk under a white flag, Thiele learned that the Norwegian senior officer had given his word that there were no mines laid and that he requested to be allowed to rehoist his flag in the morning. *Lützow*'s CO remained cautious and decided, because the situation was still unclear, that he would wait until daylight before attempting passage of the narrows.

During the night some *Blücher* survivors were received on board, and several signals received from Gruppe (Ost) concerning *Lützow*'s movements in the morning. She was not to proceed until the mine situation was clarified and, in any event, was to leave Oslo for Germany as soon as it was fully dark, then make passage at maximum speed. At 0900 the German flag rose above the Oskarsborg fortress and the ships continued passage up to Oslo, which they reached at 1143.

The town was held with very weak forces and the main naval base at Horten was occupied by only 100 men, where there was a Norwegian garrison of ten times that number. Similarly, the Drobak fortress was held by one officer and eight men! The Bolarne battery, however, remained in Norwegian hands. *Lützow*'s main task now to get her guns in working order, as she might have to fight her way past this defence on her way home. The ship eventually sailed at 1526 that afternoon, leaving *Emden* to secure the town. About two hours after sailing, information was received that Bolarne had surrendered and *Kondor* confirmed the presence of a white flag. After landing some of *Blücher*'s men at Horten to reinforce the troops there, *Lützow* proceeded, dismissing her A/S escort on passing 59°N and working up to 24 knots.

Although British submarines were known to be in the Skagerrak, Thiele believed them to be off the Swedish coast to the east on the basis of torpedo tracks being sighted there. Accordingly, he altered course westwards, intending to run due south at high speed across the dangerous open Skagerrak. It was a starless night with very good visibility and only a moderate breeze. Course was altered to 138° at 0200 and, an hour later, the ship's radar picked up a contact ahead at a range of 15,000m. This wandered to port and was eventually lost, whereupon Thiele altered course to starboard once more at 1126, to take the shortest route across to the Skagen.

The contact obtained by *Lützow*'s radar was indeed a submarine, HMS/m *Spearfish* (Lieutenant-Commander Forbes), a unit of the 6th Submarine Flotilla, which had sailed on 5 April for a Skagerrak patrol. She was on the surface some 6 miles north of the Skaw (Skagen) when her First Lieutenant sighted the bow wave of a large ship off the starboard quarter. Forbes immediately altered course to port to put the boat stern on to the enemy, which he believed to be the destroyer which had been hunting him earlier. A minute or so later, the enemy was seen to be a heavy warship (thought to be *Admiral Scheer*), whereupon the depth settings on the torpedoes were quickly altered to between 3 and 4 metres, with a speed setting of 40 knots. *Spearfish* stopped both engines to check her swing, so that the DA was not reached before the tubes were ready. Then Forbes fired his full six-tube bow salvo by eye, as it was so dark that to use the night director risked losing sight of the enemy. Immediately after firing, *Spearfish* turned away west at full surfaced speed, getting off an enemy report as she did so. After 5min 8sec running time, Forbes was rewarded by a large explosion.

Lützow was still swinging on starboard rudder when the torpedo struck aft with a heavy shock. The after compartments flooded, as the ship took up a list to port and began to settle by the stern. The rudder had gone, it was impossible to steer by hand, leaving Thiele no alternative but to steer by the propellers. This was only partially successful, as her stern was hanging off just aft of the break of the forecastle. At 0155 an urgent signal was despatched to Gruppe (Ost): 'My position is 0200 Qu 4462. Need immediate tug assistance—*Lützow*'.

The flooding was confined to compartments I to III, with damage control parties fighting to prevent the adjacent compartment flooding too. All eight diesels were serviceable for 24 knots. By 0210 all way was off the ship as compartment IV on the 'tween deck flooded. *Lützow* now stood some ten miles north-east of Skagen, drifting south-west at about 2

knots. Her position was serious as further submarine attacks could be expected and all boats were cleared for launching. The lower decks were cleared except for essential personnel, ammunition was jettisoned by 'B' turret to lighten the ship aft, and light weapons closed up in case of submarine attack. A boat was sent ashore to Skagen to summon assistance and at 0337 Gruppe (Ost) signalled that the torpedo boats *Luchs*, *Seeadler*, *Jaguar*, *Falke*, *Möwe* and *Kondor*, the 17th UJ Flotilla and the 2nd S-Boat Flotilla had been ordered to her aid. An hour later the ship's trim had been improved by transferring oil and she was now upright, although drawing some 12m aft, with the upper deck torpedo tubes under water.

Lützow was now only seven miles off the Skagen, still at the mercy of the elements but at 0505 units of the 17th UJ Flotilla hove into view, followed by ships of the 19th Minesweeper Flotilla. The sea had begun to rise and the wind had freshened to a strong breeze which did not portend well for a towing operation. To assist the helpless cruiser, a dan-layer of the 19th Flotilla came alongside to hold her head to wind, while another minesweeper attempted to pass a tow. A third vessel was secured on her starboard side and their combined efforts propelled *Lützow* at about $4\frac{1}{2}$ knots. By the start of the forenoon watch the wind was gusting to near gale conditions and the ships were working heavily, giving rise to concern that the damaged stern could break away altogether. The auxiliary minesweepers found handling *Lützow* difficult, so the appearance of a Danish tug, *Garm*, in mid-morning was a relief. Many crew members had been taken off to avoid unnecessarily endangering life in case of further submarine attack, but for the rest of the tow the weather was the enemy. *Luchs*, *Seeadler*, *Möwe* and *Kondor* had in any event now arrived to take over A/S duties from the ship's motor boat! Towards midday wind and sea began to abate and the tow continued under clear blue skies. Later in the afternoon the tugs *Wotan* and *Seeteufel* relieved the last auxiliary minesweepers as very slow progress was made down the Kattegat, with *Lützow* grounding on several occasions. Midnight on 11/12 April saw her fast aground off Laeso but she was free again some six hours later. Two more tugs arrived in mid-morning, *Norder* and *Thor* and, despite several submarine alarms, she reached the Great Belt by midnight and Kiel at 2022 on 13 April, when she secured in the Deutsche Werke yard.

Repairs were begun but it would be a long time before she was operational once more and Kpt.z.S. Thiele left the ship for a shore appointment in Norway, as Naval Commander, Trondheim. In the early hours of 9 July *Lützow* was struck by a bomb during an air raid, which penetrated the upper deck abreast 'A' turret on the starboard side before partially exploding in the 'tween deck without great effect. As repair of the torpedo damage would exceed six months, she was formally paid off on 8 August 1940. She re-entered service in 1941 but her assailant, *Spearfish*, was herself torpedoed and sunk by *U34* the week before *Lützow* paid off.

Thus, at the end of 'Weserübung' the Kriegsmarine had both Panzerschiffe in dockyard hands, one in refit, the other in repair, leaving only *Scharnhorst* and *Gneisenau* operational.

12. OPERATION 'JUNO', 1940

The strategic situation in Norway towards the middle of May 1940 was by no means clear. German forces held the south of the country and the important town of Trondheim, but further north things were still very much in the balance. In particular, the naval actions in the fjords around Narvik had led to serious German losses afloat and ashore. British, Polish and French forces were established at Namsos and Harstad, of which the latter was designated as the main base of operations. However, the German attack launched in the West, against Holland and Belgium, now affected matters in Norway, for the seriousness of the situation on the Western Front led to the Allies' decision on 24 May to evacuate Norway, but not before Narvik had been captured and the vital ore terminal destroyed. This town was actually taken on 28 May and demolition began. By the first week of June the Allied evacuation was under way.

The German command, ignorant of the true situation but aware of the pressure on its land forces in the Narvik area, decided to take appropriate action. Accordingly the SKL informed Army Group XXI in Oslo on 25 May that it intended to conduct naval operations in north Norwegian waters designed to relieve pressure on the Narvik forces. The primary targets were enemy naval forces and transports in and around Narvik, Westfjord and adjacent fjords, as well as those off Bodo and Harstad. Detailed objectives would be advised once a clearer picture of enemy dispositions were received. Army Group XXI was requested to supply details of objectives where shore bombardment would be beneficial and whatever other details of enemy forces it could provide. Admiral Raeder intended to use both his battleships as well as *Admiral Hipper* and possibly *Nürnberg* for this operation, in close co-operation with the Luftwaffe forces under Fliegerführer (Trondheim), where their main base would be. Stores, munitions, fuel and flak defences were to be built up at Trondheim for the purpose of their support. The operation was to be launched as soon as *Scharnhorst* and *Gneisenau* had completed their battle training and refit period (about 2 June) and the ships would then sail direct for Norway from the Baltic Sea.

By 31 May the SKL had still not received any information from Army Group XXI which was needed aboard the flagship by 1 June at the latest. It was now known that Harstad was the main enemy base but that was the extent of their knowledge of the Allied dispositions. Belatedly Army Group XXI signalled its requirements to the SKL on 1 June. These were, in essence, the destruction of all transports, including small vessels, in the Narvik, Namsos and Bodo areas but capture of shipping was equally desirable. Roervik was in German hands but any target in the town of Narvik (except the hospital) was worth attack.

Naval Commander (West), Admiral Saalwächter, issued operational orders on 29 May to Commander, Seagoing Forces (West), (Seebefehlshaber West), Admiral Marschall. These orders called for a surprise strike on the first and main objective, Andfjord and Vaagsfjord (i.e., Harstad). Reconnaissance had also indicated worthwhile targets in Ofotfjord. Subsidiary tasks were the covering of supply convoys from Trondheim to Saltdal, Bodo and Mo. These orders had the effect of narrowing Marschall's freedom of action for Admiral Raeder's original task was to relieve General Dietl at Narvik by engagement of British naval forces and transports in the Narvik-Harstad area. A further complication was the Führer's desire that the fleet should also safeguard the movement of the Army's relief force for Narvik then en route by road and fjord from Trondheim. Despite an interview with Raeder, Marschall's orders remained rather woolly in terms of priorities and although the Fleet Commander came away with what he believed to be the objectives of the sorties, these were not precisely what Raeder had in mind. The root cause of the problem was the clumsy chain of command, instituted in 1939, which had a shore-based command interspersed between the SKL and the commander at sea.

The forces assigned to the operation, code-named 'Juno', were *Gneisenau* (flagship), *Scharnhorst* and *Admiral Hipper*, together with the destroyers *Galster*, *Lody*, *Steinbrinck* and *Schoemann*. Co-operating were a number of Luftwaffe units: two Staffeln of reconnaissance aircraft had been sent to Stavanger to give northern cover and a Staffel of Heinkel He 115s sent to Trondheim. Luftflotte V and Fliegerkorps X agreed to give reconnaissance cover north of the latitude of Stavanger and east of 5°E; FdL (W) would give cover west of 5°E. Logistic support included the oilers *Adria* and *Samland* with the repair ship *Huascaran* ordered to Trondheim, as well as the large replenishment ships *Dithmarschen* and *Nordmark*. Turret tops and gun shields were to be painted red lead colour for air identification purposes.

The original date for the commencement of 'Juno' had been 2 July but it was not until the following evening that Admiral Marschall and his staff embarked in *Gneisenau* at Kiel. At 0800 on 4 June Marschall sailed, escorted additionally by the torpedo boats *Jaguar* and *Falke*, as well as FdM (Ost) aboard the fleet escort *F6*. *Sperrbrecher IV* led the formation as a protection against mines. The Skagen boom was cleared at 0630 on 5 June and after midday the two torpedo boats were detached to Wilhelmshaven. Three He 111 aircraft escorted the naval forces under a cloudless sky and despite a light haze the visibility was good. After passing Utsira, visibility deteriorated, giving Kpt.z.S. Netzband the hope that they would remain undetected by the RAF. In fact, no Coastal Command sorties were flown in areas likely to yield sightings of enemy forces at this time. By the early hours of 6 June the German force was to the north-east of the Viking Bank, steaming north at 24 knots. Dawn broke to a rainy day, with only mediocre visibility, as Marschall cleared the Shetland-Bergen narrows. They were still undetected and in fact during this period German code-breakers were reading British signals with considerably more success than vice versa. As evening approached, course was altered to meet the oiler *Dithmarschen*, which hove into view to port at 1925. It took an extremely long time to refuel the destroyers and heavy cruiser, this task not being completed until 1750 on 7 June. In the meantime a number of reconnaissance reports had been received, including one of a seven-ship convoy on a south-westerly course, some 110nm south-east of their position, and another reporting one tanker and accompanying escort vessel about 220nm east. The former group was a most valuable one, comprising three liners and four channel packets—*Oronsay, Ormonde, Andora Star, Royal Ulsterman, Ulster Prince, Ulster Monarch* and *Duchess of York*.

Marschall was obviously in a quandary as to where best to strike, for he took the rather extraordinary step of ordering a captains' conference aboard the flagship at 2030 that evening, to discuss the various intelligence reports received. As far as the shore targets were concerned, Marschall had very little to go on and was reluctant to hazard the fleet in confined waters for dubious reasons. Nothing was known of the actual locations of the Allied bases, other than Harstad, nor were their defences known. Such reports of enemy shipping movements that had been received, seemed to indicate an Allied *withdrawal*, but that seemed hardly possible given their capture of Narvik. Nevertheless, a signal passed to him just as the conference was ending, which indicated the presence of only one warship in Harstad, persuaded him that the Allies had in fact evacuated and that great success could be achieved in attacking the west-bound convoys. The conference broke up at 2215, the ships got under way again and *Dithmarschen* was released.

The next day dawned with cloudy sunshine and good visibility, as the ships formed a reconnaissance line steaming almost due south in line abreast at 10-mile intervals. Marschall signalled his intentions to Saalwächter at 0500: he was going to attack a convoy. The shore command, however, still required an attack on Harstad and told Marschall so in a blunt signal. In the meantime *Admiral Hipper* had sighted a tanker, escorted by one armed trawler. These proved to be the naval oiler *Oil Pioneer* and the naval trawler *Juniper*. While the heavy cruiser disposed of *Juniper*, *Gneisenau*'s secondary armament set the oiler ablaze, which was then sunk by a torpedo from the destroyer *Schoemann*.

While this little action was going on, Admiral Saalwächter ordered Marschall to leave the convoy to the heavy cruiser and proceed with the battleship to Harstad as intended. This Marschall chose to ignore. Resuming search formation once more, *Scharnhorst* and *Hipper* launched their aircraft for reconnaissance. At 0940 the cruiser's Arado reported one heavy cruiser, one destroyer and a minesweeper on a northerly course, which would later turn out to be the German's own forces! Meanwhile the empty transport *Orama* had been intercepted and sunk by *Admiral Hipper* but the hospital ship *Atlantis* was left alone. At 1330 that afternoon the cruiser and destroyers were detached to Trondheim for fuel and the battleships continued on alone. Marschall now signalled his intentions to *Scharnhorst*: he was going north to operate in the Tromsö-Harstad region. Shortly afterwards he concluded that the ships reported by *Hipper*'s aircraft did not exist, so he pressed on northwards, hoping to intercept warships revealed by his B Dienst detachment.

At 1646 a lookout at the foretop of *Scharnhorst* reported smoke bearing 60° and the sighting was passed to the flagship. Twenty-two minutes later *Scharnhorst* gave the range as 40,000 metres. Both ships closed up to action stations and flag ordered immediate notice for full speed. Radar sets were switched on for gunnery ranging as speed was increased to 24 knots. At 1710 *Scharnhorst*'s gunnery officer, F.Kpt. Löwisch, had the enemy ship in sight and reported it as having a single large funnel and probably a flight deck. At the time of first sighting the British ships, *Gneisenau* and *Scharnhorst* were steaming 345° in line ahead with the flagship leading. After altering on to 330° at 1700, Marschall made three alterations to starboard, on to 30° at 1706, 70° at 1712 and finally 150° nine minutes later, in order to close the range on the enemy, who was steering approximately 206°.

Although initially identified as *Ark Royal*, the British ship was in fact *Glorious* (Captain G. D'Oyly-Hughes), escorted by the destroyers *Acasta* (Commander C.E. Glasfurd) and *Ardent* (Lieutenant-Commander J.F. Barker). The aircraft-carrier was returning to Scapa, having landed on ten RAF Gladiators of No. 263 Squadron (N5681, N5695, N5699, N5723, N5725, N5904–5908,) and ten Hurricanes of No. 46 Squadron (L1793, L1804–1806, L1815, L1853, L1961 and L1980) from Bardufoss. She was caught completely by surprise and moreover, for some unexplained reason, had no aircraft aloft nor held in readiness for her own protection, despite having embarked six No. 823 Squadron Swordfish and Sea Gladiators of No. 802 Squadron to do so. Without aircraft with which to launch a strike, the carrier was virtually defenceless, being armed herself only with sixteen 4.7in (12cm) guns, of which only half could engage under the prevailing circumstances. Her destroyer escorts were also armed with 4.7in guns and carried eight torpedoes apiece.

The two German ships worked up to 26 then 29 knots, steaming in echelon with the flagship on *Scharnhorst*'s port quarter. Aboard *Scharnhorst* the gunnery officer, Löwisch, received orders to engage the carrier with his 28cm guns and the southernmost destroyer with his port secondary armament. At 1730 permission was given to open fire, range 14,500m, bearing 120°. The secondary guns fired first, then the heavy guns. *Glorious* made smoke and her destroyers turned to defend her, but the omens were not good for *Scharnhorst*'s third salvo had found the range.

Glorious turned south-east in a vain endeavour to escape while her two destroyers turned to protect her by laying smoke screens. They were taken under fire by the battleships' secondary armament but, handled skilfully, they were at first unharmed. *Ardent* broke out through the smoke to launch a torpedo attack but failed to score a hit as their tracks were seen and avoided. *Gneisenau* now overhauled *Scharnhorst* to lead the attack and the heavy ships' shells soon began to hit the defenceless carrier. The first hit at about 1738 penetrated the thin side of the hangar and exploded among the RAF Hurricanes; the resultant spread of fire prevented the arming of the Swordfish. Further hits on the bridge and island with the Germans' third or fourth salvo killed all on the bridge and adjacent compartments. Further hits aft doomed the carrier and she quickly took a list to starboard, wreathed in smoke but still steaming quite fast. *Scharnhorst* temporarily ceased fire but the flagship continued to shell the hapless carrier. Not until a later hit which struck a boiler room was the carrier's speed seriously reduced, making her a sitting target. At about 1800 *Ardent* again emerged from the smoke screen and fired a second salvo of torpedoes which once again were avoided. Almost immediately she was taken under fire by both ships' secondary guns and was badly hit. The 10.5cm guns had now also joined battle and by 1818 *Ardent* was in a bad way, on fire and listing. At 1822 her mast broke off and she capsized and sank. Torpedoes fired by the destroyers caused considerable manoeuvring by the German ships but as yet had no other effect.

Glorious now burnt even more fiercely and *Scharnhorst* shifted her secondary guns on to *Acasta* but the destroyer was, for the moment, out of range. However, the destroyer doubled back through the smoke and fired four torpedoes at *Scharnhorst* before seeking the protection of the smoke again. *Scharnhorst* was now manoeuvring to keep the two remaining British ships directly ahead, where the torpedo danger was least. The firing of torpedoes by *Acasta* from such an angle therefore took Hoffmann by surprise. The launching of the torpedoes was reported by lookouts in the foretop at 1833, whereupon *Scharnhorst* took avoiding action. However, it would appear that the battleship resumed her original course too soon, for at 1839 a severe shock shook the ship aft. The starboard engine stopped and her speed quickly dropped off. She turned 90° to starboard to close the flagship, while at the same time took the destroyer under fire with her 15cm guns.

Acasta's torpedo had struck *Scharnhorst* on the starboard side aft, close to 'C' turret, causing extensive flooding. 'C' turret itself had to be evacuated as smoke poured into the structure and the damage control officer ordered the after magazines and shell rooms flooded as a precaution. The Chief Engineer reported loud noises in the main thrust bearing of No. 3 (starboard) turbine and the ship's speed fell away. In compartments III and IV, the area of the hit, store rooms, magazines and fuel bunkers were flooded on the lower platform deck and the ship took on a list to starboard. No. 1 (centre) turbine room was flooding badly with water and fuel oil from ruptured bunkers and at 1905 the centre turbine stopped. In the starboard turbine room water was flooding

through from the main coupling room, but the engine still ran at 180rpm. The Chief Engineer ordered the centre turbine uncoupled and pumped oil fuel to correct the list. Meanwhile two boilers in No. 1 boiler room were shut down and the water level in the centre turbine room had reached the telephone on the bulkhead. As yet the bilge pumps were having little effect, but after ten minutes the level stabilized and began to fall. No.1 generator room was without steam. The Chief Engineer reported that maximum speed was 26 knots, 20 approximately if the bent shaft on the starboard turbine forced him to close it down as well. This state of affairs was in fact reached at 2029 and speed dropped accordingly. Attempts to re-couple the starboard shaft came to nothing as it finally seized just before midnight. Approximately 2,500 cubic metres of water were flooding various parts of the after section, causing *Scharnhorst* to trim 3m down by the stern, but counter pumping measures had reduced the list to about 1° to starboard.

Acasta, by now badly hit, still managed to engage her large adversary, obtaining one hit on the right-hand gun of *Scharnhorst*'s 'B' turret. This was to be her last effort and the destroyer sank shortly afterwards. In the course of the action *Scharnhorst* alone expended 212 main battery ammunition and 842 rounds of 15cm. The flagship fired 175 rounds of 28cm and 306 rounds of 15cm.

There were few survivors from the British ships. Just how did *Glorious* come to be in such a predicament, detached with only two destroyers for escort? The full reason for this state of affairs was never made public, despite questions being raised in the House by MPs both during and after the war. In fact, all was not well with *Glorious* for there were serious personal problems aboard her which had culminated in her Commander (Flying), J.B. Heath, being put ashore at Scapa to await court martial following disagreements with Captain D'Oyly-Hughes, prior to her last deployment to Norway. It would appear that the carrier's commanding officer had lost confidence in some of his officers and they in him, to the consequent detriment of morale. According to one witness, the reason that the ship sailed alone with out heavy escort was a request by D'Oyly-Hughes to Vice-Admiral Wells (Flag Officer Aircraft-Carriers) to be allowed to proceed to Scapa for the purpose of the forthcoming court martial. The usually given excuse of fuel shortage seems to have been a red herring. Nevertheless, to allow such a valuable ship to sail so poorly escorted on this flimsy basis is difficult to comprehend.

Be that as it may, the ship was not incapable of operating aircraft. It has been suggested that the flight deck was crowded with RAF machines, but these were in fact stowed below in the hangar. Actually, one Swordfish and three Sea Gladiators were at ten minutes' notice but not ranged on deck. It was the former and one other which the Germans saw being frantically brought up on deck at the start of the action, and these two aircraft were destroyed almost immediately by shell fire. At the time of first sighting of the German ships—when and by whom is not known because there was no lookout posted in the crow's-nest—the order

Above: *Scharnhorst* in action against *Glorious*. (USN)

Even had an earlier warning been available, false reports of German forces making for Iceland had led to *Repulse* and *Renown* being drawn off in that direction, leaving only *Valiant* to escort the evacuation convoys and she was too slow to catch the enemy battleships. Reconnaissance aircraft from RAF Coastal Command had given no warning of the fact that two German ships were loose in the North Sea and in fact this command had not even been officially informed of the evacuation. Consequently no special patrols were flown.

From the sunken carrier and destroyers, a Norwegian merchantman, *Borgund*, rescued three officers 35 ratings from *Glorious* and one rating from *Acasta* on 11 April. Five more from *Glorious* were rescued by another Norwegian ship and put ashore in Norway, where they were made prisoners, together with two men from *Ardent*, rescued from a German floatplane.

Admiral Marschall was now in a tricky situation and needed to regain a safe harbour as soon as possible. His worries showed in the constant signals to *Scharnhorst* requesting situation reports, damage repair progress and forecasts of repair durations. Two Petty Officers and 46 men had been killed by the torpedo hit and another three wounded. Hoffmann had to report that the centre turbine room was flooded with oil and water, with the auxiliaries submerged. Although it was being pumped out, he was unable to say when this would be finished. In any event, both cruising and intermediate turbines had been under water and the danger of any sea-water being left in them on the admission of HP steam was apparent. By midnight the starboard shaft could be tried again but because of loud noises was uncoupled again. Marschall was by now somewhat more reassured that he did not have a huge search operation for him launched by the Royal Navy for the B Dienst reported astonishingly little British radio traffic. The reasons for this have been discussed above. By 0950 the destroyers *Lody*, *Schoemann* and *Galster* had arrived to screen the heavy ships and, after passing down the Frohavet, the squadron reached Trondheim by the afternoon.

Scharnhorst anchored east of Munkenholmen in Trondheimsfjord and lay with three hours' notice on the port engine. A Blenheim of No. 254 Squadron, RAF, had, however, already reported her presence. While a conference was held with the port naval authorities and the staff of the repair ship *Huascaran*, divers investigated the size of the hole in the ship. It proved to measure 12m × 4m. By the following day it had become clear to Marschall that the Allies were in fact evacuating Norway and with no time to lose, he ordered a strike against the enemy shipping traffic. Accordingly, he sailed with *Gneisenau*, *Admiral Hipper* and the destroyers *Lody*, *Galster*, *Schoemann* and *Steinbrinck* at 0902 that morning. In the early afternoon the squadron had cleared the Frohavet and worked up to 27 knots.

Later in the afternoon, after the air escort had left, a surfaced submarine was seen by *Admiral Hipper* off her port quarter. It was obvious that their departure was now compromised but to compound the problem, they were also warned of enemy heavy forces operating on the convoy

was piped to range five Swordfish, but there were only three fitted with torpedo racks and of these only two reached the flight deck. *Glorious* had been caught out in a most reprehensible manner. She had been at cruising stations, steaming at 17 knots, had no aircraft aloft and the hands were at tea; in the words of one RAF survivor, almost a holiday atmosphere prevailed. Under the circumstances, it was probably as well that her captain perished, but the loss of almost all her officers left the unfortunate Commander Heath with all his detractors and supporters dead.

Glorious did attempt to radio a warning of her predicament but not until over 20 minutes after being struck by the first shell. This signal, however, was timed much earlier (1715 German time); why it was only being transmitted at 1752 is difficult to explain. The signal itself, fragmented and corrupt, was not received by any British ship and *Glorious* did not attempt to signal again until 1819. At this time she tried to signal Flag Officer (Aircraft-Carriers) but was jammed by *Gneisenau*'s B Dienst detachment. However, this signal, referring to her earlier report, was just picked up at very low strength by only one ship, the heavy cruiser *Devonshire*.

Devonshire, flagship of the 1st Cruiser Squadron (Rear Admiral J.D.H. Cunningham) stood only about 100 miles north of the carrier when she was first attacked. Unfortunately, this cruiser was on a special mission—the transport of the King of Norway from Tromso to Britain and in view of this, Admiral Cunningham decided to maintain radio silence. Not until the morning of 9 April, when the hospital ship *Atlantis* fell in with *Valiant*, did the presence of the two German battleships become known and Admiral Cunningham then reported receipt of *Glorious*'s signal. German communiques that afternoon confirmed the unpleasant facts to Admiral Forbes, C-in-C Home Fleet.

This late intelligence destroyed any chance that the Home Fleet would be able to avenge *Glorious*, despite the sailing of *Rodney* and *Renown* from Scapa Flow on the 9th—by this time the German battleships were already safe in Trondheim.

Above: The torpedo damage to *Gneisenau*, partially covered by a makeshift patch. (Bundesarchiv)

heavy ships' aircraft. By 1127 they were safely anchored off Trondheim, although they had been sighted once more by *Clyde* as they entered the Frohavet.

RAF reconnaissance flights over the port were stepped up beginning on 11 June, the day *Gneisenau* returned, mostly undertaken by No. 254 Squadron's Blenheims. A bomber strike of twelve Hudsons of No. 269 Squadron was immediately launched from Sumburgh, attacking the ships from the south with 36 250lb SAP bombs between 1523 and 1550hrs. Despite claims of hits, none of the ships was damaged but many bombs fell close to *Admiral Hipper*. Two aircraft were shot down (P5131 and N7361). The reconnaissance flight on 12 June again confirmed the presence of *Scharnhorst* but the other ships were misidentified as two cruisers and four destroyers and the following day's flight was aborted due to engine trouble.

Armed with the RAF's reconnaissance reports concerning the warships at Trondheim, Admiral Forbes (C-in-C Home Fleet) detached *Ark Royal* to launch an air strike against them. Embarked were two fighter squadrons, Nos. 800 and 803, equipped with twelve and eleven respectively Blackburn Skua II fighter/dive-bombers. Also embarked were 21 Swordfish of Nos. 810 and 820 Squadrons. In the early hours of 13 June the carrier flew off fifteen Skuas for a dive-bombing attack from a position 64°58′N. 04°38′E, each armed with one 500lb SAP bomb. Fifteen aircraft was the maximum that could be ranged under the light wind conditions and there were only that number of pilots experienced in dive-bombing. The choice of a dive-bombing attack was probably made because of the success against *Königsberg*, the failure of torpedoes in an earlier Trondheim attack (11 April) and the dive-bomber mentality of the period. This strike would be co-ordinated with an RAF attack on the airfield at Vaernes, on the northern side of the fjord, which would keep down the fighter opposition. Taking part in this attack were four Beauforts of No. 42 Squadron (L4489 was lost) and Blenheims.

By a stroke of bad luck the Beauforts flew over the light cruiser *Nürnberg* (also bound for Trondheim) east of Grip light and the resultant enemy report was received aboard *Scharnhorst* at 0234. The ships were thus in a state of alert by the time that the Skuas arrived and there were already four Bf 109s and a similar number of Bf 110s aloft. The strike force comprised six from No. 800 Squadron (Captain R.J. Partridge, RM), '6A', '6C', '6F', '6G', '6H' and '6K' and nine from No. 803 Squadron (Lieutenant-Commander J.Casson, RN), '7A', '7B', '7C', '7F', '7G', '7L', '7P', '7Q' and '7R'. Two more No. 803 machines ('7K' and '7M') were launched later as fighter cover for the fleet. The strike force climbed to 11,000ft and made landfall at 0123 north of Halten lighthouse. Crossing the coast, the Skuas flew inland for ten minutes before turning south for an approach at 10,000ft. Just before reaching the target area, No. 803 Squadron formed line ahead and No. 800 broke away for a separate attack. Most aircraft attacked *Scharnhorst* from stern to bow but Lieutenant-Commander Casson took some of his squadron around to attack from the opposite direction and the extra

routes. As a result, Gruppe (West) ordered Marschall to abandon the sortie and he turned east at 2010. The submarine was in fact *Clyde* (Lieutenant-Commander Ingram) which reported the ships as one pocket battleship and one cruiser. *Clyde* had sailed on patrol 'PO2M' from Rosyth on 4 June and while off Bjornsund on 9 June was ordered by Vice-Admiral (S/M) to proceed to the Frohavet. The German ships were too distant for a torpedo attack, but *Clyde* attempted to maintain contact on the surface at full speed, although she was unable to do so. On receipt of this report, RAF Coastal Command flew off a Sunderland of No. 204 Squadron at 1600 (British Time) with orders to search an area 15 miles either side of the reported track, between the estimated positions at 1800 and 2400hrs. However, because of the abandonment of the sortie, no sightings were of course made. At 0030 on 11 June the German force turned south to re-enter the Frohavet, escorted by two Arados from Trondheim and both

time exposed to the flak and fighters cost them dearly. Only two aircraft survived from this group. The aircraft which stayed low after bombing and used the cover of the ground mist generally escaped, but those which climbed were hit by the Bf 109s (the Bf 110s tended to hold off). Altogether, four Skuas from each squadron were lost ('6A'/L2995, '6F'/L3000, '6G', '6H', '7A', '7F', '7L' and '7Q', three of which were L2992, L2955, and L3047), including both squadron COs. By 0345 the seven survivors had landed back on *Ark Royal*. Their losses were a grievous blow to the Fleet Air Arm. The attack itself was a failure and although Admiral Wells (V.A. Aircraft-Carriers) considered two hits achieved—by aircraft '6A' and '6K'—in fact only one bomb hit and that failed to explode.

Apart from reconnaissance over-flights by the RAF, the next few days proved uneventful, except that the Arado Ar 196 catapult flights were kept busy on A/S patrols in the approaches to Trondheim. One of *Gneisenau*'s aircraft surprised a submarine on the surface, probably *Clyde*, just after midnight on 16 June and bombed it, but despite claims of a sinking the submarine escaped. A similar erroneous claim was made on 19 June off the Halten Bank.

Aboard *Scharnhorst* the engineers were endeavouring to repair the centre turbine but damage to the cruising turbine thwarted this and a specialist engineer had to be called out from Germany to uncouple it. The hole in the side was patched up and on 18 June the ship moved out into the fjord for engine trials. Above 13 knots the starboard shaft vibrated very badly and finally seized but the centre engine was found good for 15 knots. Further trials the next day resulted in the centre turbine being cleared for 24 knots. The results of the trials were communicated to the Flag and orders issued to oil from *Friedrich Brehme*, preparatory to returning to Germany for full repairs. On 20 June *Scharnhorst* sailed for home, accompanied by *Gneisenau*, *Admiral Hipper*, *Galster* and escorted herself by *Lody*, *Schoemann*, *Steinbrinck*, *Greif* and *Kondor*, together with three sweepers from the 1st Minesweeper Flotilla. *Gneisenau*'s group was intended to attack the British cruiser patrol line south-east of Iceland and act as a diversionary force to cover the crippled *Scharnhorst*'s withdrawal to the south.

Their departure went unobserved by the British, but radio traffic associated with the movement of another German warship, *Nürnberg*, was to have an effect on the battleship's movements. *Clyde*, still on patrol, had been alerted by C-in-C (Rosyth) on 18 June that a cruiser and four destroyers had left Narvik proceeding south, so Ingram positioned his boat to intercept them, should they be bound for Trondheim. This force actually comprised *Nürnberg* (K.Ad. Schmundt), the destroyer *Steinbrinck* and four ships of the 2nd Minesweeper Flotilla (*M9*, *M10*, *M12* and *M13*), returning from transporting troops and equipment of the 3rd Mountain Division northwards (Operation 'Nora'). Thus *Clyde* was now patrolling north of Kya lighthouse. It was also believed that the ships in Trondheim might attempt to break out south and three Hudsons flew reconnaissance sorties between 62°N and Lister on 18 June to meet that eventuality.

While *Scharnhorst* and her escort steamed south via Trondheimslead, Yttrefjord and Gripholmen, the flagship struck northwards and into the path of *Clyde*. This boat, one of three *Thames*-class fleet submarines completed in the mid-1930s, was armed with six bow and two stern tubes for 21in torpedoes. Ingram first sighted the enemy at 2209 on 20 June, identifying them as two capital ships and one destroyer to the south-east, range 8 miles. He immediately started an attack in rough seas and low visibility, reaching a suitable firing position some 23 minutes after first sighting. After launching his full bow salvo, at a range of 4,000 yards, Ingram went deep and altered course 60° to make his escape. Three minutes after firing, a single loud explosion was heard. The counter-attack was desultory, only about eight depth-charges being dropped, moderately close, and *Clyde* was able to get away to the west.

Gneisenau's lookouts saw the torpedo tracks far too late, only 300 metres to starboard, so that despite an emergency turn to port being ordered, one torpedo struck before the rudders began to have any effect. Two other torpedoes were seen crossing her bows. The 365kg of Torpex contained in the MkVIII** torpedo exploded with surprisingly little shock, on the starboard side close to the anchor, throwing up a column of water. The ship completed its turn to starboard with only a slight loss of speed. Visible damage was limited but the shell plating had been ripped off on the port bow opposite. Because Ingram had over-estimated *Gneisenau*'s speed and taken his point of aim ahead of the ship instead of the accepted centre, his salvo had all but missed and the damage to the battleship was limited to the mess decks forward of bulkhead 185.7. Damage control parties shored up this bulkhead while the squadron turned back towards Trondheim. Making 19 knots, the damaged ship re-entered the Schären and reached Trondheim in the forenoon of 21 June.

Divers were sent down to survey the damage and reported compartments XX and XXI completely flooded. Bulkheads and shell plating had been damaged and a number of cracks in the hull started. Once again the services of *Huascaran* were required and she came alongside on the afternoon of 25 June. Under the supervision of senior constructor Ohlerich, repairs continued until 19 July.

Meanwhile *Scharnhorst* had continued her passage home but *Clyde*'s attack report caused the RAF to fly off a Sunderland of No. 18 Group to search for *Gneisenau* and three Hudsons to patrol between 62°N and Lister as previously. At 1204 on 21 June the most northerly Hudson sighted *Scharnhorst* and her escort at 61.00N, 04.14E (i.e., off Sognefjord) and shadowed for an hour. Her sighting report was picked up, decrypted and flashed to *Scharnhorst* by Gruppe (West) at 1308. She was relieved by a Sunderland of No. 204 Squadron, which shadowed tenaciously and cunningly. Kpt.z.S. Hoffmann could only await the inevitable British air attacks and was further worried by another signal from Gruppe (West) warning him of the presence of the submarine *Severn* to the south, en route for Utsira. All ships and shore stations in Norway were warned to expect heavy air attacks. The shadowing Sunderland was eventually driven off by the combined efforts of the ship's Arado ('T3 + FM'—which tried to dive-bomb the flying-boat but lost its engine cowling instead) and Bf 109s of the air escort, one of which was shot down by the Sunderland.

The first of the expected attacks materialized at 1604 when *Steinbrinck* sighted six aircraft attacking from the port side. These were Swordfish from Nos. 821 and 823 Squadrons, FAA, based at Hatston in the Orkneys. Unfortunately they had had no recent torpedo training and this was the first such attack on a capital ship at sea. They were met by an intense barrage of flak but managed to launch their torpedoes. These were delivered in parallel tracks, with the result that *Scharnhorst* easily evaded them, while at the same time two aircraft were shot down, one by *Kondor*. Hardly had this attack died away than four Hudsons from Nos. 224 and 233 Squadrons made a high-level bombing attack with 500lb SAP bombs. Once again no hits were achieved and two of the attackers were shot down (N7246 and N7359), the other pair escaping badly damaged.

The next attempt was made by nine Beauforts of No. 42 Squadron based at Thorney Island but on detachment to Wick. This aircraft was a new type, only recently introduced into service, and although designed for the torpedo-bomber role, it was armed with bombs for its operational debut. Each aircraft carried two 500lb SAP bombs. They attacked from the port or landward side in a steep diving attack. *Scharnhorst* was forced to take violent evasive action and successfully avoided all the bombs. Flak and the defending fighters shot down three of the attackers (L4486, L4501 and L9810). It was not a very auspicious baptism of fire for the Beaufort, especially as there is reason to believe that they had been armed in error with instantaneous fused GP and not SAP bombs. If this were true, then their attack was in vain for a 500lb GP bomb could have done little harm to the battleship.

Finally, at 1749 while off Karmoy, six Hudsons of No. 269 Squadron from Wick made a high-level attack, the accuracy of which was disrupted by defensive fire and fighters. By 1805 the German air umbrella comprised ten Bf 109 fighters, two He 111s, one Do 18 flying-boat and two Ar 196s. Hoffmann considered that the air attacks were now over, but the presence of the shadower was disturbing and he was at a loss to understand why the defending fighters did not shoot it down. *Scharnhorst* anchored off Dusavik at 2207 that night and did not continue south until 0400 the following day. The thick, low cloud base was helpful to the operation but because of reports of enemy naval forces, *Scharnhorst* was not allowed to proceed to sea until released by Gruppe (West) at 0845. No further incidents occurred, the Skagen boom being cleared at 1850 and Kiel reached at 2226 on 23 June.

The day after her arrival *Scharnhorst* moved into floating dock 'C' and repairs began on the starboard shaft and No.1 turbine room. Her presence had become known in England and soon attracted the attentions of the RAF. On the night of 1/2 July five Whitleys of No. 58 Squadron (armed for the first time with 2,000lb bombs) and Hampdens of No. 83 Squadron bombed the port. *Scharnhorst* was not hit but *Prinz Eugen*, then fitting out at the Germania yard, was damaged.

One aircraft (N1461) was shot down. In a later raid by eight Whitleys on 8/9 July, *Lützow* was hit but once again *Scharnhorst* escaped damage. One aircraft from No. 10 Squadron (N1496) was lost.

Because of complications with the starboard shaft, the ship did not finish repairs until 21 November, when she sailed for Gotenhafen for trials and training. After her return to Kiel on 19 December, she was put into floating dock 'B' until 23 December for further repairs.

To return to *Gneisenau* once more, this ship was given makeshift repairs by *Huascaran* in Trondheim, where the RAF attempted to keep a close watch on her. In this they were only partly successful for the port was heavily defended and about eighteen aircraft were lost in June on this task, the brunt of which was borne by No. 254 Squadron's Blenheims. *Gneisenau* ran trials in the fjord on 20 July, this fact being reported to the Admiralty by an agent. In view of her possible imminent return to Germany, No. 18 Group, Coastal Command, despatched a Sunderland of No. 204 Squadron the next day to reconnoitre the port but because of the previous heavy losses, this type of aircraft was hardly suitable and it (N9028) was shot down by fighters. Another No. 204 Squadron aircraft was ordered to patrol off the Faeroes in case *Gneisenau* was attempting to break out of the North Sea. Further reconnaissance of Trondheim on 22 and 24 July by Blenheims of No. 248 Squadron gave no indication of the battleship's impending move, nor had her change of berth been noticed. She was now anchored at Levanger at the eastern end of the fjord.

On 25 July in the early afternoon she sailed to join Flag Officer (Reconnaissance Forces) aboard *Nürnberg* with *Admiral Hipper* and the destroyers *Lody*, *Galster*, *Jacobi* and *Ihn* off Agdenes. At midnight the heavy cruiser was detached for an operation in northern waters and the rest of the squadron continued for Germany. The B Dienst detachment reported little British radio traffic, so Kpt.z.S. Fein concluded that their departure had gone unnoticed, as indeed it had. No reconnaissance flights had been made to Trondheim on 25 June nor the following day, but on 27 June a Blenheim penetrated the area to report the presence of one battlecruiser (sic) and three small cruisers or destroyers. Actually all were merchant ships, as by this time *Gneisenau* was well on her way home. The result of this misidentification was that serious counter-measures were not launched by the British. In fact, the only untoward incident was the torpedoing of one of the escorting torpedo boats, *Luchs*, by the submarine *Thames*, which was lost before it could make a sighting report. Thus *Gneisenau* reached Kiel unmolested on 28 June.

The ship now required some three months' repair and refit, which caused problems of yard and man-power capacity because of the work being done on her sister ship. To shorten the dockyard period, it was decided not to rebuild the mast and hangar as had been done in *Scharnhorst*. She lay in Dock B at the naval yard until 21 October. On 14 November *Gneisenau* sailed for the eastern Baltic where she was engaged upon trials and training before returning to Kiel once more on 19 December.

13. OCEAN RAIDING, 1940–1941

By the spring of 1940 *Admiral Scheer* was reaching the end of her long refit and rebuilding at Wilhelmshaven Navy Yard. During the last week of April her 28cm guns were re-shipped and the masts re-stepped, but it was not until the beginning of July that her ship's company could begin to return aboard from the accommodation ship *Monte Pascoal*. Preliminary yard trials were carried out in the Jade on 20 July and a week later, Kpt.z.S. Krancke could report his vessel ready for sea once more. After such a refit, the crew badly needed training and the ship itself had yet to carry out full post-refit trials. Thus when *Admiral Scheer* did put to sea, it was eastwards to the Baltic training grounds, arriving in Swinemünde on 1 August. After various trials, including runs on the Pillau Mile (25.9 knots), minor repairs and adjustments, the ship started a series of work-up exercises with the replenishment ship *Nordmark*, with which she was to operate in the Atlantic. Towards the end of October *Admiral Scheer* was provisioned, stored and equipped for her raiding cruise and on 23 October lay at Gotenhafen fully prepared to sail.

Preparations to support the ship's break-out, her maintenance and supply on the high seas were already in train. Two weather ships were to be sailed for Jan Mayen island, carrying fuel for the He 115 reconnaissance seaplanes of 3/Kü. Fl.Gr. 506 in order to cover the approaches to the Denmark Straits, and the two oilers *Nordmark* and *Dithmarschen* were scheduled to sail two days before and 6–8 days respectively after the heavy cruiser. *Dithmarschen*, however, was only a reserve and would not sail unless *Nordmark* became unavailable. The two weather ships *Homann* and *Freese* sailed on 19 October and *Nordmark* (K.Kpt. Grau) the following day. The heavy cruiser herself sailed in the forenoon of 24 October and was joined off Gjedser by her escort, *Sperrbrecher 8*. Passing through the Great Belts, she anchored that evening off Seelandsrev and was joined by three ships of the 2nd Torpedo-boat Flotilla, led by *T10*.

Admiral Carls at Gruppe (Nord) and Krancke himself were both apprehensive about premature discovery of their mission by the British. A Petty Officer of the 2nd Torpedo-boat Flotilla had already reported it known among the civilian population of Aarhus that *Scheer* was due out on a cruise, and now reports from Luftwaffe aircraft, the submarine *U48* and B Dienst intercepts showed greatly increased enemy activity in the central and northern North Sea. Everything had been done to camouflage the departure from Gotenhafen of both the heavy cruiser and *Nordmark*, but a passage via the Belts was always open to agents' reports. Added to this, at least two British submarines were reported off the entrance to the Skagerrak. Finally, to cap it all, the weather remained disturbingly clear. However, weather forecasts for the southern North Sea for 27 October showed a welcome reduction in expected visibility and at 2218 Admiral Carls ordered *Admiral Scheer* to reverse course and make for Brunsbüttel, from whence the ship could take passage north through the German Bight. The delays caused by the unsuitable weather and the possibility of the operation being compromised meant that *Admiral Scheer* did not leave Brunsbüttel until just after 1100 on 27 October, escorted by *Sperrbrecher 12* with the 2nd Torpedo-boat Flotilla joining off Cuxhaven.

In point of fact, the British Admiralty did not suspect the possibility of a break-out by *Admiral Scheer*, but as early as 20 October analysis of radio traffic was consistent with the movement of shipping from the Skagerrak to Bergen or Stavanger and as a result a reconnaissance was requested between the Elbe and Lister light. By 23 October the indications were that a considerable movement of shipping was in train from Norway to the Skagerrak and it was also believed that a major naval unit was at Trondheim. Reconnaissance flights revealed only a little merchant shipping however. The radio traffic had died down by 24 October and no major movements were then anticipated. RAF Coastal Command patrols over the North Sea were still, at this time, primarily of an anti-invasion nature and not suitable for the detection of single ships attempting to break out into the Atlantic. No reconnaissance or bomber sorties were made to Kiel or Wilhelmshaven during the period of *Scheer*'s presence there and her sailing was not therefore noticed. The delay to her sailing actually eliminated, by chance, the only possibility of her detection because otherwise an aircraft on a sortie over Sogne Fjord on 27 October might well have seen her. When she did in fact sail, the closest any aircraft got to her was Hudson T/220 (aircraft 'T' of No. 220 Squadron) on the afternoon of 27 October, which missed her by three hours. No night patrols were flown, so the ship was able to sail the North Sea under cover of darkness.

Admiral Scheer reached Stavanger during the forenoon of 28 October and anchored in Dusavik Bay. There she lay all day until weighing at 1730 that evening. She remained undetected by the five aircraft from No. 269 Squadron which flew North Sea patrols at that time and, after detaching the torpedo boats to Bergen in the early hours of 29 October, steered generally northwards. By mid-morning she was parallel with Trondheim, steaming northwards in good visibility, beyond the range of the usual reconnaissance patrols. No special RAF reconnaissance patrols had been flown north of Trondheim as there had been no indications of enemy movements in that direction. *Admiral Scheer* was thus able to reach Arctic waters undetected. At noon on 30 October she altered course to 350°, when midway between Jan Mayen island and the north-east tip of Iceland. Throughout the day the wind, initially west-south-west Force 4, had backed and increased in strength until by late evening it had risen to hurricane force, with a correspondingly heavy sea. Visibility dropped to only $\frac{1}{2}$ mile and ice began to accumulate on the ship. Two men were lost overboard while attempting to secure some equipment on one of the 2cm guns—there was no possibility of their rescue. In such high seas the launching of a boat was impossible and the water temperature was −1°C.

The bad weather continued throughout the following day with only slight improvement. This successfully hid the ship's passage through the Denmark Straits from the only aircraft in Iceland, which were grounded by the weather. At this period the sole forces possessed by the RAF here were six Battles of No. 98 Squadron at Kaldadarnes for army co-operation duties. There was no system of patrols over the Denmark Straits. Apart from these aircraft, the Fleet Air Arm had a flight of Walrus at Reykjavik (No. 701 Squadron). By noon on 1 November *Admiral Scheer* had reached the Atlantic and was steaming south for the convoy routes.

Krancke now intended making for 53°N, 35°W and from there, striking at the assumed routes of the 'HX' convoys; this point was chosen as being equidistant from Canadian bases and the limit of escort forces range in the east. The seas, while abated now, still remained too high to operate aircraft, which reduced *Admiral Scheer*'s search range considerably, since the precise paths of the convoys were not known. It was not until the forenoon of 3 November that a ship was sighted, later identified as a tanker sailing independently; but because his orders specified that he should not compromise his presence before a convoy was attacked, Krancke left her alone. Another independent was sighted the next afternoon and similarly avoided, but it confirmed Krancke's belief that he was in the correct position.

Early on 5 November visibility was very good and seas slight. During the morning watch a shadow was sighted in the darkness, which was once again taken to be a westbound independent. The weather was now good enough for the Arado ('T3 + BH') to be employed and at 0940 it was catapulted off, returning some three and a half hours later. The aircraft captain, Ob.Lt.z.S. Pietsch, reported eight ships in convoy on an eastern course, escort not seen. The position of this convoy was some 90 miles from *Admiral Scheer*. Krancke now considered whether to make an attack on this convoy that evening or to hold contact and shadow for a dawn attack. He decided to opt for the former course and headed for the convoy. About an hour before the expected confrontation with the convoy, actually at 1427, lookouts reported smoke. This turned out to be a two-masted, single-funnel steamer sailing independently. *Admiral Scheer* could not avoid this merchantman because of the convoy to the east and was therefore forced to attack it. With her guns trained on the steamer, she flashed her to stop and ordered her to put out a boat with the ship's papers. She turned out to be the 5,389grt *Mopan* owned by Elders & Fyffes of Liverpool. After her

crew had taken to the boats, Krancke sank the banana carrier with a 10.5cm shell in the waterline. In the meantime, the mast heads of the convoy had become visible to the south, the interception of *Mopan* having cost much valuable time. Krancke had planned his approach to the convoy so that it would be difficult for it to take avoiding action and, moreover, it would be between him and the setting sun. Also the wind direction was such that it would not assist the British in laying a smoke screen. Any auxiliary cruiser could be expected to be at the head of the convoy.

The convoy was actually HX84 of 37 ships bound for England, under the escort of the auxiliary cruiser *Jervis Bay* (Captain E.S.F. Fegan). Armed with eight 6in guns, the 14,164grt ex-liner was one of 56 ex-passenger liners taken into service by the Royal Navy during 1939/40 and given 6in gun armaments for use on the Northern patrol and as convoy escorts. At best, they were morale-boosting substitutes for unavailable cruisers; at worst, death traps for their crews. Large slab-sided unarmoured vessels, they presented perfect targets for submarines and were completely outgunned by regular German surface raiders. Already *Rawalpindi* had fallen victim to *Scharnhorst* and *Gneisenau*; while seven others (*Andania, Carinthia, Dunvegan Castle, Laurentia, Patroclus, Scotstoun* and *Transylvania*) had been torpedoed by U-boats. Nevertheless, at this stage of the war, a solitary auxiliary cruiser was the most many convoys could hope for in the way of an escort.

As soon as the British ship realized that the convoy was threatened, she hauled out of line towards the enemy and ordered the convoy to disperse, requesting that the approaching warship identify herself. At 1640 Krancke did so by altering course to allow both his 28cm turrets to bear and opening fire. *Jervis Bay*'s reply was weak and short. *Admiral Scheer* now opened fire with her 15cm guns on two other targets, one the 8,073-ton tanker *San Demetrio* and the other, *Andalusian* (3,082 tons), both of which were damaged. *Jervis Bay* was no match for the German warship but her main aim was to give ships of the convoy time to scatter and thus make it more difficult for the raider to find them as darkness fell. Captain Fegan knew that there was only one possible outcome of the action—the fate of *Rawalpindi* was known only too well—but he did not hesitate to confront *Admiral Scheer*. *Jervis Bay* was soon shelled to a blazing wreck but her sacrifice enabled most of her charges to escape. Leaving the sinking AMC, the German ship went after the main target, the merchantmen, but because of the enforced delay most of the convoy escaped. After a confused action *Scheer* had sunk five ships: *Trewellard*, (5,201t) *Fresno City*, (4,995t) *Kenbane Head*, (5,225t) *Beaverford* (10,042t) and *Maidan* (7,908t).

Admiral Scheer had by now expended about half of her 15cm outfit and a good deal of 28cm. The action was bound to stir up a hornet's nest and Krancke was worried about interception by the Royal Navy, for he could not expect to be able to re-ammunition for at least seven days, until he met *Nordmark*. Accordingly he withdrew west and $\frac{3}{4}$ hour later came across another merchant vessel in the darkness and

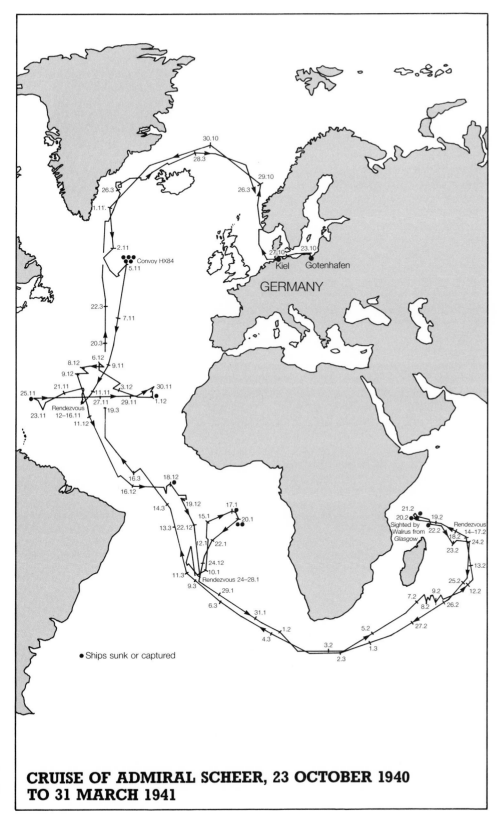

**CRUISE OF ADMIRAL SCHEER, 23 OCTOBER 1940
TO 31 MARCH 1941**

engaged her in passing. In rising seas *Admiral Scheer* steamed away south-east, to gain sea room to the south during the night, informing the SKL by radio of the success as she did so. Krancke intended now to lose himself in the wide reaches of the ocean and keep the enemy guessing, while waiting for *Nordmark* to arrive at rendezvous 'Zander' on 16 November at the earliest.

On receipt of *Jervis Bay*'s reports at the Admiralty, a search was launched for the raider and the following two 'HX' convoys were recalled to the Canadian seaboard. Admiral Forbes considered that the raider was either on a short cruise, in which case his Home Fleet could be disposed to stop her return via the Denmark Straits or if she was bound for western France. If, however, the German ship was on a prolonged cruise, his command could not assist. Nevertheless, he despatched the battleships *Nelson* and *Rodney* to the Iceland-Faeroes passage and *Hood* with *Repulse* to the approaches to western France. However, the Admiralty altered these dispositions but, as we have seen, *Scheer* was escaping south. The net result of the Panzerschiff's appearance on the convoy route was therefore considerable disruption of traffic and warship movements. Not until 17 November was the convoy cycle re-started.

Admiral Scheer steamed generally southwards until arriving at the rendezvous area on 12 November when, just after midday, the tanker *Eurofeld* hove into sight. Her captain came aboard and exchanged information, while Krancke passed over reports for *Nordmark* and a letter for *Schiff 10*, the merchant raider *Thor*, advising her captain of *Scheer*'s intentions. On 16 November the long-awaited *Nordmark* arrived and over the next few days the Panzerschiff re-ammunitioned, oiled and provisioned. *Eurofeld* was, in fact, a merchant ship caught out of home waters on the outbreak of war and for 70 days had been a fugitive from the Royal Navy. Under the circumstances her crew had done a magnificent job.

Krancke now decided to operate on the Antilles-Azores route for a fortnight. There his presence might be unexpected and there was the chance of valuable tanker traffic. If, on the other hand, little success was achieved, he would move east and concentrate on the Cape Verde-UK routes. On the afternoon of 20 November, however, he was ordered by the SKL to operate south of 42°N, to 20°W, an area not considered by Krancke, because it was the operating zone for Italian submarines based on Bordeaux. Instead, he followed his original intention and moved west. Just before noon on 24 November an independently routed ship was sighted and closed, but the quarry was alert and got off a raider 'RRRR' signal, followed shortly after by 'Suspicious ship following me'. *Scheer* ordered the merchantman to heave to under threat of opening fire, then fired a shot across her bows. This resulted in a further radio signal 'Opened fire on me' which, much to Krancke's concern, was heard being repeated by a US coastal station in Texas. Eventually, Lt.z.S.(S) Engels got aboard with a party of seamen and captured the 7,448grt *Port Hobart* out of Liverpool bound for Curaçao for bunkers and thence for Auckland, New Zealand, with a general cargo and five trainer aircraft. She had been part of a convoy until reaching 45°W, when it was dispersed. Her cargo was of little use to Germany, so Krancke sank her with charges and a 10.5cm shell. His position was now compromised again, so it was imperative that he leave for other pastures.

Steaming due east, *Admiral Scheer* now aimed for the Cape Verde islands to interdict the UK–Cape convoy routes. Krancke's tip-and-run techniques were a classic example of the raider's art—to cause the maximum disruption to the enemy. His own tally of sinkings did not need to be high; dislocation and confusion were his aims, but quite obviously, every success was a bonus, both physically and morally.

Admiral Scheer maintained her eastward passage until late on 29 November, when she began to search for targets. On 1 December smoke was sighted at 1137, but to reduce the possibility of a radio warning being sent off, Krancke decided to shadow the merchant ship until an attack could be made under cover of darkness. It was not until 2052, therefore, that a shot was fired across the enemy's bows, which resulted in the steamer's gun being manned and put into action. A brief action ensued, which ended in the steamer being hit and her crew taking to the boats. The merchant ship proved to be the 6,242grt Harrison Line *Tribesman* out of Liverpool, bound for Calcutta with a general cargo. She had not transmitted a radio warning but one boat, in which were the ship's master and chief engineer, disappeared into the darkness and if soon rescued, would yet again compromise the raider's position. After taking aboard 78 prisoners, Krancke moved away westwards again. After cruising fruitlessly in the Central Atlantic, during which time the SKL proposed that a combined operations period with *Thor* on the Cape-Freetown route would be promising, Krancke decided on 8 December to strike west again until late the following day and then to make his way to another rendezvous with his oiler.

Admiral Scheer's motors were now in need of overhaul and, after beginning his move south to the rendezvous, Krancke steamed on reduced power to allow one motor per shaft to be attended to. This was begun on 10 December and reduced the ship's maximum speed to 22 knots. At the end of the middle watch on 14 December *Nordmark* was sighted again and during the day the raider took on oil and provisions. In return, 150 prisoners were passed over to the oiler. Prisoners were, in fact, becoming a problem and to alleviate the situation, Krancke intended to move against the Cape–Freetown route, capture a ship and send it back to western France, together with the prisoners. Fully refuelled once more, *Admiral Scheer* ordered *Nordmark* to a new rendezvous in 13°S, 16°W from 30 December and carried on her cruise. Despite frequent use of her aircraft, it was not until 18 December that a ship was sighted. *Scheer* was now almost on the equator in the narrowest part of the South Atlantic, midway between South America and West Africa. Just prior to midday, the merchant ship was in sight of the raider. Krancke decided to capture her by day and accept the possibility of a radio signal being sent off because this would further confuse the enemy and perhaps draw off some of the ships which might have impeded the break-out of *Admiral Hipper* in the far north.

At 1226 *Admiral Scheer* fired a shot across the bows of the target which was zig-zagging at high speed. She quickly stopped, at the same time sending 'QQQQ' and 'RRRR' signals, together with her position, which was heard being repeated by Freetown radio. She proved to be a valuable prize, the 8,652grt *Duquesna* en route for England from La Plata. Her cargo consisted of 3,539 tonnes of frozen meat and 720 tonnes (13 million) eggs! Unfortunately the ship was coal-fired and had insufficient fuel to reach the French coast. She was, however, far too valuable to scuttle and a prize crew was

Right: The oiler *Nordmark*, one of the vital supply ships for the ocean raiders. (WBB)

therefore put aboard, under the command of Lt.z.S.(S) Blaue, with the intention of using her provisions to supply *Nordmark*, *Thor* and the raider herself.

British counter-measures on receipt of *Duquesna*'s signals included the despatch of two cruisers from Freetown, *Neptune* and *Dorsetshire*, as well as the formation of a small force off St Helena, comprising the old cruiser *Dragon*, the carrier *Hermes* and an AMC, *Pretoria Castle*. In addition, Force K (*Formidable* and *Norfolk*), which was on passage to Freetown, was diverted for the search. But the Royal Navy was spread far too thinly and had little hope of trapping the elusive *Admiral Scheer*, except by chance encounter.

Admiral Scheer meanwhile steamed further south with *Duquesna* for another rendezvous, where she expected to meet the auxiliary raider *Thor* (Kpt.z.S. Otto Kähler) as well as *Nordmark*. A small scare occurred on 20 December, when her Arado made a forced landing on the open ocean after her ninth sortie of the cruise and took some finding, but this incident revealed that Bord Fl.Gr.1/196, the aircraft's parent formation in Germany, had issued out-of-date code-books to *Scheer*'s aircraft. This only became evident when a signal from the aircraft was decoded as a warning of heavy *Japanese* naval forces! This quite naturally caused some alarm and, with the aircraft down on the sea somewhere, left Krancke in the dark and unsure whether he could risk the lost aircraft sending beacon signals. Fortunately, around sunset, a red signal flare was sighted and the aircraft with its very relieved crew was recovered safely. *Duquesna* was found again on 21 December, and the following day both the Panzerschiff and *Nordmark* re-provisioned from the captured merchantmen.

Kpt.z.S. Krancke now gave some consideration to operating in company with the auxiliary raider *Thor* but concluded that on the one hand the slow speed of the auxiliary raider would prove a millstone around his neck, while conversely, his ship, obviously a warship, would negate the auxiliary's main asset—her disguise. Even so, Krancke valued an exchange of operational experiences with his colleague in command of *Thor*. Thus, after despatching *Duquesna* to a new rendezvous in 25°S, 14°W, *Admiral Scheer* set course for rendezvous 'Friedrich' in the forenoon of 22 December. On passage 'Weihnachtsfest' was celebrated and one hundred Iron Crosses, Second Class, were awarded among the ship's company. On Christmas morning *Thor* and *Eurofeld* hove into view, with each ship giving the other a rousing three cheers. Otto Kähler of *Thor* came aboard *Admiral Scheer* for a captains' conference, while members of his crew were allowed aboard the Panzerschiff for recreational purposes. *Scheer*'s crew, however, were forbidden aboard *Thor* and also expressly forbidden to photograph her.

The SKL intended both *Admiral Scheer* and *Thor* to operate together in the South Atlantic until the end of January 1941 and signalled to that effect while the two ships lay together in this remote part of the ocean about 450 miles north of Tristan da Cunha. Operations in February were to depend upon the successes of *Schiff 33* (the raider *Pinguin*) in the Atlantic or according to the appreciations of the COs on the spot. It was also possible that another supply ship, *Alsterufer*, would join up with this raider group. *Admiral Scheer* could reckon upon returning to Germany in the new moon period towards the end of February 1941. *Thor* was to move to a more northerly operations zone at this time and work the North Atlantic, south of 40°N and west of 20°W—i.e., on the Sierra Leone (Freetown) convoy route. Kähler proved to be of the same opinion as Krancke over the question of combined operations. His ship, *Thor*, had begun her cruise on 6 June 1940 and had been at sea ever since. To date, he had sunk eight ships and fought actions with two British AMCs, *Alcantara* and *Carnarvon Castle*, damaging them both seriously. It was agreed that the SKL's instructions were not viable and that *Admiral Scheer* would operate north of 30°S and *Thor* south of 30°S until 1 February. This decided, both ships sailed in company to rendezvous again with *Duquesna*. Meeting the latter on 27 December, provisions were taken aboard, the Panzerschiff alone taking over 200,000 eggs and eight tons of frozen meat! The ship was repainted and general maintenance undertaken. Nearly 20,000 nautical miles had been steamed since leaving Gotenhafen and 36,594 cubic metres of fuel consumed. *Nordmark* re-oiled her on 28 December and on 30 December *Eurofeld* rejoined the group.

Early in the new year, on 2 January, *Admiral Scheer* steamed to 17°S 16°W to join the captured Norwegian tanker *Storstadt*, a victim of *Pinguin*; the tanker, which was later renamed *Passat*, arrived in the Gironde on 4 February. By 5 January all the engine overhauls had been completed and after topping up with oil again from *Nordmark* on 6 January, the raider was almost ready to recommence operations. Krancke informed the SKL of his intention to operate alone off West Africa and then reprovisioned for the last time from *Duquesna* before setting off. *Admiral Scheer* now steamed northwards, then north-east with the intention of hitting the Cape Town–Freetown convoy route, a decyphered signal from a merchantman, *Peshawar*, leading him to suspect the probable routeings of convoys on this track. However, despite using his aircraft frequently, nothing was sighted until mid-morning on 18 January. This proved to be a tanker which was shadowed until dusk, then attacked and captured. She was the 8,038grt *Sandefjord* owned by Viriko Redori A/S out of Cape Town bound for Freetown, with 11,000 tonnes of crude oil from Abadan consigned to Anglo-Iranian Oil at Swansea. As this cargo was of no direct use to the raider, but valuable nevertheless, the ship was despatched to France under the command of Lt.z.S. (d.R.) Götsch. *Sandefjord* was successful in reaching Bordeaux but was eventually scuttled in Nantes as *Monsun* in August 1944. In the meantime, the huge successes by *Pinguin* became known, leading to thought on the merits of further operations in these waters.

The next success occurred on 20 January and was a double event! Masts had been sighted early that afternoon when Krancke resolved to shadow until nightfall, then attack. However, an hour later a second ship was seen, forcing a re-think of the attack plan. In the event, a daylight attack was carried out, using the guise of English language signals to convey the impression that the warship was British. One of the merchant ships saw *Admiral Scheer*'s smoke and turned away but, deceived by the German's peremptory English interrogatives, allowed her too close and was soon overwhelmed, without a radio signal being sent. She was the Dutch *Barnveld*, 5,597 tons, from Tilbury, bound for Port Said and the Eastern Mediterranean via Cape Town. After sending a prize crew aboard, under the command of Lt.z.S. (S) Petersen, Krancke turned his attention to the second enemy ship, some distance away. The same technique was successful and *Stanpark* (5,103 tons) was in the bag. Her cargo consisted of cotton and potatoes from Port Sudan to Freetown. This was of no direct use to *Admiral Scheer* or Germany and Krancke ordered her to be sunk. This resulted in a series of mishaps, for the first torpedo missed, while the second struck a boat from *Barnveld* (which was just rounding the stern of *Admiral Scheer*) with its tail before it struck the water and ran amok. A third torpedo eventually struck home. Fortunately there were no injuries aboard the motor boat.

Barnveld proved to be a valuable catch. Apart from three British naval officers en route to join ships in the Mediterranean, there were also 48 Royal Marines. A more political prize was an Indian Gandhi supporter, one R. Bazay, fervently anti-British and who provided a five-page report on conditions in England when de-briefed aboard the raider. The cargo included five new Northrop Nomad light bombers, consigned to the South African Air Force at Port Elizabeth, 86 assorted army vehicles and about 1,000 tons of ammunition and equipment. After a detailed investigation of this cargo, *Barnveld* was scuttled on 21 January.

Nordmark and *Duquesna* were found again on 24 January when *Admiral Scheer* replenished her supplies, including three torpedoes and spares for the Arado. Later *Thor* and *Eurofeld* joined the fugitive group. The SKL now cancelled *Admiral Scheer*'s projected Antarctic sortie and gave Krancke freedom to choose his own area instead. He opted for a foray into the Indian Ocean where he would operate between 8 and 12 February. On transferring nearly 250 prisoners to *Sandfjord* (Lt.z.S. dR Götsch), Krancke also ordered K.Kpt. Grau of *Nordmark* to retain *Duquesna* as long as possible to supply the raiders *Kormoran* and *Pinguin* and then scuttle her. (She was in fact disposed of by the latter on 20 January). The SKL concurred with Krancke's Indian Ocean plan and issued new operational boundaries to another auxiliary raider, *Atlantis*, to avoid problems.

Admiral Scheer left the rendezvous on 28 January and steamed south-east, rounding the tip of South Africa well to the south en route for her new operational area. By 6 February she was off the southern tip of Madagascar and searching vainly for traffic on the Durban-Perth shipping lanes. No traffic was seen at all, leading Krancke to the conclusion that it was perhaps routed instead via Suez. The SKL's suggestion that it would be profitable for *Admiral Scheer* to rendezvous with *Atlantis* and later *Kormoran* was welcomed by *Scheer*'s captain therefore, because they might well have better intelligence of ship movements in these waters than he had. *Atlantis* had been working the Indian Ocean since mid-

May 1940 and had sunk twelve ships up to the end of 1940. *Admiral Scheer* made rendezvous with *Atlantis* in an unfrequented spot well to the east of Cap d'Ambre at the northern end of Madagascar on 14 February. In company with the auxiliary were the supply ship *Tannenfels*, a former 'Hansa' line merchantman taken over for supply duties in 1940, and two prizes, the tanker *Ketty Brovig* and the freighter *Speybank*. *Tannenfels* was about to be returned to Germany and she arrived in western France safely. Heavy weather prevented much personal communication between the ships as it was unsafe to work boats, but eventually a useful conference took place between Kpt.z.S. Rogge of *Atlantis* and the warship captain. Rogge recommended the northern end of the Mozambique Channel as a fruitful one and, if Krancke chose to operate there, he himself would go elsewhere. After oiling from *Ketty Brovig*, the two ships parted company on 17 February for their respective operational zones.

Acting upon Rogge's advice, *Admiral Scheer* now steamed generally westwards but it was not until the early part of 20 February that her aircraft reported a sighting. The warship herself did not sight the quarry until early afternoon, when it was seen to be a tanker steering a southerly course. Using the English signal technique, the ship was soon captured and turned out to be *British Advocate*, 6,994 tons, laden with 4,970 tons of crude oil and 4,770 tons petroleum. While this was going on, *Scheer*'s Arado reported another sighting, whereupon the prize crew were ordered to take the tanker to rendezvous with *Atlantis* at 13°S, 58°E and *Admiral Scheer* moved to intercept this new target.

A night attack on this ship revealed it to be the 2,546-ton *Gregorios C.*, a Greek out of New York bound for Piraeus via Cape Town, with a mixed cargo. Because the ship sailed under the British 'Navicert' and was carrying banned goods, Krancke sank her the following day. A new aircraft sighting came in that evening and by 1838 the ship was in sight. A flurry of English language signals now took place, bordering on farce, in which *Admiral Scheer* sought to convince the enemy that she was a Royal Navy vessel, while her quarry tried to make out that she was American. At one point the merchantman flashed to the warship 'You look like a German to me' in response to one of *Scheer*'s signals! Faced with such a suspicious target, Krancke was forced to open fire, which resulted in the stars and stripes being displayed on the ship's side and a raider signal being sent. Krancke already knew the target's identity, however, from her codes given to him at the start of the encounter, which was confirmed by the signal '*Canadian Cruiser* in 6°36'S, 47°18'E under attack by Battlecruiser'.

This was heard being repeated by other stations and obviously compromised the raider's position. Not until 3.7cm gunfire had been directed at her bridge did *Canadian Cruiser* surrender. The 7,178-ton ship had been on passage from Colochal (India) to Pensacola with a cargo of illmenite sand. Time was now pressing if *Admiral Scheer* was to be able to fit out *British Advocate* as a prize and to be at rendezvous 'Andalusia' between 5–17 March. In addition, her auxiliary machinery required overhaul prior to the break back to

Germany. Recognition of Krancke's success came with the award of the Ritterkreuz on 21 February.

The next day another ship was sighted and captured after a brief engagement of a one-sided nature with 28cm and 15cm guns, necessitated by the need to prevent the target escaping in a rain squall. This ship, the Dutch *Rantaupandjang* (2,542grt) with 3,000 tons of coal out of Durban consigned to Singapore and Sabang, was badly hit and lost one man killed, with another dying aboard the raider. She too made a raider report, before a prize crew could board her. As the cargo was of no use to the Axis war effort, Krancke sank her and prepared to move back into the Atlantic, prior to his recall home. However, the raider reports transmitted by *Canadian Cruiser* had caused Vice-Admiral Leatham, C-in-C East Indies, to set up a hunt for the German ship, although his resources were few. The cruisers *Hawkins* and *Australia* were escorting a north-bound troop convoy (WS5B) to Aden; *Emerald* and *Enterprise* were also in the northern part of the India Ocean; and the light cruiser *Glasgow* was somewhat further south. Only the latter ship was anywhere near the sinkings and even she was about 140 nautical miles to the north-west of the last reported 'Raider' position. The cruiser herself had little hope of catching *Admiral Scheer* in order to shadow her but she was equipped with an aircraft, a Walrus amphibian. This she catapulted off on the morning of 22 February to find the raider.

The Walrus sighted *Admiral Scheer* off the northern tip of Madagascar and was itself sighted by the warship at 1217. Krancke closed up flak action stations but at the same time realized that it was a reconnaissance aircraft, probably from a cruiser. *Glasgow*'s sighting report resulted in a number of warships being vectored on to her in support, including the carrier *Hermes* and the cruisers *Australia*, *Shropshire*, *Canberra*, *Cape Town* and *Emerald*, but all were some distance away. Unfortunately for the Royal Navy, the Walrus lost contact (at about 1248) when Krancke was steaming a feint easterly course with he held until dark, before resuming course for his next rendezvous.

The following day the B Dienst office reported radio signals from an enemy unit and Mauritius radio repeated an 'RRRR' report of two warships in 21°28′S, 52°10′E—about half way down the east coast of Madagascar. These, the B Dienst office suggested, were *Australia* and *Canberra* (but could not actually have been these two ships). As the position of these two warships lay across his route to rendezvous 'Hans' with *British Advocate*, Krancke cancelled this and ordered the prize to make instead direct for western France. This she successfully accomplished, arriving in the Gironde on 29 March. *Admiral Scheer* now steamed south-west to round the Cape of Good Hope once more, arriving in the South Atlantic on 3 March, after which she steamed north-west. On 6 March Krancke received a signal from the SKL informing him that three U-boats had been sailed to bring him spares for his radar set—a vital item for the hazardous homeward passage through the Denmark Straits. These boats, *U105*, *U106* and *U124*, had refuelled from *Charlotte Schliemann* in Las Palmas between 3 and 5 March. *U105* carried a complete new radar set.

At the end of the morning watch on 8 March the supply ship *Ermland* was sighted and about ¾ hour later the faithful *Nordmark* hove into view. *Admiral Scheer* transferred 148 prisoners to *Ermland*, then took aboard provisions and released her to France. After oiling from *Nordmark*, a film crew was put aboard the oiler, to recreate an attack on a merchant ship by a raider for the cinema newsreels back home. Proceeding to rendezvous 'Karin' on 9 March, *Admiral Scheer* waited the next day for the arrival of *Alsterufer*, from which she was due to take 15cm ammunition. Lying stopped, the three ships transferred munitions, stores, men and equipment by boat but Krancke was annoyed to find that *Alsterufer* was loaded with the wrong type of 15cm shells (later disputed by the Marine Arsenal). Because of this, he took some from *Nordmark* instead (she carried three 15cm guns). In addition, some new prize crews were taken from *Alsterufer*. The following day, after taking more stores, including some for her aircraft, and with her engines overhauled, the raider parted

Below: *Admiral Scheer*, seen here camouflaged after return from the Atlantic sortie. (IWM)

from her support ships to the accompaniment of rousing cheers, *Alsterufer* having been ordered to rendezvous 'Andalusia' and *Nordmark* to resupply U-boats. *Alsterufer*, incidentally, was an extremely valuable supply ship for apart from ammunition and general stores, she was also loaded with at least six cased replacement Ar 196 aircraft and spare engines. She was eventually to issue new aircraft to the merchant raiders *Atlantis* (2), *Thor*, *Pinguin* and *Orion* (one each) as well as to the Panzerschiff.

Krancke had by now decided not to undertake any more attacks on merchant shipping—his departure from the Indian Ocean had gone unnoticed and it would be foolish to advertize his presence in the South Atlantic when on the point of returning home. Accordingly, he steamed northwards, up the centre of the South Atlantic, crossing the equator in the forenoon of 15 March. That day he also received the SKL's appreciation of enemy dispoistions affecting his break back home. A day later *Schiff 41*, the raider *Kormoran* (K.Kpt. Detmers), was sighted and shortly afterwards *U124* (Kpt. Lt. Schultz) surfaced nearby. Both commanding officers came aboard the Panzerschiff for a conference on the situation in the South Atlantic and Indian Oceans. Meanwhile, fresh food was sent to *U124* and the long-awaited radar spares were taken aboard *Admiral Scheer*. At the same time it was learned that two prizes, *Portland* and *Solglimt*, had arrived safely in the Gironde and hence the prisoners from *Barnveld* were secured. After leaving the rendezvous, *Admiral Scheer* kept well in the centre of the South Atlantic until about 15°N, when she altered course due north to run up towards the entrance of the Denmark Straits, some 3,000 miles ahead. The difficult passage through British patrols in the confined area of the Denmark Straits required careful planning, especially as the heavy cruiser *Admiral Hipper* was to precede her. Once through the British patrol lines, it was still necessary to ensure that no own goals were scored; the fate of the destroyers *Leberecht Maass* and *Max Schultz* was still remembered. Thus Krancke requested confirmation that the Luftwaffe recognition sign was still red turret tops, to which the SKL replied in the affirmative.

On 24 March *Admiral Hipper* was reported successfully through the British net and *Admiral Scheer* was given clearance to return herself. After loitering for a couple of days to take advantage of bad weather, the homeward-bound raider entered the Denmark Straits on 27 March. That afternoon the radar reported a large contact and the main armament was closed up. Later a ship was sighted, thought to be a heavy cruiser, whereupon Krancke reversed course, uncomfortably aware that he was making a lot of smoke as he did so. No untoward incident occurred, however, and *Admiral Scheer* soon resumed her northward jounrney. Now the radar chose to break down at the most critical moment and another cruiser was sighted but avoided. Conditions were hardly ideal—a clear, bright sky with the Northern Lights very much in evidence! Visibility was about 12,000m. Another scare occurred on the morning of 28 March, when it was thought that they had been intercepted by a *Nelson*-class battleship, but after several anxious moments it turned out to

be an iceberg. Had it been the battleship, *Admiral Scheer* would have been finished, as there was no sea room to escape.

In point of fact, there was very little of the Royal Navy's strength in the Denmark Straits at this time, for the appearance of *Scharnhorst* and *Gneisenau* in the Atlantic had drawn off much of the hunt. Admiral Tovey had only two cruisers, *Nigeria* and *Fiji*, in the area and it may have been these which *Scheer* sighted. The RAF's presence in Iceland remained No. 98 Squadron's elderly Battles, and plans to augment them with No. 204 Squadron (Sunderland) and No. 269 Squadron (Hudson) had not yet reached fruition.

The situation was further clouded by a report on 25 March from a merchantman off West Africa that she had been shelled by a raider which was thought could have been *Admiral Scheer*.

It was actually *Komet* which was responsible, but it allayed any real suspicion that the Panzerschiff was in the process of returning home. Hence only one flight was undertaken by No. 98 Squadron on 26 March, a local reconnaissance sortie, and none at all the next day.

In the early hours of 28 March *Admiral Scheer* rounded the northern tip of Iceland and left the Denmark Straits. During the forenoon the weather blew up into gale conditions, which continued for the rest of the day, abating the following morning. By 0630 on 29 March course was altered to 160° with the weather now overcast and snowing. All RAF Coastal Command air patrols flown at this time were designed to detect break-backs through the Iceland–Faeroes or Faeroes–Shetland passages, as it was not considered likely that the hazardous Denmark Straits would be used by any returning raider. Hence all were far to the west of her actual passage and presented no threat at all. Thus *Admiral Scheer* was able to anchor safely in Grimstadfjord that day, to be greeted by visits from Viz.Ad. Schrader (Admiral Westküste) and Captain (D), 8th Flotilla (Narvik). Escorted now by *Z23*, *Z24* and *Iltis*, *Admiral Scheer* sailed again in the snow and by 1 April was anchored at Kiel-Wik. Her return was greeted with acclaim, as she had sunk or captured sixteen ships of 99,059grt. Grand Admiral Raeder, Viz.Ad. Schmundt and Admiral Guse came aboard to congratulate the crew when 40 men received the Iron Cross (1st Class) while all the rest were awarded 2nd-Class versions. The ship had been at sea for 161 days and steamed 46, 419 nautical miles. She was now much in need of a refit and preparations were begun for her docking. Krancke was promoted Konteradmiral on 9 April but remained in command for the moment.

The presence of his ship in Kiel had by now been noted by the RAF and a heavy raid was despatched on 7/8 April, consisting of 49 Whitley bombers. Two aircraft (T4298 of No. 51 Squadron and Z6468 of No. 10 Squadron) were shot down. No damage was caused to the ship. Another raid on the night of 8/9 April by 44 Whitleys was equally unsuccessful.

By this time, guns, searchlights and torpedo tubes had been lifted off by a floating crane and on 15 March the ship was moved into No. 6 dock for refit, which was scheduled to last until 23 June.

14. OPERATION 'BERLIN', 1941

Both *Gneisenau* and *Scharnhorst* were engaged on work-up and training in the eastern Baltic by the beginning of December 1940, having completed repairs to damage incurred during 'Weserübung'. Each ship took part in full and medium calibre shoots against the target ship *Hessen*, as well as tactical exercises in company with the light cruiser *Nürnberg* and units of the second Torpedo-boat Flotilla. However, exercises with U-boats revealed difficulties with the S Geräte equipment, as this failed to detect U-boats making mock attacks. The work-up exercises were completed on 18 December, when the two battleships sailed from Gotenhafen Bay at 0800 that morning, bound for Kiel, escorted by *Sperrbrecher 31* and accompanied by the fleet tender *Hela*. By noon the next day they were secured in Kiel, awaiting dockyard attention for various defects, but the programme called for their return to the eastern Baltic between 27 December and 10 January for further battle training. *Scharnhorst* undocked on 23 December and her sister the following day.

It would appear that the forthcoming sortie was to be brought forward, for on 27 December the order was issued to execute 'Berlin' on 28 December. Admiral Lütjens hoisted his flag in *Gneisenau* just prior to midday on 28 December, putting to sea almost immediately. *Sperrbrecher 13* preceded the fleet flagship, followed by *Sperrbrecher 31* and then *Scharnhorst* as the squadron threaded its way through the Danish islands. Off Seelandsrev boats of the 1st and 5th Torpedo-

boat Flotillas joined the escort, while the *Sperrbrecher* were released. The next morning, in the Kattegat, the escort was further reinforced by units of the 18th Minesweeper Flotilla. At 1900 the boom at Kristiansand (South) had been cleared and later the torpedo boats of the escort were detached to Bergen, leaving the heavy units to continue on northwards alone.

Their task was to strike against British inward-bound convoy traffic in the North Atlantic and to cause the maximum amount of disruption, loss and embarrassment to the Royal Navy, but without direct confrontation with enemy heavy units.

The operational orders originally included the heavy cruiser *Admiral Hipper*, but in the event this ship operated from Brest. The battleships' zone of operations was specified as being north of 30°N, outside the U-boats' operational area. After completion of the sortie, or in the event of repairs, replenishment or re-ammunitioning, Lütjens was ordered to put into Brest. Apart from the reserve ammunition aboard the tankers, one full outfit of 28cm, half an outfit of 15cm and a full flak outfit was to be sent to Trondheim, sufficient for one battleship, while a full outfit for one ship was to be sent to Brest.

The main target was the convoy, with a pincer attack approach to obtain maximum chance of success. It was anticipated that weakly escorted convoys would scatter on the

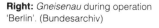

Right: *Gneisenau* during operation 'Berlin'. (Bundesarchiv)

Above: *Scharnhorst* at sea during 'Berlin'. (Bundesarchiv)

appearance of the battleships, when the aim would be to cripple as many merchantmen as possible, so that they could be sunk at leisure later, when no further mobile targets were left. On no account were sinkings to be delayed by rescue work. Independents could be sunk provided that no other tasks were on hand, and valuable ships were to be captured and sent to France in prize. Independents were to be approached under the white ensign, with guns trained fore and aft. Particular attention was to be paid to searching for confidential books, documents and codes—a copy of the British Isles tide tables for 1941 was regarded as especially desirable.

Two fast fleet oilers, *Uckermark* and *Dithmarschen* (later replaced by *Ermland*), and eight escort oilers were allocated to the sortie (*Adria, Breme, Thorn, Schlettstadt, Heide, Esso Hamburg, Weissenburg* and *Spichern*).

By the early hours of 30 December the weather conditions, while appropriate for an unobserved break-out into the Atlantic, were causing the ships some problems. A long, heavy swell with a north-westerly wind, Force 6 (just off the starboard and later port, bow), threw green seas over the bows, leaving the forward turrets standing like half-tide rocks. Spume and spray drenched the bridge personnel, despite layers of waterproof clothing. Once again the fore-end wetness of the ships was demonstrated. The flagship was

trimmed down at the bows by 87cm and even in slight seas and swell the bridge windows were threatened by seas coming over the bows. Speed had to be progressively reduced throughout the day because of the weather, resulting in costly delays to the timetable. Keeping lookout was all but impossible, and the ships proceeded almost blind. More seriously, *Gneisenau* suffered weather damage and flooding in compartment XXI where some welding split and structural damage was incurred, despite speed being reduced to only 15 knots. 'A' turret suffered the same old problems of lack of watertightness—the blast bags ripped, the periscopes leaked and water poured in through the cartridge-ejection flaps. Electrical circuits were washed out and the turret was soon awash inside as well as outside.

Both ships received orders from the flag to use the fore-peak oil bunkers first, to lighten the bows, but at 0415 Lütjens ordered the squadron into the shelter of Korsfjord where he intended to replace the blast bags and effect other necessary repairs. Luckily *Scharnhorst* was hardly affected by sea damage, having been strengthened forward after the earlier operational experiences. The ships dropped anchor off Kalvenes in Hjellte fjord at 1254. Not only had sea damage been incurred but both radar and S Geräte were defective aboard *Gneisenau*—not a good omen for the dangerous break-out. *Scharnhorst*, however, was now afflicted by that old bogey, machinery breakdowns, as the main condenser of the centre engine was reported salted up. A repair could not be anticipated in less than 48 hours. Nevertheless, later that evening, the ships weighed, intending to proceed north to Trondheim (where *Gneisenau* was to complete repairs while *Scharnhorst* continued to wait in the Arctic), but they did not sail immediately and in fact were ordered by Gruppe (Nord) to return to Kiel. The operation was to be broken off, as the delays caused by the heavy seas and the damage incurred meant that the Iceland-Faroes narrows could not be reached in darkness. Both the supply oilers, *Dithmarschen* and *Adria*, were also recalled, to Trondheim. By late on 2 January, *Scharnhorst* had anchored in the Neufahrwasser at Gotenhafen, having left her sister off Kiel, where she was to undergo repairs.

The abandonment of the sortie was a blow to Raeder, particularly as the British had no idea that the ships had even sailed. Photographic-reconnaissance aircraft had confirmed their presence at Kiel on 21 December but the next successful PR sortie of Kiel was not until 10 January, when they were no longer there. Coastal Command flights on 28 December, the day the ships sailed, were few and mainly orientated towards detecting a possible homeward-bound raider (believed to be *Hipper*). However, patrols were flown in the entrance to the Skagerrak and off Bergen, while two Beauforts of No. 42 Squadron were despatched to the Norwegian coast, but all during the morning. Later the weather closed down and prevented further flying and severely restricted No. 18 Group's sorties for the whole of the next few days, allowing the movement of the two battleships to proceed undetected.

On the material front the unsatisfactory features of German warship design were highlighted once more—unreliable machinery and wet fore-ends. There was a close parallel with the tribulations of *Admiral Hipper*'s first attempt to break out into the Atlantic in September. Finally, the curtailment of the sortie disrupted and endangered the German supply ship organization, without which the battleships could not operate.

Scharnhorst returned to Kiel on 19 January where Hoffmann immediately received orders from Lütjens to fit out as quickly as possible for a new cruise and, if necessary, sail north before *Gneisenau*, in view of the threatening ice situation in the Baltic. In fact, Raeder considered ordering *Gneisenau* to complete repairs at Trondheim to eliminate any chance of her being trapped by the Baltic ice. This proved not to be feasible and in the event it was found that *Gneisenau* could be ready to sail on 21 January and that both ships could sail together. The ice situation in the Belts was difficult, with thicknesses of up to 30cm reported. This would cause problems for the *Sperrbrecher*, reduce their effectiveness and endanger propellers.

On 22 January the Chief of Staff to Admiral Carls came aboard the flagship for a conference with Admiral Lütjens to discuss the question of co-operation with *Admiral Hipper*. The question was whether to operate the cruiser separately from the battleships, as originally envisaged, or to have all three join up. As the cruiser was already in Brest a rendezvous could only be achieved with excessive radio traffic, which was undesirable. Also *Admiral Hipper* would have to put to sea relatively early and it could not be expected that she remain undetected, even though inactive, and the consequent British counter-measures would affect the whole Atlantic before the Fleet could strike. In the end it was decided to operate separately with the cruiser not being given a release for action until Lütjens' force had made its presence felt. She was to act as a diversionary force and was therefore allowed to attack both independents and convoys. However, the option of combined operations was to be kept in mind as it had a number of advantage, including the ability to sweep a larger sea area, more forces to destroy any convoy found, and her torpedoes would be of great use. The single and major disadvantage was the cruiser's high fuel consumption, but this was not seen to outweigh the advantages.

After embarking aircraft, the two battleships sailed from Kiel in a second attempt to execute 'Berlin' on the afternoon of 22 January. Escorted this time by *Sperrbrecher 12*, and with the tug *Föhn* in attendance in case assistance in the ice was required, Lütjens proceeded down Kiel fjord and anchored that evening towards its mouth. It was cold with a slight frost, but in the fjord the ice was negligible. Passage was resumed at 0600 the next day but as the Kattegat was reached, ice conditions worsened and at 1915 *Sperrbrecher 13*, now leading the squadron, became stuck in the ice east of Anholt. Lütjens decided to dispense with her services and continued north at 18 knots, but stationed the icebreaker *Castor* astern to follow at her best speed just in case. Towards midnight the squadron anchored 8 miles north of Laeso to await the arrival of the torpedo boat escort. The Kattegat was covered in large ice floes and it was becoming colder. On the evening of 24 January reports of enemy naval movements off Stavanger led to Gruppe (Nord) recalling the squadron, apparently unaware that it was still in fact anchored and awaiting the torpedo boats. Two groups of ships had been reported, some 70nm off the coast, in about 59/60°N, which were believed to be engaged on minelaying west of Stavanger and off Korsfjord. As a result, it was decided to leave more sea room off the Norwegian coast than originally intended.

Four units of the 6th Minesweeper Flotilla arrived the next day, but ice conditions delayed the arrival of the 1st Torpedo-boat Flotilla from Kristiansand, so Lütjens remained at anchor. His decision was reinforced by the good weather conditions obtaining off southern Norway, which were unfavourable for unobserved passage. Although the British Admiralty had no direct knowledge as yet of their sailing, intelligence sources had indicated the movement of shipping along the Norwegian coast as early as 19 January and reported that on 21 January units of an unknown type were ordered from Heligoland to Bergen that day. As a result, air patrols were flown, of which those between Bergen and Stavanger might have affected 'Berlin'. However, on the evening of 25 January Intelligence informed Coastal Command that agents in Denmark had seen two heavy units, believed to be *Scharnhorst* and *Gneisenau*, passing Nyborg at 1100 on 23 January. Thus despite the age of this report, the delays in sailing from the Kattegat made it possible for the RAF to have a chance of their detection.

Lütjens eventually proceeded at 1100 on 25 January, passing the Skagen Boom at 1220. By 1930 Lindenes was passed and at 2314 course was altered to 320°. Their only escort was the torpedo boat *Falke*, *T10* having been sent into Kristiansand some five hours earlier with feed water problems. RAF PR aircraft visited Bergen, Stavanger and Haugesund, but in general bad weather grounded most Coastal Command patrols and there were no flights over the entrance to the Skagerrak. Utsira was passed at 0300 on 26 January and, nearly two hours later, *Falke* was detached to Bergen, leaving the heavy units to proceed alone.

That day flying conditions improved and all the standard Coastal Command patrols were flown but they were all too late to see the enemy ships. Blenheim D/254, flying the most northern patrol 'Trost' (between Stadtlandet and Trondheim), flew almost within sighting distance but encountered enemy fighters and took refuge in a cloud. Later, lack of cloud cover caused this sortie to be broken off. Other British precautions included a patrol off the Denmark Straits by No. 98 Squadron from Kaldadarnes and the Iceland–Faroes gap by Sunderland flying-boats of No. 201 Squadron. The intelligence reports noted earlier also led the Commander-in-Chief of the Home Fleet, Admiral Tovey, to station his forces in anticipation of an Atlantic break-out by German capital ships. Two cruisers were sailed to watch the western end of the Iceland-Faroes passage and then as a result of the definite sighting of Lütjens' force in the Kattegat, Admiral Tovey took the Home Fleet to sea at midnight on 25/26 January. This comprised *Nelson*, *Rodney*, *Repulse*, eight cruisers and eleven destroyers. They were bound for a position to the south of Iceland, from whence both possible exits to the Atlantic could be covered.

Lütjens meanwhile continued northwards and had little idea of the British counter-measures as his last, negative, reconnaissance report from the Luftwaffe had been timed at 2037/25, before the Home Fleet had sailed. The B Dienst detachments aboard reported no undue radio traffic, leading to the hope that the squadron was still not known to be at sea. The operation seemed to be proceeding to plan. Gruppe (Nord) had sailed the supply ships *Spichern* (25 January), *Schlettstadt* (16 January), *Esso Hamburg* (17 January) and *Breme* (22 January), while *Adria* awaited them far to the north. Weather reports and forecasts now indicated favourable conditions in the western and southern part of the Iceland narrows, but the ice conditions in the Denmark Straits were not known as *Uckermark*, routed that way, had not yet reported. The ships had sufficient fuel to reach either Brest or Trondheim if necessary and Lütjens resolved to steam north until position AF1563, (eta 0400/27), then decide (on the basis of the weather) which route to choose. On reaching this position, Lütjens resolved to break out south of Iceland immediately and not to refuel from *Adria* first. Accordingly, he altered course to 214° at 0400 on 27 January when standing already north of Iceland. Red turret tops and the Hakenkreuz (swastikas) were painted out.

Not until after midday did Lütjens receive warning from Gruppe (Nord) of an English unit south of Iceland, leading to the assumption that this was merely a patrolling cruiser. Admiral Tovey had actually divided his forces by now, with part being detached to Scapa to refuel, but still unknown to Lütjens a substantial force barred his way to the Atlantic. By midnight on 27 January the German squadron steamed some 60 miles off the south-east coast of Iceland, heading 234° at 27 knots. Despite the weather predictions, conditions were far from ideal. Winds and sea were slight, visibility good, with the Northern Lights playing in overcast skies. Technical problems compounded the situation for *Gneisenau*'s radar failed at this critical moment, in the narrowest part of the Iceland–Faroes gap.

At 0618, just as the flagship's radar had been repaired, *Scharnhorst*'s set detected a contact bearing 230°, range 14,400m. Her report to the flagship was followed by the closing up of action stations. A shadow was seen off to port, as Lütjens wheeled his ships 80° to starboard, obtaining a number of radar contacts as he did so. Reversing course and steaming now 090°, Lütjens ordered steam for 30 knots, to run himself out of trouble. The enemy ship was judged to be a destroyer of the *Tribal* class or a light cruiser of the 'D' class. Making smoke, the German ships retired east but no orders were given to open fire on their shadower (which was the *Dido* class cruiser *Naiad*) as with the turn 'C' turrets would not bear.

Naiad had indeed seen the German ships, turned to shadow and sent off an enemy sighting report. Admiral Tovey now ordered his heavy units in pursuit and the cruisers to maintain contact. Coastal Command was also alerted, patrols already airborne (Sunderlands Y/201, E/204 and F/204) being warned and vectored towards the sighting position, while No. 98 Squadron patrolled the Denmark Straits. All was in vain, however, for *Naiad* lost contact and Lütjens succeeded in withdrawing from a potentially serious situation. He was particularly concerned about the proximity of the Icelandic coast, reducing his room to manoeuvre, and of the possible presence of destroyers which might threaten him with torpedoes. There was no clear picture of the position in Scapa and it had to be assumed that the Home Fleet was at sea, but where? However, the B Dienst teams reported no general alarm as yet in the radio traffic being monitored. Lütjens' final decision was to hold an easterly course to disengage from the shadowers, then refuel from *Adria* before re-attempting break-out. He was tempted to try moving south or south-west to get around the southern end of the patrol line and thereby into the Atlantic, but was dissuaded from doing so by the fact that in daylight, sea and air searches would in all probability find him. He therefore steamed far to the north of the Arctic Circle, while the Home Fleet returned to Scapa.

Gneisenau's lookouts reported seeing a Sunderland at 1330, whose radio signals led to the assumption that they had been sighted. Flak gun crews were closed up but the expected attack never materialized—the aircraft had not seen them—and course was continued to rendezvous with *Adria*. Just be-

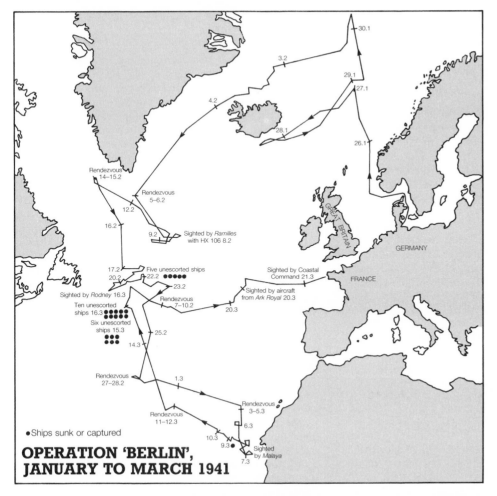

Rendezvous
14–15.2

Rendezvous
5–6.2

12.2

16.2

9.2

Sighted by *Ramilles*
with HX 106 8.2

GREAT BRITAIN

GERMANY

17.2
20.2

Five unescorted ships
22.2

23.2

Sighted by Coastal
Command 21.3

FRANCE

Sighted by *Rodney* 16.3

Rendezvous
7–10.2

Sighted by aircraft
from *Ark Royal* 20.3

Ten unescorted
ships 16.3

20.3

Six unescorted
ships 15.3

25.2

14.3

Rendezvous
27–28.2

1.3

Rendezvous
3–5.3

Rendezvous
11–12.3

6.3

10.3

● Ships sunk or captured

9.3

Sighted
by *Malaya*

7.3

**OPERATION 'BERLIN',
JANUARY TO MARCH 1941**

30.1

3.2

29.1

27.1

4.2

28.1

26.1

---

tached to search separately and so cover a wider area. Gruppe (West) assisted by supplying details of convoys, dispersal point and secret positions obtained from the prize *Storstadt*. However, the long heavy swell again made conditions aboard uncomfortable and on both ships the 15cm single mountings had to be secured. *Scharnhorst* rejoined that evening and the search was continued the next day.

At 0618 on 8 February *Gneisenau*'s radar picked up a contact to starboard, quickly followed by another at a range of 17,200m. At first these were believed to be independents, but action stations were closed up nonetheless. Visual sighting was not obtained for another two hours, when the foretop reported mastheads, evidently a convoy. *Gneisenau* continued to close until the foretop reported a 'thick' mast—possibly a warship—when course was altered, putting the convoy astern. At 0859 Lütjens signalled *Scharnhorst* details of the sighting, stating his intention to attack from the south once *Scharnhorst* had opened an attack from the north at about 1030. Two minutes later the convoy was lost to view from the flagship. *Scharnhorst* meanwhile had increased speed to 20 knots and altered course for the reported position of the convoy, sighting a ship at 0947, bearing 350°, range 28,500m.

A long, high swell was still running with good visibility, except for the occasional rain squall. There was therefore no hope of an undetected approach. A minute later many more mastheads rose over the horizon and it seemed likely that a major success was in the offing. However, it was quickly established that a warship was present, identified as *Ramilles*, a veteran ship completed in 1917 but a battleship nevertheless and armed with eight 38cm (15in) guns. Her task was to protect convoy HX106 (not HX108 as the Germans believed) from just such a marauder as *Scharnhorst*. *Ramilles* sighted the German ship, increased speed to 15 knots and closed up action stations. Hoffmann in *Scharnhorst* now engaged in a dangerous ploy on his own initiative, by closing the enemy ship until recognized as German, with the intention of then reversing course to draw off *Ramilles* and so leave the convoy open to *Gneisenau*'s attack from the south. That she had been seen was evident from the smoke from *Ramilles'* funnel as she worked up speed. Hoffmann's ploy failed, for at 1004 Lütjens, with heavy heart, ordered the attack to be broken off, after he had received *Scharnhorst*'s battleship report. Neither *Ramilles* nor *Scharnhorst* opened fire on one another as the convoy executed an emergency turn to starboard—potentially into the guns of *Gneisenau*. Instead, *Scharnhorst* withdrew as ordered, losing sight of the British battleship in a squall about 40 minutes after first sighting her. The ancient battleship had therefore saved her convoy from certain destruction—not the first time the policy of using these old warships had paid off.

Lütjens was extremely angry with Hoffmann for exercising his initiative in this manner ('a gross breach of orders'); in his interpretation of the operational orders, course was to be reversed *as soon as an enemy capital unit was sighted*. He considered Hoffmann's actions corresponded neither to his own intentions nor to his operational orders. Hoffmann argued

---

fore midnight on 28 January, Lütjens received confirmation of his sighting by *Naiad* when Gruppe (Nord) signalled the content of her enemy report—'Two suspicious ships sighted 8184AE course 60 or 70°. This was repeated by Donibristle and two aircraft were ordered to search for the Germans. By the evening of 29 January the temperature was falling fast, −7° then −12°, and in the morning of the following day, −15°C. Visibility was poor, with snow squalls and a long swell. *Adria* was located by radar and both ships oiled with some difficulty, not releasing the oiler to Trondheim until just before midnight on 1 February. Lütjens had already decided to pass south of Jan Mayen and reach the Atlantic via the Denmark Straits. After the earlier attempt, this proved an anti-climax, as they sighted no patrols and No. 98 Squadron's elderly Battles were grounded by bad weather. By evening on 4 February *Scharnhorst* and *Gneisenau* had reached the open Atlantic, meeting the oiler *Schlettstadt* the next day to fuel. After filling their tanks, the two German raiders were ready to start operations on 6 February, their first target convoy being HX108. (Details of convoys and their routes were obtained from the war diary of *Admiral Hipper*.) On the morning of 7 February *Scharnhorst* was de-

that such a statement was contained nowhere in the orders, there merely being the usual statement to the effect that *battle* with an equal enemy was to be avoided and that Lütjens' interpretation was far too restrictive for them to succeed in their task. Even so, he felt obliged to affirm that he intended no break of orders. Lütjens also reprimanded him for contacting the convoy too soon; he had specified about 1030, whereas *Scharnhorst* raised the convoy at 0950. Hoffmann countered this by pointing out that the estimated convoy position was some eight miles south of the actual position, hence his early detection. The reply from his Admiral, by open signal light, merely said, 'Urgently request you strictly conform to my orders in future'. Not a good basis on which to start operations! In fact, no damage was done, literally as well as actually, for *Ramilles* had only sighted a suspicious ship and reported her as possibly a *Hipper*-class cruiser. This accorded well with the British Admiralty's appreciation of the raider situation, for they anticipated a raider in the course of returning to Germany. The result was to draw off the Home Fleet to the north, into the southern approaches to the Denmark Straits in fact, and well away from Lütjens' force.

So *Scharnhorst* and *Gneisenau* joined up once more, empty-handed, and continued their combing of the ocean in the hope of finding a convoy that precisely fulfilled the requirements of their operational orders. The long Atlantic swell continued to plague the ships, making conditions very uncomfortable. On 10 February a signal from Gruppe (West) was intercepted, releasing *Admiral Hipper* for operations, so that an increase in the tempo of raider operations was to be anticipated. Lütjens had now searched unsuccessfully for 'SC' convoys for two days and he was pondering his next move. The *Ramilles* sighting was expected to result in a heavy escort for the next 'HX' convoys and *Admiral Hipper*'s appearance was bound to affect enemy dispositions once her presence was advertized.

He therefore decided to analyse the effects of the heavy cruiser's strike against HG53 on the north-south route, before moving himself against the 'HX' routes. The whereabouts of the Home Fleet was unknown and the position of Force H was always a source of concern. During that evening *Admiral Hipper* signalled her intention to attack HG53 about midday the next day. In the meantime, Lütjens steered for rendezvous 'Blau', an unfrequented spot in the Davis Strait to the east of Greenland's Cape Farewell, where the oilers *Schlettstadt* and *Esso Hamburg* awaited as the deep Atlantic low ruled out offensive operations anyway. As the ships steamed into the north-westerly wind, the temperature fell to −4° and it began to snow. Short steep seas and a long swell continued. By the morning of 12 February the weather had deteriorated further and speed had to be reduced to only 7 knots to avoid damage. Lütjens' fears about enemy forces were allayed some extent by the news that Force H was in Gibraltar and the news of *Admiral Hipper*'s successes against 'HG53' (actually SLS64) can only have increased his own desire for success.

The weather continued to deteriorate, giving serious concern about damage. So much so that Constructor Officer Krux suggested to Lütjens that a new course be chosen to reduce the chance of sea damage. Rolls of 50° were being experienced, the side decks going under. Questioned by Lütjens' staff, Krux stressed his concern over the rolling which, in his opinion, was such as to raise the possibility of distortion and failure of the longitudinals. He was not so much concerned with the shock and hammer from the head seas. 'B' turret structure had already moved, resulting in a fissure 1–2mm wide on the superstructure deck, which soon had a large amount of water in the sick bay. Aboard *Scharnhorst* much of the 10.5cm armament was unserviceable due to ingress of water, and a similar picture held for the RPC and fire-control systems.

By 2000hrs the west-north-westerly wind gusted Force 8–10, with large steep seas and the swell causing a reduction in speed even further to 5 knots. At this speed the ships barely had steerage way and an increase of 1 knot had to be accepted. At 2232 Lütjens ordered a new course into wind and sea, with the result that the motion became less lively, but the bows continued to slam and green seas deluged the forward turrets. No improvement was noticeable the following day; in fact the reverse, for by the time that the forenoon watch closed up, the winds had reached gale force 10, gusting storm force 11. Driving snow and hail made watch-keeping a futile misery. Towards the end of the forenoon, however, the seas began to abate and the ships did not work quite so hard. By evening it proved possible to increase speed to 10 knots. This improvement continued into 14 February, but as the ships steamed further north it got progressively colder, with ice forming on the superstructure. The thermometer registered −4°C. At the rendezvous area the swell had almost gone, thus facilitating the refuelling process. At 0847 the first oiler hove into view, followed by the second about ten minutes later. *Gneisenau* took oil from *Schlettstadt* and her sister was served by *Esso Hamburg*.

Lütjens now intended to move south again, towards his southerly replenishment ship, *Uckermark*, equip her with weather reporting cyphers, and then be in a position himself by 17 January to interdict the 'HX' convoy routes again. However, as a result of his earlier, fruitless experiences, this time he proposed to position himself further west. The target was HX111 on its fifth day out, somewhere west of 45°W. He did not have any clear intelligence as to the British policy of capital ship cover for these convoys. Agents' reports from Canada had indicated that the 3rd Canadian Division, with all its equipment and transport, was to be embarked in mid-February and that it was believed that *Repulse* was in Canadian waters for that purpose.

Lütjens sailed south once more just before midnight on 14 February to operate off the Newfoundland Banks but, apart from the occasional independent (which was avoided), sighted no targets until 22 February, when smoke was seen on the horizon. Several masts were seen and it was initially decided to catapult off one of the Arados to confirm if it was actually a convoy. However, this soon became obvious and the aircraft sortie was cancelled. The ships, then about 500 miles east of Newfoundland, were formerly part of an outward-bound convoy recently scattered. *Gneisenau* and

Above: *Myson* blows off steam on being stopped. (IWM)

Scharnhorst operated independently, the flagship firing a warning shot at the 3,237-ton *Kantara* at 1010; then, as a result of the merchantman attempting a radio signal, opened fire in earnest. Forty minutes later the target, now on fire, sank. At 1221 warning shots were fired at a second target, which also made a raider signal. 15cm and later 10.5cm guns were put into action as the range closed and the second victim, *Trelawny* (4,689 tons), was sunk.

Meanwhile *Scharnhorst* had engaged and sunk the tanker *Lustrous* (6,150 tons) in ballast to Caracas. *Gneisenau* continued her offensive, catapulting her aircraft in the search for further targets, as she engaged a third ship, the Canadian *A.D. Huff* of Montreal (6,200 tons), sinking here at 1623. After her aircraft had been recovered, the crew reported yet another steamer about 50 miles away, which they had attacked with guns and bombs, wounding some of the crew. An attempt to cut the radio aerials failed and the ship, actually *Harlesden* (5,483 tons), put out a radio signal. This resulted in some censure of the aircraft's captain, Lt.z.S. Mechel. *Gneisenau* set off in pursuit of this ship, being joined later by *Scharnhorst*. Darkness fell and it was not until 2120 that the radar aboard the flagship obtained a contact. Her sister was ordered to keep clear, as *Gneisenau* destroyed the merchantman with 15cm and 10.5cm gunfire, sinking her at 2308.

Most of the victims sent 'raider' signals and, despite jamming by the German ships, Cape Race radio station picked up some of the warnings. Thus the British Admiralty became aware of the presence of raiders off the American coast. Aircraft sorties were flown out of Halifax but the search was fruitless. Admiral Lütjens had already moved south en route for a new rendezvous with his support forces. In the evening of 26 February the oilers *Ermland* and *Breme* joined up just south of the Azores and the four ships continued passage together. *Breme* reported seeing no shipping during the five weeks that she had been on this station, which fact Lütjens noted in his War Diary with the dry comment that ships had certainly passed by and that despite the warships' morse signals, *Breme* had not seen them until they were only six miles away! *Breme* was actually stored and ammunitioned to supply *Admiral Hipper* and could only give fuel to the battleships.

By this time Lütjens had decided to attack the north-south convoy routes in about 35°N and to attempt the interception of SL67 from Freetown. To do this he had to leave the rendezvous no later than the morning of 28 February. If this proved impossible, then he would not attack SL67 as by this time he believed it would already be on the latitude of the Azores where there would be considerable danger of independents and neutrals compromising his position. In this event he would sweep south of these islands, and if SL67 were late he could still encounter it. He would also attack independents by day and groups of ships by day. South of 30°N he hoped to find better weather to allow use of the ships' aircraft.

Oiling commenced the following morning and continued, with some difficulty, into the early hours of the next day. Prisoners were sent over to *Ermland* but the ships' masters were kept aboard, as previous experience had shown that it was better to keep them separated from their men.

Lütjens now moved south-west, towards the Canary Islands, and en route on 2 March held a captains' conference aboard the flagship to outline his intentions. These were to attack the 'SL' and 'SLS' convoys off the African coast. Both ships would steam south, 40 miles apart, using aircraft to increase the swept area by about 70 miles; then at night course was to be reversed and the two ships rejoin, to reach the starting point for the following day's search. Independents were to be avoided by day but, depending on the circumstances, would be sunk if encountered by night. Enemy cruisers or patrol vessels were to be avoided so as not to compromise their position. If a number of independents were sighted simultaneously by ship or aircraft, Lütjens stated that he would decide if they were to be attacked or not—they might be a dispersed convoy. Convoys escorted by battleships were to be avoided, those escorted by cruisers were to be attacked but at long range and the escort eliminated out of danger to themselves—i.e., over 18,000m. The conference broke up just after midday and the squadron continued broadly west-south-west. Air and sea temperatures rose, the weather was fine and a general holiday atmosphere prevailed. It seemed a far cry from the North Atlantic and the Denmark Straits!

The operational area to which the battleships were moving was also worked by U-boats, of which there were three currently on station, *U105*, *U106* and *U124*. It was also possible that a rendezvous might be affected with *Schiff 10*, the raider *Thor*. As 3 March progressed the weather closed down a little and winds freshened. Under the reduced visibility conditions, the radar proved invaluable in avoiding odd independents. It remained warm, however, and in fact the high temperatures were a source of concern in the magazines and shell rooms where the cooling systems struggled to cope. The search to the west of the Canaries was proving fruitless. Despite extensive air searches, nothing had been seen and on 5 March the ships steamed south to new grounds, receiving as they did so a report of two heavy units from *U124*. As these could only be *Scharnhorst* and *Gneisenau*, speed was increased to avoid any embarrassing incident! Nevertheless, Lütjens was worried by the U-boat's presence and decided not to operate in the area until the situation was resolved. Accordingly, he turned due west at 0030 on 6 March. Eventually he was reassured and turned south once more. During the forenoon of 6 March *Gneisenau* encountered *U124* on the surface and exchanged information with her, before going their separate ways some fifteen minutes later.

More fruitless searching followed until, on the forenoon of 7 March, *Scharnhorst* sighted convoy SL67 and counted fifteen ships including, unfortunately, a battleship. On receipt of her sighting report by *Gneisenau*, Lütjens ordered her to rejoin the flag and, about 25 minutes later, his fore-top lookouts also reported the mastheads of the convoy. Lütjens reported contact with the convoy to Gruppe West, informing them that it was heavily escorted; then hauled off to await the arrival of his consort. He intended to shadow the convoy until dawn the following day, in the hope that the U-boats might have sunk or, at the very least, incapacitated the British battleship (*Malaya*). If their attack had scattered the convoy, then there might be the chance of finding part of the convoy without battleship escort. Fein could, however, see no real opportunity for his Admiral and considered that their best course of action would be to steam further south where there might be other, less well defended convoys. Thus the operational orders—in particular, the restrictions on attacking equal forces—left the battleships only the role of vulture to play; the slightest hint of the oldest enemy battleship caused the German ships to retreat and hope that the U-boats would leave a few lame ducks for them. To a certain extent, the Kriegsmarine's timidity can be understood; it had no bases nearer than western France, no repair facilities or friendly countries where refuge could be sought, so that the slightest damage was a potential catastrophe. Morale, however, was definitely affected and the fates of Admirals Boehm and Marschall made other admirals cautions about the slightest deviation from their orders. Initiative was suffocated and a price paid for it. So Lütjens waited for *Scharnhorst* on 8 March and hoped for a few crumbs from the U-boats' table.

During the night of 7/8 March *U105* (Schewe) had successfully attacked the convoy, sinking one ship of 5,229 tons, *Harmonious*. Schultz in *U124* did rather better, accounting for four ships, *Hindpool* (4,897 tons), *Lahore* (5,304) tons, *Tielbank* (5,084 tons) and *Nardarna* (7,974) tons. Neither boat saw, much less attacked, any battleship.

As yet the convoy's escort, which consisted of *Malaya*, the destroyers *Forester* and *Faulknor*, with the trawler *Celia*, had no idea of the proximity of the two German battleships, for they had not sighted them on 7 March. At 0613 Lütjens knew from a U-boat signal, that the convoy had been attacked but that contact had been lost. About four hours later he decided to search for damaged ships and closed the convoy again, having stood off to the south by some 40 miles or so the previous night. Nothing was seen until 1335, when lookouts reported a ship which two minutes later was identified from *Gneisenau* as a twin-funnelled light cruiser. It was actually *Forester* and this time the German ships were sighted. The British destroyer turned towards the suspicious ships to investigate, reporting their presence to *Malaya* as she did so. Having made her report, *Forester* reversed course to rejoin her convoy. Meanwhile *Malaya* raised steam for full speed and prepared to defend the convoy, going to action stations.

While this was going on Lütjens had ordered steam for 27 knots and his main armaments were closed up for action. For the next couple of hours or so the two sides played a cat and mouse game, each shadowing the other but without opening fire, despite being in respective gun ranges by about 1740, when the range was some 28,000m. *Malaya* had correctly identified her opponents as *Gneisenau*-class ships and launched a Swordfish floatplane, piloted by Lieutenant R.G. Brown, RN, to shadow the German force. The battleship herself returned to cover her mercantile charges. The Swordfish made very skilful use of the cloud base and kept well out of gun range of the German ships, while at the same time radio-ing reports back to *Malaya*. Lieutenant Brown lost contact about 1900 but was unable to reach *Malaya* and had to ditch. Fortunately he and his crew were later rescued by a merchant ship, *Buena Esperansa*, and put ashore in the Canary Islands. Lütjens had by now given up all hope of attacking the convoy and decided to move south to rendezvous with his oiler *Ermland*, signalling Gruppe (West) to that effect, after which he would return to the 'HX' routes. Not surprisingly, morale suffered a considerable drop as a result of the abortive attack, the second occasion when they had been driven off by a mere puff of smoke. Admiral Lütjens soon received from his B Dienst office the decrypt of *Malaya*'s sighting report, 'One large ship bearing 251°, 40 miles, course unknown. Own position 21°50'N 19° 22'W.' This was heard repeated by Sierra Leone to Gibraltar.

The British Admiralty, now alerted to the presence of these two powerful ships on the oceans, took steps to block their return to Germany and in view of the evidence that a single capital ship, however old, was sufficient to guarantee the protection of a convoy, despatched *Rodney* and the new *King George V* to escort two convoys due to leave Halifax on 17 March and 21 March. Further forces were sent into the Denmark Straits.

Lütjens was in fact steaming generally north-west, aiming for the 'HX' routes, and chanced across and sank the 8,000-ton Greek ship *Marathon*, on passage from Swansea to Alexandria via Freetown with a cargo of coal, on 9 March. The two battleships met the oilers *Ermland* and *Uckermark* in the afternoon of 11 March, spending the next couple of days oiling and reprovisioning in this remote part of the Atlantic. During the early hours of 11 March, Gruppe (West) had informed the Fleet Commander that because of the homeward passages of *Admiral Scheer* and *Admiral Hipper*, he was to operate on the 'HX' routes only until 21 March. After that date he was to move south to provide a diversion for the returning ships. Because refuelling would take until 13 March, this meant that he could not arrive on the convoy routes until 17 March, which left him only five days' operations but he considered this to be sufficient. However, shortly after they had started oiling, Gruppe (West) amended its earlier orders and allowed operations only until 17 March, after which Lütjens was ordered to attack in the Azores/Cape Verde islands area as soon as possible after that date. He was further advised that due to the impending readiness of *Bismarck* and *Prinz Eugen*, his own sortie should not be so extended that his ships could not be ready for a further sortie with the new ships at the end of April.

This upset Lütjens' plans but he decided to wait and see how replenishment went until finally formulating his plans. The main source of concern was with the ships' machinery, for although the flagship's condition was not serious, *Scharnhorst* had for some time been plagued with boiler troubles, especially in the superheaters. This already ruled out her participation in 'Rheinübung' for it was estimated that ten weeks were required for repairs. *Gneisenau* needed about a month, making it necessary to reach Brest by the end of March at the latest.

At a captains' conference aboard the flagship, Lütjens expounded his plans for the immediate future. Using both oilers to widen the search area, the battleships would scour the western part of the UK–Canada convoy routes until 17 March. The oilers were to be stationed on the wings but their low speed, only about 18 knots, might prove a handicap. That same evening, 12 March, the squadron got under way, heading for the same general area in which they had scored their first successes in February. It was on the morning of 15 March that the first contact with merchant shipping was made when *Uckermark* reported a sighting to the flagship. *Gneisenau* immediately re-coupled her centre shaft, worked up to 22 knots and steered to close the reported position of this ship, a tanker. Hardly had this ship been reached when *Uckermark* reported another tanker, some 60 miles away. The first target was stopped with a single round of 28cm and proceeded to abandon ship. She proved to be the Norwegian *Bianca*, 5,684 tons, bound for Curacao from Glasgow. Her crew were ordered back on board and an officer, Lt.z.S.(S) Westip, sent across from the battleship to assume command. He was ordered to take *Bianca* in prize to western France. *Gneisenau* now moved immediately against the second ship which was endeavouring to escape, sending 'RRRR' signals as she did so. As her maximum speed was only about 13 knots, it was not long before she too lay under the guns of the raider, having been shelled because of her radio officer's efforts. This ship was the 8,046-ton motor tanker *San Casi-*

miro on passage in ballast to load crude oil at Willemstad. Her master was taken aboard *Gneisenau* as a prisoner while Lt.z.S.(S) Grenz took over his vessel, ordered once again to make for Bordeaux.

Uckermark continued to signal new targets, now two steering west-south-west, to which the flagship now turned. The B Dienst had also reported that *San Casimiro*'s 'RRRR' signal had been repeated by Portishead radio—a disquieting fact for Lütjens as it would obviously call down a hunt. In the meantime *Scharnhorst* had intercepted and sunk the tanker *British Strength* of 7,139 tons. By 1720 *Gneisenau* had two more targets in view, both tankers, and fired warning shots across the bows of the left-hand one. The second turned away in consequence and was also fired upon. Her signals were jammed by the B Dienst aboard the flagship. Lütjens ordered the first tanker to be captured as a prize and the second sunk. The former was the Norwegian *Polykarb* (6,405 tons), registered in Kristiansand bound for Aruba from Swansea. The latter was the 6,197-ton British ship *Simnia* (6,197 tons). While all this was taking place, *Scharnhorst* accounted for the 6,554-ton tanker *Athelfoam*. After all the frustrations of the past weeks, this had been a very successful day.

Gneisenau sighted further targets in the early hours of the next day, when there was some doubt as to one being *Uckermark*. At 0330 gunfire was seen astern, this being *Scharnhorst* stopping the *Mangkhai* of 8,290 tons, formerly the German *Scheer*, captured in Macassar on 10 May 1940. Half an hour later *Gneisenau* was in action again, shelling a ship believed to be a tanker in the darkness, which was sunk after the expenditure of over 100 rounds of 15cm. The identity of this particular victim is not certain but possibly it was *Rio Dorado* (4,507 tons). The action continued throughout the morning, with *Scharnhorst* sinking *Silverfir* (4,347 tons) and *Sardinian Prince* (3,200 tons); while the flagship sank the Manchester-registered 3,648-ton *Empire Industry*, the Norwegian *Granli* (1,577 tons) bound for Georgetown, *Myson* (4,564 tons) and *Royal Crown* (4,364 tons). *Scharnhorst* also sank *Demerton* (5,200 tons). Early that evening yet another target was found, but Lütjens was suspicious of this one. She replied to the raider's gunfire and the German feared that it was a British auxiliary, possibly armed also with torpedoes However, it was only the 1,739-ton former Danish fruit carrier *Chilean Reefer*, but she received the attention of 73 rounds of 28cm and nearly 60 15cm before sinking. All the victims had come from dispersed convoys and many 'raider' signals were sent and picked up.

While *Gneisenau* manoeuvred to pick up the second lifeboat from *Chilean Reefer*, her radar office suddenly reported three contacts, one of which was soon seen to be a warship, and a large one at that. Lütjens immediately ordered full speed and turned on a southerly course, sighting *Uckermark* three minutes or so later. It was indeed a 'large warship', the battleship *Rodney*, more than a match for *Gneisenau*, with her 40cm guns (16in), even if slower. She was tasked with the escort of convoy HX114 and had already that afternoon had a suspicious ship alarm. This had turned out to be *Royal Sovereign*, yet another British battleship in the vicinity. After

Below: *Simnia* sinks. (IWM)

returning to her convoy, *Rodney* sighted the AMC *Laconia*, also part of the escort, which reported gunfire bearing 150°. *Rodney* altered course to investigate and half an hour later saw an unidentified tanker crossing her bows to port. Seven minutes later a warship could also be seen (obviously these were *Gneisenau* and *Uckermark*) and *Rodney* again altered course to close. Now a ship on fire was seen, evidently the demise of *Chilean Reefer*, and the British battleship made an enemy report. After a few minutes it became clear to the British captain that he could not hope to catch the fast German warship, so he altered course to intercept the tanker instead. *Rodney* challenged *Gneisenau* by signal lamp but was not understood, nor was the German's reply—'HMS Emerald'. Half an hour after first being sighted by *Rodney*, *Gneisenau* was lost in the darkness and smoke, as was *Uckermark* ten minutes later. It had been a very narrow escape!

Lütjens withdrew south-east at speed, receiving as he did so *Uckermark*'s correct identification of the enemy as a *Nelson*-class battleship. His main worry now was that if this was a hunting group, the other radar contacts obtained at the time of first sighting might be cruisers; in which case there was a strong chance that he would have a shadower problem. This was not the case, however, and the flagship continued through rising seas towards the rendezvous. *Scharnhorst* rejoined the flag on 18 March and later that afternoon the oilers *Ermland* and *Uckermark* were found again. Over the next two days the battleships oiled, reprovisioned and passed prisoners over to the auxiliaries. Gruppe (West) had now ordered Lütjens to operate further south, so as to create the maximum disruption to the Royal Navy's dispositions in view of the movements of *Admiral Scheer* and *Admiral Hipper* (back to Germany). But the British Admiralty could only guess where they might strike next. The general belief was that the German ships would attempt to return to Germany by the northern route and the Home Fleet's dispositions were decided accordingly.

In fact, Lütjens was bound for Brest. On 20 March, mid-morning, an aircraft was sighted fine on the bow, low on the horizon, which it was believed might not have seen them. It was, however, recognized as a carrier-borne biplane and therefore it was probable that a task force was in the vicinity. While this aircraft evidently did not sight Lütjens' squadron, its parent ship (actually *Ark Royal*) continued to fly search patrols. As the German Admiral had feared, she was accompanied by the battlecruiser *Renown*, whose path they had crossed once before. Eventually, at 1759, another Swordfish did locate them and reported their position as 46° 50′N, 21° 25′W (i.e., 600 miles WNW of Cape Finisterre), steering north at about 20 knots. Unfortunately for the British hunting groups, this signal was greatly delayed due to radio failure and, moreover, *Renown* and *Ark Royal*, which were some 160 miles south-east of that position, were unable to launch further air patrols because of weather conditions. The Swordfish from *Ark Royal* also spotted the prizes *Bianca* and *San Casimiro*, which led in turn to their interception by *Renown*, when both were scuttled by the German prize crews. *Polykarb* reached occupied France and survived until May 1945.

At this time it was still not clear whether the German ships were heading for Germany or France, so initially Coastal Command flew patrols over the Denmark Strait, but efforts were soon concentrated on the French option. Twenty-five Bomber Command Wellingtons were also held in readiness to attack, should an opportunity occur. Catalinas of No. 240 Squadron, Sunderlands of No. 210 Squadron and Whitleys of No. 502 Squadron were detailed to search the Biscay approaches but to no avail. Hudsons of No. 220 Squadron from St. Eval were tasked with a Biscay sweep and to cover the northern Biscay ports on the evening of 21 March and one of these aircraft, X/220, did in fact locate the German ships, shadowing for a while. Lütjens' B Dienst immediately deciphered the aircraft's sighting report and, his position known, decided to make direct for Brest at once. His escort, the torpedo boats *Jaguar* and *Iltis*, had already joined him and by 0330 the following day the Chausse de Seine buoy was passed, the squadron anchoring in Brest Roads at 0746. Operation 'Berlin' had been successfully concluded after 59 days at sea, having sunk or captured 22 ships totalling 115,622 tons.

Right: Success pennants hoisted, *Gneisenau* enters Brest. (Bundesarchiv)

15. 'RHEINÜBUNG', 1941

The new battleship *Bismarck*, launched in February 1939, was, by the summer of 1940, almost complete at her builder's yard, Blohm & Voss in Hamburg. A nucleus of mostly technical personnel was already aboard, having been appointed to stand by while the ship was under construction. Her commanding officer was Kpt.z.S. Ernst Lindemann, 47 years of age when appointed to command in July 1940. Born in Altenkirchen, Lindemann had joined the Imperial Navy in the spring of 1913 and saw active service during World War One. In the days of the Reichsmarine, having qualified as a Gunnery Specialist, he had held various appointments ashore and afloat, including gunnery officer of *Admiral Graf Spee*. At the beginning of the war Lindemann was posted in command of the Naval Gunnery School, from where he was appointed to *Bismarck*, the Navy's most prestigious command.

Bismarck was actually commissioned just after midday on 24 August 1940, when Lindemann officially came aboard for the commissioning ceremony. The new ship was almost immediately in action for that same night the RAF paid a visit to Hamburg. The low clouds and darkness prevented any real observation of the enemy but the light flak guns put up barrage fire. No damage was incurred by the new battleship. There were further unsuccessful raids over the next few days. Immediately after commissioning, the ship's company began their long training period and the ship's systems were tried and tested. On 27 August the port and starboard boiler plants were flashed up for training purposes, as was the midships plant the next day. Then all three plants were steamed up together. It was not until 14 September that *Bismarck* was ready to leave her builder's yard for the first time, when tugs turned her around in the river, in preparation for passage down the Elbe the following day.

A still, sunny day dawned with slight ground haze and at 1420 *Bismarck* was manoeuvred away from her fitting-out berth and shepherded down river by tugs. Marred only by a minor collision with the tug *Atlantik*, *Bismarck*'s passage down to Brunsbüttel took until 1902 when she anchored. The ship still lacked a number of essential items of equipment, notably directors and range-finders which had been delayed. Rather than waste time in the yard, it had been decided to send her to the Baltic for her work-up training to begin. Reaching Kiel fjord, *Bismarck* spent until 28 September in Kiel dockyard or its environs before sailing further east for Gotenhafen, the main training area.

In and around the Gulf of Danzig, *Bismarck* embarked on a long series of trials in conjunction with various experimental and training commands such as SVK, NEK and EKK. The whole of the ship's organization was tested—gunnery, engine room, signals, etc.—as Admiral Raeder still insisted on almost a peacetime training programme before a ship could be considered fit for front-line service. One piece of news disturbed this quiet routine. Lindemann learned of RAF bombers intruding into the area of the former 'Polish Corridor' and, mindful of the events at Taranto on 11 November 1940, expressed concern at the presence of three battleships at Gotenhafen (*Bismarck*, *Gneisenau* and *Scharnhorst*). All he could do, though, was increase the state of alert of his own flak guns.

This first work-up stage was terminated on 5 December when *Bismarck* sailed for Kiel on passage to Blohm & Voss

Right: *Bismarck* on trials prior to receiving her main range-finders. (WBB)

for final additions and modifications, arriving there on the afternoon of 9 December. Most of the ship's company were given leave while work was carried out and the return of the battleship also attracted air raids. These were ineffective but *Bismarck*'s return to the Baltic was delayed by other problems. First, the Kiel Canal was blocked by a wreck and to avoid anchoring in the exposed Brunsbüttel Roads, the ship was ordered to remain in Hamburg. The alternative, a passage around Skagen and down the Skagerrak, was vetoed by higher command. Secondly, the severe cold of the winter caused freezing-up of fresh water systems, particularly in the boiler rooms where manometers, pipes and gauges close to the outputs of boiler room fans froze solid (it was −15° outside). Similar problems were experienced by other heavy units, but it meant that the ship was unserviceable! Modifications to the pipe systems took until mid-February; by then five weeks had elapsed since her arrival in Hamburg and much valuable training time was lost. In the end it was not until the forenoon of 6 April that *Bismarck* slipped and proceeded from the Blohm & Voss yard. Off Brunsbüttel, an icebreaker and two *Sperrbrecher* came alongside as torpedo protection, before the battleship entered the locks. In Kiel, at the Deutsche Werke yard, *Bismarck* went into C Dock, where some repairs were made to the ship's bottom, paintwork refurbished and stores taken on, as well as provisions and ammunition. Two aircraft were hoisted aboard on 15 March and two days later, the ship sailed once more for Gotenhafen. Because of the earlier delays in Hamburg, some of the trials and training with the AVKS had to be foreshortened, much to Lindemann's dismay. He was also concerned about one or two machinery shortcomings, in particular the cranes, which were unreliable, and the starboard catapult which was damaged. In these early radar days, these were vital pieces of equipment for air reconnaissance. Eventually a replacement catapult was taken from *Tirpitz* and two more aircraft came aboard on 2 April, bringing the total to four, 'T3 + IH,' 'T3 + AK,' and 'T3 + DL' and 'T3 + MK' (Werk Nr. 0052, 0110, 0123 and 0150 respectively).

The ship was now stored for three months and with war correspondents, film crews, prize officers and other supernumeraries coming aboard almost daily, it was obvious to the ship's company that something was afoot. Lindemann had been told that his ship had to be ready for operations some weeks earlier than anticipated, hence the curtailment of the Ship's Gunnery Experimental Command trials (AVKS), but he himself still had no clear orders as to the task ahead. The starboard catapult was damaged again on 17 April and replaced on 20 April. Over the last few days *Bismarck* had exercised with her consort for the forthcoming operation, the heavy cruiser *Prinz Eugen*, as well as brushing up signal, A/S and flak procedures. She was now ready for action. Unfortunately, on the evening of 25 April Fleet Command informed Lindemann that the sortie would be postponed for at least seven to twelve days because *Prinz Eugen* had been damaged by a magnetic mine while en route to Kiel two days earlier. As yet the ship's company was not aware of the postponement but Lindemann feared some damage to morale if the delay were prolonged. Hence on 28 April he informed the OKM, Gruppe (Nord), Gruppe (West) and Flottenkommando that 'the ship is fully operational in respect of men and equipment and stored for three months'.

Bismarck had in fact been prepared for a new battleship sortie into the North Atlantic. The abandonment of Operation 'Seelöwe' (the invasion of England) on 14 October 1940 had left the Kriegsmarine free to concentrate upon what they regarded as their main task—war against the North Atlantic trade routes. This had begun in 1939 with the sailing of *Admiral Graf Spee* and *Deutschland* but the invasion of Norway ('Weserübung') had curtailed further sorties. Since then, damage and the need to consider the requirements of an invasion of England prevented any further strikes in the Atlantic. Now, with the fall of France, the possession of French Atlantic bases could be exploited to the full, not only by U-boats, but also by surface warships. Admiral Raeder regarded the cruises of *Admiral Scheer, Scharnhorst, Gneisenau* and even *Admiral Hipper* as highly successful and, in the light of this, issued a directive on 'Future Operations by Surface Forces' (B.Nr 1 SKL1 Op 410/41) on 2 April 1941. This considered that the sorties of the ships mentioned had had important strategic as well as tactical effects; similar sorties could be expected to affect the enemy's dispositions, both in Mediterranean and Home waters. The decisive objective was, as always, the North Atlantic trade routes. However, the enemy was well aware of this and, for example, during Operation 'Berlin' had always managed to station one battleship with each convoy, which effectively kept off the two German battleships. Even so, British resources had been stretched to do this and if more warship raiders were sent out, more convoys would have to be protected. Battleships for this could only be drawn from the Mediterranean, with consequent benefits to the Axis forces in that theatre.

At the time of the compilation of this directive, the Royal Navy had four 'R'-class battleships, *Revenge, Resolution, Royal Sovereign* and *Ramilles*, five *Queen Elizabeth*-class, *Queen Elizabeth, Valiant, Warspite, Malaya* and *Barham*, all armed with 15in guns. There were also *Rodney* and *Nelson* with 16in guns, as well as three battlecruisers armed with 15in guns, *Hood, Repulse* and *Renown*. One of the new 14in gun battleships, *King George V*, was in service and a second, *Prince of Wales*, within days of commissioning. Thus, a total of sixteen capital ships could be mustered on paper by the Royal Navy. Of these, however, *Malaya* was repairing torpedo damage from *U106* and *Resolution* torpedo damage from the French submarine *Bévéziers*. Most of the *Queen Elizabeth*-class ships were actually with the Mediterranean Fleet and not in the Atlantic. It would therefore have been difficult for Britain to increase the number of convoys given battleship or battlecruiser escort, without seriously affecting the Mediterranean Fleet. What Raeder wished to do was to disperse the enemy strength and then attack at the weak points uncovered. As both Raeder and the Royal Navy knew that reinforcements had to come from the Mediterranean, the weak points must be exposed in that theatre. Quite how Raeder would have attacked them is not obvious.

Nevertheless, Raeder based his plans on having available two ships of the *Bismarck* type to attack convoys. One would engage and sink the the escorting battleship, while the second would destroy the convoy. Unfortunately the second ship of this class, *Tirpitz*, was unlikely to be ready in time and, given Raeder's strict adherence to training schedules, could not expect to be allowed to participate, despite the keenness of her crew and captain, Kpt.z.S. Topp. Raeder was therefore forced into an intermediate solution. *Bismarck* would sail and deal with the capital ship escorts while, to accompany her, would be the heavy cruiser *Prinz Eugen*. There was actually no other choice available to him—the Panzerschiffe were too slow, the light cruisers unsuitable and the other capital ships trapped in Brest. Finally, *Admiral Hipper* was in need of a full refit after her Atlantic sortie. The choice of *Prinz Eugen* was advantageous on the one hand as her speed and quicker firing guns would be of great use against merchantmen and she was equipped with a large torpedo outfit, which her sister had made full use of already in mercantile warfare; *Bismarck* had no torpedo outfit. On the debit side, the heavy cruiser was a sprinter with unreliable and uneconomical machinery. In consequence, the replenishment tankers had to be more numerous than would otherwise have been the case. Such was the background for the participation of *Prinz Eugen* in 'Rheinübung'. Raeder had another reason for wanting the sortie to go ahead without waiting for *Tirpitz*: so far the USA had remained neutral but if that situation were to change, it might prove impossible to get battleships out at all in future.

As originally conceived, the sortie envisaged one battle group sailing from Germany, centred around *Bismarck*, while a second group consisting of *Scharnhorst* and *Gneisenau* would sail from Brest in order to obtain maximum disruptive effect and success on the convoy routes. However, *Scharnhorst* developed defects and was not expected to be operational for some months. Nevertheless, the plans were modified to include only *Gneisenau* from Brest. She would later join up with the *Bismarck* group, possibly after a sweep between the Cape Verde islands and the Azores. Hardly was the ink dry on these orders than *Gneisenau* was seriously damaged by a torpedo (see Chapter 16). Now only *Bismarck* and *Prinz Eugen* remained in the operation despite renewed pleas from the commanding officer of *Tirpitz*.

In contrast to previous sorties, this new one allowed the task force to attack escorted convoys but the task of *Bismarck* was not to destroy the enemy but to tie him down, while at the same time avoiding damage herself, so that the other ship of the task force could attack the convoy. It was stressed that the destruction of enemy mercantile traffic was the main objective. Warships were to be engaged only when the primary mission made it necessary and it could be done *without excessive risk*. The operational area was defined as the entire North Atlantic, north of the equator, outside territorial waters of neutral states. The U-boat operational area was north of 47° 30′ for the whole of the blockade zone of the British Isles, south of 42°N and east of 30°W. Both German and Italian submarines would be expected, as it was not intended to separate the operational areas of U-boats and surface forces. Previous experience had shown that the Kriegsmarine had little real information about convoy routes and timings, so that co-operation with U-boats would be mutually beneficial. Command of the operation ashore would be vested in Gruppe (Nord) until the forces at sea crossed a line between the southern tip of Greenland and the North Hebrides, after which command would pass to Gruppe (West) in Paris.

Experience during Operation 'Berlin' had underlined the need for good reconnaissance and convoy intelligence. B Dienst decrypts of Allied signal traffic were of utmost importance but it was still necessary to cover wide expanses of ocean in order to comb the anticipated convoy tracks. To this end, the squadron disposed of no fewer than seven Ar 196 floatplanes; but 'Berlin', as well as other raiding sorties, had also demonstrated the drawbacks of catapult floatplane operation. These were heavily dependent on weather conditions, which were seldom ideal in the Atlantic wastes, and moreover represented considerable danger to the parent ships while recovering their aircraft. The Kriegsmarine had little choice, however, for its only aircraft-carrier, *Graf Zeppelin*, lay unfinished. Once again the experience of 'Berlin' was called upon, in that the usefulness of the supply train for reconnaissance work was extended by the provision of special 'Scout' ships (Spähschiffe) for 'Rheinübung' (1 SKL I i 6662 G. Kdos, 4.4.41).

Two such ships were selected, *Gonzenheim* and *Kota Penang*, both motor vessels. These were to be fitted out and provisioned for a four-month sortie and carried supernumerary personnel for prize crews. In addition, they were altered to accommodate 300 prisoners. *Gonzenheim* sailed from Stettin on 11 April bound for Holland, where she was to be modified for her task at the Wilton Werft, Schiedam. Her consort was similarly treated by P. Smit at Rotterdam, the work needing two weeks to complete. Both were required to be operational by 26 April, an inordinately short time, given the important nature of the operation. They were merchant ships sailing under the Reichsdienst flag but two officers from *Gneisenau* were posted to them to ensure military discipline and conduct. Of course, they also carried naval personnel for communications purposes and prize crews.

Apart from these two ships, which had no replenishment capabilities, two fleet oilers (Trossschiffe) were detailed for 'Rheinübung'. These were *Ermland*, with a cargo of 9,366m³ of oil fuel and *Spichern*, carrying 8,000m³ of oil fuel and nearly 3,000m³ of diesel. The latter ship was designated a supply ship for U-boats also. *Ermland*'s station was in square DR16 (900nm south-west of the Azores) and *Spichern* CD64 (400nm west of the Azores). In addition, five escort tankers (Begleittankschiffe) were sailed. These were *Belchen*, stationed in AJ26 (south of Cape Farewell, Greenland), *Lothringen*, stationed east of *Belchen*, in the Davis Straits, *Esso Hamburg* in CD32 (390nm south-west of the Azores), *Breme* in DF 96 (600nm south-south-west of the Azores) and *Weissenburg* in the Arctic. There was also *Heide*, a reserve for *Weissenburg*, and *Wollin* which was to refuel the squadron in central Norway.

Replenishment was only one of the problems the SKL had to solve. Another was accurate weather forecasting. Bad weather, fog or low visibility was an essential, or at least, desirable pre-requisite, if the German ships were to evade the Royal Navy's Northern Patrol, for radar was still in its infancy and air reconnaissance would be grounded by thick weather. In fact, British radar had advanced rather more than the Kriegsmarine was inclined to believe, as will become apparent later; but nevertheless, poor weather could only benefit the 'Rheinübung' units. The vital passage was, of course, the Denmark Strait and, in order to facilitate the return of *Admiral Scheer* and *Admiral Hipper* to Germany following their raiding cruises, the SKL had early in March despatched weather ships to the Strait to report on conditions, particularly the ice edge and its extent. This was of vital importance, as the ice dictated the width of the Strait for navigation, hence room to manoeuvre and evade enemy patrols. This task could be, and was, performed by Focke-Wulf Fw 200 Condor long-range aircraft of Fliegerführer (Atlantik) but this was, at best, perfunctory, given the relations between the two services, and even so the aircraft were themselves often grounded by weather conditions.

Flag Officer (Gruppe Nord), Admiral Carls, held different opinions, fearing for the safety of the weather ships and the danger of compromising the warships' home runs, should they be discovered and their purpose revealed. He pressed for a U-boat from Stavanger to be allocated and for the future recommended the use of the ex-Netherlands submarines *UD1–UD5*. However, his views failed to carry and the 284-tonne ex-trawler *Sachsen* sailed for this task from Trondheim on 16 March. Her station was some 300nm east of Langanes peninsula. Another ship, the 344-tonne *Coburg*, was stationed well inside the Davis Strait off Resolution Island, between Canada and Greenland, where she was to be relieved later by *Sachsen*. The latter's first report was received at Gruppe (Nord) on 23 March, after which she was ordered to the Davis Straits by way of the Denmark Strait. Another report on ice conditions was signalled by aircraft of I/KG 40, operating from Trondheim on 27 March, and further details were received from the homeward-bound *Coburg*.

The activities of these little ships, operating alone for long periods in a hostile environment, both natural and man-made, deserves special mention. Theirs was a hunted existence, for their reports were intercepted by the British, who endeavoured to trap them, being well aware of the importance of their activities. *Hohmann* followed *Sachsen* to Iceland and was then relieved herself by *Ostmark*, which had sailed from Trondheim on 2 April. So that by the time that 'Rheinübung' was originally intended to be launched, only *Sachsen* and *Ostmark* would be at sea. The only other Kriegsmarine surface vessel in the Arctic wastes at this time was *Schiff 31*, formerly the British trawler *Bradman* (captured at Aandalsnes in April 1940), on a lonely mission to the north of Jan Mayen island.

The new weathership *Lauenburg* sailed from Kiel to Trondheim, ordered to relieve *Sachsen* by the end of May, and on 23 April Admiral (Westküste) was ordered to sail another

Above: *Prinz Eugen.* (Bundesarchiv)

weathership, *München*, to relieve *Ostmark* by 1 May. These details of weathership operation have been discussed not only for their importance to 'Rheinübung' but more particularly their future value to the Royal Navy and ultimately to the detriment of the Kriegsmarine itself. It had of course been realized by the Royal Navy, or its code-breakers, that these isolated, defenceless vessels were vulnerable to capture and, if this could be achieved by surprise, valuable coding data and equipment might be obtained. As a result, operations were mounted against them, the first victim being *München*. Intercepted by a force of cruisers and destroyers on 7 May, south of Jan Mayen, she was boarded by a party from the destroyer *Somali* and 'Engima' data captured before she was sunk. This, in conjunction with other captures, was to have a significant effect on British code-breaking activities ('Ultra'), although its main effect did not come until after 'Rheinübung'.

The foregoing discussion of replenishment, reconnaissance and weather problems illustrates graphically just how much auxiliary effort was required by a surface ship sortie. It contrasts fairly strongly with U-boat operations, although they did need their own supply organizations also. Further disaster struck the plans for the sortie on 22 April when *Prinz Eugen*, on passage from Gotenhafen to Kiel, was damaged by a magnetic mine, considerably disrupting the time schedule. The delay incurred was important in that the dark new moon April nights at high latitudes would be replaced be brief twilight night periods by late May, a month acknowledged to be the least favourable for break-out. The question was, should the sortie be delayed until the cruiser was repaired?

There were three options: (a) to send out *Bismarck* alone and use the coming new moon period; (b) delay until both ships were ready and the next new moon; or (c) delay only until the cruiser was repaired and ignore the moon. Admiral Carls favoured (a) but the SKL opted for (c).

On 25 April, in the light of the delay caused by the damage to *Prinz Eugen*, Grand Admiral Raeder had a conference in Berlin with Admiral Lütjens over the question of the forthcoming sortie. The latter was quite obviously unhappy at the gradual whittling down of the operation from a combined fleet sortie from both Brest and Germany to a two-ship sortie; while Raeder was keen to get the ships to sea before the USA became more actively involved. Lütjens wished to wait at least until *Scharnhorst* was repaired or even until *Tirpitz* was ready. Raeder was undoubtedly correct in not wanting to wait for *Scharnhorst*; given conditions in Brest, she might be no sooner repaired than damaged again. On the question of *Tirpitz*, there was the difference in attitudes between the Kriegsmarine (and specifically Raeder) and the Royal Navy as to just when to throw a ship into action. Given Raeder's insistence on a six-month work-up period, it was obvious that *Tirpitz* would not be allowed to participate. The secret of the decision to sail *Bismarck* and *Prinz Eugen* almost at once may well lie in Raeder's concern at the attitude of the USA, and he himself knew more about this than did Lütjens.

Raeder was actually intent on two things to improve the immediate chances of his forces, surface and submarine, in the Atlantic trade war: sanction by Hitler (a) to ignore all or part of the American neutrality patrol area; and (b) to attack US merchant ships under Prize Regulations. He saw the United States' mild reaction to the German Balkan Campaign as an encouragement that the steps he was now proposing would not result in a US entry into the war. Deep down he must have realized otherwise; hence his desire to get 'Rheinübung' to sea. He made these proposals at the Führer Conference of 20 April 1941, but barely mentioned the sortie itself. He was also concerned about repair facilities for his heavy ships, well aware of the drawbacks of the home yards and Brest. To this end he pressed for the acquisition of Spanish Ferrol! Given his pressure for the occupation of Norway and later Greece, Raeder must bear much responsibility for the misery and suffering of World War Two. Hitler, however, would not approve Raeder's plans but left him in some hope that by the time 'Rheinübung' was under way, the situation might change. Thus Raeder pressed his own views on his subordinate who came away resolved to act as ordered. As to 'Rheinübung' itself, Hitler was lukewarm, although it may well be that his thoughts were occupied by the imminent invasion of Russia, 'Barbarossa'. In the face of this colossal undertaking, it is hardly surprising that Hitler had little time to spare for his Navy Chief.

After completion of repairs to *Prinz Eugen* there were further delays so that it was not until 16 May that the Fleet command could signal 'ready for Rheinübung from midnight 17/18 May'. Gruppe (Nord) now requested Fliegerführer (Atlantik) to fly an ice reconnaissance of the Denmark Straits on 19 May, while Admiral (Norwegian) was ordered to sail *Weissenburg* and *Heide* (both with 7,000m³ of fuel and stored for a month) so as to be on station by 22 May. In western France the other oilers were sailed for their rendezvous positions and the two Spähschiffe, *Gonzenheim* and *Kota Penang*, sailed on 17 or 18 May.

The operational orders recommended a break-out as soon as the ships left Norway (if the weather was favourable) via the Iceland-Faroes gap. However, should the weather not be suitable, then Lütjens was to steam for the Arctic and rendezvous with *Weissenburg* in 70°N, 1°W (Punkt 'Hans'). There he was to top up with oil in order to make maximum use of the squadron's speed during the break-out, without regard to bunker levels. *Weissenburg* was ordered to leave her billet immediately after this and her station would then be assumed by *Heide*, coming out from the coast, to ensure a full tanker on station should the first attempted break-out not succeed.

On 1 May *Bismarck* received an inspection visit by Hitler and a large entourage of top Nazi brass, while lying in Gotenhafen awaiting orders for her departure. Admiral Raeder was not present. Karl Topp of *Tirpitz* made a plea for his ship to be included in the sortie, but to no avail, and four hours later the Führer left the ship. As a result of the delays recounted earlier, it was not until midday on 18 May that *Bismarck* moved out into the bay to top up with oil before finally putting to sea at 0200 on the following morning. 'Rheinübung' had begun.

Escorted by the destroyers *Z25* and *Eckoldt*, with *Sperr-brecher* preceding them, the two heavy units proceeded west towards the Great Belt. A third destroyer, *Lody*, joined from Kiel (the fourth, *Galster*, had the usual German destroyer problem—machinery defects). Continuing through the Belts, Kattegat and into the Skagerrak on 20 May, the squadron had the misfortune to sight, and be sighted by, the Swedish cruiser *Gotland* during the morning watch. Lütjens signalled Gruppe (Nord) with this information, concluding that his force would now be known to the enemy. Carls at Gruppe (Nord) replied, somewhat surprisingly, that, because of Sweden's strict neutrality, he did not believe that there was any great danger of their movements reaching the ears of the British. In fact, the seeds of 'Rheinübung's' failure were already sown. Carls' comments are surprising because both the SKL and he were well aware that as early as 25 January, the British Naval Attaché in Stockholm had reported to London that *Scharnhorst* and *Gneisenau* had passed through the Belts at the actual time that they did so. He remarked upon this point on 23 March, so the choice of such a compromised route was puzzling, especially as he admitted that the English spy system in Denmark and Sweden was very good.

Bismarck and her consorts cleared the boom at Kristiansand before midnight on 20 May, then altered course northwards in the early hours of the next day under clear skies and light winds. Course was altered due north at 0440. At about this time the Operations Division of the Admiralty informed HQ Coastal Command that a signal had been received from the Naval Attaché in Stockholm, to the effect that two unidentified large units escorted by three destroyers and smaller craft had passed Marstrand at about 1500 and 20 May, steering in a north-westerly direction. No. 18 Group Coastal Command was immediately ordered to fly reconnaissance patrols between Trondheim and the Naze at first light on 21 May. The B Dienst picked up and decoded the signals to these aircraft, instructing them to look for two large ships and three destroyers. However, the nearest aircraft, Blenheim H/254, was still outside visual range when the ships steamed

into Kors Fjord. *Prinz Eugen* anchored in Kalvanes Bay and *Bismarck* in Grimstadtfjord just after midday. The cruiser and the destroyers refuelled, but *Bismarck* did not. While at anchor, the distinctive black and white striped camouflage was overpainted grey. Also, unknown to them, an RAF photo-reconnaissance aircraft located and photographed *Bismarck* and a strike was launched by the RAF. This consisted of six Whitleys of No. 612 Squadron, ten Hudsons of No. 220 Squadron and two of No. 269 Squadron. However, the weather had now closed in and only two Hudsons bombed, but by this time the ships had in fact sailed.

After leaving the shelter of the Norwegian fjords, Lütjens continued north, detaching the destroyers to Trondheim at 0420 on 22 May. The weather was overcast and hazy. As yet their sailing had gone unnoticed and the RAF laid on a strike of 30 Hampdens as well as No. 42 Squadron's Beauforts at Wick, armed with torpedoes. Also on stand-by were seven Albacores of No. 828 Squadron, FAA. Bad weather grounded all this force but some limited reconnaissance flights were sent out, until 10/10 cloud at 100ft stopped all flying. Such was the desperate need of the Admiralty to determine the whereabouts of *Bismarck* that in this appalling weather a Maryland of No. 771 Squadron, FAA, took off from Hatston in the Orkneys crewed by two officer volunteers. This aircraft succeeded in locating the fjord and reporting the absence of the *Bismarck* force.

As a result, air patrols were ordered up the Norwegian coast, to Stavanger and Bergen, between the Shetlands and Faeroes, as well as between the Faeroes and Iceland by ASV-equipped Sunderlands. Catalinas flew patrols south of Iceland and the Denmark Strait was to be patrolled. Bad weather either prevented these patrols from taking off or severely curtailed them. The Royal Navy responded by sailing the battlecruiser *Hood* with *Prince of Wales* and six destroyers to Iceland, as well as alerting the various cruiser patrols. For the moment Admiral Tovey (C-in-C Home Fleet) kept his flagship, *King George V*, in Scapa Flow with five cruisers and five destroyers until the situation clarified. Back in Germany, in the course of another Führer conference on 22 May at the Berghof, Admiral Raeder briefly mentioned that *Bismarck* was at sea and managed to persuade Hitler not to recall her.

Because none of the Fleet staff nor any of *Bismarck*'s senior officers survived her eventual sinking, the intentions and thinking of Admiral Lütjens during 'Rheinübung' can only be the subject of conjecture. Even the senior surviving officer had little idea of what was said and done on her bridge in the course of the sortie. Quite when and on what grounds the Fleet Commander decided not to use the Faeroes-Iceland passage is not clear, but between midnight on 21/22 May and midday on the 22nd, he steamed due north crossing the passage to the south of Iceland. By midday he had obviously decided also not to refuel from *Weissenburg* as planned. In a signal of his intentions to *Prinz Eugen* he infers that the weather was currently suitable for a break-out, although there is no weather report at this time in the KTB of the heavy cruiser. From the courses ordered, it was obvious by now that the chosen route was via the Denmark Strait. It may

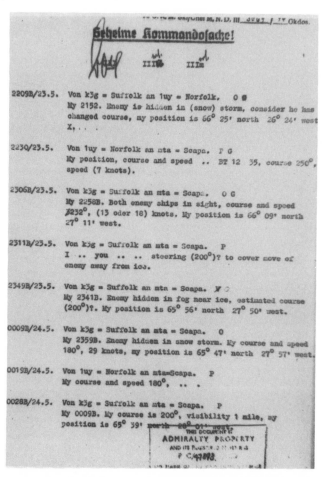

well be that his reason for doing so now was a false belief that his departure had still not been noticed by the British and he did not wish to give them any more time to realize this and station more units in the Denmark Strait during the inevitable delays in refuelling.

Throughout the afternoon and evening, therefore, the two ships steered courses to take them into the northern entrance of the Denmark Strait. As time wore on, the weather became more and more suitable for their purpose, the wind had risen and veered south-west. It was overcast and hazy. Later it began to rain. By this time orders had been given for the turret tops to be painted grey and the swastika painted out on the forecastle. There was still no firm indication of whether the British heavy forces were at sea because the same poor weather, which had grounded the RAF patrols, also affected the Luftwaffe. Such intelligence as was available seemed to indicate that as yet there was no large-scale search for them. By late evening the weather had closed down so much that *Bismarck*, in the van, could no longer be seen by *Prinz Eugen*. Visibility was only 300–400m, sometimes less. *Prinz Eugen*'s meteorologist predicted that this weather extended to the south of Greenland. In Iceland No. 269 Squadron, equipped with Hudsons, replacing the veteran Battles, but faced with

10/10 cloud, a 30m ceiling and abysmal visibility, they were rendered helpless and grounded.

An hour before midnight Gruppe (Nord) again signalled to the effect that it was believed that 'Rheinübung' was still undetected. Steaming generally west-south-west, Lütjens continued across the north of Iceland until, at about 1900, the ice edge was reached. So far, apart from a false alarm (an iceberg), no sign had been seen of enemy patrols. Further weather reports confirmed favourable break-out weather to the south, but on reaching the ice edge the horizon was light towards the ice but hazy to the east. Both ships steered a zig-zag course through the loose pack ice and snow squalls.

Suddenly, at 1922, *Bismarck* went to action station, having detected a contact with radar and hydrophones. Visual contact confirmed a warship with three funnels. It was actually the heavy cruiser *Suffolk* which had just turned south-westwards from the ice edge, when one of her lookouts spotted the German ships. She quickly regained the cover of the mist, while at the same time sending a sighting report. *Prinz Eugen*'s KTB records that the flagship fired a few salvoes at this target, but it is uncertain if this was so. In any event, *Suffolk* took up a shadowing position on the port quarter of the German pair.

An hour or so later, a second cruiser, *Norfolk* (Rear Admiral Wake-Walker), made contact and took up the port quarter billet, while *Suffolk* dropped back. *Norfolk* had, however, approached too close and was greeted by five salvoes from *Bismarck* which straddled her. As a result of the cruisers' reports, the Admiralty rearranged its dispositions in the Atlantic to meet the coming threat. At 2034 Admiral Carls at Gruppe (Nord) also received the first intimation of trouble when Lütjens' signal timed 2015 was received—'One Heavy Cruiser AD29'. He immediately alerted Fliegerführer (Nord) and Luftflotte 5 for a reconnaissance of Scapa. Seventeen minutes after receipt of Lütjens' signal, the decrypted contents of *Suffolk*'s signal were in Carls' hands also! *Bismarck* and *Prinz Eugen* were far outside effective support range by the Luftwaffe and were alone until they neared the U-boats in the Atlantic. What the enemy was doing was unclear, for the weather aborted Carls' requested reconnaissance at this critical moment.

Admiral Tovey was already at sea, having left Scapa with the Home Fleet late on 22 May. He did not receive *Suffolk*'s report and by the time he received *Norfolk*'s, his force was already steaming for the southern exit of the Denmark Strait, as he assumed this would be the German's most likely route. However, he was still well to the south-east of Iceland. Vice-Admiral Holland, on the other hand, had received *Suffolk*'s earlier report, which put the enemy about 300 miles north of him. His force, consisting of *Hood*, *Prince of Wales* and six destroyers, was therefore well placed to intercept. In addition, Coastal Command flew off Sunderlands of No. 201 Squadron from Reykjavik and Hudsons from No. 269 Squadron at Kaldadarnes to join the search.

The brief action with *Norfolk* had caused shock damage to *Bismarck*'s radar, rendering it unserviceable, with the result that *Prinz Eugen* was ordered into the lead, a move that

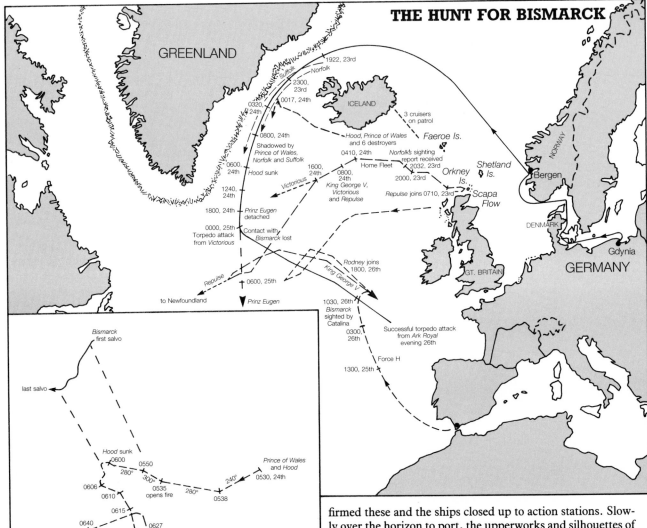

THE HUNT FOR BISMARCK

GREENLAND

1922, 23rd

Suffolk
Norfolk

2300,
23rd

0017, 24th

0320,
24th

ICELAND

3 cruisers
on patrol

Faeroe Is.

0800, 24th

Hood, Prince of Wales
and 6 destroyers

Shadowed by
Prince of Wales,
Norfolk and Suffolk

0410, 24th   Norfolk's sighting
report received   2032, 23rd

Shetland
Is.

NORWAY

0600,
24th   Hood sunk

Home Fleet

Orkney
Is.

Bergen

1600,
24th

Victorious

0800,
24th

King George V,
Victorious
and Repulse

2000, 23rd

Repulse joins 0710, 23rd   Scapa
Flow

1240,
24th

1800, 24th   Prinz Eugen
detached

DENMARK

0000, 25th
Torpedo attack
from Victorious

Contact with
Bismarck lost

Gdynia

Rodney joins
1800, 26th   GT. BRITAIN   GERMANY

Repulse

0600, 25th

King George V

to Newfoundland   Prinz Eugen

1030, 26th
Bismarck
sighted by
Catalina

0300,
26th

Successful torpedo attack
from Ark Royal
evening 26th

Force H

1300, 25th

Bismarck
first salvo

last salvo

Hood sunk
0600
0550
280°   300°

Prince of Wales
and Hood

0606
0610   0535
opens fire   280°   240°   0530, 24th

0538

0615

0640   0627

0650   0620   0624

0 1 2 3 4 5
Nautical Miles

firmed these and the ships closed up to action stations. Slowly over the horizon to port, the upperworks and silhouettes of two heavy units hove into view, although *Bismarck*'s gunnery officer would appear to have identified them initially as cruisers. They were of course *Hood* and *Prince of Wales*, but without their destroyers which had been detached.

Vice-Admiral Holland's squadron had been steaming towards the Denmark Strait, when at 2002 on 23 May he had received *Suffolk*'s sighting report of one battleship and one cruiser in a position some 300 miles north of his force. Almost 40 minutes later *Norfolk* also made a report. Improved weather conditions over the Icelandic air bases had allowed the RAF to launch air searches from Reykjavik and Kaldadarnes, towards midnight on 23 May. Sunderland Z/201 made a first sighting report in time to witness the action between the naval forces, as did Hudson G/269. On the basis of *Norfolk*'s report, Holland altered course at 295° and increased speed to 27 knots, which he estimated would lead to action in the early hours of 24 May. By midnight further reports put the enemy 120 miles from the battlecruiser force. Shortly after, however, the cruisers lost contact with Lütjens'

would have consequences later. By the early hours of 23 May the weather thickened, with fully overcast sky and driving snow. Despite this, the German B Dienst teams, who had deciphered the cruisers' reports very swiftly, showed that the course and speed alterations of the 'Rheinübung' squadron were being accurately reported. The unpleasant conclusion was that not only did the British have radar, but that it was at least as good as the German! The possible consequences of this discovery were grim. Actually both cruisers were so equipped, *Suffolk* with the new Type 284 radar and *Norfolk* with the older Type 268P. They retained contact in difficult conditions with tenacity.

Just after 0530 *Prinz Eugen*'s B Dienst team reported a new unit off to port, and, six minutes later, another, both initially believed to be cruisers. The hydrophone plots con-

force and it would appear that Holland believed that the enemy had made a major alteration of course. This led to his puzzling alteration of course northwards on to 340° at 0012 and then due north at 0017. This course was maintained until 0205 when the destroyers were ordered to continue to sweep north, while the two capital ships reversed course on to 200°. Speed was increased to 26 then 27 knots. *Suffolk* finally regained contact at 0256, her signal putting *Bismarck* about 15 miles north-west of Holland. The British ships altered course to 220° at 0321, then to 240° at 0342, and worked up to 28 knots.

At this time their respective tracks were almost parallel with the range about 20 miles. *Prince of Wales* steamed 4 cables astern of the flagship's starboard quarter. At 0535 lookouts aboard *Prince of Wales* saw *Bismarck* and *Prinz Eugen* materialize out of the mist, almost ten minutes before the Germans recorded a visual contact. She signalled to the flag, 'Enemy in sight, range 17 miles'. Seven minutes later, *Hood* reported the range as 14 miles. Holland now made what was to prove a fatal error, for two minutes after sighting the enemy, he turned 40° towards and, at 0549 a further 20° towards this, closing his 'A' arcs and placing himself at a severe disadvantage. In effect, he had allowed the enemy to cross his 'T' by his own course alterations.

At 0549 Admiral Holland ordered 'Open fire' on the leading German ship, which he believed to be *Bismarck*. *Prince of Wales*, however, had realized the error of this and took the right-hand enemy as her target. *Hood* opened fire first at 0552, just as Admiral Holland realized his mistake and ordered shift target right. One minute later *Prince of Wales* opened fire. *Bismarck* replied, followed at 0555 by *Prinz Eugen*. Both German ships took *Hood* as their target, firing four-gun salvoes, but Admiral Holland's force could only use their forward guns, due to their angle of attack. *Hood* had fired four or five salvoes before *Bismarck* replied, the German opening salvo being judged short by her gunnery officer, forward and to starboard by *Prince of Wales*. The latter's opening salvo of five 14in was over but her sixth straddled. *Prinz Eugen*'s first full broadside was of nose-fused HE because these were the ready-use shells. She was unable to observe the fall of these. A second full broadside, now base-fused HE, straddled; while one of the third was seen to hit *Hood* on the side of the boat deck in the vicinity of P3 twin 4in HA mounting. This caused a fire among ready-use ammunition cordite, probably from the UP equipment. *Prinz Eugen* now shifted target to *Prince of Wales*, until then unmolested, leaving *Bismarck* engaging *Hood*. *Bismarck*'s second salvo was a 400m bracket, of which Schneider, her gunnery officer, judged the long salvo over and the short a straddle. Her third salvo was also a straddle, with a possible hit (although the hit could well have been that of *Prinz Eugen* which started the boat deck fire). Salvo four was close short.

Admiral Holland obviously intended now to open his 'A' arcs and thus get his ships fully into action. This turn was ordered by flag hoist at 0600, indicating a further 20° to port. There is some doubt as to whether this turn was ever executed for at this moment *Bismarck*'s fifth salvo arrived.

Hood's after turrets are believed to have opened fire, suggesting that the turn had been at least started and *Prince of Wales* had just fired her ninth salvo. One or more of this last salvo from *Bismarck* struck the British flagship somewhere in the region of the mainmast, causing a colossal explosion which destroyed the 48,000-ton ship in seconds. The precise location of the hit(s), as well as the exact reason for the explosion, have been a matter for investigation, conjecture and supposition ever since 0600 on 24 May 1941. The most probable cause, however, was the ignition of the cordite stowed in 'X' and 'Y' magazines, the uncontrolled burning of which literally blew the ship apart. She sank in about three minutes, with the loss of all but three of her company of 1,418 men. *Prince of Wales* was forced to alter course to avoid the last moments of the flagship, while at the same time became the sole target of both *Bismarck* and *Prinz Eugen*.

To Lütjens it mattered not a whit how *Hood* was sunk; the important fact was that she had and a valuable material and propaganda coup had been obtained. *Prince of Wales* soon received a 38cm hit on her bridge, which did not actually detonate until emerging from the opposite side, but nevertheless it caused heavy casualties on the bridge. She quickly received six more hits, three of them 38cm, on the forward starboard 5.25in director, the aircraft crane, and one which pierced the hull below the waterline, lodging unexploded in a generator space. The 8in shells caused flooding but one failed to explode. Captain Leach now decided to break off the action as a result of this damage and because of defects in the new turrets; for most of the time only three-gun salvoes could be fired. Faced with an undamaged German force, it was undoubtedly the correct thing to do and Admiral Wake-Walker, now senior officer, concurred. Nevertheless, it required some courage on the part of Captain Leach to make it. Even so, there were some who considered she had run away.

In point of fact, the enemy was far from undamaged, having received three hits from *Prince of Wales*. One passed through *Bismarck*'s side from port to starboard in the region of compartments XX and XXI above the armoured deck and forward of the transverse armoured bulkhead. It left a large exit hole, through which tons of sea-water soon flooded the forward lower compartments. Bulkhead XX was quickly shored up but the flooding rendered unusable or inaccessible some 1,000 tonnes of fuel oil. A second 14in shell passed under the armour belt, in the region of compartments XIII and XIV, exploding in contact with the torpedo bulkhead. This resulted in flooding of No. 4 generator room and damage to the adjacent bulkheads, with the consequent slow water ingress into No. 2 boiler room on the port side. Further damage was caused to some of the double-bottom oil bunkers in this area. Finally, the third hit merely glanced the ship's boats with five men being slightly wounded by splinters.

Bismarck had expended only 93 rounds of 38cm ammunition plus an unknown number of 15cm (which had later joined in the action against *Prince of Wales*). *Prinz Eugen* had fired 178 rounds but none of hers were AP and could only have inflicted superficial damage, such as that to *Hood*'s boat

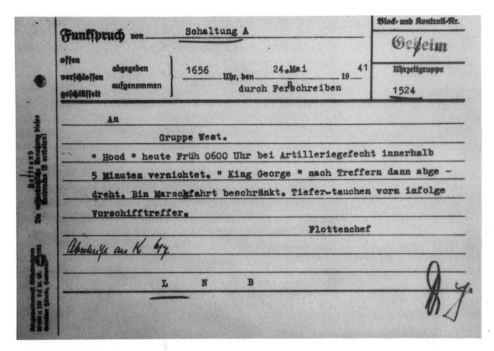

Top: Lütjens reports his success to Gruppe (West). (Author's Collection)

Above: *Bismarck* down by the bows after the Denmark Strait action. (Author's Collection)

north-eastern tip of Iceland, to cover the eventuality of Lütjens attempting to retrace his steps. Thus, in theory, Lütjens could possibly have reached home, had he decided to break off the sortie, but his every movement was being signalled and, apart from Royal Navy forces, the RAF had sent a strike force of six Beauforts from No. 22 Squadron, armed with torpedoes, to Kaldadarnes.

Back in Kiel, Gruppe (Nord) was very much in the dark, apart from knowing that 'Rheinübung' was being shadowed, now by two cruisers. A stream of decrypted shadower's reports bore mute witness to that fact. As the morning of the 24th wore on, it became evident that two more enemy units, known only by their radio call-signs 'OTT' and 'OVY', had also made contact. At 0717 a decrypted sighting report from 'OVY', giving range to *Bismarck* as 17 miles, was received by Carls. This signal was *Prince of Wales'* 0537/24. Then at 0735 Carls received another signal, this time from 'OTT', timed at 0543, reporting the range and bearing of Lütjens' force to Scapa Flow. 'OTT' was the call-sign of *Hood*. Carls was hardly surprised at the contact with Royal Navy forces, for he fully expected that the Strait would be patrolled. What he did not know was that capital ships had also intercepted *Bismarck*. It was also not known whether *Prinz Eugen* had oiled in the Arctic or perhaps from *Bismarck*, and in consequence it was assumed that Lütjens would be anxious to get her topped up. This was the reasoning behind Gruppe (Nord)'s signal to Lütjens at 1036, in which the Fleet Commander received the following:

(a) Signal position, situation and intentions (his position was already compromised).

(b) Assumed intentions—(i) drive off shadowers and allow *Prinz Eugen* to refuel. (ii) draw enemy over a U-boat patrol line.

(c) Flag Officer (U-boats) informed of situation.

(d) From 1200 command would pass to Gruppe (West).

(e) Three destroyers were at Trondheim and *Weissenburg* was on station.

A cryptic clue to what was happening fell into Carls' hands at 1116, when the B Dienst passed an appraisal to him which read, 'Unit OTT has not appeared again'. He of course had no way of knowing that *Hood* had ceased to exist hours ago. By midday the decrypted shadower's reports had enabled Carls to fix *Bismarck*'s progress accurately enough for command to be passed to Gruppe (West) on time at 1200. Still there was no word from Lütjens. Not until 1335 was a signal received from the Fleet Commander and that took until 1500 to be decoded and arrive in Carls' hands. This told him, 'Battlecruiser, probably *Hood*, sunk. Another battleship, *King George V* or *Renown*, driven off, damaged. Two cruisers shadowing'. This was timed 0632. Then at 1505 another signal from Lütjens, timed at 0801 (received at 1340), gave some amplification of the first or 0632 signal. This reported the loss of No. 4 generator room, controllable flooding in No. 2 port boiler room and his maximum speed of 28 knots. Furthermore, he reported the width of the Denmark Strait as 50nm and the presence of drifting mines. Most important of all was his disclosure that the enemy was fitted with radar.

deck. *Bismarck* and *Prinz Eugen* also fired a few rounds of 10.5cm against Sunderland Z/201, still watching the action from aloft.

Lütjens must now have been in a quandary, for although he had successfully broken out into the Atlantic, and had sunk the pride of the Royal Navy, in doing so he had stirred up a hornet's nest—the last thing that he desired. His reasons for not seeking a decisive end to the action with *Prince of Wales*, despite evidence of pressure from Lindemann to do so, can never be known. However, it was contrary to the spirit of his orders and on that count alone, it is probable that the Fleet Commander vetoed it. It would also take him back towards the cruisers, who were armed with torpedoes and *Prince of Wales* herself was still a threat. Lütjens could not afford any further damage. British countermeasures were certain and the shadowing cruisers still held contact, their efficient radar being one of the more unpleasant factors for the German admiral to consider.

The British Admiralty now concentrated all its forces into the North Atlantic, leaving only a cruiser patrol line of three ships (*Manchester*, *Birmingham* and *Arethusa*) stationed off the

Finally, he announced his intention of making for St Nazaire, while *Prinz Eugen* was to be detached for mercantile warfare.

Admiral Carls was naturally concerned over the delays in the signals reaching Gruppe (Nord), but the report of an action led him to assume it to be due to aerials being shot away. Lütjens' intentions puzzled Carls, for the damage report was sparse and rather insignificant, so why abandon the sortie? Nevertheless, he had made his own contingency plans in case Lütjens decided to return to the North Sea: the 6th Destroyer Flotilla, ordered to western France, was temporarily held at Trondheim and Flag Officer (U-boats) was requested to provide a patrol line across the Iceland–Faeroes passage. In addition, the Luftwaffe was requested to alert strike and reconnaissance forces in support of a break-back. At 1659 another signal was received from Lütjens, probably one of the brief repeats of his action report. This told of *Hood*'s sinking in less than five minutes. Half an hour later the Luftwaffe reported the results of a recent Scapa reconnaissance— admittedly under poor weather conditions. One of the ships identified was *Hood*!

Some idea of the Fleet Commander's intentions came in his 1448 signal, recorded in Gruppe (Nord)'s KTB, some $5\frac{1}{2}$ hours later. He would attempt to shake off the shadowers during the night. As an alternative, he ordered U-boats to be stationed in a patrol line on square AJ68, over which he would endeavour to draw the shadowing cruisers at daylight.

During the afternoon of 24 May *Bismarck* and *Prinz Eugen* continued south, the flagship leaving a distinct trail of oil from her damaged forward bunkers. Admiral Wake-Walker followed at a discreet distance with *Norfolk*, *Suffolk* and *Prince of Wales*. The weather was now deteriorating, to the advantage of the German ships, but the radar-equipped enemy still maintained contact. Lütjens, however, was determined to break that contact and get the heavy cruiser away on a raiding cruise. He informed Brinkmann, her captain, that at a suitable moment *Bismarck* was to take a westerly course in a rain squall, while his ship was to continue on for 3 hours. After that *Prinz Eugen* was to oil and start operations.

In the meantime Admiral Tovey, with the Home Fleet, *King George V* (Flag), *Victorious*, *Repulse* and the 2nd Cruiser Squadron, was steaming south-west, to intercept. Apart from Wake-Walker's force, Tovey could also rely on reports from RAF Coastal Command aircraft, although by now the range from Iceland was so great that only Catalina squadrons could be employed. L/240 tracked Lütjens' force during the afternoon and G/210 flew the last sortie. These aircraft were taken under fire on several occasions, without result. Eventually, at about 1540, Lütjens judged that his moment had arrived and as a squall blotted them out, ordered the separation executed. *Bismarck* increased speed to 28 knots and turned off to starboard, only to emerge from the squall in full view of her shadowers. There was no option but to rejoin *Prinz Eugen*. However, a second attempt at 1814 was successful. Having detached the cruiser, Lütjens briefly engaged *Suffolk* and *Prince of Wales* at very long range without result. He then returned to a southerly course and continued a long-range exchange of shots with *Prince of Wales*. This development was reported to Gruppe (West) but Lütjens' wording of *Prinz Eugen*'s detachment, 'will release . . . to fuel', caused uncertainty at headquarters, as to whether this in fact had taken place. It had, and, moreover, it had gone unnoticed by the British forces. *Prinz Eugen* naturally maintained radio silence.

Despite what appeared to be the successful separation, Lütjens must have despaired at ever managing himself to shake off the British cruisers, for at 2056 he radioed to Gruppe (West) that it was impossible to lose the shadowers because of their radar and that he was steaming direct for St Nazaire on account of his fuel situation. The plan to draw the enemy across the U-boats therefore fell through.

To Admiral Tovey it appeared a distinct possibility that *Bismarck* might escape and he had somehow to slow her down, so that his main force could bring her to action. To this end, he detached the aircraft-carrier *Victorious* with the 2nd Cruiser Squadron (Rear Admiral Curteiss)—*Galatea*, *Aurora*, *Kenya* and *Hermione*—early in the afternoon, for the carrier's aircraft to make a strike by torpedo. *Victorious* had embarked six aircraft of No. 800Z Squadron (Fulmar fighters) and nine Swordfish torpedo-bombers of No. 825 Squadron. This was a very meagre strike force for a Fleet carrier but the fact was that *Victorious*, like *Prince of Wales*, was a new ship and barely worked up. It had been intended that she ferry 48 crated Hurricanes to Malta by way of a work-up cruise, but in view of *Bismarck*'s appearance, this was cancelled. There had been no time to disembark all the crated aircraft, so she sailed with them and took on her few operational aircraft from Machrihanish.

When Lieutenant-Commander Esmonde took his squadron (No. 825) into the air, the weather was bad, with the flight deck pitching 10m or more and a strong north-westerly wind. Each Swordfish was armed with an 18in torpedo. The laden antediluvian-looking biplanes clawed up to 500m and set course to intercept Lütjens' force. Under the prevailing conditions, their air speed was a mere 85 knots. Fulmars were also launched for shadowing purposes. Fortunately No. 825 Squadron's aircraft were fitted with radar and with this they located *Bismarck*, but when dropping below the cloud to investigate visually, the US coast-guard cutter *Modoc* was found. *Bismarck* however, was only 6 miles to the south and spotted the aircraft as they descended.

Bismarck quickly closed up to action stations and opened up an accurate defensive fire. Esmonde's aircraft was hit some 4 miles out but continued the attack. One other lost contact but the remaining aircraft pressed home the attack. The battleship employed all her guns, including 38cm and 15cm to thwart the attack, zig-zagging at 27 knots. All eight aircraft successfully launched their torpedoes, all but one from the port side. Despite the skilled attack, only one torpedo struck *Bismarck*, the last one, on the starboard side. Unfortunately for No. 825 Squadron, this hit the main armoured belt without causing any damage. Night was now falling but Esmonde led his aircraft successfully back to *Victorious* without loss, although two of the Fulmars failed to return.

Above: Lütjens' signal despairing of losing the shadowers and reporting his intention to make for St. Nazaire. (Author's Collection)

Bismarck's gunners believed that they had shot down five aircraft and, together with the realization that the hit was not damaging, this was a great boost to morale. One man had been killed, however, and a number injured. More importantly, the high-speed manoeuvring and thus increased water pressure on the damaged hull sections (after the *Hood* action) had its effects, which were not felt immediately. In the fore-ends the collision mats parted, causing a further trim down by the bows. Amidships, the bulkhead between No. 4 generator room (already flooded) and No. 2 port boiler room ruptured further and hitherto controllable flooding became uncontrollable, with the result that that boiler room had to be shut down. Meanwhile speed was reduced to 16 knots in order to mend the collision matting at the bows.

Admiral Tovey had no way of knowing just how effective the torpedo hit might have been, except by relying upon reports from Wake-Walker's shadowers. These however now, for the first time, let him down. *Suffolk* was steaming a 30° zig-zag along the course of advance, some 10½ miles astern of *Bismarck*, regularly losing contact on one of the legs of the zig-zag but regaining it just as regularly on the other. During the middle watch on 25 May *Suffolk* found that contact was *not* regained and soon realized that the Germans had eluded them. *Bismarck* had actually made a sharp turn to starboard at about 0300, steaming first west, then gradually completing a circle around *Suffolk*, and ending up on course again for St Nazaire. As we have no means of examining any records from *Bismarck*, the events on her bridge which led to this manoeuvre cannot be established. However, it is likely that the continual observation of Wake-Walker's force over many hours had enable Lütjens' staff to gain a clear idea of the British Admiral's tactics. In particular, it was evident that

all the British ships were stationed on *Bismarck*'s port quarter. The starboard side was unguarded.

Thus *Bismarck*'s manoeuvre went unnoticed until *Suffolk* changed course, when the expected contact failed to reappear. An hour later *Suffolk* was forced to admit that contact had been lost with *Bismarck*. Assuming that their quarry had turned west, Wake-Walker turned his force south-west to continue the search. The loss of *Bismarck* was a considerable handicap to Admiral Tovey because, refuelled and with her speed possibly not impaired, the German could begin an Atlantic raiding cruise. He had to assume that *Bismarck* was making for an oiler, either south of Greenland or off the Azores. Rear Admiral Curteiss was therefore ordered to search to the west and north-west with *Victorious* and three cruisers (in case Greenland was the objective), while *Suffolk*, *Prince of Wales*, *Norfolk* and Admiral Tovey searched south-west. *Bismarck* meanwhile was steaming away south-east.

Lütjens seems to have been convinced at some time later that his manoeuvre to shake off the shadowers had not been successful, because at 0727 he reported '0700 one battleship and two cruisers still in contact', not even bothering to employ the short signal procedure normally used to avoid compromising a position. It would be interesting to know what brought him to such a conclusion, for by this time none of the former shadowers was anywhere within radar range. It could not be because, as has been suggested, radar emissions were detected which were too weak to return to the transmitting vessel, as a passive radar detector such as mettox had not yet been developed. However, it is a remote possibility that such a method had been devised by makeshift means by her radar staff, if we assume that as flagship the best personnel were drafted to her. In any event, Lütjens seems to have been greatly overawed and disturbed by the British radar; certainly he over-estimated its range. What is puzzling is the fact that commands ashore knew from B Dienst decrypts and monitoring that shadower reports had ceased after 0306 and appear to have known this long before the Fleet Commander's 0727/25. *Bismarck*'s own B Dienst must surely have reached the same conclusion.

Why then did Lütjens continue to transmit? Gruppe (West) had signalled their appreciation, that contact had been lost, to the Fleet Commander at 0846. Given these circumstances, it is at first difficult to understand just why *Bismarck* transmitted an extremely long signal at 0900, giving a detailed account of the *Hood* action, taking some 30min to transmit. However, it required considerable time for signals to be coded, transmitted and decoded, so that it is highly probable that Gruppe (West)'s appreciation arrived in Lütjens' hands some time after his 0900/25 was transmitted. To an experienced seaman, the consequences of such an inordinately long transmission by a ship not in contact with the enemy, would have been obvious. He had given himself away! It is a possibility, therefore, that this greatly affected his morale and may have been behind his address to the ship's company at noon that day. This address, couched as it was in considerably defeatist terms, not surprisingly had an equally decisive effect on the morale of the crew; the prospect

Above: Lütjens is informed of the assumption that the enemy has lost contact. (Author's Collection)

were flown against the possibility of *Bismarck* being bound for France, athwart the estimated line of advance of the enemy. Catalina Z/209 flew the southern patrol and M/204 the northern. Standing by, if anything were to come of any of these sorties, were five Beauforts of No. 22 Squadron at Kaldadarnes, eight from No. 42 Squadron and two from No. 22 Squadron at Wick, ten from No. 217 Squadron at St Eval, as well as eight from No. 42 Squadron at Leuchars. In addition, all available aircraft of Bomber Command were on standby. Six submarines were ordered to take up a patrol line off Brest and the approaches to St Nazaire. Also entering the scene was Force H, consisting of the battlecruiser *Renown*, *Ark Royal* and *Sheffield*, under the command of Admiral Somerville. Hampering search efforts was the uncertain position of many of the British units and the poor weather, with a north-westerly gale raging.

Bismarck's luck held until mid-morning on 26 May, when Catalina Z/209 caught sight of her in very poor visibility, through a gap in the clouds and almost immediately transmitted a sighting report. A few minutes later an amplifying report was also sent, but the aircraft then broke cloud cover and was seen by *Bismarck*. The battleship opened up accurate defensive fire on the aircraft, hitting it several times. After being in touch for about 15 minutes, Z/209 lost contact but her work had been done. Her sighting report was picked up and decoded both by Admiral Tovey and Admiral Saalwächter at Gruppe (West), the latter repeating it to Lütjens. When Force H received the Catalina's report, *Ark Royal* immediately launched two long-range Swordfish to shadow but it was one of her search aircraft, launched almost two hours earlier, which gained first contact. Various RAF and FAA aircraft now maintained contact for the remainder of the day, occasionally being taken under fire by *Bismarck*. Despite the relocation of *Bismarck*, Admiral Tovey could not bring her to action unless he could reduce her speed somehow. His nearest capital ship was *Renown* with Force H but, remembering *Hood*, Tovey ordered her not to engage. That in effect left only *Ark Royal*'s aircraft (30 Swordfish of Nos. 810, 818 and 820 Squadrons), for *Victorious* had long since left the scene. Accordingly, at 1450, *Ark Royal* began to launch fifteen of her Swordfish, armed with torpedoes.

In the meantime, the cruiser *Sheffield* was ordered to shadow *Bismarck*, which fact was not made known to *Ark Royal*. *Sheffield* gained contact with *Bismarck* late in the afternoon of 26 March and reported. This was duly picked up by Gruppe (West) and repeated to Lütjens. At the same time *U48* was directed to attack the cruiser. The weather was becoming worse, with high seas and low cloud. Even so, *Ark Royal*'s aircraft pressed home their attack but mistook *Sheffield* for *Bismarck*, almost doing *U48*'s work for her. Fortunately for the British, the torpedoes missed and were fitted with magnetic pistols, which proved defective, so that a second strike was ordered with torpedoes armed with contact pistols. Directed by *Sheffield*, fifteen Swordfish found *Bismarck* around 2030 that night. Despite the continual manoeuvring of the ship by Lindemann and the volume of defensive flak, one torpedo struck aft near the stern and one, possibly two,

of a fight to the last shell, victory or death, would affect most men.

Bismarck maintained radio silence after 1000 but the damage had been done. The effect was not immediately apparent because the D/F position was wrongly plotted by the British, leading to the assumption by Tovey that *Bismarck* was en route for the Iceland–Faroes narrows. All available forces were therefore concentrating to the north-east. Later some forces were ordered to act also on the assumption that the enemy *was* making for a French port. These included the battleship *Rodney* and the cruiser *Edinburgh*, while Wake-Walker in *Norfolk* tried to cover both options.

Morale aboard *Bismarck* rose a little again in the afternoon, when Lindemann attempted to reduce the effects of the Fleet Commander's address. Meanwhile the ship made steady progress south-east, until by midnight on 25/26 May *Bismarck* stood some 500nm due west of the southern tip of Iceland. During the afternoon of 25 May speed was reduced to allow damage control parties to enter the fore-ends for repairs and to attempt to use some of the previously cut off oil bunkers. At home all measures possible were being made to support the Fleet flagship, principally by the Luftwaffe; but in the end these were to be of only morale-boosting value.

On the British side, Admiral Tovey finally realized the position error, early in the evening of 25 May, at which time he was probably 100 miles or so to the north-west of *Bismarck*. RAF Coastal Command flew long-range reconnaissance sorties by Catalinas of No. 210 Squadron from Iceland throughout 25 May and into the next day, but without success. On 26 May Hudsons, Catalinas and Sunderlands searched the Denmark Strait south of Iceland and the Iceland-Faroes passage in very poor weather. In addition, two patrols

more struck the main armour belt in the midships area. All the aircraft returned safely to *Ark Royal*. Then, just as the attack finished, *Sheffield*, which had approached too close, was taken under fire by *Bismarck* but escaped unscathed, apart from splinter damage, after a few salvoes. The hit(s) amidships had little or no effect on *Bismarck* and to the chagrin of the air crews, neither did that aft, at first.

In fact, it was this latter hit which sealed the battleship's fate, for it jammed her rudders with 12° port helm on. A certain amount of shock damage was caused and the port shaft tunnel flooded. The tiller flat quickly filled with water and had to be abandoned. Flooding in adjacent compartments through started rivets and leaking cable glands, disabled salvage pumps and prevented draining out of some of the after spaces. Although damage control parties shored up some of the damaged bulkheads, the high seas defeated all attempts to place collision mats over the hole in the hull. After great effort, a hand rudder was coupled up but the water and oil in the steering gear compartments frustrated attempts to man it with crews from the secondary guns. Lindemann made great efforts to con the ship with her engines but was unable to do so. All attempts to free the rudders or to steer with the engines come to nought, and morale on *Bismarck* slumped—there was no way out.

There is some discrepancy about the jury steering attempts as, in the subsequent final investigation by the Kriegsmarine, it was stated that steering was restored and that the ship worked up to 17 knots, then 24 knots, but with a 5° list. Lütjens informed Gruppe (West) of the attack at 2054 and about 20 minutes later passed the chilling message that the ship was no longer steerable. Thus any jury steering system cannot have been in operation for long.

The Kriegsmarine was virtually powerless to relieve its flagship; the only means available were the U-boats and these could do nothing about her damage. This must have been obvious to Lütjens who, at 2140, transmitted a signal in which he vowed to fight to the last shell, adding 'Long live the Führer'. Meanwhile Admiral Dönitz (Flag Officer U-boats) ordered all boats with torpedoes to square BE6192 and a few minutes later informed them that their task was to protect the helpless battleship. Finally, at 2319, he was to order even those boats without torpedoes to the flagship. Co-operation with the Luftwaffe was, as usual, imperfect but given the ship's position, they could not mount a standing air cover for Lütjens. In any event, they could not begin to take off until about 0430 on 27 May, which meant that they could not be over *Bismarck* before 0630.

On the British side, Admiral Tovey in *King George V* had now been joined by *Rodney* and the two capital ships pursued the crippled *Bismarck*. *Rodney*, however, was badly in need of a refit and could only make 20–21 knots. In company were the destroyers *Tartar* and *Mashona*. Fuel was now a pressing problem for Tovey and until the crippling of *Bismarck* became fully appreciated, it appeared that the chase might have to be abandoned. *Ark Royal*'s air crews had changed matters in minutes. The nearest forces to *Bismarck* were Captain Vian's 4th Destroyer Flotilla, comprising *Cossack*, *Sikh*,

Maori, *Zulu* and *Piorun*, the latter a Polish ship. This flotilla made contact with the enemy about an hour before midnight and, for the next six hours or so, made numerous individual and rather unco-ordinated attacks in the dark and heavy weather. *Bismarck* was far from defenceless and took each attacker under fire, but failed to score anything but splinter hits. Under the prevailing conditions, this was hardly surprising. Equally, the destroyers achieved no success, although each expanded her full outfit of four torpedoes. Star shell was fired continually throughout the action. *Maori* made the last attack at about 0610, after which the destroyers shadowed their quarry. While their attack failed to produce any material results, it is probable that the continual action over the dark hours had an effect upon *Bismarck*'s crew, as they had little opportunity for rest, let alone sleep, that night.

Bismarck now had little way on and sometimes hove to; she could not steer and there was little point in completing high-speed circles. It was only a matter of time before the British Home Fleet caught up with the crippled battleship. As dawn broke on 27 May a north-west gale continued to blow with low cloud scudding across leaden skies. The seas remained high. *Ark Royal* was to have launched a further air strike of twelve Swordfish at dawn, but this was cancelled because of poor visibility and the field was left to the final action between the battleships.

Admiral Tovey approached *Bismarck* from west-north-west, sighting *Norfolk* (who had been shadowing since 0753) at 0820. She transmitted details of the enemy's position, course and speed to the Flag. It would appear that at this time *Bismarck* was making about 10 knots, course 330°. *King George V* and *Rodney* steamed in open order with the latter on the Flagship's port quarter. At 0842 *King George V* sighted *Bismarck* fine on the starboard bow at a range of just over 12 miles. *Bismarck* was steaming towards the British force and listed 3–5° to port. Because of haze, range-finding was difficult but *King George V* obtained a first range with her Type 284 radar and opened fire on that, one minute after *Rodney*, at 0847. *Bismarck* replied at 0849 with her forward turrets against *Rodney*. Her first salvo was 1,000m short, the second 1,000m over and the third a straddle—very good shooting. One shell missed the target by only 20m. *Rodney* also quickly found the range, obtaining at least one hit in her third and fourth salvoes, observed by *Norfolk*. However, she then re-tuned her range to one given by her main director, which was actually long and in consequence, was firing 'over' until salvo 18. This salvo produced two hits on *Bismarck*, one on the forecastle and a second on the superstructure. She continued to hit until 0902. These hits appeared to disable *Bismarck*'s forward turrets and forward fire control station.

King George V obtained her first hit about 0853 and recorded fourteen straddles in about 34 salvoes, until her 284 radar broke down at 0913, a casualty of the blast effects. *Norfolk*, to the north of *Bismarck*, opened fire at 0854 with her 20.3cm guns and *Rodney* with her 15cm secondary battery at 0858. By 0900 *Bismarck*'s replies were desultory; 'A' turret was disabled and 'B' only fired intermittently. Eight minutes

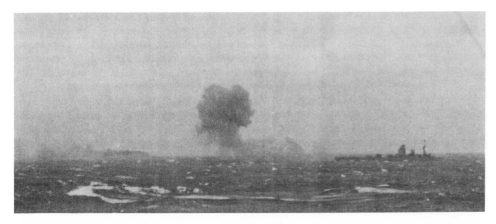

Top: *Rodney* engages the helpless *Bismarck.* (IWM)

Above: *King George V* in action. (IWM)

Right: *Lütjens'* fateful signal, 'Ship unmanoeuvrable. We fight to the last shell.' (Author's Collection)

later *Norfolk* reported that the guns of *Bismarck*'s 'A' turret were depressed and those of 'B' cocked up, indicating both turrets disabled.

After only a quarter of an hour's action *Bismarck* had lost half her fire power and most of her fire control equipment. Precise details of the damage incurred so far will never be known, for there were no survivors from the forward section. It is fair to assume, however, that she had been badly hit. Tovey now turned south, but on this course *Rodney* experienced difficulties due to swell, cordite smoke and funnel haze, so she acted independently and altered on to 040°. *Bismarck* switched control to the after director at 0910 and engaged *King George V* with the after turrets, but was able to get off only four salvoes before the director was disabled. With the turrets in local control, accuracy dropped off rapidly. At 0920 *Rodney* was re-engaged but a minute later the right gun of *Bismarck*'s 'D' turret was wrecked by a premature explosion; the left gun was able to fire two more rounds before damage forced the turret officer to cease fire. 'C' turret was silenced by a hit on its left gun at 0931. All her main armament was now out of action and the rest of the action was merely target practice. By the time that *King George V* ceased fire at 1021 and *Rodney* at 1014, the former had fired 339 rounds of 14in and the latter 375 rounds of 16in. In addition, both battleships had also fired between 600 and 700 rounds of secondary ammunition and the two cruisers *Nor-*

folk and *Dorsetshire* 527 and 254 rounds of 8in respectively. *Rodney* also fired her whole complement of twelve 24in torpedoes without managing a hit.

The effect of even a small percentage of this colossal ammunition expenditure arriving aboard *Bismarck* can be imagined. Her upper deck, superstructure and lower decks were a shambles, with huge fires raging. One of *King George V*'s shells penetrated the armour of 'B' turret and blew the back off it and *Rodney* claimed at least forty 16in hits. Despite the fires and the damage, it appeared to Tovey as if the enemy was still not sinking. So he ordered *Dorsetshire* to torpedo her. At 1025 the cruiser put two torpedoes into *Bismarck*'s starboard side, which appeared to have little effect. She then fired a third into the port side and four minutes later *Bismarck* capsized to port and sank by the stern.

Bismarck failed to inflict any real damage on Tovey's force but *Rodney* suffered considerable damage from the blast of her own guns (between 0952 and 1003, she fired full nine-gun broadsides!). The Flagship, on the other hand, experienced many defects in her 14in turrets, due to their new design.

Dorsetshire rescued 85 survivors before breaking off because of a submarine alarm. *Maori* picked up another 25. *U74* later found another three men on a raft, and on 28 May the weather ship *Sachsenwald* found another two men. Searches by the Spanish cruiser *Canarias* were fruitless—no more survivors were found.

16. THE BREST GROUP, 1941–1942

The arrival of *Scharnhorst* and *Gneisenau* in Brest on 22 March 1941 signalled a period of intense frustration for the SKL, which was to last almost twelve months. It had been their intention to refit and re-equip the two ships and then, in a combined operation with *Bismarck*, sweep the Atlantic clear of British merchant shipping, but the RAF was to negate all efforts to achieve this. As a result of their strikes, *Bismarck* was force to launch 'Rheinübung' unsupported from the south, with the consequences already described.

Although Lütjens' force had been detected on the approaches to Brest, fog had prevented this being followed up. Nevertheless, Hudson bombers of Coastal Command were put on standby at Tangmere and No. 53 Squadron's Blenheims were bombed up and ready at St Eval. In the early hours of 22 March Beauforts of No. 22 Squadron were despatched on reconnaissance to Brest, Lorient and St Nazaire, but failed to see anything because of sea fog, haze and poor visibility. Coastal Command sent out numerous sorties thereafter in an attempt to find the ships' whereabouts, but to no avail. By 24 March a Beaufort of No. 217 Squadron had established that neither was in St Nazaire and a Blenheim IV of No. 236 Squadron reported them not in Lorient. However, over Brest, cloud successfully hid the ships from this aircraft. On 26 March a Blenheim (V5648 of No. 59 Squadron) on a first-light sortie to Brest failed to return and later sorties were thwarted by 10/10 cloud.

During the afternoon of 27 March the Admiralty informed Coastal Command that they had received intelligence that the ships had arrived in Brest and it was possible that they would attempt to sail that night, on another raiding cruise. Accordingly, Hudson V/220 was flown off to carry out an ASV patrol but saw nothing. In addition, the first raid was made on Brest during the night of 27/28 March by six Blenheims of No. 53 Squadron and others of No. 110 Squadron. No damage was caused to the battleships. Adverse weather continued to defeat the efforts of the PR aircraft, until a high-level Spitfire sortie from Thorney Island brought back the first positive evidence of the battleships' presence in Brest, late on the afternoon of 28 March.

In the meantime, preparations were going ahead for the necessary refit and repairs to Lütjens' squadron. *Scharnhorst*, in particular, was badly in need of dockyard attention. All her superheater tubes were to be replaced and, among other things, torpedo tubes were installed on both ships, work which it was estimated would taken eleven weeks. There was therefore no chance of an immediate resumption of Atlantic operations, but the British High Command could not know that. Not until 1 April did a French Resistance member, a

former officer in the French Navy, get a message through to the Admiralty about the refits necessary and the fact that the ships would be immobilized for three months. Even so, because of the serious threat posed by *Scharnhorst* and *Gneisenau*, several measures were taken to prevent their leaving Brest. In the first place, the Battle of the Atlantic Directive of 9 March had switched RAF Bomber Command from concentrating upon German Reich targets to naval targets, Brest being one of these. This was not at all to the liking of the RAF, but orders were orders and thus began a long series of air raids on the battleships. Secondly, RAF Coastal Command and the Royal Navy began minelaying in the approaches to Brest and, finally, submarine patrols were instigated.

Air attacks were made on Brest on 30/31 March, 3/4 and 4/5 April by forces of 99, 62 and 49 Bomber Command aircraft. None of these scored a hit on the dry-docked ships, but one bomb was to have great significance. During the raid on the night of 30/31 March, one bomb had fallen in the dock where *Gneisenau* was berthed but had failed to explode. Three bombs had in fact fallen quite near, but it was only when the dock was being pumped out on 4 April that the unexploded bomb was discovered. Luftwaffe experts were hurriedly called in and pronounced it as a delayed-action type, which could go off at any time. Because it was felt imprudent to risk blocking the dock with a disabled ship should the bomb detonate, it was decided to move *Gneisenau* out before defusing it. Accordingly, the ship was shifted into the harbour and secured on a buoy in the Rade Abri about 400m south of the dock, on the morning of 5 April. Later a floating crane came alongside to work on the guns of SI 15cm.

Shortly after 1100 a reconnaissance aircraft was seen over the port and taken under fire but it escaped unscathed. It was a Spitfire from No. 1 PRU which brought back the first photos of the movement. A later sortie confirmed the presence of the battleship in the open harbour. The fact that the ship was now out of the dock was of great importance, for it

Left and right: *Gneisenau* under camouflage nets at Brest. (Bundesarchiv)

meant that there was a slim possibility for a torpedo attack by Coastal Command, a point which had not escaped the *Gneisenau*'s CO, Kpt.z.S. Fein. He had demanded protection for his ship while in such an exposed position but none was immediately available.

The resources of Coastal Command were not great, as far as torpedo attacks were concerned, at that moment; only No. 22 Squadron was available and its Beauforts were at St Eval in Cornwall. Nine aircraft were on line, with only six crews available. There were many problems facing the attacking force, flak batteries ashore and on the ships, net defences, the restricted room for manoeuvre and the limited zone for dropping the torpedoes. Nevertheless, an attack was ordered for the pre-dawn of 6 April. Three Beauforts were armed with parachute mines to blow up any torpedo nets, while the other three were to carry torpedoes. In the event, only four aircraft took off, the torpedo bombers and one of the mine-laden aircraft. Of these, only X/22 managed to get in an attack, which resulted in a torpedo hit, the loss of the aircraft (N1016) and the award of a posthumous VC for its captain, Flying Officer Campbell.

The aircraft was spotted by *Gneisenau* at the last moment, low down and approaching from the south over the mole. Despite the heavy flak barrage, the Beaufort successfully launched its torpedo before being shot down into the harbour. The torpedo struck *Gneisenau* on the starboard side, compartments IV and V, causing considerable damage and flooding. The outer hull and 'Wallgang' bulkhead in this region were virtually destroyed and the torpedo bulkhead from frame 51 to 62 badly distorted, its upper edge being ripped away from the armoured deck. Bulkhead 62 was damaged, as was the longitudinal bulkhead between No. 1 turbine room and the starboard shaft tunnel. The starboard shaft and bearings were also displaced. Water and oil fuel flooded through the ruptured plating and bulkheads, rapidly filling up the after flak T/S, its associated switch and amplifier rooms. Flooding was also extensive in Nos. 1 and 3 turbine rooms, No. 1 generator room and the lower rooms of 'C' turret structure.

Within 25 minutes, units of the 12th Auxiliary Minesweeper Flotilla had come alongside to act as protection against further torpedoes and five tugs stood by. In the evening *Sperrbrecher 9* lay alongside the port quarter and *Sperrbrecher 8* the starboard quarter, as further protection during the night. It was not until the forenoon of 7 April that the damaged ship could be berthed in No. 9 Dry Dock again.

The Yard Director, Admiral Stobwasser, held a conference on 8 April to discuss repairs and completion dates, but the RAF successfully intervened again on the night of 10/11 April, when 47 aircraft (nine Blenheims, 33 Wellingtons and five Manchesters) unloaded 46 tons of bombs on the dockyard. In this raid *Gneisenau* was hit by four bombs in the fore-ends. The first of these glanced 'B' turret and exploded on the starboard side of the upper deck, piercing the upper deck armour. A second passed through the hole created by the first and exploded on, but did not penetrate, the main armoured deck. The third passed through the superstructure

Above: A well known aerial view of the ships in Brest. The two battleships are in dry dock bottom left; *Prinz Eugen* lies at top right. (IWM)

Opposite page, top: Admiral Raeder leaves *Gneisenau* after inspection. (Bundesarchiv)

Centre: *Scharnhorst* in her very exposed berth at La Pallice. (IWM)

Bottom: The new torpedo tubes aboard *Gneisenau* are test fired. Note the delapidated state of the ship and the sand-bags. (ECPA)

to explode on the 'tween deck, compartment XIV, frame 148 on the starboard side. A final hit fell down a ventilation shaft on the starboard side, frame 154, exploding in a fan room in compartment XIV, adjacent to 'B' turret's barbette. Major fires broke out and some 80 men were killed and a similar number wounded. One Wellington was shot down.

When the Fleet Commander, Admiral Lütjens, came aboard on 14 April, it was estimated that about four months would be needed to effect repairs, the need for a new starboard shaft being the determining factor. 'B' turret was also now unserviceable due to the bombing and there was extensive repair work necessary in the fore-ends, where much of the crew space had been rendered uninhabitable. A full repair of the fore-ends was estimated to require about six months, but it was decided to try to cut it to the same time as that for the repair of the torpedo damage. Even the repair of the latter damage was not to be 100 per cent. Only the hull and machinery were to be fully repaired; the after fire control rooms were to be left unrepaired. However, this decision was modified later and they were partially refitted. Nevertheless, *Gneisenau* was obviously out of action for a considerable time.

Scharnhorst had so far remained unscathed and continued her refit, but measures were taken to camouflage the ships and to protect the flak guns with sand bags. Other measures were aimed at security, with French dockyard workers very much in mind. In addition, smoke-generators were being installed around the port and its approaches, the first major smoke experiment taking place on 2 May. On *Scharnhorst*, at least, extra armour plates were laid on the upper deck over the magazine spaces. Her refit was going to plan so far; repairs to her hull were expected to be complete by 9 June, guns by 13 June and machinery by 18 June.

The concentration of effort by Bomber Command between 27 March and 15 April (595 sorties, 538 tons of bombs dropped, 80 minelaying sorties, 61 mines laid) finally caused a protest from AOC Bomber Command, who succeeded getting agreement to a reduced scale of attacks with a daily PR sortie to Brest. Attacks continued to be made at a high frequency until 8 May, when they ceased until early June. Between 22 April and 7 May, 302 Bomber Command aircraft dropped 438 tons of bombs and 79 mines. In addition, Coastal Command despatched 68 aircraft with 37 tons of bombs and 61 mines. Despite the weight of bombs dropped, no hits were obtained.

By 12 June *Scharnhorst*'s new torpedo tubes had been installed and during the next few days the extra armour plate was removed. Three Arado Ar 196s arrived from Wilhelmshaven and the first trials were scheduled for 19 June. These were then postponed because of insufficient fighter cover, so it was not until the evening of 21 July that *Scharnhorst* could put to sea again. By this time *Prinz Eugen* had also arrived in Brest and had herself been badly damaged by a bomb hit on the night of 1/2 July. Brest was obviously an unhealthy place, so *Scharnhorst* was intended to spend six days further south in and around La Pallice, conducting trials and exercises to begin the long training programme so necessary for her crew after many months trapped in Brest.

Another major raid against Brest had been scheduled by the RAF, which was to have comprised several waves of bombers, escorted by long-range fighters. The operational planning called for an initial strike by three of No. 90 Squadron's Fortress I aircraft from a very high altitude, followed a quarter of an hour later by eighteen Hampdens and three squadrons of long-range Spitfires. The main force of 120 Wellingtons and heavy bombers would come in last of all. The plans had to be altered in the first place because the troublesome new Manchester bombers of Nos. 97 and 207 Squadrons had to be withdrawn because of technical problems. Then the daily PR sortie to Brest at first light on 22 July reported all the ships still in port, but its photographs were of poor quality. Because of this and also because of Admiralty suspicions of an impending move by *Scharnhorst*, a second sortie was sent but aborted due to bad weather. Finally a third sortie in the afternoon brought back photographs which, after interpretation, showed *Scharnhorst*'s berth now occupied by a tanker and two other vessels moored together to give the correct impression of length.

Because the Admiralty was already convinced of her departure, Coastal Command had been requested to fly patrols off Douarnenez, Lorient, St Nazaire and Cherbourg. Sorties planned to La Pallice and Bordeaux had to be abandoned due to cloud and icing conditions. None of the patrols sighted *Scharnhorst* and renewed PR sorties were ordered to the same ports at dawn on the 23rd. Twenty-three Beauforts and five Hudsons of Coastal Command, as well as eight Stirlings of Bomber Command, were held in readiness as a strike force, should the target be sighted. The Admiralty's appreciation of the situation was based upon PR evidence and, almost certainly, 'Ultra' intelligence, allied with new minesweeping activity and the arrival of five destroyers. It was considered that *Scharnhorst* was about to move to St Nazaire. She was

not believed to be attempting to pass back to Germany via the Channel so 'Fuller' was not put into operation. *Scharnhorst*, escorted by units of the 5th Destroyer Flotilla (*Steinbrinck*, *Ihn*, *Heinemann*, *Z23* and *Z24*), actually sailed from Brest at 2200hrs on 21 July and proceeded southwards. In doing so, she crossed one of the patrol lines set up by Coastal Command, 'Line A', then being flown by Hudson P/206. Unfortunately, this aircraft failed to sight the German force, nor detected it with ASV radar. Furthermore, due to a W/T failure, an order diverting it to patrol along the coast to St Nazaire was never received. Had it been, then it would certainly have resulted in the enemy's location.

The battleship conducted torpedo firing practice and general exercises at sea between the Roche Bonne Bank and the Ile de Ré, eventually securing alongside the mole at La Pallice in the later afternoon of 22 July. Almost immediately a camouflage company reported aboard and by darkness had fully covered the ship. The local flak regiment could muster thirty-six 8.8cm, nine 3.7cm and one hundred 2cm guns as well as twenty-seven searchlights and four Freya radar sets. Even so, the ship was in a very exposed and isolated berth.

Scharnhorst had been missed from her berth in Brest on 22 July but was not discovered at La Pallice until the forenoon of the following day by a PRU Spitfire, which was also observed by the ship. As a result of this rediscovery, Bomber Command diverted the heavy bomber component of the Brest raid to attack La Pallice instead. The first raid was made in daylight by six Stirlings of No. 15 Squadron from Wyton but only four attacked. No hits were achieved and one aircraft (N6038) ditched on return. That same night a force of 30 Whitley bombers of No. 4 Group were also despatched to La Pallice; nine No. 77 Squadron aircraft from Topcliffe and twelve No. 102 Squadron aircraft from Topcliffe and nine from No. 10 Squadron at Leeming participated. Of these, 27 attacked but scored no hits. One machine from No. 77 Squadron (Z6643) crashed on return. A further attack was made by seven Beauforts armed with 'Magnum' mines, also without result.

It was not until after midday on 24 July that a further strike reached *Scharnhorst*, this time of Halifax bombers drawn from Nos. 35 and 76 Squadrons of No. 4 Group, Bomber Command. Six aircraft of No. 35 Squadron, from Linton-on-Ouse, and nine from No. 76 Squadron, based at Middleton St George, took off for the attack, armed with 2,000lb AP and 500lb SAP bombs, but only nine aircraft attacked, dropping fifteen AP and 53 SAP bombs. The first reports of this raid approaching reached *Scharnhorst* at 1345, when the attacking force was 200–250km away. Action stations were closed up at 1400, the first aircraft being sighted dead ahead about 13 minutes later.

The flak opened up almost immediately, but at 1416 a heavy shock was felt in the ship and part of the lighting failed. Below, a sheet of flame erupted from the torpedo bulkhead opposite No. 4 generator space and a mixture of oil and water cascaded in. There were casualties among the men in these compartments and as the hatch to the next compartment could not be shut, the Electrical Action Centre was also flooded. No. 3 boiler room began to make water and the ship

Above: The bridge structure of *Gneisenau* in Brest. (ECPA)

took on a starboard list. On the upper deck, the flak guns had to go into local control and all communication was lost in the flak directors. During the next few minutes further aircraft attacked from the north-west and in the general melée at least one aircraft was seen to go down. Counter-flooding reduced the list but the ship was now in a bad way, although in no danger of sinking. Five bombs, all in one stick, had hit her starboard side. Of the bombers, No. 35 Squadron lost two aircraft (L9512 and L9527), with another written off due to damage after landing (L9507). No. 76 Squadron lost L9494, L9517 and L9529. In a simultaneous raid on Brest, 85 aircraft took part but did not hit either *Gneisenau* or *Prinz Eugen*.

After the aircraft had departed, the ship's company took stock of the damage. It appeared that *Scharnhorst* had been struck by a single stick of five bombs, all on the starboard side. The first bomb struck about frame 133 and exploded on, but did not penetrate, the armoured deck. The second passed through the ship between the torpedo bulkhead and No. 4 generator space but did not explode inside the ship. Another passed through the ship on about frame 87 to starboard, again without exploding. The fourth bomb exploded on contact with the main armoured deck about frame 52, while the last struck frame 40 and penetrated all decks and the ship's bottom without detonating. The 'tweendeck in compartments III and VIII were flooded with oil and water to

a depth of about 2m on the starboard side, No. 4 generator room and switch room were flooded, as was the starboard shaft tunnel. No. 4 magazine space, No. 2 and No. 4 auxiliary machine rooms and No. 3 boiler room were all affected by flooding. Some 3,000 tonnes of water were in the ship, of which 1,200 tonnes was the result of counter-flooding.

Kpt.z.S. Hoffmann was now in a difficult predicament, for his ship was badly damaged, obviously insufficiently protected and in an isolated berth. If he remained where he was, it was almost certain that further attacks would follow. Moreover, the dockyard facilities in La Pallice were limited. By late afternoon he considered returning to Brest that night and asked his Engineer Officer if it would be possible. This was answered in the affirmative and half an hour later he ordered steam up and recalled those crew members who were ashore.

Flag Officer (Battleships), Viz.Ad. Ciliax, returned aboard from Royan and ordered sailing at 2100. As the camouflage was being stripped off, a Spitfire was seen overhead at a very high altitude—an unpleasant portent. At 2105 *Scharnhorst* sailed, escorted once more by the 5th Destroyer Flotilla. Her sailing had been anticipated and coastal reconnaissance patrols were flown off by the RAF in consequence. However, fog and mist prevented these from sighting *Scharnhorst*, except for one aircraft. By 2200 the ship had been worked up to 22 knots and the engineering staff had succeeded in getting

Above: *Gneisenau* in the harbour. (ECPA)

all three engines steaming, although the starboard shaft was restricted to 21 knots. Pumping out the flooded compartments and shoring up the damaged bulkheads occupied the damage control parties most of the night. The morning of 27 July was foggy with some rain squalls but at 0643 a Beaufort was sighted off to starboard; it could not be engaged before it disappeared into the fog again, because of the escorting destroyer in between. Just over 20 minutes later the Beaufort reappeared, making a very low-level attack from the starboard beam. Defensive fire was opened, as the aircraft passed over *Steinbrinck*, when it dropped a 'Magnum' (a standard 1,500lb mine fitted with an impact fuse), which bounced and exploded prematurely. Almost immediately the aircraft, X/217 (AW238), was badly hit and ditched, her crew being rescued by the destroyers. No other aircraft got in an attack and at 0930 *Scharnhorst* was safely secured again on the Lannion quay in Brest.

When the damage was inspected, once the ship had been put into dry dock, the results were far from good. The structural damage was not too serious and could be made good within a reasonable time. However, it was found that major damage had been caused to her cable system, which it was estimated would require eight months repairs. Something of the order of 50 kilometres of gunnery circuitry and 150km of power supply circuitry needed replacing. This was a heavy blow to Admiral Raeder and the SKL because now

all three heavy ships at Brest were disabled. *Lützow* and *Admiral Scheer* were both in dockyard hands at home and *Tirpitz*, which was not yet fully worked up, would not be available for Atlantic employment until after 25 October. Ocean raiding by the regular warships of the fleet was obviously out of the question for a long time.

As it happened, the damage to *Scharnhorst* was the last effective blow to be struck against the Brest group by the RAF. While the dockyard pressed ahead with repairs to the ships, no major attacks were mounted by the RAF for more than a month after *Scharnhorst*'s return, except for occasional single-aircraft Fortress raids, which dropped only about 8 tonnes of bombs and caused no damage to the warships. However, these attacks did demonstrate the ineffectiveness of the 8.8cm flak at Brest which could not deal with such high-altitude attacks. Plans were therefore made to bring in 10.5cm guns.

By August it was anticipated that *Scharnhorst* would complete repairs by December, matters being partly expedited by the use of rubber-insulated cables to replace the original damaged lead-covered ones. Work on *Gneisenau* was also progressing, the new starboard shaft being given priority; installation of this was completed on 2 September. There were only two major air raids in this period, on the nights of 3/4 September by 56 aircraft and on 13/14 September by 120 aircraft, neither of which interrupted the repair programmes.

By the end of October *Gneisenau* had completed boiler trials and on 5 November could report her refit completed as far as the engineering department was concerned.

During October and November only light air raids were experienced on moon periods, usually by up to ten Stirling or Halifax bombers. However, the success of the Japanese strike against Pearl Harbor early in December had prompted the air staff to use Bomber Command for a similar purpose against Brest once more. Thus attacks were stepped up and on 17/18 December a major raid was directed against the three ships. 101 aircraft participated, dropping 138 tons of bombs. No real damage was done to the ships, except that *Gneisenau* received splinters from a near miss which caused a few casualties. A daylight raid followed the next morning, arriving over the target about 1300 hrs. It comprised nineteen Stirlings, eighteen Halifaxes and nine Manchesters. No direct damage was caused to either of the battleships, but a near miss in the dock on the port side of *Scharnhorst* caused shock and damaged the dock doors so that they could not be opened. The combined defences of the port and warships shot down five Stirlings (N3680, N6095 and W7436 of No. 7 Squadron and N3665 and W7428 of No. 15 Squadron), one Halifax of No. 35 Squadron (V9938) and a Manchester (R5795) from No. 97 Squadron. This daylight operation was code-named Operation 'Veracity I' and had an escort of ten squadrons from Fighter Command. Finally nineteen Whitley bombers attacked on the night of 18/19 December, again without success, themselves losing Z9308 and Z9277 of No. 78 Squadron.

Gneisenau undocked on 23 December and prepared for trials. However, she had to vacate her berth for *Prinz Eugen* on 6 January 1942, moving into the dry dock, where an evening raid caught her the same day. One bomb exploded in the dock between the ship and the dock wall on the starboard side, renting the hull in compartment V. As the dock was still flooded, some wing compartments outboard of the torpedo bulkhead also flooded. Although not serious, the repairs were bound to cause delay. She was repaired again by 22 January and undocked once more for trials. After gunnery exercises against moored target floats while still alongside, *Gneisenau* finally sailed for trials on 27 January, escorted by *Sperrbrecher 1* and *Sperrbrecher 9*, as well as units of the 2nd Torpedo-boat Flotilla. These lasted only eleven hours but it was all she would get. *Scharnhorst*, stuck in her dock until the doors could be opened, was nearly more permanently trapped, for on 30 December near misses hit a floating crane outside the doors, which capsized, and only quick thinking got another casualty away, otherwise the doors might not have been operable even when repaired. As it was, the dock slowly reflooded and the ship came off the blocks. In another incident, her camouflage netting caught fire, fortunately without serious consequences. Finally, she undocked on the evening of 15 January, re-ammunitioned and performed a brief gunnery shoot before departing for a short trial run on 3 February.

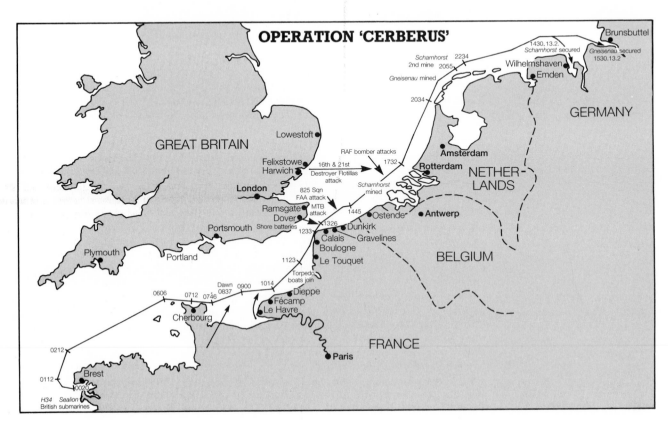

Escorted by *Beitzen* and the 2nd Torpedo-boat Flotilla, she too was only at sea for ten hours or so.

The activity surrounding the ships of the squadron had not of course escaped the cameras of the daily PRU Spitfires which, backed up by 'Ultra' intelligence, clearly indicated an imminent move. Thus the bombing raids had been reinstituted from 25 January and on 3 February the executive for 'Fuller' was issued. On 11 February PRU photographs showed six destroyers present, actually *Beitzen*, *Jacobi*, *Schoemann*, *Ihn*, *Z25* and *Z29*, as well as torpedo boats previously noted there, *T2*, *T4*, *T5*, *T11* and *T12*. Taken together with the increased minesweeping activity noted in the Channel, it was obvious that a break back to Germany via the Channel was only hours away.

The long spell at Brest was now almost over, although only the senior commanders knew it. Detachments of the ships' crews had been sent to the Baltic for periods of sea training aboard the Panzerschiff *Admiral Scheer*, in particular the 28cm turret crews, and all efforts were made to raise the general standard of the ships' companies after such a long period of inactivity. For the RAF too an onerous task was coming to an end, one which they were not sorry to lose. During the period of the ships' stay in Brest, the RAF had despatched 3,599 aircraft sorties to the port, of which 2,692 had attacked for the loss of 53 machines. 4,118 tons of bombs had been unloaded over the town, docks and ships.

With the Brest group operational once more, it had been Raeder's intention that Atlantic operations against Britain's trade routes would be resumed. However, training was a problem after such a long period in port, but it was felt that this obstacle could be overcome by short-duration strikes, using a single supply tanker. These could be launched from February 1942. Raeder put his proposals to the Führer on 13 November 1941 but failed to command Hitler's attention— he was too preoccupied with Russia. Instead, quite unexpectedly, he asked if the ships could get back to Germany by a surprise break-through up the English Channel. This somewhat disconcerted Raeder and was not at all the answer he was seeking. Nothing further occurred until 25 December, when Hitler informed his Naval Aide that in view of the continual threat of bomb damage, it was useless to keep the ships at Brest. Instead, they were to be brought back via the Channel and then employed in his new zone of destiny—Norway. Naturally this was passed on to the head of the Navy, who discussed it with his senior admirals, all of whom were against the idea. It was too risky and the crews were not trained well enough. This view eventually led Hitler to give Raeder two options: bring the Fleet back via the Channel, or scrap the heavy ships altogether. Faced with this ultimatum, Raeder had of course only one choice.

At a meeting in the Führer's Wolfschanze headquarters in East Prussia on 12 January 1942, the Navy bowed to the inevitable and accepted the task. This was given several codenames before 'Cerberus' was finalized; it was to be possibly the only occasion when co-operation between the Kriegsmarine and Luftwaffe functioned smoothly and successfully. The plan as it finally emerged was to sail from Brest at night, timed to gain full advantage of the dark period and the flood tide up Channel, risking passing the Dover Narrows in daylight to catch the British on the hop. In fact, they would do just that because the British counter-measures plan, 'Fuller', envisaged a daylight departure to pass the Narrows in darkness.

Air cover was to be provided by Luftflotte 3 under Generalfeldmarschall Sperrle at Le Touquet, later transferring to Schiphol in Holland. It was intended that at least sixteen aircraft were to be constantly over the ships; in fact, altogether, 176 fighter aircraft eventually participated, from JG 1, JG 2 and JG 26. Most were Bf 109F-2 or 'F-4 types, but II/JG 26 had re-equipped with Fw 190As by this time.

On the afternoon of 11 February Viz.Ad. Ciliax informed the ships' captains that 'Cerberus' would be executed that evening and sailing was ordered for 2030. At the last minute departure had to be postponed because of yet another air raid which had been launched by the RAF, following PR evidence of all three ships being secured alongside in the Rade Abri. Sixteen Wellingtons raided the port but inflicted no damage. Smoke generators effectively hid the ships from the aircraft and prevented a true assessment of their imminent departure. The all-clear eventually sounded at 2200 and the flagship, *Scharnhorst*, slipped at 2225. *Gneisenau* followed and groped her way through the smoke towards the harbour entrance, assuming the flagship to be clear. The latter was, however, still within the harbour and a collision was only narrowly averted. The force formed up outside the net barrage and headed seawards at 17 knots, increasing to 27 knots at 2343. It was a very dark night with a light south-westerly wind and scattered clouds. Ushant was passed at 0112 and an hour or so later Ciliax broadcast the details of the operation to the ships' companies. Course was now shaped up Channel, well clear of the Brittany coast. So far, all was quiet and the B Dienst detachments reported no undue enemy alarm. It seemed as if their sailing had gone unnoticed.

It had. An unfortunate sequence of events had led to a gap in the RAF's coverage of the approaches to Brest and the western entrance to the Channel. The routine evening patrol, Hudson W/224 had taken off from St Eval but had encountered a Ju 88 night-fighter. This was avoided but in doing so, the Hudson's ASV radar was switched off and when switched on again blew a fuse because of an operator error. Not recognizing the fault as such a simple one, the pilot returned to base and a replacement aircraft (K/224) did not take off until 2130. Although this aircraft completed its patrol, Ciliax's force was out of its ASV range by this time. The same situation applied to the next patrol, A/224, but at one point contact range was reached but on a dead astern bearing which was not effective. A second patrol line flown by G/224 also suffered ASV failure and no relief aircraft was sent out. If it had been, there was a good chance that Ciliax's force would have been found.

Having evaded the British air patrol lines, albeit unwittingly, and the submarines *Sealion* and *H34* stationed in the approaches to Brest, the German squadron skirted Alderney and passed close inshore around the Cherbourg peninsula.

Action stations were closed up before dawn, and just after dawn Bf 110 twin-engined escort fighters arrived. These were joined by Bf 109s and thereafter continuous fighter cover was provided until dusk. Luftwaffe liaison officers had been posted aboard the ships and for the one and only time co-operation between the two forces was perfect. Between 0900 and 1000 boats of the 2nd and 3rd Torpedo-boat Flotillas joined, to reinforce the escort, while up to 30 fighters circled over the squadron. It still remained quiet, with the French coast closely visible to starboard. S-boats from Boulogne further increased the protective ring around the heavy units. There was one alarm caused by the discovery of a new enemy minefield off Berck, through which a narrow channel had to be swept quickly. This was one of the fields laid down by *Welshman* which, together with *Manxman*, had laid 1,000 contact and magnetic mines in six fields between Ushant and Boulogne during the period 3–9 February.

The German force had actually been sighted by an RAF fighter patrol as it was crossing the mouth of the Somme, but the pilot reported it as a convoy under escort off Le Touquet. Only when this aircraft returned to base did it become evident that a capital ship was present. At the same time two other Spitfires flying a low-level patrol chanced across *Gneisenau* but made no report until a quarter of an hour or so later. Cap Griz Nez was rounded at about midday, at which time, the B Dienst began to report the first signs of their having been detected. Shortly afterwards, the S-boats on the port screen were ordered to lay a smoke screen, as the squadron approached the Dover Narrows. Here, between about 1318 and 1335, the Dover gun batteries engaged in a rather desultory fashion, all shells falling short. K.z.S. Fein, *Gneisenau*'s CO, could hardly believe that only one medium battery could have been brought into action at this time! After the danger zone of the batteries had been passed, the 5th Torpedo-boat Flotilla joined from Flushing. The Straits of Dover had been successfully negotiated and, in worsening weather, 'Cerberus' continued into the North Sea.

British counter-measures now began to get under way, albeit in a haphazard and faltering manner. The forces available were meagre. At Harwich the Royal Navy had six old destroyers and at Dover and Folkestone a total of eight MTBs as well as five MGBs. The Fleet Air Arm had six Swordfish of No. 825 Squadron at Manston, while Coastal Command had twelve Beauforts of Nos. 86 and 217 Squadrons at St Eval, seven more of No. 217 at Thorney Island, while at Leuchars were fourteen Beauforts of No. 42 Squadron. Bomber Command had immediately available 73 aircraft of various types, while Fighter Command had about 550 machines. At about 1328 one of the destroyers reported the presence of enemy MTBs to Lütjens and torpedo noises were heard in the hydrophone plot. These had been fired by a force of MTBs from Dover. Only five boats had sailed and one of these broke down. In the face of such a strongly defended target, all the torpedoes were fired at long range and none found its mark. S-boats as well as the destroyers *Ihn* and *Beitzen* were ordered to drive the enemy off. The next attack was from the air as six Swordfish of No. 825 Squadron

pressed home an almost suicidal torpedo attack. Met by a dense barrage of fire from the warships and fallen upon by the fighters of the air escort, all the Swordfish were shot out of the sky without obtaining a hit themselves. The leader of this formation was Lieutenant-Commander Eugene Esmonde, who was awarded a posthumous VC—the first to be won by a member of the Fleet Air Arm.

Command of the operation passed from Gruppe (West) to Gruppe (Nord) at 1516, as the weather further deteriorated. The 2nd S-boat Flotilla could not leave Ymuiden because of the weather, so that a request from the 4th Flotilla to return to base could not be allowed. The first set-back to Lütjens took place at 1530 off the mouth of the River Scheldt, when a severe explosion shook *Scharnhorst*. No. 5 Group, Bomber Command, had, between 6 and 11 February, laid 98 magnetic mines in this area (code-named 'Nectarine') using Hampdens of Nos. 49, 50 and 408 Squadrons and Manchesters of Nos. 83 and 207 Squadrons. All *Scharnhorst*'s lighting, command elements and steering failed, but damage control parties quickly got them into action once more. Leaks were reported on the port side forward and in No. 2 boiler room. It soon became evident that the situation was far from serious but Ciliax called up *Z29* and shifted his flag to her, ordering the 3rd Torpedo-boat Flotilla to stand by *Scharnhorst*. *Gneisenau* meanwhile sheered out of line, passed the stricken flagship and disappeared into the gathering gloom, squalls and low cloud having greatly reduced visibility. In accordance with the operational orders, Fein assumed command and pressed on, leaving Ciliax to chase after him in the destroyer.

The poor weather virtually nullified the RAF air attacks, which began at about 1500 by Beauforts, Hudsons, Wellingtons and other types. All these attacks were delivered piecemeal by aircraft just dropping out of the clouds to bomb whatever was below. Although the torpedo boats *Jaguar* and *T13* were damaged, the capital ships escaped. *Gneisenau* had just out-manoeuvred a torpedo attack by a Beaufort at 1640 when, three minutes later, gunfire was seen to the east. In the poor visibility, with air attacks coming from all directions, it could not at first be established what was the cause of it, but the greeny-yellow shell splashes indicated an enemy warship. Just then, three destroyers were seen dimly in the mist, whereupon a running fight developed. The destroyers were *Campbell*, *Vivacious* and *Worcester*, based at Harwich, which, together with *Mackay*, *Whitshed* and *Walpole*, had been ordered into the attack around midday. After a chase across the North Sea (during which *Walpole* had to be sent home with defects), the remaining five destroyers pressed home a determined attack. Engaged by both *Gneisenau* and *Prinz Eugen*, only *Worcester* was hit, although she managed to limp back to harbour very badly damaged. Fein ordered his own destroyers to drive off the enemy while he continued up the Dutch coast. Air attacks continued until dusk but without result.

At 2056, off Terschelling, *Gneisenau* herself was shaken by a ground mine explosion which stopped the centre engine. All engines were ordered stopped while the damage was

assessed, but it was only minor and speed was soon increased to 25 knots. *Prinz Eugen* had now become detached and thereafter proceeded independently while *Scharnhorst* was some 30 miles astern. The latter ship was in company with *Schoemann* (aboard which Ciliax had transferred after *Z29* had machinery defects) and the torpedo boats *Kondor* and *T12*. The battleship was herself having problems; first the starboard engine failed, then the port, while the Engineer Officer reported that half of the turbo-generator foundations were cracked. By 2047 ominous noises emanated from the port IP turbine, which had to be uncoupled, reducing speed to 25 knots. Machinery problems continued until 2234, when *Scharnhorst* hit a second mine north of Terschelling. All engines failed and the ship drifted helplessly for a while. It was not until just before midnight that she could continue and then only at 15 knots or so, with about 1,000 tonnes of water aboard. Tugs were despatched to her but were not required, although *Scharnhorst* did not reach Wilhelmshaven until noon the following day.

Gneisenau in the meantime reached Brunsbüttel earlier that morning, as did *Prinz Eugen*. Only the heavy cruiser was undamaged. *Scharnhorst* was quite seriously damaged but the relatively light damage to *Gneisenau* was ultimately to prove fatal. 'Cerberus' had been a huge propaganda success for Germany and an acute embarrassment to Britain. However, the success was merely tactical: it actually marked the end of ocean raiding by the capital ships of the Kriegsmarine. British losses were almost entirely borne by the RAF, whose casualties included nine Hampdens, three Wellingtons, two Blenheims, three Beauforts, four Spitfires, six Hurricanes, two Hudsons and three Whirlwinds. In addition, the Royal Navy lost six Swordfish and the destroyer *Worcester* was damaged.

RAF AIRCRAFT LOSSES DURING OPERATION 'CERBERUS', FEBRUARY 1942

Hampden bombers: AE396, AE123, AE240, P5324 (all 49 Sqn.), AT177/50, X2969/144, AE141/144, AT175/144 P4400/420, AT134/420, P1156/455
Wellington bombers: Z8714/103, Z1081/214, Z1146/419, Z1091/419
Blenheim bombers: Z7433/110, T1922/114
Hudson bombers: AM598/407, AM712/407
Beaufort torpedo-bombers: L9877/217, AW273/86, AW278/ 217
Spitfire fighters: AA722/234, AA727/234, AD195/411, AD239/118, AA921/19, AD332/19, W3565/41, W3131/401
Hurricane fighters: BE476/607, BE670/607, Z3774/1, BD949/1, BE222/607, BE498/607
Whirlwind fighters: P7050, P7093, P7106, P7107 (all 137 Sqn.)
Note: This list cannot be claimed as comprehensive. There were in any case operational losses during this attack not due to enemy action, such as two Spitfires of No. 403 Squadron, AD273 and BL337, which collided over Brightlingsea.
Royal Navy losses comprised six Swordfish of No. 825 Squadron, including V6105 'H' (Esmonde's a/c).

17. HOME WATERS, 1941–1942

With the absence of *Scharnhorst* and *Gneisenau* and the loss of *Bismarck*, there remained three heavy units in home waters early in 1941. Of these, *Tirpitz* had only commissioned on 25 February under the command of Kpt.z.S. Karl Topp. While she had been fitting out in Wilhelmshaven, RAF Bomber Command had made strenuous efforts to damage or destroy her, but to no avail, while themselves losing many aircraft. The heaviest period of attacks was between January and February 1941, 269 sorties being despatched in January and 173 the following month. The major raids took place on 15 January (96 sorties), 16 January (81 sorties) and 28 February (116 sorties). The new battleship left Wilhelmshaven for trials and working up in the Baltic on 9 March and remained in this status for first nine months of 1941.

Admiral Scheer was undergoing a major machinery overhaul following her raiding cruise, described in Chapter 13. All her main and auxiliary motors had been dismantled with pistons and pumps having been despatched to MAN at Augsburg for refurbishing. All her generators were also stripped down for repair. K.Ad. Krancke bade farewell to his command on 12 June and was succeeded by Kpt.z.S. Meendsen-Bohlken, 44 years of age from Brake in Oldenburg, who had originally joined the Navy in 1915. The ship's refit progressed relatively smoothly, so that by the first week in July, machinery trials could be begun, followed by sea trials in the western Baltic. These however revealed more problems with her motors, resulting from defective glands and seals, and the ship had to return to the yard.

In the meantime *Lützow* had completed repairs to the torpedo damage incurred in April 1940, and on 31 March 1941 was recommissioned at Kiel under the command of Kpt.z.S. Kreisch. There followed the usual storing, ammunitioning and oiling for sea, preparatory to working up. She sailed for Gotenhafen on 9 April and began her training programme in the Gulf of Danzig and off Swinemünde. It was anticipated that the ship would be deployed for action by early June, but Kreisch felt that this would not be possible and it does seem precipitate, given the Kriegsmarine's normal insistence on long work-up routines. During trials 26.6 knots was achieved on the Neukrug mile. *Lützow* was scheduled for another Atlantic raiding cruise, beginning in June, supported by the replenishment ship *Uckermark*. The latter would sail from a port in western France. However, because of the imminent invasion of Russia, Hitler vetoed all further Atlantic sorties for the moment, effectively disrupting the plans of the SKL. Nevertheless, they felt that they were justified at least in transferring the ship to Nor-

way, the first stage of the operation, after which they hoped that the situation in the East would have stabilized enough to persuade the Führer to allow the sortie to proceed.

Despite her captain's misgivings, *Lützow* was ordered to Norway on 6 June (Operation 'Sommerreise'), and on the afternoon of 10 June she sailed from Gotenhafen bound for operational deployment in Norwegian waters; Kreisch informed his ship's company of the move that day. The following day the light cruisers *Emden* and *Köln* joined, both being bound for Oslo on training duties; *Sperrbrecher 18* provided the escort. A shortage of destroyers and torpedo boats forced this combined movement. *Lützow* had been ordered to be off Kristiansand two hours before dawn on 13 June. To comply, it was necessary for the Great Belt to be transitted at 15 knots, the Kattegat at 18 knots, thereafter increasing to 20 knots (*Leipzig*'s maximum). After detaching the two light cruisers, passage would be continued with the destroyers at 24 knots. On the evening of 10 June *Galster* joined off Fehmarnsund, followed later by *Eckoldt*, *Z23* and *Z24*. Finally, *Lody* joined with Captain (D6) Kpt.z.S. Schulze-Hinrichs.

Admiral Carls at Gruppe (Nord) had wished further to reinforce the escort with the former Norwegian torpedo boats which had comprised the 7th Torpedo-boat Flotilla until their transfer to BdU for training use but the SKL denied his request. Based on earlier experiences, Carls thought it unlikely that *Lützow* would succeed in leaving the Baltic undetected and anticipated that any such sighting would result in increased British activity in the Denmark Strait and south of Iceland. To ambush these patrols, he wished to station U-boats to intercept them. Unfortunately he had no U-boats under his direct control and BdU could only allocate two. Furthermore, there were problems in providing the necessary air cover for the transfer. Luftwaffe 5 reported being able to provide only four Bf 109s and two Bf 110s at Mandal, eight Bf 109s and two Bf 110s at Stavanger, with four more of the latter at Herdla. However, in agreement with Abschnittskommandeur–Jutland, further forces were transferred temporarily from Denmark to south Norway (six Bf 110s).

Just before midnight on 11 June *Sperrbrecher 18* was detached and passage speed could be increased to 15 knots as planned. The following day speed was increased to 20 knots during the forenoon watch. A straight course was being steered, while two Ar 196s provided air escort. Shortly after midday four Bf 110s joined and at 1336 the Skaw was passed. Problems of communication were being experienced with the air escort, a sign of the imprecise co-ordination between the

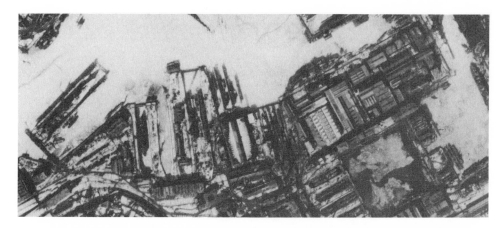

two services. Towards evening the two light cruisers, the Arados and two of the Bf 110s were detached, leaving *Lützow* to press on with her destroyers. Two Bf 110s and four Bf 109s remained as air cover. Towards midnight Gruppe (Nord) signalled that an enemy aircraft (probably Blenheim T1955 of No. 235 Squadron) had been shot down by a Bv 138 off the entrance to the Skagerrak, a welcome piece of news, as it could mean a gap in the enemy's reconnaissance patrols.

In point of fact, this action was of little consequence, for the British Admiralty had been aware of an impending move from the early hours of 11 June, almost certainly as a result of 'Ultra' intelligence and possibly derived from the requests to the Luftwaffe for air cover. British cryptographers were considerably more successful with Luftwaffe code-breaking at this time than with naval codes, and it is likely that the signals between Luftflotte 5 and units in Denmark were monitored. It was believed that the transfer in question was *Tirpitz* and fourteen aircraft then on routine patrol off south Norway were alerted. Reconnaissance patrols were ordered to Kristiansand, Bergen and Stavanger by 1000hrs, as well as increased surveillance of the seas off Iceland. Five torpedo-armed Beauforts were sent to Wick, two flying-boats to Sullom Voe and another to Iceland. By early evening of 11 June the Admiralty was able to supply positive evidence to the RAF that the unit in question was *Lützow* and that she had left the Kiel bay area north-bound about 0900 that morning. Counter-measures were therefore reorganized on a new time scale, assuming a mean speed of advance of 20 knots. In addition, the Home Fleet sailed from Scapa, bound for the south-west corner of Iceland—exactly as anticipated by Admiral Carls but he lacked the means to attack it. *Fifteen* minutes after *Lützow* passed the Skaw, the Admiralty informed the RAF of the fact *without any visual contact having been made with the enemy* and air dispositions were altered accordingly. Five Beauforts of No. 22 Squadron from Wick and nine of No. 42 Squadron from Leuchars were airborne before midnight on 12 June, but two of the former returned due to defects.

Lützow passed on under overcast skies and rain squalls. A west-south-west wind blew, approaching gale force. Throughout the night of 10/11 June and subsequently, the B Dienst detachment aboard *Lützow* had been registering greatly increasing radio traffic to and from No. 18 Group, RAF Coastal Command, the reasons for which have already been explained. However, it was not until 0015 on 13 June that a sighting report was picked up which, when decyphered twenty minutes later, read '1 cruiser and 4 destroyers in 57°48 N, 06°50E Course 270°'. The aircraft's radio call-sign was 'w8n', actually Blenheim W/114 which had sighted an enemy aircraft and turned to attack it. While in the course of this, it saw *Lützow* and her escort, which actually had no air cover at this time, or so Kreisch believed. From British reports, however, there would appear to have been two Bf 109s and two Bf 110s with the ships at the time of first sighting by W/114. Kreisch immediately warned his destroyers to expect an air attack around dawn and ordered his own flak closed up from dawn. At the same time he sent an urgent request to

Luftflotte 5 for fighter cover. It was unfortunate that he also had to reduce speed to 21 knots at this time because his destroyers could not keep up in the rising seas. The first visual contact with the enemy was made at 0115, when a fleeting glance was obtained of two low-flying aircraft which could not be identified. These may have been No. 22 Squadron machines, but they were thought to be German aircraft returning to base.

It was Beaufort W/42 which made the first offensive contact with *Lützow*, having crossed her course and turned back at the Norwegian coast. On the homeward leg the pilot chanced across the ship's wake through a gap in the clouds, circled back and made an unobserved torpedo attack, which scored a hit. A few minutes later another Beaufort, Y/42, also attacked but missed, followed by R/42 which made two runs but could not get the torpedo to release. Two late take-offs from No. 22 Squadron were unsuccessful; one failed to locate the target, while the second, C/22, made an attack but missed and was shot down by a Bf 109. (This aircraft was either W6521 or W6522, both of which were lost that day).

Lützow was caught completely unawares, despite having seen an unidentified aircraft only a quarter of an hour before the successful attack. Action stations were not closed up and Kreisch had retired to his sea cabin leaving the Commander, K.Kpt. Knocke, with the watch. When an aircraft was seen again at 0218, it was at first thought to be German but a challenge from destroyer *Z23* went unanswered, following which a splash was seen in the water. Knocke immediately ordered 'hard to port' but the Second Torpedo Officer, Lt.z.S. Euler, called out for an alteration to starboard because of the track of the torpedo. This Knocke ordered but the ship was still answering to port and the torpedo (dropped at a range of only about 600m) struck before this helm order took effect. It exploded adjacent to No. 2 motor room, throwing No. 2a motor off its foundations. Both Nos. 1 and 2 motor rooms, as well as No. 1 gearing room, began to fill and there was also extensive flooding in the wing spaces between compartments VI and VIII, which had been empty. The torpedo bulkhead in No. 1 motor room and No. 1 gearing room was badly distorted and nearly 1,000 tonnes of water flooded into the ship. She quickly took up a threatening port list of

18–20°, with the upper deck awash and all engines stopped—those on the starboard side because the list prevented their lubrication systems working. Until the list was reduced to about 10° by counter-flooding, the starboard machinery was useless. The water continued to rise in No. 2 motor room which had to be abandoned 36 minutes after the explosion. Fortunately, there had only been three casualties and they had only light wounds. To add further to the ship's problems, the shock of the explosion set off the smoke-generating equipment and she quickly became wreathed in smoke, leading some of the attacking Beauforts to report her well on fire. The Damage Control Officer, Kpt.Lt. (Ing) Ritzmann, was an experienced officer—he had been aboard the ship at Ibiza before the war and at Oslo in 1940—and quickly and efficiently set about securing the ship. Counter-flooding gradually reduced the list to 8–10°, but at the cost some 1,200 tonnes of water in the ship.

Meanwhile Kreisch, after his rude awakening, signalled his predicament to Gruppe (Nord) and then ordered *Eckoldt* to prepare to tow the stricken ship to Egersund. He was keenly aware of the danger to his ship, unprotected as she appeared to be by Luftwaffe cover. However, an attempt to launch her own Arado as cover had to be abandoned due to the list, damaged crane and lack of compressed air. His intentions were to make for Egersund under tow if his main motors could not be started but if they could, then he would make for Stavanger, which was some 40nm away but offered better repair and defence possibilities than Egersund. However, while the destroyer was still getting out her towing gear, the Engineer Officer, K.Kpt. (Ing) Pennekamp, reported No. 3 motor room and its two motors serviceable and only a few minutes later could make a similar report about No. 4 motor room. Kreisch altered his plans and cancelled the proposed tow, intending now to proceed under his own power back into the Baltic. By 0320 the ship was under way at a speed of 12 knots.

The situation was still acute for the whole generating outfit of the ship was in a very fragile state and might leave the ship without power at any moment, one reason for making a bee-line to Stavanger. On the other hand, the ship could only be fully repaired in Germany and Kreisch felt it unlikely, given the shortage of destroyers and torpedo boats, that the five he had with him now could be made available again later, should he stay in Norwegian waters. He therefore decided to make for home, close under the coast and with his destroyers protecting the starboard flank. His fears were of course justified because the RAF had launched further attacks against *Lützow*. Nine Blenheims of No. 114 Squadron and three Beauforts, all armed with bombs, had taken off from Leuchars but of these, only Blenheim D/114 located the enemy. This aircraft made a brave, lone attack but did not obtain any hits with her two 500lb bombs before escaping back into the clouds. A final strike by three No. 22 Squadron Beauforts from North Coates failed to locate *Lützow*.

That his force was being shadowed was only too apparent from the B Dienst reports which were quickly passed to Kreisch, with decrypted shadowing reports. Hudson Z/220 sighted her about 0420 and maintained contact for two hours or so before Blenheim X/248 took over. Bomber Command had agreed to send out a heavy bomber strike if *Lützow* could be precisely pinpointed and early in the afternoon four Stirlings were flown off, but in view of the doubt as to exactly where the target would be, they were subsequently recalled. Photo-reconnaissance sorties were despatched to likely Norwegian ports to no avail, the last sighting being by Blenheim S/248 in mid-afternoon when *Lützow* was well inside the Skagerrak. Thus the major air attack feared by Kreisch never materialized and his ship berthed in Deutsche Werke at Kiel late on the afternoon of 14 June, tugs bringing her in on the last leg because of fears that her generators were about to fail altogether.

Operation 'Sommerreise' ended therefore in failure with *Lützow* yet again badly damaged by a torpedo, which would take many months to repair. Naturally, close investigation of the incident followed, which was centred upon the poor communications or indeed lack of ability to communicate with the Luftwaffe air umbrella. The speed at which the British became aware of the ship's movements and intentions was extremely disconcerting and boded ill for future ventures of this kind. It is surprising that, knowing how easy it was for the B Dienst to decrypt RAF codes, no one questioned whether or not the same was being done to Luftwaffe and

Kriegsmarine codes. An investigation was later conducted as a result of mounting U-boat losses in unexplained circumstances, but this concluded that code-breaking was not responsible. Evidence to the contrary was surely available as early as the *Lützow* incident. Finally, it was left to Admiral Carls at Gruppe (Nord) to make the only questioning comment about the ship's poor state of alert, given the circumstances. So *Lützow* once again passes out of the narrative and Kpt.z.S. Kreisch was posted away as head of the German Training Group to the Royal Romanian Navy.

After the torpedoing of *Lützow*, the SKL earmarked *Admiral Scheer* in her place, together with the same supply ship, *Uckermark*, in the hope that she could be ready for operations by the end of August 1941. This soon slipped to September and even later. By the end of October the sortie was scheduled for the second half of November or early December. *Scheer*'s commanding officer was due to attend the preliminary operation conference at Gruppe (Nord) on 25 October, and early in November Gruppe (West) was ordered to equip *Scheer*, *Uckermark* and the raider *Thor* with the necessary chart portfolios for western France. Delays continued as, towards the end of that month, Raeder was still considering the issue and would make a decision by December. By this time the programme called for *Scheer* to be available for Atlantic deployment from the end of February 1942 and *Lützow* by the end of March.

The problems experienced in co-operation and communications with Luftwaffe units led to some exercises aimed at improving matters. *Admiral Scheer*, however, which had been engaged in gunnery work-up exercises in the Mecklenburger Bight during July and August, had reported very good liaison with the Air Force at Grossenbrode which had provided air targets and, in particular, air torpedo attack simulation; the latter assumed greater importance following *Lützow*'s torpedoing. The expertise of the British torpedo aircrews had been an unpleasant shock, coming as it did on top of the *Bismarck* episode. It was therefore intended that air-sea liaison be further refined, but because of the invasion of Russia, the eastern Baltic was less secure than previously for major units on exercise. It was therefore decided that *Admiral Scheer* would be sent to Oslo to continue work-up and, at the same time, would conduct further Luftwaffe co-operation exercises with units in Denmark en route. Before this could be done, the ship had to spend a period in dockyard hands at Kiel because of defects in her auxiliaries. In fact, because of delays in the delivery of certain parts, it was not anticipated that she would be fully operational until the first quarter of 1942.

Admiral Scheer eventually sailed from the Mecklenburger Bight on 4 September, accompanied by *T2*, *T8* and *T11* as well as *Sperrbrecher 132*, *Vp1601* and *Vp1604*.

It was a calm, bright, moonlit night and it was no surprise therefore that, at 0308 on 5 September, the B Dienst team reported to the captain that they had picked up a sighting report: 'To 18 Group, Aircraft Ja8p 5.9 0230 hrs 1 cruiser and 3 destroyers Brg 180° 5nm 58° 07N, 09.00 E'. Meendsen-Bohlken immediately ordered cessation of the zig-zag and

steamed at high speed directly for Oslofjord, not even stopping to take on pilots. By 0735 *Admiral Scheer* was passing Askholm—the grave of *Blücher*—and at 1000 secured in Oslo. Torpedo nets and camouflage netting were quickly in place. At 1304 the first air raid warning sounded.

Admiral Scheer had first been seen by chance on the afternoon of 4 September by an aircraft of Bomber Command which was returning to Britain. As a result of this, Coastal Command sent a Hudson of No. 220 Squadron to patrol the Skagerrak as far as 10°E from midnight on 4/5 September and it was this machine which made the above sighting report. Subsequently, a PR flight to Oslofjord found the ship berthed there and bombing raids were launched against her. On 6 September four B-17 Fortress I bombers of No. 90 Squadron took off from Kinloss and arrived over Oslo around midday. All their bombs missed. One aircraft (AN533 ex 40-2071) was shot down by fighters. Another raid took place in the early hours of 7 September; one of the aircraft was claimed by the ship's light flak. It was obviously an unhealthy place to be, and without the protection of the flak defences of the major Reich ports, so *Scheer* was ordered home again and sailed that afternoon. She thus missed another Fortress raid launched against her on 8 September, which resulted in two more losses to fighters (AN525 ex 40-2057 and AN535 ex 40-2075). Yet again the watchfulness of the British forces had been demonstrated, as well as the selective nature of these attacks—the presence of the training cruisers at Oslo had never provoked a bombing raid, but as soon as *Admiral Scheer* appeared, so did the bombers. Nevertheless, the sortie did improve air-sea liaison and this was to aid the smooth functioning of the air cover for 'Cerberus' in February 1942.

Shortly after *Admiral Scheer*'s return to the Baltic, fears began to grow that the Red Fleet might make an appearance on the open sea and possibly attempt to break out of the Baltic altogether (which was the reason for stationing the old pre-dreadnoughts in the Belts). To meet this possibility, almost all the operational heavy units and such screening vessels as could be scraped together were assembled to form the 'Baltenflotte'. Under the command of Viz.Ad. Ciliax with his flag in *Tirpitz*, this also included *Admiral Scheer*, the light cruisers *Nürnberg*, *Köln*, *Leipzig* and *Emden* as well as the destroyers *Z25*, *Z26* and *Z27* with the torpedo boats *T2*, *T5*, *T8* and *T11*. All except *Köln* and *Emden* formed the Northern Group, which was to be based in the Aaland Islands. The fleet sailed from Swinemünde on 23 September and the next day was anchored in Foegloe Fjord at the entrance to the Gulf to Finland, well placed to intercept any break-out attempt. It soon became clear, however, that the massed Ju 87 Stuka raids on Kronstadt by StG 2 between 21 and 24 September had severely crippled the Red Fleet—the battleships *Marat* and *Oktyabrskaya Revolutsiya* both being sunk or damaged, as were many other ships.

As any break-out now seemed unlikely, it was decided to reduce the Baltenflotte to a cruiser force and prevent any unnecessary risk to the capital ships from the few operational Red submarines. *Tirpitz*, *Admiral Scheer* and two torpedo

boats were ordered to sail for Germany on the evening of 25 September, leaving a Northern Group in the Aaland Islands; this consisted of *Nürnberg*, *Köln* and the three destroyers with two minesweepers of the 1st Flotilla and five boats of the 11th UJ Flotilla. The Southern Group comprised *Leipzig*, *Emden*, three boats of the 2nd Torpedo-boat Flotilla and a couple of minesweepers. On return, *Tirpitz* sailed to Gotenhafen, while *Admiral Scheer* proceeded to Hamburg for further work on her machinery. She spent the remainder of 1941 in the Baltic on training and work-up exercises, as did *Tirpitz*, major operations in Atlantic waters having been vetoed by the Führer in view of the invasion of Russia.

On the morning of 13 February 1942 *Scharnhorst* and *Gneisenau* arrived back in German waters following the completion of 'Cerberus'. The former put into Wilhelmshaven but *Gneisenau* passed through the Kiel Canal and by 15 February was in Floating Dock 'C' at Deutsche Werke. *Scharnhorst* joined her in the early hours of 26 February, having been ordered by the SKL on the 18th to complete her repairs in Kiel. Both ships were damaged and needed refits which would require considerable dockyard attention. Also present under repair at this time was the unlucky *Lützow*, but *Tirpitz* had by now left for Norwegian waters and *Admiral Scheer* was anchored off Brunsbüttel in the Elbe. Even so, the concentration of three of the five remaining heavy units of the fleet in Kiel—already an attractive target for the British because of the U-boat building yards at Germania—caused considerable concern to Admiral Carls and the ships' commanding officers. Nor had it gone unnoticed by RAF PR sorties and the British, still smarting from the 'Cerberus' escapade, made a concerted effort to destroy the core of the Kriegsmarine's fleet.

Gneisenau's refit was scheduled to be completed by 6 March, during which time bomb damage in compartment V was to be repaired, the machinery overhauled and the screws changed. At the same time, Starboard IV 15cm was to be inspected because of problems. By 24 February this refit was making good progress and it was expected that a day could be shaved off the dockyard period. However, in the early hours of 25 February there was an air raid upon the port, bombs near-missing the dock. One Stirling (N6067 of No. 15 Squadron) was lost in the attack. It was an unpleasant portent, for there was a second raid that night by a force of Wellingtons, Hampdens and Halifaxes. Thirty-one aircraft took off but only twelve claimed to have attacked the prime target.

It was enough, for at 2315 one bomb hit *Gneisenau* in the vicinity of 'A' turret which caused large casualties to the turret crew and the damage control parties below. The bomb struck and penetrated the upper deck forward of 'A' turret and was deflected aft by the longitudinal armoured bulkhead at frame space 185.6, subsequently exploding on the armoured deck by a hatch and ventilation trunk, in the seaman petty officers' mess. The vertical bulkhead was ruptured and fire spread to the forward crew space through this hole, but the bomb did not penetrate the armoured deck. This was distorted by the force of the explosion. However, the hatch to the 28cm magazine is believed to have been open (it could not

Above: *Gneisenau* lies disarmed at Gotenhafen on 1 August 1942. (IWM)

subsequently be found) and the flash and splinters entered the magazine.

About 25 minutes after this first hit, a second huge explosion occurred, thought initially to be a second bomb hit. It was subsequently decided that this was in fact caused by the ignition of fuel gas and fumes in the tank spaces by the earlier bomb hit. This explosion ignited and blew out all the contents of the magazine and a huge jet of flame issued from 'A' turret which was totally burned out. The upper deck was torn up and peeled back like an opened tin as far as 'A' turret and was severely distorted as far as the rear of 'B' turret. The turret itself jumped 60cm. Below, bulkheads were demolished and a large hole blown in the handling room, although no cartridges in this space ignited. The shell room and double bottom were also wrecked and the outer bottom plating pierced by splinters. Damage control parties flooded the sections aft of 'A' turret (i.e., 'B' magazine and shell rooms) as well as 'A' reserve magazine, thus preventing further explosions. A huge fire raged within the fore-ends, and on deck burning camouflage materials added further to the inferno. Well over 100 men were killed, including the Engineer Officer. The fire burned for almost three days before it could be fully extinguished. Some 3,000 tonnes of water were in the ship, from flooding and fire-extinguishing activities. Accommodation spaces for about 600 men had been rendered totally uninhabitable. Work began to clean up the mess and damage, but it was immediately apparent that the ship would be out of action for a long time.

Admiral Carls was naturally worried about further raids (there was another on the night of 27/28 February by Hampdens and Manchesters) and was concerned for the safety of *Scharnhorst*. He wished to send her to Gotenhafen to complete her repairs, but Hoffmann objected because the ship could not move under her own power and to arrange a tow would cost a good deal of valuable time, extending the refit accordingly.

Gneisenau in the meantime continued her salvage operations. She was undocked on 9 March, and on 18 March Fein was informed that the Führer had decided that the ship was to be rearmed with three twin 38cm turrets, which would necessitate her being de-commissioned for at least twelve months. This task was to be undertaken by the dockyard at Gotenhafen and preparations began immediately for her

transfer there. *Gneisenau* departed from Kiel on the morning of 4 April, escorted by the icebreakers *Castor* and *Stettin*, as well as the pre-dreadnought *Schlesien*. The severe winter ice frequently stopped *Castor* and progress was exceedingly slow. On 5 April *Castor* had to be detached because of recurrent machinery defects and *Schlesien* took the lead, only to be stopped herself by the heavy ice after a short time. As a result of the ice problem, it was not until mid-morning of 6 April that *Gneisenau* was secured in Gotenhafen. Although not appreciated at the time, it was to be her last movement under her own power. Kpt.z.S. Fein was promoted Konteradmiral on 1 April and on 11 April was relieved by K.Kpt. Kähler as commanding officer, Fein being appointed Admiral Commanding (Norway) as Chief of Staff.

Preparations were going ahead for *Gneisenau*'s conversion to 38cm guns: the foreship was to be rebuilt, new mainmast fitted, the main flak control position rebuilt and the after TS fully refitted. All superheater tubes were to be renewed, air pre-heaters renewed, the turbines opened up and the diesel generating capacity increased. In the meantime, all the flak guns were to be landed for use ashore and the 15cm guns removed from their mountings. The lifting of the damaged turrets caused problems because cutting torches had to be used and there was a considerable fire risk due to oil being present.

On 1 July 1942 *Gneisenau* was paid off. She never again recommissioned because the Barents Sea débâcle in December that year resulted in Hilter's orders to scrap the big ships. Work ceased and the ship lay forlorn and rusting until scuttled on 28 March 1945.

Scharnhorst remained in Kiel for her refit. Extra armour plates were laid on deck for protection, as had been done in Brest, and the ship escaped serious bomb damage, although she did suffer minor damage and some casualties in an air raid on 12 March. By the end of that month the refit period was expected to last ten weeks in dock, with a further three weeks needed after. She had serious problems with her turbines and extensive re-cabling was also needed. Hoffmann too was promoted Konteradmiral on 1 April, like his colleague in *Gneisenau*, and left the ship the same day to assume a post with the Baltic Command, prior to taking up the appointment of Admiral Commanding (Netherlands) in July. His successor was Kpt.z.S. Hüffmeier, formerly captain of the light cruiser *Köln*. Despite delays caused by the winter weather conditions and the discovery that eight boilers needed re-tubing, *Scharnhorst* was undocked on 16 June. Machinery trials then revealed further turbine problems, this time in the port LP astern drum, and it was feared the other turbines might also be affected, the cause being suspected as the mining during 'Cerberus'. In the event, these fears proved unfounded and on 16 August the ship sailed for Gotenhafen and work-up, in company with *Greif*, *T8* and *T110*. She remained in the eastern Baltic on trials and training duties for the remainder of the year, the only incident being a minor collision with *U523* on 16 September. In January 1943, after fleet exercises, *Scharnhorst* was ordered to Norway for operations.

18. NORWAY AND THE ARCTIC, 1942

With *Tirpitz* now fully worked up, there was the question of her active employment to be considered. Unfortunately, the loss of *Bismarck*, the entrapment of the Brest Group and the torpedoing of *Lützow*, caused Hitler to be very nervous about allowing his capital ships back on to the open oceans. In addition, the complex chain of supply and replenishment ships set up for 'Rheinübung' had long been rolled up by the Royal Navy and to re-establish another would be difficult and time-consuming. However, Raeder had a practical answer to the problem—ever since the Lofoten and Vaagso raids during 1941, Hitler had been sensitive to the possibility of a British landing in Norway. Raeder therefore proposed that *Tirpitz* be sent to Norway, where she would act not only as a deterrent to any such adventure, but would also be ideally placed to interdict the Allied convoys to North Russia. The preoccupation of the Führer about an invasion of Norway is interesting and intriguing. It is highly unlikely that any such operation was ever planned but the various Command War Diaries, particularly that of Gruppe (Nord), contain frequent references to 'reliable agent's reports' of planned operations, troops being loaded, ships being assembled, etc. All these reports fuelled Hitler's belief in such an operation and one could ask if this was indeed the purpose of the reports—who was controlling the agents? After some hesitation, Hitler agreed to *Tirpitz*'s deployment but stipulated that the SKL must guarantee her arrival undamaged (!) and that she was not to attack convoys known to be accompanied by aircraft-carriers.

By the time that Hitler's decision had been made known to the SKL (12 January), *Tirpitz* had already sailed west from Gotenhafen and had to be held for 24 hours pending release by the SKL. The operation was code-named 'Polarnacht'. Gruppe (Nord) had proposed to the SKL that on completion of a safe passage to Trondheim, *Tirpitz* be immediately sent out on a three- to four-day sortie against the 'PQ' convoys. The SKL was lukewarm about the idea, pointing out that weather conditions favourable for the passage to Norway would be unfavourable for offensive operations. There was also the question of destroyers and the Kriegsmarine's shortage of these valuable ships. Any sortie without a screen would be dangerous, especially at night, as it was known that the convoys were protected by heavy cruisers and destroyers. In the end, the SKL agreed, on condition that the target must be located and known in advance and that all available intelligence and reconnaissance means (i.e., aircraft, B Dienst and U-boats) be used to gain a clear picture of the situation. Destroyer escort must be available, which in turn meant only a short-duration sortie given the short legs of these ships.

Not surprisingly, much thought was given to the best route to Trondheim. A passage through the Belts, Kattegat and Skagerrak was immediately ruled out as it was believed, quite rightly, that the ship would be reported by agents in Sweden. The alternative was to use the Kiel Canal and then the North Sea route, but this exposed the ship to air attack for a longer period. There were also problems with the deep draught of the ship in the shallow North Sea rivers, which could not be ignored. At one stage it was considered sending her north with only part-filled bunkers, but this was vetoed. Despite the disadvantages of the North Sea route, this was the one chosen and an elaborate cover plan prepared to send *Tirpitz* to Wilhelmshaven for a refit. Plans to provide an air umbrella of fighters were thwarted by the local Luftwaffe command's reluctance to send liaison officers to briefings and planning conferences without the express permission of Goering. The operational orders for 'Polarnacht' were issued on 2 January. Sailing would only go ahead if the weather conditions were favourable. Interestingly, these orders contained the possibility of an attack being made on a worth-while target en route, subject to Gruppe (Nord) approval and sufficient fuel being left to the destroyers.

After all the worry and concern, the operation passed off quite uneventfully. *Beitzen* with Captain (D5) and *Z29* joined off Kiel and in the German Bight both *Jacobi* and *Heinemann* joined the screen. The squadron was not sighted by air patrols and by 17 January *Tirpitz* lay berthed in Assenfjord, an arm of Trondheimsfjord. Unfortunately, her destroyers were forced to return to Germany the following day, as they were required to escort 'Cerberus' through the English Channel. Thus, although *Tirpitz* was now in an operational theatre, she was immobilized through lack of escorts. An 'Ultra' intercept the next day told the British that she had arrived in Norway, but it was not until midday on 23 January that she was finally located by photo-reconnaissance aircraft; she was now camouflaged by nets.

Her presence in Norway posed a serious threat to the Royal Navy at a time when it was already over-stretched—war had by now broken out in the Far East. In consequence, Churchill himself expressed a keen interest in the destruction of the ship. Once again, however, berthed as she was some 46 miles? from the sea, the only means of attack was the RAF. The first raid was launched on 29/30 January by nine Halifax and seven Stirling bombers, but these were unable to locate the target. One Halifax (L9581/76) ditched on return. *Tirpitz* remained within Trondheimsfjord for the remainder of the month, only undertaking short-duration training trips in the sheltered waters, having no escorts. However, on the evening

of 20 February Gruppe (Nord) ordered her and the 2nd Torpedo-boat Flotilla (*T5*, *T4* and *T12*) to one hour's notice from 2000hrs on 21 February and immediate notice for steam from 0400 on 22 February. The reason was the impending movement of Flag Officer (Battleships), Viz.Ad. Ciliax, to Trondheim aboard *Prinz Eugen* and accompanied by *Admiral Scheer*. *Tirpitz* was to be held ready in the event of their needing support. She sailed at 0620 on 21 February and about two hours later was on station off the entrance to Trondheimsfjord, together with *T5* and *T12*.

Viz.Ad. Ciliax sailed from Brunsbüttel with *Prinz Eugen* and *Admiral Scheer* two hours before midnight on 20 February, bound for Trondheim—Operation 'Sportpalast'. The weather was favourable, with 9/10 cloud and occasional snow squalls. In the early hours of the following morning, their escort joined, the destroyers *Beitzen*, *Schoemann*, *Jacobi*, *Ihn* and *Z25*, together with the 5th Torpedo-boat Flotilla, *Seeadler* and *Falke*. Once again the British Admiralty became aware of the operation through 'Ultra' intercepts and on 20 February requested Coastal Command to institute reconnaissance patrols, as well as alert the torpedo-bomber squadrons.

At 1210 on 21 February *Admiral Scheer* reported to the Flag that an aircraft had been sighted to starboard, possibly an enemy patrol. It was actually Hudson H/53 which immediately transmitted an accurate position and sighting report. This was in turn decoded by the B Dienst team and

reported to Ciliax about fifty minutes later. Ciliax reversed course shortly afterwards, breaking off the operation, intending to return to Germany. If he had continued, there were still six hours of daylight left for the enemy torpedo-bombers to get in an attack and his intelligence sources also believed that *Duke of York* and *Rodney* were at sea. Not yet having reached Limfjord, he had a considerable distance to cover before the safety of the Norwegian Leads could be reached. The reversal of course was judicious, for the Beaufort strikes sent out, failed to find the squadron in consequence; and a shadowing aircraft, which might have reported the new course, was shot down by Bf 110s during the evening.

At 1727 Ciliax was most surprised to receive a signal from Gruppe (Nord) ordering him to reduce speed and prepare to reverse course again after dusk. He believed that despite the lack of enemy signal traffic, counter-measures had been launched by the British and that if the operation were resumed, it would involve considerable risk. He signalled his thoughts to Admiral Carls but no comment was received. Course was duly reversed at 1938, when the 5th Torpedo-boat Flotilla was detached to Heligoland. By 0815 on the morning of 22 February, the squadron had stopped to pick up pilots off Karmsund and shortly after resuming passage, sighted four Beaufighters of No. 248 Squadron, which had been despatched to attack Stavanger-Sola airfield and chanced across the ships. At 0827 a lone Bomber Command Manchester made an unsuccessful attack before making off.

second wave of seven machines from No. 817 Squadron left the deck a little later, two of which were fitted with radar. No. 832 Squadron obtained radar contacts of about 0300, but weather conditions were so bad that nothing could be seen visually. In fact, this was almost certainly Ciliax's squadron. Defeated by the weather conditions, both Albacore squadrons made for Sumburgh as ordered but two aircraft collided and crashed, while the CO of No. 832 flew into the sea and was lost. Ciliax's escape was only temporary however, for one of the above-mentioned submarines, *Trident*, torpedoed *Prinz Eugen* at 0703 and badly damaged her. *Admiral Scheer*, 700 metres astern, escaped and proceeded to join *Tirpitz* in Assenfjord at 1448, where the damaged cruiser eventually arrived later that evening.

There was now a respectable force available to the Kriegsmarine in Norwegian waters, allowing for the damaged *Prinz Eugen*. *Tirpitz* and *Admiral Scheer* were both fully worked up and operational while five destroyers and three torpedo boats were available for screening purposes. Raeder in fact had great plans for Trondheim for he envisaged the building of a large German town on Gulosen Fjord to service and support a shipyard which was to take over the construction of the ships originally intended to be built in Kiel under the 'Z' plan. This yard was to have been *five* times the size of the Deutsche Werke yard in Kiel and was to have capability of laying down one *H*-class battleship per year, as well as refitting two capital ships and two-dozen U-boats at the same time. This grandiose plan had been put before Hitler on 21 July 1941 and approved; Albert Speer had been instructed to go ahead with its planning, but nothing ever came of it for various reasons, not least the chronic oil shortage which began to be felt from about the spring of 1942 and the fateful decision in 1943 to scrap the fleet following the 'Regenbögen' debacle.

Ciliax hoisted his flag in *Tirpitz* on 24 February and on 6 March sailed on his first offensive operation with the new battleship. The sortie was precipitated by a Luftwaffe reconnaissance aircraft which had reported a convoy south-east of Jan Mayen island, early on the afternoon of 5 March. This was reported to consist of fifteen merchantmen, escorted only by a cruiser (actually *Kenya*) and a couple of destroyers—an ideal target for *Tirpitz*. Ciliax sailed at midday with *Z25*, *Jacobi*, *Schoemann*, *Ihn*, *T5* and *T12*, but later that evening *Jacobi*, *T5* and *T12* were detached to Trondheim. His orders included the avoidance of action with superior enemy forces and the engagement of equal forces only so far as it was necessary to achieve the main objective, the destruction of the convoy. The action was to be so manipulated that while *Tirpitz* destroyed the cruiser, the destroyers would take care of the enemy destroyers, which experience had shown would act with skill, cunning and aggressiveness to protect their charges. Ciliax stressed that German training was not to be assumed as giving them an advantage. Only when the escort was destroyed would the merchant ships be sunk, and then calmly with a shooting gallery approach.

Ciliax's plans began to go awry early on, for his departure had been observed by the submarine *Seawolf*, whose report

By 0932 Haugesund was abeam and just after midday the ships were secured in Grimstadfjord, where the destroyers were to oil. While there, a PR Spitfire was seen overhead. Passage was resumed that evening and an hour before midnight Ciliax was entering the open sea at 24 knots. The 23rd dawned with very poor visibility and snow squalls. All the destroyers were lost to view and it was only with some difficulty that *Z25* and *Schoemann* were closed up on the Flagship.

In the meantime, Admiral Tovey, who had intended an attack on Tromso with the Home Fleet, changed his mind and despatched *Victorious* with *Berwick* and four destroyers to a position off Stadtlandet to attack the German force at 0100 on 23 February. Four submarines were also stationed off the approaches to Trondheim. In appalling conditions, *Victorious* managed to launch a strike of ten Albacores of No. 832 Squadron, but only one was equipped with ASV radar. A

reached Admiral Tovey just after midnight, 6/7 April. *Seawolf* had sailed from Lerwick on 1 March for her twenty-fifth war patrol and by lunchtime on the 6th was in the vicinity of Kyr lighthouse at the northern end of the Frohavet—the normal exit from Trondheim for the Kriegsmarine's surface forces. That evening a flying-boat was sighted and then smoke was seen to the south, which ten minutes later could be resolved as the foretop and funnel of *Tirpitz*. The enemy squadron was about ten miles away, steering east at about 26 knots, shaping to pass inshore of Kyr. *Seawolf* was not in an attack position but immediately turned north hoping to cut the German force off, should it delay leaving the coast until after dark. This proved impossible, so at 1940 (British time; i.e., German −1 hour) she surfaced and sent a sighting signal.

The Home Fleet comprised two battleships, the battle-cruiser *Renown*, the carrier *Victorious*, one cruiser and twelve destroyers. Bad weather prevented the carrier from using her aircraft, as it also prevented *Tirpitz* from using hers. Ciliax had no knowledge at all that such a powerful fleet was at sea and so near to him; if he had, the operation would have been abandoned immediately. The convoy which started the chain of events was PQ12, which was scheduled to cross the returning QP8 at noon on 7 April, so there were actually two convoys at sea; but Ciliax did not know this either. Actually Tovey, Ciliax and the two convoys were all only about 80 miles from one another, but the weather conditions prevented their meeting. On the morning of 7 April Ciliax detached his destroyers to sweep northwards while he proceeded more north-westerly. At 1728 a signal was picked up by his B Dienst team from the 2,815-ton Russian *Ijora*, saying that she was being attacked, obviously by the destroyers. The German Admiral immediately assumed that this signal would alert the Royal Navy who would then order the convoy to alter course and at the same time launch a hunt for his ships. Tovey had indeed picked up the signal but its position was not clear and his searchers were too far south.

In the meantime, Ciliax attempted to oil his destroyers in the night but because of sea conditions and darkness, this proved impossible and at 2113 *Ihn* was detached to Harstad to oil. Conditions were no better the following morning because of snow squalls and icing. *Tirpitz* turned north, seeking the elusive convoy to the south of Bear Island but found nothing except *U403* which was also groping about in the dark, having little to go on; news that there were three U-boats at sea was disquieting to Ciliax as misidentification was not an unknown occurrence. By 0740 attempts to refuel the destroyers had been abandoned and they were detached to Tromso to oil, leaving *Tirpitz* alone. Mid-morning on 8 April, *Tirpitz* turned east-south-east and midday had an encounter with an Fw 200 Condor, with which signals were exchanged. Surprisingly, this aircraft had not detected PQ12, which at noon stood only about 70nm north-west of *Tirpitz*. Ciliax realized that his intelligence data were insufficient and that the longer he stumbled about in the Arctic without destroyers, the more likely it would be that the Home Fleet would find him. Resolving to break off the sor-

tie, he signalled Gruppe (Nord) at 2149 to that effect and steamed south. *Ihn* rejoined the Flag at 0800 the following day.

Once again, 'Ultra' intelligence revealed Ciliax's move and Tovey was able to alter course towards the Lofoten Islands and increase speed. *Victorious* launched six Albacores to search for *Tirpitz* on the morning of 9 March, again in very poor weather conditions, and at 0910 lookouts in *Tirpitz* sighted aircraft which they identified as Albacores. It was Albacore 'F' which first spotted the German battleship and she was quickly joined by a second. Their sighting report was immediately relayed to the strike force of twelve Albacores of No. 817 (five aircraft) and No. 832 Squadron (seven aircraft) which had been launched about fifty minutes after the reconnaissance aircraft. *Tirpitz* launched her own Arado as makeshift fighter cover and prepared for the inevitable torpedo strike. This arrived at 1015, but although the German reports record it as being pressed home with great determination and courage, it was in fact poorly executed because of strong head winds and the inexperience of the squadron commander. By skilful manoeuvring, Topp avoided all the torpedoes, while at the same time *Tirpitz* shot down two of her attackers; three were actually claimed, with one probable. A unique opportunity had been missed by the Fleet Air Arm and one which would never occur again. By midday *Tirpitz* was entering Vestfjord, where she was relatively safe from attack and during the afternoon both *Z25* and *Schoemann* rejoined. *Tirpitz* anchored in Bogen Bay and was ordered to remain there for the moment by Gruppe (Nord). *T5* and *T12* also joined her escort. Shortly before midnight on 12 March *Tirpitz* sailed again and 24 hours later was berthed in Faettenfjord, without having been intercepted by British forces. The operation could hardly have been called a success; only one ship had been sunk for a good deal of priceless fuel expended, while the attack on *Tirpitz* had been an unpleasant shock.

For *Admiral Scheer* it was disappointing not to have been included in the sortie, but her captain realized that with the vast difference in speed between her and *Tirpitz* combined operations were not really feasible. Nevertheless, he knew it important to get his ship and crew into action as soon as possible on morale grounds alone and he put forward a number of ideas as to her effective employment. These were essentially to deploy the ship further north, where she could lurk in the fjords and strike at short notice against close targets where speed would not be a serious problem. The long haul north to the convoy routes obviously meant that her speed was a handicap if based on Trondheim. Both BdS and Gruppe (Nord) basically agreed, but the shortage of both oil fuel and destroyers prevented a solution at least until the end of April. In consequence, *Admiral Scheer* remained berthed in Lofjord, where she was joined on 21 March by *Admiral Hipper*, and it was not until 14 April that *Scheer* managed to get in one day's training—the first since 23 February!

Concentrated at this time in the Trondheim area were *Tirpitz*, *Admiral Scheer*, *Admiral Hipper* and *Prinz Eugen*, the latter still under repair. The RAF now returned to the fray and launched a series of attacks against this valuable target towards the end of March. On the night of 27/28 March 43 sorties were despatched, of which sixteen bombed. All of these bombed blind through the smoke screen except one which attacked *Admiral Scheer* and *Prinz Eugen*. The following night Nos. 4 and 5 Groups of Bomber Command sent 34 aircraft (including eleven Lancasters), of which 27 claimed to have bombed; one Halifax was lost (W1044 of No. 10 Squadron). A repeat attack on 30/31 March by another 34 Halifaxes of No. 4 Group was thwarted by the weather and no fewer than five Halifaxes were shot down (R9438, R9496 and W1015 of No. 35 Squadron, R9453/76 and W1043/10). A month later, after photo-reconnaissance had shown all four units still in their usual berths on 27 April, operation 'Bluebeard' was launched against the ships in Trondheim. On the night of 27/28 April 32 Halifaxes of No. 4 Group and twelve Lancasters of No. 5 Group attacked *Tirpitz*. The Lancasters were drawn from Nos. 97 and 44 Squadrons, while the Halifaxes were from Nos. 10, 35 and 76 Squadrons (ten, eleven and eleven machines respectively). These flew from forward airfields at Lossiemouth, Tain and Kinloss.

An unusual feature of this attack was the employment of the 1,000lb spherical mine by Nos. 10 and 35 Squadron aircraft. This was intended to explode below water and it was hoped that such an explosion would have more effect on the hull than current AP bombs were having on the armoured deck. Because many missed and hit the shore, their spherical shape gave rise to the belief that they were intended to roll down the sides of the fjords and under the ships!

The raid was another failure as one of the Halifaxes did not get airborne and of the remainder, only 22 aircraft claimed to have bombed the primary target—*Tirpitz*. One attacked an unidentified ship, one an alternative target, while three jettisoned their bombs. Two No. 35 Squadron aircraft and two from No. 10 Squadron were missing from this raid. Of the Lancasters, only three machines of No. 97 Squadron bombed the main target, one bombed Vaernes airfield, one jettisoned and one was missing. Five aircraft of No. 44 Squadron bombed the prime target and one jettisoned its bombs. The following night No. 4 Group repeated the attack with 23 machines from Nos. 10, 35 and 76 Squadrons, of which nineteen bombed. Again, no results were obtained and two more Halifaxes were shot down. The aircraft lost on these sorties were W1037 and W1041 of No. 10 Squadron, W1048, W1053, W1020 and W7656 of No. 35 Squadron; while the lone Lancaster lost was L7572 of No. 97 Squadron. Interestingly, W1048 'S'-Sugar' was recovered almost intact from Lake Hoklingen in Norway during 1973.

The build-up of the fleet in Norwegian waters continued, with the last remaining operational unit in home waters, *Lützow*, having been ordered north on 6 May 1942. This unfortunate ship had only completed the repairs necessitated by the torpedo hit of June 1941 in January and then proceeded to Swinemünde on the 24th of that month to begin working up. The winter of 1941/42 had been the worst for a decade and the severe icing of the Baltic had halted all sea training. As a result, *Lützow* lay trapped and idle in Swinemünde until 2 April. When she was able to put the sea, a brief period in Danziger Werft was needed to install Fu.M.B. equipment. Grand Admiral Raeder paid a visit on 21 April when he was pressed to send the ship raiding on the oceans again. Although he agreed with the idea, his hands were tied and nothing was to come of it. After a brief work-up, *Lützow* sailed west on 15 May, escorted by *Z29*, *Beitzen* and *F1*, being joined later by *Z27* and *Lody*. Operation 'Waltzertraum' was under way.

The next morning the squadron passed east of Anholt and Laeso in the Kattegat and were joined soon after by a fighter escort. At 1030 an aircraft was briefly spotted on the horizon to the west and about two hours later the B Dienst reported that the aircraft had made a sighting signal: '1 Battlecruiser

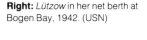

Right: *Lützow* in her net berth at Bogen Bay, 1942. (USN)

and 5 Destroyers in 57°30′, 11°15′E course 350° 15kts'. Once again the operation had been detected. Actually, this had been rather fortuitous for the British as it was an aircraft of Bomber Command, returning from other duties, which had first spotted the wake of a fast vessel in the Great Belt in the very early hours of 16 May. This report reached Coastal Command at 0755 (British Time). Air patrols were alerted accordingly, resulting in the sighting report already described. It had been expected that *Lützow* would attempt to move to Norway but it was not known when. Nevertheless, certain dispositions were made by Coastal Command to attack her the moment it was possible. To this end, the Beauforts of Nos. 42, 86 and 217 Squadrons were moved north to Leuchars, Wick and Sumburgh. Of these, No. 42 Squadron was earmarked to deal with *Lützow*, the simultaneous move south by the semi-repaired *Prinz Eugen* (see *German Cruisers of World War Two*) having forced a division of the meagre RAF torpedo strike force.

Throughout the afternoon of 16 May it was evident that shadowing aircraft held continuous contact with 'Waltzertraum' and at 1450 Gruppe (Nord) ordered course to be reversed. This was executed about half an hour later but at 1600 Gruppe (Nord) warned K.Ad. Bey, Flag Officer (Destroyers), who was in fact the senior officer in command of 'Waltzertraum' at this stage, to be prepared to steer north again from about 2000 so as to be in Kvarenes Fjord by 0400/17. (This was the tactic that had succeeded with 'Sportpalast'.) At 2015, the squadron duly reversed course again and at 0520 the next day was anchored in Kvarenes Fjord. There *Lützow* received a new Arado to replace the one damaged by her own flak on passage. Reports were also received about a major but unsuccessful air attack on *Prinz Eugen*. Not until almost midnight on 18 May did *Lützow* resume passage north and by 0800 she was abeam of Lervik. The weather was favourable for her passage, it was overcast and hazy with poor visibility, so Stange intended to press on, passing Stadtlandet by day, since low clouds covered the mountain tops. However, further intercept sighting reports caused him to change his mind and at 1058 *Lützow* reversed course to lie up in Grimstad Fjord.

In fact, her earlier reversal of course in the Skagerrak had already thrown the RAF off the scent and the strike by No. 42 Squadron was therefore cancelled. When she was detected again on 18 May, the fourteen Beauforts despatched to attack failed to locate her. *Lützow* eventually left Grimstad Fjord at 1700/19 and arrived without further incident in Lofjord at mid-morning the following day. There she remained, until sailing for Narvik at 2300 and 24 May, some four or five days earlier than expected. Stange assumed the reasons for this to be the expected sailing of a 'PQ' convoy. By midnight on 25 May *Lützow* had joined *Admiral Scheer* in Bogen Bay.

The usefulness of this large force in Norway was more illusory than real, for the fuel position was critical and all operations had to be carefully weighed to see if the fuel expenditure was worth while. Sea training under way had to be slashed drastically, with a resultant decline in efficiency. In April, for instance, stocks of fuel in Norway amounted to only just over 11,000 tonnes ashore and a further 27,000 tonnes in tankers. The Kriegsmarine's total fuel stock was 140,000 tonnes, of which only 110,000 tonnes was usable—and that had to serve all commands, including Gruppe (Sud) in the Mediterranean.

Nevertheless, the sailing of convoy PQ17 was judged to be a target worthy of the fuel expenditure entailed and Raeder resolved to attack it with all the forces at his disposal. *Tirpitz* lay in Trondheim with *Admiral Hipper* and four destroyers, while at Narvik were *Admiral Scheer*, *Lützow* and six destroyers. Once again, however, Raeder found that he did not have a free hand to deploy his ships as he wished. The Führer had his own restrictions to place on their operation. Of these, the major one was his insistence that the presence or otherwise of a carrier with the convoy must be established before the fleet was to be sent into action. This quite obviously could not be ascertained quickly and, to gain time, Raeder moved the fleet north to a better waiting position until the necessary clearance could be given. Thus 'Rösselsprung', the planned attack on PQ17, got under way late in the afternoon of 2 July, when the Fleet Commander, Admiral Schniewind, sailed from Trondheim with *Tirpitz*, *Admiral Hipper*, four destroyers and the torpedo boats *T5* and *T17*.

The original intention had been for *Tirpitz* to lie in wait in Vestfjord and Kummetz's ships in Altenfjord until the convoy passed 5°E, then sail to join forces some 100 miles north of North Cape. The convoy was to be attacked between 20° and 30°E. (The essential elements of this plan had, however, been in British hands since 18 June via an interception of the land line to northern Norway by the Swedes, who passed the information to the British Naval Attaché in Stockholm).

Viz.Ad. Kummetz, Flag Officer (Cruisers), in command of the northern force, sailed from Bogen Bay in the early hours of the following morning with his flag in *Lützow*, accompanied by *Admiral Scheer*, the oiler *Dithmarschen* and five destroyers of the 8th Flotilla. Their intended passage was from Ofotfjord via Tjeldsund to Altenfjord. The weather was overcast, with low clouds and fog. At 0242 the jinx struck *Lützow* yet again when, in the narrow Tjeldsund where it was thick with fog and a stern current was running, the unfortunate ship ran aground. *Scheer*, which could neither see the casualty nor anchor in the fairway, had to press on blindly at slow speed, hoping that the same fate did not overtake her. After a few minutes, *Lützow* was sighted listing slightly to port and with damage to her bottom in compartments IX and X. As she was now unable to participate in 'Rösselsprung', Kummetz shifted his flag to *Admiral Scheer*. The unhappy *Lützow* was sent back to Narvik with her crew's morale plummeting. Schniewind also had his problems as three of his destroyers, *Lody*, *Galster* and *Riedel*, had also run aground on uncharted shoals in Gimsöystraumen early in the afternoon of 3 July. Despite these mishaps, he continued north and joined Kummetz's force in Kaafjord the following morning, the change in plans having been brought about by Hilter's continuing delay in giving Raeder permission to attack.

On the British side, too, there was indecision and some confusion. Had *Tirpitz* sailed and, if so, where was she? A PR

Above: *Admiral Scheer* in 1942/43. (WBB)

Spitfire which overflew Assenfjord just after midday on 3 July had recorded the heavy ship's absence, but reconnaissance of Bogen Bay was inconclusive and it had to be assumed that all four heavy units might be at sea looking for PQ17, or using it as an excuse for passing one or both of *Lützow* and *Admiral Scheer* into the open Atlantic on raiding cruises again. 'Ultra' intelligence sources had, since 3 July, been giving evidence of a German concentration of forces planned for Altenfjord, but concrete evidence that *Tirpitz* had sailed to attack PQ17 was lacking. 'Ultra' knew, by the evening of 4 July, that she was at anchor in Altenfjord and there were none of the tell-tale signs such as increased radio traffic to indicate that she might now have actually sailed towards the convoy. Unfortunately for the British, the First Sea Lord, Admiral Pound, distrusted his intelligence staff on this occasion and decided himself that *Tirpitz had* sailed. It is unlikely that the earlier evidence from Sweden regarding the German plan weighed heavily with him.

The result was tragic, for at about 2100 on 4 July a signal was sent ordering the convoy to scatter. The defenceless merchantmen were slaughtered by U-boats and aircraft in an episode which is, and has been, the subject of books in themselves and which brought considerable acrimony and accusation between Royal, Merchant and US Navies, for ships of the latter force were involved in the cover for PQ17. The full ramifications of the event on the Allied side are outside the scope of this book, where only the German naval moves will be considered.

It was not until the forenoon of 5 July that Hitler allowed 'Rösselsprung' to proceed, false sightings of aircraft-carriers and battleships by U-boats and the Luftwaffe having further confused matters. In fact, by this time it had become evident that the covering force was withdrawing west, that the convoy had split up and had also begun to suffer heavy losses. Most important of all, it was now known that no carrier was in the vicinity and as a result, there were many regrets that the Fleet had not been in a waiting position to interfere directly after the attacks by torpedo aircraft. Schniewind sailed at 1055 that morning (pre-empting any sailing orders such was his frustration), with *Tirpitz*, *Admiral Scheer* and *Admiral Hipper*, together with seven destroyers and two torpedo boats. This force was split into two groups, the flagship with

Admiral Hipper and four destroyers, Kummetz leading the remainder. At 1200 Gruppe (Nord) signalled Schniewind to proceed with the sortie. Off Rolvsoy, the Soviet submarine *K21* reported having made a torpedo attack on *Tirpitz* and at 1925 *Tirpitz*'s B Dienst service passed a decrypt of a signal repeated by Cleethorpes radio of a 1700hrs sighting report detailing two battleships and eight destroyers at 71°25′N, 23°40′E. This was thought to be originally from a Soviet source. Whoever had originated it, the fleet had been discovered at sea. About half an hour later a further signal of the same nature was intercepted from Murmansk, which emanated from a patrolling British aircraft. Finally, two hours later, another report from the British submarine *P54* was intercepted. Torpedo boats *T15* and *T7* were detached to Kirkenes at 2056, but the stream of reports from U-boats and aircraft regarding the steady destruction of PQ17 boded ill for the continuance of 'Rösselsprung', and so it proved. Raeder decided that, in the light of the success achieved already against the convoy, the possible risk to the fleet was no longer worth it. At 2142 Gruppe (Nord) signalled to Schniewind 'Break off'. Course was reversed and by 1030 the following day, the fleet was back in Kaafjord.

Morale was at rock bottom, a factor of considerable concern to the various commanding officers who pressed several options for going out after the remainder of the dispersed convoy. Requests were passed to Gruppe (Nord) but denied because with 27 ships out of the original 38 sunk and the remainder scattered, it was not considered worth while, and that evening the fleet sailed south for Bogen Bay again, where they arrived the following day. The abandonment of the operation was questioned from the lowest seaman to the Flag Officer himself, as Schniewind remarked. '. . . without some offensive spirit, warlike operations cannot be carried out with hope of success'. The fact that the mere suspicion of *Tirpitz* being at sea had led directly to the destruction of PQ17 was of no consolation to the men of the 1st Battle Group.

Among those turning their minds as to exactly how some warlike operations could be launched was Meendsen-Bohlken of *Admiral Scheer*, who suggested that it was likely that the losses sustained by PQ17 would force the Allies to route independents and small fast convoys along the ice edge to Russia, and discontinue the large convoys. These, he felt, would make ideal targets for his type of ship. Flag Officer (Cruisers), Ad. Kummetz, however was doubly cautious about the idea. In the first instance, sea room was greatly restricted and under these conditions, gun-power and radius of action were of little use. Secondly, there were always destroyers present, which presented a definite threat during the long Arctic nights. Carls at Gruppe (Nord) concurred but kept open the idea for future plans.

Lützow sailed from Narvik on 9 July bound for Germany and repair yet again. She reached Trondheim the next day but did not finally sail from there until 9 August, escorted by *T7*, *T15* and *F1*. Despite attempts at interception by two submarines and aircraft of No. 18 Group, *Lützow* reached Swinemünde unharmed on 12 August.

During the summer of 1942 the SKL were still actively working on getting one or both of the former Panzerschiffe out on to the oceans again. The operational areas seen as best suited to surface ocean raiders were the South Atlantic, the Indian Ocean and parts of the Pacific, although a complicating factor in the latter two theatres was the fact that they were agreed Japanese spheres of influence. On the other hand, the Pacific War had greatly reduced the Allied forces in the South Atlantic, where escorts were now sparse, and it was also considered possible that German successes in the region could bring political benefits as far as relationships with Chile and Argentina were concerned.

The condition of the two ships, *Lützow* and *Admiral Scheer*, dictated to some extent the type and duration of sortie planned, in particular the diesel generator installations. These had always been a source of concern and *Lützow* still had all eight of her original generators. For a six-month sortie it would have been necessary to replace at least half of these, but replacement motors would not be available before the early part of 1943. She could not therefore be available for operations before autumn 1943. *Admiral Scheer*, however, had already received four new diesel generators and could be sent out on a six-month sortie with some confidence, espe-

cially if, as was discussed, she could put into a Japanese dockyard for overhaul during the cruise. As this was politically and technically questionable, and because she could not be fitted with another four diesel generators before March 1943, it was decided instead to send her out on a short-duration cruise.

The time-scale for this sortie into the South Atlantic envisaged a break-out in November 1942, being on station during January and February and returning in March 1943. The potential results were seen as outweighing the dangers of the outward and inward passages. It was intended that the ship would return home to Wilhelmshaven for a six-week machinery overhaul prior to the sortie, following the completion of Operation 'Wunderland'. Unfortunately, the plans were cancelled because Raeder was unable to get sanction for the sortie when he met the Führer on 26 August—nothing was to shake Hitler's belief in Norway being the Zone of Destiny.

Meendsen-Bohlken himself continued to question the role of his ship in northern waters where her particular merits were of little use. Perhaps she would be better based in western France from where she could fall upon the Allied Atlantic traffic? Such an idea made sense to a degree, but it ignored the painfully learned lessons of the dangers associated with Brest as a base of operations. It also ignored Hitler's belief in the destiny of Norway and therefore remained but a dream. Nevertheless, he was granted his wish to take *Admiral Scheer* into action, for on the afternoon of 16 August the ship slipped and proceeded from Skjomenfjord, escorted by units of the 5th Destroyer Flotilla to execute Operation 'Wunderland'.

This was a curious operation for a strike against convoy traffic in the Kara Sea. It had originally been intended for both *Lützow* and *Admiral Scheer* together, so it was not a quick post-'Rösselsprung' morale-booster; its aim was to engage convoys from the east. This was the odd part, as no traffic was known, intelligence in the Kara Sea area scanty in the extreme, charts old or unreliable, and the area had already proved fruitless for *Admiral Hipper* in the summer of 1940.

Below: The Soviet *Alexander Sibiriekov* on fire and sinking after shelling by *Admiral Scheer* in August 1942. (USN)

Schiff 45 (the raider *Komet*) had made similar observations the same year but admittedly the USSR was not then at war. On the other hand, there were not likely to be any cruisers or capital ships about . . .

With such sparse information about his operating theatre, *Scheer*'s captain had obtained some changes to the plan after discussion with Admiral (Nordmeer), K.Ad. Nordmann, aboard *Tanga* prior to the sortie. The auxiliary vessels *Schiff 13* and *Schiff 24*, whose task was ice reconnaissance, would be replaced by two U-boats (*U251* and *U601*), which carried better radio equipment and would be better able to avoid enemy patrols. In addition, Bv 138 flying-boats were to make long-range reconnaissance flights over the Kara Sea, using the U-boats for refuelling purposes, thus extending their range. This was an ingenious idea but the five Bv 138s flown off on initial reconnaissance had to abort because of fog, and one of the trial attempts to refuel from *U255* led to the aircraft capsizing. In the event, *Scheer* saw or heard nothing from the aircraft throughout the sortie.

By midday on 17 August *Scheer* stood south-east of the bleak and inhospitable Bear Island, steaming north-east. There the destroyers were detached to return to Altenfjord. Visibility was poor, ideal for remaining undetected. In the early hours of the next morning there was a brief alarm when a ship was sighted looming out of the mist and evasive action had to be taken to avoid being seen, as *Scheer*'s captain decided not to compromise his position by attacking it. If it was indeed a ship, then it was probably a Soviet independent. At 0505 the ice edge was reached, where course was altered due east across the north tip of the lonely Hope Island, towards Cape Zhelaniya, the northern tip of Novaya Zemlya. Icebergs were a continual hazard. Early on the morning of 19 August, the ship's Arado seaplane was catapulted off on the first of many ice reconnaissances and shortly afterwards *U601* was sighted. Her captain, Kpt.Lt. Grau, came aboard for an hour's conference. After a couple of hours in company, *U601* departed and a little later the island of Novaya Zemlya was seen far away in the distance. The aircraft was employed all day, mainly in attempts to establish the ice edge and conditions, but its use was greatly hampered by the unreliable nature of its magnetic compass in these northern latitudes. Restricted to remaining in visual contact with the ship, the seaplane's reconnaissance abilities were limited.

On the afternoon of 19 August Meendsen-Bohlken attempted to penetrate the pack ice north of Uyedinyeniya Island (in 82°E). This he succeeded in doing between two major ice fields, but by evening he decided that the ice would prevent his reaching the Wilkitzky Strait, the ultimate aim and the entrance to the Laptev Sea. Reversing course, *Scheer* extricated herself and met *U251* which she re-stored and provisioned. The U-boat reported that the cruiser's funnel smoke had been visible miles away—which had been remarked upon before during Atlantic raiding. Leaving the U-boat, *Admiral Scheer* explored the southern edge of the ice field around Uyedinyeniya Island and encountered an unmarked shoal which caused some excitement. (A $4\frac{3}{4}$-fathom bank is marked on modern charts.) As the ship

pressed further east, the invaluable aircraft returned on the evening of 20 August with news of a nine-ship convoy led by a two-funnelled icebreaker (actually *Krassin* and *Lenin*). Unfortunately, the convoy's position was only generally known and fog prevented *Scheer* finding it in the end. For four fruitless days, she searched the desolate, icy and poorly charted waters, south-west of the Wilkitzky Strait between Severnay Zemlya and Cape Chelyuskin on Kharitona Laptev land. Her furthest east was about 96°E! Finally, on the morning of 25 August, the faithful Arado ('T3 + EK') crash-landed and became a total loss.

Deprived of his best means of reconnaissance, *Scheer*'s captain withdrew generally south-west, closing the Russian mainland. That afternoon, in a brief action, she encountered and sank the icebreaker *Alexander Sibiriakoff* (1,384 tones) which had been en route to erect a weather station at Cape Molotov on Severnay Zemlya. Twenty-two prisoners were taken. The next plan was to attack Port Dickson radio station at the entrance to the Gulf of Yenisey. *Scheer* steamed west again, between Uyedinyeniya Island and Arctic Institute Island, before turning south into the Gulf. Half an hour before midnight on 26 August, the radio masts hove into view and, in the early hours of the following day, *Scheer* went into action against the radio installations, port facilities and shipping in the harbour. In an action lasting just over an hour the Gunnery Officer, K.Kpt. Schumann, had to opportunity to ply his trade at long last. Considerable damage was done to various installations and claims were made to have sunk a 5,000-tonne tanker and to have damaged other ships, including an icebreaker, *Taimyr*. As far as is known, only the patrol vessel *SKR-19* (*Dezhnev*) and the steamer *Revolutsioner* (433 tonnes) were damaged. Seventy-seven rounds of 28cm were fired and in total 379 rounds of 15cm and 10.5cm.

Scheer now steamed north, rounded the northern tip of Novaya Zemlya and re-entered the Arctic Ocean. No other traffic was seen and late on 28 August Admiral (Nordmeer) ordered 'Wunderland' broken off. The following evening destroyers met the returning cruiser in the Barents Sea and by the evening of 30 August *Admiral Scheer* was secured in Skjomenfjord. There was little to show for her sortie, the results were less than hoped for but given the circumstances, especially the virtual lack of any concrete intelligence about shipping movements in the area, *Scheer* was judged to have done as well as could be expected. The beneficial effect on morale was incalculable.

On 20 October *Admiral Scheer* left Kaafjord southbound, accompanied by the 5th Destroyer Flotilla, joining *Tirpitz* off Narvik three days later, arriving in Trondheim on 24 October. She was due for a refit and continued her passage south to Germany on 6 November, escorted by the 8th Destroyer Flotilla (*Z23*, *Z28* and *Z29*), reaching Swinemünde on the 12th. Meendsen-Bohlken was relieved as captain on 29 November on his posting as Naval Commander (Tunisia), being succeeded by F.Kpt. Grüber (the Commander) temporarily. *Admiral Scheer* moved to Wilhelmshaven in December and began her refit in the Naval Yard.

Tirpitz, meanwhile, was still in northern waters, having

Above: *Tirpitz* in Bogen Bay, 17 July 1942. (IWM)

out that this would be *Tirpitz*'s second winter in the Arctic, with no home leave, no action and little opportunity even for exercises. On 18 October *Tirpitz* was ordered to Trondheim and, after participating in an exercise commanded by Viz.Ad. Kummetz as a cover, sailed south on 23 October, accompanied by *Admiral Scheer, Z23, Z28, Z29, Beitzen* and *Eckoldt* (Operation 'Globus I'). She reached her berth in Faettenfjord by the evening of 24 October without major incident.

The whereabouts of *Tirpitz* was a continual source of concern to the British Admiralty who organized many reconnaissance sorties by Coastal Command and sent submarines to patrol the waters off her base. Her move to Trondheim soon became known and previously laid plans were put into operation to attack her within the confines of her lair. Thus, on 25 October, the executive for Operation 'Title' was given.

This was a plan to attack the ship using chariots, the two-man torpedo-like submarines originally developed by the Royal Italian Navy and used by them with some success in the Mediterranean. The scheme involved the use of a typical Norwegian motor fishing vessel (*Arthur*), under which were slung two chariots. Each chariot carried a detachable warhead in the nose which would be clamped to the hull of *Tirpitz*. It was an ingenious plan which all but succeeded, for having penetrated Trondheimsfjord, the wires holding the chariot parted when *Arthur* was only a few miles from *Tirpitz*. The party of British and Norwegians scuttled the fishing vessel and made for the Swedish border, but at the frontier one was injured in a gun battle and subsequently captured by the Germans. As a result of Gestapo interrogation, this man gave some details of the operation before being murdered.

The first *Tirpitz* knew of the attempt against her was just before midnight on 5 November; thereafter special measures were taken to detect any further attempts at sabotage or other means of covert attack. Added urgency to these measures was provided by reports of the sabotage operation against shipping in Bordeaux on 12 December, by British Commandos in canoes. For the moment however, no other attacks were made against her and her refit needed completion. The RAF had other priorities and the earlier losses did nothing to encourage further attacks. Ironically, by December 1942 the German fighter defences in Norway were at a low ebb, and tightly stretched. IV/JG 5 was tasked with defending fleet bases in Norway. Its staff flight and 10./JG 5 had twelve Fw 190s and six Bf 109s at Lade, while defending the Narvik area were seven Fw 190s of 12./JG 5 at Bodo and four more at Oerlandet. Finally, in the Arctic were nine Fw 190s of 11./JG 5 at Banak and four at Alta. Only 75 per cent of these aircraft, however, were operational, with a similar number of pilots.

By the end of December *Tirpitz* began to re-calibrate her guns after the refit and was preparing for her post-refit trials. However, she was not expected to be operational again until mid- to late January 1943. Topp was promoted Konteradmiral on 1 February but remained in command until the arrival of Hans Meyer, latterly the captain of *Köln*, on 22 February. K.Ad. Topp then took up a post within the Construction Office (K-Amt) at OKM.

returned to Bogen Bay on 8 July 1942, following the abortive operation against PQ17. She was in need of a refit and at the beginning of September 1942 was out of service for fourteen days because of urgent repairs to her diesel generators. In fact, the dockyard refit in Germany planned for the winter of 1942/43 never took place because, on 11 September, the OKM signalled that Hitler wished the ship to remain in Norwegian waters, so any home refit before April 1943 was out of the question. In consequence, Topp was asked to detail what refit tasks could be performed while the ship remained in the Arctic. The reply was that a considerable amount of work was necessary on her weapons, fire control systems and machinery, much of which could not be fully undertaken in Norwegian waters because of the lack of floating crane facilities. If repairs had to be carried out in the north, Trondheim was preferred because of its better protection against both submarines and aircraft. Topp also pointed

19. 'REGENBÖGEN', 1942

After completion of repairs following her second torpedoing, *Lützow* spent a period in the eastern Baltic working up. Stange was still in command but had to lament the fact that one-third of his officers were new and inexperienced, while over a quarter of the crew were new men with very little training. Of the officers vital to fighting the ship in action, only the second Gunnery Officer was experienced. This was a common problem in the Kriegsmarine, where the turnover of crews was always high. Unfortunately, Stange himself had never seen action and the general lack of experience in the wardroom may well have contributed to later events.

Lützow sailed from Gotenhafen on 8 December bound for Norway (Operation 'Prometheus') escorted by the destroyers *Galster*, *Riedel* and *Z31*. Poor visibility and heavy weather made their passage an uncomfortable one but it had the advantage of preventing their being sighted by the RAF. Because of weather damage and shortage of fuel, *Galster* had to be detached to Trondheim, but the remainder of the squadron reached Bogen Bay without incident on the afternoon of the 12th. A few days later Operation 'Rudelsburg' saw their transfer further north, sailing from Narvik on 16 December and arriving in Kaafjord on the 18th. *Lützow*'s presence in the far north was soon noted and gave cause for concern to Admiral Tovey, who assumed that she was preparing to break out into the Atlantic. He therefore reinstituted patrols in the Denmark Strait and despatched the new battleship *Anson* to Hvalfjord in Iceland.

The forces in Kaafjord, however, remained inactive until, on 30 December, a signal was received by Gruppe (Nord) at 1050 from *U354* reporting a convoy 50nm to the south of Bear Island, steering east. A few minutes later this was amplified by a further signal giving the convoy composition as six to ten steamers and only a weak escort. The U-boat was ordered to remain in contact with the convoy and shadow. In the meantime it had been ascertained by radio intelligence that two British light cruisers were in Murmansk, but otherwise there was no evidence of any heavy covering group for the convoy being at sea. The conditions could not have been better for meeting the almost impossible restrictions laid down by Hitler—no aircraft-carrier, no heavy ships, a weak escort and a shadowing U-boat.

As a result of this information, Admiral Carls telephoned the SKL in Berlin suggesting that the forces under Kummetz's command be sailed to execute 'Silberstreife/ Regenbögen' (these being the code names for two of the Arctic convoy attack plans). At the same time he ordered Kummetz's ships, *Admiral Hipper* and six destroyers, to three hours' notice. Just after midday one of the staff officers at

SKL telephoned to say that *Lützow* could also participate at the discretion of Carls. Admiral (Nordmeer), Admiral Klüber, and Kummetz were now ordered to put *Hipper* and the destroyers at immediate notice for sea. At the same time *U354* reported further details of the convoy and intimated the possible presence of a light cruiser. This caused Carls some concern, for it was known that two enemy cruisers had been present in Murmansk; as early as the afternoon of 27 December the War Diary of Admiral (Nordmeer) recorded a B Dienst decrypt reporting their sailing. In fact, Klüber correctly guessed their task—to meet and escort into Murmansk the convoy being shadowed by *U354*.

About an hour later Klüber telephoned Admiral Carls with a proposal to reinforce the attack with *Lützow*, to which there was no immediate answer. Within half an hour, however, he received agreement to sail *Lützow* as well. The inclusion of the light cruiser *Köln* was vetoed on the grounds that her seaworthiness was poor and that she might be more of a hindrance than an asset. *Lützow*'s fire power would be useful, despite her low speed. Later that same afternoon Carls also decided that it would be opportune to use the sailing of 'Regenbögen' to pass *Lützow* out into the Arctic for a long-planned mercantile warfare sortie. Permission was requested from the SKL for this. Admiral Fricke soon telephoned to stress that *Lützow* was not to be risked unduly during 'Regenbögen' but did not veto her proposed sortie; whereupon Carls informed Admiral Klüber that the cruise planned for *Lützow* would go ahead following the successful completion of 'Regenbögen'. The SKL's agreement was received early that evening. Thus the attack on convoy JW51B (or PQ20 as it was referred to by the Kriegsmarine) lacked a single clear objective and *Lützow* was saddled with a dual-purpose mission, just as she had been during 'Weserübung' in 1940.

The raiding cruise intended for *Lützow* was Operation 'Aurora', a four- to six-week sortie in the Arctic Ocean. Her operating area was to be north of 70°N (i.e., the latitude of Altenfjord) and between 5° and 35°E. This was essentially the Barents Sea with Bear Island as its centre point. Her task was the location and destruction of enemy mercantile traffic (weakly escorted convoys and independents). She was, as usual, ordered to avoid contact with anything of heavy cruiser size and above and be prepared to break off the sortie at any time ordered by Gruppe (Nord). As if completely to negate any chance of results, she was further ordered to avoid obtaining such success that enemy counter-measures might be taken against her! That a captain be expected to put to sea and fight under such terms is beyond comprehension, but such were the restrictions being placed on the Kriegsmarine's heavy ship commanders.

The SKL gave Viz.Ad. Kummetz (Flag Officer Cruisers) the go-ahead for the sortie at midday on 30 December. Kummetz flew his flag in the heavy cruiser *Admiral Hipper* and had with him in the Arctic as well as *Lützow* six destroyers, *Eckoldt, Beitzen, Riedel, Z29, Z30* and *Z31*.

It was a cold, overcast day with snow showers in Kaafjord as the ships' captains reported aboard the flagship for a pre-sortie conference. Kummetz outlined his plans for the attack. In essence, these were to utilize the brief hours of daylight in these high latitudes to destroy the convoy and to avoid the dangers of an enemy destroyer torpedo counter-attack during the long Arctic night. To do this, he intended to employ his own destroyers as scouts and then, when the convoy had been found, use them to shadow until dawn. Only then would the heavy units close the convoy and begin the destruction of its escort. After the escort had been disposed of, the merchant ships would be easy prey. As usual, the operational orders included the instruction to avoid superior enemy forces and eschew risks to the heavy units. The conference lasted about an hour, after which the captains repaired to their ships and began preparations for sailing.

The convoy reported and shadowed by *U354* was JW51B, which consisted of fourteen ships escorted by six destroyers and five other vessels. The 'PQ' number sequence had been discontinued after the traumatic events of PQ17. After pressure from Admiral Tovey, it had been decided that the convoy would be split into two parts, of which the sailing of the first, JW51A, on 15 December had remained undetected. Part of the escort for this convoy had been the cruisers *Sheffield* and *Jamaica* under the command of Admiral Burnett (which were the two cruisers referred to as being in Murmansk in the earlier B Dienst reports). In command of the close escort of JW51B was Captain R.St.V. Sherbrooke in *Onslow*. Also part of the screen were the destroyers *Oribi, Obedient, Orwell, Achates* and *Bulldog*, together with the minesweeper *Bramble*, the two corvettes *Hyderabad* and *Rhododendron* and two trawlers, *Ocean Gem* and *Vizalma*. *Sheffield* and *Jamaica* had been ordered to sail right through to Murmansk with JW51A and not, as previously, turn back at 25°E. This was to prove a fortunate decision on the part of the Admiralty, as the two cruisers were detailed to support JW51B as well. Distant cover was to be provided by units of the Home Fleet, including *Anson, Cumberland* and three destroyers stationed to the east of Jan Mayen. The convoy had sailed from Loch Ewe on 22 December and initially had a quiet passage, but after six days a storm had scattered the merchantmen, with the result that part of the escort had to be detached to round up stragglers.

Kummetz sailed early on the evening of 30 December and by midnight stood about 40nm north of the island of Söröy.

Already his operational orders were being made even more restrictive for that evening a signal had been received from Admiral Klüber which stated 'contrary to operational orders for contact with enemy: Exercise discretion if faced with enemy of equal strength—unnecessary risk to the cruisers undesirable'. The wording quoted in the War Diary of Admiral (Nordmeer) does not quite correspond with that given in Kummetz's diary, but the meaning was almost the same and had been prompted by *his* senior officer, Admiral Carls at Gruppe (Nord), that afternoon. However, Admiral Kurt Fricke, the Kriegsmarine's Chief of Staff, who had made the original telephone call to Carls, had merely said that the cruisers must not be exposed to too great a risk and that abandonment of the sortie must be held in mind if the escort proved unexpectedly strong.

Outside the shelter of the fjords, the seas were rough and the young inexperienced crews began to suffer. Snow showers were intermittent and it was getting colder as the squadron pressed on to the north-east. Fortunately they were not sighted by the four British submarines then on patrol, *Graph, Unruly, Trespasser* and *Seadog*, because of the weather conditions. To assist Kummetz, *U354* had been ordered to transmit homing signals every half hour from 0200/31. However, about an hour and a half later she was forced to dive and could no longer transmit. *Lützow* was already experiencing problems as it took the best part of two hours (due to errors by seasick signal staff) to decode a signal from Kummetz which detailed his orders for the search for the convoy. Thus she knew only half an hour after the intended executive time that the reconnaissance formation was to be begun at 0230. Kummetz's plan was to string the destroyers out in line abreast, to sweep a path some 85nm wide to the north-east, thereby passing astern of the convoy, and thus have it against the lighter eastern horizon when the attack was launched. *Admiral Hipper* was stationed ten miles behind the north-western flank, *Lützow* behind the south-eastern flank.

At 0245 the executive was given, whereupon all the ships hauled off on to their respective courses and positions, so as to be at the designated point at 0900, when the sweep would turn due east. At 0545 Stange of *Lützow* received a signal from Admiral (Nordmeer) detailing the plans for 'Aurora,' with the additional proviso that at least half her ammunition and torpedoes remained after 'Regenbögen'. Stange evidently knew nothing of the plan until this signal and remarked that he had had no opportunity even to discuss the matter with his senior officer, Kummetz. He had little information as to enemy dispositions and had no knowledge of any routes used by merchant ships. At the right opportunity, he intended to signal Kummetz to this effect.

On the change of watches at 0800, *Lützow* stood about 110nm north of Tanafjord. The seas had abated somewhat and the winds veered and dropped a little, carrying the occasional snow shower with them. Almost immediately, she received a signal from Kummetz reporting contact with the enemy, whereupon she altered course east, then to 033°, and increased speed to 24 knots to close the reported position, which was about 80nm to the north. This would involve some three hours' steaming, unless *Hipper* forced the convoy further south. This was what Kummetz intended for he signalled Stange to the effect that, at dawn, he would attack from the northern flank of the convoy. In these latitudes there were but four hours or so of daylight or twilight—little time to get in a decisive attack—and Stange regretted that he was so far south and not faster. It would be dark again by 1200.

Having found the convoy, *Admiral Hipper* withdrew to await the dawn and ordered the destroyer *Eckoldt* to shadow it. The main body of the convoy, which was what had been sighted, comprised twelve merchant ships and eight escorts sailing on an easterly course. About 45 miles to the north were the trawler *Vizalma* and a straggler, while the minesweeper *Bramble* was approximately fifteen miles north-east of the convoy. Also at sea were Admiral Burnett's cruisers, some 30 miles north of the convoy. None of the British forces knew the precise positions of any of the others at this time. Between 0759 and 0820 the destroyers *Eckoldt*, *Beitzen* and *Z29*, the northernmost trio, assessed the size of the convoy, while at the same time were sighted but not reported by the corvette *Hyderabad* which assumed that they were the expected Russian destroyers. A little later *Obdurate*, on the starboard beam of the convoy, also saw the strange destroyers and reported to Captain (D). She was immediately ordered to investigate and the escort was alerted. After some difficulty, the destroyers were identified as German and a very brief and indecisive exchange of fire took place.

Lützow meanwhile continued to close at 26 knots, passing *U354* on the way until, at 0922, the foretop reported a shadow 10° off the port bow. Six minutes later gunfire was seen over the horizon and then *Z31* also reported contact with a group of ships. Kummetz now ordered the 1st Division of destroyers to close up on *Admiral Hipper* and the 3rd Division (*Z31*, *Z30* and *Riedel*) to close on *Lützow*. However, of the latter, only *Riedel* could be seen by *Lützow* for the moment. Stange briefly considered using his aircraft but discarded the idea because of the time needed to recover it and the alternative of a flight back to Kirkenes could not be done in the little daylight remaining. Finally, at 0948, *Lützow* herself made contact with the convoy fine on the port bow. Shortly after that she received a signal from Kummetz, standing north of the convoy, reporting himself in action with it. *Lützow*'s lookouts now reported an aircraft sighted off the port bow, but it was not visible from the bridge. In fact, there was an aircraft groping about in the gloom which observed *Admiral Hipper*'s open actions with the convoy's escort and saw the convoy itself, but was only able to distinguish shapes by the light of the star shells being fired down below. The report from this aircraft was not received from Fl.Fhr.Nord (Ost) by Admiral (Nordmeer) until *eleven* hours later. While perhaps not materially altering the situation, it was further evidence of the poor communications between the two services.

The three destroyers eventually joined and were stationed astern where they could neither protect *Lützow*'s flank nor probe the convoy's position. At 1042 an unidentified enemy vessel was sighted to port, whereupon Stange altered course 20° away as the snow and poor visibility rendered it impossible to identify the ship, and he was in some fear of a torpedo attack. His radar was reporting numerous contacts at ranges between 6,200m and 14,000m, but he had no idea what they were—they might have been *Hipper* and her escort. Here it is worth noting that no PPI screen had been developed by the Kriegsmarine nor an action plot, so that determining the relative positions, courses and speeds of the antagonists was very much a matter of guesswork.

Gunfire was seen on the port quarter at about 1050, but because of the light it could not be established if it were friend or foe. This was probably the Flagship engaging the minesweeper *Bramble*, which was subsequently sunk by *Eckoldt*. Because of the uncertainty, Stange was reluctant to enter the snow squall which hid the convoy from view, as he considered there to be a high risk of torpedo attack at short range by one of the escorting destroyers. Instead, he decided to loiter outside and hope for an improvement in conditions. Thus, at 1052 he altered course south-eastwards, effectively running parallel to and north of the convoy, since the appearance of *Admiral Hipper* in the north had caused exactly the action that Kummetz had predicted—the convoy Commodore turned the convoy south.

Unfortunately for Stange his ship was now too far east and instead of the merchantmen running directly into *Lützow*, they passed unseen round her stern. Stange continued this

Below: *Lützow* in Norwegian waters. (WBB)

course until 1106, when due east was steered to remain in clear weather and keep free of the convoy's smoke. Ten minutes later *Hipper* was sighted in action off the port quarter. As Stange now saw no chance of closing the convoy from the east because of visibility conditions, he changed his plans and circled back to the north-west, intending to attack the convoy from the northern side with *Admiral Hipper*. It appears that he was also concerned about losing contact with the Flagship in the approaching darkness.

Kummetz now ordered *Lützow* and her destroyers to attack the van of the convoy while he would attack the stern. As *Lützow* moved north-west, an enemy ship (probably *Hyderabad*, which again failed to report, or *Rhododendron*, which did) was seen briefly in the mist on the starboard bow, but there was no time to open fire on it. *Z31*, however, engaged a target at this time with three salvoes. The destroyers *Riedel*, *Z30* and *Z31* now trailed forlornly astern of *Lützow*, unable to play any active part in the confused action. Finally, at 1138 the convoy emerged from the snow squall to the south, although individual ships could not be clearly distinguished because of the escorts' smoke screen. Now surely *Lützow* could go into action at last.

Four minutes after the convoy left the shelter of the squall, *Lützow* opened fire with her main armament at a range of 16,000m. It was the first time since 1939 that she had fired her 28cm guns in anger. The grey Arctic twilight rendered the identification of targets all but impossible, while ice on the range-finder and periscope optics prevented any visual estimation of range, so radar had to be used instead. The difficulty of observing targets or fall of shot resulted in the 15cm guns ceasing fire after only one salvo, while the 28cm also ceased fire at 1148. Flash from the muzzles of 'A' turret also made control difficult. Some of the convoy escorts replied with gunfire, but their shells fell well short. These ships were probably *Obedient*, *Obdurate* and *Orwell*, armed only with 4in guns.

Continuing generally north-west, *Lützow* engaged further targets in the convoy with both main and 15cm armament between midday and 1205, claiming some hits with the 15cm. *Riedel*, trailing astern of *Lützow*, fired a few rounds into the smoke-obscured convoy but soon ceased fire, as did *Z30*. Targets remained elusive and evasive in the prevailing conditions, especially as the convoy Commodore ordered an emergency turn to starboard. While this was going on, a ship was seen to the north on fire and quickly exploded. This was almost certainly the unfortunate *Eckoldt*, which had mistaken the cruisers *Sheffield* and *Jamaica* for *Admiral Hipper*. These two British cruisers had made contact with *Admiral Hipper* about an hour earlier, tracked her and then surprised the German Flagship on her disengaged side, badly damaging her. Stange, however, knew nothing of this as yet; his last signal from the Flag merely told him that *Admiral Hipper* was in action against the convoy from the north and that *there were no cruisers present*. Only minutes after this signal, the first shells struck Kummetz's flagship and at 1203 Stange received orders to break off the action. Accordingly, he withdrew westwards at speed but at 1222 observed two ships on his starboard beam, at first believed to be German ships. It quickly became evident that they were not, but before Stange had a chance to fire, the British cruisers had opened an uncomfortably accurate fire on *Lützow*. Fire was returned at 1228 with both main and secondary armament at a range of 15,400m, but without effect before the threat of a torpedo attack caused Stange to turn away, whereupon the cruisers became lost in the mist.

Stange considered himself extremely lucky not to have been hit in this encounter, so accurate was the firing by *Sheffield* and *Jamaica*. In the brief series of encounters which comprised the battle of the Barents Sea, *Lützow* had expended only 86 rounds of 28cm and 76 15cm shells, causing only minor damage to one merchantman. The two British cruisers held on to the west for a while, but as it became obvious that the enemy was withdrawing, Admiral Burnett turned south after losing contact so as to keep between the convoy and the enemy force. Kummetz decided not to detach *Lützow* to Operation 'Aurora' because of the belief that the two cruisers were maintaining contact; he later amplified his reasons, citing the impossibility of conducting extended operations during the almost perpetual Arctic night at this time of year when luck would play a greater part than skill. In addition, the ice edge severely restricted evasion room when confronted with an enemy hunting force. In view of the large amount of ammunition remaining to *Lützow*, this decision was later questioned, in particular Kummetz's right to veto 'Aurora'. Schniewind, the Fleet Commander, agreed with him, but Admiral Carls did not. Early the following morning, Kummetz's force was back at its moorings in Kaafjord and the acrimony was about to begin.

The subsequent events concerning the investigation into the affair by the various parties concerned—Raeder, the SKL, Flottenkommando, Gruppe (Nord), Befehlshaber der Kreuzer and Admiral (Nordmeer)—have already been discussed in *German Cruisers of World War Two* so will not be repeated here. Suffice it to say that it resulted directly in Grand Admiral Raeder's resignation, following Hitler's orders to scrap the heavy ships because of their lamentable performance on this and a number of previous occasions. The fact that the Führer himself was responsible for many of the initiative-destroying restrictions placed upon the Fleet was of little consequence—Raeder could not convince Hitler that the Fleet had its uses because he no longer had his ear. Despite a long and reasoned protestation dealing with the Fleet, its history, traditions and achievements, the head of the Navy failed to make the Führer understand that the latter's restrictions were the root cause of the problem, even after pointing out the offensive successes achieved up until the *Bismarck* sortie. It was following the unfortunate 'Rheinübung' operation that Hitler had begun to impose his restrictions.

Yet Raeder failed to understand the situation at the Führer HQ, or did not wish to understand—he kept himself and the Navy aloof from politics, probably as a result of experiences in 1918/1919, to the ultimate detriment of the Navy itself. The political infighting and jockeying for position around the

Above: Admiral Kummetz's flagship at the battle of the Barents Sea. (IWM)

Führer was endemic and Raeder's non-participation meant that others became favoured—Goering in particular. Thus all Raeder's attempts to obtain carriers, for example, came to nought, having belatedly realized their importance because Goering's voice carried more weight. Nor was Raeder without his own faults: he was stubborn and did not encourage his commanders voicing unwelcome opinions. This was the reason that Boehm and Marschall were sacked; in the case of the latter, it was precisely because he exercised his initiative that Raeder replaced him, which leads to the suspicion that caution might well have prevailed, even if Hitler had not laid down the guidelines. Was Hitler just the excuse? With so few ships available anyway, they were less expendable and commanders were not likely to be allowed a free hand in their employment.

Eventually Grand Admiral Raeder tendered his resignation and once assured that it was meant, Hitler accepted it. Two suggestions were put forward as successors: Rolf Carls, in command of Gruppe (Nord), a 'big ship' man; and Karl Dönitz, Flag Officer (U-Boats). The latter was chosen.

Admiral Dönitz arrived at the Führer HQ on 25 January 1943, being promoted to Grand Admiral and Head of the Navy on 30 January on Raeder's official retirement. The latter was appointed Inspector-General of the Navy, a sham post, to disguise the rift at the top. Dönitz was immediately presented with Hitler's three-point plan for the Navy:

(1) All construction and conversion of heavy units to cease immediately.

(2) Battleships, Panzerschiffe, heavy and light cruisers to be paid off, except where required for training.

(3) The spare dockyard capacity, manpower and weapons to be released to U-boat production and maintenance.

Although item (1) affected only ships under conversion (principally *Graf Zeppelin* and *Gneisenau*), as there had been no work on new construction of capital ships since the beginning of 1940, the order was the death-knell for the surface fleet. Surprisingly, because Dönitz was a U-boat man, this

did not happen quite as Hitler had intended. Barely a week after his appointment, Dönitz returned to the Führer and presented him with his plans for the fleet. These detailed the timetable for paying off the major units but not, as Hitler envisaged, their breaking up or disarming. *Gneisenau* had already been paid off, *Leipzig* would be decommissioned that month, *Admiral Hipper* and *Köln* in March, the two pre-dreadnoughts by May, and *Scharnhorst* by 1 July 1943. Finally, *Tirpitz* was to be paid off in the autumn. *Prinz Eugen*, *Admiral Scheer*, *Lützow*, *Nürnberg* and *Emden* were to remain in commission with reduced complements, as a training squadron. Hitler seems to have accepted this plan without too much dissention. Then, at a subsequent meeting on 26 February, Dönitz informed the Führer that *Admiral Hipper*, *Leipzig* and *Köln* had already been paid off, but that he considered it unnecessary to pay off the remaining ships as he felt that they still had important tasks in Norway and that he proposed to send *Scharnhorst* to that theatre shortly. Hitler received these proposals with some amazement, for they were contrary to those laid down in Dönitz's own plans of early February!

The new C-in-C was clever in his treatment of the Führer however—yes, he had paid off some ships, his most useless ones. *Admiral Hipper* was damaged as a result of the Barents Sea action, *Leipzig* had been ineffective since 1939 and *Köln*, well no one could find a use for her anyway. Also by referring to a move to Norway, Dönitz was playing to Hitler's own theories about its importance. Moreover, the personnel released from the decommissioned ships could be used to top up shortages in the modern and effective units because only a small proportion of the released personnel were suitable for U-boat duties anyway. Suitable candidates had long since been commandeered out to that arm. Despite another long monologue from the Führer on hearing these plans, Dönitz got his way and the three above-mentioned units were the only ones actually decommissioned under the plan, and they all went back into service later in 1943/44.

20. NORTHERN WATERS, 1943-1944

At the turn of the year, 1942/43, *Scharnhorst* was in the eastern Baltic, engaged upon training and working up. It was intended, as has been recounted, to transfer her to Norway for operational duties, despite the original instructions of the Führer to have her paid off. Her orders for Norway in fact pre-dated Raeder's resignation and Dönitz was merely letting already laid plans run their course. On 6 January *Scharnhorst*, *Prinz Eugen*, *Emden*, destroyers and torpedo boats began a couple of days' Fleet exercises under the Fleet Commander, Admiral Schniewind, to hone the crews into trained units, but with so few days spent at sea this was difficult. The fuel shortage was now so serious that every possible measure was taken to economize even zig-zag courses were banned except in situations of acute submarine danger.

As regards the movement of *Scharnhorst* to Norway, Admiral Carls proposed to base her at Altenfjord with Flag Officer (Cruisers), Admiral Kummetz, while *Tirpitz* was to be moved to Bogen Bay as Schniewind's flagship. The latter assumed that this division of forces was the result of 'Regenbögen', when Kummetz's force was judged to have been too weak (yet the escort it was fighting consisted only of a handful of destroyers and a couple of cruisers!), but in his view, because the main task of the Battle Group was defensive (countering any Allied landing), such a division of forces was undesirable. Actions against the convoys would necessarily be restricted during the long Arctic nights, especially after the 'Regenbögen' debacle. He suggested that they keep both *Tirpitz* and *Scharnhorst* together, which was eventually agreed to by Gruppe (Nord).

The code-name for *Scharnhorst*'s move was 'Fronttheatre' but the actual operation could not be executed yet, first because of problems with *Scharnhorst*'s turbines and secondly because of the perennial oil shortage. The oil allocation for 'Fronttheatre' had not yet arrived in Gotenhafen and, as a result, oil had to be obtained from *Schlesien*, *Schleswig-Holstein* and *Emden*, as well as from Swedish tankers! Thus, when the SKL authorized the move on 8 January, it could not begin until the following day because of the laborious task of oiling from the ships of the training squadron. Schniewind, however, shifted his flag from *Hela* to *Scharnhorst* that afternoon, while final preparations were being made. Twenty-four hours later he sailed, accompanied by *Prinz Eugen* and the destroyers *Jacobi*, *Ihn* and *Z24*. *Z37* and *Steinbrinck* could not sail because of defects; orders were therefore passed to *Galster* and *Z25* in Bergen to sail south and meet 'Fronttheatre' on its way north.

The weather was disturbingly fine with very good visibility which boded ill for an undetected break-out. In the early hours of 11 January the squadron cleared the boom at Seelandsrev and after daybreak fighter cover formed up over the ships. So far they appeared not to have been detected but at 1300 the B Dienst team on the Flagship reported hearing transmissions from four aircraft. Then, a quarter of an hour later, lookouts saw a twin-engined aircraft to the north-west. Only ten minutes elapsed before Schniewind was reading the B Dienst decrypt of its report: 'J9zp 1311 1 battleship, 1 cruiser, 1 destroyer brg 110° 3nm Course 280° 57°45'N, 10°25'E'. Flak crews were immediately closed up as the squadron opened up into an aircraft defence formation.

Though the Fleet commander could not know it, the aircraft's presence was not fortuitous. *Scharnhorst*'s movements in the eastern Baltic had been noted as early as 5 January by 'Ultra' intelligence sources and radio traffic intimated that a move to Norway might be imminent. As a result, RAF Coastal Command moved No. 16 Group's No. 236 Squadron (Beaufighters) to No. 18 Group on detachment to Wick. Their task was to reconnoitre the area between Heligoland and the Skagerrak. In addition, two Lancasters laid mines in Haugesund on the night of 8/9 January. Further indications of an operation in progress were the activation of navigational beacons in Denmark, increased aircraft activity and photographs of two destroyers moving south (actually *Galster* and *Z25*—see above). Throughout 10 and 11 January decrypts of all the German squadron's signals passed into the Admiralty's hands as it sailed into the Skagerrak. Short of a drastic deterioration in weather conditions, Schniewind had no chance of passing north undetected and little hope of arriving undamaged because the British knew his times and movements almost as soon as he did. Apart from the air patrols, two submarines, *P55* and the Norwegian *Uredd*, were positioned to intercept and a destroyer sweep was laid on.

The aircraft report referred to above emanated from Beaufighter P/236. A second aircraft, U/236, was diverted as well but saw nothing. In turn, the B Dienst deciphered all the RAF reports and radio instructions to the submarines to a greater or lesser degree. Each side of course was blissfully unaware that the other was reading its signals! Six Whitley bombers of No. 612 Squadron, twelve Hampdens of No. 455 Squadron and six of No. 144 Squadron were sent out to locate and attack the German squadron but saw nothing, losing Hampdens R/455 and P/455 later in crash landings.

The reason that they were unsuccessful was that at 1555, about one hour after their first being sighted, Gruppe (Nord) ordered Schniewind to reverse course and then, at 1700, the attempt was abandoned altogether. Under the extremely good weather and visibility conditions, the Fleet commander considered it impossible to reach Norway unseen—the enemy aircraft had seen him at a range of 40,000m, then reported with astonishing accuracy indicative of a very experienced crew! Carls' orders specified a return to Gotenhafen, but Schniewind suggested anchoring in the western Baltic to await a turn in the weather and thereby save precious fuel. However, Carls decided, undoubtedly correctly, that the risk was just not worthwhile for a non-urgent transfer.

On 21 January a new code-word was issued for the transfer, 'Domino', and on the afternoon of 23 January Schniewind shifted his flag once more to *Scharnhorst*, sailing less than two hours later. Once again the details of the sortie were known in essence almost immediately by the Admiralty, thanks to 'Ultra'. A strike force comprising twelve Beaufighters of No. 489 Squadron and a similar number of Hampdens from No. 455, plus aircraft from Nos. 235 and 236 Squadrons (Beaufighters), was ordered to readiness and PR sorties were laid on. As the stream of decrypted German signals reached RAF and Admiralty planners, dispositions were altered accordingly. In the meantime, Schniewind continued passage under 10/10 cloud but extremely good visibility. By early afternoon the air cover had arrived and destroyers from Kristiansand (*Jacobi*, *Z24* and *Z25*) had just joined. These in fact had been spotted by a PR Mosquito earlier.

A quarter of an hour later a low-flying aircraft was detected to the north-west, while the FuMB office reported continuous radar pulsing on enemy aircraft radar frequencies. Finally, at 1425, the inevitable occurred when the B Dienst decoded a sighting report: '5rvs 1424 hr 2 cruisers 5 destroyers 270° (position corrupt)'. The sender was Mosquito 'S' which belonged to No. 540 Squadron, which had been formed from PRU flights at Benson and tasked with the reconnaissance of Norway. Twenty-three Hampdens and fifteen Beaufighters were flown off from Wick and Leuchars, but failed to contact the enemy because yet again course was reversed by Schniewind, this time immediately on receipt of the B Dienst report. By late afternoon on 27 January the ships were back in Gotenhafen once more. The Admiralty also became aware of this but anticipated further attempts to reach Norway.

In February the question of paying off the Fleet affected discussions concerning the future deployment of *Scharnhorst*. This ship was due to be paid off by 1 June 1943 (vide KTB Flottenkommando), but Dönitz proposed that in the meantime she should still be sent to Norway as planned. The Fleet Commander, Schniewind, was in agreement, seeing a number of advantages, particularly the combination of *Tirpitz* and *Scharnhorst* as a powerful task force. It would have a beneficial psychological effect on their crews and counter, to some extent, the paying off of other units, which the enemy could not fail to get wind of. On the other hand, if the decommissioning timetable was to be adhered to, *Scharnhorst* would have to be back in Gotenhafen by 1 May at the latest, which only allowed two months in Norway. There was also the question of fuel to be considered and the shortage of destroyers and torpedo boats. Perhaps, thought Schniewind, the

date could be put back to September or October so that both *Tirpitz* and *Scharnhorst* could return together, thus economizing on oil fuel for the escorts? Already the Führer's intentions were being side-stepped! Dönitz obtained the necessary approval for the transfer of *Scharnhorst*, but *Prinz Eugen* had been allocated to the Ausbildungsverband (Training Squadron) and was no longer to be sent to an operational theatre.

On 2 March 1943 Hüffmeier travelled to see Schniewind at Gruppe (Nord)/Flotte to be briefed for his move north—Operation 'Paderborn'—and the following day *Scharnhorst* put to sea for exercises with *Prinz Eugen*. These were continued the next day but on their completion *Scharnhorst* set course west. After lying at anchor in the Mecklenburger Bight, she finally began 'Paderborn' on the afternoon of 6 March, escorted by *Z28*. *Beitzen* joined the following morning and passage was continued north through the Kattegat in good weather and moderate visibility. The escort was increased by the arrival of *Ihn* and *Steinbrinck* from Kristiansand (South) on the evening of 7 March with, as yet, no indication that the squadron had been detected by the British.

Actually, 'Ultra' intelligence derived from fighter concentrations in southern Norway had indicated a possible movement on 6 March. Two Beaufighters of No. 235 Squadron were sent to patrol from Bergen to Kristiansand (S) but saw nothing. *Scharnhorst*'s movement was confirmed by the Admiralty early the next day and there were fears of an Atlantic break-out. As a result, steps were taken to intercept her off northern Norway and to protect convoy RA53. Later it was known that *Scharnhorst* had not proceeded as far as had been thought and patrols were redeployed accordingly. Early on 8 March a BOAC aircraft en route from Sweden to Leuchars reported seeing what was probably *Scharnhorst* in the Skagerrak the previous evening, but weather conditions prevented further effective reconnaissance of the Norwegian coast. Not until 13 March was it known definitely that the ship had joined other major units in Narvik.

Thus, unlike the earlier attempts, 'Paderborn' progressed smoothly, mainly due to adverse flying weather conditions, and in the early hours of the 8th units of the 3rd Torpedo-boat Flotilla further reinforced the escort. During that day a south-westerly gale blew, making conditions difficult for the escorts, several of whom lost men overboard and suffered weather damage. As the day passed on, weather conditions worsened, with the wind reaching storm Force 10, and continued thus until Bogen Bay was reached on the evening of 9 March.

Having successfully concluded 'Paderborn', it was now the turn of *Tirpitz*, also ordered to Bogen Bay—Operation 'Rostock'. She was to come under the command of Flag Officer (Cruisers), Viz.Ad. Thiele, who had succeeded Kummetz on 19 February. Unfortunately for Thiele, Dönitz had, as a result of the conference with Hitler over the sailing of *Scharnhorst* to Norway, decided that the post required an officer experienced in Arctic waters command at Flag level. Obviously the situation was delicate, there could be no risk of an operation failing because of inexperience, and there was presumably no time for Thiele to find his feet. The latter was therefore shocked to be informed that he was to be posted elsewhere, only two weeks after taking up the position. In his own words 'it hit him hard'. Kummetz returned on 13 March, while Thiele became Flag Officer (Training Squadron). His big opportunity was not to come until the last few months of the war.

Tirpitz left Altenfjord on the morning of 11 March, being joined by her escort later, *Jacobi*, *Galster*, *Jaguar* and *Greif*. After anchoring overnight off Hamnesliera, passage was continued uneventfully the next day and by the early hours of 13 March *Tirpitz* was secured in her net-protected berth in Bogen Bay. Admiral Kummetz's flag was broken out that morning and *Tirpitz* assumed the role of flagship for the not inconsiderable force now stationed in the Narvik area: *Tirpitz*, *Scharnhorst*, *Lützow*, *Nürnberg* and the destroyers *Jacobi*, *Galster* and *Z28*, as well as the torpedo boats *Jaguar* and *Greif*. The oil shortage remained acute, however, and with only three destroyers available, the screening forces were very weak.

Tirpitz's quiet passage north was the result of a wrong assumption by the British Admiralty. They were aware of the progress of the refit, its completion and her sailing on 11 March, but believed that she was bound for Germany. Consequently all counter-measures were designed with this in mind, thereby missing *Tirpitz* altogether. Not until 13 March was she found in Narvik, which caused the postponement of Russian convoys RA54 and JW54 (due to sail on 27 March), and on 16 April the Admiralty announced that the Russian convoys had been cancelled altogether. Such was the threat posed by Admiral Kummetz's force.

Their stay in Bogen Bay was brief, for after a few days of exercises Kummetz cleared the boom an hour before midnight on 22 March and set course for Altenfjord with *Tirpitz*, *Scharnhorst*, *Lützow* and the destroyers *Jacobi*, *Galster*, *Steinbrinck*, *Riedel*, *Z28* and *Z31*. The weather was thick and the execution of Operation 'Silesia' passed unnoticed by the British, so by the early hours of 24 March Kummetz could signal his safe arrival in Altenfjord. Shortly after her arrival, *Scharnhorst* suffered an explosion in one of her store rooms holding chemicals. The explosion took place in compartment III on the starboard side, above the armoured deck. The force of the explosion vented itself upwards into the technical rates mess, killing seventeen men and injuring about twenty more. The casualties were high because it was evening meal time. The incident was believed to be a sabotage attempt, possibly instigated in Gotenhafen, although this was never proved. Despite the damage, the ship remained operational.

The primary task of the squadron at this period was to attack the Russian convoys; the defence of Norway was a secondary role. Kummetz was concerned that his lack of destroyers, currently only four serviceable, negated his ability to launch any offensive sortie and said as much to Ad. Klüber, Admiral (Nordmeer). Also, the lack of Luftwaffe strike forces further reduced his freedom of action because it was necessary that any enemy carrier be neutralized prior to his making a move. Klüber agreed, but could do little to improve matters.

Both Kummetz and Klüber were keen to get the fleet into action and erase the problems brought about by the failure of 'Regenbögen'. The offensive spirit was there, as was recognition on the part of Higher Command that the Flag Officer at sea should have realistic orders, not being so tied by risk considerations that his force was impotent. Detailed operational orders were issued in April 1943 for the next strike against the Russian convoys; code-named 'Ostfront' (formerly 'Skagerrak'), it reflected some of this new-found freedom for the commanders at sea. The whole of the task force in northern waters was to be committed to this attack, *Tirpitz*, *Scharnhorst* and *Lützow*, seven destroyers of the 5th and 6th Flotillas, as well as two torpedo boats of the 3rd Flotilla. Unfortunately, the Allies refused to oblige and suspended the convoys, leaving the German fleet without a target. The enforced idleness in barren, virtually uninhabited Arctic fjords, Altenfjord in particular, during the long polar nights sapped morale. At least in Trondheim and, to a lesser extent, Bogen Bay, there were small towns within the vicinity for rest and recreation. In Alta there was nothing.

The idea of Operation 'Aurora' had not been completely abandoned; it was still alive in January 1943 but its code-name had been changed to 'Hektor'. Nothing further appears to have been pursued on this operation, but a repeat of 'Wunderland' evoked a great deal of discussion in staff circles during the spring and summer of 1943. This was subsequently allocated the code-name 'Hussar' and was also referred to as 'Dudelsack' and 'Südwind'. Stange was obviously keen to get *Lützow* to sea and pressed for the sortie to be approved but the SKL were lukewarm to the idea, while Admiral (Nordmeer) considered that the use of U-boats would be a more effective and economical solution. The SKL in fact believed that *Admiral Scheer*'s sortie in 1942 would have led to Soviet reappraisal of defences in the Kara Sea, thus compromising a second attempt.

One of the problems was reconnaissance and intelligence, for it was extremely difficult to find enemy targets in the cold and icy wastes of the Kara Sea. The use of Bv 138 flying-boats of 3(F)/SAGr 130 in co-operation with *Lützow* received some attention, but this had failed during 'Wunderland' in 1942 and there was little expectation that it would be any better now. The maximum range of this aircraft was 1,440nm with a tankage of 5,200 litres, but this was achievable only by using a catapult take-off from one of the Luftwaffe catapult ships. If the machine had to take off from the sea, its fuel load was restricted to only 3,000 litres, reducing its range to only 960nm. Not only this, but the aircraft was of a troublesome nature, prone to defects, and could not take off in sea conditions above state 3. All these considerations meant that a substantial base back-up would be needed of personnel, spares and fuel, which would have to be transported to a suitable location by *U255* and *U601*.

In the event, despite some exercises, mainly of a communications nature between aircraft and *Lützow* in July, the idea was dropped. Instead, it was proposed to send three destroyers with *Lützow* as well as an oiler which was to be based off Franz Josef Land to support the strike force. Stange had already suggested equipping his ship with a Focke-Achgelis Fa 330 Bachstelze towed autogyro (of the same type as issued to U-boats in the Indian Ocean) to increase his circle of observation. The prospect of being towed 150m in the air, in sub-zero conditions, surrounded by icy water cannot have led to much enthusiasm on the part of those who were to pilot it!

Yet another variation of the plan called for the use of *Scharnhorst* in lieu of *Lützow* on the grounds that her better speed would give the advantage of a faster strike and withdrawal rate, but this advantage was more than offset by her greater fuel consumption. As always, this was the dominant consideration. The basic fact remained that the volume and routeing of traffic along the Soviet Union's Arctic coast had never been accurately ascertained, so in the end it was decided to send U-boats to operate there and, at the same time, mine these waters. From July seven boats were despatched on this duty, with the additional task of reconnoitring for the possible use of the Battle Group. Concurrent with this, U-boats had also reported increased activity on Spitzbergen, where there was an Allied presence, believed to be a weather station. Recent reports, however, indicated that perhaps there was more military activity than had previously been thought. Although a detailed reconnaissance by *U355* at the beginning of August reported this military presence to be insignificant, the possibility of an operation against Spitzbergen became the subject of considerable discussion.

Initially a raid by a force of six destroyers carrying troops was envisaged, but Gruppe (Nord) suggested using a couple of auxiliaries instead—as ever, fuel was the problem. However, Kummetz then proposed employing both *Tirpitz* and *Scharnhorst* to support the destroyers and using the sortie for training purposes, for which the August manoeuvres' oil allotment would be used. Although Schniewind and Kummetz disagreed over the precise quantity of fuel required, the matter was put to the SKL, who deferred the matter until September because of the fuel situation. At the same time they ruled out using the destroyers alone or with the auxiliaries and also the use of *Lützow* with destroyers. If the operation was to take place, it would be by the whole Battle Group or by U-boats alone. There for the moment matters rested. The code-names 'Sizilien/Zitronella' were allocated for the plan.

At the beginning of September the SKL ordered *Lützow* home to refit at Libau, but Kummetz still hoped in the meantime to send her into the Kara Sea. Unfortunately, the U-boats in the area had reported little traffic and it was believed that most of the Allied supplies to the USSR were being routed through Persia and the Far East with the 'Arctic Highway' route very much a secondary option. *Lützow*'s deployment was to be held open until 15 August in the hope of a convoy sighting by the U-boats, but after that the ice situation would become unfavourable and the ship's refit imminent.

At the beginning of September the attack on Spitzbergen was finally approved and early on the evening of the 6th both *Tirpitz* and *Scharnhorst* left their net-protected berths and proceeded out of the fjords. Accompanying them were the 4th (*Z29, Z33, Z31*), 5th (*Z27, Steinbrinck, Z30*) and 6th (*Galster, Lody, Riedel*) Destroyer Flotillas. Embarked on the 4th Flotilla was landing force 'Grün' and on the 5th Flotilla force 'Rot' comprised of men from the 349 Grenadier Regiment based in Alta. Late that night the ships passed down Stjernsund and reached the open sea just after midnight. The weather was fair with good visibility but a low off Iceland promised to alter things later. Bear Island was passed about 1400 on 7 September. As yet there was no indication of any unusual activity on the part of enemy radio traffic which might point to their sailing having been detected. That evening a signal was received from Admiral (Nordmeer) to the effect that a Spitfire had overflown Alta during the afternoon, but nothing seems to have resulted from its sortie. Soviet aircraft also flew one that day and noted the ship's absence.

Just after midnight Spitzbergen was sighted off to starboard, when action stations were closed up. Three hours later the ships entered Eisfjord where the destroyers were released to their objectives, zero hour for the landing being 0500. Green Harbour radio station was heard to transmit a warning of three cruisers and seven destroyers in the fjord, which *Tirpitz* unsuccessfully attempted to jam. The signal was later heard repeated by Reykjavik. *Tirpitz*, screened by *Galster* and *Riedel*, supported the 4th Destroyer Flotilla (Grün), its objective being Adventsburg, Kap Linne and defence of the entrance to Eisfjord, while *Scharnhorst* and *Lody* covered the 5th Flotilla in its assault at Longyearbin and Grummantsbyen. Both ships launched their aircraft on spotting, strafing and bombing sorties, while the ships' guns assisted in the destruction of coal installations, loading facilities and accommodation blocks. Soon the area was well on fire, smoke obscuring much of the small settlements.

There were few defences but these put up a spirited resistance and damaged several of the destroyers, *Z29* having to call for gunfire support from *Tirpitz* at one point. By 0500 (the landing had been advanced by half an hour) the resistance had virtually ceased and all troops had been landed. Even so, the fact that Green Harbour's signal had got through caused Kummetz to urge haste in the operation and at 0600 signalled *Scharnhorst* to order completion of reembarkation by 0900 at the latest. *Tirpitz* received thirteen prisoners (all Norwegian except one Englishman) from the destroyers as well as a number of wounded sailors and 70 surplus troops from *Z33*, before sending a last eight rounds of 38cm into Barentsburg and leaving Gronfjord. *Scharnhorst* too had completed her task and withdrew, joining the flagship an hour or so later.

British counter-measures were not extensive. As nothing further could be heard from Spitzbergen, the submarine *Tantalus*, then on patrol west of Bear Island, was ordered at 0427 (British Time, two hours behind German) to close Eisfjord with utmost despatch.

Tantalus's patrol position was rather an odd one but because she was a new boat, having only commissioned in June, this was perhaps a work-up patrol. On 6 September she had been in the close vicinity of the northern tip of Bear Island; had she remained there twenty-four hours longer, she could not have failed to see the German squadron. As it was, she had begun to move away north-west and missed a unique chance.

The cruiser *Belfast* and destroyer *Impulsive* sailed from Iceland and the Home Fleet moved out of Scapa, but no contact was made with the German squadron which, by the evening of 9 September, was safe back in Alta. As far as the Kriegsmarine was concerned, the sortie had been a welcome success; morale improved tremendously and even if the Flag Officers knew that it really was only a realistic exercise, it had served its purpose.

Two further operations of a similar nature were also discussed after the completion of 'Sizilien'. These were 'Aussenjade', a raid against the Soviet base at Beluschja, and 'Borkumrif', a raid against Jokanga. The objectives were to destroy defences and harbour installations, sink patrol and coastal defence forces, and destroy merchant shipping. Both operations were to be carried out by *Tirpitz* and *Scharnhorst* with eight destroyers. 'Aussenjade' was calculated to require 6,100³ of oil, 'Borkumrif' 7,000m³; or, if both were combined, 8,300m³ were required in total. Admiral Schniewind, however, considered that the base at Beluschja was of little importance but that that at Jokanga was. He recommended the use of destroyers to lay mines instead of employing the Fleet. pointing out that no new operation was needed for psychological or morale purposes after 'Sizilien', although the use of *Lützow* (which had not participated) and three destroyers might be considered on psychological grounds only. There was no possibility of any great material success, the ship was slow and hence more at risk from counter-measures. The SKL agreed and nothing came of the idea; in fact, they had already, on 10 September, ordered *Lützow* home to refit.

On 23 September the former Panzerschiff sailed from Langfjord escorted by *Steinbrinck*, *Jacobi*, *Ihn* and *Z27* (Operation 'Hermelin'). Yet again 'Ultra' gave warning of this movement as a result of various intercepts, including the movement of Bf 110s of 13./JG 5 to Bodo from Kirkenes and the despatch of the oiler *Schleswig* to Alta. Re-disposition of various Bf 110 units along the coast as far as Bergen showed that *Lützow* was to return to the Baltic and not merely as far as Trondheim. Despite this and other intelligence, British counter-measures were disorganized and unco-ordinated, with the result that *Lützow* was not actually spotted until the morning of 27 September, when she was sighted by Beaufighter Y/404 south of Stadtlandet. Problems of serviceability, lack of crews and poor co-ordination between the Royal Navy and the RAF prevented any serious strike from getting airborne until after midday, when twelve Tarpons (Grumman Avengers) of No. 832 Squadron took off. These failed to find *Lützow*, which continued south unmolested and reached Gotenhafen on 1 October, but only after the entrance to that port had been swept *ten* times because of mines laid previously by the RAF. This failure to intercept *Lützow* led to a searching enquiry into Admiralty-Coastal Command co-operation and tactics, which bore fruit later when the strike wings became effective.

Tirpitz and *Scharnhorst* remained in the Arctic, still a thorn

in the side of the Admiralty. It had been intended to follow up the chariot attack of October 1942 with another, this time using X-craft, the new midget submarines. These were true submarines of about 30 tons displacement, crewed by four men and armed, not with torpedoes but with large 2-ton explosive charges which were carried on the beam. There were released under the target where their explosion would have the maximum effect. *Tirpitz* could have been reached by these craft under their own power were she still in Trondheim, but Altenfjord was a different matter. Thus Operation 'Source', as it was named, had to be altered slightly, in that the midget submarines would be towed to the Arctic by S- and T-class submarines.

Six X-craft were detailed for the attack, of which three had *Tirpitz* as their target (*X5*, *X6* and *X7*), *Lützow* one (*X8*) and *Scharnhorst* two (*X9* and *X10*). The attack was scheduled for the morning of 22 September. Problems during the passage north caused the loss of *X9* and the scuttling of *X8*, leaving only four boats available for the attack. Furthermore, *Lützow* was no longer in Altenfjord and *Scharnhorst* was exercising away from her berth; only *Tirpitz* remained as a target.

The 22nd September began much as any other day in the boring routine of *Tirpitz*, but at 0905 a petty officer reported seeing a black U-boat-like hull inside the nets about 20m from the shore. Five minutes passed while the man had doubts—was it a porpoise? Deciding that it was not, he reported to the Commander and the Flak Officer when the object was seen again on the port side. A boat was ordered away, armed with hand grenades with which to attack it. At 0920 the order to close W/T doors was given when the submarine was seen again in the vicinity of 'A' turret, being attacked by the picket boat. Finally the submarine found-

ered, its crew being picked up by the boat. Meyer did not know what the enemy submarine (actually *X6*) had done below his ship but, from the bearing of the prisoners, its task had been completed. He gave orders for the hull to be searched and for steam to be raised immediately, so as to be able to clear the nets.

Five minutes later a second midget submarine was sighted just outside the nets and was engaged with light flak. It was obviously as dangerous now outside the nets as it was inside, so the only option left to Meyer was to heave in his anchor cables and attempt to move the ship away from the suspected mine positions. This second submarine was actually *X7*, which was on her way *out* of the nets, having laid her charges before *X6*. There were therefore eight tons of Amatex lying on the bottom under *Tirpitz*. Emergency stations was piped and a tug belatedly closed the nets, but another fifteen minutes elapsed before the ship was fully closed up.

At 1012 two rapid and large detonations took place, causing the hull to jump and whip with tremendous force. All the lighting failed and the fire sprinklers came on. The port engine was out of action, No. 2 generator room and the after T/S were making water, and there was much secondary damage throughout the ship. Both aircraft which were not in the hangar were damaged. *X7* now surfaced again and was finally sent to the bottom by gunfire. Two of her crew escaped. Fifteen minutes later a third boat was seen and sunk by depth-charges from the picket boat belonging to *Z27*. This submarine was *X5*, which was never seen again.

Because of the shifting of the ship's position, the force of the explosions did not have quite the effect desired by the British, but it was serious enough. *Tirpitz* was out of action as a fighting unit for a considerable length of time. The explo-

sions had taken place in the vicinity of compartment VIII and there was about 800m³ of water in the ship, but she was in no danger of sinking. The complete machinery installation was out of action for the present and only one boiler flashed up. Part of the electrical installation was also out of action, but the most serious damage was incurred by the armament and fire control systems. 'A' and 'C' turrets had been lifted off their roller paths and dropped down again, while all directors were disabled. One man had been killed and 40 wounded. The damage to the ship was such that there was no question of her being moved to Germany for repair. Instead, the work had to be carried out on the spot; no simple task given the complete absence of facilities in Kaafjord.

With the immobilization of *Tirpitz* and the transfer of *Lützow* south to refit, there now remained only *Scharnhorst* as an effective capital ship in Arctic waters. Of the destroyer force, only the 4th Flotilla were still with Flag Officer (Cruisers) in Altenfjord—*Z29*, *Z30*, *Z33*, *Z34* and *Z38*. This drastic reduction in the Kriegsmarine's strike force allowed the British Admiralty to restart the Arctic convoys in November, the first outward bound one, JW54A, sailing on the 14th. This was followed by JW54B a week later and in December by JW55A. The sailings of the convoys became known to the Germans who were discussing the tasks for the fleet in the winter of 1943/44. It was intended to maintain the battle group at *Tirpitz* and *Scharnhorst* (with the addition later of *Prinz Eugen*) and at least five destroyers, but because *Tirpitz* would not be fully repaired until about March 1944, the main task of this force was to be defensive—i.e., to counter any enemy landings. Actually the priorities were:

(a) To counter any attempted landing in northern Finland, Norway or Jutland.

Below: *Scharnhorst* in 1943. (WBB)

(b) To attack the Arctic convoy traffic.

(c) Mining or bombardment of enemy bases and routes.

(d) To act as a fleet in being, thus tying up enemy ships.

No small consideration was the fact that in the long Arctic winter nights, German radar inferiority would put them at a serious disadvantage. There were other problems too: the strength of the U-boat flotilla in the Arctic was at a low ebb, Luftflotte 5 had been denuded of bombers and had only limited numbers of reconnaissance aircraft and, finally, but probably more significant, 'Ultra' intelligence was now working very efficiently. There were also personnel difficulties because, in November, Viz.Ad. Kummetz had reported sick and departed on extended leave. The actual reasons for his departure are not clear but the result was that K.Ad. Bey, Flag Officer (Destroyers), was appointed as his stand-in, despite this officer's complete ignorance of capital ship operations. He was a destroyer man pure and simple, who was not aided at all by the fact that Kummetz's staff was in the process of falling apart. Many of its officers were being reappointed elsewhere, so the confusion that met Bey when he arrived in Kaafjord and boarded *Tirpitz* on 7 November can be imagined. Not only had Kummetz departed, but Kpt.z.S. Huffmeier had been promoted to Konteradmiral and left the ship on 14 October to take up a post at OKM. He was succeded by Fritz Hintze, formerly head of the Torpedo Department at the experimental establishment at Eckernförde. Until the summer of 1942, however, he had been the Navigating Officer of *Admiral Hipper*. Thus, not only was the flag officer inexperienced, so also was the ship's commanding officer who had no knowledge of Arctic operations.

It is possible that, in view of the shortages and difficulties facing the Battle Group at the end of 1943, Bey and his superiors expected little or no action until the spring of 1944; in which case, the new Flag Officer's inexperience can be seen in the light of his being merely a temporary appointment. The use of the Fleet during the dark Arctic winter had always been discounted.

Now a new factor entered into play. As a result of reverses on the Eastern Front, Hitler had issued his Führer Directive No. 51, which stressed the importance of the victory in the East and which called on all measures to ensure it. The implications for the Kriegsmarine were obvious—the Russian convoys had re-started and their supplies would be of decisive importance to the fighting along the Eastern Front. Despite the willingness to fight, on behalf of the ships' commanding officers, the directive could not have come at a worse time for the force in northern waters, for the reasons already given.

The first indications of a new convoy being prepared reached Admiral Schniewind in Kiel on 18 December as a result of enemy radio traffic. Whether the Battle Group would be employed against it remained to be seen. Whether this radio traffic actually referred to the new convoy is not clear, because the three ships' names deciphered did not sail with either JW55B or RA55A. Air reconnaissance sorties were essential to establish the composition, course, speed and escort strength of any convoy before the surface forces could

be committed; but here Schniewind ran into the long-standing problem of co-operation with the Luftwaffe. Luftflotte 5 calmly informed him that because of the reduction in its forces and the withdrawal of its bomber squadrons, any reconnaissance flying was not worth the wear and tear on men and machines, if the Navy was not intending a surface attack anyway. Schniewind was furious and pointed out that U-boats would engage in any case and that they also needed intelligence. If the convoy got through undamaged, the Navy would accept no censure.

While this was being resolved, a Ju 88 found a convoy on the morning of 23 December about 400nm east of Bodo. This, Schniewind calculated, could be entering the Barents Sea by about midday on 26 December. The only odd thing was its proximity to the Norwegian coast, which Schniewind attributed to Allied knowledge of Luftwaffe weakness in the region. On the other hand, he considered the possibility of its being a lure, designed to entice out the Battle Group, which would in turn be destroyed by an as yet undetected but suspected heavy covering force, while another, west-bound, convoy slipped past unmolested. Since the west-bound convoy would consist of empty ships, the reasoning behind Schniewind's assumptions must have been faulty. Later that day further aircraft reports gave better details of the convoy, which comprised seventeen merchant ships and three tankers, escorted by three or four cruisers and nine destroyers or corvettes. Experience told Schniewind that the heavy covering force would be about 300nm away from the convoy.

The convoy was, in fact, JW55B, part of a double operation, its counterpart being the west-bound RA55A. JW55B had sailed from Loch Ewe on 20 December and comprised nineteen ships escorted by two corvettes, a minesweeper and ten destroyers. The cruiser covering force (Force 1), formed by the 10th Cruiser Squadron (Vice-Admiral Burnett), consisted of *Belfast*, *Sheffield* and *Norfolk* which had sailed from Kola Inlet; while the distant, heavy cover was formed by Force 2, *Duke of York* (Admiral Fraser, C-in-C, Home Fleet), the light cruiser *Jamaica* and four destroyers. Force 2 sailed from Iceland to cover JW55B between 27° and 38°E, then intended to return to Scapa as cover for RA55A.

Meanwhile the communications lines between Altenfjord, Narvik, Kiel and Berlin were humming with activity, as doubts about the execution of Operation 'Ostfront' in its proposed form began to surface. Bey was extremely doubtful about the plan for an attack in the dawn twilight because light conditions would not offer much hope of success for surface gunnery. He was of the opinion that a sortie by the destroyers alone would be more fruitful. Schniewind agreed with Bey; the guidelines laid down by the SKL envisaged the use only of destroyers during the winter months. Unfortunately there were few of these. If, as was also suggested, *Scharnhorst* were sailed to a waiting position off the Polar coast, she would require two destroyers as escort herself, leaving only three with which to attack the convoy. A further complication was the weather which was deteriorating, a storm-force wind being forecast. Luftflotte 5 now injected a little more hope from the point of view of reconnaissance when it signalled—in contrast to its earlier predictions—that it could provide continuous shadowing of the convoy, continuous but not complete coverage for the location of enemy heavy forces, and a close escort for the outward-bound task force. As Schniewind said, it was better than hoped for.

On the evening of 24 December radio transmissions were intercepted which suggested, from bearings, that there was another enemy group some 180nm astern of the convoy, or, because of the acute angle of the fix, 100–200nm to the north or north-west. Another possibility was that there were actually two separate enemy groups. Schniewind seems not to have placed much importance on these, but the staff of Admiral (Nordmeer) immediately assumed it to be the usual heavy covering force which accompanied the Russian convoys. It is almost certain that this was in fact Force 2. Schniewind now proposed sailing *Scharnhorst* to attack the convoy, to which the SKL agreed at 1433 on Christmas Day. Moments later, the executive signal 'Ostfront 25' was given to Bey. Hardly had the operation been given the go-ahead, than Flieger-führer (West) signalled that, because of weather conditions, no further reconnaissance sorties could be flown. Once the convoy had crossed a line between North Cape and Bear Island, the reconnaissance responsibility would pass to Luftwaffe Command (Finland), whose forces included the Ju 88s of 1.(F)/124 and the Bv 138s of 3.(F)/130, both based at Kirkenes.

By evening the weather had deteriorated further, a southerly gale (Force 8–9) being forecast, veering south-westerly and decreasing Force 6–8 by the next morning. On the Polar coast of Norway, it was gusting 6-8 with driving rain and snow. It was also snowing in the Barents Sea. Under the prevailing conditions, the staff at Admiral (Nordmeer) considered the operation questionable because of the difficulties of reconnaissance and because it would be almost impossible to fight the ships in the heavy seas. They proposed that the sortie be cancelled. Schniewind duly passed this recommendation on to the SKL, but Dönitz ordered 'Ostfront' continued. The Fleet Commander now wired the SKL with the proposal that *Scharnhorst* should sail alone because the enemy destroyers would be just as handicapped by the weather as his own, but this merely resulted in Dönitz leaving the final decision to Bey. Thus as the hours ticked away to the sailing time, practically all the staffs and commanders had grave reservations about the launching of 'Ostfront'. Dönitz, however, was adamant, probably because he could not afford to back down from a political point of view. The result was to be a suicide mission for *Scharnhorst* and most of her crew.

A major, perhaps *the* major, factor in the loss of *Scharnhorst* was that, once again, the British knew all about 'Ostfront', its intentions and timings, through 'Ultra' intercepts. One of the reasons why 'Ultra' knew so much was the fact that when Bey was aboard *Scharnhorst*, communications with Schniewind, the Luftwaffe, Admiral (Nordmeer), etc. had, of necessity, to be by radio; and radio transmissions were being routinely decoded by this time. If this was not exactly instantaneous, it was at least fast enough for tactical purposes. Communications with the immobilized *Tirpitz*, on

the other hand, were by land-line and teleprinter—altogether much more secure. Thus all the pre-operational signals between 20 and 25 December were available to the British Admiralty. All they needed now was a time of sailing. The order 'Ostfront 1700', issued by Admiral (Nordmeer) at 1637, was in the hands of Admirals Fraser and Burnett early the next day.

K.Ad. Bey sailed with *Scharnhorst* on the evening of 25 December in accordance with his orders, accompanied by the destroyers *Z29*, *Z30*, *Z33*, *Z34* and *Z38*. Still assailed by doubts about the whole plan, he made one last attempt to clarify his orders as he proceeded down the fjords to the sea. Nothing came of his signal because it did not reach its destination for *five* hours and was not understood when it did. The open sea was reached about 2200 and course continued northwards in heavy seas at 25 knots. The destroyers, never renowned for their seakeeping abilities, now began to work badly; on *Z38* a number of men were injured because of the ship's movement.

Bey had no precise idea just where the convoy was; all he knew in the early hours of 26 December was that the Luftwaffe shadowing aircraft had lost contact with JW55B early the previous evening. By 0700 hours, Bey assumed that he was in the general vicinity of the convoy and ordered a sweep across its estimated course. Accordingly, he turned on to 250° at a speed of 12 knots. With the five destroyers strung out in line abreast and the battleship behind, Bey steamed south-west. It soon became apparent that the destroyers could not hold this speed and a reduction to 10 knots had to be ordered. After about half an hour, Bey estimated his position to be about 40nm south-east of Bear Island, whereupon action stations were closed up. Now, as a result of signalling problems, the destroyers continued to sweep south-west but *Scharnhorst* altered to the west and thereby lost contact with her destroyers. In the meantime *U716* made a sighting report of JW55B which was received by *Scharnhorst*, which then altered course to the north-east as a result.

The situation for Bey could not have been worse. His destroyers had become separated from the Flag and were sweeping a parallel but reciprocal course to that of the convoy. The most north-westerly destroyer, *Z38*, was still more than 15 miles from the convoy's track. In fact, the convoy itself was diverted north out of harm's way to leave the field clear for the antagonists. Approaching from the south-east was Admiral Burnett and his cruisers, while from the south-west the battleship *Duke of York* was closing in.

At 0840 *Belfast* gained radar contact with *Scharnhorst* and the range closed rapidly as the two forces converged. Just over forty minutes later *Sheffield* sighted the German battleship, and only another three minutes later *Belfast* fired star shell to illuminate the target. *Norfolk* then fired six broadsides by radar 284, hitting *Scharnhorst* twice, one shell striking the foretop where it destroyed the radar and caused casualties to the men on the flak control position. The second shell, which apparently failed to explode, hit the battery deck in compartment IX between P III 15cm and the torpedo tubes.

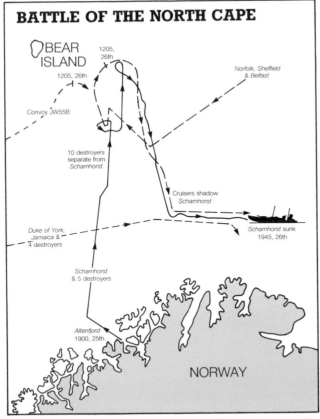

BATTLE OF THE NORTH CAPE

BEAR ISLAND

1205, 26th

1205, 26th

Convoy JW55B

10 destroyers separate from *Scharnhorst*

Norfolk, Sheffield & Belfast

Cruisers shadow *Scharnhorst*

Scharnhorst sunk 1945, 26th

Duke of York, Jamaica & 4 destroyers

Scharnhorst & 5 destroyers

Altenfjord 1900, 25th.

NORWAY

None of the other cruisers fired at this time because the line of bearing formation caused their guns to be masked by *Norfolk*. The German ship, sailing without her radar operating and enveloped by snow squalls, was taken completely by surprise. She quickly hauled away to the south, on which course only her after turret could bear and her return fire was inaccurate. Bey sent a signal to Gruppe (Nord) at 0955, reporting himself under radar-directed fire from cruisers. This arrived in a somewhat corrupt form and Schniewind was uncertain if it meant that Bey had contacted the convoy itself or just a cruiser covering force. In the meantime, the shore-based B Dienst service had been reporting numerous shadowing signals from the force in contact with *Scharnhorst* addressed to Scapa but also to another unknown unit, whose call sign was 'DGO'. Schniewind considered these signals to be either from a cruiser to the convoy or from a cruiser to its flag. A third possibility had also to be considered—that 'DGO' was actually the heavy covering force. This appreciation was not relayed to Bey and because of the haste in sailing, there had been insufficient time to embark the usual B Dienst detachment. He remained in the dark, in more ways than one.

Other snippets of information feeding into Flottenkommando at Kiel supported the suspicion that a heavy force was in the vicinity of *Scharnhorst*. Fliegerführer (Lofoten) reported at 1306 that a Bv 138 had detected a number of enemy units by radar in position AC4776 and shadowed them until contact was lost around dusk. Given the conditions under which this aircraft operated and the possible importance of its discovery, it was quite extraordinary that this signal was only passed to Flottenkommando at 1306; the aircraft report was timed at 1012, *five hours* earlier. A second and more detailed report from which Schniewind would have almost certainly deduced the presence of a capital ship force was not received by the Navy until well after the action was over.

As it was, Schniewind decided that these contacts might well be *Scharnhorst*'s destroyers returning because of the heavy seas. The whereabouts of the 4th Destroyer Flotilla was known neither to Bey nor Schniewind, nor anyone else for that matter. Admiral (Nordmeer) was then ordered to ask Bey if the destroyers had been ordered to return, but no clear answer was received. All that was known was that *Scharnhorst* signalled at 1525 that she was retiring at 27 knots, position AC4526. Later that afternoon the B Dienst reported a further stream of contact signals from the shadowers, which were relayed to *Scharnhorst*. However, Bey knew only too well that he was being shadowed; it was knowledge of the other, heavy, enemy force that he badly needed. Back in Kiel, Schniewind could only follow the track of events by means of B Dienst decrypts and the occasional signal from Bey.

At 1656 Bey signalled himself in action with heavy units, position AC4677, by which time Schniewind knew the position to be extremely serious. The question was, how could the battleship possibly be helped? As in the *Bismarck* sortie, nearby resources were few except that in this instance *Scharnhorst* should have had destroyers with her; but where were they? Schniewind desperately needed to get them to the flagship but first they had to be found. At 1834 a signal was despatched to the 4th Flotilla 'Scharnhorst in action Q AC4677. Signal position'. Eventually a reply was received, which showed the destroyers to be north-west of *Scharnhorst*, still intent on looking for the convoy. Now, however, the convoy was of secondary consideration and Schniewind needed to divert all destroyers and U-boats to the flagship. By 1918, when Bey's signal about fighting to the last shell arrived, it was obvious that the situation was critical. In consequence, the destroyers, which could not reach the battle in less than ten hours, were ordered home and the U-boats of Group Eisenbart ordered to the last known position of *Scharnhorst*. It was to no avail for, just as in the case of *Bismarck*, a signal was decoded by the B Dienst at 2032, which read 'English unit DGO 1919 to LFV finish her off with torpedoes'. *Scharnhorst* had gone down in the Barents Sea.

Moving back in time now, the action can be followed at sea. After the initial contact and brief engagement, *Scharnhorst* retired south-east at speed and then, after losing the shadowers with her superior speed, turned north-east in an attempt to attack the convoy from the north. Burnett, however, still tracking by radar, guessed the intention and moved to position his cruisers between the enemy and the convoy. Bey's destroyers had been ordered to attack the convoy in the position reported by *U277* at 0945 and had to reverse course into the heavy seas. *Scharnhorst* was now approaching the convoy from the north-east, while Burnett's cruisers, reinforced by the arrival of the destroyers *Musketeer*, *Matchless*, *Opportune* and *Virago*, sought to regain contact with her. This was achieved just after midday when *Sheffield* gained radar contact. All three cruisers engaged with broadsides while the destroyers were ordered to make a torpedo attack.

Scharnhorst immediately turned away to the north-west and opened fire herself, straddling *Virago*. *Sheffield* and *Belfast* fired full broadsides at first, but *Norfolk* had only 'A' and 'B' turrets bearing. This ship, using non-flashless cordite, received most of *Scharnhorst*'s attention and was hit on 'X' turret barbette, disabling the turret. A second hit was scored amidships. All her radar sets were knocked out and a number of casualties incurred. *Sheffield* was straddled and hit by a few shell splinters. The destroyers also engaged as they chased the battleship. This phase of the action lasted some 23 minutes, several hits being scored on *Scharnhorst*, which reported herself in action with *heavy* units—leading Schniewind to assume that the Home Fleet had caught up with her already. No one now knows just what damage was caused to *Scharnhorst* at this stage. It now appeared to Bey that he had outrun the cruisers and, as they were no longer visible, that they were not in contact with him.

Such was not the case, for Burnett kept his ships just outside visual range and tracked by radar. B Dienst reports showed Schniewind that the cruisers were still in contact and these signals were relayed to Bey. However, it was not until late afternoon that the full gravity of his situation became clear to him, when *Belfast* fired star shell to illuminate for Admiral Fraser in *Duke of York*, whose flagship opened fire with 14in (35.5cm) broadsides at a range of 11,000m at 1649. Her first broadside straddled *Scharnhorst* which, caught completely unawares, had her turrets still trained fore and aft. *Scharnhorst* turned north to escape the battleship's gunfire but immediately ran into *Belfast* and *Norfolk* of Force 1, which also engaged the German battleship.

By this time *Scharnhorst* had been hit twice by *Duke of York* and once by *Jamaica*. The former's first hit struck in the vicinity of 'A' turret on the starboard side, disabling it. Flash from this hit blew back to 'B' turret, whose magazine was flooded for safety. The second hit struck the quarterdeck and caused damage and casualties to the exposed crews of flak guns. After the fires had been extinguished, 'A' and 'B' magazines were drained but 'A' turret appears to have remained disabled. Nevertheless, after the inital shock, *Scharnhorst*'s main turrets fired accurately, frequently straddling *Duke of York* and putting two shells into her masts, but these failed to explode. The destroyer *Savage* was also engaged and near-missed, while Force 1 was briefly fired upon before *Scharnhorst* pulled out of range.

Now it became a duel between the two capital ships, but in the darkness *Duke of York*'s radar-directed fire was much more telling. A hit on the ventilation trunking of 'B' turret of *Scharnhorst* made it untenable due to cordite smoke, and another destroyed SI 15cm gun and its magazine crew. Yet another passed through the belt armour into No. 1 boiler room, cutting the HP steam pipes to the turbines, whereup-

on speed fell away to 10 knots. The time was now about 1820 and Bey had just signalled Gruppe (Nord) that the enemy was firing by radar from a distance of over 18,000m. His position was AC4965, course 110°, speed 26 knots. Now reduced to a crawl, another signal was despatched at 1825, 'We shall fight to the last shell'. The reduction in speed allowed the destroyers to gain some ground, despite *Scharnhorst*'s engineering staff isolating the damage and getting the speed back up to 22 knots.

The destroyers *Savage* and *Saumarez* closed up astern of *Scharnhorst* while their division mates were off to starboard. The former pair were taken under ragged and ineffective fire by the battleship's light guns. *Saumarez* returned the fire while *Scorpion* and the Norwegian destroyer *Stord* fired eight torpedoes each, as well as opening fire with their guns. Despite turning away, *Scharnhorst* was probably hit by one of *Scorpion*'s torpedoes and this turn had put her in a good position for the other two destroyers. *Savage* fired eight and *Saumarez* four torpedoes, of which it is believed three hit. *Saumarez* had herself been hit by several shells, including 28cm, but these did not explode. Nevertheless, the resultant splinters caused considerable damage and casualties, particularly among the torpedo men.

One of the destroyer's torpedoes struck *Scharnhorst* on the starboard side just forward of the bridge and three hit the port side. Serious flooding resulted, there was much shock damage and her speed was again reduced. This enabled *Duke of York* to re-engage, hitting the German ship heavily. Aboard *Scharnhorst* some ammunition from 'B' turret, now also evacuated, was transferred to 'C' turret, the only 28cm in action. By 1911 *Scharnhorst* could only manage 10 knots and was listing to starboard. Four minutes later *Belfast* rejoined the action, scoring two hits with her third broadside. Shortly after that *Scharnhorst*'s 'C' turret fell silent, leaving only a couple of 15cm in action. Fraser now ordered *Belfast* up to sink her with torpedoes, the cruisers firing three torpedoes but without hitting. *Jamaica* fired two and also missed, then obtained two hits with her starboard tubes. *Scharnhorst* could still reply with parts of her armament but without effect.

The destroyers *Musketeer*, *Matchless*, *Opportune* and *Virago* now arrived on the scene, firing nineteen torpedoes at the virtually stopped and defenceless *Scharnhorst*, which by this time was making only about 3 knots, with her starboard rail submerged. Five hits were claimed in this attack. The German ship was now obscured by a dark pall of smoke, so that an explosion at 1945, heard but not seen, was assumed to be her magazines exploding.

Thus no enemy saw *Scharnhorst* sink in the icy waters of the Barents Sea, leaving only thirty survivors, despite a long search by the British destroyers and cruisers. Admiral Bey and all his officers were among those who perished, so a detailed record of events on *Scharnhorst*'s last sortie can never be made. A huge amount of ammunition was expended by the British ships in sinking *Scharnhorst*; *Duke of York* alone fired 446 rounds of main armament. In addition, no fewer than 55 torpedoes were fired in this action, of which eleven were claimed hits.

21. ECLIPSE OF THE BATTLESHIPS, 1944–1945

Opposite page, top: *Tirpitz* on 30 April 1944. (IWM)

Centre: *Tirpitz* in Kaafjord, 2 June 1944. (Bundesarchiv)

Bottom: Two minutes later during smoke-generator trials. Note that the wind hardly seems in a suitable direction! (Bundesarchiv)

The directive to scrap the heavy ships at the beginning of 1943 had an immediate effect upon *Admiral Scheer* and *Lützow*, both of which returned to Home Waters that year with the intention that they be employed as training ships with the Ausbildungsverband. This withdrawal to the Baltic and the crippling of *Tirpitz* meant that, after the loss of *Scharnhorst*, the task of eliminating the remaining German capital ships fell to the Allied air forces. Even though it was extremely unlikely that these ships would ever again appear on the open seas to challenge Allied superiority, some considerable effort was still expended to destroy them.

The main purpose of these attacks was not always the sinking of a capital ship; often it was in conjunction with the more important task of destroying U-boat construction.

Thus a raid on Wilhelmshaven on 22 March 1943 had, as its objective, the destruction of U-boats and building yards, although this dockyard was not a major U-boat construction centre. However, *Admiral Scheer* lay in No. 5 dock under refit and was a worthy target this time for a force of sixty-nine B-17 Fortresses of the USAAF's 1st Bombardment Wing and fifteen B-24 Liberators of the 2nd Bombardment Wing, 8th Air Force; 224 tons of bombs were dropped for the loss of one B-17 and two B-24s. No damage was done to the warship but Flottenkommando immediately ordered her east into the Baltic further away from the Allied airfields.

In the autumn of 1943 a PR sortie to Gotenhafen on 7 October revealed *Admiral Scheer* being manoeuvred by tugs in the port, having last been seen in Swinemünde on 18 August. Also present was *Lützow*, together with *Emden* at the Polish wharf, *Nürnberg* and *Leipzig* alongside the Romanian wharf, and *Prinz Eugen* lying off. *Gneisenau* was noted completely camouflaged and the two elderly pre-dreadnoughts *Schleswig-Holstein* and *Schlesien* were also present. All the Kriegsmarine's remaining large units bar two were here in one port. Not surprisingly, an Allied air raid took place. This was undertaken by the 8th USAAF on 9th October with 41 B-24s of the 2nd Bomb Division (93rd, 44th, 382nd and 392nd Bomb Groups) and the 1st and 3rd Bomb Divisions (92nd, 96th, 305th, 306th and 308th Bomb Groups) with 109 B-17s. The B-24s were tasked with bombing Danzig, the B-17s Gotenhafen, the former dropping 86 tons and the latter 272 tons of bombs for the loss of two and six aircraft respectively. Despite all the bombs, no worthwhile military target was hit but this, the first daylight raid so far east, came as an unpleasant surprise to the Kriegsmarine.

It was still *Tirpitz*, however, which commanded most of the attention, at least as far as the Royal Navy was concerned. Alone in Arctic Norway following the loss of *Scharnhorst*, she continued repairs to the damage caused by the X-craft attack in the autumn of 1943. This repair work was carried out in arduous conditions without any of the dockyard facilities normally obligatory for such a major task, which included the construction of a 34m-long cofferdam under the ship. Code-named Operation 'Paul', advance parties of specialists began arriving from 11 November and were accommodated aboard the repair ship *Neumark*, which was secured alongside *Tirpitz*, whose double aircraft hangar was emptied and converted into a workshop. A second repair ship, *Huascaran*, arrived in Kaafjord on 25 November, followed by *Pernambuco* (with materials) and *Monte Rosa* (with 250 workmen) by the end of that month. Repairs could now begin in earnest.

Defence was however a problem as, with the loss of *Scharnhorst*, Altenfjord's protection consisted only of *Tirpitz*'s 'B' turret, two 15cm guns and the floating torpedo batteries *Lillan* and *Drott*, which had been brought up from Trondheim. There was a serious fear that *Duke of York* might appear in the fjord, and the unpleasant fact was that none of the torpedo tubes aboard *Lillan* and *Drott* was at the moment effective. By early January 1944 four 38cm guns and four 15cm were operational aboard the battleship. A 20-tonne floating crane had arrived but not the vital 100-tonne crane, which meant that some of the necessary work was impossible. Despite all the difficulties, the repair work progressed well and by mid-March 1944 *Tirpitz* was ready for trials. Between 15 and 16 March the ship ran full power and gunnery trials in Stjernsund and Vargsund escorted by *Z30* and *Z38* under poor and snowy weather conditions. By this time, the ship was fully effective, except for the centre turbine, which needed opening up because of noises. This, however, was expected to be rectified by early April. Both Schniewind and Dönitz recognized the magnificent work done by the repair staffs and the ship's own company and sent their congratulations. By the end of March, a week earlier than expected, all three engines were serviceable and the ship was an operational unit once more.

Meanwhile British intelligence had been keeping a watching brief on the ship's progress, both by means of 'Ultra' and by agents' reports from the local Norwegians. No attacks were launched in this period except for a raid by fifteen Soviet bombers on 10 February (only four found the target), which was unsuccessful. The Royal Navy had, however, been planning an attack themselves with aircraft of the Fleet Air Arm, which was to take place on 4 April. As a result of 'Ultra' intelligence, a change in *Tirpitz*'s plans had become known to Admiral Fraser (C-in-C Home Fleet), which led to this attack being brought forward by 24 hours. Code-named

Thetis

← Kaafjord

6 32

Operation 'Tungsten', the attack involved two fleet carriers, *Victorious* and *Furious*, as well as four escort carriers, *Emperor*, *Pursuer*, *Searcher* and *Fencer* (the latter being for A/S duties). Embarked in this group of carriers were 39 Barracudas, 28 Corsairs, 20 Hellcats, 14 Seafires and 40 Wildcats, of which the actual strike force were the Barracuda dive-bombers of Nos. 8 and 52 TBR Wings, which would be covered by Corsair, Hellcat and Wildcat fighters.

In the early hours of 3 April, some 120nm north-west of Kaafjord, No. 8 TBR Wing (Nos. 827 and 830 Squadrons) took off with an escort of about forty fighters (whose task included the suppression of enemy flak and control positions). A second strike of Barracudas from No. 52 TBR Wing was launched about an hour later, also with fighter escort. One Barracuda (LS580/829) crashed on take-off but the remaining forty dive-bombers attacked.

For *Tirpitz* it was intended that the day would be spent on further trials and exercises and the appearance of a PR Spitfire over her berth the previous day had already been forgotten. At 0530 the battleship was ready for sea, her programme for the day including a run on the degaussing range and a full power trial. The first indication of anything untoward came at 0642, when a report was received of approximately thirty aircraft about 80km north of Alta, flying south. One minute later the air-raid warning signal was given and the smoke generators started. *Tirpitz* was by this time practically clear of her nets, the port anchor secured and the starboard up and down with cable still out. Six fighters now attacked from astern, strafing the ship with machine-gun fire, to knock out her flak and control positions. At 0630 the Barracudas made their first attack, dive-bombing with 1600lb AP, 500lb SAP or 500lb MC bombs. The ship's flak was only partially effective and in the absence of any defending fighters, the Barracudas bombed from below 1,000m, which increased their accuracy but prevented the AP bombs from achieving their full penetration potential.

There were no fighters to defend *Tirpitz* because the fighter units of Luftflotte 5 had been greatly reduced, the unit based at the Alta strip having long departed. Such fighter strength as remained in the Arctic, the Bf 109s of III/JG 5 at Petsamo and the Bf 110s of 13.(Z)/JG 5 at Kirkenes, totalled only some forty machines and was fully employed on the battle front, east of Kirkenes. Apart from the battleship's own defences, there were also the two flak cruisers *Nymphe* (in Kvanikbucht) and *Thetis*, both armed with six 10.5cm SKC/32, six 2cm/38 and two 4cm Flak/28; these two vessels were, respectively, the former Norwegian coast defence ships *Tordenskjold* and *Harald Haarfagre*, which had been rearmed by the Germans. Ashore in the Alta area were five batteries equipped with guns of between 7.5cm and 15.5cm calibre, while to seaward in the Oksfjord region there were four batteries of between 14.5cm and 15.5cm. Some light flak also existed.

The success of the attack was undoubtedly due to surprise, for the smoke defences had not fully developed before the bombers arrived and when it did it greatly hampered control of the flak guns. Heavy losses were incurred by the crews of

Tirpitz's unshielded 3.7cm and 2cm weapons. Both the forward flak control positions and the main control positions were early victims of the fighters' machine-guns and, until the after position could take over, the ship's defences fired in erratic local control. An early bomb hit on the bridge injured the ship's Captain, whereupon the Navigating Officer assumed command. Altogether, five AP and four HE bombs appear to have hit the ship in the first attack, causing serious structural damage to the upperworks, fires and many casualties. By 0645 a lull developed, when Kpt.z.S. Junge (the Commander) took over the ship and the wounded were seen to.

Tirpitz by this time had drifted broadside on in Kaafjord, with her bows west, close in shore. The starboard anchor was dropped and two tugs came alongside to pass tow lines to bow and stern. The time was now 0725. Eight minutes later the second wave of bombers arrived, whereupon the tugs promptly slipped and fled, while a furious barrage fire was opened up. Five more hits were obtained in this attack, causing further damage to the upper decks. Two Barracudas (LS551/829 and LS569/830) were shot down in the attack, one of which crashed near *Neumark*'s berth and was partially salvaged later. One Hellcat fighter was also lost.

In total, *Tirpitz* was hit by four 1,600lb AP bombs, five 500lb SAP and five 500lb MC bombs, mostly on the starboard side, none of which penetrated the main armoured deck. Some 438 casualties were incurred, of which 122 were fatal. Her upperworks were a shambles, hangars burned out and aircraft wrecked. The last of many fires was not extinguished until later that evening. In addition, the supply ship *C.A. Larsen* was set on fire and damaged but not sunk, while the fighters shot up *UJ1212* in Stjernsund, *UJ1218* in Kaafjord, as well as the merchant ship *Dollart* off Loppa.

The whole process of repair had to be begun again and it was to be many months before *Tirpitz* would be operational once more. Further strikes against her had to be cancelled because of bad weather, so that it was not until July that she was attacked again, this time by 44 Barracudas of Nos. 820, 826, 827 and 830 Squadrons, with an escort of 48 fighters. This operation, 'Mascot', was launched on 17 July but failed because the battleship's early warning system had been greatly improved. A similar operation, 'Goodwood', on August 22, 24 and 29 also failed for the same reasons.

Next, it was the turn of the RAF, but because of the distance to Kaafjord their attack had to be mounted from North Russia. Thirty-six Lancasters of Nos. 617 and 9 Squadrons flew out from Lossiemouth on 10 September, bound for Archangel, but six had to be abandoned when they became lost and crash-landed (LL884, LM448, NF938, NF985 and PD211 of No. 9 Squadron and ME559 of No. 617 Squadron). Thirty-eight aircraft, operating from Yagodnik, attacked *Tirpitz* about midday on 15 September. Twenty-one of these were armed with the fearsome 6-ton 'Tallboy' bomb and six with JW mines. The latter were 400lb bomb-mines filled with 90lb of Torpex which parachuted down. Designed for use in at least 14m of water, this weapon was intended to oscillate between the bottom and surface for two hours before

finally sinking. These caused the Germans much puzzlement when they examined them later. The final aircraft (of No. 463 Squadron) carried camera crews.

Unfortunately, complete surprise was not achieved and bombing had to be carried out through the smoke. Seventeen 'Tallboys' and 72 JW6s were dropped but only one, a 'Tallboy', hit. This passed through the bows and exploded beneath the keel, making a huge hole in the ship, some 10m by 16m and about 1,000 tonnes of water flooded into the ship. The shock of the explosion was felt throughout and much internal damage was done. All her engine foundations were sheared, the hull damaged below water as far aft as 'A' turret and the upper deck buckled. She was neither seaworthy nor battleworthy. Little damage had been done to the armament, except for four 3.7cm and three R.A.G. forward. None of the attackers was lost in the raid although one (PB416/617) was missing on the flight home.

Tirpitz was now finished as a seagoing fighting unit. Repairs of any permanent or major nature were impossible, given the situation now in the far north. Dönitz however still believed that the ship had a role to play in the defence of

Norway against the always expected Allied landing. In consequence, temporary repairs were made to the bows, after which she was to be employed as a floating battery west of Lyngenfjord. The 1st Battle Group would then be dissolved and K.Ad. Peters would haul down his flag. At midday on 15 October, *Tirpitz* left Kaafjord for the last time. Escorted by the flak cruisers *Nymphe* and *Thetis*, three AFPs and four minesweepers, she made her sorry way out towards the sea, at a speed of 8 knots—about all the bows would take—and arrived in Sandesund the following morning. The 1st Battle Group actually ceased to exist on 20 October, Peters greatly regretting that, since his assuming the post on 6 June, he had had no opportunity of leading it into action.

The new berth for *Tirpitz* was in the lee of Hacköy Island, about four miles west of Tromso. Her arrival had been duly noted both by agents and PR aircraft. It was immediately realized that, with some modifications, Lancasters could now reach her from RAF bases; the somewhat dubious assistance of the Soviets was no longer needed. It was necessary, however, to change the Merlin engines of Nos. 617 and 9 Squadrons' aircraft to Merlin 24s and to remove the mid-upper turrets and armour plate to enable the aircraft to make the 2,252-mile round trip. Even so, a Wellington long-range fuel tank and a Mosquito tank had to be added to carry the extra fuel.

On 29 October nineteen Lancasters, accompanied once again by one from No. 463 Squadron to photograph results, attacked *Tirpitz* in her new berth. No hits were scored but near misses distorted one of the shafts and some flooding occurred. One aircraft (NF920/617) was damaged by flak and crash-landed in Sweden. Not until 12 November did another attack take place, again with the same squadrons. *Tirpitz*, anchored, was caught in fine, sunny weather, with no cloud, no smoke defences and no fighter protection. She fired three 38cm salvoes and then opened fire with the rest of her armament in a futile attempt to defend herself. No. 617 Squadron dropped their 'Tallboys' first, followed by No. 9 Squadron.

The first warnings of aircraft had reached the ship at about 0800, when *Tirpitz* was immediately connected to the main air-raid centre at Tromso. About a quarter of an hour later, fighter protection was requested and the ship closed up to action stations. Tromso air-raid sirens sounded at 0854 and at 0915 the British aircraft were sighted. Five minutes later the request for fighter protection was repeated and Fw 190s of JG 5 at Bardufoss scrambled immediately. No one, however, had informed the Luftwaffe of the battleship's move to Tromso. The 10.5cm opened up about 0934, followed by the 3.7cm and 2cm a couple of minutes later. One 'Tallboy' (approximately the fourth dropped) certainly struck the ship and probably two more. The definite hit struck her port side near the catapult, in the wing compartment of the port turbine room, penetrating all decks and armour. Another bomb fell in the sea abreast the after range-finder on the port side, causing a great flash of light, while the next four bombs fell inside the net area. The ninth bomb fell abreast 'D' turret and seconds later developed a huge black column of smoke, followed separately by the flash of an ammunition explosion

amidships, not connected with a bomb hit. Many other bombs fell scattered around the ship's berth. Huge quantities of water were thrown over the ship, which quickly listed 35°. Counter-flooding orders were given but could not be carried out and abandon ship was ordered. The list to port continued until the ship was at 60°, where it remained briefly. Now a huge explosion occurred in the vicinity of 'C' turret, which lifted the whole rotating mass bodily out of the ship, after which *Tirpitz* rolled over until her upperworks struck the sea bed.

Later examination showed the ship's side to be torn away between frames 98 and 132, but forward of this there was only shrapnel damage. The precise cause for the explosion in 'C' turret was never ascertained. It was probable that the after turbine room (Mitte) and the after centre boiler room quickly flooded, and all spaces to port of the centre-line between frames 83 and 154.5. This immediate flooding was sufficient to cause the 35° list, given that the ship was low on fuel and stores, therefore riding light. Flooding continued, causing the list to increase to 60°. At this time it was calculated that some 17,000 tonnes of water may have been in the ship, which would normally have continued right over, but it is believed that soft mud on the bottom may have checked her until 'C' turret exploded. Loss of life was heavy, including the Commanding Officer, Kpt.z.S. Weber, who had taken over from Junge on the ship's arrival in Tromso. Now only the two former Panzerschiffe remained to the Kriegsmarine, both in Baltic waters.

In the Baltic the beginning of 1944 at first saw little change in the pattern of the Kriegsmarine's activities, which, as far as the remaining heavy ships were concerned, were mainly of a training nature. *Lützow*, now commanded by Kpt.z.S. Knocke (formerly her Commander during 1941/43), underwent a three-month refit at Libau, between the end of 1943 and mid-March 1944; while *Admiral Scheer* (Kpt.z.S. Rothe-Roth) had also been under refit until 13 January. Both ships had been part of the Ausbildungsverband since their return from the Norwegian front, as had *Schlesien* and *Schleswig-Holstein* since 1941. In their role as training ships, none could be described as effective fighting ships because large numbers of cadets under instruction replaced regular crew members. Moreover, because of the fuel shortage, some of the training

ships spent little time at sea. In the case of the Panzerschiffe, *Lützow* appears to have carried out the sea-training, while her sister went to sea much less. Similarly, *Schleswig-Holstein* was, until February 1944, employed mainly as a stationary training hulk, after which she was reactivated and employed in a similar manner to her sister. The fact that these elderly vessels still retained a coal-firing ability was of significance in their continued employment.

As the year progressed, the situation on the Eastern Front began to deteriorate and it became likely that a more active role for the Fleet would come about. In consequence, plans were laid for the formation of a 2nd Task Force (the 1st was still centred around *Tirpitz*) and, if necessary, a 3rd Task Force. However, for the moment, there matters rested. Nevertheless, the Soviet offensive against the Finns on the Karelian Front at the eastern end of the Gulf of Finland in the early summer of 1944 caused some concern and it was felt expedient, from a political point of view, to demonstrate to Finland some visible evidence of German support. Light forces were sent into the Gulf and a heavy force to the western entrance of the Gulf. This latter was code-named 'Rotbuche', under which a base was to be established in the Aaland Islands. Taking part in this were *Lützow*, *Prinz Eugen*, the fighter direction ship *Togo*, as well as destroyers and torpedo boats. Fighter cover was to be provided by the Fw 190s of I/JG 54 at Turku in Finland. Net-protected berths were laid out and the flak defences in the islands augmented. *Lützow* sailed from Gotenhafen, escorted by *T3*, *T4* and *T12* on 24 June, but the crisis was only of short duration and she set sail for home again on 8 July.

By this time the situation on the Eastern Front around Riga, capital of Latvia, was becoming critical and the plans for the formation of the 2nd Task Force were put into operation. Viz.Ad. Thiele, currently Flag Officer (Training Squadron), was earmarked for the post of Flag Officer (2nd Task Force), while either Schniewind or Viz.Ad. Kreisch (Flag Officer—Destroyers) would command the future 3rd Task Force, if and when it was formed. Thiele was duly appointed on 17 July and on 29 July he was ordered by Dönitz to cover the evacuation of all German dependants, surplus personnel and wounded from Riga. *Lützow* sailed with the 2nd Torpedo-boat Flotilla (*T4*, *T1*, *T9* and *T12*) to accomplish this task, but before the Gulf of Riga was reached, the situation stabilized and she was instead stationed off the Irben Straits—the entrance to the Gulf of Riga. However, as this involved both the use of scarce fuel and exposure to possible submarine attack, the ship was ordered into Libau, where she could bolster that port's flak defences.

The increasing threat and effectiveness of Soviet air attacks was now being felt throughout the Baltic and Gulf of Finland and a programme of augmenting the ships' flak outfits was put in hand. *Lützow*, as the most valuable of the heavy ships, was high on the priorities for refit and was ordered home from Libau on 28 August to begin her rearmament. In the next few weeks at Gotenhafen, she received four single 4cm Flak 28, which supplanted two of the old 3.7cm twins and two of the 2cm MGC/38 singles. Then after investigation it was found to be possible to fit two more, for a total of six 4cm. Twin 2cm LM44 mountings with shields supplanted the single 2cm but no shields were yet available for the remaining 3.7cm twins. Not until some time later were these mountings landed for the fitment of shields.

Schlesien too had received some attention to her outfit, having two 4cm Flak 28, four 3.7cm SKC/30 in twin mountings and twenty 2cm (2×4, 6×2). *Schleswig-Holstein* on the other hand had not yet been improved. Their planned outfits were:

Schleswig-Holstein	6, 10.5cm SKC/32gE (6×1)
	6, 4cm Flak 28 (6×1)
	4, 3.7cm SKC/30 (2×2)
	24, 2cm (3×4, 6×2)
Schlesien	6, 10.5cm SKC/32gE (6×1)
	10, 4cm Flak 28 (10×1)
	22, 2cm (4×4, 3×2)

Both were to receive FuMO25 radar and a comprehensive FuMB outfit. At the end of October 1944, orders were given that the night range-finders and other control gear were to be landed by the three U-boat depot ships in Gotenhafen for installation aboard the old battleships. *Schlesien* began her refit at Gotenhafen on 15 July and *Schleswig-Holstein* in the same dockyard on 27 September. Both ships were also being re-equipped for icebreaking duties in the new year, a task which assumed greater importance as the year progressed and the Baltic States became cut off. Maintenance of the lines of communication between Gotenhafen, Libau and Memel was vital but, unlike the situation in earlier winters, this task would now have to be carried out in all probability under air attack. Hence the flak up-grading of the old Linienschiffe.

Lützow returned to the Aaland Islands at the end of September when, as part of a force which included *Prinz Eugen*, *Z25*, *Z35*, *Z36*, *T1* and *T8*, she helped cover the evacuation of the remaining German forces from the northern end of the Gulf of Bothnia. This operation was uneventful and the ship was back in Gotenhafen by 25 September. Action was imminent however, because on 10 October the Red Army reached the Baltic coast between Libau and Memel, cutting off German forces in Kurland. Now enemy formations were within the range of the guns of the fleet and Admiral Meendsen-Bohlken (who had relieved Schniewind

as Fleet Commander on 31 June), prepared to commit his remaining ships to the desperate land battles on the Eastern Front.

Only *Lützow* and *Prinz Eugen* were considered fully effective, *Admiral Scheer* had long been employed on training duties with the Ausbildungsverband (K.Ad. Rogge since 30 September), while *Admiral Hipper* had been paid off or under refit for a long time. None of the light cruisers was considered of much use in the forthcoming tasks. Thus the brunt of the work initially fell to *Lützow* and *Prinz Eugen*, supported by the few remaining torpedo boats and destroyers. *Admiral Scheer* was ordered to prepare for more active duty and exchange her AP ammunition for HE as soon as possible, but for the present she would not be able to participate in the initial shore bombardments. *Lützow* conducted battle practice shoots against *Hessen* at the beginning of October, before joining *Prinz Eugen* for exercises at sea, preparatory to going into action on bombardment duties. The duties of the Task Force were laid down as follows:

(1) To engage the Red Fleet if it were to break out of Leningrad.

(2) To support the Army.

(3) Special operations in the Aaland Sea.

The first was unlikely, the third only a minor requirement. It was the second task which was the more important, but it presented difficulties because of the mine, submarine and air attack dangers. *Lützow* sailed from Gotenhafen on 10 October, exercised with *Prinz Eugen* briefly in the foggy Baltic autumn weather before proceeding towards the Lithuanian coast. The task was to disrupt Soviet army concentrations north and south of Memel.

As the coast was closed around midday on 11 October, the sounds of gunfire could be heard but the hilly and wooded coast north of Memel could not be distinguished through the fog and rain. At 1336 *Prinz Eugen* opened fire but *Lützow* was unable to do so herself until 1356 because of target selection problems. Throughout the day targets all around Memel and inland were engaged by the ships, using main and secondary guns. Cease-fire was eventually ordered at 2340 before the ships withdrew from the coast. After a night spent steaming about at sea, Viz.Ad. Thiele took the Task Force back inshore the following day to resume its bombardment, this time with the assistance of forward observers ashore, in support of the 7 Panzerdivision, 28 Army Corps. There was no opposition from the shore and only slight air attacks—communications and visibility caused most of the problems—but by late afternoon Thiele signalled the Army that the ships had completed their task, setting course to return to Gotenhafen.

This was the first time that *Lützow* had seen action since 'Regenbögen' in December 1942 and it had a significant effect upon the morale of her crew. After replenishing ammunition and fuel, it was intended that a repeat strike would be launched immediately but there was a delay with the 28cm ammunition and, as a result, *Prinz Eugen* left without *Lützow*. Ammunition was currently a problem, there being available only about $3\frac{1}{2}$ outfits each for *Lützow* and

Top: *Schleswig-Holstein* after the war. (WBB)

Above: *Admiral Scheer*, 1944/45. Note 3.7cm gun on 'B' turret and Vierling at the break of the forecastle. (WBB)

Opposite page, top: *Lützow* at Swinemünde, 16 April 1945. (PRO)

Centre: *Lützow* on 19 April 1945 after the Lancaster raid. Note the bomb craters and the salvage craft alongside the ship. (PRO)

Bottom: *Lützow* after hostilities. (WBB)

Admiral Scheer. Further supplies were being sent up from the arsenals, while further quantities were being returned from Norway. *Lützow* finally rejoined Admiral Thiele off Memel on 14 October. Most of the bombardment on the 15th, however, was carried out by *Prinz Eugen*, *Lützow* having been ordered to reserve hers for a later operation planned for 17 October. As a result, she only fired 30 rounds against one target.

Viz.Ad. Thiele shifted his flag to *Lützow* on 17 October and sailed the following day, only to anchor in the bay while orders were clarified. Thus it was not until the evening of 22 October that *Lützow* sailed, escorted by *Z28*, *Z35*, *T21*, *T13* and *T20* for another bombardment of the Memel area. *Prinz Eugen* could not participate because of a collision with *Leipzig*. *Admiral Scheer* and *Admiral Hipper* were both ordered to prepare for active duty but in the event neither participated for the moment. *Lützow*'s first task was in the Memel area

again, after which she was to assist the hard-pressed defenders of the narrow Sworbe peninsula. Her attack began on the morning of 23 October and continued until that afternoon, engaging with both main and secondary guns. Transferring to the Sworbe peninsula, bombardment was continued at 0710 on 24 October. In the course of this action, heavy air attacks were fought off without damage, except for *Z28*, which was hit by several bombs. The task was completed by midday, after some 300 rounds of 28cm had been fired into the Sworbe alone and, with the thanks of Generalleutenant Schirmer of 23 Infantry Division, *Lützow* returned to Gotenhafen.

In November both *Lützow* and *Admiral Scheer* received shields for their 3.7cm SKC/30 guns, as they prepared for action again. The latter got her first chance of action when, on 21 November, she sailed with *T3* and *T12* to participate in Operation 'Hammer'—bombardment duties off the Sworbe. That evening *Prinz Eugen* hove into view, whereupon Admiral Thiele shifted his flag to *Admiral Scheer*. The next day *Admiral Scheer* opened fire in earnest, using her own aircraft for spotting. Shore batteries returned the fire, straddling but not hitting the ship. Some 143 rounds of 28cm and 374 rounds of 15cm were fired. This action continued the following morning when not only the shore batteries replied, but there were also concentrated air attacks, during one of which the ship's Arado was shot down. A huge quantity of ammunition was expended that day, but towards late afternoon information was received that the Sworbe was to be evacuated that night. *Admiral Scheer* stood by overnight, joined the following morning by *Lützow*, but the evacuation passed off uneventfully and their services were not required. After their return to Gotenhafen on 25 November, both ships were ordered to remain at twelve hours' notice.

On the night of 18/19 December Bomber Command despatched a raid of 236 Lancaster bombers against Gotenhafen, which caused considerable damage and loss to ships and harbour installations. Among the ships hit was *Schleswig-Holstein*, part way through her refit by Deutsche Werke. The ship was in the process of running basin turbo-generator trials, had her full crew aboard and was closed up for action. The first bomb struck in compartment IV, exploding in the port engine room, the second in compartment III, the midships engine room, and the last in compartment II on the waterline abreast 'B' turret. This last bomb passed through the ship's bottom without exploding. In the midships engine room, the destruction of the main condenser flooded the space with live steam, which forced its evacuation. Flooding in No. 1 boiler room put out the only two boilers flashed up and bombs on shore had destroyed power and fire-fighting mains. With the loss of both turbo-generators, all power was lost and the lighting failed. A list to port of 11° was controlled to 4° by counter-flooding, but there was serious flooding aft and the stern settled on the bottom. A large number of casualties were suffered. The next day a salvage ship came alongside to pump out flooded compartments, but further fires broke out which were later extinguished. Salvage attempts were broken off on 26 December

when the whole ship settled back on to the bottom. A month later she was ordered to be paid off and on 26 January 1945 decommissioned. *Lützow* escaped damage in this raid, although the steamer *Warthe* just astern was badly hit and sunk. The British lost four aircraft in this raid, LM671, NG114, NN726 and PB723.

Because of the danger of further air raids, both *Lützow* and *Admiral Scheer* were ordered to Pillau immediately after the raid, where they remained until into the new year.

At the end of January 1945 and into the first week of February, both *Lützow* and *Admiral Scheer* were engaged in supporting the Army against the Soviet advance into East Prussia. However, on 6 March both ships sailed west, escorted by *Z34*, *Z43*, *T33* and *T23*. *Lützow* and the escorts put into Swinemünde the next day but *Admiral Scheer* continued to Kiel where she was due for a refit. Even in this dark hour, the refit schedules were adhered to. In mid-March *Schlesien* was also in action against land targets in the Kolberg-Gotenhafen area, from 15 to 21 March when, her ammunition exhausted, she returned to Swinemünde with wounded evacuees. *Lützow* returned to the Gotenhafen area on 21 March and, until 8 April, engaged many targets in and around Danzig Bay, often under air attack and shore bombardment herself. Having shot off all her ammunition and in need of refuelling, she returned to Swinemünde.

The presence of the heavy ships in Swinemünde in between bombardment duties was known to British intelligence and a series of raids was launched against that port and its environs. The first took place on 13 April by 34 Lancasters, but the attack was unsuccessful due to cloud. A second raid was made on 15 April, again by day, in which twenty Lancasters participated, seventeen of which carried 'Tallboy' bombs. Again no hits were achieved because the weather was too thick to bomb. Finally, yet another daylight raid was launched by No. 617 Squadron, this time on the 16th, using eighteen Lancasters, fourteen of which had 'Tallboys.' Escort was provided by Mustangs of Nos. 442 and 611 Squadrons. Near misses from these heavy bombs caused flooding in *Lützow*'s hull and she gradually settled to the bottom. One Lancaster, EG228, was shot down. This was not quite the end of *Lützow*'s career, however, because the water was very shallow. Most of her armament was still effective and from the end of March to 3 May 1945 she bombarded Soviet positions around Swinemünde until her ammunition was exhausted. Wrecked by her crew, the deserted hull became burned out and was subsequently raised and probably scrapped by the Russians.

Schlesien also bombarded Soviet positions from Griefswalderbucht but on 2 May she was mined by an RAF air-laid magnetic mine. Badly damaged, the ship was towed into Swinemünde and allowed to settle on the bottom. By this time the port was being abandoned, so she did not go into battle again. *Admiral Scheer* under refit at Kiel had been hit by five bombs during a 600-bomber raid on the night of 9/10 April, which capsized her so that not a single ship above the size of a cruiser remained to the Kriegsmarine at the capitulation.

POSTSCRIPT

Why did the Kriegsmarine's assault upon the ocean sea lanes fail yet again? In 1917/18 the U-boats had all but strangled the supply routes to Great Britain, but they were eventually defeated by the anti-submarine forces of the Royal Navy and the institution of the convoy system. In this earlier conflict, the High Seas Fleet played no role on the oceans; only a handful of cruisers on distant stations achieved any great success for a brief period in the opening years of World War One. Perhaps the major strategic factor associated with Germany's problem in dealing with Great Britain was geographical—the enemy lay squarely across Germany's exits to the world's oceans, and while this was not an insurmountable obstacle in the days before aircraft and radar, it nevertheless inhibited Germany's courses of action.

Obviously this situation still obtained in 1939, with the added problems of the development of aircraft and radar. Furthermore, even the few overseas bases possessed by Germany in 1914 no longer existed, thus forcing any ocean sortie by capital ships to be one of a nomadic nature, dependant upon a chain of supply and replenishment ships. The latter had been developed with some enthusiasm by the Kriegsmarine during the late 1930s but were never to attain the technology and efficiency of the US Navy's Pacific support operations in 1943–1945. The Royal Navy, with many bases available, neglected replenishment at sea until forced to reconsider this practice when it became more closely involved in the Pacific War in 1944/45.

For the Germans, the supply of spares, provisions, fuel and ammunition was however only one of the factors to be considered. The most pressing problem by far was the possibility of serious action damage or major mechanical breakdown while on the high seas. With no friendly bases to put into, it is easy to see why action was not pursued to the end on many occasions when the Royal or US Navies would have done so. There was the possibility that a U-boat requiring repair could put into a benevolent neutral port for a few days for repair without being noticed, or perhaps lie up in some unfrequented bay, but this could never have been an option for a capital ship, as the *Admiral Graf Spee* episode showed. The U-boats were also much more numerous and therefore expendable, which the capital ships were not, and little political damage would be done if a submarine had to be scuttled because minor repairs were simply impossible several thousand miles from Kiel.

Thus, even when a ship evaded the Royal Navy's blockade of the entrances to the North Atlantic, the conduct of mercantile warfare on the oceans remained a difficult task. Admiral Raeder's efforts to base capital ships in Norway and western France would have made the reaching of the oceans that much easier, but it was not that simple because air power had become a significant factor, as the experiences of the Brest Group showed. His attempts to obtain bases even further south in Spain or the Spanish Atlantic Islands, out of range of Bomber Command, came to nought on political grounds and even had he succeeded, the likely consequence would have been the stationing of Bomber Command squadrons in Gibraltar.

Air power in fact played a major role in the failure of the Kriegsmarine's capital ships to prove other than nuisance value on the high seas. They did get to sea, they did sink shipping and they caused a good deal of disruption to the Royal Navy's plans, but their results were disproportionate to the efforts expended, especially if they are compared with the U-boats, and even the latter felt the impact of air power from 1943 onwards. The failure of the Kriegsmarine to see the implications of air power at sea was not unique; many other navies had been similarly disposed. Where Germany was concerned, the combination of the Versailles Treaty, a 'battleship-minded' Naval Staff and an egotistical Luftwaffe C-in-C, led to the Kriegsmarine being a very late entry into the field of aircraft-carrier construction—too late as it turned out. Had *Graf Zeppelin* gone to sea with *Bismarck*, it is likely that No. 825 Squadron would have been destroyed in May 1941, as it was later to be in February 1942 during 'Cerberus'—and *Bismarck* might well have had a long and successful cruise. However, even allowing for the presence of air cover, the basic problem remained—no overseas dockyards, with all that that implied. As the war dragged on and no quick victory was evidently going to be achieved, other important factors emerged, which greatly restricted the employment and prospects for the capital ships. These were oil and intelligence.

Germany had no indigenous oil reserves of any note and was forced to obtain oil where she could. After 1941 Russian oil was no longer available, leaving only the Romanian oil fields and, moreover, Germany was forced to supply oil to the Royal Italian Navy as well. The result was that from the beginning of 1942, great economies had to be made in fuel usage, with every movement, exercise or operational sortie being critically examined to assess if the possible successes justified the oil expended. This of course had a knock-on effect, in that training and efficiency suffered drastically.

In the field of intelligence, both sides were reading the other's signals from the beginning of the war. In the first two years or so the Kriegsmarine appears to have had the upper hand, often, for example, knowing the exact disposition of

British submarines. However, as the 'Ultra' intelligence department became more and more effective, the situation reversed and soon the British were reading even the small print of the Kriegsmarine's operational orders. Thus no German warship could make any operational move without the Royal Navy and its sister arms being made aware of the fact, which completely negated any attempt at a surprise entry on to the North Atlantic sea lanes. This failure to accept that their codes could have been broken is probably the most damning indictment of the Kriegsmarine Naval Staff, for it led directly to the collapse of their most effective weapon—the U-boat offensive. It is astonishing that, despite doubts about the security of codes and investigations into the matter, no radical changes were made to codes. Given the fact that this was no less than a matter of national security, codes should have been changed *on suspicion* that they had been compromised. For this omission, Admirals Raeder and Dönitz must ultimately be held responsible.

In summary, therefore, it is evident that in the early years of the war, while capital ships could reach the oceans, their activities were restricted by the absence of base and repair facilities, which resulted in timid employment and a corresponding lack of success, commensurate with their poten-

tial. Later on they were unable even to reach the oceans because of 'Ultra' intelligence and shortage of oil fuel. Deprived of air cover because *Graf Zeppelin* had been abandoned, they did not even have the option of fighting their way out. Even if they had been able to do so, the absence of base facilities still remained, and with the entry of the USA into the war, the Kriegsmarine was even more outnumbered. The result was that the ships remained for the most part idle after December 1942, while the morale and efficiency of their crews fell drastically.

The inescapable conclusion is that the construction of the capital ships was a futile exercise of national prestige, in an age when possession of battleships, irrespective of their usefulness, was an indication of world status. With the lessons of World War One there for all to see, it would have been more advisable to have built a large force of destroyers, torpedo-boats, S-boats and escorts to secure the long coastline from Spain to North Cape, and to conduct the ocean war purely with U-boats, having diverted all the efforts expended in capital ship construction to that end. This was actually done, but 1940 was far too late and Admiral Raeder did not have the political weight to secure the Kriegsmarine's full share or more of the scarce resources.

Below: *Gneisenau* scuttled as a blockship at Gotenhafen. (USN)

APPENDICES

1. SHIPS' TECHNICAL DATA

SCHLESWIG-HOLSTEIN and SCHLESIEN
Displacement:
Full load: 14,800 tonnes (*S-H*); 14,400 tonnes (*S*).
Standard: 13,191 tonnes.
Length: 126.6m (oa); 125.9m (wl).
Beam: 22.2m.
Draught: 8.35m.
Machinery:
Eight oil- and four coal-fired marine boilers (*S-H*). Eight oil-fired only (*S*).
Three-cylinder triple-expansion engines.
Three shafts, 16,000ihp = 17 knots.
Oil fuel: 950m³ (*S*); 1,009m³ (*S-H*).
Coal: 400 tonnes (*S*); 436 tonnes (*S-H*).
Endurance: 4,000nm at 9 knots (*S*); 3,400nm at 9 knots (*S-H*).
Armament:
Four 28cm SK L/40 in Dreh. LC/01 (2×2).
Ten 15cm SK L/45 (10×1).
Four 8.8cm SK L/45 in MPL C/13 (4×1).
Four 3.7cm SKC/30 in Dopp LC C/30 (2×2).
Four 2cm MG C/30 (4×1).
Protection:
Deck: 40mm (67–97mm sloped).
Belt: 240mm max.
Conning tower: 300m.

DEUTSCHLAND
Displacement:
Full load: 15,200 tonnes.
Standard: 11,700 tonnes.
Length: 186.0m (oa), (187.9m after 1940/41 refit), 181.7m (wl).
Beam: 20.7m.
Draught: 5.81/7.25m.
Machinery:
Eight MAN 9-cylinder double-acting two-stroke diesels, four per shaft.
Two shafts; 41,500bhp = 26 knots.
Diesel oil: 3,347m³ max. (3,114m³ usable); 3,229m³ normal (3,003m³ usable).
Endurance: 18,650nm at 15 knots, 7,149nm at 26 knots.
Armament:
Six 28cm SK C/28 in Dreh. LC/28 (2×3).
Eight 15cm SK C/28 in MPL C/28 (8×1).
Six 8.8cm SK C/31 in Dopp L C/31 (3×2).
Eight 3.7cm SK C/30 in Dopp LC/30 (4×2).

Ten 2cm MG C/30 (10×1).
Eight 53.3cm torpedo tubes (2×4).
Two aircraft, one catapult.
Note: It is evident from design sketches that this ship was originally to have had four 8.8cm SK C/25 in two twin mountings, but this weapon was not successful. Also, at the time of design the 2cm and 3.7cm guns were not available.
Protection:
Deck: 45mm.
Belt: 80mm.
Conning tower: 150mm.
Turrets: 140mm.

ADMIRAL SCHEER
Displacement:
Full load: 15,900 tonnes.
Standard: 11,700 tonnes.
Length: 186.0m (oa); (187.9m after 1940 refit), 181.7m (wl).
Beam: 21.4m.
Draught: 5.81/7.25m.
Machinery:
As *Deutschland* but 44,200bhp.
Diesel fuel: 3,333m³ max. (3,100m³ usable); 3,217m³ normal (2,992m³ usable).
Endurance: 17,460nm at 15 knots; 6,960nm at 27 knots.
Generating capacity 2,800 kW.
Armament: as *Deutschland*.
Protection:
Deck: 40mm.
Belt: 80mm.
Conning tower: 150mm.
Turrets: 140mm.

ADMIRAL GRAF SPEE
Displacement:
Full load: 16,200 tonnes.
Standard: 12,100 tonnes.
Length: 186.0m (oa), 181.7m (wl).
Beam: 21.7m.
Draught: 5.80/7.43m.
Machinery: As *Admiral Scheer*, except generating capacity 3,360kW.
Armament: As *Admiral Scheer*, except 10.5cm SK C/33 from completion.
Protection:
Deck: 45mm.
Belt: 100mm.
Conning tower: 140mm.

SCHARNHORST and GNEISENAU
Displacement:
Full load: 38,100 tonnes.
Standard: 35,540 tonnes.
Length: 229.8m (oa), (234.9m after 1939 refit), 226.0m (wl).
Beam: 30.0m.
Draught: 9.10/9.90m.
Machinery:
Twelve Wagner boilers (52kg/cm² at 450°C).
Three-shaft geared turbines (Brown-Boveri-*Scharnhorst*, Deschimag-*Gneisenau*).
166,500shp = 32 knots (*Scharnhorst*).
153,990shp = 30.7 knots (*Gneisenau*).
Oil fuel: 5,960m³ max. (5,540m³ usable); 5,355m³ normal (4,980m³ usable).
Endurance: 9,020nm at 15 knots, 2,210nm at 32 knots (*Scharnhorst*); 8,380nm at 15 knots, 2,900nm at 30.7 knots (*Gneisenau*).
Armament:
Nine 28cm SK C/34 in Dreh LC/28 (3×3).
Twelve 15cm SK C/28 in Dreh LC/34 and MPL C/35 (4×2 and 4×1).
Fourteen 10.5cm SK C/33 in 8.8 Dopp LC/31 (7×2).
Sixteen 3.7cm SK C/30 in Dopp LC/30 (8×2).
Ten 2cm MG C/30 (10×1).
Three aircraft, two catapults.
Protection:
Deck: 105mm.
Belt: 320mm.
Conning tower: 220mm.
Turrets: 360mm.

BISMARCK and TIRPITZ
Displacement:
Full load: 50,900 tonnes (*Bismarck*); 52,700 tonnes (*Tirpitz*).
Standard: 41,700 tonnes (*B*); 42,343 tonnes (*T*).
Length: 248m (oa), 240.2m (wl).
Beam: 36.0m.
Draught: 8.7m/10.8m.
Machinery:
Twelve Wagner boilers (58kg/cm², 450°C).
Three-shaft Brown-Boveri geared turbines, 163,000shp = 30 knots.
Oil fuel: 7,900m³ (*Tirpitz*, 8,297m³ max. (7,717m³ usable), 7,944m³ normal,

(7,388m³ usable).
Endurance: 8,410nm at 15 knots, 3,740nm at 30 knots (*Bismarck*); 10,200nm at 16 knots (*Tirpitz*).
Armament:
Eight 38cm SK C/34 in Dreh LC/34 (4×2).
Twelve 15cm SK C/28 in Dreh LC/34 (6×2).
Sixteen 10.5cm SK C/33 in Dopp LC/37 (foremost 4 in *Bismarck* LC/31).
Sixteen 3.7cm SK C/30 in Dopp LC/30 (8×2).
Twelve 2cm MG C/30, (12×1).
Six aircraft; two catapults.
Protection:
Deck: 120mm.
Belt: 320mm.
Conning tower: 350mm.
Turrets: 360mm.

SCHLACHTSCHIFF 'H'
Displacement:
Full load: 68,000 tonnes.
Standard: 56,200 tonnes.
Length: 227.8m (oa); 266m (wl).
Beam: 37.6m.
Draught: 9.6/11.2m.
Machinery:
Twelve MAN 9-cylinder double-acting two-stroke diesels.
Three shafts, 165,000bhp = 30 knots.
Diesel oil: 10,000m³ = 16,000nm at 19 knots.
Armament:
Eight 40.6cm SK C/34 (4×2).
Twelve 15cm SK C/28 in Dreh LC/34 (6×2).
Sixteen 10.5cm SK C/33 in Dreh LC/38 (8×2).
Sixteen 3.7cm SK C/30 in Dopp LC/30 (8×2).
Six 53.3cm torpedo tubes (under water).
Six aircraft.
Protection:
Deck: 120mm.
Belt: 320mm.
Conning tower: 385mm.

SCHLACHTSCHIFF 'O'
Displacement:
Full load: 38,200 tonnes.
Standard: 32,300 tonnes.
Length: 256.5m (oa), 246.0m (wl).
Beam: 30m.

Draught: 9.6m/11.2m.
Machinery:
Eight MAN 24-cylinder double-acting two-stroke 'V' motors.
Four Wagner boilers.
Two shafts 116,000bhp (diesel) plus one shaft 60,000shp (turbine) = 33.5 knots.
5,100m³ fuel = 14,000nm at 19 knots.
Armament:
Six 38cm SK C/34 in Dreh LC/34 (3×2).
Six 15cm SK C/28 in Dreh LC/34 (3×2).
Eight 10.5cm SK C/33 in Dreh LC/38 (4×2).
Eight 3.7cm SK C/30 in Dopp LC/30 (4×2).
Six 53.3cm above-water torpedo tubes.
Four aircraft, one double catapult.
Protection:
Deck: 110mm.

Belt: 180mm.
Conning tower: 200mm.

KREUZER 'P'
Displacement:
Full load: 25,689 tonnes.
Standard: 22,145 tonnes.
Length: 230m (oa), 223 (wl).
Beam: 26m.
Draught: 7.2m/8.0m.
Machinery:
Twelve 9-cylinder MAN double-acting two-stroke 'V' motors.
Three shafts, 165,000bhp = 33 knots.
5,000m³ diesel fuel = 15,000nm at 19 knots.
Armament:
Six 28cm SK C/34 in Dreh LC/34 (3×2).
Four 15cm SK C/28 in Dreh LC/34 (2×2).

Eight 10.5cm SK C/33 in Dreh LC/38 (4×2).
Four 3.7cm SK C/30 in Dopp LC/30 (2×2).
Six 53.3cm under-water torpedo tubes.
Two aircraft, two catapults.
Protection:
Deck: 100mm.
Belt: 120mm.
Conning tower: ?.

GRAF ZEPPELIN
Displacement:
Full load: 33,550 tonnes.
Standard: 23,200 tonnes.
Length: 250m (oa).
Beam: 27m.
Draught: 6.4m/8.5m.
Machinery:

Sixteen La Mont boilers (70kg/cm² at 450°C).
Four-shaft Brown-Boveri geared turbines 200,000shp = 33.8 knots.
6,740m³ oil fuel.
Endurance: 8,000nm at 19 knots.
Armament:
Sixteen 15cm SK C/28 in Dopp MPL C/36 (8×2).
Twelve 10.5cm SK C/33 in Dopp LC/37 (6×2).
Twenty-two 3.7cm SK C/30 in Dopp LC/30 (11×2).
Seven 2cm MG C/30 (7×1).
Forty-two aircraft.
Protection:
Deck: 60mm.
Belt: 100mm.
Conning tower: 150mm.

2. CONSTRUCTION, COMMANDERS AND FATES

SCHLESIEN
Laid down: 1905
Launched: 28.5.06
Commissioned: 5.5.08
Builder: Schichau (Danzig)
Commanding Officers (Reichs- and Kriegsmarine only):

Kpt.z.S. Wilhelm Canaris	1932 to	1934
Kpt.z.S. Heinrich Ancker	1934 to	1936
Kpt.z.S. Thilo von Seebach	1936 to	1937
Kpt.z.S. Friedrich Wilhelm Fleischer	1937 to	1938
Kpt.z.S. Werner Lindenau	1938 to	1939
Kpt.z.S. Kurt Utke	1939 to	11.39
Kpt.z.S. Günther Horstmann	11.39 to	.....
Kpt.z.S. Isenlar (acting)	1.41 to	6.41
Kpt.z.S. Werner Lindenau	6.41 to	.....
Kpt.z.S. Ernst von Studnitz	1.42 to	6.42
(No commanding officer from June 1942)		
Kpt.z.S. Franz Friedrichs	9.42 to	2.43
(No commanding officer from February 1943)		
Kpt.z.S. Alfred Roegglen	6.43 to	.....
Kpt.z.S. Hans-Eberhardt Busch	Autumn 1944 to	Loss

Fate:
Mined off Usedom 2.5.45 and scuttled in Swinemünde 4.5.45. Wreck broken up post-war, 1949–56.

SCHLESWIG-HOLSTEIN
Laid down: 8.05
Launched: 17.12.06
Commissioned: 6.7.08
Builder: Krupp, Germania (Kiel)
Commanding Officers (Reichs- and Kriegsmarine only):

Kpt.z.S. Friedrich Götting	1932 to	1933
Kpt.z.S. Karl Georg Schuster	1933 to	1935
Kpt.z.S. Günther Krause	1935 to	1937
Kpt.z.S. Hans Feldbausch	1937 to	1938
Kpt.z.S. Gustav Kieseritzky	1938 to	1939
Kpt.z.S. Gustaz Kleikamp	1939 to	12.40
Kpt.z.S. Alfred Roegglen	12.40 to	5.41
Kpt.z.S. Walter Hennecke	5.41 to	10.41

F.Kpt. Rigauer (acting)	10.41 to	.....
(Officers appointed as necessary 1942 to 1944)		
K.Kpt. Bürklen	2.44 to	Loss

Fate:
Badly damaged at Gotenhafen by RAF air raid 18.12.44. Paid off 26.1.45 and scuttled 21.3.45.

DEUTSCHLAND
Ordered: 17.8.28
Laid down: 9.2.29
Launched: 19.5.31
Commissioned: 1.4.33
Builder: Deutsche Werke (Kiel)
Yard number: 219
Commanding Officers:

Kpt.z.S. Hermann von Fischel	4.33 to	1935
Kpt.z.S. Paul Fanger	1935 to	1937
Kpt.z.S. Paul Werner Wenneker	1937 to	12.39
Kpt.z.S. August Thiele	12.39 to	4.40
K.Kpt. Weber (acting)	14.4.40 to	6.40
Kpt.Lt. Heller (acting)	16.6.40 to	8.8.40
(Ship paid off 8.8.40 to 31.3.41)		
Kpt.z.S. Leo Kreisch	31.3.41 to	1.42
Kpt.z.S. Rudolf Stange	5.1.42 to	11.43
(Vacant from November 1943)		
Kpt.z.S. Bodo-Heinrich Knocke	1.44 to	Loss

Fate:
Renamed Lützow 15.11.39. Badly damaged by RAF bombers at Swinemünde 16.5.45. Scuttled 4.5.45 and broken up post-war.

ADMIRAL SCHEER
Ordered: 1931
Laid down: 25.6.31
Launched: 1.4.33
Commissioned: 12.11.34
Builder: Wilhelmshaven Navy Yard
Yard number: 123
Commanding Officers:

Kpt.z.S. Wilhelm Marschall	12.11.34 to	.....
Kpt.z.S. Otto Ciliax	9.36 to	10.38
Kpt.z.S. Hans Heinrich Wurmbach	10.38 to	24.10.39

Kpt.z.S. Theodor Krancke	25.10.39 to	12.6.41
F.Kpt. Gruber (acting)	1.6.41 to	12.6.41
Kpt.z.S. Wilhelm Meendsen-Bohlken	12.6.41 to	1.11.42
F.Kpt. Gruber (acting)	1.11.42 to	2.43
Kpt.z.S. Richard Rothe-Roth	2.43 to	3.44
Kpt.z.S. Ernst-Ludwig Thienemann	3.44 to	4.45

Fate:
Bombed and sunk while under refit at Deutsche Werke, Kiel 9.4.45. Wreck broken up in situ post-war.

ADMIRAL GRAF SPEE
Ordered: 28.8.32
Laid down: 1.10.32
Launched: 30.6.34
Commissioned: 6.1.36
Builder: Wilhelmshaven Navy Yard
Yard number: 124
Commanding Officers:

Kpt.z.S. Konrad Patzig	6.1.36 to	1937
Kpt.z.S. Walter Warzecha	1937 to	1938
Kpt.z.S. Hans Langsdorff	1938 to	Loss

Fate:
Scuttled in the River Plate estuary off Montevideo, Uruguay, 17.12.39.

SCHARNHORST
Ordered: 25.1.34
Laid down: 30.6.34, relaid 15.6.35
Launched: 3.10.36
Commissioned: 7.1.39
Builder: Wilhelmshaven Navy Yard
Yard number: 125
Commanding Officers:

Kpt.z.S. Otto Ciliax	7.1.39 to	23.9.39
Kpt.z.S. Kurt Hoffmann	24.9.39 to	31.3.42
Kpt.z.S. Friedrich Hüffmeier	1.4.42 to	13.10.43
Kpt.z.S. Fritz Hintze	14.10.43 to	Loss

Fate:
Sunk in action with HMS Duke of York and units of the Home Fleet off North Cape 26.12.43.

GNEISENAU
Ordered: 25.1.34
Laid down: 8.12.34, relaid 6.5.35
Launched: 8.12.36
Commissioned: 21.5.38
Builder: Deutsche Werke (Kiel)
Yard number: 235
Commanding Officers:
Kpt.z.S. Friedrich Förste   21.5.38 to   12.39
Kpt.z.S. Harald Netzbandt   12.39 to   1940
Kpt.z.S. Otto Fein   8.40 to   11.4.42
K.Kpt. Kähler (acting)   15.4.42 to   1.7.42
Fate:
Badly damaged at Kiel by RAF bombers, 26–27. 2.42. Transferred to Gotenhafen for rearming with 38cm guns but work stopped January 1943. Scuttled as a blockship at Gotenhafen 27.3.45 and broken up post-war.

BISMARCK
Ordered: 16.11.35
Laid down: 1.7.36
Launched: 14.2.39
Commissioned: 20.8.40
Builder: Blohm & Voss (Hamburg)
Yard number: 509
Commanding Officers:
Kpt.z.S. Ernst Lindemann   20.8.40 to   Loss
Fate:
Sunk in action with HMS *King George V* and *Rodney* in the North Atlantic 27.5.41.

TIRPITZ
Ordered: 14.6.36
Laid down: 2.11.36
Launched: 1.4.39
Commissioned: 25.2.41
Builder: Wilhelmshaven Navy Yard
Yard number: 128
Commanding Officers:
Kpt.z.S. Karl Topp   25.2.41 to   21.2.43
Kpt.z.S. Kans Meyer   22.2.43 to   5.44
Kpt.z.S. Wolf Junge   5.44 to   11.44
Kpt.z.S. Robert Weber   11.44 to   Loss
Fate:
Sunk by RAF bombers off Tromso 12.11.44.

GRAF ZEPPELIN
Ordered: 16.11.35
Laid down: 28.12.36
Launched: 8.12.38
Commissioned: —
Builder: Deutsche Werke (Kiel)
Yard number: 252
Fate:
Scuttled incomplete at Stettin 24.4.45. Refloated by the Soviets 1946/47. Probably sank in tow en route to Russia 1947.

FLUGZEUGTRÄGER 'B'
Ordered: 11.2.35 (hull), 16.11.35 (machinery)
Laid down: 30.9.36
Launched: —
Commissioned: —
Builder: Krupp Germania (Kiel)
Yard number: 555
Fate:
Broken up on the slipway 1940.

3. ARMAMENT

40.6cm SK C/34 ('H' class)
Gun:
Calibre	406.4mm
Muzzle velocity	810m/sec
Barrel length	52 cal/21,130mm
Bore length	48.6 cal/19,750mm
Barrel life	200 rounds
Weight of breech and barrel	159,900kg
Maximum range	36,400m at 30°

Ammunition: see separate table.
Mounting:
Elevation/depression	+30°/−5½°
Training limits	290°
Elevation rate	?
Training rate	?
Weight of gun cradle	59,900kg
Turret weight	1,475,000kg

Armour:
Face	385mm
Side	240mm
Roof	130mm

38cm SK C/34 (*Bismarck* and *Schlachtschiff 'O'*)
Gun:
Calibre	380mm
Muzzle velocity	820m/sec
Barrel length	51.66 cal/19,630mm
Bore length	48.43 cal/18,405mm
Barrel life	250 rounds
Weight of breech and barrel	111,000kg
Maximum range	35,550m at 30°

Ammunition: see separate table.
Mounting:
Elevation/depression	+30°/−5½°
Elevation rate	6°/sec
Training rate	5°/sec
Turret weight	1,052,000kg

Armour:
Face	360mm
Side	220mm
Roof	130–180mm
Rear	320mm

28cm SK C/34 (*Scharnhorst. Kreuzer 'P'*)
Gun:
Calibre	283mm
Muzzle velocity	890m/sec
Barrel length	54.47 cal/15,415mm
Bore length	51.25 cal/14,505mm
Barrel life	300 rounds
Weight of breech and barrel	53,250kg
Maximum range	40,930m at 40°

Ammunition: see separate table.
Mounting:
Elevation/depression	+40°/−8°
Elevation rate	8°/sec
Training rate	7.2°/sec
Turret weight	750,000kg

Armour:
Face	360mm
Side	220mm
Roof	150mm

28cm SK C/28 (*Deutschland* class)
Gun:
Calibre	283mm
Muzzle velocity	910m/sec
Barrel length	52.35 cal/14,815mm
Bore length	49.13 cal/13,905mm
Barrel life	340 rounds
Weight of breech and barrel	48,200kg
Maximum range	36,475m at 40°

Ammunition: see separate table.
Mounting:
Elevation/depression	+40°/−10°
Turret weight	600,000kg

Armour:
Face	140mm
Side	85mm
Roof	85–105mm

28cm SK L/40 (*Schlesien* class)
Gun:
Calibre	283mm

Muzzle velocity	820m/sec
Barrel length	39.58 cal/11,200mm
Bore length	36.75 cal/10,401mm
Barrel life	—
Weight of breech and barrel	45,300kg

Ammunition: see separate table.
Mounting LC/01:
Elevation/depression	+30°/−4°

15cm L/45 in MPL C/16
Gun:
Calibre	150mm
Muzzle velocity	835m/sec
Muzzle energy	1,610mt
Barrel length	45 cal/6,558mm
Barrel life	1,400 rounds
Length of rifling	5,095mm
Type of rifling	45/30 increasing towards muzzle
Number of grooves	48
Weight of breech and barrel	5,730kg
Maximum range	16,800m

Ammunition:
Weight of shell	45.3kg
Weight of charge	3.90kg (base fuse HE), 4.09kg (nose fuse HE)
HE charge	Fp02
Length of shell	612mm (HE base fuse), 609.2mm (HE nose fuse)
Weight of cartridge	22.7kg
Length of cartridge	865mm
Propellant	RPC12 or RPC38
Fuses	f2, S/60 or C/27

Mounting:
Elevation/depression	+27°/−10°
Weight of cast gun cradle	2,345kg
Total weight of mounting	11,386kg

Note: Schlesien and *Schleswig-Holstein* original armament.

15cm SK C/28 in Dop.L.C/34

Gun:

Calibre	149.1mm
Muzzle velocity	875m/sec
Muzzle energy	1,770mt
Barrel length	55 cal/8,200mm
Liner length	52.4 cal/7,816mm
Constructional gas pressure	3,050kg/cm²
Barrel life	1,100 rounds
Recoil force at 0° elevation	52,000kg
Length of rifling	6,588mm
Type of rifling	Cubic parabola 50/30 cal
Number of grooves	44
Weight of breech and barrel	9,080kg
Maximum range	23,000m
Construction	Jacket with loose inner sleeve. Rhein-Metall thread. Vertical sliding wedge breech. 2 hydraulic brakes and air recuperator

Ammunition:

Weight of shell	45.3kg
Weight of charge	3.058kg or 3.892kg
HE charge	Fp02
Length of shell	4.5 cal/655mm or 4.6 cal/678.9mm
Weight of cartridge	23.5kg
Length of cartridge	865mm
Propellant	RPC/32
Fuses	C/27

Mounting:

Elevation/depression	+40°/−10°
Training limits	±360° = 720°
Elevation change per handwheel revolution	1.04° (8° power)
Training change per handwheel revolution	1.09° (9° power)
Weight of cast gun cradle	2,440kg
Weight of base	2,835kg
Weight of pedestal	41,830kg
Weight of training gear	2,350kg
Electric power	10,300kg
Weight of shield	32,480kg
Total weight of mounting	*Bismarck:* 116,250kg (with R/F), 110,000kg and 108,000kg (Short barbette). *Scharnhorst:* 120,000kg.
Armour	*Bismarck:* Front, 100mm; side and rear, 40mm; roof, 40mm. *Scharnhorst:* Front, 170mm; side, 60mm; roof, 30–50mm; rear 70mm. The 15cm SK C/28 guns in the Panzerschiffe were carried in MPL/28 shielded mounts weighing 24,830kg, while those in *Scharnhorst* were MPL/35 which had larger shields and weighed 26,710kg. The armour thickness of both was 20–60mm. Elevation was +35°/−10°. *Graf Zeppelin* had Dopp MLC/36 mountings of 47,600kg weight.
Armour type	Whn/A, KCn/A

10.5cm SK C/33

Gun:

Calibre	105mm
Muzzle velocity	900m/sec
Muzzle energy	625mt
Barrel length	65 cal/6,840mm
Liner length	60.5 cal/6,348mm
Constructional gas pressure	2,850kg/cm²
Barrel life	2,950 rounds
Recoil force at 0° elevation	1,300kg
Length of rifling	5,531mm
Type of rifling	Cubic parabola 55/35
Number of grooves	36
Weight of breech and barrel	4,560kg
Maximum range	17,700m (horizontal), 12,500m (80°)
Construction	Jacket with loose inner sleeve. Vertical sliding wedge breech

Ammunition:

Weight of shell	15.1kg	
Weight of charge	5.2kg	
HE charge	Fp02	Propellant charge (tracer)
Length of shell	459mm (L4.4HE)	438mm (L4.0 tracer)
Weight of cartridge	6kg	6kg
Length of cartridge	769mm	769mm
Propellant	C/32	C/32
Fuses	Time S/30	Time S/6
Weight of complete round	26.5kg	23.5kg
Length of complete round	1,163mm	1,142mm

Mounting:	**8.8cm Dop.L C/31**	**10.5cm Dop.L C/37**
Elevation/depression	+80°/−8°	+80°/−10°
Training limits	±360° = 720°	±360° = 720°
Elevation change per handwheel revolution	1.33° (10°/sec power)	1.76° (12°/sec power)
Training change per handwheel revolution	1.5° (8°/sec power)	1.5° (8.5°/sec power)
Weight of cast gun cradle	1,455kg	1,455kg
Weight of base	2,300kg	
Weight of pedestal	7,150kg	7,000kg
Weight of sight	745kg	560kg
Electric power	1,295kg	1,295kg
Weight of shield	6,130kg	5,270kg
Total weight of mounting	27,350kg	26,425kg
Armour	Front 15mm; side and deck 10mm	Front 20mm; side and deck 10mm and 8mm; rear 8mm
Armour type	Whn A	Whn A

10.5cm SK C/32ns in 10.5cm MPL C/32ge

Gun:

Calibre	105mm
Muzzle velocity	780m/sec
Muzzle energy	475mt
Barrel length	45 cal/4,740mm
Liner length	42 cal/4,400mm
Constructional gas pressure	2,850kg/cm²
Barrel life	4,100 rounds
Recoil force at 0° elevation	22,600kg
Length of rifling	3,694mm
Type of rifling	Cubic parabola 45/30cal
Number of grooves	32
Weight of breech and barrel	1,765kg
Maximum range	15,175m
Construction	Monobloc jacket with drawn-on vertical sliding wedge breech. Rhein-Metall thread

Ammunition:

Weight of shell (HE)	15.1kg
Weight of charge	3.8kg
HE charge	Fp02
Length of shell	459mm
Weight of cartridge	4.6kg
Length of cartridge	657mm
Propellant	RPC/32
Fuses	Time S/30, inst C/28
Weight of complete round	24.0kg
Length of complete round	1,050mm

Mounting:

Elevation/depression	+70°/−10°
Elevation change per handwheel revolution	3°

Training change per handwheel revolution	3°
Weight of cast gun cradle	655kg
Weight of pedestal	2,100kg
Weight of sight	350kg
Electric power	210kg
Weight of shield	1,670kg
Total weight of mounting	6,750kg
Armour	Front 12mm; side and deck 4mm
Armour type	Wsh

Note: Schlesien and Schleswig-Holstein as rearmed

8.8cm FLAK L/45 in MPL C/13
Gun:

Calibre	88mm
Muzzle velocity	790m/sec
Recoil force at 0° elevation	13,200kg
Weight of breech and barrel	2,500kg

Ammunition:

Weight of shell	9kg
Weight of charge	2.35kg

Mounting:

Elevation	+70°/−10°

Note: Original fitting in Deutschland. Still in Schlesien and Schleswig-Holstein during the war.

8.8cm SK C/25 in 8.8cm Dop.L C/25
Gun:

Calibre	88mm
Muzzle velocity	1,060m/sec
Barrel length	6,340mm/72 cal
Liner length	6,625mm/75 cal
Constructional gas pressure	3,100kg/cm²
Barrel life	600 rounds
Recoil force at 0° elevation	13,000kg
Weight of breech and barrel	5,980kg
Maximum range	17,600m (horizontal), 13,650m (vertical)

Ammunition:

Weight of shell	9kg
Weight of charge	4.53kg
Length of shell	385.5mm
Weight of cartridge	13.5kg
Length of cartridge	1,227mm

Mounting:

Elevation/depression	+85°/−10°
Training limits	±360° = 720°
Elevation change (power)	10°/sec
Training change (power)	10°/sec
Weight of cast gun cradle	1,030kg
Weight of base	3,900kg
Weight of pedestal	12,155kg
Weight of sights	910kg
Electric power	695kg
Weight of shield	1,170kg
Total weight of mounting	28,950kg
Armour	Front, side and deck 8mm
Armour type	Panzerstahl

Note: An unsuccessful gun intended for Deutschland and the 'K'-class cruisers

8.8cm SK C/32 in 8.8cm Dop.L C/32
Gun:

Calibre	88mm
Muzzle velocity	950m/sec
Barrel length	76 cal/6,690mm
Liner length	72 cal/6,340mm
Constructional gas pressure	3,150kg/cm²
Barrel life	3,200 rounds
Recoil force at 0° elevation	7,800kg
Weight of breech and barrel	3,640kg
Maximum range	17,200m (horizontal), 12,400m (vertical)

Ammunition:

Weight of shell	9kg
Weight of charge	3.1kg
Length of shell	397mm
Weight of complete round	15kg/932mm

Mounting:

Elevation/depression	+80°/−10°
Training limits	±360° = 720°
Elevation change per handwheel revolution	3.6° (10°/sec power)
Training change per handwheel revolution	2.5° (—)
Weight of cast gun cradle	1,775kg
Weight of base	815kg
Weight of pedestal	6,257kg
Weight of sights	745kg
Electric power	1,280kg
Weight of shield	5,830kg
Total weight of mounting	23,650kg
Armour	Front 12mm; side and deck 10mm
Armour type	Whn A

Note: Carried by the Panzerschiffe after the failure of the SK C/25 model. Replaced the temporary 8.8cm Flak L/45.

4cm FLAK 28 (BOFORS)
Gun:

Calibre	40mm
Muzzle velocity	854m/sec
Barrel length	2,249mm
Length of rifling	1,932mm
Barrel life	10,000rounds

Ammunition:

Weight of shell	0.955kg
Weight of charge	0.303kg
Vertical range	7,000m approx.

3.7cm SK C/30 in twin mounting C/30
Gun:

Calibre	37mm
Muzzle velocity	1,000m/sec
Muzzle energy	38mt
Barrel length	83 cal/3,074mm
Bore length	80 cal/2,960mm
Constructional gas pressure	3,450kg/cm²
Barrel life	7,500 rounds
Recoil force at 0° elevation	1,000kg
Length of rifling	2,554mm
Type of rifling	Cubic parabola 50/35
Number of grooves	16
Weight of breech and barrel	243kg
Maximum horizontal range	8,500m
Maximum vertical range	6,800m (tracer 4,800m)
Construction	Monobloc barrel with drawn on breech ring. Vertical sliding block breech. Hydraulic brake and spring recuperator

Ammunition:

Weight of shell	0.742kg
Weight of charge	0.365kg
HE charge	Fp02
Length of shell	162mm
Weight of cartridge	0.970kg
Length of cartridge	381mm
Propellant	RPC/32
Weight of complete round	2.1kg
Length of complete round	516.5mm
Fuses	E.nose fuse C/30; nose fuse C/34; Ers St C/34 (tracer)
Duration of tracer	12 sec
Rate of fire	160rpm cyclic, 80rpm practical

Mounting:	
Elevation/depression	$+85°/-10°$
Training limits	$\pm 360° = 720°$
Elevation change per handwheel revolution	$3°$
Training change per handwheel revolution	$4°$
Weight of cradle, brake, etc. (swinging mass)	243kg
Weight of cast gun cradle	152.5kg
Weight of base	71kg
Weight of pedestal	2,162kg
Weight of sight	87kg
Weight of electric power	630kg
Complete mounting	3,670kg

Note: The standard pre-war light flak gun which was not replaced until the last years of the war. It proved too slow in action, being only semi-automatic.

2cm C/30 in 2cm Pedestal L/30
Gun:

Calibre	20mm
Muzzle velocity	835m/sec
Barrel length	65 cal/1,300mm
Bore length	65 cal/1,300mm
Constructional gas pressure	2,800kg/cm²
Barrel life	22,000 rounds
Recoil force at 0° elevation	250kg
Length of rifling	720mm
Weight of breech and barrel	64kg
Maximum horizontal range	4,900m
Maximum vertical range	3,700m

Ammunition:

Weight of shell	134g
Length of shell	78.5mm
Weight of charge	39.5g
Weight of complete round	320g
Length of complete round	203mm
Rate of fire 20-round magazine	280rpm cyclic, 120rpm practical

Mounting:

Elevation/depression	$+85°/-11°$
Training limits	none
Weight of cradle, brake, etc. (swinging mass)	43kg
Weight of mounting without sights	282kg
Weight of complete gun	420kg

2cm C/38 in 2cm Pedestal L30
Gun:
As 2cm C/30, but recoil force at 0°, 290kg; weight of barrel and breech 57.5kg.
Ammunition:
As 2cm C/30, but rate of fire improved to 480rpm cyclic, 220rpm practical.
Mounting:
As 2cm C/30, but weight of complete gun, including spent cartridge net 416kg.

2cm FLAK 35, Vierling L38
Guns:
Four 2cm C/38 barrels.
Ammunition:
As 2cm C/38, but rate of fire 1,800rpm cyclic, 880rpm practical.
Mounting:

Weight of cradle and brake	410kg
Weight of mounting less sights	828kg
Weight of sights and training gear	96.6kg
Weight of power training	31.5kg
Weight of armour	500kg
Weight of complete gun	2,150kg

TORPEDOES

Calibre	533mm
Type	G7a
Fuel	Compressed air
Warhead	430kg TNT
Speed/range	30 knots = 15,000m
	40 knots = 5,000m
	45 knots = 4,500m
Gyro angling	Up to 90° left or right in 1° steps
Depth setting	Up to 52m in 1m steps

SHIPBOARD AIRCRAFT
Heinkel He 60C

Type	Two-seat catapult reconnaissance floatplane
Powerplant	One 660hp BMW VI 6,0 ZU
Performance	Max. speed 225km/hr at 1,000m
	Cruising speed 190km/hr at 1,000m
	Service ceiling 5,000m
	Range 950km
Weights	Empty 2,725kg
	Loaded 3,425kg
Dimensions	Span 12.9m
	Length 11.5m
	Height 4.9m
Armament	One flexible 7.9mm MG

Arado Ar 196A-3

Type	Two-seat catapult reconnaissance floatplane
Powerplant	One 960hp BMW 132K
Performance	Max. speed 310km/hr at 4,000m
	Cruising speed 253km/hr
	Service ceiling 7,000m
	Range 1,070km
Weights	Empty 2,990kg
	Loaded 3,730kg
Dimensions	Span 12.4m
	Length 11.0m
	Height 4.45m
Armament	Two fixed MG FF 20mm cannon and one 7.9mm MG. Two flexible 7.9mm MG in rear cockpit. Two 50kg bombs.

Heinkel He 114A-2

Type	Two-seat catapult reconnaissance floatplane
Powerplant	One 960hp BMW 132K
Performance	Max. speed 335km/hr at 3,500m
	Cruising speed 290km/hr
	Service ceiling 4,800m
	Range 1,050km
Weights	Empty 2,315kg
	Loaded 3,400kg
Dimensions	Span 13.6m
	Length 11.09m
	Height 5.15m
Armament	Two 7.9mm MG. Two 50kg bombs

Arado Ar 197

Type	Single-seat carrier-borne fighter
Powerplant	One 880hp BMW 132 De
Performance	Max. speed 400km/hr at 2,500m
	Cruising speed 355km/hr
	Service ceiling 8,000m
	Range 695km
Weights	Empty 1,840kg
	Maximum 2,475kg
Dimensions	Span 11m
	Length 9.2m
	Height 3.6m
Armament	Two fixed 7.9mm MG in fuselage
	Two fixed 2cm cannon in upper wing 200kg of bombs

Fieseler Fi 167

Type	Carrier-borne torpedo reconnaissance bomber
Powerplant	One 1,100hp Daimler-Benz 601B
Performance	Max. speed 325km/hr
	Cruising speed 270km/hr
	Service ceiling 8,200m
	Range 1,500km
Weights	Empty 2,800kg
	Maximum 4,850kg
Dimensions	Span 13.5m
	Length 11.40m
	Height 4.8m
Armament	One fixed forward-firing 7.92mm MG17
	One flexible rear-firing 7.92mm MG15
	One 1,000kg bomb or one 765kg torpedo

Junkers Ju 87B

Type	Carrier-borne dive-bomber
Powerplant	One 1,200hp Jumo 211B Jumo 211Da
Performance	Max. speed 340km/hr (at sea-level)
	Cruising speed 282km/hr
	Service ceiling 8,000m
	Range 790km
Weights	Empty 2,710kg
	Maximum 4,340kg
Dimensions	Span 13.8m
	Length 11.1m
	Height 4.01m
Armament	Two fixed 7.9mm MG17 in wings
	One flexible 7.9mm MG15 in rear cockpit
	500kg of bombs

Ju 87C, the naval version, was a modified Ju 87B with folding wings, slightly higher weights and presumably a little lower performance.

Messerschmitt Bf 109T

Type	Single-seat carrier-borne fighter
Powerplant	One 1,200hp Daimler-Benz DB 601N
Performance	Max. speed 568km/hr at 6,150m
	Cruising speed 483km/hr
	Service ceiling 10,500m
	Range 660km
Weights	Empty 2,000kg
	Maximum 2,954kg
Dimensions	Span 11.18m
	Length 10.38m
	Height 2.6m
Armament	Two 7.9mm MG17 in fuselage
	Two 7.9mm MG17 or 20mm cannon in wings

Arado Ar 195

Type	Carrier-borne attack/reconnaissance
Powerplant	One 880hp BMW 132 De
Performance	Max. speed 280km/hr
	Cruising speed 250km/hr
	Service ceiling 6,000m
	Range 650km
Weights	Empty 2,380kg
	Maximum 3,745kg
Dimensions	Span 12.50m
	Length 10.5m
	Height 3.6m
Armament	One fixed forward-firing 7.9mm MG17
	One flexible rear-firing 7.9mm MG15
	One 800kg torpedo or 500kg bomb

MAIN ARMAMENT AMMUNITION

40.6cm SK C/34 ('H' class)

	Weight	Length	Charge	Fuse
Pz.gr. L/4.4(mh)	1,030kg	1,786mm		Bdz 38
Spr.gr. L/4.6(mh) Bdz	1,030kg	1,867mm		Bdz 38
Spr.gr. L/4.4(mh) Kz	1,030kg	1,949mm		Bdz 38
Ad.gr. L/4.2(mh) Kz and Bdz	600kg	1,705mm		Hbgr Z40K or Dopp Z45S90 and WZ40K
Spr.gr L/4.1(mh) Bdz and Kz	610kg	1,644mm		Bdz 38, Kz 27

(Last two for coast defence use only.)

Cartridge	Weight	Propellant filling
Main (cased)	219kg	128kg, RPC/38
Forward (bagged)	134kg	134kg, RPC/38

38cm SK C/34 (Bismarck and Schlachtshiff 'O')

	Weight	Length	Charge	Fuse
Pz.gr. L/4.4(mh)	800kg	1,672mm	18.8kg = 2.35%	Bdz 38
Spr.gr. L/4.5(mh) Bdz	800kg	1,710mm	32.6kg = 4.1%	Bdz 38
Spr.gr. L/4.6(mh) Kz	800kg	1,748mm	64.2kg = 8.0%	Kz 27
Spr.gr. L/4.5(mh) Bdz and Kz	495kg	1,710mm		Hbgr. Z40K Dopp Z45K Bdz 40K
Spr.gr L/4.4(mh) Bdz and Kz	510kg	1,672mm		Kz 27, Bdz 38

(Last two for coast defence use only.)

Cartridge	Weight	Propellant filling
Main (cased)	182.5kg	112.5kg, RPC/38
Forward (bagged)	99.5kg	99.5kg, RPC/38

28cm SK C/34 (Scharnhorst, Kreuzer 'P')

	Weight	Length	Charge	Fuse
Pz.gr. L/4.4(mh)	336kg	1,245mm	6.6kg = 2.0%	Bdz 38
Spr.gr. L/4.4(mh) Bdz	315kg	1,245mm	16.0kg = 5.1%	Bdz 38
Spr.gr. L/4.5(mh) Kz	315kg	1,273mm	21.8kg = 6.9%	Kz27

Cartridge	Weight	Propellant filling
Main (cased)	124kg	76.5kg, RPC/38
Forward (bagged)	42.5kg	42.5kg, RPC/38

28cm SK C/28 (Deutschland class)

	Weight	Length	Charge	Fuse
Pz.gr. L/3.7(mh)	300kg	1,047mm	7.84kg = 2.6%	Bdz 38
Spr.gr. L/4.2(mh) Bdz	300kg	1,188mm	16.94kg = 5.65%	Bdz 38
Spr.gr. L/4.2(mh) Kz	300kg	1,188mm	23.33kg = 7.8%	Kz27

Cartridge	Weight	Propellant filling
Main (cased)	189.5kg	71.0kg, RPC/38
Forward (bagged)	36kg	36.0kg, RPC/38

28cm SK L/40 (Schlesien class)

	Weight	Length	Charge	Fuse
Pz.gr. L/2.6	240kg	736mm		Bdz 36
Spr.gr. L/2.9	240kg	821mm		Bdz 36
Spr.gr. L/4.4(mh) Bdz and Kz	284kg	1,245mm		Bdz 36 or KzF Spr.gr mbh or Dopp Z 160AZ

4. ELECTRONIC INSTALLATIONS

RADAR SETS

Aerial	Designation (i)	Designation (ii)	Fitted to	Wave Length	Pulse Frequency	Power		Range	Accuracy	
Rotating pillar	FuM021		Destroyers	81.5cm	500	1kW	(Gema)	14–18km	±3°	
Above range-finder	FuM022		Battleships and Heavy Cruisers	81.5cm	500	1kW	(Gema)			
Combined radar and range-finder	FuM023		Battleships and Heavy Cruisers	81.5cm	500	8kW	(Gema)			
Rotating pillar	FuM024		Torpedo boats, Light Cruisers and Destroyers	81.5cm	500	8kW	(Gema)	15–20km	±0.3°	
Rotating pillar	FuM025		Torpedo boats, Light Cruisers and Destroyers	81.5cm	500	8kW	(Gema)	15–20km	±0.3°	
Above range-finder	FuM026		Battleships and Heavy Cruisers	81.5cm	500	10kW	(Gema)	20–25km	±0.25°	
Combined radar and range-finder	FuM027		Battleships and Heavy Cruisers	81.5cm	500	15kW	(Gema)			
Double Fixed	FuM028		Type 37 Torpedo boats				(Gema)			
Fixed reflector and electronic sweep	FuM029		U-boats							
Rotating reflector	FuM030	40G (gU)	U-boats	81.5cm	500	8kW		6–8km	±5°	Luftwaffe set. 'Hohentweil'
	FuM061	FuG200U	U-boats	54cm	50	30kW		8–10km	±3°	(Lorentz)
Extendable reflector, Rotating vertical Polarizing	FuM062	FuG200S	S-boats							(Lorentz) 'Hohentweil'
	FuM063		Surface ships			30kW		12–20km	±2°	(Lorentz) 'Hohentweil'
	FuM071	FuG202	S-boats and VP	63cm	2640					(Telefunken) Luftwaffe set 'Lichtenstein'
	FuM081		Prinz Eugen (Land use?)			15kW		20–30km	±5°	'Hohentweil K'
	FuM0221	FuSe64								'Mannheim'
	FuM0212,213 and FuM0214	FuSe65	Flak Cruisers and Land use							(Telefunken) 'Würzburg-Riese'

Other Sets:

Vertical Polarized Diodes. 2 groups of 16 dipoles each	FuM01									1,000Hz and 2,000Hz
	FuM02									'Calais' 500Hz

RADAR TRANSMISSION RECEIVERS

Designation (i)	Designation (ii)	Manufacturer	Fitted to	Frequency Range	Code
FuMB1	R 600A	Metox		500/113 M/C	'Metox'
FuMB2		Sadir		120/666 M/C	
FuMB3		RPZ		220/180 M/C	
FuMB4	RSI/5UD 42	Rhode & Schwarz	All	470/90 M/C	'Samos'
FuMB5		Rhode & Schwarz	classes	1,500/400 M/C	
FuMB6		Rhode & Schwarz	of	250/160 M/C	
FuMB7		Telefunken	ships	3,700/3,000 M/C	'Naxos I'
FuMB8	Wanz G	Hagenuk		250/166 M/C	'Cypern I'
FuMB9	Wanz G	Hagenuk		156/254 M/C	'Cypern II'
FuMB10				100/400 M/C	'Borkum'
FuMB26	Naxos II			7,500/15,000 M/C	'Tunis'
FuME1	FuKG 41g	Elac	Individual	380/361 M/C	'Wespeg' 21/14/7 Signals/min. 79–83cm
FuME2		Elac	Large Vessels	400/353 M/C	'Wespeg (2)'

AERIALS FOR FuMB

Designation	Constructors	Fitted to	Frequency	D/F Accuracy	Code
Mb Ant 1	Naval Shipyards	S-boats	233–166	±5°	
Mb Ant 2	Naval Shipyards	U-boats			'Biscay Cross'
Mb Ant 3	Naval Shipyards	Various	400–100	Omni-dipole	'Bali' round omni-directional dipole
Mb Ant 4	Naval Shipyards	Various	400–100	±5°	'Sumatra' loop dipole, 45° Polarization
Mb Ant 6	Naval Shipyards	Various			'Palau' double butterfly dipoles
Mb Ant 7	Naval Shipyards	Large Vessels	400–100	±3°	'Timor' vertical and horizontal butterfly loops

REFERENCES AND BIBLIOGRAPHY

OFFICIAL SOURCES

German War Diaries (Kriegstagebücher or KTB)
(a) *Commands:*
Gruppe (Nord), Gruppe (West), Gruppe (Ost), MOK (Nord), MOK (Ost), Flottenkommando, Kampfgruppe, Befehlshaber der Schlachtschiffe, Befehlshaber der Panzerschiffe, Befehlshaber der Kreuzer, Admiral (Nordmeer), Befehlshaber der Aufklärungsstreitkrafte
(b) *Ships:*
Admiral Graf Spee, Admiral Scheer, Deutschland/Lützow, Scharnhorst, Gneisenau, Bismarck, Tirpitz, Schlesien, Schleswig-Holstein, Nürnberg, Admiral Hipper, Prinz Eugen

Documents
Plattenliste für die Vertikalpanzerung des Panzerschiffes 'Ersatz Preussen'
Das Panzerschiff 'A' und die Vorentwürfe von 1920 bis 1928—Sandhofer, Militärgeschichtliche Mitteilungen, 1968
Entwicklung der Panzerschiffe der 'Deutschland' Klasse; von Ministerialdirektor Presse, 1 August 1944
Panzerschiff *Deutschland*—Tabelle zur Zeichnung, Panzeranordnung TS4/25078
Panzerschiff 'A'. The Military, Political and Strategic Considerations which Led to its Construction (2.11.28), RM20/1568
Schiffesbuch II *Deutschland*, TS298/57406
Panzerschiff 'Ersatz Lothringen'—Bauvorschrift für die Hauptmachinenanlange
Schiffesbuch II *Admiral Scheer*, TS46/24161
Plattenliste für die Vertikalpanzerung des Panzerschiffes 'Ersatz Braunschweig'
Erpobüngen-Panzerschiff *Admiral Graf Spee*, schlussbericht, TS176/24483
Ship Replacement Conference, 28 June 1932, RM20/993 & 994
Schiffesbuch II *Admiral Graf Spee*, TS46/24159
Waffenanlage *Admiral Graf Spee*,

TS176/24483
Umarmierungsplänen, *Scharnhorst* and *Gneisenau* (25.5.38), RM20/880
Ersatz Elsass, RM20/994
Schiffesbuch II, *Scharnhorst*, TS298/57407
Schlachtschiff *Gneisenau*—Geschutz Material der SA & MA, Band I, TS21/29498
Enstehungsgeschichte für die Schlachtschiffe F & G
Erpobungsbericht—*Bismarck*, TS268/16178
Bauvorschrift-Waffenanlage *Bismarck*, TS131/22065
Bauvorschrift-Schiff *Bismarck*, TS131/22064
Kaliberfragen Panzerschiffe D & E (4.4.35), AIVa 1330/35
Gewichtsliste *Admiral Scheer*, TS122/24479a
Gewichtsliste *Scharnhorst*, TS122/24481a
Gewichtsliste *Tirpitz*, TS/24482a
Waffenanlage *Graf Zeppelin*, TS131/22068
Flugzeugträger, TS1216/23369
Trägerflugzeug, TS25/27496
Handbuch der Deutschekriegschiffstypen, Heft 1, MDiv 401, 1944
Unterlage u. Richtlinien zur bestimmung der Hauptkampfentfernung und der Geschosswahl, Heft (a), OKM, 1940
Konstruktion Rheinmetal-Borsig: Angeben über Marinegeschütz

British		
Repulse	Report of proceedings 8.4.40	(ADM199/474)
Renown	Report of proceedings 8.4.40	(ADM199/474)
Rawalpindi	Report of proceedings 23.11.39	(ADM199/725)
Clyde	Patrol Report 20.6.40	(ADM199/1877)
Seawolf	Patrol Report 6.3.42	(ADM199/1836)
Spearfish	Patrol Report 11.4.40	(ADM199/1843)
Triton	Patrol Report 8.4.40	(ADM199/1847)
Trident	Patrol Report 8.4.40	(ADM199/1864)
Rodney	Ship's Log March 1941	(ADM53/115027)
Ramilles	Ship's Log February 1941	(ADM53/114929)
Malaya	Ship's Log March 1941	(ADM53/114600)
Tantalus	Ship's Log September 1943	(ADM53/18192)

Air Historical Branch Narrative History:
Bomber Command (AIR41/40)
Coastal Command (AIR 41/47, /48, /73)
3 Group Operational Record Book (AIR25/51, /52)
4 Group Operational Record Book (AIR25/93)
5 Group Operational Record Book (AIR25/109A)
Evaluation of Captured Enemy Aircraft (AIR40/133)

Published Sources
Air-Britain. *RAF Serial Registers L*, 1979; *N*, 1979; *P*, 1978; *R*, 1980; *T*, 1981; *X/Z*, 1984; *AA/AZ*, 1985; *BA/BZ*, 1986
Anon. *Die Versunkene Flotte*. Stalling, 1961
Apps, Lt.Cdr. Michael. *Send Her Victorious*. Wm. Kimber, 1971
Barker, R. *The Ship Busters*. Chatto & Windus, 1957
Bowyer, C. *The Wellington Bomber*. Wm. Kimber, 1986
Bredemeier, Heinrich. *Schlachtschiff Scharnhorst*. Heyne-Buch, 1982
Breyer. *Battleships and Battlecruisers*. Macdonald, 1973
Breyer, S. & Koop, G. *Von der Emden zur Tirpitz*. Verlag Wehr und Wissen, 1982
Brown, David. *Carrier Operations in World War II*. Ian Allan
Busch, Fritz-Otto. *Prinz Eugen*. Futura, 1975
Campbell, J. *Naval Weapons of World War Two*. Conway Maritime, 1985
Cooper, A.W. *Beyond the Dams to the Tirpitz*. Wm. Kimber, 1987
D'Eyncourt, Sir Eustace T. *Notes on some Features of German Warship Construction*. Proc. Inst. Naval Arch., 1921
Gomersall, B. *The Stirling File*. Air-Britain, 1987
Goodall, S.V. *The ex-German battleship Baden*. Proc. Inst. Naval Arch., 1921
Hadeler, Wilhelm. *Der Flugzeugträger*. Lehmanns Verlag, 1968. *Project Sketches of Air Support Ships in the German Navy of the Second World War*. Translated

from Marine Rundschau, 1972
Halley, James. *The Squadrons of the Royal Air Force*. Air-Britain, 1985. *The Lancaster File*. Air-Britain, 1985
Harris, Gp. Capt.P.I. *Wilhelmshaven Disaster*. Flypast, June 1983
Hastings, Max. *Bomber Command*, Michael Joseph
Hendrie, Andrew. *Seek and Strike*. Wm. Kimber, 1983
Kennedy, Ludovic. *Menace—the Life and death of Tirpitz*. Sidgwick & Jackson, 1979
Lewin, R. *Ultra goes to War*. Hutchinson, 1978
Mullenheim-Rechberg, Baron von. *Battleship Bismarck*. Triad, 1982
Nesbit, Roy Conyers. *Woe to the Unwary*. Wm. Kimber, 1981. *The Torpedo Airmen*. Wm. Kimber, 1983
Roberts, N. *The Halifax File*, Air-Britain, 1982. *The Whitley File*, Air-Britain, 1986
Rohwer, J. & Hümmelchen, G. *Chronology of the War at Sea*, Vols. I & II. Ian Allan, 1974
Roskill, S. *The War at Sea*, Vols I to III. H.M.S.O.
Schofield, Vice-Admiral B.B. *The Loss of the Bismarck*. Ian Allan
Showell, Jak P. Mallman. *The German Navy in World War Two*. Arms & Armour Press, 1979
Smith, J.R. & Kay A. *German Aircraft of the Second World War*. Putnam, 1978
Sturtivant, Ray. *The Squadrons of the Fleet Air Arm*. Air-Britain, 1984
Thetford, Owen. *Aircraft of the Royal Air Force since 1918*. Putnam, 1971. *British Naval Aircraft since 1912*. Putnam, 1971
Watts, A.J. *Loss of the Scharnhorst*. Ian Allan, 1970
Weal, E.C. *Combat Aircraft of World War Two*. Arms & Armour Press, 1977
Winton, J. *Find, Fix and Strike*. B.T. Batsford
Woodward, D. *The Tirpitz* Wm. Kimber, 1955
Whitley, M.J. *Destroyer! German Destroyers in World War Two*. Arms & Armour Press, 1983. *German Cruisers of World War Two*. Arms & Armour Press 1985.
Graf Zeppelin. Warship, Vols. 31 & 33, Conway.
Hümmelchen, G. *Die deutschen Seeflieger*. Lehmanns Verlag, 1976
Jung et al. *Die Deutschen Kriegschiffe 1815–1945*, Vol. I. Lehmanns Verlag